# COINS AND MONEYS OF ACCOUNT

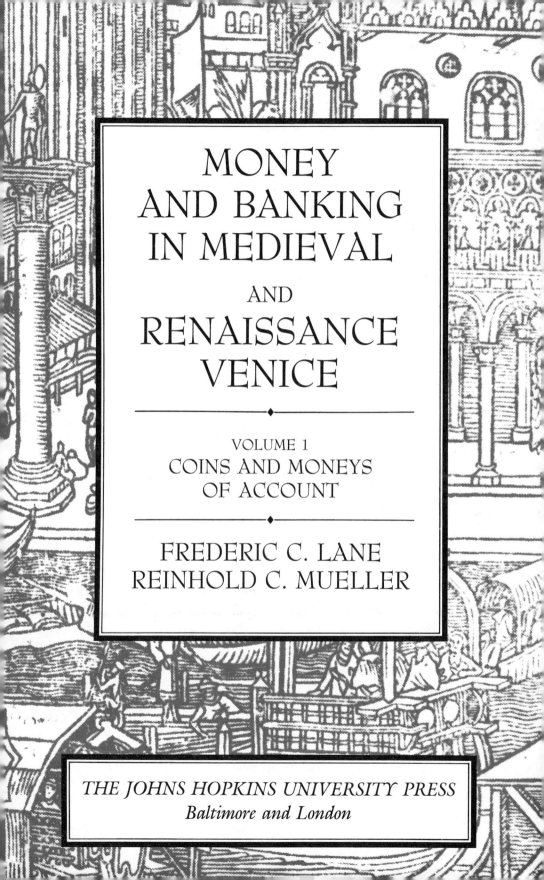

# MONEY
# AND BANKING
# IN MEDIEVAL

## AND

# RENAISSANCE
# VENICE

VOLUME 1
COINS AND MONEYS
OF ACCOUNT

## FREDERIC C. LANE
## REINHOLD C. MUELLER

THE JOHNS HOPKINS UNIVERSITY PRESS
Baltimore and London

*This book has been brought to publication
with the generous assistance of
the National Endowment for the Humanities
and the Gladys Krieble Delmas Foundation.*

*Front case stamping:* Silver mezzanino of Andrea Dandolo.
See p. 343 for a full description.

The Johns Hopkins University Press, 701 West 40th Street
Baltimore, Maryland 21211
The Johns Hopkins Press Ltd, London

Library of Congress Cataloging in Publication Data

Lane, Frederic Chapin, 1900–1984
Money and banking in medieval and Renaissance Venice.

Bibliography: v. 1, p.
Includes index.
Contents: v. 1. Coins and moneys of account.
1. Money—Italy—Venice—History.   2. Banks and
banking—Italy—Venice—History.   3. Venice (Italy)—
Economic conditions.   I. Mueller, Reinhold C.   II. Title.
HG1040.V46L36  1985       332.1'0945'31       84-47947
ISBN 0-8018-3157-1 (v. 1)

The paper in this book is acid-free and meets the guidelines for permanence
and durability of the Committee on Production Guidelines for Book
Longevity of the Council on Library Resources.

Photographs of the Byzantine coins were provided courtesy of the
Dumbarton Oaks Collection, Washington, D.C. Photographs of all others
were provided by the Museo Bottacin, Padua, and were photographed by
the Gabinetto Fotografico, Museo Civico di Padova. (All other credits are
specified in the captions.)

# CONTENTS

CONTENTS

CONTENTS

vii

CONTENTS

# ILLUSTRATIONS

## COINS

*Note: Coins are generally pictured in actual size and threefold enlargement; captions do not repeat silver contents, for which see tables A.2 and A.3.*

LIST OF ILLUSTRATIONS

# TABLES

# PREFACE

*Pecunie nostri dominii sunt nervi
immo animo huius rei publice*

HIS ASSERTION, that "the moneys of our dominions are the sinews, nay even the soul, of this republic," made in a decree of the Venetian Senate in 1472 reforming accounting procedures, epitomizes the conscious concern of a leading Renaissance state for its money—both as coin and as money of account. *Pecunie* meant debits and credits as well as the coins used to pay debts and collect credits. Such concern was not unique to Venice but that city's central position in the bullion trade of medieval Europe gave her decisions an importance transcending even her general commercial eminence and imperial position.

Our two-volume history deals with *pecunie,* not so much as individual coins (although the coins are fully described and illustrated), as with their utilization in effecting payments. It deals, furthermore, with the production of coins and the connection between production and the bullion trade; with Venetian monetary policy in the context of the Mediterranean and European worlds; with banking and exchange operations in the Venetian economy. The division of material between this first volume, entitled *Coins and Moneys of Account,* and the second volume, *The Money Market,* is partly topical, partly chronological. All the main themes are introduced in volume one, and some, such as the industrial organization of the mint and the penetration of Venetian coins into areas previously part of the Byzantine Empire, are carried through the fifteenth century, while others, such as the flows of bullion, monetary policies, and the relative value of the moneys of Venice and of its chief trading partners, are cut off at about 1400. A terminal date of the early fifteenth century for much of the first volume was suggested by the subject matter itself, since it was at that time that the myriad and confusing medieval moneys of account were finally simplified into two basic kinds, which then dominated accounting calculations until the early sixteenth century. Volume two developes the themes of banking and foreign exchange in Venice from the origins, while carrying the problems of the bullion trade and monetary policy to the late fifteenth century.

As a whole, our volumes—and especially the general treatment in part 1 of this first volume—are aimed at a mixed audience composed both of economists sufficiently interested in basic monetary problems to want to look back to see what money has been, and to historians sufficiently interested in the men and women of medieval and early modern times to wish to understand their money. Some sections are, to be sure, too detailed to hold the attention of readers not specialists in Venice. They seemed necessary, however, to make the exposition convincing and comprehensive and more useful to experts in special aspects of Venetian commerce or art. Numismatists also may find our economic-historical approach to coins useful to their science and their interests.

Although such Venetian coins as the gold ducat and the silver grosso are well known, there is little general understanding of the other coins or even of the ways in which ducats and grossi were evaluated when used to pay prices and to settle contracts stated in moneys of account. During many years when we were focusing on other than monetary problems— either maritime trade and industrial organization, or banking and the administration of familial and charitable trust funds—we used the documents on monetary history published by Roberto Cessi in 1937, but without feeling sure that we understood adequately the moneys referred to in those documents. Professor Cessi was a trailblazer at a time when the lay of the land was little known. Hoping to build on his and others' work, we decided about twelve years ago jointly to attempt a study in which explanation of Venetian moneys would be the center of attention.

One cause of misunderstandings in Venetian monetary history has been the large gaps in the Venetian archives. Mint archives comparable to those of England or Florence or the Low Countries have not survived in Venice. Even basic registers of governmental decrees are missing for several crucial decades of the fourteenth century. Monetary policies and especially monetary practices have had to be reconstructed indirectly from such varied sources as merchants' manuals, account books and commercial letters, notarial registers, and general fiscal and commercial legislation. Such sources, at the same time, have been important in analyzing the relations between changes that occurred in Venice and those that occurred in the lands of its trading partners.

The monetary histories of Venice's trading partners have attracted much attention recently and a large number of important publications have appeared in the last decade: by Bernocchi, Cipolla, and de la Roncière on Florence, by Felloni and Lopez on Genoa, by Munro and Spufford on England and Flanders, by Kellenbenz and von Stromer on Germany, to mention only a few. These works and others that were appearing—some while this book was in press—tempted us to delay publication so as to be able to make extensive revisions. Fearful, however, that one delay would lead to others, we decided instead to prepare this volume for publication before completion of the entire joint project, in order to contribute now to the wider discussion with our stress on the pivotal role played by Venice in the big changes in bimetallic ratios which took place in the fourteenth century and their effect on the practical meaning of moneys of account.

When we decided upon our collaborative effort in 1972, it was agreed that Lane would concentrate on moneys of account and on the policies and organization of the mint, while Mueller would focus on banking and exchange. As a result, the first volume is largely Lane's, while the second volume will be largely Mueller's. This volume nonetheless is co-authored: what each wrote the other worked over carefully, adding material from primary sources and secondary works. As regards the original research for this volume, it may be said that Lane utilized the archival sources that had attracted his attention while studying naval and maritime history and the history of accounting while Mueller gleaned material from estate papers, the appeals for pardons and reductions of sentence registered in the Grazie series, and decisions of the commercial court of the Giudici di Petizion. Both authors exploited the well-known registers of the deliberative organs of the state. Of course, each placed at the disposal of the other the notes made in long years of research. Most of the volume at hand was first drafted by Lane, while Mueller wrote chapter 5, sec. iv; all of chapter 6; chapter 11, secs. i and ii; chapter 16, secs. iv and v; appendix A, sec. ix; appendix C, sec. ii; and appendix D (with respective tables) and transcribed the documents printed in appendix G; he also produced the graphs and most of the illustrative material.

Chapter 20, by Lane, appeared as "La mobilità e l'utilità delle monete di conto" in *Rivista di storia economica*, n.s., 1 (June 1984):9–31 and in English in its International Issue (December 1984).

We owe an inestimable debt to many friends, colleagues, and students with whom our discussions of monetary problems in historical context started much more than a decade ago. Several have at one time or another placed at our disposal the results of their research prior to its publication. Notable, among many, are E. Ashtor, Ph. Braunstein, C. M. Cipolla, J. Day, R. and F. Edler de Roover, P. Grierson, R. S. Lopez and G. Airaldi, G. Ravagnani, J. F. Richards, L. Buenger Robbert, P. Spufford, A. Stahl, and U. Tucci. Special mention should be made of Giorgetta Bonfiglio-Dosio who provided us with typescript copies of her fine critical edition of the *Capitolare dalle broche* while it was still in press. It permitted us to check our earlier readings of this record of the operation of the mint and to exploit it more fully; she also allowed us to use her unpublished article on the workers at the mint. Our collection of domestic exchange rates was enriched by the quotations passed on by S. Collodo, B. Kohl, J. Law, and G. M. Varanini.

Others have read drafts of our work at various stages of completion. First to be mentioned should be Richard Goldthwaite and John Munro who carefully read a nearly complete manuscript at an advanced stage and prepared extensive and extremely helpful commentaries, regarding both the big questions and important details. Each helped us in our attempt to relate Venetian experiences to the better known experiences of other areas, in particular Florence, England, and the Low Countries.

Our exploration of monetary history also put us in the debt of experts in the field of numismatics, in which we could do little more than pose questions. Drafts of individual chapters and subsections were kindly read and commented upon by G. Gorini, P. Grierson, and A. Stahl. The great majority of the coins pictured in this volume were selected with the help of Andrea Saccocci from the numismatic collection of the Museo Bottacin in Padua, of which he is curator; he also very generously agreed to write the numismatic descriptions of those coins. (P. Spufford and A. Stahl—both of whom have important works on monetary history and exchange in press—provided helpful suggestions for rendering the descriptions in English.)

Mueller is especially grateful for a fellowship from the Harvard University Center for Italian Renaissance Studies at I Tatti, Florence, in 1975–76, which enabled him to study at the Datini archives in Prato, benefiting from the expertise of Luciana Frangioni and Marco Spallanzani, whose friendly help has remained constant. Again in 1978–79 Mueller was able to absent himself from teaching, this time thanks to a fellowship from the American Council of Learned Societies. The results of the research of those years, as of the generous grants of computer time and assistance at the University of Arizona, will be more obvious in the second volume.

Steadfast friends at the Computer Center of the University of Venice gave of their time and patience in the preparation of the long table of exchange rates (D. 3) and graph 3.

Our years of research were greatly facilitated by many archivists, librarians, and employees, not only, but most especially, in Venice. To mention only some of those at the archives at the Frari: L. Lanfranchi, B. Lanfranchi Strina, M. F. Tiepolo, and F. Zago.

As is surely usual for prolonged projects of this scope, the persons closest to the authors absorb the greatest amount of punishment. Essential support, critical readings with a view to our varied audiences, deadline-pace typing (handled at early stages by Lilly Lavarello), and the like were provided by Richard Altobelli, Jonathan Lane, Susanne Lane, and Laura Lepscky Mueller.

Our thanks go also to members of the Department of History at the Johns Hopkins University for aid volunteered and rendered at crucial stages in the preparation of the copy.

The Johns Hopkins University Press, finally, has shown itself to be full of encouragement, help, and hospitality.

Westminster, Massachusetts,
   and Venice
1984

# ABBREVIATIONS

*For full titles and facts of publication see Bibliography.*

| | |
|---|---|
| *Annales, ESC* | *Annales, économies, sociétés, civilisations* |
| ASF | Archivio di Stato, Florence |
| ASP | Archivio di Stato, Prato |
| ASV | Archivio di Stato, Venice |
| *AV* | *Archivio veneto* |
| Bernocchi | Bernocchi. *Le monete* |
| *BG* | *Bilanci generali* |
| BMCV | Biblioteca del Museo Civico Correr, Venice |
| BMV | Biblioteca Nazionale Marciana, Venice |
| *Cap. Broche* | Bonfiglio-Dosio, ed. *Il "Capitolar dalle broche"* |
| *Cap. Fontego* | Thomas, ed. *Capitolare dei Visdomini del Fontego* |
| Cipolla, *I movimenti* | Cipolla. *Studi di storia della moneta.* Vol. I, *I movimenti* |
| *CNI* | *Corpus Nummorum Italicorum* |
| *DMB* | Center for Medieval and Renaissance Studies, ed. *Dawn of Modern Banking* |
| *DMC* | Cessi, ed. *Deliberazioni del Maggior Consiglio* |
| DF | Documenti finanziari |
| *DQ* | Lombardo, ed. *Le deliberazioni del Consiglio dei Quaranta* |
| *EcHR* | *Economic History Review* |
| Einaudi in *Enterprise* | Einaudi. "The Theory of Imaginary Money" |
| EPHE-6 | Ecole Pratique des Hautes Etudes, VIe Section, Paris |
| FSV | Fonti per la Storia di Venezia |

| | |
|---|---|
| *JEcH* | *Journal of Economic History* |
| *JEEcH* | *Journal of European Economic History* |
| MC | ASV, Maggior Consiglio, Deliberazioni |
| *NAV* | *Nuovo archivio veneto* |
| Papadopoli | Papadopoli. *Le monete* |
| *PMV* | Cessi, ed. *Problemi monetari veneziani* |
| *PRV* | Luzzatto, ed. *I prestiti della Repubblica di Venezia* |
| PSM | ASV, Procuratori di San Marco |
| *RES* | Cessi, ed. *La regolazione delle entrate e delle spese* |
| *RIN* | *Rivista italiana di numismatica e scienze affini* |

*Abbreviations used in descriptions of coins:*

| | |
|---|---|
| AE | Aes (copper, bronze) |
| AR | Argentum (silver) |
| AV | Aurum (gold) |
| B | Billon |
| *Obv.* | Obverse |
| *Rev.* | Reverse |

*Additional abbreviations used only in table D.3 are explained in app. D, below.*

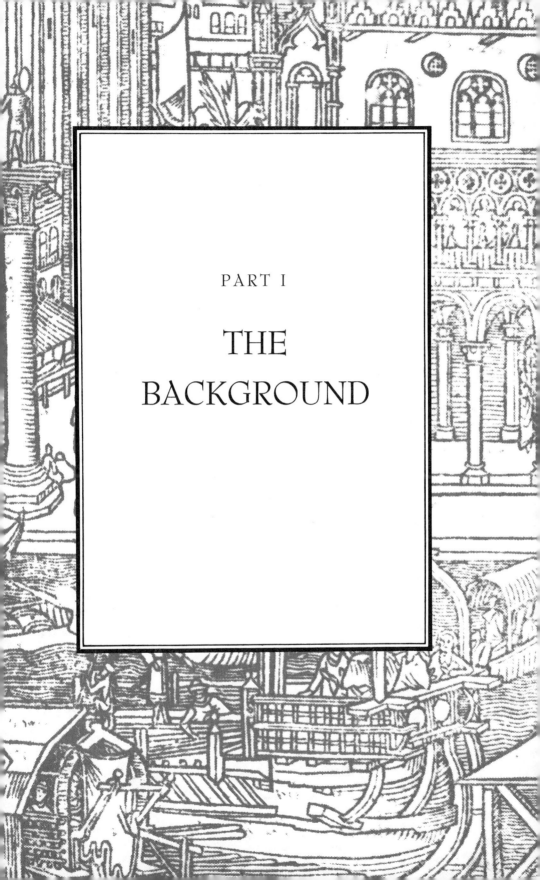

PART I

# THE
# BACKGROUND

# 1

# WHAT MONEY IS AND WAS

## i. SOME ECONOMISTS' ANSWERS

RELATING THE MONETARY EXPERIENCE of medieval Venice to that of Europe and the Mediterranean generally requires explaining some distinctions about the meaning of "money," not for the sake of a foray into monetary theory, but in order to clarify terms that are in common usage but are employed with varying, often ill-defined, meanings by numismatists and economic historians.

The connections between coins and moneys of account raise questions that are central to many problems of medieval monetary history. The conventional definition of "money" as a medium of exchange and a standard of value dodges essential questions about that relationship by assuming that one thing performs the two functions, although conceptually and historically the two are separable. Moreover, both "medium of exchange" and "standard of value" are sufficiently ambiguous to make "moneyness" only a matter of degree. Theorists concluded some time ago that many things have been "more or less" money;[1] estimates of the size of the money supply have distinguished between M-1*a*, M-1*b*, M-2, and so on.

Some ambiguities of the expression "medium of exchange" can be

---

[1]Albert Gaylord Hart, *Money, Debt, and Economic Activity* (New York, 1948), 5; idem, in *International Encyclopedia of the Social Sciences,* ed. David L. Sills (New York, 1968), s.v. "money." Later, Milton Friedman similarly in *Encyclopaedia Britannica, Macropaedia,* 15th ed. (1980), s.v. "money."

avoided by referring to "means of payment." But to serve as a medium of exchange a means of payment must be generally accepted within a community. Nowadays, government-backed paper generally serves that purpose, and coins serve only to make small change. Paper money printed by governments is accepted without distinctions based on who is paying or being paid. Because creditors are legally obliged to accept it in payment of debt, it is called legal tender.[2] Official designation of legal tender, however, does not alone determine what means of payment is the common medium of exchange at any particular time and place. Custom is equally important. Bank deposits are now counted in calculating the total stock of money. Checks and electronic devices for transferring bank deposits, which banks are obligated to pay in legal tender, are the most commonly used means of payment and are even accepted by some governments in the payment of taxes.

In the Middle Ages also, custom as well as law determined which means of payment were so widely used that they functioned as media of exchange. Paper money circulated only in China, and in Europe checks were not generally accepted. Metallic coin was the chief means of payment, and governments declared some coins to be legal tender, others not. The extent to which the legal tender was supplemented through custom by other means of payment varied greatly from place to place. There was much offsetting of one claim against another even in country villages, but only in busy commercial centers such as Venice could debtors make payments by transfers of bankers' promises. Some other forms of credit were also transferred to meet obligations, but credit was far less important than coin.[3]

While some economic theorists define money in terms that make its use as a means of payment the essential quality,[4] others consider its essential quality to be its functioning as a standard of value.[5] If the latter is the

---

[2]The definition of J. Keith Horsefield ("The Beginnings of Paper Money in England," *JEEcH* 6 [1977]:117)—"anything which is generally acceptable in final settlement of debt"—includes more than legal tender but much less than is nowadays generally included in figures on the money supply.

[3]Abbot Payson Usher, *The Early History of Deposit Banking in Mediterranean Europe*, Harvard Economic Studies, 75 (Cambridge, 1943; reprint, New York, 1967), 176–86.

[4]D. H. Robertson, *Money*, rev. ed. (Chicago, 1949), 2–3: "In this book, the term money will be used to denote anything which is widely accepted in payment for goods or in discharge of other kinds of business obligations." Hart (*Money, Debt, and Economic Activity*, 4) wrote: "Money is property with which the owner can pay off a definite amount of debt—with certainty and without delay, even though he is dealing with a stranger." Walter Eucken, *The Foundations of Economics*, trans. T. W. Hutchison (London, 1950), 159–72, assumes that money is a means of payment, which he calls a means of exchange, and recognizes it as potentially and often historically distinct from the "scale of reckoning."

[5]Rupert J. Ederer, *The Evolution of Money* (Washington, D.C., 1964), 7–16. J. M. Keynes, *A Treatise on Money*, 2 vols. (London, 1930), 1:3–4, although defining "money itself" as the

essential quality, then money existed before there were any coins and when exchange could still be called barter. Extensive barter brings into use some kind of a unit of reckoning.[6] Occasional exchanges can take place without such a unit, of course, as when a farmer swaps a horse for two cows. But if a number of items are exchanged by barter at the same time, even though no money changes hands as a means of payment, the bargainers generally agree to evaluate all the items being exchanged in some unit—to say, for example, that one cow equals two cowhides, one horse equals four cowhides, and so on, without an actual cowhide ever being involved. They could exchange dozens of different articles, each evaluated in cowhides, concluding with a few minor swaps thrown in to balance their accounts. If they concluded all their bargaining in one afternoon, the result would be the same as it would have been if they had used as their unit of reckoning some purely abstract unit or a symbol, such as a notch in a stick of wood, the worth of each object bartered being measured in notches.

It might be said as a matter of logic that any unit of reckoning thus used in comparing the values of articles being exchanged functions as a standard of value, even if only for a few hours in a single afternoon.[7] But the social importance of the unit of reckoning as a standard of exchange values depends on its being used for a substantial period of time. It could serve a useful function even if it were employed only for several days or weeks, as at a medieval international trade fair. But defining money as a standard of value suggests units of reckoning used continuously over many years. Some definitions of money recognize the importance of time by adding that it is "a medium for deferred payments and a store of value."[8] Just as means of payment have been called more or less money according to how universally they were accepted, so units of account used to compare exchange values might be called more or less money according to the length of the period of time during which the same unit was used.

In analyzing many situations in economic history it is perfectly practical to regard the medium of exchange and the standard of value as one and the same. Commonly used means of payment generally become standards of value. But economic theorists agree that the two are distinct

means of payment, first stated: "Moneys of Account, namely that in which Debts and Prices and General Purchasing Power are expressed, is the primary concept of a Theory of Money." He added: "Money Proper in the full sense of the term can only exist in relation to a Money of Account." Hart, s.v. "money," offered a kind of compromise, saying that the best definition of the noun *money* "seems to be an extremely liquid asset, measured in a standard unit of account and capable with certainty of discharging debts expressed in that unit." It would seem to follow that for anything to be *completely* money, there would have to be complete certainty, a certainty more complete than was common in medieval and early modern times.

[6] Ederer, *The Evolution of Money,* 31–33.
[7] Ibid., 11.
[8] Roy Harrod, *Money* (London, 1969), 3–4.

conceptually,[9] and in some historical situations they can be seen to be distinct.[10] A recent clinching example was provided by the German inflation of 1924. If asked the price of a book, the bookseller looked first at its price marked in dollars or gold marks. But he did not expect payment in dollars or gold marks. He looked next at his bank's latest report of the exchange rate on paper marks, a report received fresh at least once a day (on some days every hour, if personal memory can be trusted). From the two figures, the bookseller calculated how many paper marks he expected his customer to pay. In medieval and early modern times also, the "money" changing hands was in many cases distinct from the "money" in which prices were recorded. Obligations and prices stated in monetary terms were often paid in kind, that is, in grain, chickens, or even labor, not in coin.[11] Many big deals between wholesale merchants were essentially barter, as is clear from bookkeeping records of transactions concluded orally on Venice's Rialto. The payments recorded in ducats were made, the entries specify, in itemized amounts of such commodities as cotton and copper at specified prices. Moreover, the whole history of Venetian money illustrates how complex and changeable were the links between the standards of value and the various coins and other means of payment.[12]

[9]Keynes, *Treatise on Money*, 1:3–4: "Money of account is the *description* or *title* and the money is the *thing* that answers to the description. If the same thing always answered to the same description the distinction would have no practical interest. But if the thing can change whilst the description remains the same, then the distinction can be highly significant." Cf. Harrod, *Money*, 4; Hart, *Money, Debt, and Economic Activity*, 6–10; Robertson, *Money*, 4; and Eucken, *Foundations of Economics*, 159–63.

[10]George N. Halm, *Monetary Theory* (Philadelphia, 1942), 2–3, gives the example of a primitive tribe in which goats are the standard of value and a judge must decide whether a particular goat "is or is not too old and too scraggy to constitute a standard goat. . . ." The example shows, he says, "that the medium of exchange may be strictly speaking, a concrete thing, whereas the unit of account may be an abstract quantity. If, however, the units of the medium of exchange are practically identical (for example units of weight of a precious metal or pieces of paper bearing a certain imprint), there is not much sense in being too particular about this distinction. The unit of the medium of exchange becomes at the same time the unit of account, that is, we calculate in terms of units of the medium which we actually use." Whether the "units of the medium of exchange" were practically identical during the centuries when coin was the chief means of payment is questionable, since coins of the same denomination varied significantly one from another and from the standard set for freshly minted coin.

[11]On the extent of the use of money in exchange see Carlo M. Cipolla, *Money, Prices, and Civilization in the Mediterranean World, Fifth to Seventeenth Century* (Princeton, 1956), somewhat revised as *Moneta e civiltà mediterranea* (Venice, 1957). A pithy survey of the origin of coinage and its development in the West is in Philip Grierson, *Numismatics* (New York and Oxford, 1975), 5–38.

[12]Luca Pacioli, in his famous treatise on double-entry bookkeeping, wrote that payments could be made in nine ways: cash, credit, barter, assignment in bank, and combinations of these (*Summa de arithmetica, geometria, proportioni e proportionalità* [Venice, 1494], fol. 200v, excerpted in Florence Edler, *Glossary of Mediaeval Terms of Business Italian Series, 1200–1600* [Cambridge, Mass., 1936], 33).

## ii. MONEY OF ACCOUNT AND TRIMETALLIC COINAGE

Present-day coins have inscriptions stating their value: one cent, five cents, a quarter dollar, a dollar. Medieval coins generally had no inscriptions stating their value. Their names were derived from the title of the ruler who issued them or from the image they bore: ducats if the ruler was a duke; reali or imperiali if issued in the name of a king or an emperor; crowns, angels, or eagles if distinguished by the prominence of such an image in the design of the coin. When counted out in a payment, the coins were evaluated in denominations that did not appear on the coins: they were valued in pounds, shillings, and pence, or other terms, just as we evaluate nickels and dimes in dollars and cents. They were evaluated in moneys of account whose names differed from those of most of the coins used as the means of payment.

In much of Europe the names of the units of account used in evaluating coins were derived from the monetary system created by Charlemagne. The Carolingian reforms provided for the coinage of only small silver pieces called denarii, of which 240 were struck from the pound weight, the Roman libra. They declared that 12 of these denarii should be equal in value to 1 Roman solidus. Accordingly, 240 denarii = 20 solidi = 1 libra, and these denominations were used to indicate standards of value, although no solidi or libre were then coined.[13] The system was adopted in Saxon England, and it survived in Britain as pounds, shillings, and pence (£, s., and d.) until their meanings were changed by the adoption of the decimal system in 1971.

With the dissolution of the Carolingian Empire, control over coinage passed to local authorities. Feudal lords, communes, and territorial princes minted pennies of various weights, fineness, and insignia. Many different libre came into use in keeping accounts. Each libra was counted as 20 solidi and 240 denarii, but each had a different exchange value. At first that value depended on the amount of silver in the particular denarii (the only coins issued) of which 240 composed the particular libra. Later other coins became important in determining the relative values of the many different libre and solidi (pounds and shillings).

To call pounds and shillings money when there were no coins with that name may be misleading. Anyone who thinks that money is essentially a means of payment may well prefer to call them denominations of account, as was suggested by Abbott Payson Usher.[14] That practice would suffice in describing a simple monetary system in which every denomination of account referred to a coin of the same name or a well-known

[13]Cipolla, *Money, Prices, and Civilization,* 38–41; idem, *Le avventure della lira,* 2d ed., rev. (Bologna, 1975), 13–17; Harry A. Miskimin, "Two Reforms of Charlemagne: Weights and Measures in the Middle Ages," *EcHR,* 2d ser., 20 (1967):35–53.

[14]Usher, *The Early History,* 201.

multiple of that coin. This was the case in medieval England, where *denarius* was the Latin name of the penny coin and *solidus* referred to 12 pennies, *libra* to 240 pennies. But before long, most countries used, at least to some extent, coins whose names were different from those of the denominations of account. Moreover, the monetary denominations used in contracts were recognized in law as having continuity of meaning even though both the name and the content of the coins in common use as payment had changed.

Any denomination used in contracting obligations and keeping accounts might logically be called a money of account in a broad sense. The expression "money of account" is well established in the literature. It will be used here to show that a standard of value is involved. Some historians call money of account only those denominations of account (serving as standards of exchange value) that do not refer to coins in use, although sometimes they have the same names.[15] Carlo Cipolla called moneys of account "ghost moneys" because these denominations of account did not in the main refer to anything visible and tangible. It enabled him to emphasize correctly that "the values attributed to the two 'moneys,' the real coin and the ghost, were not the same."[16] Such ghosts play very active roles in Venetian history.

Three kinds of money were distinguished by Tommaso Zerbi in describing the practice of medieval Milanese bankers and administrators:

1. Any coin actually used in making payments he called "moneta effettiva." Many coins were not identified with any denomination used in accounting. They were commonly designated by the symbol pictured on the coin (e.g., the Visconti serpent) or by the coin's legal value (e.g., the sesino, i.e., sixpence). They were then evaluated in other units.
2. Those coins that in specifiable years and sectors of the economy constituted the basic or link coins of moneys of account he called "moneta numeraria." They were the kinds of coins that parties to a transaction understood would be used in stating a price or in counting out the payment of a debt defined in a money of account. Thus a debt in lire imperiali would be paid in gold florins or ducats in a large wholesale transaction, whereas in a retail sale it would be paid in silver grossi in one period, in sesini in another, in pegioni in yet another. In buying bread, still another moneta numeraria might be understood. Which coin was used depended on which was the link coin of that money of account at a given moment.

[15]Raymond de Roover so used it in his *The Rise and Decline of the Medici Bank, 1397–1494,* Harvard Studies in Business History, 21 (Cambridge, Mass., 1963), 33, and in *The Bruges Money Market around 1400,* Verhandelingen van de Koninklijke Vlaamse Academie voor Wetenschappen, Letteren en Schone Kunsten van Belgie, Klasse der Letteren, 30, no. 63 (Brussels, 1968):39.

[16]Cipolla, *Money, Prices, and Civilization,* 38–39.

3. Denominations of account used to reduce to a common standard of value all the various coins handled constituted moneys of account ("monete di conto") in his view. In given periods and definable kinds of transactions, they corresponded to known coin or coins as defined by common understanding or as actually stated. In Milanese usage, there were three moneys of account: the lira imperiale, which Zerbi describes as "amphibious," since it could be paid in either silver or gold; the fiorino di moneta, which was based on silver and was used in large banking and commercial firms; and the lira terzuola, which was used in household accounts.[17]

In France the livre tournois was used by the kings to reduce to a common standard all the different kinds of moneys used in French provinces. Moneys of account of local usage are called in French mere "systèmes de compte"; only the livre tournois and the livre parisis, also used by the French kings but less extensively, are commonly called "monnaies de compte."[18]

Because of the different meanings that leading historians of money have given to the term "money of account" and equivalent expressions in other languages, it seems worth repeating that in this book the term is applied broadly. Here it includes both denominations of account for which there were corresponding coins and ghost moneys, that is, denominations of account for which there were no corresponding coins. Thus, it includes various ghosts, such as what Zerbi called monete di conto; the systèmes de compte of the French, as well as their monnaies de compte; but also a unit like the Venetian ducat, which, as we shall see, was both a money of account and a moneta numeraria. All these denominations of value used in setting prices, imposing obligations, or making contracts are here considered moneys of account.[19]

As more different kinds of coins came into common use, the need for using moneys of account as common measures in which to state their

[17]*Moneta effettiva e moneta di conto nelle fonti contabili di storia economica* (Milan, 1955), 13–22, 33–37, 75–76, and on the contrast between imperiali coins and imperiali of account, 57–58. See also below, chap. 5, sec. ii.

[18]Philippe Wolff, *Commerce et marchands de Toulouse, vers 1350–vers 1450* (Paris, 1954), 306–11; Etienne Fournial, *Histoire monétaire de l'occident médiéval* (Paris, 1970), chap. 7, "Monnaie et systèmes di compte."

[19]It is used in the broad sense by Peter Spufford, *Monetary Problems and Policies in the Burgundian Netherlands, 1433–1496* (Leiden, 1970), chap. 1, and by Herman van der Wee, "Monetary, Credit, and Banking Systems," in *The Cambridge Economic History of Europe*, vol. 5 (Cambridge, 1977), 290–94 (although his brief general description focuses on northern Europe and ignores the extent to which gold coins such as the florin and ducat were the basic or link coins of separate moneys of account in southern Europe). Choosing the same broad sense for the term, Keynes wrote: "Money of account, namely, that in which debts and prices and general purchasing power are expressed" (*Treatise on Money*, 1:3); cf. above, n. 9.

9

relative value increased. Foreign as well as domestic issues circulated extensively in commercial centers because the political fragmentation accompanying the development of feudalism placed mints operating under practically independent princes, barons, bishops, or cities within relatively few miles of competing mints. Until the fifteenth century it was quite exceptional that an area as large as England should contain only mints that were under the firm control of a single monarch. Especially in the two regions of most intense exchange, northern Italy and the Netherlands, cities as close together as Venice, Padua, and Verona or Bruges, Antwerp, and Calais had different moneys of account and different coins. Under these conditions, efforts to prevent the use of foreign coins as media of exchange were unsuccessful. Each jurisdiction had its own money of account which was used to evaluate various coins for legal purposes, and international merchants used a money of account of their choice to evaluate the many coins and the other foreign moneys of account with which they dealt.

Within many of these independent monetary jurisdictions, the coinage of a single type, the pennies derived from Charlemagne's denarii, had by the fourteenth century been supplemented by coins of greater value. The silver content of the traditional pennies had diminished precipitously almost everywhere after the breakup of the Carolingian Empire. England was exceptional. There the weight (1.5 grams) and the fineness (0.925) of the penny changed little from A.D. 991 to A.D. 1343. Although its weight was diminished gradually during the next two centuries, its fineness was maintained so consistently that *sterling* became a synonym for high quality and reliability.[20] But on the Continent most pennies minted in the twelfth century contained more copper than silver. Whereas Charlemagne's denarii contained about 1.7 grams of fine silver, those minted in Pavia in the 1160s were so debased that they contained only 0.2 grams, and those minted in Verona 0.1 grams.[21]

Because its penny had not been debased, England was relatively late in feeling the need of new and larger types of coins. English groats worth 4 pennies were not issued regularly until after the rise in prices following the Black Death of 1348. They were of sterling fineness and equal in weight and in legal value to 4 pennies. What came to be called a shilling, equal to 12 pennies, was first coined in 1504. The need for larger silver coins was felt much earlier in Italy. Of several efforts to introduce a larger silver coin the most successful was the coinage by the Venetians about 1200 of what was called the "grosso" or, occasionally, the "matapan." Somewhat heavier

[20]John Craig, *The Mint: A History of the London Mint from A.D. 287 to 1948* (Cambridge, 1953), xv, 45–46, 98–100; A. E. Feavearyear, *The Pound Sterling: A History of English Money* (Oxford, 1931), 8, 350.
[21]Cipolla, *Le avventure della lira,* 25–27.

and finer than the English penny (2.178 grams, 0.965 fine), the grosso was immediately and widely used within both Venice and its trading area. Soon there were many other issues of this new type, that is, coins that were more than 90 percent fine silver and worth at least as much as a solidus, that is, 12 pennies, usually more.[22] In this introductory chapter they will be referred to generally as "groats," here used in a generic sense.

In France the many kinds of pennies issued by the great feudal lords were only gradually replaced by royal issues of pennies. In addition, in 1266 Louis IX introduced a large groat weighing 4.22 grams of 0.958 pure silver and valued at 1 sou (solidus) of the livre tournois.[23] It is commonly called the gros tournois.

In the meantime, gold coins were being issued by Byzantine and Moslem mints, and some of them were used in the West, especially in ports such as Venice; and some gold was coined in Sicily, Naples, and Spain. But gold coins were of such high value that their use was restricted, although they became more important in international trade after Genoa and Florence both minted pieces of pure gold in 1252.

These developments gave Europe a trimetallic monetary system in that there were three kinds of coin to be evaluated in money of account: black money, white money, and yellow money. Debased pennies, along with the many issues of half-pennies and even smaller denominations, were called black because they were composed largely of copper and quickly darkened. The alloy from which they were made was usually less than 1/5 silver. White money, in contrast, revealed its high silver content by shining white when rubbed. If it turned red when rubbed, revealing a copper content, it was said to blush for shame. The yellow money minted in western Europe was as nearly pure gold as was technically feasible.

Instead of this threefold division, a twofold division is commonly made, especially in connection with moneys of account in Italy.[24] It distinguishes between moneta piccola and moneta grossa. The former was the money used in local markets and retail trade; the latter was the money used in interregional trade and in large governmental dealings. But the distinction was not always clear-cut, nor were the uses of the two kinds of coin entirely separate. Moreover, although black money was always part of

---

[22]For a broad survey of the coins of many countries see Peter Spufford, "Coinage and Currency," an appendix to vol. 3 of *The Cambridge Economic History of Europe* (Cambridge, 1963), 576–602.

[23]Fournial, *Histoire monétaire,* 86–88; Thomas N. Bisson, "Coinages and Royal Monetary Policy in Languedoc during the Reign of St. Louis," *Speculum* 32 (1957):443 ff.

[24]Cipolla, *Le avventure della lira,* 49–51; idem., *Studi di storia della moneta,* 1, *I movimenti dei cambi in Italia dal secolo XIII al XV* (Pubblicazioni dell'Università di Pavia; Studi nelle Scienze giuridiche e sociali 101, Pavia, 1948), cited hereafter as Cipolla, *I movimenti* in order to identify it among Cipolla's many publications.

the moneta piccola and gold was always part of the moneta grossa, white money was partly one and partly the other; that is, some silver coins circulated only locally, some were issued primarily for international payments, and some served in both capacities, more or less, in varying degrees at various times, as did the Venetian groats (grossi).[25] It is difficult to apply this dichotomy to medieval England and France, where for centuries the official moneys of account were all based on silver coins. Even in Italy, where the distinction is obvious, it is worthwhile to distinguish also the coins and moneys of account based on fine silver from the black money on the one hand and the gold money on the other. Coins more than 9/10 pure silver were important in international exchanges and wholesale trade generally. A threefold distinction is necessary in order to analyze separately (1) the effects of changes in the relative value of gold and silver and (2) the effects of debasement or deterioration of the silver or billon coins.

A list of the coins changing hands in a transaction in Normandy in 1473 is illustrative of the diversity of coins used in large payments in the later Middle Ages. Nine kinds of coins were itemized, including many French gold écus, two English gold nobles, some English groats, many of the various French silver coins of about the same value, some Flemish and German silver, and some silver issued by the duke of Brittany. Each variety was carefully rated in livres tournois, and the total was rounded off to 400 livres by adding 7s. 2d., described only as "white money now current."[26]

In smaller transactions, including wage payments, black, white, and yellow money were all probably used when they were available. Consider, for example, a payday about 1420 at the Venetian arsenal, where a skilled craftsman earned about 20 soldi a day.[27] At the end of a five-day week, when he was owed 100 soldi, he could be paid with 1,200 black pennies, with 25 silver groats, or, since gold ducats were then selling at about 100 soldi, with 1 yellow ducat. A paymaster was extremely unlikely to count out 1,200 pennies to scores of workmen. If he gave each a gold ducat—also unlikely—it was not what the craftsman wanted for buying bread. But an energetic craftsman on piece rates who had earned 165 1/2 soldi in a good week might receive 1 gold ducat, valued at 100 soldi; 16 silver groats, valued at 64 soldi; and 18 billon pennies, valued at 1 1/2 soldi, giving him

[25]The coins received in papal tax collection in Tuscany in 1296 were 42 percent gold, 50 percent good silver, and only 8 percent billon, but the percentage of billon varied from 1.1 percent in Lucca to 38.7 percent in Siena (John Day, "La circulation monétaire en Toscane en 1296," *Annales, ESC,* 23 [1968]:1054–66).

[26]Michel Mollat, *Le commerce maritime normand à la fin du Moyen Age* (Paris, 1950), 381–82. In 1614 a contemporary estimated that there were 400 varieties of coins circulating in the Low Countries and 82 in France (Barry E. Supple, "Currency and Commerce in the Early Seventeenth Century," *EcHR,* 2d ser., 10 [1957]:240n).

[27]Cf. below, chap. 12, sec. iv.

his total of 165 1/2 soldi, which was written in the paymaster's accounts as 8 lire 5 soldi 6 denari di piccoli.

### iii. MEDIEVAL MONETARY DOCTRINES

While our craftsman at the Venetian arsenal would have had to accept his pay by tale, that is, by counting out the different coins, whatever their condition, in large payments it was common practice to weigh coins and value them according to their weight, assuming that their fineness was known. This practice reflected a deeply rooted feeling that the value of a coin was determined by its metallic content. Governments made efforts to have their coins circulate at the values that they chose to give them as legal tender, but the values that they set in money of account were supplemented or contested in the market place by standards of value expressed in units of weight of gold and silver.

This metallistic conception of money is one form of what today is commonly called a commodity theory of money and is contrasted with a state theory of money. According to a nineteenth-century formulation of the state theory, money is whatever the state declares to be money, namely, whatever it declares to be valid for keeping accounts and paying debts, and it is worth whatever the government says it is worth.[28] Emile Bridrey called its medieval equivalent the feudal theory of money. According to this theory, money of account was a measure, comparable to a foot or an ounce. Just as fixing the length of a foot or a yard was a lord's prerogative, so could he fix the value of coins in libre, solidi, and denarii. In this sense, money was in the lord's domain.[29]

In spite of the prevalence of the "feudal" legal conception, the feeling that metallic content determined the "real value" of money was reflected not only in the extensive use of payment by weight rather than by tale but also in the possibility of adjusting prices according to the kind of coin offered in payment. Moreover, the commodity (or metallistic) theory of money was clearly and forcefully formulated by theorists, both churchmen and lawyers. Churchmen, by profession concerned with justice, challenged the right of princes to devalue their coinage just as they wished. In deferred payment of debts and the fulfillment of other obligations, justice depended, they said, on paying the same value as the specie received or originally promised. Lawyers cited texts from Roman law requiring that

[28]Usher, *The Early History*, 194–96; Ederer, *The Evolution of Money*, 22, 100, 136.

[29]*La théorie de la monnaie au XIVe siècle. Nicole Oresme. Etude d'histoire des doctrines et des faits économiques* (Paris, 1906), 112–40. Thomas N. Bisson, *Conservation of Coinage* (Oxford, 1979), 7, prefers the label "proprietary," objecting to "feudal" because rights to income from coinage were not given in fief. See also R. Cazelles, "Quelques réflexions à propos des mutations de la monnaie royale française (1295–1360)," *Le Moyen Age* 72 (1966):83–105.

whoever had borrowed good wine must repay with wine of similar value, not new wine for old, and applied the same principle to debts contracted by exchange of coin: debtors should pay back money of the same "goodness" as that received or contracted for.[30]

The fundamental problem lay in the changes in the value of money that could take place between the date of a contract and its maturity. That forced theorists to analyze devaluation by looking more closely at the nature of money. John Buridan, rector of the University of Paris in the early fourteenth century, applied the Aristotelian distinction between four causes, saying: the material cause of money is a rare material; the efficient cause is the state; the final cause is the needs of men, who exchange goods; the formal cause is the sign of value. (As John T. Noonan writes, "this succinct statement will not be improved by the later scholastics.") Buridan proceeded to say that money is sometimes weak and sometimes strong, thus seeming to recognize that money had a value that could change even apart from official action. At the same time, he held that the prince could alter the value of money only if the community as a whole would benefit.[31] Buridan's more famous disciple, Nicole d'Oresme (d. 1384), also emphasized that the prince's authority over money and his decisions to alter its value should not be exercised for his own gain—even though he held that money was not a commodity to be hoarded or loaned but a sign to serve as a measure of value.[32]

[30]Usher, The Early History, 220.

[31]John T. Noonan, The Scholastic Analysis of Usury (Cambridge, Mass., 1957), 67–68.

[32]Timothy J. Reiss and Roger H. Hinderliter, "Money and Value in the Sixteenth Century: The Monete Cudendo Ratio of Nicholas Copernicus," Journal of the History of Ideas 40 (1979):296–97. Cf. Charles Johnson, ed. and trans., The De moneta of Nicholas Oresme and English Mint Documents (London, 1956), chaps. 1, 4, 5, 10. For a different view of Oresme and a survey of other sources see Marie-Odile Piquet-Marchal, "Doctrines monétaires et conjonctures aux XIVe et XVe siècles," Revue internationale de l'histoire de la banque 4 (1971):327 ff. For other introductions to the very extensive and somewhat controversial literature see Julius Kirshner, "Raymond de Roover on Scholastic Economic Thought," in Raymond de Roover, Business, Banking, and Economic Thought in Late Medieval and Early Modern Europe: Selected Studies of Raymond de Roover, ed. Julius Kirshner, intro. essays by Julius Kirshner and Richard A. Goldthwaite (Chicago, 1974); Jean Favier, "Etat et monnaie," in La moneta nell'economia europea, secoli XIII–XVIII, ed. Vera Barbagli Bagnoli, Papers presented at the seventh "Settimana di Studio" of the Istituto Internazionale di Storia Economica "Francesco Datini," Prato, 1975 (Florence, 1982), 171–84, which, although it lacks notes or bibliography, is rich in ideas about the connections between monetary doctrines and their application at times of recoinage; and Gino Barbieri, "Le dottrine monetarie dal XIII al XVIII secolo (schema di una ricostruzione panoramica)," Economia e storia 22 (1975):319–55, also in Barbagli Bagnoli, ed., La moneta nell'economia europea, 309–49. As regards the case of France see Cazelles, "Quelques réflexions"; and J. P. Cuvillier, "Notes on the Royal Coinage in France from the Fourteenth to the Fifteenth Centuries," JEEcH 8 (1979):117–30. Finally, for Lombardy in the fourteenth and fifteenth centuries see Gigliola Soldi Rondinini, "Politica e teoria monetarie dell'età viscontea," in Barbagli Bagnoli, ed., La moneta nell'economia europea, 351–408, somewhat revised in Nuova rivista storica 59 (1975):288–330.

Such opinions, based on justice and morality, did not directly challenge the prince's power to fix and change the value of the coins he minted, but they could affect the way judges might decide a dispute over the fulfillment of an obligation, such as how a dowry or a legacy had to be paid. Moreover, they set a standard of justice that princes were urged to keep in mind in planning the output of their mints and that was given lip service at least by the magistrates of such city republics as Florence or Venice.

# 2

# SEIGNIORAGE AND INTERNATIONAL FLOWS OF SILVER AND GOLD

## i. SEIGNIORAGE

SINCE MEDIEVAL GOVERNMENTS expected mints to produce revenue, a mint paid out for a given weight of silver or gold bullion somewhat fewer coins than the number made from the bullion. Some writers call the whole difference between what the government paid for the bullion and the value of the coins made from it seigniorage, but that is misleading. The mint's total charge included the costs of making coins as well as a "seigniorage," which was the profit made by the government.[1] Seigniorage was a kind of tax justified on the ground that issuing coinage was one of the rights of government belonging to a territorial lord, a "seigneur." Even medieval Venice, which as a merchants' republic had a tradition of collecting little seigniorage, expected to collect some profits on its coins.

A government's readiness to coin unlimited amounts of a specified metal at fixed rates is sometimes loosely called "free coinage." Free coinage in the literal sense, however—that is, coinage at government expense—began only at the end of the fifteenth century, and then only for a few coins, as when Venice's Council of Ten ordered that suppliers of gold to the mint be paid the whole 67 ducats made from a mark of gold.[2]

---

[1] See below, app. A, n. 1, on the meanings of *seigniorage, brassage,* etc.
[2] See below, chap. 10, sec. iii.

For many medieval rulers, especially the several princes crowded closely together within approximately the area of modern Belgium, their mints became a major source of revenue. The existence of independently directed mints within short distances of each other led to many "wars" fought with coins instead of swords and spears.[3] Each prince tried to coin as much as possible so as to increase his total receipts from seigniorage. Within his own territory he had a legal monopoly of the production of coins, but his ability to act like a monopolist in setting the price of his product, that is, his mint charges, was in fact limited by the competition of the mints of neighboring princes, each of whom was likely to use his legal monopoly of coinage within his own territory as a base for attacking the monopoly of his neighbor.

The competition between mints sometimes took the form of cheaper products, that is, of coins inferior in fineness but similar or even identical in appearance to those of a country into which they were introduced. That kind of competition was considered an act of hostility close to armed conflict. The prince who succeeded in getting his inferior coins accepted in neighboring countries could increase the flow of precious metal to his mint.

Another way in which a prince might induce bullion to flow to his mint rather than to that of a neighbor was to offer a higher price for the metal. A higher mint price might be offered either directly or by lowering a minting fee expressed as a percentage of the coins minted. Such a lowering of the amount charged for the service of turning bullion into coin required a reduction in the rate of seigniorage. It might increase the amount of bullion attracted by the mint sufficiently that the total revenue obtained by a prince or city-state from its mint was increased.

## ii. EXPORTS AND IMPORTS OF BULLION AND COIN

When a prince's territory contained mines, he could of course order coined in his mints all the silver and gold produced, but his powers of policing did not always enable him to cope with the lure of higher mint

---

[3]Some examples involving Flanders and Brabant are analyzed in Henri Laurent, *La loi de Gresham au Moyen Age: Essai sur la circulation monétaire entre la Flandre et le Brabant à la fin du XIVe siècle* (Brussels, 1933); John H. Munro, *Wool, Cloth, and Gold: The Struggle for Bullion in Anglo-Burgundian Trade, 1340–1478* (Toronto, 1972); and Spufford, *Monetary Problems and Policies*, 75, where the author comments, "Coinage in a medieval state could not be a placid affair, but was a perpetual struggle with neighbors, mitigated only by occasional monetary conventions. To this struggle the rather grandiose name of "Guerre Monétaire" has been applied. The term is perhaps too strong, for political enmity is not necessarily implied; the struggle for bullion was as likely to occur between political allies as between political enemies." The concept was developed by Albert Girard, "Un phénomène économique: La guerre monétaire (XIVe–XVe siècles)," *Annales d'histoire sociale* 2 (1940):207–18. He included competition in attracting gold by coining with higher gold-silver ratios.

prices elsewhere. Even the ruler of a kingdom rich in the minerals had to moderate his claims for seigniorage to take account of the better prices his subjects might get for bullion by smuggling it to another country. Miners and powerful landlords in a producing area had an interest in marketing at the best possible price. The sovereign might be more interested in the expansion of minting than in the expansion of mining, but both he and the mines' workers and owners had reason to favor the export of gold and silver to a wide market.

The centers of consumption, such as England, Flanders, and France, saw things differently. Veins of gold and silver west of Germany had been practically exhausted by the fourteenth century. Metal for the mints of those countries came either from recoinage or from the importation of bullion or coin. Although each country welcomed imports of bullion, almost all forbade the export of uncoined silver or gold and in general also of good coin, so that the international flow of the precious metals had to penetrate many customs barriers, at each of which existed the risk of confiscation.

The restrictions varied from country to country, with England and Venice presenting contrasting extremes. England forbade the use of foreign silver coins; Venice permitted many to circulate so long as they were up to the standard of the country minting them. Indeed, like most Continental countries, Venice could not exclude foreign coins or compel their prompt presentation to the mint for recoinage as successfully as could seagirt England. After 1299, England forbade the export of silver either uncoined or coined. Although exceptions were made for some years and by licenses for some purposes and persons, the historian of the pound sterling summarized the emphasis of English policy by writing: "For a long period death was the penalty for those found exporting good English money."[4] Venice, in contrast, sought profit as an international intermediary and thus permitted supply and demand to govern its bullion market. It even encouraged the export of silver bullion as well as of good gold and silver coin.[5] The policies of most countries were intermediate between English bullionism and Venetian permissiveness but were closer to the former.

---

[4]Feavearyear, *The Pound Sterling*, 3–4. Cf. Craig, *The Mint*, 55; and John H. Munro, "Bullionism and the Bill of Exchange in England, 1272–1663: A Study in Monetary Management and Popular Prejudice," in *DMB*, 173–74. Edward Ames, in "The Sterling Crisis of 1337–1339," *JEcH* 25 (1965):496–522, tabulates licenses and regulations and shows ingenuity in compiling figures indicating periods of relatively active exports, although his general analysis is flawed by his not recognizing the gold basis of the Florentine lira a fiorini, on which see below, chap. 4, n. 9, and chap. 13, sec. iii. For the general problems of the period see Michael Prestwich, *The Three Edwards: War and State in England, 1272–1377* (London, 1980).

[5]See below, chap. 9, sec. iii, and on foreign coins in Venice, chap. 13, sec. i.

As a practical matter the prohibitions on the international flow of precious metal were of limited effectiveness. From the centers of production in eastern Europe silver found its way to England, on the western edge of the European commercial network. Large quantities of foreign coins were acquired by the London mint for recoinage so as to increase the English currency.[6] In spite of legal barriers, shipment of precious metal was an essential element in medieval international commerce.

In that trading system as a whole, the bullion flows were only occasionally dominated by the efforts of princes to increase their revenues through manipulation of mint prices and the fineness of their coins. Short-term movements of specie were occasioned by the need for coins as ready cash for military outlays or, especially at Venice, for the preparation of seasonal commercial voyages. In the long run, precious metal was attracted to mints in countries that regularly offered for sale commodities in demand elsewhere, as were the tin, wool, and cloth of England, or in countries that after years of good harvest had surplus grain for export. The silver obtained by the export of English wool is an especially well-documented example. The scale of such international flows of precious metals can be indicated by a few figures from England and Venice in years of peak coinage. For a half-dozen years at the beginning of the fourteenth century, the English mint coined into English pennies over 40,000 kg a year of foreign coin.[7] For 1423 the yearly product of the Venetian mint was re-

---

[6]C. G. Crump and C. Johnson, "Tables of Bullion Coined under Edward I, II, and III," *Numismatic Chronicle,* 4th ser., 13 (1913):200–245, as summarized in Harry A. Miskimin, "Monetary Movements and Market Structure—Forces for Contraction in Fourteenth and Fifteenth Century England," *JEcH* 24 (1964):477. Crump and Johnson indicate (p. 202) that foreign silver was distinguished by a different mint charge. It was identified as coming from Bruges, Ghent, and Brussels or was simply called "Baudekin" silver.

[7]Terence H. Lloyd, "Overseas Trade and the English Money Supply in the Fourteenth Century," in *Edwardian Monetary Affairs (1279–1344),* ed. Nicholas J. Mayhew, British Archaeological Reports, 36 (Oxford, 1977), 96–124. Lloyd's table 1 gives the annual output for the years 1303–9 as 105,730 pounds (47,896 kg), of which 99 percent was from foreign coin. Reservations concerning Lloyd's estimates, as presented here and in his *The English Wool Trade in the Middle Ages* (Cambridge, 1977), were expressed by John Munro in "Bullionism," 178 n. 22; in "Mint Policies, Ratios, and Outputs in the Low Countries and England, 1335–1420: Some Reflections on New Data," *Numismatic Chronicle* 141 (1981):71–116; and most recently with improved tables of coinage in England and the Low Countries in his "Bullion Flows and Monetary Contraction," in *Precious Metals in the Later Medieval and Early Modern Worlds,* ed. John F. Richards (Durham, N.C., 1983) (for more on the volume edited by Richards see below, chap. 9, n. 1). There is no doubt, however, that large amounts of silver were imported to England, obviously more in some years, less in others. Mavis Mate, in "High Prices in Early Fourteenth Century England: Causes and Consequences," *EcHR,* 2d ser., 28 (1975):4, reports that an Italian who had been master of French mints for twenty years estimated that during that time nearly 100 tons of silver had been exported from France. Cf. Harry Miskimin's view, as cited below in chap. 4, n. 9.

ported to be about 4,000 kg of gold ducats and about 10,000 kg of silver coin made from imports.[8] Although the estimates involve a large margin of error, they leave no doubt that when the balance of trade was favorable, gold or silver was imported. An international flow of bullion or coin was essential in creating a balance of payments when the balance of trade was distinctly favorable or unfavorable.

The balance of trade itself depended on the exchange not only of commodities but also of services. In applying to medieval and early modern Europe the dictum that to obtain precious metals a country without mines had to export more goods and services than it imported, it is necessary to stretch the meaning of "services." It has to be stretched to cover more than the shipping and financial operations that economists now usually include as supplements to the merchandise trade balance. In medieval and early modern times, "services" included military activities that were hardly distinguishable from plunder or piracy, like that by which the admirals of a heroic naval tradition added to the money supply of Elizabethan England![9] Important also in balances of payments were the ransoms that kings or lesser warriors who had been captured in battle had to pay for the "service" of being released, as well as the tolls or gifts that international traders paid in many forms for protection (or for the benefits of not being plundered) and for advantages that princes gave some merchants over competitors. Between the badly policed and intermittently warring feudal states the most obvious flows of specie arose from the use or restraint of force in ways that we can call "services" only ironically and in order to emphasize the importance of military events in connection with changes in the flows of specie.[10]

Even more important in many regions during the later Middle Ages were the international payments made for the "services" of the popes. The religious services rendered by the Church all over Europe were of course paid for locally. The transfer of a part of that income from local churches to the papal court became an important part of the international flow of specie.[11] Some of the money that the popes drew to Rome or Avignon was used for the political purposes of particular pontiffs, for the pope was

[8]According to a senatorial decree of 1419, the normal imports of silver amounted to 40,000 marks. On its agreement with the figures included in the oration of Doge Mocenigo, see below, app. B, sec. iii.

[9]Keynes wrote, "The boom period in England definitely began with the return of Drake's first important expedition" (*Treatise on Money*, 2:156n).

[10]See Frederic C. Lane, "Economic Consequences of Organized Violence" and related essays reprinted in his *Profits from Power: Readings in Protection Rent and Violence-Controlling Enterprises* (Albany, 1979).

[11]Yves Renouard, *Les relations des papes d'Avignon et des companies commerciales et bancaires de 1316 à 1378*, Bibliothèque des Ecoles Françaises d'Athènes et de Rome, 151 (Paris, 1941), 32–39; William E. Lunt, *Papal Revenues in the Middle Ages*, 2 vols. (New York, 1934), 34–56.

a temporal ruler, but as a whole it was claimed as payment for the very extensive administrative and doctrinal functions performed by the pope as the head of the Church and for his broad cultural functions within western Christendom.

If the three kinds of services mentioned above—the ecclesiastical, the military, and those that we think of as economic services in the ordinary sense—together with the relation between the value of the commodities exported and the commodities imported, left the country with a surplus, then its balance of trade was "favorable." It was owed additional payments in the form of gold or silver in order to complete the balance of payments.

## iii. EFFECTS OF MINT CHARGES

Whether in a particular historical case international payments were immediately balanced by a shipment of precious metals into the country with a favorable balance of trade depended on many factors, one being the level of the mint charges in the countries having a favorable balance. By asking too high a seigniorage, a prince might discourage the import of gold or silver and encourage instead other forms of importation. A low seigniorage and a favorable trade balance was the combination most likely to attract precious metal into the country.

The interactions between the seigniorage, the flows of precious metals, and the flows of other commodities can be illustrated by imagining an Italian who acquired silver in Germany and was deciding to which of two countries, say, France or England, he should ship his bullion. If the seigniorage in England and France were such as to make the mint charge in England 10 percent and in France 2 percent or even 9 percent, a reason for shipping to France seems obvious. But in reality, even if silver supplied the only significant currency in both countries, as was the case for many centuries, there were other considerations to be weighed. He had to think of what he could do with the coin he received for his bullion. The best way to get the funds back to his own country would be to use the coins to buy something he could import into Italy at a profit, let us say wool. His choice of where to send his bullion would be determined partly by where wool or some other desired commodity could be bought most cheaply. To be sure, if the difference between the seigniorage in France and England was as much as 8 percent, he might calculate that it would pay to send the bullion for coinage at the cheaper rate and then export the coins to the country where wool was cheapest. He might compare (*a*) the differences in mint charges with (*b*) the differences in the price of wool and (*c*) the costs of transporting bullion or coin, including smuggling charges. After bills of exchange came into use in the fourteenth century, he could use the exchange rates quoted in bills of exchange in calculating which was the better market. Those rates would be used in figuring out the specie points, namely, the mint prices that in the light of shipping costs would make shipments of specie profitable.

Mint charges and mint prices (which reflected the mint charges) represented only one among several sets of prices determining the flow of coin or bullion, as of other commodities, but they were one factor. Charging low seigniorage was one way in which a ruler of a country with a favorable balance of trade could encourage the importation of gold and silver.

In contrast, if a country had an unfavorable balance of trade, even the low mint charge made possible by low seigniorage would not attract precious metal. Its merchants would not be importing specie but instead would be picking out for export the heaviest of the coins in circulation. In that situation a high seigniorage was more helpful. It made culling coins for export less profitable and helped keep within the country its stock of specie.

High seigniorage discouraged export of coins because it increased the difference between their exchange value and that of the metal they contained. In general, coins were worth more than bullion for the same reason that gold or silver jewelry cost more than bullion of the same weight and fineness: the coins incorporated more labor. On the other hand, the size of the spread between the value of coins and that of bullion depended also on the demand for coin. For export and perhaps for hoarding, bullion might seem better, but coins were preferred in making most payments in the country in which they were legal tender. Some coins, such as gold crowns, were useful as royal gifts; others, such as small bits of black money, for other purposes, such as paying for being ferried across Venice's Grand Canal. So different coins can be said to have had different demand schedules, but the exchange value was always above the metallic value.

A high seigniorage added to the spread between the price a mint paid for bullion and the legal value of the coin made from the bullion. A merchant culling coins for export had to calculate their value as bullion. In fact, when he sold overseas, the foreign mint or moneychangers would ignore legal values and treat the coin as bullion. A small difference between the price offered for bullion abroad and that offered at the mint of his own country would not be an incentive to export. If the export was to be profitable, the price at the foreign mint or on the international bullion market had to be sufficiently above the domestic mint price to cover the whole mint charge, seigniorage included, as well as the costs and risks of transport and smuggling.[12] Consequently, the higher the seigniorage, the greater had to be the contrast in bullion prices at the two mints before specie would flow from the one country to the other.

[12]Munro, "Bullionism," 174.

Thus a high seigniorage had different effects according to circumstances. For a country with a favorable balance of trade, or with its trade nearly in balance, a low seigniorage encouraged the import of gold or silver. For a country with an unfavorable balance of trade, a high seigniorage increased the amount by which the international market price for bullion had to rise above the domestic mint price before culling coins for export became profitable.

In any case, a high seigniorage increased the chances of counterfeiting and also of invasion by foreign coins manufactured more cheaply by a foreign mint, perhaps coins inferior in fineness to those of which they were imitations, perhaps coins being minted somewhat more cheaply because they were minted in a country where lower seigniorage permitted a lower mint charge.

The deleterious effects of a monetary war were most severely felt in a country suffering from a trade balance so unfavorable that its best coins were being culled for export. The lack of good currency then made it easy to introduce counterfeits and inferior foreign issues. While complaints about the scarcity of good coins multiplied, exporting merchants were blamed for not bringing back bullion and were accused of importing useless luxuries instead. Rulers were under pressure to do something to improve the coinage.

# 3

# RECOINAGE: REVALUATIONS AND DEVALUATIONS

### i. REASONS FOR RECOINAGE

OMPLAINTS ABOUT SHORTAGES of coins were so common as to create the impression of a general insufficiency, not merely of local shortages caused by the flows of specie now from this country, now from that, in response to a change in the balance of trade or in mint policy. Many historians assert that medieval Europe as a whole suffered chronically from a scarcity of precious metals. But scarcity was always relative. What is relevant are the changes both in the quantities available and in the need for using coins as means of payment. In general, it may be said that before the large importations following the discovery of America, Europe's demand for coins increased faster than its supply of metals from which to mint them.

Indeed, during some centuries, especially in the early Middle Ages, the amount of precious metal available probably decreased. Wear and tear, clipping of the coins in circulation, and losses by shipwreck, by unrecovered hoarding, or by other misadventure gradually reduced an existing supply unless or until mines and imports provided replacements.[1] While a

---

[1]Philip Grierson, in his chapter "Numismatics" in *Medieval Studies,* ed. James A. Powell (Syracuse, 1976), 125, estimates the loss of weight by wear as about 0.2 percent a year for a coin in active circulation, while allowing that it could be half or twice as much. Grierson rejected as "unproven and indeed altogether improbable" (p. 132) the contention of C. C. Patterson in "Silver Stocks and Losses in Ancient and Medieval Times," *EcHR,* 2d ser., 25

region was exporting more precious metal than it imported, and quickening commerce demanded more coin, the amount of specie in the region became less adequate.

During the dissolution of the Carolingian Empire, inadequate supply in that sense was a main cause of the decline in the amount of silver in the coins in use on the Continent. The above-mentioned debasement of imperial pennies by Italian mints from the ninth century to the twelfth has usually been attributed to the greed and competition of local lords, but it probably was in the public interest, because it met a growing need for coin that arose from the increased use of markets and the general expansion of trade.[2] Until new silver mines were discovered or exports expanded enough to attract specie, increasing the number of coins depended on diminishing their silver content. Even if the governments did not reason that way, they may have been responding to the need for an increase in the circulating medium.

Greed, or the necessity of having money in order to stay in power, had certainly been one factor in that debasement, and it appears clearly in the continuation through later centuries of the decline in the metallic equivalents of most moneys of account. Even when they were not driven to debasement by monetary wars against rival mints, princes yielded to the temptation to issue inferior coins to pay armies or other creditors with whom they had previously contracted in terms of coins of higher weight and fineness. One way to obtain the metal was to order a general re-

---

(1972):207–8, 220, that irrecoverable loss of silver from all causes was in the Roman Empire about 2 percent a year, so that "stocks unsupported by mine production would vanish in about a century after production ceased, for the half-life would be thirty five years." Earlier, Grierson had suggested that it was normal for a type of coin to remain in circulation for a century after coinage of that type had ceased, provided its value as legal tender was higher than its commercial (i.e., metallic) value ("Problemi monetari dell'Alto Medioevo," *Bollettino della Società Pavese di Storia Patria* 54 [1954]:74–75). For early medieval Europe and the Caliphate, Patterson estimated at about 1 percent the "Silver Loss Constant." Peter Spufford, *Monetary Problems and Policies,* 11, estimates the deterioration through normal wear and tear as 1 percent a year. John Craig, *The Mint,* xvi, 26–27, 60, estimated that the average loss by wear and tear in fifty years was 10 percent of the bulk, enough to obliterate the design, and that in the fourteenth century the loss after thirty years would be 10–20 percent. Nicholas J. Mayhew, "Numismatic Evidence and Falling Prices in the Fourteenth Century." *EcHR,* 2d ser., 27 (1974):1–15, adds some evidence to make Patterson's conclusion seem credible but focuses his evidence on "wastage," in which he includes "silver taken in and out of England" (p. 4). Although this conception of "wastage" is pertinent to his concern with falling prices, it raises quite different problems. For wear alone he accepts the figure of 2 percent to 2.75 percent per decade, close to Grierson's. Cf. Munro, "Bullionism," 178–79. The extreme contrasts among these estimates arises from ambiguity as to whether the estimate of the deterioration of the currency includes only the results on coin of abrasive handling or also clipping and sweating and the whole process of culling for hoarding or export.
[2]Carlo M. Cipolla, "Currency Depreciation in Medieval Europe," *EcHR,* 2d ser., 4 (1963):413–22.

coinage. The ruler declared that after a stated date all previously issued coins would no longer be legal tender and ordered them all brought to the mint. He paid for them by issuing new pennies or groats which contained less precious metal than the old but which were given the same legal value in the money of account. When rulers debased their coins in this way while keeping a traditional design and weight in order to deceive, they put themselves in the same class with counterfeiters, as churchmen sometimes told them. Indeed they were also denounced as counterfeiters for less deceitful devaluations.[3]

Circumstances quite independent of any prince's strivings for more revenue also induced devaluations. The more intensely coins were used, the more difficult it became for a government, even when guided by concern for justice and the general welfare, to avoid gradual devaluation. A persistent factor throughout the Middle Ages and in early modern times was the inaccurate technique used in minting and the resulting physical condition of the coins in circulation. Until the rolling mill and the balance press began to be used, the coins were not uniform in weight as they came from the mint. They were made from blanks, of which a specified number were cut from a specified weight of gold or silver. The blanks were made approximately circular and were then struck by iron or steel dies. This technique of coinage resulted in significant differences among even freshly minted coins. Some of the coins in circulation were sure to be of less weight than others. Also, it was difficult to tell whether a coin had been clipped or sweated (that is, whether particles had been removed from it by shaking it in a bag with other coins). Filing or cutting off of the edges of coins was not easily detected until milling of the edges was introduced in the sixteenth and seventeenth centuries.

Merely from use, the silver and billon coins that passed frequently from hand to hand lost weight. Once somewhat inferior coins were accepted, it was difficult to decide where to draw the line. That was one reason why large payments were made by weighing coins, not by tale, that is, not by counting coins.

When even new coins of the same design and denomination differed one from the other in weight, the better coins were likely to be taken out of circulation. Those who received them put the full-weight pennies or shillings aside, perhaps to be saved for spending later, while the poorer pennies or shillings were spent as quickly as possible. The bankers and goldsmiths, or whoever acted as moneychangers, were experts at culling, that is, at picking out the best coins in each new batch they received from

[3]As was Philip IV of France, somewhat unjustly according to Armand Grunzweig, "Les incidences internationales des mutations monétaires de Philippe le Bel," *Le Moyen Age* 59 (1953):125–31; and Jean Favier, *Philippe le Bel* (Paris, 1979), 148–49.

the mint and leaving only lighter specimens in common circulation. Coins so worn or clipped that their inferiority was evident were accepted in payment because merchants eager to sell might find no buyers unless they would accept them. Employers had nothing else to give workmen when payday came around. Even tax collectors sometimes had to take them or nothing. The town clerk of Rouen reported in 1467 or 1468 that he had been obliged to accept coins at higher than their legal rates because otherwise he would not have been paid by the townsmen.[4] Under these conditions, and without any clear line dividing full-weight and light-weight coins, there was a persistent tendency towards deterioration of the coinage actually in use.

This tendency led to two evils generally deplored. First, deterioration enabled some men to profit by taking advantage of others. An ignorant workman or a farmer from the back country suffered in the situation described by Thomas Babington Macaulay in famous pages from his *History of England*. He was speaking of the late seventeenth century, but similar situations occurred in earlier centuries and in many countries:

> Fresh wagon loads of choice money still came forth from the mint . . . and . . . vanished as fast as they appeared. Great masses were melted down; great masses exported; great masses hoarded: but scarcely one new piece was to be found in the till of a shop, or in the leathern bag which the farmer carried home from the cattle fair. . . . It was a mere chance whether what was called a shilling was really a tenpence, a sixpence, or a groat. . . . The evil was felt daily in almost every place and almost every class, in the dairy and on the threshing floor, by the anvil and by the loom, on the billows of the ocean and in the depth of the mine. Over every counter there was wrangling from morning to night. The workman and his employer had a quarrel as regularly as the Saturday came round. On a fair day or a market day the clamors, the reproaches, the taunts, the curses, were incessant; and it was well if no booth was overturned and no head broken. No merchant would contract to deliver goods without making some stipulation about the quality of the coin in which he was to be paid. . . . Where artisans of more than usual intelligence were collected together in great numbers, as in the dockyard at Chatham, they were able to make their complaints heard and to obtain some redress. But the

[4]Mollat, *Le commerce maritime normand*, 381.

ignorant and the helpless peasant was cruelly ground
between one class which would give money only by tale and
another that would take it only by weight.[5]

Also generally deplored as an evil consequence of the deterioration
of the coins in circulation was the resulting devaluation of the money of
account. Prices and debts were of course fixed in moneys of account, and
when the sellers or creditors were forced to accept inferior coins at the
values legally assigned to full-weight freshly minted coins, they were acknowledging by their actions that the money of account was really of less
value, in metal, than the laws stipulated. Moreover the effects of deterioration of coins in circulation, if they were not checked by recoinage, were
cumulative. In the situation described by Macaulay, wear and tear, sweating and clipping, and hoarding and culling for export were estimated by
contemporary experts to have reduced the silver content of the coin in
circulation by at least 10 percent, perhaps by 50 percent, below mint
standard.[6]

Deterioration was most likely to occur when a country had to export
specie for any reason, such as paying the cost of a war or importing grain
after a bad harvest. Under those conditions the best pieces were not merely
hoarded as reserves in treasure chests; they left the country altogether.

Scarcity of coin was more generally felt when the metal exported
was silver. Since silver was coined into smaller denominations than was
gold, it was employed in a wider range of transactions. Gold was used
more for storing away wealth and had a lower velocity of circulation.
When an unfavorable balance of trade or some political payments caused
the silver coins to be culled out and melted down for export, there was
both a very real and a very apparent reduction in the circulating medium.[7]
Evident also was increased use of counterfeits, inferior foreign coins, and
clipped specimens—abuses that served to ease somewhat the deflationary
impact.

## ii. ALTERNATIVES IN RECOINAGE AND GRESHAM'S LAW

Once the coins in circulation had deteriorated, how could a government remedy the situation? In minting new coins it had to make a choice
among difficult alternatives.

Should it mint at the old standard or at a lowered standard? If the

---

[5]*The History of England from the Accession of James II*, 5 vols. (Boston, 1856–61), 4:495–502.

[6]J. Keith Horsefield, *British Monetary Experiments, 1650–1710* (Cambridge, Mass., 1960), 26,
says that the average weight of silver coin had fallen about 50 percent. Cf. Feavearyear, *The
Pound Sterling*, chap. 6.

[7]Supple, "Currency and Commerce," 244.

new coins were of the old standard, the operation was called a restoration of the currency. But if there were a great many debased, underweight coins in circulation and they were permitted to continue to circulate at face value, a new issue with the same legal value in money of account as the older issue would be culled for hoarding or export. Experience with that effect led to the formulation of the law mistakenly attributed to Sir Thomas Gresham: "Bad money drives out the good."[8] (Gresham was well aware of the "law," but he was far from the first to understand it.)

Gresham's law would not operate if the old issues could be removed from circulation. That could be done by ordering all the old issue, or all depreciated coins, turned in for reminting. Obedience could be induced by paying for them their full face value, just as governments nowadays accept old, worn-out bank notes in exchange for new ones. But to give out good coins for a lot of debased, underweight coins could prove expensive. Venice did it to some extent on some occasions, as we will see, but the practice did not often appeal to governments that expected coinage to be a source of revenue.

Governments generally preferred to declare the old issues to be no longer of any value as legal tender and to treat them as bullion when they were turned in to the mints, paying for them according to the weight and fineness of the individual coins. Demonetizing old issues in this way was not always effective in putting them out of circulation, but insofar as it was, it placed the cost of restoring the currency on those who held the deteriorated coins. The more bad money there was in circulation, the more unpopular was such a measure. This method was successfully used in England for the seven recoinages undertaken between 1100 and 1300.[9] But in the earlier of those centuries, England was much less urbanized than northern Italy and did not need large quantities of coin, nor was it wearing coins down by hard usage to the same extent. The lack of public protest suggests that relatively few people then held depreciated English coin, for when they hoarded, they hoarded the better specimens. In contrast, at the

---

[8]Raymond de Roover, *Gresham on Foreign Exchange: An Essay on Early English Mercantilism with the Text of Sir Thomas Gresham's Memorandum for the Understanding of the Exchange* (Cambridge, Mass., 1949), 91–93; Marc Bloch, *Esquisse d'une histoire monétaire de l'Europe*, Cahiers des *Annales*, 9 (Paris, 1954), 62. These lecture notes of Bloch's, edited posthumously by Lucien Febvre and Fernand Braudel, have recently been published in Italian, with a preface by Ugo Tucci: Marc Bloch, *Lineamenti di una storia monetaria d'Europa* (Turin, 1981). It should be noted that several passages in these lectures are identical with passages in Marc Bloch's "Mutations monétaires dans l'ancienne France," also published posthumously, in *Annales, ESC,* 7 (1953):145–58 and 433–56 (e.g., *Esquisse,* 73–74, and "Mutations monétaires," 450–51).

[9]Craig, *The Mint,* xvi, 26–35, 38; Feavearyear, *The Pound Sterling,* 9–13. Michael Prestwich, "Edward I's Monetary Policies and Their Consequences," *EcHR,* 2d ser., 22 (1969):406–7, 413–14, emphasizes the amount of foreign coins among those reminted.

recoinage of 1696, of which Macaulay wrote, when the old silver coins were demonetized there were loud protests.[10] And in busy commercial centers such as Venice it was difficult to enforce prohibitions against the circulation of coins even after the particular type had been demonetized.

There were two other ways of avoiding the unwanted operation of Gresham's law. The government could let the old, deteriorated coins circulate but declare that these issues would henceforth have less value in the money of account than previously. This was called "crying down" the currency. At the same time coins of an entirely new type might be issued, or there might be a new minting of coins of the old standard. Suppose groats had traditionally been worth 10 denarii. If new groats were also declared worth the traditional 10 denarii, old groats might be declared worth only 8 denarii. Then anyone who had saved 24 of the old groats thinking that the 24, being worth 240 denarii, would enable him to pay off a debt of 1 libra, or to buy an article customarily priced at 1 libra, would be told that the coin he had saved would no longer suffice for the debt or the purchase. He would feel cheated by the government. Lowering the value of the coins in circulation was also intensely unpopular. It was probably most detested by those who had reason to fear that they would continue to be paid in the coin that had been cried down while they were required to pay debts, prices, and dues in "restored" coin.[11]

The least unpopular alternative was to issue new coins that contained less fine metal than the previous issue of that denomination. If the coins in circulation had so depreciated by culling, wear and tear, and clipping as to average only 90 percent of their original weight, then minting the new issue with only 90 percent as much fine silver as the previous issue would enable the new coins to circulate on a basis of equality with the old. This is the alternative that we will find was used by Venice in the century 1350–

[10]Horsefield, *British Monetary Experiments*, gives fully and sympathetically the arguments against the method used.

[11]Joseph R. Strayer, *The Reign of Philip the Fair* (Princeton, 1980), 395–96; Cazelles, "Quelques réflexions," 256–62. Edmund Fryde recounts the riots unleashed in fourteenth-century Paris by brusque attempts to return to "good currency." Riots took place in 1306, for example, when a *renforcement* contained the provision that landlords could exact in reinforced currency "the same inflated rents as had been current during the period of monetary depreciation" ("The Financial Policies of the Royal Governments and Popular Resistance to Them in France and England, c. 1290–c. 1420," *Revue belge de philologie et d'histoire* 57 [1979]:836, reprinted in Edmund B. Fryde, *Studies in Medieval Trade and Finance* [London, 1983]). Aldo De Maddalena suggests that while debasements were favored by debtors generally and revaluations indeed drew violent reactions from the lower and indebted urban classes, the rural poor—who he says had a different concept of good and bad money—reacted mildly or not at all to revaluations ("Uomini e monete preindustriali: Personaggi in cerca d'autore," in Barbagli Bagnoli, ed., *La moneta nell'economia europea*, 506–7; see also Bloch, *Esquisse*, 72–73).

1450.[12] This alternative steadily lowered the legal equivalent in fine silver of the money of account. Or one might say that it merely registered devaluations that had already taken place in fact through the deterioration of the previous issues by wear and tear, clipping, faulty minting, and culling.

Governments became interested in recoinage especially when foreign silver or billon coins began circulating extensively. Even if they were not inferior imitations minted by a rival prince or city-state as instruments of attack in a monetary war, foreign coins were generally considered objectionable. Counterfeits among them were harder to identify and their silver content less well known. Merely passing a law against the circulation of foreign coins was less effective than providing coins to take their place. If the foreign coins were being used to pay debts and prices fixed in the local money of account even if they contained only 90 percent as much fine metal as similar domestic issues, then a government might issue new coins containing somewhat less fine metal than both the older local issues of the same denomination and the foreign coins that were being used in their stead. The new issue could then function as "bad money" and drive out the foreign coins.

This possibility calls attention to an ambiguity in the meaning of the adjectives *good* and *bad* as they are used in Gresham's law. In the case just imagined, the foreign coins would be "good" in the sense that they would contain more precious metal than the new coins issued at less than the old standard. The new coins would be the "bad" by that standard. But in the eyes of legislators, the money they wanted to drive out, and in many cases did drive out by issuing new coins containing less fine metal, was "bad" because it was foreign and because it included many pieces clipped and worn in varying degree and counterfeit products difficult to distinguish from good coin, so that the type as a whole was unreliable, allowing many chances to swindle the unwary. Yet, by crying down the value of the whole foreign issue or forbidding its circulation altogether, the government made it "good money" in the sense that its value as legal tender became less than the value of its metallic content. The new issue was "good" in the sense that it was a product of the domestic mint, as near to standard weight and fineness as the technique and administrative efficiency permitted, and that it had not as yet been clipped, worn, or copied by counterfeiters. But it was "bad" in the sense that must be given that word in Gresham's law, if the law is to be valid, for compared with its legal value, it contained less precious metal than the coin it was intended to replace.

Governments generally preferred a recoinage that lowered the metal-

---

[12]On actual rates of deterioration and devaluation in Venice and the complications involved see below, chap. 18, sec. i.

lic content of commonly used coin. Such a recoinage was less expensive than redeeming the old coin at its legal value. It did not damage the government's prestige as much as a lowering of the official value that the government had previously bestowed on its coin would have done, and it aroused less opposition. Many new issues of less weight merely confirmed a diminution through wear, clipping, and culling of the coins already in use and therefore of the metallic equivalent, practically speaking, of the money of account. But it made official a lowering of the metallic content of the standard of value and was in a sense inflationary.

The inflationary effect undoubtedly benefited the government financially in one way: it made easier servicing and paying off the long-term government debt, which in the case of Venice was substantial. But whether a devaluation was followed by depreciation in the purchasing power of the monetary units depended on many factors, of which changes in the metallic equivalents of moneys of account was only one.

"Without a study of prices, monetary history is never completely understandable," wrote Marc Bloch.[13] Available archival sources have not been found, however, to provide the basis for creating price series for medieval and Renaissance Venice. In this respect, as in many, many others, Venetian economic and social history stands in sharp contrast to that of Florence, where public and private archives have provided new and extensive data recently compiled by Richard Goldthwaite, Charles M. de la Roncière, and Giuliano Pinto.[14] In fact, no student of Venice has so far succeeded in producing a study of prices, much less of wages, for the centuries preceding 1550. Even for the later centuries of the republic's history, scholars have been forced to turn to Chioggia and Udine as the market places nearest to the capital city with extant documentation exploitable for series that might show movements parallel to those in Venice. An ambitious study of data from those towns—a study not yet fully published—was undertaken under the direction of Fernand Braudel by Ruggiero Romano, Frank Spooner, and Ugo Tucci. Only one preliminary article and two overviews based on that research have appeared.[15]

[13]*Esquisse,* 92.

[14]Richard A. Goldthwaite, *The Building of Renaissance Florence: An Economic and Social History* (Baltimore, 1980); Charles M. de la Roncière, "Florence: Centre économique regional au XIVe siécle," thesis in 6 vols. (Aix-en-Provence, 1976, typescript), of which two-thirds was published as *Prix et salaires à Florence au XIVe siècle, 1280–1380,* Collection de l'Ecole Française de Rome, 59 (Rome, 1982); Giuliano Pinto, *La Toscana nel tardo Medio Evo: Ambiente, economia rurale, società* (Florence, 1982).

[15]Ruggiero Romano, Frank C. Spooner, and Ugo Tucci, "Le finanze di Udine e della Patria del Friuli all'epoca della dominazione veneziana," *Memorie storiche forogiugliesi* 44 (1960–61):235–67. A long series of grain prices for Udine, beginning already in 1450, has long been available in Guid'Antonio Zanetti, *Nuova raccolta delle monete e zecche d'Italia,* 4 vols. (Bologna, 1775–89), 2:295 ff.; Fernand Braudel, "La vita economica di Venezia nel secolo XVI," *La civiltà veneziana del Rinascimento* (Florence, 1958); and Fernand Braudel and Frank

For Venice, Maurice Aymard found a substitute for market prices of wheat in officially fixed prices for the period 1560–1630.[16] For wages the only solid series constructed to date is that by Brian Pullan for the building trades during the period 1550–1630.[17] Studies of wages in earlier centuries are based on sources still too fragmentary to build a series,[18] and their indication of the purchasing power of money needs to be supplemented by more such studies as those of Bartolomeo Cecchetti, of Gino Luzzatto for 1343, and of Philippe Braunstein for 1378–81.[19]

In the absence of wage and price series for Venice in the centuries dealt with in this book, our investigations may be considered a preliminary first step towards eventual studies of wages and prices—an essential preliminary to the extent that they clarify the changing denominations, of money of account and of coin, in which wages and prices were recorded.

### iii. VOCABULARY

In the following descriptions of changes in coins and moneys of account, some words frequently treated as more or less interchangeable

---

C. Spooner, "Prices in Europe from 1450 to 1750," in *The Cambridge Economic History of Europe,* vol. 4 (Cambridge, 1967). Since then, series of wheat prices have been compiled for other cities of the Venetian Terraferma: G. Lombardini, *Pane e denaro a Bassano tra il 1501 ed il 1799* (Vicenza, 1963); Gigi Corazzol, *Fitti e livelli a grano: Un aspetto del credito rurale nel Veneto del '500* (Milan, 1979), with a series for Padua for the period 1500–1594; for Verona beginning in 1500, see the long appendix to Giorgio Borelli's first contribution in *Uomini e civiltà agraria in territorio veronese,* ed. Giorgio Borelli (Verona, 1982).

[16]*Venise, Raguse et le commerce du blé pendant la seconde moitié du XVIe siècle,* EPHE-6, Ports-routes-trafics, 20 (Paris, 1966). Most recently Ivo Mattozzi, "Il politico e il pane a Venezia (1570–1650)," *Società e storia* 20 (1983):271–303.

[17]"Wage-Earners and the Venetian Economy, 1550–1630," *EcHR,* 2d ser., 16 (1964), reprinted in Brian Pullan, ed., *Crisis and Change in the Venetian Economy in the 16th and 17th Centuries* (London, 1968).

[18]Frederic C. Lane, *Navires et constructeurs à Venise pendant la Renaissance,* EPHE-6, Oeuvres étrangères, 5 (Paris, 1965); idem, "Wages and Recruitment of Venetian Galeotti, 1470–1580," *Studi veneziani,* n.s., 6 (1982):15–43; Andrè Wirobisz, "L'attività edilizia a Venezia nel XIV e XV secolo," *Studi veneziani* 7 (1965):307–43.

[19]Bartolomeo Cecchetti, "Saggio sui prezzi delle vettovaglie e di altre merci in Venezia nei secoli XII–XIX," *Atti del R. Istituto Veneto di Scienze, Lettere ed Arti,* 4th ser., 3 (1874):1465–91; Gino Luzzatto, "Il costo della vita a Venezia nel Trecento," *Ateneo veneto* 125 (1934), reprinted in his *Studi di storia economica veneziana* (Padua, 1954); Philippe Braunstein, "Pénurie et cherté à Venise pendant la guerre de Chioggia (1378–1380)," *Beiträge zur Handels- und Verkehrsgeschichte,* 17–31, Grazer Forschungen zur Wirtschafts- und Sozialgeschichte, 3. It is generally assumed that the cost of living was higher in Venice than in Terraferma cities (see Cipolla, *Le avventure della lira,* 58 and 74 n. 29). In fact, wage rates in the building trades were so much higher in Venice than in Milan in the 1460s that Francesco Sforza, who had purchased an unfinished palace on the Grand Canal, was advised to hire workers in Milan and send them to Venice, thus to save 30–50 percent on labor costs (see Anne Markham Schulz, *Niccolò di Giovanni Fiorentino and Venetian Sculpture of the Early Renaissance* [New York, 1978], 3).

will be used with differentiated meanings as follows:[20] (1) *Devaluation* will be used broadly to cover any reduction in the weight of pure gold or silver contained in a coin or represented by a unit of a money of account. (2) *Debasement* will be used in a restricted sense to mean a reduction in fineness, that is, in the percentage of pure gold or silver in a coin. In a contrasting usage, John Munro carefully defines *debasement* almost exactly as *devaluation* is defined above. His definition contributes to the clarity of his own discussion of the motivation of princely policies.[21] However, analyzing the various causes, results, and forms of devaluation frequently calls for distinguishing debasement from other factors in devaluation, namely: (3) *deterioration* of coin through usage, clipping, and culling, which reduced the weight of the coins in circulation; and (4) *lightening* a coin by reducing its legal weight without reducing its fineness. At a time when many payments were made by weight, making a coin lighter carried less implication of deception than did debasement, and it is distinct from deterioration in that it refers to official acts and legal specifications.

Determining whether a "devaluation" referred to was a reduction in the value of a coin or of a money of account requires close attention to the individual case. Contemporary descriptions are likely to cause confusion.[22] References to strengthening or weakening the money do not always make clear whether by "money" they mean coins or money of account. In English, "crying up" the legal values of coins was called an enhancement of the currency; "crying down" the coins was called an abatement. Similarly, in French "hausser la monnaie" was called "un surhaussement" or "une augmentation," and in Italian "alzare la moneta" meant "un alzamento" or "aumento." These terms referred to raising the value of coins in moneys of account.

But meaning could be reversed. "Crying up" the coins made the units of the money of account worth less precious metal. Therefore, the money of account could be described as weakened and changed from strong money (Fr. "monnaie forte," It. "moneta forte") to weak or base money (Fr. "monnaie faible," It. "moneta debole"). From that point of view, crying up the coins was a weakening (Fr. "affaiblissement" or "diminution," It. "indebolimento" or "peggioramento") of the money of account. On the other hand, a crying down of the coins was for the money

---

[20]These are the meanings more carefully defined by Horsefield, *British Monetary Experiments*, 23–24.

[21]Munro, *Wool, Cloth, and Gold*, 13.

[22]A striking example is Luigi Einaudi's comment on Paul Harsin's interpretation of Bodin in *Paradoxes inédits du Seigneur de Malestroit touchant les monnoyes, avec la response du Président de la Tourette*, ed. Luigi Einaudi, Collezione di scritti inediti e rari di economisti, ed. Luigi Einaudi, 3 (Turin, 1937), 36n.

of account a restoration (Fr. "renforcement," It. "rinforzamento").[23] One way of speaking treated coins as "real money"; the other way of speaking treated the money of account as "real money." The linguistic ambiguity is evidence of a conceptual ambiguity about just which money was "real." It stirred Marc Bloch to remark challengingly in a lecture delivered before 1940: "Quand et dans quels milieux exactement s'est faite l'inversion du vocabulaire? Je l'ignore et je regrette de l'ignorer."[24] Bloch's challenge has not been answered.

[23]Luigi Einaudi, "The Theory of Imaginary Money from Charlemagne to the French Revolution," in *Enterprise and Secular Change: Readings in Economic History,* ed. Frederic C. Lane and Jelle C. Riemersma (Homewood, Ill., 1953), 248–49, a translation of Einaudi's "Teoria della moneta immaginaria nel tempo da Carlomagno alla rivoluzione francese," *Rivista di storia economica* 1 (1936):18–19, translated by Giorgio Tagliacozzo, and ed. with the assistance of Raymond de Roover, cited hereafter as Einaudi in *Enterprise.* Cf. de Roover, *Gresham,* 72.

[24]*Esquisse,* 40–42.

# 4

# BIMETALLISM AND MULTIPLE MONETARY STANDARDS

## i. MEANINGS OF BIMETALLISM

T WAS THE SILVER COINAGE that because of deterioration or debasement needed recoinage from time to time. Gold coins were made and kept more uniform and were used principally though not exclusively by sophisticated international merchants and government officials. Very few gold coins circulated in western Europe during the early Middle Ages, and those few were Byzantine or Moslem or imitations thereof. When in the thirteenth century gold coins were minted in northern Italy and then beyond the Alps, they were given legal values in the already existing moneys of account, which had been derived from the traditional silver coins. If those legal values had been maintained and observed in practice, the old moneys of account would have become equally based on both silver and gold. That is, debts recorded in moneys of account would have been payable with coins of either metal at the legally established rates. The traditional moneys of account would have expressed bimetallic standards. But the value of the gold coins in the established money of account changed as a result of changes either in the relative value of the two metals or in the content of the silver coins. Then either the gold coin was allowed to become the basis for a new money of account or the government adjusted the values and content of the coins in an effort to maintain a single, bimetallic standard.

"Bimetallism" is a concept loaded with emotion and confusion in American usage because of its role in the class struggle and the party politics that culminated in the victory of the gold standard in 1896. A bimetallic standard had been formulated in 1792, when the U.S. dollar was ordered minted containing 371 1/4 grains of pure silver and a ten-dollar gold piece was ordered containing 247 1/2 grains of pure gold. That bimetallic dollar as money of account set the bimetallic ratio at 15 to 1 (371.25/24.75). In practice, not those coins but a mixture of Spanish coins and American paper currencies variously discounted served as the chief means of payment for many decades.[1] During a period when silver was plentiful the ratio was raised to 16 to 1. Later the discovery of gold in California and Australia made gold worth less. As a result, virtually all silver coins disappeared from circulation, and in the 1850s the United States was on a gold standard with a subsidiary silver coinage.[2] After the Civil War came a reversal. New mines, especially in Nevada, made silver so plentiful that it was not worth 1/16 as much as gold. Even when a considerable amount was bought by the government, the price internationally kept on falling, especially after the new German Empire adopted a gold standard in 1871. In fear of losing all of its gold, the American government in the midst of the very severe depression following the panic of 1893—finally stopped its purchase of silver altogether. Not only silver miners but bankrupt farmers and unemployed workers blamed the government's adherence to a monometallic gold standard for their misery. They placed passionate hope for relief in bimetallism, which was then defined as "the free and unlimited coinage of both gold and silver into full legal-tender coins."[3]

That definition is useful in identifying bimetallism as a cause, a hope, perhaps a program; but it does not suffice to identify it as a condition of affairs distinct from other monetary arrangements.[4] In describing historical situations, a bimetallic monetary *system* is to be distinguished from a bimetallic monetary *standard*.[5] Europe in the fourteenth century had a bimetallic system in that both gold and silver coins were in use. Also there was a widespread feeling that both gold and silver should be legal tender

[1]Arthur Nussbaum, *A History of the Dollar* (New York, 1957), 52–57; Paul Studenski and Hermann E. Kroos, *Financial History of the United States* (New York, 1952), 62 ff.

[2]David A. Martin, "1853: The End of Bimetallism in the United States," *JEcH* 33 (1973):826.

[3]Wharton Barker, *Bimetallism, or the Evils of Gold Monometallism and the Benefits of Bimetallism* (Philadelphia, 1896), in the brief foreword facing p. 1.

[4]In the general account of the struggle in Samuel Eliot Morison and Henry Steele Commager, *The Growth of the American Republic*, 2 vols. (New York, 1937), vol. 2, chap. 11, esp. 248–49, "bimetallism" also refers primarily to the cause or program. Cf. the careful definition by D. A. Martin ("1853: The End of Bimetallism," 525 n. 2): "Bimetallism required a fixed mint ratio, free coinage, unlimited legal tender for both monies, and the right to convert all coin to bullion at the pleasure of the holder."

[5]Thus Robertson (*Money*, 56–57) emphasized that France after 1803 had a bimetallic *system* but had first a silver and then a gold *standard*.

and that there should be some clarity about their relative values. But their relative values kept changing, and their coinage was not free and unlimited. Only in a few states and for relatively short periods was there a unified monetary standard based on a clearly defined bimetallic ratio.

## ii. THE INSTABILITY OF A BIMETALLIC STANDARD

Bimetallic ratios in Europe varied as much in the later Middle Ages as at any time before the late nineteenth century, as is indicated in table 1. These bimetallic ratios are, before 1800, those found at Venice, but the ratio varied not only from decade to decade but also from place to place. Shortly before 1350 the bimetallic ratio was as high as 20 to 1 in some places north of the Alps, while it was only 11 or 12 to 1 in Genoa or Rome.

The relative values of gold and silver varied according to changes in demand as well as changes in supplies. Changes occurred not only in the productivity of mines and the openness of routes to the mines but also in the extent to which gold or silver was wanted for jewelry or other forms of ostentation, or for political payments (for which gold was generally preferred), or for coin for mercantile use.

When such factors produced a change of the bimetallic ratio in one region, commerce made effects of the change felt elsewhere. The intensification of trade in Europe during the late Middle Ages radiated to all surrounding regions the impact of changes in the bimetallic ratio. No important participant in international commerce could maintain a bimetallic standard unaffected by the values being set on gold and silver by its trading partners.[6]

To be sure, the effects were felt much more slowly between, say, 1350 and 1450 than between 1750 and 1850. In the earlier century the difference between the ratios in two countries had to be wider before the undervalued metal was exported. In medieval Europe, not only was the shipment of specie illegal at many frontiers but high rates of seigniorage reduced the profits on exporting the coin of one country in order to sell it as bullion to the mint of another country.[7] The difference in bimetallic ratios had to be all the more substantial if silver coin was to be exported in order to obtain gold. Bimetallic ratios are usually stated by comparing coined silver with coined gold, as in the statement above about the bimetallic value of the U.S. dollar in 1792. But between silver bullion and coined gold the ratio was considerably higher. It was even somewhat higher between uncoined silver and uncoined gold because the expense of

[6]For example see below, chap. 19.
[7]Cf. above, chap. 2. Raymond de Roover (*Gresham*, 77–83, 138–40) explains the relations between seigniorage and specie points under conditions like those of the Middle Ages with reference to theoretical explanations provided by Jacob Viner, *Studies in the Theory of International Trade* (New York, 1937), 78, 129, 378.

TABLE I.

Secular Changes in Bimetallic Ratios, 1200–1900

| Year | Ratio | Year | Ratio |
|------|-------|------|-------|
| 1200 | 10  | 1570 | 11 |
| 1250 | 8.5 | 1640 | 14 |
| 1280 | 10  | 1700 | 15 |
| 1310 | 14  | 1800 | 15 |
| 1350 | 10  | 1850 | 16 |
| 1400 | 11  | 1890 | 20 |
| 1500 | 11  | 1896 | 30 |
| 1520 | 12  |      |    |

SOURCES: Andrew M. Watson, "Back to Gold—and Silver," *EcHR*, 2d ser., 20 (1967):23–27; William A. Shaw, *The History of Currency, 1252–1894* (New York, 1895), 69–70, 157; J. Lawrence Laughlin, *History of Bimetallism in the United States* (New York, 1897), 288–92; Studenski and Kroos, *Financial History*, 218–20, 187; Davis R. Dewey, *Financial History of the United States* (New York, 1934), 406–7; below, table 12.
NOTES: The ratios, in rounded figures, indicate how many units of silver could be bought with one unit of gold. All dates are approximate.

coining, as well as the seigniorage, was higher on silver than on gold.[8] Consequently, to export silver coin for sale profitably as mere bullion, in order to have gold instead, a merchant would have to find a market in some place where the value of silver compared with that of gold was considerably higher than in the place where he was assembling silver coins for export.

Although international flows of specie did not respond as sensitively as they did later to differences in bimetallic ratios, in such medieval centers as Venice the responses themselves were similar. International trade was sufficiently intense and variable that businessmen sometimes found it necessary or profitable to settle foreign balances by a shipment of specie. In such situations merchants were well enough informed to send whichever of the two metals was the more highly valued in the receiving country.[9]

[8]See below, chap. 5 and app. C, sec. i.
[9]Harry A. Miskimin, "Le problème d'argent au Moyen Age," *Annales, ESC,* 17 (1962):1125–30, contains a simplified summary of one of the theses developed in Miskimin's *Money, Prices, and Foreign Exchange in Fourteenth Century France,* Yale Studies in Economics, 15 (New Haven, 1963), 90–117, namely, that years of increase in the coinage of silver or gold in England, France, or Flanders correlated with years of decrease of its coinage in the others *or* with increases in the coinage of the other metal. Some of the years witnessed large movements of gold for political reasons. But, Miskimin concluded, "the mechanism that controlled specie movements must be sought in the balance of trade not simply in international speculation" (117–18). Cf. below, chap. 5, n. 34. Edward Ames, in "The Sterling Crisis of 1337–39," finds good evidence with which to identify periods in which specie was exported. Ames fails, however, to consider possible changes in the relative value of gold and silver as a

When differences in bimetallic ratios were large and persistent, merchants collected for export coins of the metal more highly valued elsewhere. As soon as their market value as bullion exceeded their legal value, they became "good" money in the sense in which that term is used in Gresham's law and were subject to being driven out by "bad" money made of the metal that was legally overvalued. With bimetallic ratios changing as much as 20 percent within a decade or two during the later Middle Ages, the export of undervalued coins repeatedly destroyed efforts to maintain a stable bimetallic standard.

A somewhat similar element of instability affected efforts to maintain a single monetary standard based on both silver and billon. Many billon coins were more than 75 percent copper, and while their silver content, even if it was less than 25 percent, was important in determining their market value, it was not the only factor determining the rates at which they would be given or taken by a moneychanger in return for white money.[10] Just as a bimetallic standard based on an established relation between the values of gold and silver was often upset by increased supply of one or the other of the metals, a standard based on an established relation between silver and billon coins was often upset by an increased supply of billon coins. The problem arose in Venice in the thirteenth century before gold was coined there. A very early Venetian monetary standard was bimetallic in that it was based on both pennies that were 25 percent silver and groats that were 96 percent silver. It later turned into two monetary standards, one based on the penny, the other on the groat.[11]

### iii. ALTERNATIVES TO A BIMETALLIC STANDARD

When a bimetallic standard disintegrated because of a change in the supply of one or the other of the different kinds of coin on which it had been based, it was replaced by (1) the demonetization of one coin (or metal) so that the other provided the only monetary standard, which was thus made monometallic, or (2) two separate monetary standards, gener-

---

factor in fluctuation of exchange rates or the movement of precious metals between countries, because in his table 1 he considers the Florentine money used in the accounts he studied to have been based on silver. In his source (Armando Sapori, ed., *I libri di commercio dei Peruzzi* [Milan, 1934]), it is repeatedly and clearly identified as *£, s.,* and *d.* a fiorini, which was a money of account based on gold, as Raymond de Roover clearly explained in his *Rise and Decline of the Medici Bank,* 33, and as is fully confirmed by Giulio Mandich in "Per una ricostruzione delle operazioni mercantili e bancarie della compagnia dei Covoni," in *Libro giallo della compagnia dei Covoni,* ed. Armando Sapori (Milan, 1970), and by Mario Bernocchi in Bernocchi, 3:264–67. Ames's article was reprinted as an example of the possibilities of "the new economic history" in *Essays in Quantitative Economic History,* ed. Roderick Floud (New York, 1974).

[10]See below, chap. 5, sec. i.

[11]See below, chap. 8, sec. iii.

ally one based on silver, the other on gold. England's adoption of the gold standard (described below in chapter 5, section ii) is an example of the continuance of a traditional or established money of account to express a single unified standard that became monometallic. In Venice and Florence, in contrast, the disintegration of a bimetallic standard was followed by the use of distinct standards, one based on silver, the other on gold. Their use and their relation to each other were complicated in some periods by efforts to maintain a stable or official relationship also between silver and billon coins. Between 1300 and 1500, Venice employed an unusually large number of moneys of account. Although analyses of specific historical situations come in later chapters, it seems worthwhile to analyze here by simplified examples of accounting practices the way in which changes in coins produced new moneys of account or changed the relations of old moneys of account to basic coins.

Consider a merchant keeping accounts in lire worth 20 soldi and 240 denari at a time when two coins were in circulation, a penny of cheap alloy and a groat of pure silver. Assume that the groat contained 12 grams, that the penny contained 1 gram of fine silver, and that the groat was officially valued at 12 pennies. There was then a single monometallic standard of value: 1 lira = 240 grams of coined silver. Suppose the penny was then debased, so that a penny contained only 0.8 grams of silver, while the groats still contained 12 grams each. How then would the merchant keep his accounts?

In entering in his books transactions in which both pennies and groats had been paid or received, he had a choice between two options. His choice presented the issues thought about more or less precisely by everyone handling coins and relating them to standards of value. The merchant might consider that the money of account he had been using was based on the penny and that since the groats he was offered were now 15 times the metallic value of the penny, he would enter them on his books as worth not 12 times as much as a penny but 15 times as much, namely, as 15 pennies. Or, alternatively, the merchant might consider that the money of account he had been using was and had been based on the groat and decide that he would continue to enter a groat on his books as worth 12 pennies. But he would then consider penny coins to be at a discount. He would accept them as worth less than 1 penny. He would enter them in his books as worth 1/15 of a groat, or 4/5 of a penny.

In real situations approximating this oversimplified example, some merchants decided one way, some the other. As a result, what had been a single standard of value based on both coins divided into two standards of value, one based on the penny, the other on the groat. The penny became the basic or link coin of one money of account, the groat the basic or link coin of the other money of account.

What determined a merchant's choice? It was essentially a choice between coins. Which did he handle most and consider basic for his business—the penny or the groat? His decision would be influenced by the government's regulation of the value of the two coins as legal tender and by the nature of his business activity. Whichever coin he chose, he would treat it as the constant and the other as having variable value, so that he allowed a premium, or applied a discount, just as he discounted or gave a premium for foreign coins that came into his hands.

Merchants who commonly used both gold and silver coin confronted the same kind of choice when a previously established relation between the two different kinds of coins was upset by a change in the bimetallic ratio. Consider a merchant who kept accounts in a lira of 20 soldi which had for a decade been worth 1 gold crown containing 4 grams of gold and also worth 10 silver groats each containing 4 grams of silver. When he received a gold crown, he recorded a receipt of 20 soldi, and when he received 10 silver groats, he recorded also the receipt of 20 soldi. Since that gave the same value (20 soldi) to 4 grams of gold and 40 grams of silver, it reflected a bimetallic ratio of 10 to 1.

$$1 \text{ crown} = 20 \text{ soldi} \quad = 4 \text{ grams gold}$$
$$10 \text{ groats} = 20 \text{ soldi} \quad = 40 \text{ grams silver}$$
$$1 \text{ gram gold} = 10 \text{ grams silver}$$

Suppose that the bimetallic ratio rose to 12 to 1, so that the 4 grams of gold in the crown became worth 48 grams of silver, the amount of silver contained in 12 groats. The merchant would then have to decide whether to consider the lira in which he kept his books to be based on the gold crown or the silver groat. If he decided to consider that the money of account he was using was based on the silver groat, he would still enter groats as worth 2 soldi each, but he would record the receipt of a gold crown as the receipt of 24 soldi. His alternative was to consider that the money of account he was using was based on gold. Choosing that option, he would record the gold crown as still worth 20 soldi but would thereafter record the receipt of a silver groat, not as 2 soldi, but as only 40/24 soldi, that is, 1 2/3 soldi, which he would record as 1 soldo 8 denari. If he kept the value of the gold crown steady at 20 soldi, he was making that the link coin of his money of account. If he kept the value of the silver groat at 2 soldi, the same as before, and recorded a premium for the gold crown, he was making the groat the link coin of his money of account. Faced with historical situations, some merchants decided one way, some the other; and governments decided that some accounts should be linked to gold, others to silver. What had been one money of account was divided into two divergent standards of value and two moneys of account based on quite different coins.

As more and more mints produced all three types of coins—billon, fine silver, and gold—situations arose favoring the simultaneous use of three kinds of money of account: one based on black pennies, another based on silver groats, and the third based on gold coins. Retailers and day laborers considered pennies the basic coin in their accounting if they handled them more than any other coins. Wholesale merchants generally preferred the groats, not only because they frequently used them in making and receiving payments within their city but also because groats were more highly esteemed than pennies as "real money," a real store of value. Merchants engaged in foreign trade had reasons for treating gold as basic, at least if they traded in areas that also used gold, but in other regions, or in the same region at different times, they might prefer to treat large silver coins as those to which they tied their moneys of account.

In northern Europe the minting of gold coins began much later than in Mediterranean lands, and moneys of account based on gold were little used until late in the Middle Ages. The most important moneys of account were generally based on silver coin.[12]

Not for long, and not in many places, did three moneys of account have a distinct existence, each linked definitely to one of the three different kinds of coins. By various methods (some of which will be described below), governments tried to tie the diversely based moneys of account together into a single monetary standard. Their efforts at combining those based on billon with those based on silver were frequently successful because the line between black money and white money was in many places not sharply drawn, and the relative value of the black money was much affected by a government's control over the amount issued. It was more difficult to combine a money of account based on gold with a money of account based on silver into one standard, since a government could do little to affect changes in the relative value of the two metals.

Freezing the relations of several moneys of account was made difficult by the persistent depreciation of the money of account most closely linked to small coins. The billon and small silver coins passed so frequently from hand to hand that they deteriorated by use even when they were not debased and overissued, as they often were for fiscal reasons. Devaluation of a money of account based on black money created pressure for a similar devaluation of the money of account linked to silver in order to preserve the traditional relation between those two standards of value. But any such devaluation of the silver coinage and the money of account based on it upset the established relation between the silver money and gold money. Moneys of account based on white money were thus constantly under pressures from two sides: pressures arising from devaluations of the black money and the smaller pieces of white money and pressures arising from changes in the relative market value of gold and silver.

[12]A few based on black money are also distinguishable (Hans van Werveke, "Monnaie de compte et monnaie réelle," in *Revue belge de philologie et d'histoire* 13 [1934]:124–25; Wolff, *Commerce et marchands de Toulouse*, 311).

# 5

# METALLIC VALUES
# AND EXCHANGE VALUES

## i. METALLIC EQUIVALENTS AND LINK COINS

INETEENTH-CENTURY ARGUMENTS about whether the dollar was a bimetallic standard illustrate the difficulties that can arise in determining the metallic equivalent of a particular money of account at a particular time. Calculating the metallic equivalent of a money of account of centuries ago in a country where several moneys of account had been in use during decades of changes in trimetallic coinage is unavoidably complicated.[1]

Estimates of metallic equivalents are needed, however.[2] The monetary regulations in a city such as Venice cannot be understood without considering how the men making the regulations thought their coins were related to their moneys of account. Also, any comparison of prices at different times is likely to be very misleading if it does not consider whether or not there were changes in the meantime in the metallic equivalents of the moneys of account in which the prices were recorded. And comparisons of prices in different places, or any other international monetary comparisons, are meaningful only if the metallic equivalents are also

---

[1]Herman van der Wee, *The Growth of the Antwerp Market and the European Economy*, 3 vols. (The Hague, 1963), 1:107–22.

[2]On the general problem of converting prices from money of account into their equivalents in pure silver see Aldo De Maddalena, *Prezzi e aspetti di mercato in Milano durante il secolo XVII* (Milan, 1949), 62–66; see 73–79 for his solution.

compared, unless, to be sure, records of exchange rates are available. For most of the Middle Ages and for most places, records of exchange rates are not available, and when they are, they merely add a new dimension. The relation of metallic values to exchange rates then becomes one of the major problems in monetary history.

In seeking metallic equivalents, one encounters the problem of allowing for the deterioration of coins through use, clipping, and culling. The difference between the weight legally prescribed for the mint and the average weight of those in circulation was frequently 10 percent and could be much more, as illustrated in chapter 4.

For most of the Middle Ages most calculations can be based on the legally prescribed weight because so many payments, especially large payments, were made not by counting coins but by weighing them. Especially in the eastern Mediterranean and southern Italy many mints made little effort to issue coins that were all of the same weight. An extreme example, not typical but illustrative of possibilities, is the tarì of the kingdom of Naples and Sicily: some monarchs issued some tarì that were eight times as heavy as others. As a result, a unit of weight, the ounce (oncia) became the money of account, and although it was divided into 30 tarì of account for fractional calculations, the number of actual tarì coins needed to make an oncia was determined by weighing, not by counting, coins.[3] At Constantinople the bezant, or perpero, was based on Byzantium's traditional chief coin, but contracts often specified those of the "old" or of the "correct" weight. The money of account referred to a coin of a legally prescribed weight, although most of those in circulation were lighter. In such cases the design that distinguished one coin from another was supposed to indicate a uniform content of gold or silver but did not guarantee a uniform weight.

In northern Italy and western Europe, however, efforts were made to manufacture coins that were all of the same weight. The range of variation permitted in minting was smallest for the most precious coins, those of gold. Until 1321 Venice permitted its silver coins of high reputation, its grossi, to be used in making payment by weighing them. Although in their manufacture specialized craftsmen were employed in efforts to make them all of equal weight, in fact many of those circulating were so far underweight, presumably from clipping, wear and tear, and culling, that when payment by tale was made obligatory in 1321, creditors were obliged to accept at full value any grossi that were not more than 10 percent underweight.[4] That would seem to raise the question, Was the

[3]Robert S. Lopez, *Settecento anni fa: Il ritorno all'oro nell'occidente duecentesco*, Quaderni della *Rivista storica italiana*, 4 (Naples, 1955), 11–12. See also Carmelo Trasselli, "Le aree monetarie nel Mediterraneo centro-occidentale (secc. XIII–XVI)," in Barbagli Bagnoli, ed., *La moneta nell'economia europea*, 54, 60–63.

[4]*PMV*, doc. 79; and below, chaps. 13, sec. iv, and 14, sec. i.

silver equivalent about 1300 of a lira di grossi 240 times the fine silver content legally prescribed for the grosso, namely, 504 grams (240 × 2.1) or somewhere between that figure and 10 percent less? The relevance of the question may well depend on the problem being investigated. In regard to the bimetallic ratio in Venice in the 1320s, some of the very high prices for gold at that date may need to be discounted to allow for the deterioration of the grossi in actual use in those years. An example in England of extreme variation in barley prices in 1299–1300 is explained by Michael Prestwich as partially the result of the circulation at the time of much lightweight foreign coin.[5]

Determining which was the link coin on which a money of account was based is relatively easy if in such sources as account books one coin was always given the same value in the money of account, while other coins were valued variously from time to time. As is obvious from the simplified examples given in chapter 4, coin of which the value in the money of account was invariable was the basic, link coin.

But that leaves open several questions:

1. What if the records repeatedly name as constant in value a coin that was not in use at the time? In that case, one possibility is that an amount of gold or silver in a coin no longer in use is the basis of the money of account. A debtor could call for payment of that amount of precious metal. Although it was known that the coin was no longer available, its metallic value still determined the metallic value of that money of account. It might be called a bullion-based money of account.[6]

For such a bullion-based money of account, it is often necessary to identify the coin no longer in use that determined the amount of metal the user of the money of account had in mind. Some coins of relatively high value that enjoyed a high reputation either because of the prestige of the government that issued them or because for a long time they had been maintained at a high standard were sufficiently memorable that they, as ghosts, provided an unchanging bullion base for long-lived moneys of account. Their weight and fineness can be learned from surviving specimens or possibly from documents.

2. What if a coin's name was a word that did not refer to any coin? It was a misnomer if it had come to be used merely as a designation of a denomination in a money of account. An example is the word *grossi* as used about 1500 in the Venetian lira di grossi, where *grossi* does not refer to current coins of that name or even to the coins from which the

---

[5]"Edward I's Monetary Policies," 411–12. Cf. Munro, "Bullionism," 179, 183.

[6]This type of money of account is called Type A by Hans van Werveke in "Monnaie de compte e monnaie réelle," 123. Examples are the écus of Philippe of Valois and Louis of Bavaria. Cf. J. P. Cuvillier, "Notes on the Royal Coinage."

expression originated. "Grosso" had become a denomination of account meaning 1/24 of a ducat; a "lira di grossi" in 1500 meant, not 240 grossi coins, but 10 ducat coins.[7]

In such a case the fact that "grosso" had an invariable value in the accounting tells nothing about the metallic equivalent of the money of account. That metallic equivalent has to be sought through the entries that refer to coins, not to mere denominations of account. Ducats were real gold coins. Equating the lira di grossi of that date with 35.5 grams of gold is an acceptable inference from the constancy with which 1 ducat containing 3.55 grams of gold is equated with 2 soldi of the lira di grossi.

3. What if the evidence from account books and from the administrative or legislative records is unclear and somewhat contradictory? In that case it is essential to compute the metallic content of all the coins that were in use and to compare their relative metallic values and their relative legal values. It is useful to take as a preliminary hypothesis the belief that the coin that was most overvalued legally was the basic coin. Unless there is reason to believe the contrary, it is reasonable to conclude that the basic coin was the coin of which the metallic value was lowest in relation to its value as legal tender when making payments recorded in that money of account.

The reasonableness of this conclusion can be made clear by reconsidering the simplified example described in the discussion in chapter 4 of how changes in coinage produced new moneys of account. Suppose pennies that were worth 1 denaro each and had previously contained 1 gram of silver each were debased to contain 0.8 grams, while groats worth 12 denari continued to be coined containing 12 grams of silver each. Before the debasement of the pennies, either 20 groats or 240 pennies—in either case 240 grams of silver—had been worth 1 lira of account. If the legal value of the coins was left unchanged, after the pennies were debased to contain only 0.8 grams of silver the lira could be paid with only 192 grams of silver (240 × 0.8) when paid in pennies, while 240 grams would still have been required legally to make the payment in groats (20 × 12). Under these conditions, the merchant who had incurred a debt of 1 lira had reason to pay it in pennies, and the creditor would be obliged to accept the payment in settlement of the debt, since the pennies were legal tender for 1/240 of a lira. Groats would then command a premium, and pennies would become the basic link coin of the money of account.

Further questions arise when such analysis leaves two or three coins with equal claim to be the link coin for the same money of account, as when both or all three have invariable values in the entries in an account book.

[7]See below, chap. 16.

*a.* There is no problem if the two or three coins were of the same metal and fineness and their differences in weight corresponded to their differences in value, as did the English groats and shillings when they were minted to supplement the English penny. The metallic equivalence of the denominations of account are the same whichever coin is used in the calculations.

*b.* If two coins, one of silver, the other of gold, both appear to be established by law as link coins for the money of account, as a silver one-dollar piece and a gold ten-dollar piece were for the U.S. dollar in 1792, it is pertinent to inquire whether both coins were in fact commonly used at those values in making payments, as would be the case if there was effectively a bimetallic standard, or whether at the time being studied the gold coin or the silver coin had practically disappeared from circulation, as was the case in the United States in the 1850s, so that although the monetary standard was by law bimetallic, it was in practice monometallic.[8] If in the period being studied the payments recorded in the money of account were in fact being made practically all in one kind of coin or the other, then the coin actually in use should be used in calculating the metallic equivalent of the money of account at that time.

*c.* The most difficult cases are those involving two or more coins, some of fine silver; some of billon; and some with a silver content, placing them on the border line between white money and black money. Such cases arise when account books and administrative records show that pennies and groats were both accepted for years at unvarying values. It is then necessary to amend the preliminary hypothesis formulated above according to which the coin with the lowest *metallic* value compared with its legal value is to be considered the link coin. It has to be amended to say that the coin with the lowest *market* value compared with its legal value is to be considered the link coin. The amendment is necessary to take into consideration that the market value of the black money was almost always higher than its metallic value.

One reason why the market or exchange value of black money was normally higher than its comparative metallic value was the higher cost of manufacture. The cost of the copper was relatively unimportant because a pound of silver was worth more than a hundred times as much as a pound of copper.[9] But making black money worth 100 soldi took more labor than did making white money of the value of 100 soldi. Accordingly, even when the percentage of seigniorage on the two kinds of coins was the same, the mint charge for manufacturing billon pennies was about 6 percentage

---

[8]Martin, "1853: The End of Bimetallism," 826.
[9]On copper prices see below, app. C.

points above the mint charge for manufacturing groats of pure silver, about 8 percent instead of 2 percent, at least in that proportion.[10] In comparing the values of the two kinds of coins, the value of the large amount of labor that was embodied in the pennies should be added to the value of the silver they contained. Their added labor cost was a part of a coin's intrinsic value in the literal sense of *intrinsic*, but since that word is customarily used to refer to the metallic value of a coin, the full intrinsic value will be referred to below as the "cost value" (cost value = metallic value + cost of manufacture).

Quite distinct from the cost value thus defined was the exchange value, commonly called the market value. The exchange value was affected by such extrinsic factors as utility or scarcity and by custom or official values.

More often than not, the exchange value of billon and copper coins was higher than their cost value. They met a demand for coins to use for small payments or charities, as well as in making change. For such purposes coins of pure silver were impractical. Copper had to be used in order to make a coin of small denomination large enough to handle. Once people were used to such a coin, the demand for it gave it a value far above its intrinsic worth, provided it was not issued in too large amounts. Since their market value depended on supply and demand, billon coins could and generally did circulate at more than their cost value.

In this respect, black money resembled the coins of base metal that in a modern monetary system are defined as "token coinage." Token coins now are legal tender for small sums only but can be exchanged at government agencies and at government expense for currency of larger denomination that is fully legal tender. Early attempts to issue token money had limited success. The cost of redeeming such tokens at face value was excessive, and the very idea of token money was contrary to the prevailing commodity theory of money and to princely expectations that coinage should produce revenue, not add to governmental expenses.[11] All things considered, medieval coins of low metallic value are best described not as token coinage but as subsidiary coinage serving the functions later served by token coinage.

Billon coins were kept in a subsidiary position and above their intrinsic value most of the time by the inconvenience of using them in large payments and by the coinage of a relatively small amount compared with the need. The inconvenience is evident if one imagines counting out the number of Venetian piccoli required about 1500 to pay the sum of 1 lira di

[10]Usher, *The Early History*, 198–201; Bernocchi, 3:38–40; and for the comparative mint charges at Venice see below, chap. 18, sec. i, and app. A.

[11]Joseph J. Spengler, "Coin Shortage: Modern and Premodern," *National Banking Review* 3 (1965):210–12; Usher, *The Early History*, 196, 231–33; Feavearyear, *The Pound Sterling*, 157–59.

grossi: 14,880 piccoli.[12] Payments with large numbers of small coin could be made—and in one period in Venice were made—by preparing them in paper packages![13] But that was a sign of the very unsatisfactory state of the coinage.

The most important reason why black money was confined as much as it was to a subsidiary position in the thirteenth and fourteenth centuries was the failure of mints to turn out more of it. Thus it had scarcity value. Moneyers much preferred making the more highly valued silver coins. Both moneyers who were entrepreneurs operating mints and craftsmen who shaped and struck the coins objected to turning out coins of low value, from which they gained little, considering their labor and the number produced. Left to themselves, they would not have produced as many as were needed. Mints met the public demand for such coins only when governments required them to do so, either by contracts or by minting regulations.[14] They produced excessive amounts only when governments tried to add to their income from seigniorage by ordering both large production and the acceptance of the billon coins at legal values far above their cost of production.

Seigniorage was rooted in the ability of governments to have coins accepted at the values officially set. Seigniorage may be regarded as an appropriation by governments of all or part of the value the coin derived from being both useful and of limited quantity. Those qualities affected a coin's exchange value, and a government's monopoly of the right to determine official values as legal tender enabled it to take a kind of monopolist's profit, which was one of the elements represented in the exchange value.

In calculating the relation of black money to the metallic equivalent of a denomination of account, allowance must be made for both the cost value and the scarcity value of the billon coins. A minimal value for a billon coin can be calculated from its metallic content, but its maximum value might be much higher. For example, if a penny contained 1/36 as much silver as a groat, a moneychanger was fairly sure to offer a groat for 36 of them. On the average he would probably offer a groat for 34 pennies because the large costs of labor in minting pennies raised their intrinsic value to 1/34 that of a groat. And if pennies were in short supply, he might well give a groat for 32 pennies. His decision was also influenced by the values prescribed by law and the extent of the laws' enforcement. In short,

---

[12]At that time the metallic base of the lira di grossi a oro was 10 ducats and the value of the ducat in silver or billon coin was stabilized at 124 soldi. $10 \times 124 \times 12 = 14{,}880$.

[13]Papadopoli, 1:383 n. 5; Reinhold C. Mueller, "L'imperialismo monetario veneziano nel Quattrocento," *Società e storia* 8 (1980):288 n. 21, which also describes fifteenth-century limitations on their use as legal tender.

[14]Usher, *The Early History,* 198; Spengler, "Coin Shortage"; Spufford, *Monetary Problems and Policies,* 44–45; and below, chap. 10, sec. v.

four kinds of value—metallic, cost, official, and utility or scarcity—are worth distinguishing in explaining a fifth value, exchange value.

Efforts to have a single unified monetary standard that was bimetallic or trimetallic were affected by these labor costs and scarcity values. Compared with their exchange value, gold coins cost less to make than did silver coins. A bimetallic ratio calculated from a mint's prices for gold bullion and silver bullion was higher than the ratio calculated from the gold and silver content of coins. A difference of 2–3 percent could result from a difference between the manufacturing costs of gold and silver coin. Larger differences were created when a government set seigniorage high or low so that the total mint charge would increase its revenue or attract more of the desired kind of metal, either gold or silver.[15]

Even more allowance for the lower mint charge on gold must be made in comparing billon coins in order to discover the bimetallic ratio prevailing in a particular period, since minting billon cost more than minting fine silver.[16] In Venice and Florence the distinction is usually clear: black money contained less than 25 percent silver—generally much less—while white money was almost always more than 90 percent fine. Silver made into billon coin gained more in exchange value than silver coined into grossi. But the problem is complicated in many places by the lack of a clear distinction. Any coin containing less than 50 percent fine silver may be called billon,[17] and in Flanders, for example, many coins had a silver content ranging between 25 percent and 80 percent.[18] At Venice, such coins of intermediate fineness, important for a time in adjusting to rapid changes in the relative value of gold and silver, were minted only for some fifteen years in the mid-fourteenth century.[19]

Other factors also determined the immediacy of effects of changes in

[15]Francesco Casaretto, *Le monete genovesi in confronto con le altre valute mediterranee,* in Atti della Società Ligure di Storia Patria, 55 (Genoa, 1928), chap. 6 and p. 174 n. 2. Casaretto compared silver values and exchange values of coins in the twelfth century and estimated that the difference was highly variable and as much as 25 percent for Genoese silver or billon coins and only 2–5 percent for gold coins. He estimated, accordingly, that the billon coin exchanged for gold coin at a price 20 percent above that at which silver bullion exchanged for gold bullion (p. 63). But for coins of fine silver the difference was less. The estimate of a difference of 2–3 percent is based partly on the differences in mint charges on gold, fine silver, and billon as tabulated in Bernocchi, 3:38–40, and partly on the implications of decrees of the Venetian Senate analyzed below in app. C.

[16]Cf. the bimetallic ratios given in table A in Bernocchi, 3:302–3.

[17]Grierson, *Numismatics,* 193.

[18]On Flemish groats see Raymond de Roover, *Money, Banking, and Credit in Mediaeval Bruges: Italian Merchant-Bankers, Lombards, and Money-Changers. A Study in the Origins of Banking* (Cambridge, Mass., 1948), table 10, p. 224.

[19]The only such Venetian coins produced before 1500 were the soldino (0.670 fine) and the mezzanino (0.780 fine), minted between 1331 and 1347 (see chap. 15, sec. iii and app. A, sec. vi).

bimetallic ratios or the introduction of new coins. Most of all, a legally overvalued coin cannot safely be considered the link coin determining the metallic content of the money of account unless there is evidence that it was also "the real coin which at the time predominated as the means of cash payment in the particular line of business and therefore was the coin referred to explicitly or implicitly in setting prices" (Zerbi's definition of what he called moneta numeraria).[20]

## ii. NEW LINKS FOR MONEYS OF ACCOUNT

Although the libre, solidi, and denarii used in Western Christendom in the year 1000 referred to moneys of account based on the denarii derived from the Carolingian monetary system, by 1300 so many other coins had come into use and the denarii were so debased generally that the old moneys of account had become linked more tightly to other coins.

The English development, however, was unique in this respect, because English pennies (i.e., denarii) continued to be made of fine silver during the centuries in which those on the Continent were being debased. Even in the fourteenth century, except in a very few years, the English penny's fineness was maintained, and its weight was not substantially reduced until mid-century.[21] When larger English silver coins were issued—groats in 1279, shillings in 1504—they were also of sterling fineness and were made exactly 4 or 12 times the weight of the penny. Until the late seventeenth century the English £, s., and d. constituted a money of account based on the silver coins of that integrated series. When gold coin began circulating extensively, the gold pieces were given various values in that money of account. The gold coins, insofar as they were made legal tender, were generally undervalued until gold began to fall in value compared with silver about 1690. For some years around 1700 the largest silver coin, the sovereign, was worth 20 shillings, and the most used gold coin, the guinea, was worth officially first 22 shillings and then 21 shillings, 6 pence. For decades England in effect used a bimetallic standard.

When that bimetallic standard disintegrated, the result was a monometallic standard which, rather surprisingly, turned out to be a gold standard. As supplies of gold increased, it became clear that the guinea was overvalued. Isaac Newton, in a famous report submitted when he was director of the mint in 1717, calculated accurately the extent to which gold coin was then overvalued. As a result, the guinea was revalued to 21 shillings. Contrary to what Newton had expected, it kept that value when gold continued to fall in value during the rest of the century. The silver

[20]*Moneta effettiva*, 18; and cf. 74.
[21]Feavearyear, *The Pound Sterling*, 350; and a table kindly furnished by John Munro, "The Alterations of the English Coinage, 1279 to 1526."

content of 21 shillings became worth more abroad than the gold content of 1 guinea, although it was worth less than that in England. Large silver coins disappeared from English circulation as silver was shipped to India, while gold was arriving from Brazil.[22] Practically, England shifted to a gold standard a century before the fact was given legal recognition in the Act of 1819, when specie payment was resumed after the Napoleonic Wars.[23] Thus England kept its single monetary standard in spite of changes in the coins used.[24]

In contrast to the unity of money of account preserved in England, a multiplicity of moneys of account developed in the Italian cities—even within the same city—even before they had begun coining gold. Venice's money of account was based on both a billon penny and a groat of fine silver in the first half of the thirteenth century. If billon and fine silver are considered two separate metals, as they are by some scholars, Venice then had a bimetallic standard. When that standard broke down, diversely based standards emerged to distinguish a standard of value based on the billon penny and a standard based on the silver groat.[25] The money of account based on black money was called the "pound of small pennies" (lira di piccoli) to distinguish it from newer moneys of account called a "pound of groats," or more literally translated, the "pound of large pennies" (lira di denari grossi), and a "pound paid in large pennies" (lira a grossi).

Later—much later in some places—as the metallic value of piccoli became infinitesimal, all moneys of account became linked to newer coins of higher value than 1 piccolo, even the money of account that kept the name lira di piccoli. Indeed, long before piccoli coins had gone out of use, the word *piccoli* had taken on a new meaning. It was used to designate a denomination in a money of account: that is, in many usages it was understood that the word *piccoli* denoted not the coins that were called by that name but a subdivision of the lira, namely, 1/240 of a lira, the value of which depended not on the piccolo coin but on some other coin. To be sure, which meaning the word had is doubtful in some cases in the fourteenth century, but there are innumerable instances in later centuries when *piccoli* in "lira di piccoli" did not refer to coins in use.[26]

In Milan and many other cities of northern Italy the money of

[22]Feavearyear, *The Pound Sterling*, chap. 7 and pp. 45, 63; Horsefield, *British Monetary Experiments*, xii, 75–83; Bloch, *Esquisse*, 79–80; Li Ming-Hsun, *The Great Recoinage of 1696–1699* (London, 1963), 143–73.

[23]Jacob Viner summarized the situation thus: "England . . . although legally on a bimetallic basis had for some time been in effect on a gold standard basis, since the mint ratio of silver to gold was such as generally to undervalue silver and keep it out of circulation" (*Studies*, 123, citing R. G. Hawtry, *Currency and Credit*, 3d ed. [1928], 320–32).

[24]Feavearyear, *The Pound Sterling*, 2.

[25]See below, chap. 8, sec. iii.

[26]Papadopoli, 2:323–35, 375–81.

account derived from the pennies coined since Carolingian times by imperial mints was called the lira imperiale, divided into soldi and denari imperiali. Originally the metallic equivalent of that lira had been the content of
240 denarii, but before the end of the thirteenth century the denarius had
become so debased that the metallic equivalent of the lira imperiale depended instead on that of larger coins such as the sixpence (sesino), which
was about 50 percent silver, and the groat (grosso), of higher fineness,
worth 24 denari imperiali.[27] A different money of account based on a kind
of half-penny called the terlino or terzuolo was also used, but it was
stabilized with 2 lire terzuole consistently worth 1 lira imperiale.[28] After
the gold florin had been given varying values in the lira imperiale for
decades, and then stabilized at 32 soldi imperiali for quite a while, it
became the basis of another money of account (as explained below in
chapter 19, section iv).

In Florence a multiplication of moneys of account began very soon
after the minting of gold. At first, in minting the gold florin in 1252,
Florence created a bimetallic standard by giving the gold florin the same
value as 20 of the silver groats, also called florins at that time, each of
which was worth 1 soldo. A single denomination of account, the lira, then
equaled both 1 gold florin, containing 3.55 grams of gold, and 20 silver
florins, each containing about 1.59 grams of silver, a bimetallic ratio of 8.96
to 1.[29] That bimetallic standard was extremely short-lived, however, for
gold soon rose in value, and two moneys of account based on two quite
distinct standards of value were used. A money of account based on the
gold florin was adopted for big business affairs, officially and in practice. A
money of account called the lira di piccioli was used in local trade and
became linked to both billon and silver coins. There was no stable market
value or legally declared relationship tying the gold florin and the silver
coinage into a single standard of value, for the price of the gold florin in
lire and soldi di piccioli fluctuated freely and frequently in response to
market conditions.[30]

In Venice, a similar separation between the money of account based
on gold and that based on silver or billon developed more slowly and
intricately but was clear-cut by the early fifteenth century. (That separation
will be explained in detail below, in chapter 16.)

In Milan, Florence, and Venice, the simultaneous use of both a
money of account based on gold and a money of account based on silver
led to adoption of a standard way of expressing the value of the gold

[27]Cipolla, Le avventure della lira 54–55; Zerbi, Moneta effettiva, 27, 32–37.

[28]Zerbi, Moneta effettiva, 23–26.

[29]Robert Davidsohn, Forschungen zur Geschichte von Florenz, 4 vols. (Berlin, 1896–1908),
4:321; Bernocchi, 3:75–78, 140–42, 149–63, 263, 268, and 4:iv–vi. The process is explained
more fully below, in chaps. 13, sec. iii, and 19, sec. iii.

[30]Bernocchi, 3:76–79, 139–68, 263–68.

TABLE 2.

Coins Issued by Louis IX of France, 1266

| Coin | Weight | Fineness | Value in Money of Account (deniers tournois) |
|---|---|---|---|
| Denier | 1.13 g | 0.299 (0.338 g silver) | 1 |
| Gros | 4.22 g | 0.958 (4.04 g silver) | 12 |
| Ecu | 4.20 g | 1,000 (4.20 g gold) | 120 |

SOURCE: Fournial, *Histoire monétaire*, 86.

money compared with that of the silver money. This domestic exchange rate consisted of the fluctuating price of the florin or the ducat stated in the silver-based lira di piccoli. Sometimes and in some places, such as Milan, domestic exchange rates were occasionally decreed by government authorities, but in other cities, most notably Florence, they were set by market action and then officially and regularly registered. The term "domestic" (as used in appendix D) serves to distinguish those quotations of local moneys from the rates of foreign exchange, that is, from the prices of foreign moneys in local moneys of account (and of local moneys in foreign moneys of account).

In France, the pennies (deniers) that had been the basis of the livre tournois, the most used money of account, were so debased by the time of Louis IX that they were 2/3 copper. In his reform of 1266, Louis coined a groat, famous as the gros tournois, which was 96 percent pure silver, and an écu of almost pure gold. He linked all three coins to the livre tournois, with 1 livre tournois equal to 80.8 grams of silver or 8.4 grams of gold (see table 2).

Some years later we find the gros worth 13 deniers and Louis's écu, because of the rise in the value of gold, worth much more than 120 deniers. What then determined the metallic value of the livre tournois? Seemingly the denier, because 240 deniers were still counted as 1 livre. But the gros seems to have acquired the value of 13 or 13 1/3 deniers tournois without any alteration of its silver content, and it was the gros that became the basic or link coin of the livre tournois. Only the higher labor value of the denier and its utility in small payments for a time enabled both the gros and the denier to function as basic coins in the trimetallic pattern set by Louis IX.[31]

[31] Fournial, *Histoire monétaire*, 86, 88. Marc Bloch wrote, "Le denier, très vite, est tombé au rang d'une monnaie d'appoint: entendez d'une sorte de monnaie de confiance, dont la valeur nominale était toujours beaucoup plus considérable que ne l'eût comporté, dans l'échelle générale des valeurs monétaires, la quantité de metal précieux qu'elle contenait" (*Esquisse*, 45; and "Mutations monétaires," 150).

The manipulation of the coinage under Philip IV complicated the French system. Beginning in 1295 he raised sharply the rating of such coins as the gros and the écu in the money of account. Then he lowered the amount of fine metal in the silver and billon coins. In 1306 the debased issues were cried down to lower values in livres tournois, and coins of "the good old" standard were issued.[32]

In the innumerable subsequent changes, French monetary ordinances employed for all the silver and billon coins a formula that produced a figure called the "pied de monnaie." It expressed the legally stipulated relation between the weight of a coin, the proportion of fine silver it contained, and the legal value assigned the coin. This gave a unified monetary standard, because the relation was the same in coins of both high and low denominations if they were minted with the same pied de monnaie.[33]

Its use did not solve the problems created by many devaluations. The pied de monnaie was changed frequently, especially in the periods of disaster during the Hundred Years' War. The higher the pied de monnaie, the lower the amount of silver represented by a livre tournois. It became necessary to specify at a particular time whether the livre tournois being used was based on those current coins with a high pied de monnaie or those with a low pied de monnaie. Restorations of the currency were called a return to the good money of St. Louis, and although these revaluations did not raise the metallic standard quite that high, they made it high enough to make worthwhile distinguishing it from the debased money it was supposed to replace. That distinction created two concurrent kinds of livres tournois, "monnaie forte" and "monnaie faible." One is tempted to say that there was "no fixed rate of equivalence between coins in use and money of account."[34] At least monnaie forte and monnaie faible

[32]Fournial, *Histoire monétaire*, 30, 89–93; Edouard Perroy, "Le 'décrochage' des monnaies en temps de mutations: Le cas des viennois faibles en 1304–1308," *Le Moyen Age* 64 (1958): 438–39.

[33]The formula is $P = TC/5t$, where $T$ is the number of coins cut from a mark, $C$ is the legal value of the coin, $t$ is the fineness, and $P$ (the pieds) is 1/5 the value in sous tournois of the coins obtained from a mark of silver *argent le roi*, i.e., 0.958 fine (Fournial, *Histoire monétaire*, 30–31, 135. Wolff, *Commerce et marchands de Toulouse*, 303–13, gives the clearest explanation. See also Miskimin, *Money, Prices, and Foreign Exchange*, 32–33).

[34]C. W. Previté-Orton, *A History of Europe from 1198–1378* (London, 1951), 268. References to monnaie faible and monnaie forte refer generally to the money of account (e.g., Fournial, *Histoire monetaire*, 29), but a debased coin is also called "plus faible" (ibid., 31; cf. above, chap. 3, sec. iii). In his table 1, pp. 100–101, Fournial tabulates the effects on the metallic equivalents of the sous tournois of the 86 changes in the pied de monnaie between 1330 and 1360. On the maze of French coinage in this period see also Bloch, *Esquisse*, 37, 40, 45, 46; Miskimin, *Money, Prices, and Foreign Exchange*; Cuvillier, "Notes on the Royal Coinage," 118–30; John Bell Henneman, *Royal Taxation in Fourteenth Century France: The Development of War Financing, 1322–1356* (Princeton, 1971), 331–48; idem, *Royal Taxation in Fourteenth Century France: Captivity and Ransom of John II, 1356–1370*, Memoires of the American Philosophical Society, 116 (Philadelphia, 1976), 313–16, including tabulations of the prices of silver bullion and the value of the coin made from it.

changed their metallic values whenever a revaluation or devaluation changed the pied de monnaie.

More similar to the developments in Italy was the creation later in France of new moneys of account named after the gold coins on which they were based. Their subdivisions were given the names of silver coins, but the values of these subdivisions depended on the gold coin. For example, the écu became a money of account based on the gold coin bearing the imprint of a shield. It was divided into 18 gros, of which the value had no fixed relation to any coin called a gros but was instead always 1/18 of the value of the golden écu.[35]

In the busiest monetary center of the north, Bruges, in the county of Flanders, a fief of the king of France, the money of account most used in the thirteenth century was the "livre parisis," which was tied to the French livre tournois (1 d. parisis = 1.25 d. tournois). But Flanders was practically independent, and by 1317–19 its livre parisis became tied to a Flemish "groot," with 1 groot equal to 12 deniers parisis. Soon, a money of account more obviously linked to the Flemish groot, the pound groot (that is, 240 groots), became the most used in Bruges and also elsewhere in the Low Countries.[36]

Black moneys underwent a kind of resurrection as link coins in some countries in the fifteenth or in the sixteenth century, when for fiscal reasons they were coined in excessive quantities and given value as legal tender higher than their metallic value. When white money was scarce and black money plentiful, black money operated as bad money according to Gresham's law, driving out coins whose silver content was worth more than their legal value. As larger and larger quantities of black money were issued by princes desperately short of funds, the money of account based on the black money declined more and more from the values it had had as long as the issue of black money had been limited. A value higher than its metallic equivalent had depended on the basic coin's having been issued in limited quantity, and the extent to which it lost value depended on the amount of overissue.

In the latter part of the fourteenth century, both white and black money were much debased in Flanders. Although the groot was established as the link coin of the pound groot, much black money was accepted at values above its metallic worth. In commenting on that situation, one

---

[35]Edouard Perroy and Etienne Fournial, "Réalités monétaires et réalités économiques," *Annales, ESC*, 13 (1958): 538; Wolff, *Commerce et marchands de Toulouse*, 112; Fournial, *Histoire monétaire*, 142–44.

[36]Substantial differences between French and Flemish monetary systems came only in 1337 (de Roover, *Money, Banking, and Credit*, 211, 221–23; Hans van Werveke, "The Economic Policies of Governments: The Low Countries," in *The Cambridge Economic History of Europe*, vol. 3 [Cambridge, 1963], 357; idem, "Monnaie de compte et monnaie réelle," 133–34; van der Wee, *Growth of the Antwerp Market*, 1:107–8).

expert on Flemish coinage, Herman van der Wee, emphasized that the market value of copper coins could differ from their low metallic value to such an extent that the metallic content did not determine the value of a money of account based on such coins. When black money drove coins of fine silver out of circulation, the value of the money of account, according to his interpretation, "was then determined by the value attached to the money remaining in circulation, . . . i.e., the inflated black money." Its silver content was so heavily overvalued that linking it with the money of account on the basis of its intrinsic silver value was impossible. The situation became comparable, writes van der Wee, to an "inflation of what we would call fiduciary money." Then its value did not correspond to its metallic content, "just as in the case of an inflation of paper money the value of the money of account is not determined by the price of the paper material."[37] Similarly, Ugo Tucci, describing the debasements in Italy, says that the black money became a kind of fiduciary money.[38]

The value of the money of account in those circumstances depended largely on the quantity issued, that is, on the number of the base coins in circulation, as does the value of modern fiduciary money. That idea was not unknown to medieval shopkeepers and moneychangers, as Carlo Cipolla has shown in his analysis of the legislation at Florence in 1378–82. When the lower middle and working classes of Florence desired to lower the value of the gold florin compared with that of the quattrino, the black money in which they received payment (or rather the base coin of the money of account in which their payment was calculated), they voted to retire from circulation and melt down a stipulated number of quattrini every two months until the florin fell from 75 to 70. The scheme did not succeed, in part because the Florentine currency probably became permeated (anew) by Pisan quattrini, which flowed in to replace the Florentine quattrini withdrawn, and in part because of the strong opposition of the

[37]Herman van der Wee, in his critical review of Raymond de Roover's *The Bruges Money Market around 1400*, in *Business History Review* 43 (1969):375. While de Roover characterized black money as token money (p. 38), he also called it a "perpetual threat to the stability of medieval currency systems." Yves Renouard, "Le commerce de l'argent au Moyen Age," *Revue historique* 203 (1950):41–52, reviews—and follows—de Roover. Peter Spufford, *Monetary Problems and Policies*, 40, analyzing an inflation in the Netherlands later in the century, says that the money of account then became based on the black money, not on the better silver coins. He considers the money of account "securely anchored" to the black money, which he calls a "third metal, 'bad' silver." He does not say how much pure silver was represented by the units of account or what the bimetallic ratio was between "'bad' silver" and better silver, nor does he discuss the possibility that the relative value of the black money depended less on its metallic value than on the quantity circulating.

[38]"Le monete in Italia," in *Storia d'Italia*, vol. 5, *I documenti* (Turin, 1973), 568–70. The basic general issue, namely, the relation between the values of moneys of account and the metallic content of coins, is reconsidered below, in chap. 20.

upper classes, who restored oligarchical rule in early 1382 and hastened to repeal the deflationary law.[39]

The extent to which the values of moneys of account in the late medieval and early modern periods came to depend less on the metallic content of particular coins and more on the quantity of coins issued and on the faith people had in the money will be examined from a different angle below, in chapter 20.

## iii. HABIT VERSUS CALCULATION

While mintmasters and moneychanging bankers figured down to small fractions the changing content of the moneys in which they dealt, most everyday usage was governed by ignorance and custom. As W. Stanley Jevons wrote more than a hundred years ago, when gold and silver coins were still in use, "The great mass of the population who hold coins have no theories, or general information whatever, upon the subject of money. They are guided entirely by popular report and tradition. The sole question with them on receiving a coin is whether similar coins have been readily accepted by other people. . . . By far the greater number of people possess no means of learning the metallic, or even the legal, value of an unfamiliar coin. Few people have scales and weights suitable for weighing a coin and no one but an assayer or analytical chemist could decide on its fineness. . . . People in general accept coin simply on the ground of its familiar appearance." On the other hand he also wrote: "Though the public generally do not discriminate between coins and coins, provided there is an apparent similarity, a small class of money-changers, bullion dealers, bankers or goldsmiths make it their business to be acquainted with such differences and know how to derive profit from them."[40]

For the history of money in Venice, or in any country, a persistently recurrent problem is discerning the effects of these two contrasting attitudes: that of what Jevons called "the great mass of the population" and that of the "small class who make it their business to be acquainted with . . . differences of fineness and weight." The problem is all the more persistent because the contrast was not absolute in practice. No clear-cut line separated the "mass" from the "small number." Some differences between coin and coin could be detected by the eye, by ringing, or by biting. Visible insignia were much more important to some people than to others. Coins accepted in some social circles and for some uses might be

---

[39]Carlo M. Cipolla, *Il fiorino e il quattrino: La politica monetaria a Firenze nel 1300* (Bologna, 1982), 98–103.

[40]W. Stanley Jevons, *Money and the Mechanism of Exchange* (London, 1876), 78–80.

rejected in other circles or for other uses. Custom ruled in some situations, rational calculation in others; but a few generalizations may be hazarded.

The coins of small denomination were those most ruled by custom. Their metallic value was normally lower relative to the costs of their manufacture than was the case for coins of larger denomination. They passed most rapidly from hand to hand, suffered most from wear and tear, and were the least affected by international trade balances. They were the most expensive to melt or to export, especially if the export was forbidden, as it was in most countries. Only if the market price for silver bullion rose very far indeed above the mint price would it pay to cull them for export. But once their use had become customary, they could circulate domestically at a legal value far above their intrinsic or metallic worth.

Did the force of custom enable coins of larger denominations also to circulate at traditional and legal values far above their metallic worth? To the extent that it did so, custom overrode the commodity conception of money and turned coins into a kind of fiduciary money. Coins were accepted in payment because of the receiver's *fiducia* that he would be able to make payments with them.

This was a new, third level of faith in "money." At the first level, represented by the first coins, faith in the fineness of the metal was all that was asked for by the imprint placed on it by the authority who minted it. The amount of the metal had to be determined by weighing the coins. At a second level, coins could be counted out with faith that they were of a standard weight, at least approximately. At the third level, coins were accepted, not because of faith in the amount of precious metal they contained, but because of faith that they could be used to make payments similar to those in which they had just been accepted.

Just when that third level of faith was attained is disputable. Opinions vary on the extent to which coins were accepted at legal or customary values above their intrinsic values in medieval and early modern Europe. On so broad a question it is not surprising to find contradictory evidence. One indication of the relative force of faith or custom versus that of calculation is the behavior of prices when the metallic equivalents of the moneys of account were reduced, either by crying up the link coins or by reducing the amount of silver in the coins. After a detailed study of the reaction of grain prices to such devaluations in fourteenth-century France, Harry A. Miskimin concluded that changes in metallic value were quickly reflected in prices—a triumph of calculation over custom.[41] But that was "certainly not true in 1305" nor of land rents generally, commented Joseph Strayer,[42] and efforts of the king's agents to prevent prices from respond-

---

[41]*Money, Prices, and Foreign Exchange*, 61–64; he also concluded that "prices existed in many currencies simultaneously."

[42]In his review of Miskimin's *Money, Prices, and Foreign Exchange*, in *JEcH* 24 (1964):409.

ing to changes in the currency were sometimes quite successful later in the century, according to R. Cazelles.[43] In the much later debasement of the coin in England begun by Henry VIII, perhaps the most thoroughly studied example, not all prices rose in proportion to the decline in the metallic value of the currency.[44] Miskimin's flat statement that "since all money was taken and given as metal, it was presumably all equally good" does not apply universally.[45] Sometimes some prices responded quickly to changes in the coinage, sometimes some prices did not. A comparison of cases suggests that much depended on the people's recent experience. Many rapid changes in the content and official values of coins destroyed a people's faith in what the government declared to be the value of its money, as happened in some decades in fourteenth-century France. On the other hand, when the content of coins and their values had been fairly constant for a generation or more, custom had more power. Then custom supported the people's faith that they could use the money they accepted in payment to make payments of equivalent value themselves. Such faith gave coins some of the characteristics of fiduciary money.

## iv. PAPER MONEY AND BANK CREDITS

If pieces of metal were accepted at values determined not by their content but by their imprint, why could not the government issue pieces of paper that would be accepted in payment at values determined not by their content but by their imprint? In the seventeenth and eighteenth centuries governments began to do exactly that in effect, but the first widely accepted paper money depended as much on faith in bankers as on

[43]In his "Quelques réflexions," 255.

[44]J. D. Gould, *The Great Debasement: Currency and Economy in Mid-Tudor England* (New York and Oxford, 1970), 86, concluded that "it is not true either that the proportion in which coinage was debased invariably reflected an equiproportional increase in the supply of money, or that the increase in the supply of money necessarily resulted in an equiproportional rise in the price level." Such specific price series as those for grain, masons' wages, and cloth behaved differently. And "coins of differing de facto mint equivalents circulated . . . at the same level of value." Similar conclusions were reached by Christopher E. Challis, "The Circulating Medium and the Movement of Prices in Mid-Tudor England," in *The Price Revolution in Sixteenth-Century England*, ed. Peter H. Ramsey (London, 1971), 117–46. Regarding England in 1690, Horsefield (*British Monetary Experiments*, 26) says: "Clipped coins in use circulated at their full nominal value."

[45]*Money, Prices, and Foreign Exchange*, 117. In the same summary section, entitled "Not a Conclusion," he also wrote: "These facts would seem to eliminate Gresham's law as the instigator of coinage movements," a statement that also seems too sweeping or at least much subject to misinterpretation, even if one grants what seems to be his main point, that international arbitrage based on comparison of mint prices for bullion was not the "instigator of currency movements" (Cf. Harry A. Miskimin, "L'applicazione della legge di Gresham" [Paper presented at the fourth "Settimana di Studio" of the Istituto Internazionale di Storia Economica "Francesco Datini," Prato, 1972]; and above, chap. 4, n. 9).

faith in governments. The bank notes issued by the Bank of England bore not the imprint of the royal ruler but the bank's promise to pay.[46] When the Bank of England was founded in 1694, bankers' promises to pay had been serving as an important means of payment for three or four centuries, most notably at Venice. Venetian bankers' promises had not taken the form of paper money that passed from hand to hand. Instead, sums owed by a banker as recorded on his books had been transferred upon oral order from one creditor to another. While coin dominated in small transactions, bank credits had become the form of money most extensively used in big commercial and governmental operations.

True banking had developed, it is now generally agreed, not from moneylending or pawnbroking, but from the manual exchange of coins.[47] The local moneychanger turned banker was often the principal supplier of bullion and scrap coin to the mint, and it was often he who first received and first handled the imperfect products of the mint's craftsmen. It was he who had the first chance to cull overweight coin; who knew both local and foreign coins of whatever sort better than did any other merchants, as well as the moneys of account based on them; who could distinguish legitimate from counterfeit coins; and who knew bullion prices and domestic and foreign exchange rates and how to profit from differences between and among them. It was the local banker, accordingly, who was able to impose some kind of order in the confusion arising from an endless variety of coins and from multiple moneys of account. While receiving coins in deposit, he created a substitute superior to specie for many purposes, namely, bank money.

The banker created this surrogate for specie in the following manner. He accepted good, bad, and average coins and sorted them out with two purposes in mind. In order to determine how much he would credit the depositor, he assessed their weight and fineness and evaluated them in a money of account, discounting some because they looked worn or sweated and perhaps allowing a premium on heavy specimens. He knew that he could later find occasion to put some light coins back into circulation, while those that were too mutilated or too obviously clipped could be sold by weight to the mint at the price of bullion. The heaviest coins he

[46]Although the issue of bank notes by the Bank of Stockholm occurred earlier, the issues of the Bank of England gained much wider circulation (Shepard T. Clough and Richard T. Rapp, *European Economic History*, 3d ed. [New York, 1975], 187–92). The bills of credit issued by the Province of Massachusetts in 1690 and then widely imitated in other colonies were a slightly earlier form of paper money, less acceptable in European financial centers than on the rapidly growing frontier, where the needs for new forms of money as means of payment were greatest (Richard Sylla, "Monetary Innovation in America," *JEcH* 42 [1982]:23–26; for the multiplicity of forms invented in the Colonies, see William Letwin, "Monetary Practice and Theory of the North American Colonies during the 17th and 18th Centuries," in Barbagli Bagnoli, ed., *La moneta nell'economia europea*, 439–69).
[47]See below, chap. 6, n. 45.

put aside, perhaps to be sold later at a profit or exported. His total evaluation of the coins received, arrived at in agreement with the depositor, he registered in his books in the denominations of the most prestigious local money of account. That credit to the depositor's account constituted a claim to ownership of the value of the deposit, an amount the banker was obligated to pay to its owner on request. He could pay either by giving back specie or by adhering to an order from the depositor to transfer the claim to another party. The claim could—and did—become a means of payment when the depositor transferred all or part of the claim to a third party. That third party obviously had to agree to accept the banker's promise to pay. His faith—his *fiducia*—in the solvency of the banker and thus in his ability to convert the claim into cash on demand made the claim fiduciary money in the current sense—a means of payment based on a promise.

Faith in a banker's promise, as well as the possibility of avoiding the cost and loss of time involved in evaluating the various kinds and qualities of coins that made up any payment in cash and the possibility of avoiding the headache involved in calculating continuously the relationship between coin and money of account, helped the banker to wean his clients away from the use of specie and to accustom them to leaving their deposits as much as possible intact in order to utilize them for making payments by transfer of the claim from account to account on the banker's books. The facility and security that his service offered enabled the banker to concentrate in his hands both the circulating capital of businessmen and the savings of commercially inactive persons. The banker, or more correctly the banking system, thus functioned as a socializer of the liquid wealth of many different persons and acted as a clearing house and as a common bookkeeper for the entire business community.[48] Since the banks had to retain only a fractional cash reserve in order to meet daily demand, they contributed to the transformation of wealth into productive capital by lending the excess reserves to other businessmen and by investing directly in commerce and manufacture.

It is well known that within a banking system bank loans can have the effect of creating money or credit, via the mechanism of multiple

[48]The role of banks in "socializing" capital is described in V. I. Lenin, *Imperialism: The Highest Stage of Capitalism* (New York, 1939; reprint, 1970), chap. 3. For Lenin, completion of the process of course had to await the extensive concentration of capital by international monopoly banks under "finance capital." The function of clearing house and common bookkeeper is discussed by Karl Marx in *Capital,* trans. Ernest Untermann, vol. 3 (Chicago, 1909), 711–13. Cf. G. Rodkey, in *Encyclopedia of the Social Sciences,* ed. E. R. A. Seligman and Alvin Johnson (New York, 1930–35), s.v. "bank deposits." For these themes see also Reinhold C. Mueller, "The Role of Bank Money in Venice, 1300–1500," *Studi veneziani,* n.s., 3 (1979), 47–96, esp. 94–96. The concept of the claim is developed by K. Brunner and A. H. Meltzer in "Uses of Money: Money in the Theory of an Exchange Economy," *American Economic Review* 61 (1971):784–805.

expansion.[49] The extent to which banks in medieval and early modern Europe created credit is even more obscure than the extent to which today's banks do so. The inference that they did create credit, that is, that they did expand the money supply beyond the total value of coins issued and circulating, is based on the proven existence of certain essential preconditions: bankers operated on a system of fractional cash reserves; they granted lines of credit to individuals, companies, and governments, often in the form of bank money; they sometimes monetized government debt in this way; and finally, they were welded into a banking system by a more or less functional arrangement of interbank accounts.[50]

Moreover, the factor of credit creation, combined with the cost of "telling" the coins at the time of deposit and withdrawal, and the tendency for the demand for coin to exceed supply at least occasionally contributed to the tendency of bank money to separate from its metallic base and to become a new standard of value, as well as a separate means of payment. Businessmen therefore sometimes specified whether a payment was to be made by transfer of bank money or in cash. Bankers could turn the differential, or "agio," between full-weight coins and bank money into a source of profit.

In the market places of medieval and early modern Europe, banks and the means of payment that they created played an important role in mediating and facilitating transactions. Even though bank money circulated primarily by oral order and therefore almost exclusively in the local market place, it helped to overcome the inconveniences caused by the at best unpredictable availability of good coins. The easily transferable bank deposit or claim, registered in a widely used money of account, was the forerunner of the bank note.

---

[49]The theoretical maximum expansion of credit is the reciprocal of the reserve ratio, so that a reserve ratio of 1 to 3 can lead to a threefold expansion of the money supply (see, for example, Lester V. Chandler, *The Economics of Money and Banking*, 3d ed. [New York, 1959], chap. 5).

[50]de Roover, *Money, Banking, and Credit*, chap. 13, "Bank Deposits As Money," and p. 320. For a contrary opinion see Ederer, *The Evolution of Money*, 113, 116, 121, where the definitions are extremely restrictive.

# 6

## THE RISE OF BANKERS

### i. ENGLAND'S PLACE IN BANKING HISTORY

ACAULAY WROTE THAT when the Bank of England was founded, "all the goldsmiths and the pawnbrokers set up a howl of
rage."[1] Anglo-Saxon historians and Anglo-American economists alike have long looked upon London's goldsmiths as the "pioneers
of bankers and financiers."[2] It is true enough that in England goldsmiths
performed many banking functions, but they began doing so only at the
beginning of the seventeenth century—many centuries after the development of banking in Italy.

The reasons for the late development in England of deposit banking
are many and complex, and no attempt will be made to deal with all of
them in the present context. Two factors, however, seem particularly
worthy of consideration. First of all, in late medieval England the exchange of foreign coin for sterling was a royal monopoly, closely con-

---

[1]Quoted in R. D. Richards, "The First Fifty Years of the Bank of England (1694–1744),"
in *History of the Principal Public Banks,* ed. J. G. van Dillen (The Hague, 1934; reprint,
London, 1965), 257. The author shows, however, that only a minority of the goldsmith-
bankers opposed the institution of a national bank of issue, as a threat to their survival.

[2]For one example of many see Ellis T. Powell, *The Evolution of the Money Market, 1385–1915:
An Historical and Analytical Study of the Rise and Development of Finance as a Centralised, Co-
ordinated Force* (London, 1915), 11.

nected with the mint at the Tower of London.[3] As was mentioned in the preceding chapter, deposit banking is now generally explained as an outgrowth of the moneychanger's service of exchanging coins from different mints and of different metals. For a long time, the royal monopoly of exchange in England, therefore, closed to the enterprise of private individuals the one area of economic activity most crucial to their development into bankers. The royal monopoly, along with the isolated geographical position of England, rendered monetary circulation more controllable, and moneychangers less necessary, than on the Continent.

Another factor that reduced the need for professional moneychangers and promoted the activity of goldsmiths was the attraction Englishmen of wealth felt towards gold and silver plate. Ownership of objects made from precious metals had the advantage, especially in feudal society, of serving both as a store of value and as a conspicuous display of wealth. A large market for the wares produced by goldsmiths existed in most periods in medieval and early modern England.[4] Successful members of the goldsmiths' guild in London became dealers in precious metals, and they seem occasionally to have extended credit in the course of business.[5] This widespread demand for gold and especially silver plate developed in the context of the English bullionist mentality, which had its origins in a national trade policy. It was reflected in an endless series of statutes passed between 1275 and 1663 that basically sought to ensure an influx of bullion and to inhibit its export.[6]

[3]The office of king's exchanger, established about 1344, was initially held by royal license as a farm, with bases in London and some provincial centers. Between 1380 and 1505, however, the office was held by the "master-worker" of the mint, who thus combined the roles of mintmaster and buyer of foreign coins that constituted a supply of bullion for the mint; he had to show a profit in both roles. In that period the exchange was located on Lombard Street; users paid a kind of brokerage fee (Thomas F. Reddaway, "The King's Mint and Exchange in London, 1343–1543," *English Historical Review* 82 [1967], 1–23, esp. 8–11; Michael Prestwich, "Italian Merchants in Late Thirteenth and Early Fourteenth Century England," in *DMB*, 99). Many of the prohibitions that simply forbade the importation of coins were aimed primarily at keeping out counterfeit and clipped coins (see Munro, "Bullionism," 187–90 and his app. A).

[4]See the general comments on hoarding in John H. Munro, "Monetary Contraction and Industrial Change in the Late-Medieval Low Countries, 1335–1500," in *Coinage in the Low Countries, 880–1500*, ed. Nicholas J. Mayhew, British Archeological Reports, International series, 54 (Oxford, 1979), 102–3. Of course in England as everywhere, there were periods when hoards were monetized: during the dissolution of the monasteries under Henry VIII and during the Civil War a century later as a means of financing the Royalist cause (Reddaway, "The King's Mint and Exchange," 23; Powell, *Evolution of the Money Market*, 34; and Christopher Hill, *The Century of Revolution, 1603–1714* [London, 1961], 214).

[5]George Unwin, "London Tradesmen and Their Creditors," in *Finance and Trade under Edward III*, ed. George Unwin (Manchester, England, 1918), reprinted in George Unwin, *Studies in Economic History: The Collected Papers of George Unwin*, ed. Richard H. Tawney (London, 1927), 107–9.

[6]Munro, "Bullionism." The proto-mercantilism of Edward III's staple policy was moti-

The contrast between a late feudal monarchy like England and the highly commercialized city-states of Italy on this score is neatly drawn in a "relation" prepared by the secretary to the Venetian ambassador Andrea Trevisan, resident in England in 1497–1498.[7] One of the aspects of English economy and society that struck him particularly—as it did his successors—was the concern for extravagant display and the ubiquity of silver plate as the primary form of conspicuous hoarding. This situation he attributed to the favorable balance of trade enjoyed by England and to the bullionist concern for prohibiting the reexportation of coin and bullion accumulated within the country as a result of the positive commercial balance.

Extravagance was everywhere manifest to this Venetian observer: in the churches, monasteries, and convents—from the richest to the poorest; in the wardrobes of feudatories and ecclesiastics (the Venetian ambassador in 1531 estimated the value of Cardinal Wolsey's holdings of plate at 150,000–200,000 ducats); in the houses of London merchants. No one was considered a person of consequence, he said, who did not have in his house plate worth at least £100 sterling, equal to 500 scudi d'oro, and even the humblest innkeeper supposedly set his table with silver plates and cups. It was thus logical, although hardly less surprising to our observer, to find fifty-two goldsmith shops on the Strand alone, "so rich and full of silver vessels, large and small, that in all the shops of Milan, Rome, Venice and Florence put together I do not think there are as many of such grandeur as are to be seen in London."[8]

Of course there is some exaggeration in the Venetian diplomat's description. Some bullion occasionally had to be exported, in response to a particular monetary policy or to fluctuations in rates of foreign exchange, not to speak of the need for provisioning armies on the Continent, a need that could not always be met on the foreign exchange market.[9] More significant, however, is the Venetian's perception of a contrast between

---

vated, according to the parliamentary rolls, by the desire "to replenish the realm with Money and plate of gold and silver" (discussed by George Unwin in "The Economic Policy of Edward III," in Unwin, *Finance and Trade,* reprinted in his *Studies,* 128).

[7]*A Relation or rather a True Account of the Island of England . . . about the Year 1500,* ed. and trans. C. A. Sneyd (London, 1847), 28–29, 77–78 (n. 40), reprinted in facsimile in Luigi Firpo, ed., *Relazioni di ambasciatori veneti al Senato,* vol. 1, *Inghilterra* (Turin, 1965), with an introductory note concerning the attribution of the anonymous text; original pagination is maintained. The text of 1531 is Firpo, *Relazioni,* no. 3.

[8]*A Relation,* 42–43 (also quoted in Reddaway, "The King's Mint and Exchange," 23). In the 1560s there were 90–100 goldsmiths in Cheapside and an increasing number on Lombard Street (Powell, *Evolution of the Money Market,* 53–54. In general see F. J. Fisher, "The Development of London as a Centre of Conspicuous Consumption in the Sixteenth and Seventeenth Centuries," reprinted in *Essays in Economic History,* ed. E. M. Carus-Wilson, vol. 2 [London, 1962], pp. 197–207).

[9]Munro, "Bullionism," esp. 212.

the England he observed and the Venetian scene, where the exportation of bullion to the Levant was a natural and accepted phenomenon and where conspicuous hoarding among active merchants was as a result more contained.[10] For him, the bullionist mentality and the tendency to hoard that paralleled it belonged to another world. And indeed it is surprising to learn that no less a figure than Sir Thomas Gresham, the royal agent on the money markets of London and Antwerp, remembered for the monetary law that bears his name, had invested his patrimony largely in gold chains, as was discovered at his death in 1579.[11]

The England of these traditions did not know—or need—the services of the local deposit and transfer banker. The nonexistence there of deposit banks similar to those operating in Venice and other major market places on the Continent is evidenced by the absence of references to such institutions in the handbooks of accounting produced as late as the Elizabethan period. When Luca Pacioli's famous tract on double-entry bookkeeping, published in Venice in 1494, was translated into English in 1588, the section relating specifically to banking was omitted as irrelevant.[12]

Partial banking functions were therefore handled by a cluster of financial intermediaries: the merchant—first foreign, then English—who dealt also in bills of exchange; the scrivener, who, while primarily a writer of bonds and contracts, was the first to accept fungible deposits of money and make them available as investment credit; and the goldsmiths, as craftsmen and bullion merchants.[13] But even taken together they did not constitute a banking system and therefore created no ready alternative to coin, as deposit banks created bank money. English merchants reacted to this handicap and to national bullionist policies by assigning and discounting such credit instruments as letters obligatory and bills of exchange long before endorsement became widespread.[14]

Goldsmiths began to take on new functions only under Elizabeth and developed rapidly into bankers only in the Cromwellian and Restoration periods. It was only in the late sixteenth century, according to R. D.

[10]This is not to say that Venice's conception of coin and bullion as exchange commodities was considered the norm by contemporaries. The Florentine polemicist and Medici partisan Benedetto Dei (d. 1492) praised Florence's exports of woolens and silks to the Levant, while disparaging Venice's export of ducats (Giustiniano degli Azzi, ed., "Un frammento inedito della cronaca di Benedetto Dei," *Archivio storico italiano* 110 [1952]:109).

[11]Powell, *Evolution of the Money Market,* 34; cf. de Roover, *Gresham,* 17–30. In the seventeenth century the East India Company exported bullion, an activity that needed the careful defense of Sir Josiah Child (Hill, *Century of Revolution,* 214).

[12]R. D. Richards, *The Early History of Banking in England* (London, 1929), 21.

[13]Ibid., 2–20, 223–30. It is worth remarking that Richards begins his classic history with a brief consideration of banking in Venice in order to underscore the contrast with developments in England.

[14]Munro, "Bullionism," 212–15; van der Wee, "Monetary, Credit, and Banking Systems," 347–54.

Richards, that goldsmiths, after a long tradition of handling bullion, took up the manual exchange of coins and began accepting deposits of money and valuables, albeit only as nonfungibles and merely for safekeeping. But even these services were by no means habitual. As late as the early decades of the seventeenth century many London merchants deposited their specie and bullion for safekeeping at the Tower of London, where Elizabeth had concentrated the national mint. However, Charles I's seizure in 1640 of private stores kept there for a total of £200,000 sterling certainly encouraged merchants to turn away from royal institutions and to seek out the private goldsmiths as safe depositories.[15] Rapid modernization in English banking took place in the last decades of the seventeenth century under the stimulus of the whole gamut of new opportunities that opened up in the course of the so-called Puritan or bourgeois revolution. It was then that goldsmiths began issuing the negotiable promissory notes for which they are best known.[16]

## ii. INTERNATIONAL BANKERS

Since England developed native operators on the money market only in the sixteenth and seventeenth centuries, she had to rely on foreigners in the preceding centuries. Those foreigners were primarily Tuscan merchants, whose numerous financial activities led to their being called bankers or merchant bankers by modern historians.

It is not uncommon to apply the term "banker" to any person of the medieval and early modern period who dealt in money—whether coin or its surrogates—or provided financial services. It is much more useful, however, to conceive of the ancestors of modern bankers in terms of a tripartite division: international bankers, pawnbrokers, and local deposit bankers.[17] Each was involved in a different kind of credit. The first were

[15]Richards, *Early History of Banking*, 35–36; Hill, *Century of Revolution*, 219.

[16]Richards, *Early History of Banking*, esp. 223–30; van der Wee, "Monetary, Credit, and Banking Systems," 347–54.

[17]These distinctions were already clearly made by Gino Luzzatto, in *Enciclopedia italiana* (Rome, 1929–36; reprint, Rome, 1949), s.v. "banca—dal medioevo ai nostri giorni"; and they became practically codified by de Roover in his *Money, Banking, and Credit*, passim. See also his "New Interpretations of the History of Banking," reprinted in his *Business, Banking, and Economic Thought*; idem, "Early Banking before 1500 and the Development of Capitalism," *Revue internationale d'histoire de la banque* 4 (1971):1–16, which is an expanded version of "Banking and Credit in the Formation of Capitalism," *Fifth International Conference of Economic History, Leningrad 1970* (Paris, The Hague, New York, 1979), vols. 4–5, pp. 9–17; and idem, "La structure des banques au Moyen Age," *Third International Conference of Economic History, Munich 1965* (Paris, 1974), vol. 5, pp. 159–69. Henri Lapeyre, "La banque, les changes et le credit au XVIe siècle," *Revue d'histoire moderne et contemporaine* 3 (1956):284–97, basically accepts de Roover but creates a fourth category for public banks, which here will be treated as an outgrowth of local banks. Jacques Heers, *Gênes au XVe siècle: Activité économique et problèmes sociaux*, EPHE-6, Affaires et gens d'affaires, 24 (Paris, 1961), 91–92, found the

merchants who, *inter alia,* made short-term credit available in the course of their international transfers of funds; the second extended consumption loans on collateral; the third accepted deposits, transformed them into bank money which was readily available for making payments via transfer, and created credit by lending on current account.

Specialization among these categories was by no means complete, and the division is not intended to imply a rigid exclusiveness. An individual or a company might be involved in some way in functions relating to all three categories: international bankers sometimes established local deposit banks; they and local bankers occasionally extended consumer credit on collateral, although not as openly as the pawnbroker; and local deposit banks turned to long-distance commerce as one way of investing deposits. Distinctions among these categories probably meant little outside the commercial community. The general public tended to classify all dealers in money as usurers.[18] However, in many medieval towns and cities, most clearly in Bruges, the principal functions of each category were considered quite separate juridically.

International bankers and pawnbrokers have caught the attention of modern historians, much as they held the attention of inhabitants of the medieval world, haves and have-nots alike. By contrast, the least colorful, the local moneychanger and deposit banker, will be accorded pride of place here. In the traditional historiography of banking, Venice is identified with the giro bank. During the seventeenth century, giro banks continued the most basic of the operations performed as early as the fourteenth century by local deposit bankers, most intensely and notably at Venice. The government-operated giro banks of the later century were but emaciated descendents of medieval private bankers who had used their transfers of deposits to add bank credit to the money supply and who therefore deserve to be called, in one sense of the term, the first true bankers.[19]

The size and extension of the networks created by international bankers, however, attracted much more attention than did giro banks in the fourteenth century as well as later. International bankers needed large organizations to carry on their extended operations, and in order to mobi-

division not in accord with the situation in Genoa. The division was most recently accepted by Robert S. Lopez, "The Dawn of Medieval Banking," in *DMB*, 7. Finally, see Raymond Bogaert, "Ursprung und Entwicklung der Depositenbank im Altertum und Mittelalter," in *Essays zur historischen Entwicklung des Bankensystems,* by Raymond Bogaert and Peter Claus Hartmann (Mannheim, 1980).

[18]Iris Origo, *The Merchant of Prato: Francesco di Marco Datini* (London, 1957), 151. See also Jacques Le Goff, "The Usurer and Purgatory," in *DMB*, 25–52, and in his recent opus, *La nascita del purgatorio* (Turin, 1983).

[19]As Henri Lapeyre puts it, the local deposit banker was the only banker properly so called ("La banque, les changes et le credit," 286–89, 296).

lize the necessary capital, they developed forms of business organization that constitute a major contribution to the development of capitalism and were used later by all kinds of bankers.

The companies that led in international banking were originally family partnerships. When outsiders were taken in as partners, they generally accepted the directorship of the family nucleus. While most companies were small, the most famous were extraordinarily large, as were in the first half of the fourteenth century the Florentine firms of the Bardi, the Peruzzi, and the Acciaiuoli, which the chronicler Giovanni Villani called the "Pillars of Christendom," and later the Alberti and the Medici. An idea of their size can be gained from the lists of branch offices that they maintained in some 8 to 16 cities and from the number of employees operating the branches: in 1336 the Peruzzi had a staff of 88; in 1341 the Acciaiuoli had a staff of 53; and in 1469 the Medici personnel numbered about 60 (50 salaried factors and 10 managers and partners).[20] The home office was generally housed in the family palace. Branch offices were usually small, and the employees of all firms from a single city of origin felt the need to join together into a corporation, or "nazione," for mutual assistance against their hosts. The business of the foreign nazioni was generally transacted, not in private offices, but in a public Bourse, or exchange. The magnificent palace built by the Medici in Milan in the 1450s to house their branch office, however symbolic of economic and political power, was an exception.[21]

The legal structure of these big inland firms of international bankers differed from the temporary venture partnerships that predominated among merchants in such maritime cities as Venice. Tuscan companies preferred setting a period of three to five years for the life of a partnership, which could of course be renewed in similar or modified form for another period of years after the balance was cast and profits (or losses) were distributed. Before the failures of so many Florentine companies in the 1340s, the large partnerships preferred a unitary legal structure whereby the home office directly controlled the whole network of branches, which were run largely by salaried employees, sometimes by full partners. After the bankruptcies and the Black Death, large firms like those of Francesco Datini and the Medici evolved a more flexible form of business organization somewhat resembling a holding company whereby the central office established a new partnership, a separate legal entity with separate capital

---

[20]Raymond de Roover, "The Organization of Trade," in *The Cambridge Economic History of Europe*, vol. 3 (Cambridge, 1963), 85–86.

[21]On the Florentine nazioni see Goldthwaite, *The Building of Renaissance Florence*, 34–41. For proud comments by Benedetto Dei on the far-flung Florentine "banchi" see degli Azzi, "Un frammento inedito," 208 f. Only the portal of the Medici branch in Milan remains, preserved at the Castello Sforzesco (see de Roover, *Rise and Decline of the Medici Bank*, 263).

and separate liability, for each foreign branch. In practice, however, the legal structure used by international bankers made little difference in the daily task of entrepreneurial decision making; and the communication of decisions remained slow and problematical, whether branches were run by employees or by partners.[22]

International bankers mobilized capital by pooling funds. They formed partnerships with designated capital funds in which they owned shares according to the portions invested; a majority of the shares was usually held by members of the family that gave its name to the company. Working partners either received a salary or their input was capitalized and assigned a share in the capital fund; they were forbidden by the articles of association to invest personally outside of the firm. Profits and losses were divided among the partners in proportion to their share in the capital. Liability was technically unlimited for all partners until the spread in fifteenth-century Tuscany and Genoa of the accomanda form of organization, whereby silent partners, liable only up to the amount of their investment, were admitted. Up until the middle of the fourteenth century the partners often assigned 1 to 1 1/2 percent to the Lord God ("Messer Domenedio"), who thus became a shareholder with an interest in the success of the company; when profits were divided, his portion was rendered to the poor.[23]

Above and beyond the capital fund, or "corpo," of the partners was another more flexible fund which enabled the further accumulation of investable capital. It was called the "sopracorpo" and consisted of a kind of time deposit that earned interest, or "discrezione," at a rate of 8, 10, or 12 percent per annum. As Raymond de Roover has explained, these investments "fuori del corpo" were of three kinds: funds provided by partners in addition to their shares in the corpo; reinvested earnings; and deposits by outsiders, who were often aristocrats and clergymen or in general persons not directly active in business. These deposits must be contrasted with the demand deposits of the local banks, for they were not readily transferable, nor could they normally be withdrawn on short notice.[24]

---

[22]de Roover, "The Organization of Trade," 75–90.

[23]Ibid., 76–77. On the structure of the early firms see Armando Sapori, *La crisi delle compagnie mercantili dei Bardi e dei Peruzzi* (Florence, 1926); and Michele Luzzati, *Giovanni Villani e la compagnia dei Buonaccorsi* (Rome, 1971). For "véritables sociétés par actions" in Genoa see Heers, *Gênes au XVe siècle*, 151, 200–206.

[24]de Roover, *Money, Banking, and Credit*, 31–42. There was room for flexibility within generally accepted guidelines, as the following example shows. Late in the year 1400 the Datini firm in Florence negotiated a deposit from a third party for the firm of the heirs of Zanobi Gaddi, which needed operating capital. The sum deposited was 1,200 florins, at 8 percent interest. Upon learning the conditions, the manager of the Gaddi firm in Venice voiced serious objections in his next letter: while the rate of interest was reasonable ("el detto pregio è ragionevole"), the depositor had been given the unusual option to withdraw on only 15 days' notice, in contrast to the prevailing practice of fixing the term of the certificate at 4–6

As generic businessmen or hommes d'affaires, international bankers compiled diversified portfolios by investing in long-distance trade, local manufacture (usually in textiles), government bonds, tax farming at home and abroad, maritime insurance, provisioning of armies, and international transfer of funds. Some opened local deposit banks in their home city as part of their diversified investments and as a means of increasing the funds at their disposal. Such a decision signified their willingness to undertake daily and apparently petty tasks such as exchanging coins for a fee, but their subsidiary local banks were important in the creation of long-term credit. In their international activity, which covered from one end to the other the known commercial world, they developed and perfected the bill of exchange as a means of transferring credit balances over long distances without the risk and cost of transporting specie. They also utilized the bill of exchange as a means for very extensive short-term lending and borrowing. Some firms in fact specialized in foreign exchange and created, through their transactions in bills, sophisticated money markets that registered slackness or intensity in the supply and demand both of credit and of specie.[25] These markets made it possible for merchants to function as collection agents for the papal Curia, to transfer money to cover purchases made abroad, to ransom feudal lords captured in war, to provision armies on the march, and to extend credit to other merchants or to princes. All these elements were combined into a single network of regional and international debits and credits, held together with constant letter writing.

Best known perhaps are the contacts between international bankers and foreign princes, always in need of credit. The majority of loans made to foreign rulers might more accurately be called the purchase of futures. Such loans were made only in exchange for trade privileges and were generally recouped in raw materials such as wool or via contracts making the bankers collectors of taxes or customs. As Richard Goldthwaite has recently remarked, such merchants and international bankers had as much need of the prince as he had of them.[26]

Thanks to studies by such historians as Armando Sapori, Yves Re-

---

months, with a given number of days' notice due prior to withdrawal at the end of that time. A fixed term, he wrote, normally covered periods of variable interest and profitability ("grasso e magro") and inhibited the depositor from seeking to withdraw his funds on short notice in order to reinvest them elsewhere at a higher return. As negotiated, the manager continued, the agreement permitted the depositor to withdraw at will, forcing his own firm to seek alternative sources of credit on the foreign exchange market at higher rates of interest (ASP, Datini, b. 713, letter of the Commissaria Gaddi to Florence, 23 December 1400).

[25]See Reinhold C. Mueller, "'Chome l'ucciello di passagio': La demande saisonnière des espèces et le marché des changes à Venise au Moyen-Age," in *Etudes d'histoire monétaire*, ed. John Day (Lille, forthcoming); and below, vol. 2.

[26]Richard A. Goldthwaite, "Italian Bankers in Medieval England," review of *Bankers to the Crown: The Riccardi of Lucca and Edward I*, by Richard W. Kaeuper, in *JEEcH* 2 (1973):763–71, esp. 767.

nouard, Raymond de Roover, Richard Kaeuper, and Michael Prestwich, we have become familiar with the Tuscan firms that acted as financial agents for the Curia and the English crown: the Bonsignori of Siena, the Ricciardi of Lucca, the Frescobaldi, Bardi, Peruzzi, Alberti, and Medici of Florence, along with dozens of smaller companies. Their ability to transfer capital enabled them to extend credit in one place and collect in another. They invested in high-quality raw wool and woolen cloth, with which they supplied industries in Florence. While advances made to English kings were recouped by customs privileges or by liens on royal revenues, of which they organized the collection, these firms also advanced money to nobles and monasteries whose lands and hands produced the wool in which they were interested.[27]

Even though Edward III's reneging on huge outstanding loans was only one of several causes of the famous Florentine bankruptcies of the 1340s, the Italian international bankers thereafter withdrew from involvement with royal finances. Some of their functions in England were taken over by the English Company of the Staple, which was granted monopoly rights on the export of wool precisely in order to constitute a source of royal credit. But once again, in the mid-fifteenth century the London branch of a Florentine firm, this time the Medici firm, became sufficiently involved in loans to the king and noble factions that the home office was forced to close the branch in 1477.[28]

Other countries produced international bankers who thrived especially after the Florentine firms had begun to decline: Jacques Coeur in France; the Fuggers, Welsers, and others in southern German cities. The Germans made huge profits in mining, but most of their mining rights were acquired in the traditional manner, by lending money to the Hapsburgs and territorial lords. Florentine and Genoese international bankers survived throughout most of the sixteenth century as specialists in the speculative credit operations concentrated at the great exchange fairs.[29]

The long involvement of the Tuscan firms with the ecclesiastical and secular princes of Europe has tended to overshadow their presence in

[27]Besides the studies of de Roover cited in n. 17 above, extensive bibliographies and broad historical overviews of international bankers are provided by Jacques Le Goff, *Marchands et banquiers du Moyen Age* (Paris, 1956); and by Armando Sapori, *La mercatura medievale* (Florence, 1972).

[28]On the Company of the Staple and credit to the crown see A. B. Hibbert, "The Economic Policies of Towns," and Edmund B. Fryde and M. M. Fryde, "Public Credit, with Special Reference to North-Western Europe," in *The Cambridge Economic History of Europe*, vol. 3 (Cambridge, 1963), pp. 336 and 467, respectively; on the return to old practices by the Medici see the latter, 470–71, and de Roover, *Rise and Decline of the Medici Bank*, 332–38.

[29]See Jean-François Bergier, "From the Fifteenth Century in Italy to the Sixteenth Century in Germany: A New Banking Concept?" in *DMB*, 105–29.

nearly every major market place in western Europe. Dozens of such firms operated also in Venice, despite the importance of that city's own merchants and bankers and its concern for protecting the interests of its own citizens. How the operations of international bankers meshed with those of Venice's deposit banks will be analyzed in volume 2 when we describe the Venetian foreign exchange market, which was organized and operated almost exclusively by Florentine international bankers.

### iii. CONSUMER CREDIT

The second category of dealers in money very much in the public eye comprises pawnbrokers. Consumption credit was necessary for survival for the poor, whether their need was temporary or continuous, and for the "magnificentia" of the highborn who felt the need to maintain a style of life above and beyond their means. While in the countryside petty landowners and sharecroppers could put up land and agricultural produce for loans extended usually by nonprofessional lenders,[30] urban populations needed the services of professionals who would lend—at interest—on the security of personal property. In economic terms, their lending activities consisted merely in transferring purchasing power, which was itself consumed in the use, in contrast to the lending activities of both international bankers and local deposit bankers.[31]

The Church came to consider legitimate many forms of credit on which the lender took what we today would normally call interest. But the contractual forms considered acceptable in themselves, or regarding which exceptions or "titles" to taking interest existed, all involved investment credit and served the interests of merchants and entrepreneurs and were therefore not available to the poor. In most cases, some kind of risk or uncertainty for the lender was involved, an important factor in the considerations of theologians and canon lawyers. No risk factor existed in the case of the "mutuum," an illegal loan at interest generally secured on personal property, and it was therefore unequivocally judged sinful by the Church. Public or manifest usurers were excommunicated by the Third Lateran Council in 1179 and were considered by the general public—and

---

[30]There is a vast literature on rural credit. Here it will suffice to mention two recent studies on the Veneto and Tuscany: Corazzol, *Fitti e livelli a grano;* and Giuliano Pinto, "Note sull'indebitamento contadino e lo sviluppo della proprietà fondiaria cittadina nella Toscana tardomedievale," *Ricerche storiche* 10 (1980):3–19, reprinted in his *La Toscana nel tardo Medio Evo.*

[31]Lester Chandler (*The Economics of Money and Banking,* 34 ff.) makes the point that consumption loans can benefit the debtor to the extent that he can go into debt to meet extraordinary needs at one moment and then repay with money that has less utility to him later—a notably abstract way of contrasting the different needs of the poor when starving and when well employed.

especially by those who had recourse to their services—as infamous by virtue of their very profession.[32]

Civil authorities realized that the ecclesiastical prohibition against usury did not attenuate the need, and they were often forced to license the operation of pawnbrokers within their jurisdiction. Such secular acceptance of manifest usury was attacked in 1311–12 by the Council of Vienne, which charged with heresy anyone who held that usury was not a sin and therefore strongly condemned civil authorities who licensed pawnbroking. But the Church's decisions could do little to change civil policy in this regard. The public need remained, and some control was better than none. In fact, the license or charter constituted a source of revenue for the government, a guarantee of legal protection—however tenuous—for the pawnbrokers, and it offered a certain degree of governmental control over this important social function.

Licensed or not, pawnbroking remained essentially illegal, and Christian usurers still had to face the spiritual forum of confession in which restitution was a precondition for absolution. Episcopal courts were happy to agree on a forfeit covering uncertain usury ("male ablata incerta"), since those sums went to the bishop rather than to verified victims of gouging. Only after restitution was made or provided for was burial in hallowed ground permitted. Jewish lenders, obviously not bound by canon law, could simply be expelled if their services were deemed dispensable.

Interest rates were often high. In Bruges in the fourteenth and fifteenth centuries the legal rate was 43.33 percent per annum. It was normal there and elsewhere to extend loans to a maximum of about 60 percent of the value of the item pawned in order to guarantee recuperation of principal, interest, and fees from the sale of the item in case of nonpayment.[33] In regions where families of Jewish lenders entered the market for consumption credit, they were often able to offer lower rates of interest than individual Christian usurers and thereby cut the latter out of the market. Charters granted to Jews fixed maximum rates of interest but then helped the lenders maintain the lower rates by according them a monopoly of business in the area.

During the early centuries pawnbrokers were generally Christians and very often Italians. Italians who traveled to other countries and to the fairs were generically called Lombards. The so-called Lombards active in Bruges in the fourteenth and fifteenth centuries were in fact originally from Asti and Chieri in Piedmont.[34] Pawnbrokers in the Veneto and

---

[32]Noonan, *The Scholastic Analysis of Usury*; Gabriel LeBras, in *Dictionnaire de théologie catholique*, ed. A. Vacant, E. Mangenot, and E. Aman (Paris, 1903–72), s.v. "usure."

[33]de Roover, *Money, Banking, and Credit*, 132–33.

[34]Ibid., 101. See also Jacques Heers, *Il clan famigliare nel medioevo* (Naples, 1976), 291–93, where the author shows that pawnbrokers sometimes belonged to solid family companies

Friuli in the thirteenth and early fourteenth centuries were known as Tuscans. But none was a member of the great families of international bankers discussed previously.[35] Sooner or later, at least in Italy, the Christian pawnbrokers were replaced by Jews, whose souls were not endangered by the anathemas pronounced by the Church. In Florence itself for a very long time the pawnbrokers were Christians, licensed and controlled by a foreign judge.[36] When the Medici took over the reins of power in 1434, that judgeship was suppressed, and negotiations were begun to replace the Christians with Jews, who finally agreed in 1437 to handle the business of pawnbroking in that important commercial and industrial capital.[37] In much of Italy, however, families of Jews had taken over moneylending much earlier. Jews connected with the Curia Romana moved northward from Rome as far as Tuscany as early as the second half of the thirteenth century. After the pogroms connected with the Black Death, Jews moving southward from Germany began supplanting Christian usurers in northern Italy, and particularly in the Veneto. It was then, as we shall see, that Venice first came into contact with professional Jewish lenders.[38]

The role of pawnbrokers was more important in social terms than in economic terms. While professional moneylenders can be found extending credit to merchants on a personal guarantee rather than on collateral, this was more the exception than the rule. They provided no other banking services, such as exchange of currencies or acceptance of deposits, which were reserved to deposit bankers. The latter usually had to be citizens of the town in which they wished to open a bank, while Jews, by contrast,

and gives the example of the Gallerani of Siena, active in London, Paris, and the fairs of Champagne in the thirteenth century, and other "veritable tribes," such as the Vagnon and the Pelletta, who operated networks of pawnshops throughout Piedmont. On the tendency of the "merchant-banker-Lombards" of Asti to lend to princes and to buy up fiefs see Alessandra Sisto, *Banchieri-feudatari subalpini nei secoli XII–XIV,* Pubblicazioni della Facoltà di Lettere e Filosofia, Università di Torino, 14/1 (Turin, 1963).

[35]Exceptionally, a member of the Gianfigliazzi family was condemned by Dante (*Inferno,* 17) and is identifiable on the basis of the coat of arms on his moneybags (see also Sapori, *La mercatura medievale,* 138 n. 1).

[36]The licenses, which have never been studied, were granted by the Commune upon payment of a "fine"; they netted some 3,000 florins per year for the communal treasury (see, for example, ASF, Provvisioni, reg. 61, fol. 74 [20 June 1373], and ibid., Esecutore degli Ordinamenti di Giustizia, n. 265 [CRIA n. 2900], acta civilia for the year 1357, a volume that contains dozens of decisions for and against the pawnbrokers. Other volumes of these acts contain complete lists of the licensed pawnbrokers).

[37]Essential bibliography in de Roover, "New Interpretations," 213.

[38]See the papers presented by Philippe Braunstein, Michele Luzzati, Brian Pullan, Renata Segre, Ariel Toaff, and Gian Maria Varanini at the session dedicated to "Prestatori e banchi di pegno a Venezia e nel Dominio" and organized by Reinhold C. Mueller, at the convention "Gli Ebrei e Venezia (secoli XIV–XVIII)," Fondazione Giorgio Cini, June 1983, forthcoming.

were rarely accorded full citizenship. Pawnbrokers were therefore not strictly speaking ancestors of the deposit bankers.

Shortly after the middle of the fifteenth century the observant Franciscans began a movement aimed at supplanting the usury of Jewish "infidels" with public nonprofit pawn banks, or "monti di pietà," which were supposed to serve the needs of the poor. By offering loans on collateral at only about 5 percent interest, these institutions were supposed to undersell the Jews. Fighting fire with fire, the Franciscans proposed to eliminate usury, in the sense of exorbitant interest, with moderate interest. Local governments that supported the institutions could therefore terminate their charters with the Jews and expel them from their territory. Monti di pietà were established in cities and towns throughout Italy within the half-century following institution of the first monte in Perugia and its approval by the Venetian pope Paul II (Barbo) in 1467. Franciscan preaching caused many expulsions, often accompanied by the unleashing of popular furor against the hated usurers. But the monti di pietà in fact rarely succeeded in supplanting the Jews, for they were much less flexible in meeting the needs of different kinds of borrowers. Venice supported both the activities of Jews and the monti di pietà in her dominions, while seeking as long as possible to keep the capital city itself free of both.[39]

The later history of the monti di pietà is rather curious. In Italy they tended early to become centers of political and economic power for local families and factions and moved ever further away from their original, pious goals. When this development had become irreversible and the monti took on the role of public banks, countries of western and northern Europe became interested in the earlier program. They sought in the sixteenth century to follow the original Italian example, not so much against Jews as against Christian usurers. In 1572 a monte di pietà was established in Bruges.[40] At about the same time, a French observer was sent to Italy to study the institution and the feasibility of introducing it to France.[41] And English economic writers like Malynes began proposing the introduction of the "mounts of charitie" as antidotes to usury in the early seventeenth century—long before Cromwell made it possible for Jews to return to England.[42]

---

[39]See Brian Pullan, *Rich and Poor in Renaissance Venice: The Social Institutions of a Catholic State, to 1620* (Oxford, 1971), 431–75.

[40]de Roover, *Money, Banking, and Credit,* 101.

[41]Léon Poliakov, *Les banchieri juifs et le Saint-Siège du XIIIe au XVIIe siècle* (Paris, 1967), 274 ff.

[42]Richards, *Early History of Banking,* 12–13. For the situation in Spain see Felipe Ruiz Martin, "Demanda y oferta bancarias, 1450–1600," in *Mélanges en l'honneur de Fernand Braudel,* 2 vols. (Toulouse, 1973), vol. 1.

## iv. LOCAL DEPOSIT BANKS

The third and truest ancestor of modern banking, the deposit bank-er, is the most difficult to describe in general terms because of the pecu-liarities of each local situation. All observers seem to agree, however, on the essential nature and on the origins of deposit banking. "The essential function of a banking system is the creation of credit," wrote Abbott Payson Usher in the first sentence of his projected history of deposit banking. No matter what other functions a system of individual bankers performed nor what the peculiarities of its procedures and forms were, the primary activity was "the creation and transfer of credit, whether in the form of the current accounts of depositors or in the form of notes."[43] As explained above, the creation of money is made possible by the acceptance of deposits on current account and their transfer in bank. The more clients develop the habit of paying by transfer, the more of the original deposit the banker can lend or invest. After setting aside a reserve with which to meet demand for cash withdrawals, the banker can invest and lend the excess reserve at the same time that the depositor can use his claim against the banker for paying his own debts. A system of bankers holding ac-counts with one another creates money or credit by the mechanism of multiple expansion, thus adding to the total money supply.[44]

The second point of general agreement concerns the origins of de-posit banking. While international banks originated in the traffic in for-eign exchange ("cambium per litteras"), local banks developed in connec-tion with the manual exchange of coins ("cambium minutum").[45]

When moneychangers began accepting money on deposit from their clients, they transformed themselves into bankers. But they never dropped the function of moneychanging, because it was an important source of profit. Therefore, contrary to the assertions of persons like Francesco Ferrara, who insisted that an operator had to be called "bancherius" before

---

[43]Usher, *The Early History*, 3; also Abbott Payson Usher, "The Origins of Banking: The Primitive Bank of Deposit, 1200–1600," *EcHR* 4 (1934):399–428, reprinted in Lane and Riemersma, eds., *Enterprise and Secular Change*. Cf. Federigo Melis, "La grande conquista trecentesca del 'credito di esercizio' e la tipologia dei suoi strumenti fino al XVI secolo" (Paper presented at the fourth "Settimana di Studio" of the Istituto Internazionale di Storia Economica "Francesco Datini," Prato, 1972).

[44]De Roover, *Money, Banking, and Credit*, chap. 13; idem, "Early Banking before 1500," 4.

[45]The idea that deposit banking grew out of moneylending was held by André-E. Sayous, "Les operations des banquiers italiens en Italie et aux Foires de Champagne pendant le XIIIe siècle," *Revue historique* 170 (1932): 6. In this respect he was followed by Renée Doehaerd, *Les relations commerciales entre Gênes, la Belgique, et l'Outremont d'après les archives notariales genois au XIIIe et XIVe siècles*, 3 vols., Institut Historique Belge de Rome, Etudes d'histoire écono-mique et sociale (Rome and Brussels, 1941), 2:101. Since then the question has been laid to rest (see de Roover, "Early Banking before 1500").

the change in his functions from that of "campsor" to that of banker could be considered complete, no simple or immediate shift in nomenclature occurred. Local usages differed, and changes took a long time. The term "bancherius" was probably first encountered in Genoa, which preserves the earliest solid documentation regarding local banks. But as Robert S. Lopez has shown, even in the first century of the documented history of Genoese banking, 1150–1250, the functions of international banker, moneychanger, local banker, minter, and lender were not differentiated and were often performed by the same person or firm. Thus the terms "nummularius," "cambiator," "campsor," and "bancherius," as used in Genoa and elsewhere, were practically synonymous and applied to mere moneychangers as well as to deposit bankers.[46] In time, the first two terms tended to be used more for changers of coins, the latter two for deposit bankers.[47] Florentines used the term "tavoliere" as the Italian equivalent of "campsor" for all members of the Cambio guild, whether they emphasized manual exchange or deposit banking. Beginning in the late fourteenth century, the Florentines started applying the term "cambiatore" to specialized dealers in bills of exchange, who in the sixteenth century became universally known as "cambisti." It took a century in Venice, as we shall see, before a relatively clear distinction was made between "campsor" and "bancherius," the latter term being reserved then for the Rialto's distinctive transfer banks, or "banchi di scritta." But extreme caution must be exercised before drawing conclusions regarding functions performed merely on the basis of nomenclature. A final caveat might be instructive: in papal usage, the international bankers who handled papal business, whether the Bonsigniori in the thirteenth century or the Fuggers in the late fifteenth century, were called "campsores domini pape."

The deposits that moneychangers accepted were basically of two kinds. For the commercially inactive client, such as a widow, or for a person who wished to set aside money for a specific future purpose, such as a dowry, the campsor would create a conditioned deposit—which we would call a time deposit—payable when the conditions were fulfilled, on which he might offer to pay a return.[48] From active merchants, in contrast, he received unconditional deposits payable on demand. Such deposits on current account were available as a ready means of payment by

---

[46]Robert S. Lopez, *La prima crisi della banca di Genova (1250–1259)* (Milan, 1956), 22 and n. 4. The same text was published as "I primi cento anni di storia documentata della banca a Genova" in *Studi in onore di Armando Sapori* (Milan, 1957), 1:215–53, but without notes or documents. See also Carmelo Trasselli, *Note per la storia dei banchi in Sicilia nel XIV secolo*, Banco di Sicilia, Fondazione "I. Mormino," Quaderno no. 1 (Palermo, 1958):10–13.

[47]Alessandro Lattes, *Il diritto commerciale nella legislazione statutaria delle città italiane* (Milan, 1884), 199 and 212–15, nn. 5, 6, 10.

[48]"Conditioned deposit" is a term used by Usher in *The Early History*, passim.

transfer from one account to another on the banker's books. They did not earn interest. By tacit understanding, the depositor permitted the banker to use the money that he had deposited or that was credited to his account by transfer in return for safety and the service of transfer.

The transfer of accounts on bankers' books, or "giro di partite," from which the term "giro bank" derives, was the hallmark of Venetian banking. While Venetians took the service for granted, foreigners, used to other practices, sometimes remarked on the particular advantage of avoiding the use of specie when dealing at the Rialto banks. Deposit banks in other cities had a similar potentiality, but different structures and different needs caused giro to be less characteristic of deposit banks in some cities than in others, less used in Tuscany than in Bruges or Barcelona or Venice.[49]

The fact that deposit and transfer banking, that is, the use of bank money, was less important at the "tavole" of Florence than elsewhere probably depended on some four factors. First, it was a practice, supported by both guild and communal statutes, for Florentine merchants generally to offset a debit with one firm by assigning it a credit with another firm. Initially the debtor was supposed to guarantee the solvency of the merchant on whose books the assignment was made, but soon the only legal criteria were the agreement of the beneficiary of the assignment and the correctness of the accounting entries involved.[50] Using offsets as a means of avoiding the use of specie became ingrained in Florentine business practice, among big and small operators alike.[51] But it did not permit the creation of credit in the strict sense, which requires the concentration of deposits in a specialized banking system, although examples of overdrafts can be found even in the process of offsetting. Second was the opportunity open to many active and inactive persons to deposit money in the sopracorpo of their own or others' international banking firms. This kind of deposit at interest, or discrezione, which was not readily transferable, took the place of the conditioned deposit of the local banker. A third factor was the location of the moneychangers' stalls. At least in the thirteenth century and in the first half of the fourteenth century, while offsetting was becoming a habit, the tavole of Florentine moneychangers were situated in four separate locations: the Mercato Vecchio, the Mercato Nuovo, Or San Michele, and Oltr'Arno. Such dislocation made interbank clearance cumbersome and the welding of individual banks into a system more problematical. Even though the local tavole run by international firms like the Uzzano and the Medici

[49]Federigo Melis, *Note di storia della banca pisana nel Trecento* (Pisa, 1956), chap. 8; and Luzzatto, *Enciclopedia italiana*, s.v. "banca."

[50]Lattes, *Il diritto commerciale*, 135 n. 26, with specific references to the relevant guild and communal statutes; see also Federigo Melis in *Documenti per la storia economica dei secoli XIII–XVI*, Pubblicazioni dell'Istituto Internazionale di Storia Economica "Francesco Datini," Prato, 1st ser., 1. (Florence, 1972), 83.

[51]Goldthwaite, *The Building of Renaissance Florence*, 306–13.

tended to locate exclusively in the area of the Mercato Nuovo, the habit of offsetting was perhaps too firmly entrenched to be replaced by transfers at the local banks.[52] Fourth and finally, it is worth noting that at least in certain periods Florentine international bankers preferred to pay the value of bills of exchange in cash rather than by offset or by bank transfer, a propensity reflected in accounting entries that expressly name the employee who brought ("rechò") or took ("portò") the specie to the other party.[53] By contrast, Florentine firms active in Venice, as we shall see, as well as in Bruges and Barcelona, drew and remitted by transferring money on the current accounts that they kept with local bankers.[54] In short, Florentines in Florence probably did not use bank money with any regularity.

So important was the mediation of deposit bankers in other commercial centers that when they were in financial trouble or altogether in decline, city governments stepped in to provide the service of deposit and transfer at public banks. Such a move was discussed at Venice as early as the fourteenth century, but its first public giro bank was instituted only at the end of the sixteenth century.[55] The first medieval public bank was founded at Barcelona in 1401 and survived the vicissitudes of centuries. It did not have a monopoly of deposit banking, but some functions, such as the payment of bills of exchange, were concentrated there. The Taula, or Bank of Deposit, was not authorized to extend credit to private parties but did so especially in certain periods. On the other hand, it was intended to extend credit to the city government and to administer its floating debt. It was even a kind of bankers' bank to the extent that private bankers deposited their reserves there.[56] Valencia followed Barcelona's example by establishing a public bank in 1408. Its Taula de Canvi purported to be a "safe and useful office for merchants, private parties and foreign businessmen, and a protector of pilgrims and travelers, widows and orphans." But despite its good intentions, it was dissolved in 1416.[57] At just about the same time, Genoa's famous Casa di San Giorgio founded the Banco di San

[52]The difficulty of clearing accounts by oral order in Florence probably promoted the early use of written orders or cheques (see ibid.; and Marco Spallanzani, "A Note on Florentine Banking in the Renaissance: Orders of Payment and Cheques," *JEEcH* 7 (1978):145–68).

[53]See, for example, ASF, Archivio Mediceo avanti il Principato, filza 133, no. 1, ledger of Averardo de' Medici, Florence, 1395.

[54]de Roover, *Money, Banking, and Credit,* 57–58. It should be noted that three- and two-party bills of exchange were often intended merely to offset a debit with a credit in the same foreign city named or to mask a loan at interest; for such fictitious exchanges no transfers in a bank took place, and a simple entry in the merchant's accounts is the only evidence of the operation.

[55]Ugo Tucci, "Il Banco della Piazza di Rialto, prima banca pubblica veneziana," reprinted in his *Mercanti, navi, monete nel Cinquecento veneziano* (Bologna, 1981).

[56]Usher, *The Early History,* pt. 2; Manuel Riu, "Banking and Society in Late Medieval and Early Modern Aragon," in *DMB,* 131–67.

[57]Riu, "Banking and Society," 156.

Giorgio in 1407. It was meant primarily as a tool for controlling monetary circulation. As a transfer bank it served the needs of the funded debt, for shares and interest on shares of the Casa were transferred on the books of the Banco and constituted bank money. But the Banco did not succeed in its aims and was suppressed in 1444 after considerable difficulty.[58] Barcelona remained unique, then, and the foundation of the more famous public giro banks had to await the late sixteenth and seventeenth centuries.[59]

Today to speak of banks conjures up images of skyscrapers reflecting the power of private initiative and of large regulatory agencies instituted to represent the interests of the state and of depositors. In the medieval and early modern period, banks were miniscule in physical terms, but their importance in monetary terms made some form of guild control or of governmental supervision necessary.

The tables of moneychangers and bankers were located in the center of business districts. They took up little space: a booth or stall in a public square; a small ground-floor room, perhaps connected to a small back room, in a public building or in a private palace. In some cities, such as Bruges, Milan, Genoa, and Venice, the local government owned and rented out the locales to moneychangers. In other cities, such as Florence, locales were rented out privately.

In Bruges, stalls located on the Wisselbrugge and at the adjoining Waterhalle were rented out by the city, but only to persons who had purchased (or whose forebears had acquired) the right to exchange money from the counts of Flanders. The latter viewed manual exchange and banking as part of their feudal prerogative, like the right to mint coins. Of the 4 privileges held in fief beginning in the early thirteenth century, 3 were for stalls and 1 was for a mobile unit. In the course of the thirteenth century some 10–15 further stalls were opened and licensed by the original fief holders, but in the fifteenth century the number seems to have dropped back to the 4, who insisted on their monopoly rights.[60] Other

[58]Heinrich Sieveking, "Das Bankwesen in Genua und die Bank von S. Giorgio," in van Dillen, ed., *History of the Principal Public Banks,* 21–23; idem, *Genueser Finanzwesen,* vol. 2, *Die Casa di S. Giorgio,* Volkswirtschaftliche Abhandlungen der Badischen Hochschulen, 3 (Freiburg, 1899). (Since Heers, in *Gênes au XVe siècle,* was interested in the mid-fifteenth century almost exclusively, he did not deal with the operations of the Banco di San Giorgio.)

[59]See the collection of essays edited by van Dillen, *History of the Principal Public Banks;* and now also Domenico Demarco, "Origini e vicende dei banchi pubblici: I banchi napoletani" (Paper presented at the fourth "Settimana di Studio" of the Istituto Internazionale di Storia Economica "Francesco Datini," Prato, 1972).

[60]de Roover, *Money, Banking, and Credit,* 174–77. James I of Aragon also considered the royal right to establish exchange tables in the cities of his domain parallel to his right to mint coins (1247) (see Charles Du Resne Du Cange, *Glossarium medie et infinae latinitatis,* rev. ed., 10 vols. [Niort, 1883–87], s.v. "tabula" ["tabulam tenere cambii"]. On the royal monopoly in England see above, sec. i).

nearby towns had different systems: in Lille moneychangers' locales were
situated in a building on the market place, which was in the domain of the
count of Flanders, while in Ghent the count had conceded his rights to the
town government.[61] A diploma of Philip the Fair of 1304 restricted the
activities of moneychangers in Paris to part of the pons magnus; in the rest
of the domain, moneychangers having royal authorization operated at
public "tables" (1305).[62]

Communal traditions in Italy had promoted the privileges and jurisdictions of city governments in the regulation of moneychanging as in
minting. Milan is said to have built a special structure for banks.[63] The
statutes of the Cambio guild of Bologna speak of the rental of stalls
situated in a special area ("infra confines cambii").[64] In Genoa the government rented out stalls located under a loggia at Piazza Banchi until it
burned down in 1415, but even thereafter the 6–12 bankers active at any one
time were located close to the Casa di San Giorgio.[65] In both Palermo
and Messina there were "contrade dei banchi."[66]

In Florence the Cambio guild set certain rules regarding the renting
of quarters by moneychangers, but it was the individual tavoliere who
contracted directly with the landlords of palaces adjacent to the market
places for the ground-floor space they needed. Leaving such matters to
private initiative was characteristic of Florence.[67]

[61]de Roover, Money, Banking, and Credit, 177; van Werveke, "The Economic Policies of
Governments," 358–59.

[62]Du Cange, Glossarium, s.v. "cambium publicum" and "tabulam tenere cambii."

[63]Lattes, Il diritto commerciale, 215 n. 15. In January 1410, Milanese campsores were ordered
to move their banks to the area called "il Broletto"; if their bank was "cum tapedo," they were
taxed £10,000 on that occasion; if "sine tapedo," the tax was 1,000 florins (Soldi Rondinini,
"Politica e teoria monetarie," 304).

[64]A. Gaudenzi, ed., Statuti delle società del popolo di Bologna, 2 vols., Fonti per la Storia
d'Italia (Rome, 1896), 2:106–7.

[65]de Roover, Money, Banking, and Credit, 199; Heers, Gênes au XVe siècle, 92–95.

[66]Trasselli, Note per la storia dei banchi in Sicilia nel XV secolo, pt. 2, I banchieri e i loro affari,
Banco di Sicilia, Fondazione "I. Mormino," n.s., Quaderno no. 6 (Palermo, 1968):164, 181;
and below, n. 68.

[67]The earliest statutes of the Cambio guild in Florence permitted moneychangers to
transact business at home as well as at the table (Saverio La Sorsa, L'organizzazione dei
cambiatori fiorentini nel medio evo [Cerignola, 1904], 50–51 and cap. 82; the statutes were since
published in a critical edition, Statuti dell'Arte del Cambio di Firenze [1299–1316], ed. Giulia
Camerani Marri [Florence, 1955]). Some accounts showing the payment of rent by bankers
for their locales at the Mercato Nuovo are extant (see de Roover, Rise and Decline of the Medici
Bank, 19–20. See also ASF, Magistrato dei Pupilli avanti il Principato, vol. 4, fols. 160r–v,
which shows that banks owned by the estate of Johannes Guidonis Pescie were rented to the
de' Ricci, Alberti, Portinari, and da Uzzano for 45 and 50 florins per year during the last
quarter of the fourteenth century; in vol. 2, fol. 52v, the rent of a tabula in the Mercato Nuovo
belonging to the estate of Bartolomeo di Ser Spinello is documented. Cf. Charles M. de la
Roncière, Un changeur florentin du Trecento: Lippo di Fede del Sega [1285 env.–1363 env.],
EPHE-6, Affaires et gens d'affaires, 36 [Paris, 1973], 69–70). In Barcelona, local bankers

Licensed moneychangers usually distinguished themselves from retail merchants and others by draping a colored cloth over their table. Such was the case in Tuscany, Lombardy, and Aragon.[68] Only one mention has been found of a moneychanger in Venice having such a cloth; there it may not have been obligatory but merely traditional.[69] The moneychanger-banker or his factor could be found seated at his table, on top of which he kept a pouch for coins and an account book for entering deposits and transfers. That was the way he was pictured in the earliest statutes of the Cambio guild of Florence: "sedentes ad tabulam cum tasca, libro et tapeto."[70] Pen and ink, an assay scale, and some kind of abacus completed the necessaries of the profession.[71]

Moneychangers and early bankers formed guilds in perhaps a majority of Italian cities during the thirteenth century.[72] One of the best-known guilds, even though in a market city of secondary importance, is that of Perugia. For most people, its fame derives from its beautiful guildhall, perhaps the only one remaining in Italy today.[73] One of the earliest, on the other hand, is the Cambium Sancti Martini of Lucca. As early as 1111, Lucchese moneychangers had to take an oath, the text of which was affixed to the facade of the cathedral. They swore to commit "no theft, nor trick, nor falsification." Evidence of the existence of a guild dates from the early thirteenth century.[74] Statutes for the "società dei cambiatori" in Bologna were drawn up in 1245. They reveal that by that time Bolognese bankers were not only changing coins but accepting deposits and making transfers between merchants and other bankers.[75] Venice's neighbor

---

began by doing business in their dwellings, until they were all required to relocate at or near the exchange (Usher, *The Early History,* 12–13).

[68]Lattes, *Il diritto commerciale,* 201 and 216 n. 17; Riu, "Banking and Society," 143; Usher, *The Early History,* 239. In Palermo, privately owned banks in the "contrata campsorum" were distinguishable by tellers' windows ("finestralia") (Trasselli, *Note per la storia dei banchi in Sicilia nel XIV secolo,* 19, 21, 23, 27). In Venice, shipmasters set up tables similarly identifiable by distinctive insignia when they hired crews at San Marco.

[69]ASV, Avogaria di Comun, reg. 3647, fol. 106 (30 July 1421): during a scuffle over an exchange of coins at a bank at San Marco, some coins spilled from a bag "super tapeto banchi."

[70]de Roover, *Rise and Decline of the Medici Bank,* 17.

[71]See the sixteenth-century paintings of moneychangers by M. van Reymerswael reproduced in de Roover, *Money, Banking, and Credit,* 206, 270; see also 200–201 and 216 n. 26.

[72]La Sorsa, *L'organizzazione,* 23–24.

[73]Raffaello Marchesi, *Il cambio di Perugia: Considerazioni storico-artistiche* (Prato, 1853).

[74]Thomas Blomquist, "The Dawn of Banking in an Italian Commune: Thirteenth Century Lucca," in *DMB,* 57. The text of the oath is in La Sorsa, *L'organizzazione,* 29.

[75]Armando Sapori, in *Enciclopedia italiana* (Rome, 1929–36; reprint, Rome, 1949), s.v. "cambiatori"; Gaudenzi, ed., *Statuti delle società del popolo,* vol. 2, esp. caps. 34, p. 73, and 62, p. 86. The latter reads, "de rationibus reddendis, ubi dicitur de facto cambii, in eis non solum inteligantur in simplici facto cambii, id est de una moneta vel re cambianda pro altera, sed de

Padua also had a guild ("fratalea campsorum") from an early date, but Venice had none.

The earliest extant statutes of the Florentine Arte del Cambio, one of the seven major guilds of that city, date from 1299, although the existence of a guild is documented at least by 1234.[76] It is clear from the statutes as well as from the matriculation lists of individuals and partnerships that the guild was concerned, not with international banking, which was completely unregulated, but exclusively with moneychanging and local deposit banking.[77] As mentioned above, several international banking firms like the Medici firm operated local moneychanging and deposit banks at the Mercato Nuovo and for that reason had to be members of the Cambio. Many members, however, were small operators.[78] Goldsmiths were probably part of the guild until the late thirteenth century, when they joined the Arte dei Medici e Speziali. On the other hand, in the fourteenth century the Cambio incorporated some refiners of silver and maintained a special matriculation for brokers, who were to bring business to members of the Cambio. Pawnbroking was strictly forbidden to members. The guild itself performed some functions in the market place—for a fee. It weighed gold and silver, checked weights and measures, and weighed coins brought to it, cutting up those that were illegal.[79]

---

omni re et debito ad quod et quam campsores se constituerint vel in libris suis scripserint debitores. . . ."

[76]La Sorsa, *L'organizzazione,* pt. 4.

[77]de Roover, *Rise and Decline of the Medici Bank,* 16; in polemic with La Sorsa, idem, "La struttura della banca fiorentina nei secoli XIV e XV e la tesi Salvemini-La Sorsa," *Economia e storia* 11 (1964): 190–98.

[78]de la Roncière, *Un changeur florentin;* Lippo the moneychanger was not even a member of the Cambio! (see p. 93 n. 2). See also Richard A. Goldthwaite's article on the banchi al minuto in fifteenth-century Florence, forthcoming in *JEEcH.*

[79]La Sorsa, *L'organizzazione,* 57–58, 68–69, 80–81. The guild had to employ brokers, some twelve of whom were members of the guild in the early fourteenth century, although enrolled in a special category; they directed manual exchange business (technically buyers and sellers of gold and silver coin) to the moneychangers and collected a brokerage fee of 1 soldo di piccioli per 100 florins (6 denari di piccioli per party to a transaction) (see Francesco Balducci Pegolotti, *La pratica della mercatura,* ed. Allan Evans [Cambridge, Mass., 1936; reprint, New York, 1970], 196; cf. de Roover, *Rise and Decline of the Medici Bank,* 17 and n. 56, where the brokerage fee is seen as the banker's commission fee). A practical example is illustrative of the procedure followed. On 9 April 1397 the Datini branch in Florence brought to the guild 350 florins tale which had been culled by the branch in Pisa and sent to Florence; weighing and evaluation at the guild showed there to be 8 different types and conditions of coins; only 5 coins were standard, or "pari," whereas all the rest were heavy ("meglo"), resulting in an addition of almost 9 florins in gold value to the tale value (2.57 percent). For this service, and for the brokerage fee charged on converting 220 lire in silver coin into 57 gold florins, the accountant recorded expenses of 8 soldi di piccioli, thus: "Abatiamo per senseria de'fiorini e della moneta s. 4, e per la pesatura al peso dell'arte, s. 4" (ASP, Datini, reg. 595 [a ricordanza], fol. 12). The coffers of the guild, finally, also received income from fines levied for use of illegal weights and measures (La Sorsa, *L'organizzazione,* 80–81).

Both where guilds predominated and where they did not exist, communal governments stipulated certain preconditions for legitimate operation of a bank. An oath to observe guild statutes and/or the monetary ordinances of governments was required of moneychangers just about everywhere in Italy, as well as in other places, such as Bruges.[80] Moreover, concern for the trustworthiness of a banking operation and the desire to reassure if not protect depositors caused governments and guilds alike to insist on the prior posting of surety in some form, whether real or personal, before a banker could begin operation.[81] The suitability of the surety and sometimes of the candidates themselves might be examined by councils or magistracies, as was the case in Venice in the fifteenth and sixteenth centuries. As in Venice, very high bonds were required also in Genoa and Palermo beginning in the mid-fifteenth century.[82]

The relationship of moneychanger-bankers to their local government was often ambiguous and never easy, whether bankers were organized in guilds or not. Expertise was useful but could involve conflicts of interest. There are cases in which governments deposited cash in private banks, as at Cremona and Milan in the late fourteenth century. The practice was forbidden in Perugia in 1342.[83] In other cases, local bankers were asked to serve as collectors, fiscal agents, or administrators of public funds.[84]

[80]Lattes, *Il diritto commerciale*, 219 n. 26; de Roover, *Money, Banking, and Credit*, 182–83; for Padua, Luigi Rizzoli and Quintillio Perini, *Le monete di Padova* (Rovereto, 1903), doc. 35; for Catalonia, Usher, *The Early History*, 237.

[81]Lattes, *Il diritto commerciale*, 202–3, 219–20, nn. 26, 33. On the bond posted by moneychangers in Pistoia according to their guild statutes of 1296 see David Herlihy, *Medieval and Renaissance Pistoia; The Social History of an Italian Town, 1200–1430* (New Haven, 1967), 161–62 and n. 36; for Sicily see Trasselli, *I banchieri*, 53–55, 61. In Catalonia, a statute of 1301 (reconfirmed in 1359) seems to consider the bond a kind of insurance: "quod aliquis non teneat tabulam cambii in aliquo loco Cataloniae nisi prius eam assecuraverit pro mille marchis argenti. . . . Et qui dictam securitatem, sub dicta forma, non praestiterint, non audeant tenere in sua tabula tapits, vel alios pannos . . ." (Latin partially in Du Cange, *Glossarium*, s.v. "cambiare: cambitor"; in English in Usher, *The Early History*, 239–40). Assurance of correctness and reassurance of clients are implied in the statutes of Marseilles (n.d.): "quod nullus possit vel debeat esse campsor vel nummularius nisi fuerit civis Massiliae et satisdederit idonee [sic] per 300 marchas, scilicet quod bene et fideliter exerceat officium suum et tute et secure cum eo contrahatur" (Du Cange, *Glossarium*, s.v. "cambiare: campsor"). In Siena in 1383, in the wake of a series of bankruptcies, bond was set at £4,000: "E gli ufiziali della Mercanzia di Siena féro lege che nisuno tenesse banco se prima no ne avesse dato la ricolta di IV milia lire" (A. Lisini et al., eds, *Cronache senesi* [Bologna, 1931–39], Rerum Italicarum Scriptores, 2d ed., 15:697). In general, on requirements to post bond and their ineffectiveness in protecting depositors see de Roover, "Early Banking before 1500," 15.

[82]For the fourteenth century see Raffaele Di Tucci, *Studi sull'economia genovese del secolo decimosecondo. La nave e i contratti marittimi. La banca privata* (Turin, 1933), 126; on the fifteenth see Heers, *Gênes au XVe siècle*, 94, which insists that the sums were no longer symbolic, if they had been so previously; the same is true for Sicily, where after about 1460 a guarantor was liable "ut bancus" in case of failure of the bank (Trasselli, *I banchieri*, 53–55, 61).

[83]Lattes, *Il diritto commerciale*, 223 nn. 49–50.

[84]de Roover, *Money, Banking, and Credit*, 280. In Florence the Medici were official *ca-*

Much more frequently governments looked to local banks to supply cash and open lines of credit. In Florence not only international bankers but also the Arte del Cambio, as the representative of local bankers, lent money to the government.[85] The case of Venice became extreme: Rialto bankers advanced money to the Signoria continually, especially during the fifteenth century.

Relations between bankers and local mints varied. In most cases, local bankers were purveyors of bullion to the mints. But some city governments institutionalized cooperation with moneychangers as a group in order to utilize their expertise in regard to the production of coins, while others sought to avoid too close a relationship with the local mint, since conflicts of interest could give individual bankers an unfair advantage over other merchants. Genoa in the twelfth century, Bologna, Florence, and Lucca in the thirteenth, Perugia and Padua in the fourteenth institutionalized the relationship. The Bolognese statutes of 1246 call for selection by lot from among the members of the moneychangers' guild of a supervisor of the mint ("suprastans monete"), and the consuls of the guild had the duty of seeing to it that "moneta parva et etiam grossa" be produced. That probably meant, if operation of the mint was let on bids to entrepreneurs, as it was in the following century, that the guild would be involved in negotiations with prospective bidders.[86] Operation of the Florentine mint was not farmed out, and the Cambio guild was directly involved in two ways. First, of the two official mintmasters ("domini monete auree et argentee"), one came from the Cambio, the other from the Calimala. The Cambio's representative was selected by the directory of the guild and was named by the heads of the seven major guilds. The guild furthermore had to provide from its membership three "sententiatores auri," who were the immediate directors of production and who tested the purity of the coins. The role of the guild in the operation of the mint was therefore essential, and supervision of its work was restricted to periodical visits by the Capitano del Popolo, a foreign official called in to verify the tests.[87]

It is assumed from negative evidence that Lucca had once had a

*merlenghi* of the Magistrato dei Pupilli and of the Parte Guelfa. In Palermo a banker was regularly chosen by the government as "depositario generale" (Trasselli, *I banchieri,* 57–58).

[85] La Sorsa, *L'organizzazione,* 75; Lattes, *Il diritto commerciale,* 209, 231 n. 81.

[86] Gaudenzi, ed., *Statuti delle società del popolo,* 2 cap. 69, p. 91.

[87] La Sorsa, *L'organizzazione,* 44–45 and pt. II; Bernocchi, 3:5–10. In Padua, a technical committee was composed of two members of the goldsmiths' guild and two of the moneychangers' guild (Rizzoli and Perini, *Le monete di Padova,* 59 and doc. 16). Mint activity was carried out in the houses of goldsmiths and moneychangers, according to Roberto Cessi, "Documenti inediti sulla zecca padovana dell'epoca carrarese," *Bollettino del Museo Civico di Padova* 9 (1906): 110, and "Nuovi documenti sulla zecca padovana dell'epoca carrarese," ibid., 10 (1907):147.

somewhat similar arrangement at the mint. In the statutes of the Commune of 1308, however, members of the moneychangers' guild were expressly prohibited from holding any office in the Lucchese mint. Thus Lucca passed from a policy of close cooperation, under a regime dominated by merchant bankers, to a policy of considering the activities of campsor and mint official as mutually exclusive. Concern for conflict of interest was raised, it has recently been explained, by the more popular regime that had come into power in Lucca in 1300.[88] At Venice, similarly, a concerted effort was made to keep distinct the two roles of banker and official or supervisor of the mint. As in many other respects, Venice found distinctive solutions to monetary problems that were common to western Europe.

[88]Blomquist, "The Dawn of Banking in an Italian Commune," 61.

# 7

# VENICE'S PLACE
# IN MONETARY HISTORY

### i. A BULLION MARKET IN A MERCHANTS' REPUBLIC

ONETARY PROBLEMS RESEMBLING those of the modern period are encountered more in medieval Venice than in most of medieval Europe because of the peculiarity and extent of Venice's international trade and its form of government.

In the sparsely settled agricultural areas that dominated the map of medieval Europe, the peasantry constituted far and away the majority of the population, and men lived largely on what they or their village produced. In Venice and several other cities in which population was densely concentrated, commercial activity governed the production and distribution not only of luxuries but also of such necessities as salt and grain. The commerce of these cities was international, which meant that Venice from its beginning was involved in trade between areas having different monetary systems. Not only in dealing with England and Egypt but also in settling balances with such nearby cities as Padua, Udine, and Bologna familiarity with foreign coins and monetary systems was required. The Rialto attracted foreign coins as well as foreign merchants. Similarly international was the trade of the few western medieval cities that can be considered in one way or another as outstanding as Venice for the sophistication of their commercial life: Pisa, Genoa, Florence, Barcelona, Bruges, and Antwerp. Among such cities, Venice was distinctive as a bullion market. Florence and Genoa are more famous as the homes of international banking houses, but neither approached the position that

Venice attained as a center through which silver and gold were imported and exported.

Venice was also distinctive politically. Earlier and more completely than any other city, it established its autonomy, its freedom from either the western or eastern empire and from any tribal or feudal monarchy. It was a self-governing city-state, the only city-state that became a major bullion market, unless seventeenth-century Amsterdam is considered an independent city-state instead of a part of the emerging Dutch nation-state.

Venice's being a unit no larger than a city-state enabled the Venetians to develop republican institutions in which monetary policies were decided by debates and by votes in elected councils. In the large feudal monarchies where the monetary systems of such modern nations as France and England had their roots coinage was controlled by a prince and his monarchic instruments of government. In Venice the doge was exalted as the symbol of the republic, and his name (or initials) appeared on Venice's coins, but after 1172 Venice's doges executed the decisions of councils of which the doge was only one member, although for some centuries the most important member. Those councils represented an upper class that identified its interests with those of the Venetian city-state.

In the feudal states a ruler's primary interest in monetary policy was fiscal. He operated his mint as a source of revenue more or less restrained by the teaching of the churchmen and lawyers about his obligation to do justice and by powerful subjects' opposition to change. Clergy, nobles, and burghers through their representative estates protested with some success against debasements and devaluations by which a prince might enrich himself at their expense.[1]

In Venice the pressures determining policy had a different pattern. Governmental revenue certainly was a concern of the ruling councils, but it was only one concern among many. The upper class represented in the governing councils benefited from the financial health of the state, for it received from the state military and diplomatic support in private enterprises. Indeed, the members of the upper class who served on the councils were probably those most concerned with that aspect of their class interests. But the class to which they belonged—many of them individually and through their close relatives—was interested in monetary policy not only as an indirect way of advancing the fortunes of its members by increasing the power of their republic. It was interested also in the effects of particular monetary measures on the profits of their commercial ventures. The members of the upper class were merchant-nobles. They might, for example, gain or lose if a new kind of coin raised or lowered the prices they had to pay for cotton or spices in Syria. Moreover, quite apart from

[1]See Bisson, *Conservation of Coinage.*

such particular interests which might affect governmental policy, they were all in a position to see that debasement or devaluation or the raising of the seigniorage on a particular coinage might in the long run do less to increase the government's revenue than would the maintenance of Venice's reputation as an international trade center, a "world market." Even in a fairly short run—a decade or less—the loss or gain in general revenue from the turnover on the Rialto, consumption of wine in the taverns, and other incidentals of being a world market were weighed against a variety of other considerations in determining policy.

This mixture of pressures, some arising from special interests and some from differing conceptions of the general interest, adds to the modernity of medieval Venice. And because Venice was a republic and not a monarchy, policy was determined by the votes of the majority in the councils. In that respect, Venice was like other Italian city-states of the later Middle Ages. In the communes of Florence and Genoa also, innovations in monetary matters were debated and voted upon in fairly large legislative bodies. Even so, the making and execution of monetary policy at Venice seems somewhat more modern because governmental functions there were more unified. At Florence and Bologna, for example, communal councils made the major decisions, but the formulation and the administration of the regulations governing the mint were partly in the hands of semiautonomous guilds of merchants or bankers.[2] At Venice they were in the hands of officials and committees chosen by the Commune's integrated network of councils headed by the doge.

## ii. THE REPUBLIC'S GOVERNING INSTITUTIONS

The first coins issued at Venice were denarii bearing the names of Germanic emperors. The first of a new and better series, a series that bore the names of Venetian doges (as well as of San Marco), was issued by Doge Sebastiano Ziani, (1172–78) the same doge whose election marks the establishment of the principle that the doge should never act contrary to the advice of the appropriate council.[3] Sebastiano Ziani was elected after a

[2]See above, chap. 6, sec. iv.

[3]On relations between Venice and the Empire, see Gerhard Rösch, *Venedig und das Reich: Handels- und verkehrspolitische Beziehungen in der deutschen Kaiserzeit,* Bibliothek des Deutschen Historischen Instituts in Rom, 53 (Tübingen, 1982). Ziani's predecessor, Vitale Michiele II (1156–72), had already issued a coin bearing his name (Papadopoli, 1:35–71; and Franco Panvini Rosati, *La monetazione comunale in Italia,* Archivio di Stato di Bologna, Quaderni della Scuola di Paleografia ed Archivistica, 5 [Bologna, 1963], 6, 12). It was called a mezzo denaro by Papadopoli (1:67); but Ottorino Murari argued persuasively that it was the last in a series of debased Venetian denari derived from those "bearing the names of Germanic emperors. The new series which Sebastiano Ziani initiated was patterned on the less debased Veronese denari, which were the coins then most used in Venice. Michiele's coin was about half the value of the new coins" ("Il cosidetto mezzo-denaro o bianco del Doge Vitale

revolution that completed Venice's evolution from a dukedom into a commune. For about two centuries after becoming practically independent of both the Carolingian and Byzantine empires, Venice had been ruled by dukes who almost succeeded in making that position hereditary. Under these dukes Venice negotiated trade treaties with the Holy Roman emperors, who were supreme over the rest of northern Italy; established a Venetian lordship in Dalmatia; and gained a privileged position in Greece and the Aegean as allies of the Byzantine emperor. When the maritime power of the Byzantine Empire was undermined by the conquests of the Seljuk Turks in Asia Minor and of the Normans in southern Italy, Venice obtained extensive and profitable trading privileges from Alexis Comneni, the emperor of the Greek dynasty that beat back those foes. It was while the Comneni dynasty was ruling in Constantinople (1081–1204) that Venice grew into a major commercial center and naval power, profiting from the exceptional economic growth of western Europe in the twelfth century and from the favored position Venetians had within the Byzantine Empire, in the region the Venetians called Romania (and it is so called here [see map 2]). It was the failure of the doge Vitale Michiele II to force the Comneni emperor in 1170–72 to renew these Venetian privileges in Romania that ignited the revolution that elevated Sebastiano Ziani to the dogeship.

Even before 1172 the doge had been flanked by six councillors. This Ducal Council was elected by a general popular assembly, which also elected the doge. After 1172 a committee dominated by the same leaders who formed the Ducal Council nominated the doge, and his election by the popular assembly became a mere formality. Once they controlled the choice of the doge, the leading families chose only men whom they thought they could count on never to act against the advice of his councillors. His obligation to do so was affirmed in law, in his oath of office, and in practice.[4]

This limitation on the doge's power did not prevent forceful personalities among the doges of the next century and a half from dominating the government. Sebastiano Ziani dominated partly because of his great wealth and partly because of his enhancement of the power and prestige of

Michiele II," *RIN*, 5th ser., 15 [1967]:115–22). The supposed coinage of leather money by Doge Domenico Michiele (1117–30) is a myth thoroughly explored and exploded by Philip Grierson in "Deux fausses monnaies vénitiennes au Moyen Age," *Schweizer Münzblätter*, August 1954, 86–90.

[4]Giovanni Cassandro, "Concetto, caratteri e struttura dello stato veneziano," *Rivista di storia del diritto italiano* 36 (1963), also published, but without notes, in *Bergomum* 38 (1964): 33–55; Frederic C. Lane, *Venice: A Maritime Republic* (Baltimore, 1973), chap. 8. For a quite recent survey and a useful bibliography of over 100 pages see Giorgio Zordan, *L'ordinamento giuridico veneziano: Lezioni di storia del diritto veneziano, con una nota bibliografica* (Padua, 1980).

Venice through skillful diplomacy. The culmination of his own prestige came when he presided at the peace conference held in Venice in the year 1177, at which pope and emperor, after a bitter war, met and embraced. The ensuing Peace of Constance (1183), negotiated between the emperor and the Lombard cities, united in a league of which Venice was not a part, contained a clause that was important for the history of minting: the emperor renounced imperial claims to the authority to grant or withhold coinage rights in Italy. Many Italian communes, even those that considered themselves within the Holy Roman Empire, as Venice did not, had been minting their own coins for some time, and this concession by the emperor of their right to do so, each in its own way, merely reduced the predominance of mints that had previously enjoyed imperial privilege. There was then an increase in the output of other mints, including that of Venice.[5]

The next dominating doge, Enrico Dandolo, managed Venetian interests so skillfully during the overthrow of the Byzantine Empire in the Fourth Crusade that he laid the foundations of a Venetian maritime empire which partially replaced the Byzantine. In making Venice's contract to provide shipping for the Crusaders and in committing the Venetians themselves to participate in the crusade, he acted with the advice and consent not only of the small Ducal Council but of a much larger council of notables, and he then expounded their decisions to a popular assembly to receive its acclaim. His monetary innovations (which will be described in the next chapter) were probably approved similarly, although the contemporary chronicles do not give such detail on the monetary matters as they do on diplomatic and military decisions.

The popular assembly faded away, and the basic legislative and electoral authority passed to a Great Council of several hundred notables chosen from all six sections of the city. Until the early fourteenth century the basic regulations about the currency, for example, the decision to mint the gold ducat, were made by the Great Council.

The doge and the six Ducal Councillors managed the Great Council by formulating the proposals submitted to it. The doge presided over its meetings, as he did also over the meetings of the many smaller councils that gradually took over most of the functions of the Great Council when its membership became too large for effective debate and its main function became electing officials.

About 1300 the most powerful of the smaller councils, called the Quarantia because its members numbered forty, in addition to judicial and

[5]Cipolla, *Le avventure della lira*, 47–48; and Louise Buenger Robbert, "The Venetian Money Market, 1150–1229," *Studi veneziani* 13 (1971):35–36, which also cites the sources for the Peace of Constance. For the effects of the Peace of Constance on minting activity in Italy see Panvivi Rosati, *La monetazione comunale*, passim.

constitutional powers, was entrusted with special responsibility for the mint. After 1331 it shared that responsibility with a somewhat larger council that had been created to handle commercial and foreign affairs, a council later called the Senate. For some decades the Quarantia acted sometimes alone, sometimes in joint sessions with the Senate, which ultimately absorbed its legislative and administrative functions.[6]

When the Quarantia acted alone, it was managed by three Capi, or Heads. In many important matters the three Heads of the Quarantia met with the doge and his six Ducal Councillors. Those ten officials together constituted what was called the Signoria. Presided over by the doge, the Signoria was the supreme executive body, but it ruled by coordinating and executing the decisions of larger councils, not by deciding major issues by itself. Later, *Signoria* was used to refer to the government as a whole, but at least until 1432, Venice as a political organization called itself a commune. When the mint made a profit, that was revenue for "the Commune." Public property was distinguished from private property by being called "di Comun." Sovereignty resided in the Commune, certainly not in the top executive council composed of the doge, his six councillors, and the three Heads of the Quarantia.[7]

The change from "Comune Venetiarum" to "Serenissima Signoria" expressed a pride in rulership that arose not only from becoming the capital city of a colonial empire with domination over Istria, Dalmatia, and Greek islands ("il dominio da mar") and over cities and regions on the Italian mainland ("la Terraferma") but also from the fact that the monopoly of power within Venice was held by a self-conscious ruling class. A nobility largely constituted during the thirteenth century became hereditary early in the fourteenth; thereafter it reaffirmed and glorified its status.

Back in the thirteenth century, craftsmen such as the silversmiths, including those who performed the manual labor of shaping and striking coins, banded together into guilds with certain limited powers of self-government. But unlike many Italian communes, Venice had no guild of moneychangers and bankers. In communes where there was such a guild, it often had a role in administering the mint and regulating the currency.[8] In Venice, in contrast, the administration of the mint and the policing of

[6]Enrico Besta, *Il Senato veneziano (origine, costituzione, attribuzione, e riti)*, Miscellanea di storia veneta, 2d ser. 5 (Venice: Deputazione di Storia Patria, 1899), esp. 126; also Giuseppe Maranini, *La costituzione di Venezia*, 2 vols. (Venice, Perugia, and Florence, 1927–31; reprint, Florence, 1974), vol. 1, *Dalle origini alla serrata del Maggior Consiglio*, 303, 309–10, and vol. 2, *Dopo la serrata del Maggior Consiglio*, 144–45.

[7]Antonio Battistella, *La Repubblica di Venezia nei suoi undici secoli di storia* (Venice, 1921), 322–23; Cassandro, "Concetto, caratteri e struttura." Only in 1462 was the term "signoria" substituted for "comune" in the doge's election oath, or "promissio" (Samuele Romanin, *Storia documentata di Venezia*, 10 vols. [Venice, 1853–61; reprint, Venice, 1925], 4:312).

[8]See above, chap. 6, sec. iv.

moneychangers and silver merchants were directed by the Signoria and subordinate officials chosen from among the members of the ruling class. The richest Venetians had acquired their wealth from overseas trade. They and the inheritors of much real estate stood outside and above the guildsmen and dominated the wholesale markets. Among them were the bullion merchants and bankers, as well as the operators of shipping lines and the big importers of spices or cloth. This group controlled the governing councils so completely that they felt no need for any separate guild organization. To be sure, there was at least one early doge, Lorenzo Tiepolo (1268–75), who took particular care to be popular with guildsmen. The monetary policies of his dogeship may well have had the interests of the craftsmen and shopkeepers in mind, as well as those of the international traders and shippers who dominated as the ruling class.[9]

An important step in the consolidation of the ruling class was the so-called "serrata" of the Great Council under Pietro Gradenigo (1289–1311). While the membership of that council was greatly enlarged from a few hundred to well over 1,000, the membership was made lifelong and hereditary and was thus "closed" or, one might say, "locked in." During the next few decades admission of new families was made more and more difficult. Hitherto the line between noble and non-noble had been indistinct; thereafter it became clearly defined by membership in the Great Council. Election to all the other governing councils and to important and lucrative offices such as mintmaster was restricted to nobles thus defined.[10] Nobles numbered about 1,200 adult males in a city of about 120,000 inhabitants and included leading bullion merchants and local bankers, as well as leaders in long-distance trade and the foremost admirals and politicians.

Within that ruling class, control centered in a smaller group which concentrated power more firmly through the Council of Ten. Created originally to punish and prevent domestic subversion, the Ten expanded their functions in the later fifteenth century at the expense of the Senate after the Senate had been enlarged to over 100 and had become the main theater for debates on foreign affairs and financial policy generally, as well as on coinage. When quick action was needed to meet the emergencies of international power politics, the doge and his councillors met with the Ten to take the action they felt to be immediately necessary for national security. Its jurisdiction was stretched to cover financial integrity. After a vain attempt was made to reassert the authority of the Great Council in

[9]See below, chap. 8, sec. i.

[10]Lane, *Venice: A Maritime Republic*, 111–13; idem, "The Enlargement of the Great Council of Venice," in *Florilegium Historiale: Essays presented to Wallace K. Ferguson*, ed. J. G. Rowe and W. H. Stockdale (Toronto, 1971); Guido Ruggiero, "Modernization and the Mythic State in Early Renaissance Venice: The Serrata Revisited," *Viator* 10 (1979).

1456, the Council of Ten in 1472 asserted unchallenged responsibility for regulating coinage and for administration of the mint.[11]

This pyramid of governing councils—the Ducal Council, the Ten, the Quarantia, the Senate, the Great Council—was geared together by temporary ad hoc committees which often included magistrates concerned with administering the regulations under review, as well as delegates from several councils. These ad hoc committees usually included also temporary advisers or commissioners called wise men ("savii") chosen by the council most concerned and authorized to formulate motions dealing with a recognized problem. Some savii chosen by the Senate became fixtures from an early date, as did the Savii ai Ordini, who drafted for the Senate the regulations about the voyages of the merchant marine, and the more important Savii Grandi, who handled dispatches and instructions for ambassadors. Later the Savii di Terraferma were created to deal with the armies and other problems on the mainland. When these savii elected by the Senate met with the Signoria, they constituted the Pien Collegio. Subordinate and sometimes temporary collegi of changing membership including the nobles whose present or past offices gave them special competence in the matter at issue were appointed from time to time to decide or recommend regarding difficult questions. One such was the Collegio delle Biave, the major supervisory board concerned with provisioning the city with grain; because of the importance of various means of payment in the grain trade, of twenty ex-officio members one was an assayer, one a mintmaster of silver, and one a mintmaster of gold.[12]

In deciding monetary policy, such special temporary committees were likely to include experienced members of the Quarantia and the Senate, which would make the final decision, and some at least of the mintmasters.[13] The Venetian mints—a silver mint and a gold mint—were managed by salaried officials, who hired the moneyers and other craftsmen who shaped and struck the coins. The mintmasters were all nobles, clearly superior in status in the fourteenth century to the skilled artisans and concerned not with the technical processes as much as with buying bullion and keeping accounts. They were members of separate boards, one supervising the silver mint, the other the gold mint, and only rarely acted jointly except through ad hoc committees.

To prevent men in public office from becoming too powerful, modern governments rely in part on a separation of powers which dis-

---

[11]Gino Luzzatto, *Storia economica di Venezia dall'XI al XVI secolo* (Venice, 1961), 218; Mueller, "L'imperialismo monetario," 292–93; and below, vol. 2.

[12]Marin Sanudo il giovane, *De origine, situ et magistratibus urbis venetae ovvero la città di Venetia (1493–1530),* ed. Angela Caracciolo Aricò (Milan, 1980), 128–29.

[13]For example, see below, vol. 2, on the collegi created to reform the gold mint in 1410–21. On the mintmasters see this volume, chap. 12, sec. i.

## A BUREAU OF THE PROCURATORI DI SAN MARCO

A manuscript illumination of the late fourteenth century depicts the
Procuratori paying a legacy to the monastery of San Maffeo di Murano.
*Left to right:* a bookkeeper, a gastaldo, two Procuratori,
a lay brother, and a notary.

*Seminario Patriarcale, Venice, Catastico di S. Maffeo di Murano.*
*Photograph by Böhm.*

tinguishes between the executive, the legislative, and the judiciary
branches. The Venetians had other ways of dividing up power. The Great
Council, in addition to passing basic laws, sat in judgment in some special
criminal cases and under a "gratia" procedure regularly granted pardons
and mitigated or confirmed penalties pronounced by specialized magistracies.[14] Both the Senate and the Great Council not only passed laws
but also chose officials, such as the mintmasters, who were charged with
the execution of the laws.

To prevent individual abuses of power, the Venetians conferred
power only on committees, not on individual nobles. The mintmasters,

---

[14]Carlo Guido Mor, "Il procedimento 'per gratiam' nel diritto amministrativo veneziano
del sec. XIII," in *Cassiere della bolla ducale: Grazie—Novus liber (1299–1305)*, ed. Elena Favaro,
FSV (Venice, 1962).

like the members of almost all committees, served for short terms. The general rule that applied to all councils and chief magistrates (except the Great Council and the doge) limited the term of office to a year or two and, except in the case of senators, forbade immediate reelection to the same office. Colleagues, short terms, and liability of prosecution at the end of the term of office if the office had been misused were the Venetian guarantees against arbitrary use of individual power.

An exceptional life status was enjoyed by senior nobles elected Procuratori di San Marco. Their office was next to the mint and administered not only the funds assigned for the upkeep and operation of San Marco but also the safekeeping of coin collected for the Commune by various agencies, much of it coin accumulating for specified purposes, such as the periodic payment of interest on the public debt. In addition, they handled a great deal of paper work and coin as administrators of bequests, both many that named them as the trustees of legacies to minors and many that were left in perpetuity to religious and charitable institutions. As the number of public and private trust funds that they administered grew, and the honor of the office was more and more desired by leading nobles, the number of Procuratori was increased from two before 1259 to six in 1319 to nine in 1443.[15]

Among the many more or less permanent commissions and magistracies created to put decrees into effect, the division of authority was seldom clearly defined or enduring, especially in regard to enforcement. It was common practice to encourage several different offices to be active in punishing offenders by offering monetary reward to those officials who condemned the offender. A widely applied general practice awarded a third of the fine collected to the accusor, a third to the agency condemning the offense, and a third to the Communal treasury. A decree of 1338 restricting the sale of silver named twelve different magistracies as enforcement agencies eligible to receive a third of the fines they inflicted, including not only several specialized agencies for the Rialto market but also local police authorities.[16]

In spite of this application to public service of an appeal to the competitive spirit and to private interest, enforcement may well have been extremely lax in many cases. A zealous magistrate might add to his income. Whether his zeal added to his reputation among his fellow nobles and aided his political advancement or created instead a host of vindictive personal enemies must have varied with the popularity and practicality of

---

[15]Reinhold C. Mueller, *The Procuratori di San Marco and the Venetian Credit Market: A Study of the Development of Credit and Banking in the Trecento* (New York, 1977), chap. 1. For their keeping cash on hand which the government used when it had a special need to make payments in coin see, for example, below, chap. 13, sec. iv. For the importance in their operations of the changing values of moneys of account see chap. 20, n. 24.

[16]Doc. 3 in app. G (from ASV, Secreta, Capitolare dei Capi Sestiere, cap. 34, fols. 50–52).

the decree he was empowered to enforce and with other circumstances. It may well have been true for centuries before 1500, as a cynical diarist of that date lamented, that Venetian nobles were more interested in currying favor with each other than in enforcing the law.[17] Descriptions of Venice's monetary policies in ensuing chapters cannot avoid many assertions of the prohibition of this or that practice when the only evidence that it "was forbidden" is the text of a law, and "was forbidden" should not be taken by the reader to mean that there is good evidence that the law was enforced. In innumerable cases evidence is lacking, and the degree of enforcement is an open question.[18]

The maze of magistracies and councils through which any Venetian noble had to work to assert his ideas regarding public policy makes it difficult to follow the lines of political conflict concerning monetary matters. Advocates of hard money, of a higher or lower price for silver, or of tighter restrictions on banking can be discerned in some of the records. Occasionally a particular policy innovation or reform can be attributed to a particular doge or a particular organ of the government, such as the Quarantia or the Council of Ten, but we lack descriptions of debates before the sixteenth century, and even then we depend on personal reports such as those of the diarist Marino Sanuto. Venetians made no official record of the arguments advanced for or against proposals, unless they were embodied in the preambles to motions. They left no minutes comparable to the *Consulte e pratiche* of Florence. Records of the Senate's *Deliberazioni* help by recording defeated motions as well as those passed, but they begin to be complete only in 1333; and those of the Quarantia are even more incomplete, indeed entirely lacking for the early decades of the century, when the Quarantia was most active in formulating monetary regulations.[19] Motions passed or defeated sometimes refer to the general

[17]Robert Finlay, *Politics in Renaissance Venice* (Rutgers, 1980), 8–10, 219, and passim. Any assumption that the Venetian nobles always acted with patriotic and lawful devotion to the public welfare is an ingenuous distortion of Venetian idealizations of the constitution, which supposedly restrained their avarice and selfish ambitions. Cf. Donald E. Queller and Francis R. Swietek, "The Myth of the Venetian Patriciate: Electoral Corruption in Medieval Venice," in their *Two Studies in Venetian Government*, Etudes de philosophie et d'histoire, 33 (Geneva, 1977).

[18]Document 5 in app. G is an example of how the pardoning power of the Great Council could defeat strict literal enforcement by minor magistrates, perhaps overzealous in their eagerness for a share of the fine.

[19]The notes of Marino Sanuto on registers of the Quarantia, most of which are now missing (notes currently in ASV, Quarantia Criminal, b. 14bis), are of little help, since Sanuto's interests resembled those of a modern journalist more than those of a modern economist. He tends to note sexual offenses, unusual punishments, and the misdeeds of his and others' ancestors, and he is only secondarily interested in matters relating to money and banking. The lacunae in the series are analyzed by Antonino Lombardo in his "La ricostruzione dell'antico archivio della Quarantia veneziana," in *Miscellanea in onore di Roberto Cessi*, vol. 1 (Rome, 1958), pp. 239–57, and in *DQ*. On the Senate and other series see Andrea

considerations or pressures justifying monetary policy—concern for a particular branch of trade or for Venice's position as a world market, concern for revenue or for prestige—but conclusions regarding incentives or motives affecting particular decisions have to depend heavily on analyses of attendant circumstances.

Da Mosto, *L'Archivio di Stato di Venezia*, Bibliothèque des "Annales Institutorum," 5, bks. 1 and 2 (Rome, 1937).

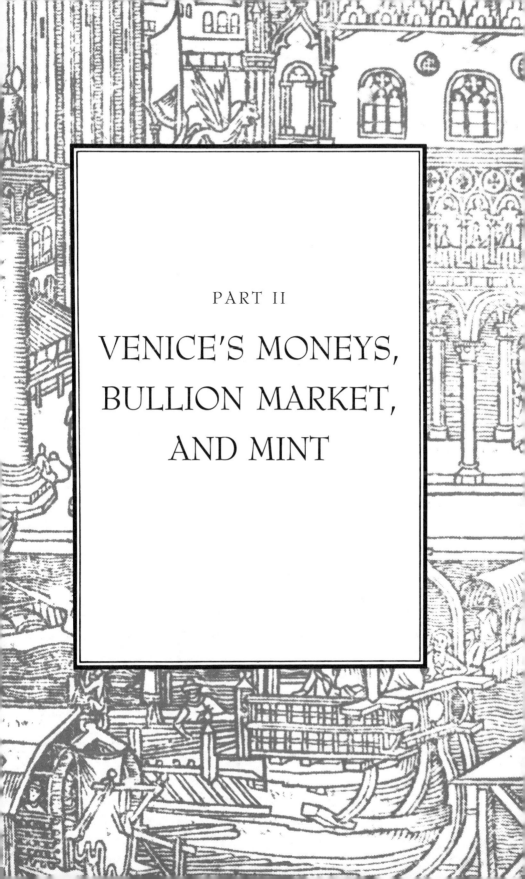

PART II

# VENICE'S MONEYS, BULLION MARKET, AND MINT

# 8

# THE FIRST COINS
# AND MONEYS OF ACCOUNT

## i. MONEY IN VENICE BEFORE 1192

ROM THE INCEPTION of their city Venetian businessmen and politicians dealt in two monetary systems, one based on gold, the other on silver. That experience prepared them for their future role as middlemen able to profit in the bullion trade from handling both metals.

Before they made themselves independent, the Venetians were part of the Roman empire and its eastern continuation, which still called itself Roman but which we call Byzantine. While they were developing the beginnings of their own institutions, their economic life was closely connected with that of Byzantium.

The most important coin in the Roman-Byzantine system was the gold solidus minted by Constantine in A.D. 309 and thereafter by succeeding emperors in Constantinople according to the same standard for more than seven centuries. Since 72 solidi were minted from 1 pound of gold and the Roman pound equaled 327.4 grams, theoretically the solidus should have weighed 4.55 grams. It was as nearly pure gold as was practical. Surviving specimens indicate that the actual weight or fineness was slightly less, so that the average solidus between A.D. 303 and A.D. 1034 contained in fact 4.4 grams of pure gold.[1] This coin acquired from the

[1]Philip Grierson, *Byzantine Coinage,* Dumbarton Oaks Collection, 41 (Washington, D.C., 1982), gives a general view, as does Philip D. Whitting, *Byzantine Coins* (London, 1973), with

Greek word for coin the name nomisma. In somewhat altered form it later became known as the hyperpyron ("hyperperum" in Latin), or in Italian, "perpero." In English the name bezant is often applied to it and also to many coins made in imitation of it. Here we will call nomismata (sing., "nomisma") the Byzantine gold coins issued before a Comnenian reform of 1092 and perperi those of later date.[2]

For accounting purposes the nomisma was divided into smaller denominations of account as follows:

$$1 \text{ nomisma} = 12 \text{ miliaresia}$$
$$1 \text{ miliaresion} = 24 \text{ follis}$$
$$1 \text{ nomisma} = 288 \text{ follis}$$

During the centuries, these fractional denominations were only intermittently and in variable degree represented by coins. When they were represented by coins, it was mainly by coins of bronze of which the value depended on how many of them the government declared were needed to equal 1 nomisma. Until the twelfth century at least, this was true of coins of small denominations containing silver.[3]

Additional denominations of account, also based on the nomisma, developed out of the system of weights used in minting. On the one hand the Roman pound (libra) was used as a denomination of account equal to 72 nomismata; on the other hand the weight of a perpero was divided into 24 carats (keratia), and these carats were also treated as monetary units of account.

---

beautiful illustrations. Michael F. Hendy, *Coinage and Money in the Byzantine Empire, 1081–1261*, Dumbarton Oaks Studies, 12 (Washington, D.C., 1969), 5, gives the weight of the nomisma as 4.4 grams. Grierson, "Coinage and Money in the Byzantine Empire," in *Moneta e scambi nell'alto medioevo*, Atti delle settimane di studio, 8 (Spoleto, 1961), 414–15, rejects the suggestion that the difference of 1/10 of a gram was due to seigniorage. His general treatment implies that minting was not at all a source of revenue for Byzantine emperors but an expense that was either covered by the terms on which they required payments to be made to them in gold or accepted as incidental to the prestige of putting their image on golden coins (p. 423). A gold coin weighing 1/7 less and called the "mancus" or "solidus mancosus" was coined in the Byzantine-ruled parts of Italy and was used at Venice (Grado and Istria) in the ninth century (Philip Grierson, *Dark Age Numismatics: Selected Studies* [London, 1970], no. 3, pp. 102–3).

[2]See below, in this chap. at n. 22, and chap. 13, sec. ii.

[3]Hendy, *Coinage*, 5, 7; Grierson "Coinage and Money," 412; A. Andreades, "De la monnaie et de la puissance d'achat des métaux précieux dans l'Empire Byzantine," *Byzantion* 1 (1924):80–81. See also the references to perperi and carati in doc. 4 (1196) in Gino Luzzatto, ed., *I prestiti della Repubblica di Venezia nei sec. XII–XV*, DF, ser. 3, vol. 1 (Padua, 1929), cited hereafter as *PRV*, pp. 17–24, which are clearly references to a money of account, not to coins. Some other uses of "bezant" and "perpero" as money of account are explained in Robert S. Lopez and Irving W. Raymond, *Medieval Trade in the Mediterranean World* (New York, 1955), 14, 170.

In addition to coins of pure gold, the Byzantine emperors issued other coins that were of the same weight but of a mixture of gold and silver and called electrum. The division into carats was used to guide the mixing of gold and silver in stipulated proportions. The nomismata contained, before 1034, as nearly as possible 24 carats of gold. A coin of almost the same weight but containing only about 6 carats of gold and 18 carats of silver was worth about 1/3 as much.[4]

Except for this use of silver in electrum and in a silver wash on coins that were at least 90 percent bronze, the Byzantine emperors for a time after the year 1000 practically ceased coining silver.[5] Coinage was of course an imperial monopoly, and all export of gold or gold coins by private parties was illegal, although in some centuries the emperors themselves sent much abroad for military and diplomatic purposes. Each emperor reminted with his own image as much as he could of the gold coinage of his predecessors. His name on gold coinage was the sign and symbol of his sovereignty.[6] At Venice after 1000, nomismata were considered foreign coins, but many Venetian merchants trading within the Byzantine Empire—that is, in the Greek islands, in southern Italy, and in the Balkans—were thoroughly accustomed to using them as standards of value and means of payment.

In contrast to the Byzantine system of gold coins and the associated denominations of account, the Venetians adopted from the Carolingian west the monetary standard based on silver and expressed in pounds, shillings, and pence, or (as it seems more appropriate to call them in this chapter) libre, solidi, and denarii. As in the Carolingian Empire, at Venice the first coins minted were denarii, and the libra was a denomination of account equal to 240 denarii. Although the first denarii minted at Venice bore the names of Germanic emperors, that did not signify recognition of the sovereignty of the western emperor over Venice. It was a concession to the need of issuing coins that would be accepted in the neighboring lands of northern Italy that did recognize the emperor's authority.[7] Venetians referred to their own money of account as the "pound composed of pennies of our own mint" ("libra denariorum nostre monete"), or the "pound of Venetian pennies" ("libra denariorum venetialium" or "venetorum"), or the "pound of Venetian [pennies]" ("libra venetialium"), abbreviated

---

[4]Hendy, *Coinage*, 18, 25.

[5]Grierson, *Byzantine Coinage*, 11.

[6]Grierson, "Coinage and Money," 420, 423; Hendy, *Coinage*, 8. Hoarding gold was forbidden, and even goldsmiths were not allowed to have more than a pound in their possession at one time (Hendy, *Coinage*, 312).

[7]Cipolla, *Le avventure della lira*, 13–46; Papadopoli, 1:1–73. Cessi, introduction to *PMV*, v–xvi.

in contemporary documents as "lib. ven."[8] It is generally referred to below as the traditional Venetian libra or simply as the lib. ven.

Denarii coined by official imperial mints, however, especially that at Verona, were more used in Venice before 1183 than were coins minted in Venice itself. Obligations were recorded more frequently in libre denariorum veronensium than in libra denariorum venetialium or lib. ven. At one time the Veronese denarius was worth 2 Venetian denarii, but shortly before 1180 the denarii of the two cities had the same value.[9]

The metallic value of this lib. ven. can be estimated either in bullion or in coin, that is, from the number of lib. ven. needed to buy a mark of silver bullion or from the amount of fine silver contained in the 240 denarii of 1 libra. A will made in 1154 indicated that 10 lib. ven. were equivalent in value to a mark of silver bullion, presumably of pure silver.[10] The denarii that had been minted in Venice earlier and were still in circulation at that time are called Henricus denarii because they bear the name of an emperor Henry (III, IV, or V). Of the surviving specimens the lightest contains 0.091 grams of fine silver.[11] Ten lib. ven. of such coins would contain 218.4 grams silver (2,400 × 0.091), slightly more than the mark in use at that time.[12] Since the process of coinage was expensive, coined silver was generally worth more than silver bullion. Accordingly, one is led to suspect that the equation of 1 mark with 10 lib. ven. was not a current market price of silver bullion but a conventional way of reckoning.

The denarius coined under Sebastiano Ziani (1172–78) and continued little changed by his successor weighed 0.362 grams and was 0.270 fine, so that its content in fine silver was 0.098 grams.[13] Consequently, 10 lib. ven. of these denarii contained 235.2 grams of silver, and weighed considerably more than the mark of the silver bullion considered equal in value to 10 libre in the testament of 1154! However, 235.2 grams were about the weight of the Venetian mark at a later date (see app. A, note to table A.1).

At the same time, the Venetian mint was coining somewhat heavier

---

[8]These forms are given by Robbert in "The Venetian Money Market." Cessi, in *PMV*, xv, gives various forms. It is "libre denariorum venecialium" in Raimondo Morozzo della Rocca and Antonino Lombardo, eds. *Documenti del commercio veneziano nei secoli XI–XIII*, 2 vols., Documenti e studi per la storia del commercio e del diritto commerciale italiano, ed. F. Patetta and M. Chiaudano, 19–20 (Turin, 1940), vol. 2, doc. 534.

[9]Robbert, "The Venetian Money Market," 16–17, 26–27, 32–34. On the libra of Verona see also Cipolla, *Le avventure della lira*, 25–26, 47; and Tommaso Bertelè, "Moneta veneziana e moneta bizantina (secoli XII–XV)," in *Venezia e il Levante fino al secolo XV*, ed. Agostino Pertusi, 2 vols. (Florence, 1973), vol. 1, pt. 1, pp. 10–11.

[10]Robbert, "The Venetian Money Market," 53–54.

[11]Ibid., 28.

[12]See below, note to table A.1.

[13]Robbert, "The Venetian Money Market," 30–31, 94; Papadopoli, 1:69–87, esp. 73 and 78.

## DENARO OF SEBASTIANO ZIANI

This type of denarius or denaro (later called the piccolo) was first minted during the dogeship of Sebastiano Ziani (1172–78).

*Obv.:* +**.SEB.DVX.** Cross patée in a circle.
*Rev.:* +**.S.MARCVS** Cross patée in a circle.

B, *14 mm (cup-shaped), 0.336 gr. Museo Bottacin, inv. no. 1 (Papadopoli, 1: 74 no. 1).*

coins that were almost pure copper, being only 5–7 percent fine silver. Numismatists have called them mezzo-denari, although their intrinsic value was nearer 1/3 of a denarius.[14] The smallness of all three coins can be visualized by recalling that an American silver dime weighed about 2.5 grams, seven times as much as Ziani's denarii.[15]

While these two coins—the denaro and the "mezzo denaro"—were the only Venetian issues, Venetian money began ousting the money of Verona. In the decade between 1184 and 1194, Venetians changed from stipulating most payments in libre veronensium and instead specified that they be in libre venetialium. One reason for the change may be that the mint at Verona lost prestige as a mint of the Holy Roman Empire after the Peace of Constance in 1183 and became merely the mint of a rival city. Essential to the shift also, presumably, were the indemnities paid at about that time by the Byzantine Empire and the trade relations that drew silver to Venice so that Sebastiano Ziani and his immediate successor could issue large numbers of the new type of denarius, a type that Venetians could regard as their own.[16]

Thus, in the twelfth century Venetians were familiar with two monetary standards, an eastern standard based on a gold coin (the nomisma) and a western standard based on a billon coin (the denarius). The monetary standard based on gold was most used in distant overseas trade; the monetary standard based on billon silver was most used locally, for commerce with the mainland and in the state's official business.

A loose union of the two monetary standards was attempted from time to time. Intermittently 1 nomisma was considered equal to 2 lib. ven. (40 solidi).[17] While that relationship prevailed, a unified monetary standard may be pictured as follows:

$$1 \text{ nomisma} = 2 \text{ lib. ven. (40 solidi)} = 480 \text{ denarii ven.}$$

With the nomisma containing 4.4 grams of fine gold and the 480 denarii of Ziani containing 47.04 grams of fine silver (480 × 0.098), the bimetallic ratio between the two kinds of coin was 10.7 to 1.[18] Between uncoined silver and coined gold the relation was 10.8 to 1, when 1 mark of silver

---

[14]Robbert, "The Venetian Money Market," 29.

[15]In 1892–1970 (R. S. Yeoman, *A Guide Book of United States Coins,* 27th ed. [Racine, Wis., 1974], 108–11).

[16]Robbert, "The Venetian Money Market," 30–37, 54–55, 92; Papadopoli, 1:69–87.

[17]Robbert, "The Venetian Money Market," 92; Bertelè, "Moneta veneziana," 11–13, 32–34; *BG,* vol. 1, doc. 3, p. 19 (1152); *PRV,* doc. 4 (1196); *PMV,* xiv n. 2 (1152).

[18]C. Desimoni, "La moneta e il rapporto dell'oro all'argento nei secoli XII al XIV," *Atti della R. Accademia dei Lincei, Classe delle scienze morali,* 5th ser., 3 (Rome, 1896):18–19, concluded that the bimetallic ratio in the second half of the twelfth century was 9.5:1 to 10:1. Andrew Watson's recent compilation, in "Back to Gold," indicates large variations from one country to another. He concludes that it was "generally between 9 and 10" (p. 23).

(238.5 grams) was equated with 10 lib. ven., and 10 lib. ven. with 5 nomismata (perperi) (5 × 4.4 = 22 grams).[19]

This unitary bimetallic system of monetary values, in which the relations between the denominations are arithmetically convenient, was not established by law. It is presented here only as a kind of ideal that may have existed in men's minds in the Venetian-Byzantine trading area. It does not claim to picture accurately a ratio used in exchange at any particular date or legally pronounced, but it may well picture a rough average of situations that occurred during some centuries. Moreover, some such picture may have been in the minds of those who used these units of account, although in dealing with particular coins and weights in particular situations they expected to depart from it and were alert to do so in ways from which they could profit. In practice the relations of the moneys of account to the actual coins and the bars of bullion that were used as means of payment were unstable.

The instability of the relations between the standards of value and the means of payment were a source of profit to experts and of concern to statesmen. Among the sources of instability four must be kept in mind: (1) changes in the content of the gold coins; (2) changes in the content of the silver coins; (3) long-term changes in the bimetallic ratio because of changes that affected the relative value of gold and silver, changes either in supply (as from mining) or in demand (as in their uses); (4) short-term changes in trade balances that were settled by the export or import of coins or bullion.

Changes in the best-known gold coinage began during the reign of the Byzantine emperor Michael IV (1034–41). He issued some nomismata that contained as few as 19 1/2 carats of gold. Under his immediate successors the debasement was much more extreme; the weight of the nomisma was kept at 4.4 grams, but its gold content fell as low as 6 carats in 1081.[20]

The issuance of so many coins all called nomismata converted the nomisma that was in use as a standard of value into a disembodied money of account. The nomisma of 24-carat gold, after it was no longer coined and had practically disappeared from circulation, continued to be the standard of value. The value of each new issue of debased nomismata was estimated according to its metallic content, and the estimate was expressed in terms of denominations of account that remained tied to the old, standard nomisma no longer coined, namely, in miliaresia and follis conceived as subdivisions of the standard nomisma of pure gold.[21]

Alexius I Comnenus restored order to Byzantine coinage about 1092,

[19]Robbert, "The Venetian Money Market," 53–54, 91–93. But cf. below, app. C.
[20]Hendy, *Coinage*, 5–6, where he summarized the basic articles about the debasement, those by Philip Grierson.
[21]Ibid., 6–9.

but he did not restore fully the gold standard. He began issuing a new type of nomisma called the hyperpyron, or by Italians, the perpero. These perperi were of the traditional weight, 4.4 grams, but contained only 20 1/2 carats fine gold, with 2 1/2 carats silver, so that their metallic value was almost exactly 7/8 that of the predebasement nomisma.[22] Coins of this content were issued for some time, so that the money of account used in the Byzantine Empire shifted its base from the old nomisma to the new Comnenian type. One miliaresion came to mean 1/12 of the Comnenian perpero, while 1 carat came to mean 1/24 thereof. For example, a mixture of gold and silver so largely silver that its intrinsic value was about 1/3 that of the perpero was now valued as 4 miliaresia.[23]

At Venice also the perpero became a similar money of account based not on the coins of the old standard containing 4.4 grams of fine gold but on those of the Comneni worth 7/8 as much. Clearly this happened at Pisa,[24] but evidence seems unclear concerning the date at which Venetian mentions of perperi refer to the moneys of account based on coins worth 7/8 of the old nomisma. A number of references before 1204 refer very explicitly to "old perperi." But in the mid-thirteenth century, even the most highly valued perperi seem to be those of the Comnenian standard.[25]

Meanwhile the relation between the Venetian libra and the Byzantine perpero was altered by the changes that Doge Enrico Dandolo (1192–1205) made in Venetian silver coinage.

## ii. THE MONETARY REFORMS OF ENRICO DANDOLO

Enrico Dandolo's first step, at the beginning of his dogeship, was conventional. He coined denarii of the same type and weight as those of

[22]Grierson, *Byzantine Coinage*, 9; Hendy, *Coinage*, 10–17, 34, 46. That is, in the 4.4 grams, 3.75 were gold, 0.46 silver, and the rest copper. Hendy figured the value of the Comnenian perpero as 7/8 of that of the original nomisma by considering the silver worth 1/10 as much as the gold, so that 2 1/2 carats of silver added the equivalent of 1/4 carat of gold, making the coin worth 20.75/24 of 4.4 grams of gold.

[23]Hendy, *Coinage*, 17–18, 25 for table, 35–36 for convincing texts that must refer to the Comnenian hyperperon, not the predebasement nomisma.

[24]Ibid., 18, 37.

[25]Robbert, "The Venetian Money Market," 23, 76–77. Hendy's explanation (p. 36) of "perperi auri boni veteres pesantes," which is that *veteres* refers to the weight, does not seem compelling. References to "veteres" without "pesantes" occurs in G. L. F. Tafel and Georg Martin Thomas, eds., *Urkunden zur älteren Handels- und Staatsgeschichte der Republik Venedig mit besonderer Beziehung auf Byzanz und die Levante vom IX. bis zum Ausgang des XV. Jahrhunderts*, 3 vols. in 2, Fontes Rerum Austriacarum, Diplomata et acta, 12–14 (Vienna, 1856–57; reprint, Amsterdam, 1964), vol. 1, doc. 69, p. 178; and in the second mention of perperi in Raimondo Morozzo della Rocca and Antonino Lombardo, eds., *Nuovi documenti del commercio veneto dei secoli XI–XIII*, Monumenti storici, n.s., 7 (Venice: Deputazione di Storia Patria, 1953), doc. 21.

Sebastiano Ziani but of only 25 percent fine silver instead of 27 percent.[26] This slight debasement was probably no more than the deterioration that Ziani's issues had undergone through wear and tear, so that if Dandolo had minted coins at the old standard, there would have been danger of their being culled for hoarding or export.

Enrico Dandolo's major innovation was the minting of a larger coin of almost pure silver. Although for some time after its appearance it was called a ducat, that name was later appropriated by Venice's gold coin which also depicted the doge receiving the symbol of his authority from St. Mark. Dandolo's new coin, although sometimes called a matapan, is most commonly and properly known as the grossus or grosso.[27] Weighing 2.19 grams, with a fineness of 0.965, as high as could be consistently maintained, it contained 2.1 grams of pure silver.[28]

Although the grossus was "good money" in the sense of being almost pure silver and of more dependable weight and fineness as it left the mint than any other issue, it had the effect of devaluing somewhat the lib. ven. The weight of the grossus suggests that it was expected to be worth 2 solidi (24 denarii), but it was almost immediately declared worth 26 denarii. With the grossus at that value, 1 lib. ven. (240 denarii) paid in grossi had a content of 19.38 grams of fine silver, less by 10 percent than the 22–23 grams, which had been the silver equivalent when the lib. ven. was represented by 240 denarii of the mint standard of Sebastiano Ziani. The metallic equivalent in grossi was less than the metallic equivalent in denarii even during the few years in which the lib. ven. had been represented by 240 of the slightly debased denarii issued by Enrico Dandolo.[29] Indeed, if Dandolo had continued to mint denarii like those issued at the beginning of his dogeship, as well as grossi, merchants would have had reason to cull the better denarii for hoarding or export, since debts in Venice recorded in

[26]Louise Buenger Robbert, "Reorganization of the Venetian Coinage by Doge Enrico Dandolo," *Speculum* 49 (1974):50; idem, "The Venetian Money Market," 94; Bertelè, "Moneta veneziana," 12, which gives slightly lower weights, saying that Ziani's denari contained 97 millesimi, those of Dandolo 90 millesimi di fino; Papadopoli, 1:78, 86.

[27]Papadopoli, 1:81–86; Philip Grierson, "The Origins of the Grosso and of Gold Coinage in Italy," *Numismaticky Sbornik* 12 (1971–72):33–37; idem, *Monnaies du Moyen Age* (Fribourg, 1976), with colored illustrations, 162. On Grierson's different dating of the issue see below, n. 33. He explains the name matapan as from the Arabic word for a person sitting down, as is the Christ enthroned on the reverse. Martin da Canal, *Les estoires de Venise: Cronaca veneziana in lingua francese, dalle origini al 1275,* ed. Alberto Limentani, Civiltà veneziana, Fonti e testi, 12 (Florence, 1972), p. 46, refers to the grossi as "mehailles d'argent que l'en apele ducat."

[28]Papadopoli, 1:84–86; the reference there to "sterlino," however, is to be explained with reference to silver bars, not grossi, as will be shown below, in chap. 10, sec. i. See also Robbert, "Reorganization," 49; Cessi, introduction to *PMV,* xx n. 2; and Luzzatto, *Studi,* 262.

[29]Robbert, "The Venetian Money Market," 45.

lib. ven. could have been paid with less silver by using grossi. The grossi were "bad money" and the denarii "good money" in the sense of Gresham's law. Dandolo prevented such a wasteful operation for the Venetian mint by stopping coinage of any denarii. He coined half-pennies, and to provide small change he struck a new coin, the quartarolus, mostly copper, worth 1/4 of a denarius.[30]

These monetary changes have usually been associated with the Fourth Crusade. That seems correct insofar as the enormous payments in silver made by the Crusaders from France, the intense economic activity created by their demands, and the booty from the crusade were the circumstances that made possible and profitable the minting of millions of the new coins. The 40,000 marks of silver that the Crusaders paid, while not all that they had promised, was enough to coin much more than 4 million grossi.[31] Without some such flow of silver to the mint, Dandolo would not have been able to flood with his new issues the city of Venice, nearby cities that furnished supplies, and the ports at which the fleet anchored and bought supplies.

But there is some reason to believe that the decision to mint the new type of coin was made before the agreement in 1201 with the Crusaders. The two earliest chronicles to describe the first minting of the grossus disagree as to the date of the event. Doge Andrea Dandolo dated it 1194, years before Enrico Dandolo concluded Venice's contract with the French knights.[32] Although Andrea Dandolo wrote long afterwards, he constructed his account of Venetian history with full access to official records and the aid of a staff and with a lawyerlike concern with accuracy in details, so long as they did not put Venice in an unfavorable light.[33] Moreover,

---

[30]Robbert, "Reorganization," 50–51; Papadopoli, 1:85. The quartarolus may be considered token coinage because, being only 0.003 fine, its intrinsic value was minimal, as was that of the smallest Byzantine coins of the time, the copper or lead tetartera, on which see Philip Grierson, *Byzantine Coins* (London, Berkeley, and Los Angeles, 1982), 219.

[31]Donald E. Queller, *The Fourth Crusade* (Philadelphia, 1977), 36–47. Queller seems to give *payment* a narrower meaning than do Edgar H. McNeal and Robert Lee Wolff, who wrote that of 94,000 marks promised, 34,000 remained outstanding (see their chapter in *The Later Crusades, 1189–1311*, ed. Robert Lee Wolff and Harry W. Hazard, vol. 2 of *A History of the Crusades*, Kenneth M. Setton, general editor [Madison, Wis., 1969], 162, 167).

[32]Andrea Dandolo, *Andreae Danduli Chronica per extensum descripta*, ed. E. Pastorella, Rerum Italicarum Scriptores, 2d ed. (Città di Castello and Bologna, 1938–58), vol. 12, pt. 1, p. 273, where Dandolo also refers to the grossi as matapani.

[33]Girolamo Arnaldi, "Andrea Dandolo doge-cronista," in *La storiografia veneziana fino al secolo XVI: Aspetti e problemi,* ed. Agostino Pertusi, Civiltà veneziana, Saggi, 18 (Florence, 1970). See also Giorgio Ravagnani, in *Dizionario biografico italiano*, s.v. "Dandolo, Andrea" (Rome, forthcoming). In contrast, Martin da Canal says that the grossi were minted after the conclusion of the contract with the Crusaders (*Les estoires,* 44–47). Da Canal wrote nearly a hundred years earlier than Andrea Dandolo, to be sure, but that was still 60–70 years after the first coinage of the grossus, and it was not based on any firsthand knowledge. His

concern with the coinage was by the time of Andrea Dandolo a Dandolo family tradition. Dandolo doges dominated Venetian coinage for about a century and a half, as we shall see. After Enrico Dandolo coined the first grosso, Giovanni Dandolo minted the first gold ducat; Francesco Dandolo minted the first of a new series of silver coins, the mezzanino and the soldino; and Andrea Dandolo himself during his dogeship (1343–54) presided over a refinement of that silver series and the beginning of a new kind of black money of major importance in Venetian colonies. The credibility of his statements about the earlier changes in the coinage is greater because of the role his Dandolo clan played in Venetian monetary history. While it seems likely, then, that the decision about the new coin or coins had already been made in 1194, large numbers of grossi were probably minted only after work had begun on the fleet for the Crusaders, so that in popular tradition the coinage of the grosso was considered a result of the contract made with the Crusaders.

The exact date, of course, is of minor importance. More interesting are the circumstances that may have motivated Enrico Dandolo and that gave his innovation far-reaching effects. The size of the crusading effort of 1201–4 and its resounding economic success, in brilliant contrast with its abject failure to achieve its avowed religious aim, certainly magnified the effects of Enrico Dandolo's monetary reforms but did so by accelerating monetary trends already in existence. Examination of the monetary developments during the last decades of the twelfth century reveals several good reasons for Venice to issue this new type of coin at that time.

Enrico Dandolo may have judged as undesirable the repeated devaluations of the denarii that would be necessary to prevent new issues from exceeding in intrinsic value the coins already in circulation which had been worn down by wear and tear. He may have desired a more stable standard of value and introduced a larger coin of almost pure silver because he considered it the appropriate means of establishing the more stable standard.

In paying for food supplies and raw materials in the nearby Italian cities, a larger silver coin would have a certain obvious convenience. Several of the imperial mints had recently issued new kinds of denarii contain-

---

narrative has been proved quite unreliable on many subjects (see Gina Fasoli, "La 'Cronique des Veniciens' di Martino da Canale," *Studi medievali*, 3d ser., 2 [1961]; Alberto Limentani, "Cinque note su Martino da Canal," *Atti dell'Istituto Veneto di Scienze, Lettere ed Arti, Classe di scienze morali, lettere ed arti*, 124 [1965–66]:262–85; and Antonio Carile, *La cronachistica veneziana [secoli XIII–XVI] di fronte alla spartizione della Romania nel 1204* [Florence, 1968], 177–78). Da Canal's version was accepted by Grierson in "The Origins of the Grosso," 37, and in *Monnaies*, 162, and is used by Donald E. Queller, "A Note on the Reorganization of the Venetian Coinage by Doge Enrico Dandolo," *RIN* 77 (1975):167–72, to date the coinage of the grosso in 1201.

ing about twice as much silver as the pennies most in use, although none as large and of as fine silver as Dandolo's grossus.[34] He may have surmised correctly that a yet larger coin made of practically pure silver would have an even better chance of acceptance. And if Venetians could get their large coin accepted at the valuation they were setting on it, they could pay customary prices with less silver.[35]

For everyday use in the exchanges within Venice itself there was also increasing need for coins larger than the denarii parvi. Even in the payment of wages a larger silver coin could be used, as becomes evident if coins are compared with wage rates. Scattered statements about wages are indicative, despite the large margin of error involved in their use. The earliest, of 1224, give 2–3 solidi a day as the pay for bowmen and first-class seamen.[36] In coin, that meant 24–36 denarii parvi, or about 1–1 1/2 grossi. A planner of military expeditions about a century later allowed approximately 1 1/2 grossi a day for the lowest-paid oarsmen, 2 grossi for bowmen, and 3 grossi for mates.[37] Master shipwrights were paid at about the same rate as bowmen and first-class seamen, at least in later centuries. If the master carpenters and caulkers who built the fleet for the knights of the Fourth Crusade were paid, say, 2 solidi per day, and paid once a week after working 6 full days in that period of peak employment, they were due approximately 12 solidi a week. Twelve solidi (of the lib. ven.) could be paid with 144 denarii parvi, or by counting out 576 of the quartaroli newly minted by Dandolo, or, most easily, by handing over 5 grossi and 14 parvi (144/26 = 5 + [14/26]). Even if this very rough estimate should exaggerate the weekly wage twofold, it still indicates the usefulness of grossi in meeting a shipyard's payroll.[38]

[34]Cipolla, *Le avventure della lira,* 32–37; Grierson, "The Origins of the Grosso," 36–37.
[35]Robbert, "Reorganization," 55.
[36]Louise Buenger Robbert, "A Venetian Naval Expedition of 1224," in *Economy, Society, and Government in Medieval Italy: Essays in Memory of Robert L. Reynolds,* ed. David Herlihy, Robert S. Lopez, and V. Slessarev (Kent, Ohio, 1969), 144.
[37]Marino Sanuto ("Torsello"), *Liber secretorum fidelium crucis super Terrae Sanctae recuperatione et conservatione,* in *Gesta Dei per Francos,* ed. J. Bongars, vol. 2 (Hanover, 1611; facs. reprint, Jerusalem, 1972), p. 75, cap. 20; and Franco Cardini, "I costi della crociata: L'aspetto economico del progetto di Marin Sanudo il Vecchio (1312–1321)," in *Studi in memoria di Federigo Melis,* vol. 2 (Naples, 1978), pp. 179–210. For further references to seamen's wages see Frederic C. Lane, "Venetian Seamen in the Nautical Revolution of the Middle Ages," in Pertusi, ed.,*Venezia e il Levante,* 1:423–24 n. 4.
[38]da Canal, *Les estoires,* 46, considers the need for coins to pay shipwrights employed in building ships for the Crusaders to be the reason for issuing the new coin. Louise Buenger Robbert, in addition to other, better arguments in support of Dandolo's date, suggests that the coin created for that purpose was not the grossus but the quartarolus ("Reorganization," 52–53; cf. idem, "The Venetian Money Market," 34, 39–44, 46–47). Queller, on the other hand (in "A Note on the Venetian Coinage"), questions her interpretation. Neither calculates the coins that would be used in paying craftsmen on a weekly basis, as was later the practice in the Venetian arsenal (cf. above, chap. 1, sec. ii).

## DENARO GROSSO OF ENRICO DANDOLO

This large silver coin, introduced by Enrico Dandolo (1192–1205), imitated the design of the Byzantine gold hyperpyron.

*Obv.:* **+.H.DANDOL². DVX .S.M.VENETI** St. Mark hands the banner to the doge; both face front.

*Rev.:* Christ enthroned; flanked by I̅C̅ X̅C̅ (the Greek abbreviation for Jesus Christ).

*AR, 20.8 mm, 2.177 gr. Museo Bottacin, inv. no. 5 (Papadopoli, 1: 86 no. 1).*

The above calculation demonstrates the difficulty of classifying Dandolo's grossus as either moneta grossa or moneta piccola. That distinction became important and relatively clear in fifteenth-century Italy. It had existed earlier when the chief coin in Venice larger than a denarius parvus was the golden nomisma of the Byzantine emperors, each one of which was worth hundreds of times as much as a denarius parvus. Those denarii minted by Sebastiano Ziani had been on the border line between white money and black money, since they were only 27 percent silver. The real need for an intermediate coin was met by Dandolo's grossus of almost pure silver. When the perpero was quoted in Venice at 40 solidi of the lib. ven., its usual value, it was worth 480 times as much as a denarius parvus but only 18–20 times as much as the denarius grossus (480/26). Thus the grossus was neither moneta grossa nor moneta piccola but occupied an intermediate position.

That simplified distinction reemerged at least relatively clearly in later centuries and affected the moneys of account, as will be explained in later chapters, but it cannot usefully be applied to thirteenth-century Venice. Immediately after its coinage the grossus was linked to the money of account already linked also to the parvus, and the grossus was extensively employed both within the city and in international trade or in the settling of international accounts.

Indeed, Enrico Dandolo was probably most concerned with Venice's Levantine trade and the need of making payments in the Greek lands then called Romania. That he had his eye on its use in the east is indicated by the design and value of the new coin. Its style copied important features of Byzantine coinage. On one side was Christ the Redeemer enthroned; on the other side were two figures, not the emperor and St. Michael to be sure, but the doge and St. Mark, the latter presenting the doge with a symbol of his authority.[39]

Moreover, changes were occurring in the Byzantine monetary system between 1190 and 1198 that favored the introduction of such a silver coin. In the twelfth century, after the Comnenian monetary reforms, the Byzantine money of account, the hyperpyron or perpero, became based on a coin of the same name which had the traditional weight of 4.4 grams and in which gold constituted 20 1/2 carats. Coins of intermediate value were made of electrum in which there was more silver than gold.[40] Coins of smaller denominations were practically token money; their value depended on the number legally specified as worth 1 perpero. They were composed mainly of bronze, but some were made white by means of a silver wash. Among these whitish issues was one called a trachy. (This

[39]Papadopoli, 1:81–82; Grierson, *Monnaies,* 162; idem, *Byzantine Coins,* 234–37 and pl. 68, nos. 1128, 1129, 1133, 1134.
[40]Hendy, *Coinage,* 5, 14–15, 18–19.

GOLD HYPERPYRON OF EMPEROR ISAAC II (1185–95)

*Dumbarton Oaks Collection, Washington, D.C. (Hendy, Coinage, 143 and pl. 20).*

billon trachy has to be distinguished from a coin made of electrum also called a trachy). Before 1147 the billon trachy was in effect token coinage. It was valued officially at 1/48 of a perpero and passed from hand to hand at that value, even though the metal it contained was worth less than half that much. Suddenly about 1147 its value as legal tender was reduced; 120 were required to pay 1 perpero. Since its silver content was also reduced at that time, its value as legal tender was still above its value as metal.[41] But between 1190 and 1198 the legal value of this billon trachy was cut again, down to only 1/184 of a perpero.[42] The metal in 184 billon trachea was then on the verge of being worth more than the metal in 1 perpero. At such a low official valuation, the metallic value was higher than the official value, or at least the metallic value of some specimens was higher.[43] To correct that situation, the Byzantine government did its best to call in the pieces of higher metallic value, and the authorities themselves clipped them to bring their intrinsic value down to their official value.[44] In the situation that developed in the 1190s, the Byzantine billon coinage no longer functioned as token coinage; there was a direct connection between its intrinsic value and the value at which it was accepted in exchange.

This change in the Byzantine monetary system made the 1190s a particularly good time for the Venetians to launch a large silver coin for use in their overseas trades. That Venice coined the grosso in the same decade when the billon coinage of the Byzantine Empire was acquiring a value affected by its silver content seems more than merely coincidental.

By minting the grosso, Venetian authorities accentuated a general trend towards greater use of silver coins in the Levant. This increased use of silver tended to raise its value compared with that of gold. The trend was to the Venetians' advantage, because they were relatively well supplied with silver bullion. As German miners increased production, Venice obtained silver not only from the knightly lords of the Fourth Crusade but also from many Western travelers to the Levant and from Western purchasers of spices and silks. Supplies of gold were also increasing about 1200, but mainly from African sources and mediated by Pisan, Florentine, and Genoese merchants. Venetians had every reason to encourage the increasing use of silver, since silver coins made it easier for them, who

[41]Ibid., 160–61, 170; Grierson, *Byzantine Coinage,* 11–12.

[42]Hendy, *Coinage,* 171. Cf. Grierson, *Byzantine Coins,* 216, 218.

[43]Hendy, *Coinage,* 21, gives the silver content as 6.3 percent, and on pp. 416–17 he gives weights of between 2.87 and 5.85 grams, with the median near 4 grams. With about 0.24 grams of fine silver in the average coin as a result, 184 of these billon coins contained 44.16 grams of silver and 681.84 grams of copper. Even without being able to calculate the value of the copper, one can say that the metal in 184 of them was worth more than 1 perpero (worth about 3.85 grams of gold) whenever the bimetallic ratio was less than 11.5.

[44]Hendy, *Coinage,* 180–81, 313–14; Grierson, *Byzantine Coins,* 236–37.

CLIPPED TRACHY OF EMPEROR ALEXIUS III (1195–1203)

Many of the billon coins of that time are so neatly clipped that the clipping is believed to have been done officially.

*Dumbarton Oaks Collection, Washington, D.C. (Hendy, Coinage, 151 and pls. 22–23).*

received silver from Germany, to pay for purchases in the Byzantine Empire.

Although the utility of the new coin is evident, the reasons for its valuation in money of account at 26 denarii of the lib. ven. are doubtful. Was 26 denarii its original value or an adjustment from 24 denarii made shortly after it was issued? Two explanations are offered, one looking towards the Italian mainland, the other towards Byzantium. The first suggests that the weight of the grossus was designed to make it worth 2 solidi of the lib. ven. when the lib. ven. was based on pennies of Verona or those of Venice issued by Sebastiano Ziani. Then in practice it was found equal in metallic content to 26 of the pennies actually circulating in Venice about 1200, namely, the somewhat debased pennies (denarii) issued by Enrico Dandolo and old pennies worn down by wear or clipping.[45] The other explanation also assumes that the weight of the grossus was designed to make it worth 2 solidi of the lib. ven. but compares that with the value of 1 Comnenian perpero, which was 40 solidi of the lib. ven. The metallic value of 1 Comnenian perpero and of 20 grossi was the same when the bimetallic ratio was just about 11 to 1.[46] The ratio 11 to 1 is plausible for 1190.[47] But the value of gold was falling during the first half of the thirteenth century.[48] It may well have become clear very soon after 1200 that not 20 but 18 1/2 silver grossi equaled in metallic value the gold content of the perpero. The grossi would have that value if the bimetallic ratio went down to about 10 to 1.[49] Since 18 1/2 grossi equaled 40 solidi when the grossus was valued at 26 denarii, giving the grossus a value of 26 denarii made it easier to maintain the traditional relationship between the Byzantine perpero and the Venetian libra, namely 1 perpero = 2 libre (40 solidi).[50] The falling value of gold thus appears an adequate reason for crying up the grossus from 24 to 26 denarii.

[45]Robbert, "Reorganization," 56–57.

[46]The Comnenian perpero contained 3.75 grams of gold and 0.46 grams of silver (see above, n. 22). Twenty grossi contained 42 grams of silver (2.18 × 0.965 × 20). Subtracting the 0.46 grams of silver in the Comnenian perpero leaves 41.54 grams of silver as equivalent in value to 3.75 grams of gold, a ratio of 11.08 to 1. In his introduction to *PMV*, xxxiii, Cessi wrote that the grosso was intended to equal 2 soldi "al corso orientale," but he valued the perpero at 36–39 solidi. (Cessi of course wrote without the benefit of the studies of Hendy and Bertelè.) On the perpero's varying values later see below, chaps. 13, sec. ii, and 14, sec. iii.

[47]In 1190, Emperor Frederick Barbarossa, while traveling through the Balkans, made a contract to get Byzantine coins in return for marks of uncoined silver at the ratio of 1 to 11.2 (Hendy, *Coinage*, 21–23).

[48]Desimoni, "La moneta e il rapporto dell'oro all'argento," 9–19.

[49]Deducting from the amount of silver in 18 1/2 grossi the 0.46 grams of silver in the Comnenian perpero leaves only 38.4 grams of silver as equivalent in value to the 3.75 grams of gold in the Comnenian perpero. This gives a bimetallic ratio of 10.2 to 1 or 10.3 to 1.

[50]If the value of the grossus had been set at 24 denarii, then 18 grossi would have been worth only 432 denarii (36 solidi). When it was set at 26, the 18 grossi were worth 468 denarii (39 solidi); thus, even at 26 denarii, 18 1/2 grossi were required to achieve the value of 480 denarii (40 solidi).

Exchange with perperi was all the more important because grossi were sent into Romania in large quantities. Indeed they became widely used throughout the Levant, as well as in the regions that came under Venetian control as a result of the Fourth Crusade.[51] Under the Latin emperors at Constantinople and under their Greek rivals at Nicaea and other places, perperi coins declined more and more in gold content, in reliability, and in prestige,[52] while Venetian grossi were kept up to the standard established under Enrico Dandolo, so that during the thirteenth century they partly displaced the perperi as the basis for an international standard of value for the region.

### iii. THREE MONEYS OF ACCOUNT

Although the coinage of the grossus had no immediate effect on the traditional Venetian libra, in time it led to the use of three distinct kinds of libre, as shown in table 3. The difference between libre grossorum and libre ad grossos is linguistically slight in their Italian forms—lire *di* grossi and lire *a* grossi—and has been overlooked by some scholars, but it is mathematically large. One lira di grossi, in fact, was worth more than 26 lire a grossi. How the distinction between the two originated may seem complicated, but for understanding the Venetian monetary system between 1250 and 1450 it is essential to recognize the differences.

For more than sixty years the grossus was the only silver coin minted in Venice. A little silver—very little—went into black money, the fractional coins—namely, the blancus, worth 1/2 or 1/3 of a denarius parvus, and the quartarolus, worth 1/4. They were mainly copper, containing fine silver amounting at best to only 1/20 of their weight. The coinage of denarii was not resumed until the time of Doge Lorenzo Tiepolo, 1268–75.[53]

After the coinage of grossi, the traditional Venetian libra was sometimes called the libra denariorum parvorum because it was conceived as composed of 240 of the small, old denarii, now called parvi. Clearly distinct was a new money of account called the libra grossorum, conceived as composed of 240 of the large, new coins, the grossi (sometimes called denarii grossi, since "denarius" was used as a generic term). But references to this new money of account for high denominations are rare for that period. When "lib. ven." appears without further specification, one may assume that the libra denariorum parvorum, the traditional Venetian libra, is meant.

During the sixty years when no denarii parvi were coined, the value of this Venetian libra compared with the values of the moneys of other

[51]Bertelè, "Moneta veneziana," 6.
[52]Ibid., 66, 71–88; Hendy, *Coinage,* 247–54.
[53]Papadopoli, 1:89–109; Robbert, "The Venetian Money Market," 29, 38, 45.

TABLE 3.

Values of Grossi and Piccoli in Three Moneys of Account, after 1282

| | Value in Denari of Which 240 Denari = 1 Lira | | |
|---|---|---|---|
| Coin | Lira di Piccoli | Lira di Grossi | Lira a Grossi |
| Grosso | 32 denari | 1 denaro | 26 1/9 denari |
| Piccolo | 1 denaro | 1/32 denaro | (26 1/9)/32 denari |

countries depended on the grossus.[54] In that sense one may say that the lib. ven. became linked to the grossus. Or better, one might say that in this period the traditional Venetian libra was based on both coins, on the old denarii surviving from earlier coinages and on the new grossi. Both might be used in paying a debt recorded in the traditional libra. After the pennies of Ziani's type had been worn, clipped, and culled for twenty to sixty years they may well have averaged even less than 90 percent of their weight when first issued, so that the silver content of 26 old parvi was not more than that of 1 new grossus. Presumably in about 1240 or 1250 a common way of paying 1 Venetian libra was to hand over 9 grossi and 6 parvi: $(9 \times 26) + 6 = 240$. Both coins supported a single monetary standard of value which was expressed in a single money of account in which 1 libra represented just about 20 grams of silver (see table 4).

During the 1250s the unity of this traditional money of account began to crack. The grossus began to rise in value compared with the parvus. A specification that 1 libra ad grossos had the value of 9 grossi and only 5 parvi (instead of 6) appears in connection with a law of 1254 concerning usury.[55] That new equation had the effect of giving to 1 grossus the value of 26 1/9 parvi, since $240 - 5 = 235$ and $235/9 = 26$ 1/9. The introduction of this awkward figure suggests that the grossus was rising, perhaps because of increased deterioration of the parvi, and that an effort was being made to prevent such a rise. The result was that for about a decade the value of the grossus coin was in law not 26 times that of the

[54]Papadopoli, 1:86, 122–23; Robbert, "Reorganization," 49.

[55]The exact date and language of the law is doubtful. Cf. *DMC*, vol. 2 (Bologna, 1931), pp. 222 and 369; ASV, Giudici del Piovego, b. 1 (capitolare), cap. 1, first entry after the formal oath of the magistrates; and *Novissimum statutorum ac venetarum legum volumen duabus in partis divisum Aloysio Mocenigo* (Venice: Pinelliana, 1729), 221. But a legal specification that 9 grossi 5 parvi equaled 1 libra is the only satisfactory explanation of the awkward fractional valuation of the grossus as 26 1/9 denarii ad grossos (see Frederic C. Lane, "Le vecchie monete di conto veneziane ed il ritorno all'oro," in *Atti dell'Istituto Veneto di Scienze, Lettere ed Arti, Classe di scienze morali e lettere*, 117 [1958–59]:55–56, an article that analyzes pertinent passages in a manuscript of Thomas E. Marston subsequently given to the Library of Yale University. It has been published as the *Zibaldone da Canal, manoscritto mercantile del sec. XIV*, ed. Alfredo Stussi, FSV [Venice, 1967]).

## TABLE 4.

### Values of Coins and Moneys of Account, 1172–1331

| | Coins | | | | Moneys of Account | | | | |
| | Silver Content (In Grams) | | | | Fine Silver Equivalent (in grams) | | | | |
| Period | Piccoli | Grossi | Ratio | Legal Value of the Grosso in Piccoli | Lira di Piccoli[a] | Lib. ven.[b] | Lira a Grossi[c] | Lira di Grossi Manca[d] | Lira di Grossi Complida[e] |
|---|---|---|---|---|---|---|---|---|---|
| 1172–92 | 0.098 | | | | | 23.5 | | | |
| 1194–1202 | 0.091 | 2.1 | 23:1 | 24–26 | | 21.8 | | | 504 |
| 1202–54 | 0.091f | 2.1 | 23:1 | 26 | | 21.8–19.4 | | | 504 |
| 1254–68 | 0.091f | 2.1 | 23:1 | 26.III | 21.8f | | 19.3 | 501.9 | 504 |
| 1269–80 | 0.072 | 2.1 | 29.2 | 28 | 17.3 | | 19.3 | 501.9 | 504 |
| 1282–1331 | 0.058 | 2.1 | 36.2 | 32 | 13.9 | | 19.3 | 501.9 | 504 |

[a] 240 piccoli.
[b] 240 piccoli or 9 grossi 6 piccoli.
[c] 9 grossi 5 piccoli.
[d] 239 grossi.
[e] 240 grossi.
[f] Only old issues circulating.

125

parvus coin but 26 1/9 times. In practice the number of small coins a moneychanger would give for 1 of the larger, more purely silver grossi must have varied with the conditions of the coins and the bargaining positions of the parties to the exchange. But the law determined the way accountants figured and the way in which calculations were made in the settlement of debts recorded in the traditional lib. ven. During the 1250s and 1260s the usage was established that when grossi were used in payment, they were valued at 26 1/9 of the denarii of which 240 constituted the lib. ven. If parvi were used, they were of course worth just 1 of the denarii of that traditional libra.

The relative values of parvi and grossi changed more radically when Lorenzo Tiepolo (1268–75) began the new coinage of parvi with a reduced weight, which "weakened" their silver content to about 0.075 grams.[56] The grossus was then declared worth officially 28 parvi of the new issue, and it soon rose even higher. Its rise above the rate of 28 parvi to 1 grossus was probably accelerated in the practice of moneychangers by the coinage of large numbers of the new parvi under the inflationary policy that seems to have been pursued by the popular doge Lorenzo Tiepolo. After his death the coinage of parvi was severely restricted. But their silver content was again diminished. Their legal value was set at 32 to a grossus in 1282.[57] The legal values of the grossus and the parvus thereafter remained stabilized at that level.

While the value of the denarii parvi thus declined from 1/26 to 1/32 of a denarius grossus, the traditional Venetian libra acquired two distinct names. When a debt or a price that was stated as a certain number of lib. ven. was to be paid in parvi, the libra was called a libra parvorum. It was then clear that the payment should be made with 240 parvi coins. When a lib. ven. was to be paid in grossi, it was called a libra ad grossos.[58] It was then clear that the payment required was 9 5/26 grossi, or 9 grossi 5 parvi. This libra ad grossos was sometimes (although rarely) called the "libra

[56]Assay of coins in Papadopoli's collection showed that these piccoli were almost exactly 1/4 silver and weighed just about the same as the piccoli issued after 1279 under instructions stipulating that 786–790 be coined from each mark of alloy (Papadopoli, 1:109–12, 326; cf. CNI, 50–51. Cf. also below, app. A, n. 18).

[57]Papadopoli, 1:120–23; and below, chap. 10, sec. v.

[58]References to the libra denariorum parvorum or libra parvorum are found as early as 1212 and 1223, but only to distinguish that libra from the libra grossorum, although references to the latter are rare before 1229. When "lib. ven." without other specification is used before 1252, one may assume that it refers to the libra parvorum (Robbert, "The Venetian Money Market," 47 and n, 48; Papadopoli, 1:128). The earliest clear reference we have found to libre ad grossos is in 1276 in the papers of the estate of Marco Querini, son of Giovanni, in PSM, Ultra, b. 113. Its use earlier seems implied by the regulation for paying customs in DMC, 2:285 (9 April 1271). Early but not precisely datable references to it are in the Capitulare Visdominorum Ternarie, BMV, Ms. Lat., cl. V, cod. 6 (2380), fols. 1, 10. After 1280, references to libre ad grossos in the estate papers in the archives of the Procuratori are common.

## DENARO PICCOLO OF LORENZO TIEPOLO

This new type of piccolo was introduced during the dogeship of
Lorenzo Tiepolo (1268–75).

*Obv.:* +LA.TE.DVX Cross patée in a circle.
*Rev.:* +.S.MARCVS Cross patée in a circle.

B, *13.2 mm (cup-shaped), 0.262 gr. Museo Bottacin, inv. no. 46 (Papadopoli, 1: 113, no 5).*

parvorum ad grossos," which might be translated as "the pound of pennies
paid in groats."[59] The longer name served only to distinguish clearly the
libra ad grossos from the libra grossorum, which was about 26 times as
large. The payment of 1 libra grossorum called for the payment of 240
grossi coins.

The libra grossorum and the libra ad grossos thus were both based
on the same coin, the grossus, and between 1254 and 1282 there had been
no change in the number of grossi required to pay either a libra grossorum
or a libra ad grossos. After 1282 also, until the coinage of the old grossus
was discontinued in 1356, the number of grossi legally required to pay
either a libra ad grossos or a libra grossorum remained unchanged. That
meant that just as the grossus was always counted as 1 denarius of the libra
grossorum, the grossus was also always counted as 26 1/9 denarii of the
libra ad grossos: $[240/9] - [5/9] = 26.666 - 0.555 = 26.111$, or $[240 - 5]/9$
$= 26.111$.

Just as the relation between the libra ad grossos and the grossus
remained unchanged, so the relation between the libra parvorum and the
parvi coins remained unchanged: 1 libra parvorum = 240 parvi. In con-

---

[59]It is called the "libra parvorum ad grossos" in Favaro, ed., *Cassiere della bolla ducale,* doc.
62 (1300). "Soldi di piccoli a grossi" are mentioned in the context of Venice in Cesare Ciano,
ed., *La "pratica della mercatura" datiniana (secolo XIV),* Biblioteca della rivista *Economia e
Storia,* 9 (Milan, 1964), 65–66. Roberto Cessi, in his introduction to *PMV* (p. xxxiv), described the lira a grossi as a lira di piccoli calculated on the basis of the original value of the
piccoli relative to the grosso. His conclusion is here modified to indicate that the value of 1
grossus as equal to 26 1/9 denarii was not "the original value" but a value fixed by law at the
time when the grossus began rising in value compared with the denarius parvus.

## QUARTAROLO OF LORENZO TIEPOLO

The quartarolo contained only a trace of silver and had the legal value of 1/4 of a piccolo.

*Obv.:* **+ .LA.TEVPL?.DVX.** Within the circle, **V.N.C.E.** forming a cross.
*Rev.:* **+ .S.MARCVS.** Within the circle, a cross, with a lily in each quadrant.

B, *15.9 mm, 0.659 gr. Museo Bottacin, inv. no. 47 (Papadopoli, 1: 113 no. 5).*

trast, the relation between the libra parvorum and the grossus did change. After 1282 a libra parvorum could be paid with only 7 1/2 grossi, instead of the 8 1/2 (240/28 = 8.57) required about 1270 or the 9 6/26 required about 1250.

After 1282 there was no further change in the legal value of the grosso in relation to that of the libra parvorum; it remained at 32 denarii parvi per grossus as long as the old grossus was coined. Even in the practice of moneychangers there were only relatively small departures from that figure until the 1330s, although the parvi coined between 1282 and 1331 contained 13 percent less silver than they should have contained if the silver content of 32 parvi was to equal that of 1 grossus (see table 4).

With this separation of the libra parvorum from the libra ad grossos, Venice had two legal standards of value, one based on billon, the other on silver. At least during the years 1254–82, when the relations between them were changing, these two moneys of account constituted two separate standards of value. After 1282 the success in maintaining the parvus at 1/32 of a grossus reestablished a single legal silver standard.

Although one might describe the distinction between the libra parvorum and the libra ad grossos as the addition of a new money of account, it is best described as a splitting of the old Venetian libra, the lib. ven. Calling it a split in the previously used money of account directs attention to a vital question: What happened to obligations, wages, and prices that previously had been set in the Venetian libra, the lib. ven.? were they paid as if the traditional libra had become a libra ad grossos or as if it had become a libra parvorum?

In the course of the next twenty years, the way that question was answered made a difference of about 30 percent in the silver content of the coins represented by the moneys of account. After 1282 a holder of government bonds ("imprestiti") due 1 libra of interest would receive coin containing 13.92 grams (240 × 0.058) of silver if the "libra" of account were considered a libra parvorum, or 19.3 grams (240 × [2.1/26.111]) of silver if it were considered a libra ad grossos (see table 4). A seaman or a shipwright whose wages remained at a customary rate and added up to 50 libre in a year would receive 696 grams of silver if the "libre" were considered libre parvorum, 965 grams of silver if they were considered libre ad grossos. Clearly it was in the interest of creditors to have their credits recognized as libre ad grossos. It was in the interest of employers to have the wages they were accustomed to paying calculated as if they had been in libre parvorum. To some extent these interests dominated both in practice and in the provisions made by the government to regulate the transition.

An important body of creditors were the holders of government bonds. The bonds had been floated by imposing loans on the well-to-do. Venice's rulers were men of wealth. It is not surprising that the lib. ven.

recorded in the Loan Office (Officium Imprestitorum) were considered libre ad grossos.[60]

At about the same time, the salaries of government officials also were fixed in a money of account based on the grosso, either by interpreting the traditional salary in libre as meaning libre ad grossos or by specifying the salary for new offices in a designated kind of libra. For the latter purpose, both the libra grossorum and the libra ad grossos were used.[61] A salary or account recorded in libre ad grossos or libre grossorum would be paid in grossi, or if it were paid in another coin, it would be paid in an amount determined by the values of these coins compared with that of the grosso.

Not only at the Loan Office and in the payment of salaries to high officials was the old money of account transformed into libre ad grossos at the end of the thirteenth century. But the same development probably occurred also in most other accounts of a kind in which payments had in practice been in grossi. This seems to have been true of all payments made in the Levant, and it is significant that in 1275 the Great Council ordered that all payments made for the Commune "beyond-the-sea," even those to sailors and oarsmen, be made in grossi.[62] Within Venice some tax payments were levied in denarii parvi, but when the tax on the butcheries was auctioned in 1285, the payment was specified in libre ad grossos, and most taxes thereafter were in libre ad grossos.[63]

For retail trade within the city, prices were set in libre parvorum. A law of 11 December 1269 ordered that all transactions ("mercate") of 50 libre or less (except those in gold, silver, pearls, and precious stones) be made with "denarii parvi," naming the amount in libre and solidi.[64] This law might indeed be said to have created the libra parvorum (later called the lira di piccoli) as a new money of account based on the new (that is, lighter) denari parvi being coined by Doge Lorenzo Tiepolo at that time, while the old Venetian libra clung to the grossus and continued its life as the libra ad grossos. Certainly the libra parvorum became the money of account usually used in setting prices in the retail trade. It was used also in setting wages.[65] And because it was sometimes used in setting rents, it was

[60]Gino Luzzatto, *Il debito pubblico della Repubblica di Venezia dagli ultimi decenni del XII secolo alla fine del XV* (Milan, 1963), 8–9 n. 2, 150. This book is a reprint of Luzzatto's introduction to *PRV* of 1929.

[61]Roberto Cessi, ed., *La regolazione delle entrate e delle spese (sec. XIII–XIV)* in DF, ser. 1, vol. 1, pt. 1 (Padua, 1925), cited hereafter as *RES*, docs. 6, 9, 11, and others of ca. 1300.

[62]*PMV*, doc. 23.

[63]*BG*, vol. 1, doc. 55. In 1339 the tax on wool was fixed in libre ad grossos (ibid., doc. 64). Many provisions of that year specified whether taxes were in grossi or piccoli.

[64]*DMC*, 2:393, immediately after the law of 6 December, which set the current price of the grossus as 28 denarii parvi.

[65]See for example the accounts for stonecutters working in Vicenza in the 1340s in PSM, Misti, b. 4, published by Rodolfo Gallo in "Contributi alla storia della scultura veneziana. Andriolo de Santi," *AV* 44–45 (1949); and below, chap. 12, sec. iv.

TABLE 5.

Relative Values of Four Moneys of Account
in Use ca. 1250–1350

| |
|---|
| 1 lira di grossi manca = 239/240 lire di grossi complide |
| 1 lira di grossi complida = 26 1/9 (26.111) lire a grossi |
| = 32 lire di piccoli |
| 1 lira a grossi = 1/26.111 (0.0383) lire di grossi complide |
| = 1.226 lire di piccoli |
| 1 lira di piccoli = 0.82 lire a grossi |
| = 1/32 (0.031) lire di grossi complide |

sometimes used also in evaluating real estate (even buildings of great value), although rents could also be recorded in lire grossorum. In levying forced loans real estate was assessed in libre ad grossos.[66]

The change in the relative values of the grossus and the denarius parvus affected in a minor way the money of account of largest value, namely, the libra grossorum. Its relation to the traditional Venetian libra had been established as 1 to 26. If it kept that relationship with the libra ad grossos after the latter had been declared worth 9 grossi 5 parvi, then the libra grossorum could be figured to be worth only 239 grossi instead of 240, for (26 × 9) + 5 = 239.

This difficulty was solved by distinguishing between two kinds of libre grossorum, or lire di grossi, to use the Italian name. One, the "lira di grossi manca" (the short pound), was equal to 26 lire a grossi (libre ad grossos) and to 239 grossi. In contrast, the libra grossorum of 240 grossi was called the "lira di grossi complida."[67]

Thus there were four kinds of libre (or lire) to be distinguished: libre grossorum of two kinds: (1) lire di grossi manca and (2) lire di grossi complida; (3) libre ad grossos, or lire a grossi; and (4) libre parvorum, or lire di piccoli. Although the Latin forms in use when the distinction originated—namely, "libre ad grossos" and "libre grossorum"—are more easily distinguished visually than the Italian forms—"lire a grossi" and "lire di grossi"—we will generally refer to them hereafter by the Italian names used in later centuries. The relationship among these four lire is summarized in table 5. Their values then in grossi were:

1 lira di grossi manca = 239 grossi
1 lira di grossi complida = 240 grossi
1 lira a grossi = 9.19 grossi
1 lira di piccoli = 7.5 grossi

[66]Luzzatto, *Il debito pubblico*, 146.
[67]Lane, "Le vecchie monete di conto," 53–57; Mandich, "Per una ricostruzione," 106.

The lira a grossi, like all other lire, was divided for purposes of calculation into 20 soldi and 240 denari, but none of these denominations of account was represented by any coin. The value of a denaro a grosso was determined by the fact that 240 denari a grossi formed a lira a grossi and 26 lira a grossi were worth 239 grossi coins. In this complicated relationship, lire, soldi, and denari a grossi were all based on the grosso.

The denaro a grossi is a glaring example of what Carlo Cipolla suggests calling a ghost. It might even be called a specter, a spook haunting the arithmetical accuracy of Venetian accounts. It was not the equivalent of any coin, past or present. It was not the multiple of the smallest unit in the Venetian moneys of account, the denaro of the lira di piccoli. One denaro a grossi equaled about 1 1/5 denari piccoli ($32/[26 \, 1/9] = 1.226$), but the relation could not be reduced accurately to any convenient fraction. A fourteenth-century manual of mathematics, not using decimals, calculated 8 denari a grossi as equal to 10 piccoli, and 9 denari a grossi as equal to 11 piccoli.[68]

These complications seem an obvious reason for an increasing use of the lira di grossi, at least in private contracts. Lire, soldi, and denari di grossi formed the money of account most frequently referred to in the earliest surviving Venetian notarial registers.[69] Only sometimes is libra complida specified, but whether libra manca is to be understood in all the other cases is doubtful. Commercial loans and partnerships were commonly contracted for a single year or voyage, and renewals gave opportunity for specifying the kind of lire involved. All three kinds of lire were commonly used in such contracts in the first decades of the fourteenth century.[70] Although those based on the grossi were more common, many refer to the libre parvorum or "ad parvos."[71] The same is true of many contracts concerning dowries and legacies. Contracts in which the kind of lire or soldi is not specified are not rare; they are usually for relatively large figures, which suggests that lire di piccoli are meant. But with reference to the testaments, judges ruled in 1396 that when simply "libre" was written in a will, it was to be understood as "libre ad grossos."[72] And the libra ad

[68]BMV, Ms. It., cl. IV, cod. 497 (5163), fol. 12.

[69]Manuela Baroni, ed., *Notaio di Venezia del secolo XIII (1290–1292)*, FSV (Venice, 1977); Maria Francesca Tiepolo, ed., *Domenico prete di S. Maurizio, notaio di Venezia (1309–1316)*, FSV (Venice, 1970).

[70]Tiepolo, ed., *Domenico prete di S. Maurizio*. Andreina Bondi Sebellico, *Felice de Merlis, prete e notaio in Venezia ed Ayas (1315–1344)*, vol. 1, FSV (Venice, 1973), where libre ad grossos are specified in docs. 106, 108, 455, and 464; libre denariorum venetialium grossorum in docs. 116, 118, 456, and 457; libre denariorum venetialium in docs. 109, 113, 115, and 453.

[71]Assuming that "libre parvorum" (Tiepolo, ed., *Domenico prete di S. Maurizio*, doc. 10), "libre ad parvos" (ibid., doc. 400), "libre parvulorum," and "libre ad parvulos" (Baroni, ed., *Notaio di Venezia*, doc. 162) mean the same thing.

[72]See below, app. G, doc. 7; and Reinhold C. Mueller, "The Procurators of San Marco in the Thirteenth and Fourteenth Centuries: A Study of the Office as a Financial and Trust Institution," *Studi veneziani* 13 (1971):207n.

grossos was used by many government bureaus besides the Loan Office and was used in calculating exchanges with Levantine moneys.[73]

The wide use of the lira a grossi in spite of its mathematically inconvenient relation to the coins in use and to the other moneys of account seems to have been due to two qualities that only this lira of account combined: (1) being derived from the traditional libra of Venice, so that it was regarded as a continuation of the age-old standard of value; and (2) being based on the grosso, a fine silver coin of unchanged weight and fineness and associated in the minds of the Venetians with national success, prosperity, and financial soundness.

[73]See below, chap. 16, sec. v, on conversion of officials' accounts at the end of the fourteenth century.

# 9

# THE BULLION TRADE
# AND MARKET ORGANIZATION

HE EXPORT AND IMPORT of gold and silver have been determined for most countries by the need of settling trading balances created by the exchange of other goods and services or by a government's expenditures or receipts outside its borders. Venice was an exception: the export and import of precious metals were part of its merchandise trade balance. Imports of spices, silk, cotton, and so on, were paid for by exporting metals, including much silver and gold, along with copper, iron, tin, and lead, all of which had been imported precisely for reexport.

The transactions and shipments were in private hands, although they were fostered and regulated by the government. In the later Middle Ages, Venice became the world's leading bullion market, probably handling more exchange of precious metals than any other city in the world. In arranging exchanges of gold and silver between regions that differed one from another in their demand for and supply of these precious metals, the Venetians acted as middlemen and, as in other branches of trade, enjoyed middlemen's profits.

## i. THE GEOGRAPHY OF BULLION FLOWS

The mineral resources of the Mediterranean region had been intensively exploited in the ancient world and were relatively exhausted before the Roman Empire disappeared. As population and trade expanded in the Mediterranean and especially in Italy after A.D. 1000, the demand for specie increased. The demand for gold, silver, and copper called for import from other regions, even from very distant regions. During the early Middle Ages, new supplies of silver came chiefly from inner Asia; Afghanistan, eastern Iran, and Transoxiana provided Islam with large quantities. While some of this silver flowed across Russia to the Baltic, most of it was coined in the Islamic states to the east and southeast of the Mediterranean.

In the twelfth century, after the flow from central Asia had stopped, western Europe became the main source of new supplies. Part of the newly mined silver went into the currencies of France, England, and Germany, but part was distributed around the Mediterranean by Italian ships. New supplies of gold also began arriving from a region outside the Mediterranean basin, from south of the Sahara. Some of the caravan routes by which it reached the Mediterranean had their terminus in Morocco, some in Algeria and Tunis, some in Egypt. Over the centuries the western African ports sent gold northward and eastward through Spain or through Sicily or directly by sea. Thus after 1100 the main flow of precious metals moved from west to east: from western and central Europe and the western Mediterranean on the one hand to the Middle East on the other. Much was hoarded within the Arab lands, but the flow continued eastward into India. The spices and drugs that came from India and the East Indies were to a large extent paid for with gold, silver, and copper.[1]

Within that general pattern, details changed in ways important for Venetian coinage. The output of silver mines rose or declined from decade to decade, or shifted from one locality to another, as from Saxony to Tyrol or to Bosnia. In some periods the gold produced in the kingdom of Hungary had decisive influence; in most periods it was of much less significance than that coming from Africa. Changes occurred in demand as well as in supply. One of the most consequential was the variation in the

---

[1]Robert-Henri Bautier, *The Economic Development of Medieval Europe* (London and New York, 1971), 161–69; John U. Nef, "Mining and Metallurgy in Medieval Civilization," in *The Cambridge Economic History of Europe*, vol. 2 (Cambridge, 1952), 430–34; E. Ashtor, *Les métaux précieux et la balance des payements du Proche-Orient à la basse époque*, EPHE-6, Monnaie, prix, conjonctures, 10 (Paris, 1971); idem, *A Social and Economic History of the Near East in the Middle Ages* (Berkeley, 1976), 83, 175; E. W. Bovill, *Caravans of the Old Sahara* (London, 1933); idem, *The Golden Trade of the Moors*, 2d ed. (New York and Oxford, 1969); Artur Attman, *The Bullion Flow between Europe and the East, 1000–1750,* Acta regiae societatis scientiarum et litterarum gothoburgensis, Humaniora, 20 (Göteborg, 1981), 10–16; and Richards, ed., *Precious Metals*. Since Richard's volume of the papers presented at a conference at the University of Wisconsin in 1977 appeared after our book was written, we could not benefit fully from it, although the content of some of the papers was made available to us in advance of publication through the generosity of the authors. On demands for and supplies of precious metals in the Mediterranean see Thomas Walker, "The Italian Gold Revolution of 1252: Shifting Currents in the Pan-Mediterranean Flow of Gold," 29–50; Louise Buenger Robbert, "Monetary Flows—Venice, 1150 to 1400," 53–78; and on trans-Saharan supplies also Philip D. Curtin, "Africa and the Wider Monetary World, 1250–1850," 231–52.

demand for silver coinage. In some periods the mints of the Moslem countries at the eastern end of the Mediterranean preferred gold or copper.[2] In various times and places particular coins also enjoyed popularity out of proportion to their comparative metallic value. And even when the centers of demand and supply remained fixed, the routes connecting supply to demand could shift dramatically with the use of different passes through the Alps or different trails across the Sahara to different ports of outlet. Wars or crop failures turned cities that had been exporters of gold or silver into importers of the same metals.

Such temporary shifts did not change the general pattern. That framework of exchange was reflected by bimetallic ratios. Generally, gold had a higher value in northern and western Europe than around the Mediterranean and was valued more highly compared with silver in the western Mediterranean than in the Levant. But there were sudden shifts in bimetallic ratios just as there were in trade routes.[3]

## ii. THE ASCENT OF THE VENETIAN MARKET

A shift that occurred between ca. 1170 and ca. 1220 pushed Venice to prominence in the bullion trade. The mines that had been most important when Europe had begun replenishing its supply of silver had been in western Europe—in the Harz Mountains (Goslar), the Black Forest, the Vosges, the Jura, the lead-silver mines of England,[4] and perhaps silver mines in Sardinia or Tuscany.[5] In 1170 the discovery of a rich lode of silver at Freiberg in Saxony (on the edge of the Erzgebirge, which separate Saxony from Bohemia) started a frenetic search for new mines comparable in its time to the gold rush of 1849 to California.[6] The discovery and exploitation of new sources of metals—copper and some gold, as well as silver—carried German miners through the kingdoms of Bohemia and Hungary to important finds in the Carpathians, Transylvania, and the

[2]Watson, "Back to Gold," 22–30; Ashtor, *Social and Economic History*, 80–86, 290–92, 305–6. Ashtor there seems to assume that the amount of production of gold or silver coin depended only on the supply of bullion, without considering whether one kind of metal may have been preferred to another at various periods, whether as a form of display, a means of hoarding, or as a medium of payment. See also Boaz Shoshan, "From Silver to Copper: Monetary Changes in Fifteenth Century Egypt," *Studia Islamica* 56 (1982).

[3]Watson, "Back to Gold," 22–39.

[4]Nef, "Mining and Metallurgy," 435; Hermann Kellenbenz, *Deutsche Wirtschaftsgeschichte*, 2 vols. (Munich, 1977–81), 1:107–8; Louis F. Salzman, *English Industries of the Middle Ages* (London, 1913), chap. 3; John W. Gough, *The Mines of Mindip* (Oxford, 1930), 56–58; Marc Bloch, "Le problème de l'or au Moyen Age," *Annales d'histoire économique et sociale* 5 (January 1933), 6–7, trans. in Marc Bloch, *Land and Work in Medieval Europe: Selected Papers* (London, 1967; New York, 1969), chap. 7.

[5]Bernocchi, 3:59; Tucci, "Le monete in Italia," 543–44.

[6]Nef, "Mining and Metallurgy," 437.

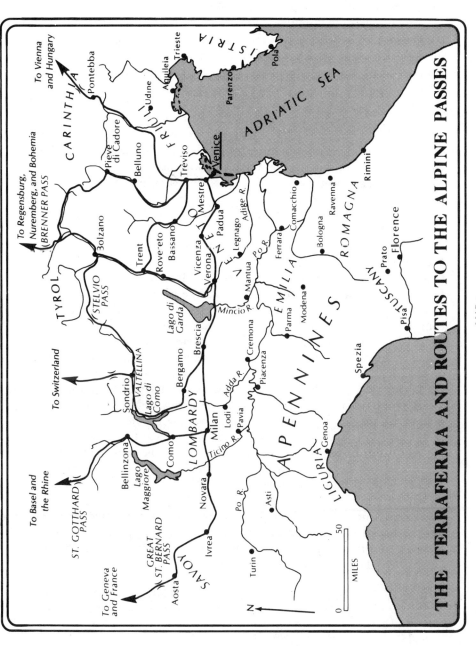

To Vienna
and Hungary

To Regensburg,
Nuremberg, and Bohemia
(BRENNER PASS)

Pontebba

Aquileia
Trieste
ISTRIA

CARINTHIA

Udine
Parenzo
Pola

FRIULI

ADRIATIC SEA

Pieve
di Cadore

Belluno

Treviso

Mestre
Venice

Rimini

Bolzano

Trent

Rove-eto
Bassano

Vicenza
Padua
Adige R.

Legnago

Comacchio
Ravenna

ROMAGNA

TYROL

STELVIO
PASS

Verona

Mantua
Po R.
Ferrara

EMILIA

Bologna

Prato
Florence

TUSCANY

To Switzerland

Lago di
Garda

Mincio R.

Modena
Parma

Pisa

Brescia

Bergamo

Cremona

APENNINES

Spezia

VALTELLINA

Sondrio

Adda R.

Piacenza

Lago di
Como

Lodi

Milan

Pavia

Como

LOMBARDY

Ticino R.

Genoa

LIGURIA

To Basel and
the Rhine

Bellinzona

Lago
Maggiore

ST. GOTTHARD
PASS

Novara

Po R.

Asti

GREAT
ST. BERNARD
PASS

Ivrea

SAVOY

Turin

To Geneva
and France

Aosta

N

50

MILES

0

THE TERRAFERMA AND ROUTES TO THE ALPINE PASSES

MAP I

137

eastern Alps. During the rest of the Middle Ages Europe obtained silver and copper mainly from eastern central Europe.

Venice profited from this shift because of its location. At the northern end of the Adriatic, it was closer to the mines than any other port through which the products of German miners could reach the metal-hungry Mediterranean. Other cities, such as Genoa, were as well or better placed to balance larger imports from the Levant by sending in return the product of the burgeoning textile industry of Flanders. For Venice, metals from central Europe were as important as western woolens in fueling its eastern trade. Venice's rise to commercial prominence in the thirteenth century was based not only on the growth of its trade overseas through the efforts of Venetians but also on the growth of metal production in Europe, an achievement not of Venetians but of German miners and merchants.

The products of the German mines and foundries were brought to Venice by German traders, and as mining expanded, it was financed also by leading merchants of such southern German cities as Regensburg, Vienna, and later, above all, Nuremberg. At about the time of the Fourth Crusade the richest foreigner in Venice was Bernard the German, who seems to have made his fortune marketing the silver from mines in the eastern Alps.[7] Indeed, the analyst of his wealth suggests that Bernard's company had a monopoly supplying Venice with silver. Although evidence of any such "monopoly" is lacking, Bernard's testament (dated 1213) certainly proves his outstanding wealth; before his death it was partly invested in real estate within Venice, as was much of the wealth made in the Levant trade by Sebastiano Ziani and his son Pietro, two of the few Venetians to whom similar wealth can be imputed. Not all the silver minted at Venice during Bernard's lifetime was shipped from Germany, as is clear when one recalls the many marks of silver that French Crusaders brought to pay Enrico Dandolo for the outfitting of the Crusader's fleet in 1200–1202; but Bernard's huge fortune and his loans to the Venetian Commune highlight the prominent role of German silver in the vigorous growth of Venice at the opening of the thirteenth century.[8] By 1221–25 many merchants from various cities of southern Germany and Austria were trading in Venice, bringing copper, linen, and other products, as well as silver, and they were given special privileges and supervision in the German warehouse, the Fondaco dei Tedeschi.[9]

[7] Wolfgang von Stromer, *Bernardus Teotonicus e i rapporti commerciali tra la Germania meridionale e Venezia prima della istituzione del Fondaco dei Tedeschi,* Centro Tedesco di Studi Veneziani, Quaderni, 8 (Venice, 1978), 7–15.

[8] Cf. Lane, *Venice: A Maritime Republic,* 60–73.

[9] Heinrich Simonsfeld, *Der Fondaco dei Tedeschi in Venedig und die deutsch-venezianischen Handelsbeziehungen,* 2 vols. (Stuttgart, 1887; reprint, Aalen, 1968), 2:8, 103; Philippe Braunstein, "Remarques sur la population allemande de Venise à la fin du Moyen Age," in *Venezia*

VIEW OF THE RIALTO, CA. 1500

Detail from Jacopo de' Barbari's woodcut showing the Rialto
bridge, with the Fondaco dei Tedeschi on the right and, across the
bridge, the area where bullion was weighed, assayed, and auctioned
and where bankers had their tables.

*Photograph by Giacomelli.*

That warehouse for the Germans became a conspicuous symbol of
the way Venice tied the mineral-rich lands beyond the Alps to the Mediterranean. It was located close to the Rialto bridge, at the bend in the
Grand Canal where the river barges and barks from the mainland met
small seagoing craft and lighters which came up the Grand Canal from
Venice's inner harbor at San Marco. It was a customs house as well as a
hotel and warehouse. Like the spaciously rebuilt sixteenth-century structure now occupying that site (and serving as the central post office), the

---

*centro di mediazione tra oriente e occidente (secoli XV–XVI): Aspetti e problemi,* ed. H. G. Beck,
M. Manoussacas, and A. Pertusi, 2 vols., Civiltà veneziana, 32 (Florence, 1977), 1:233–43;
idem, "Wirtschaftliche Beziehungen zwischen Nürnberg und Italien im Spätmittelalter,"
*Beiträge zur Wirtschaftsgeschichte Nürnbergs* 1 (1967):377–406; Karl-Ernst Lupprian, "Zur
Entstehung des Fondaco dei Tedeschi in Venedig," in *Grundwissenschaften und Geschichte.
Festschrift für P. Acht,* Münchner Historische Studien, Abteilung Geschichtliche Hilfs-
wissenschaften, 15 (Kallmünz, 1976), 128–34; Rösch, *Venedig und das Reich,* 85–96. Not to be
forgotten are the documents in *DMC,* 2:298–303; and the introductory comments of Georg
Martin Thomas, ed., in *Cap. Fontego,* xii–xv.

THE INTERIOR OF THE FONDACO DEI TEDESCHI

Surrounding the central courtyard were storage areas and lodgings
for German merchants.

*Soprintendenza per i beni ambientali e architettonici di Venezia, Gabinetto
fotographico.*

early Fondaco grouped several floors of rooms around a central courtyard
which had direct access to the Grand Canal. Boatmen were under strict
orders to take all arriving German merchants and their wares directly to
the Fondaco (or Fontego, as Venetians called it) without any stops to see
old Venetian friends who would have benefited from a first look at what
the importers had to offer that year. At the Fondaco, noble superinten-
dents and subordinate doorkeepers, inspectors and brokers enforced Venetian customs duties and marketing regulations. The Fondaco dei
Tedeschi symbolized not only Venetian linkage of north and south; as
customs house it also symbolized the Venetians' resolve to be intermediaries so as to make profits from the linkage.[10]

Of course Venice could not prevent the Germans who came south
across the Alps from taking their silver to Milan to supply its mint or that
of Genoa or Florence.[11] Until Venice acquired its mainland empire about
1400, it could not even prevent the Germans from offering gold or silver

[10]Karl-Ernst Lupprian, *Il Fondaco dei Tedeschi e la sua funzione di controllo del commercio
tedesco a Venezia,* Centro Tedesco di Studi Veneziani, Quaderni, 6 (Venice, 1978).
[11]See below, chap. 17, sec. i.

for sale in the mainland cities through which they passed on the way to Venice, such as Verona, Treviso, and Padua. But none of those nearby cities could offer as big a market as was offered by the Venetian merchants who bought to ship overseas, nor could the Germans find there comparable opportunities to invest in such products as spices and silks for their return journey across the Alps. In the thirteenth century Venetians were forbidden to go to such cities to buy from the Germans and to provide facilities there for purchase by the Germans of Levantine wares.[12] Thus, even before Venice acquired the direct political power to enforce staple rights over the Veneto, it knew how to mobilize the commercial power of its merchants in order to induce Germans to come to the Rialto to sell.

At the end of the thirteenth century the Venetian bullion market became less exclusively dependent on German suppliers. Silver brought by sea, mainly by Ragusans, began arriving from new mines opened up in the Balkans. During the first quarter of the fourteenth century silver mines in Bohemia and Hungary produced more plentifully than ever. After a decline later in that century, silver production turned up again in the next century, accompanied by high copper output, especially from mines in the Carpathians, which were exploited by German capitalists for export.[13]

As a market for gold, Venice was less important in the thirteenth century than were western Italian cities such as Pisa, Genoa, and Florence because the western Italian cities had closer commercial ties to Sicily, Spain, and the ports of western north Africa, Islam's Magrib, which the Venetians called Barbaria (see map 2). In most centuries those ports were the main outlets into the Mediterranean for gold from the rich deposits of the western Sudan. Less abundant supplies reached Venice from Hungary late in the century and from Black Sea ports. From Constantinople and Greece old Byzantine issues came to Venice for recoinage. Only during the 1330s and 1340s, however, did Venice shoot ahead as a market for gold.

Venice's role as a gold market expanded during the fourteenth century because of the improvement of Venetian connections with Egypt and increased gold production in the Kingdom of Hungary. A diversion of trade from the caravan routes of the western Sahara to routes that led from the headwaters of the Niger and Senegal rivers east and north to

---

[12]*DMC*, 2:62 (no. lxxii [1272]) and 3:389 (no. 90 [1295]), with more severe penalties and mention of selling pepper.

[13]Wolfgang von Stromer, "Oberdeutsche Unternehmer im Karpatenraum, 1335–1435," in *Fourth International Conference of Economic History, Bloomington, 1968,* EPHE-6, Congrès et colloques, 14 (Paris, 1973), 119–22; idem, "Oberdeutschland als Geld- und Wechselmarkt," in *Fifth International Conference of Economic History, Leningrad, 1970,* EPHE-6, Congrès et colloques, 15 (Paris, 1976), 4:133–34; idem, "Nuremberg in the International Economics of the Middle Ages," *Business History Review* 44 (1970):210–25; idem, "Hartgeld, Kredit und Giralgeld. Zu einer monetären Konjunkturtheorie des Spätmittelalters und der Wende zur Neuzeit," in Barbagli Bagnoli, ed., *La moneta nell'economia europea,* 111–17 (with bibliography updated to 1980).

Egypt worked to Venice's advantage. Her commercial relations with Egypt were as good as those of any of the competing Italian cities— indeed they were generally better—either indirectly through Crete and Cyprus or directly by well-protected convoys. (The increases in gold supplies for the Venetian mint and the measures by which the Venetian government facilitated their arrival and utilization are described below, in chapter 17.) By the fifteenth century, when the gold supply from the Sudan shifted its routes back to the caravan trails of the western Sahara and increased in volume, Venice had acquired naval and commercial strength which enabled her to obtain a large share through the ports of Barbary.[14]

In the earliest surviving estimate of the total commercial turnover on the Rialto, 1/5 involved imports of gold and silver.[15] Equal in importance to her access to supplies of precious metals was Venice's ability to furnish the bullion merchants with the merchandise that they wanted in exchange. At first that meant supplying spices, silks, and other specialties of eastern origin. Later it meant supplying also some raw materials, such as cotton for Germany's fustian industry, and high-quality products of Venice's own industries, such as glass or scented soaps. While gold and silver attracted each other, both were attracted by Venice's ability to offer—more plentifully than could any other medieval city—all kinds of desired wares in return. Given this magnetism, Venice was well supplied with silver from across the Alps and through Dalmatia and gold from varying directions by its well-organized galley fleets; the latter also assured opportunities to export specie to other major commercial centers. Thus through the fifteenth century the Venetian bullion market maintained the prominence that it had gained in the thirteenth century as a market for silver, in the fourteenth as a market also for gold.

### iii. THE MARKET FRAMEWORK

Sellers of bullion were drawn to Venice not only by its location and the merchandise that it offered for sale but also by the mixture of freedom and restrictions in the Venetian market.

Importers were subject to one very conspicuous restriction: they were required to offer their bullion for sale to Venetians, just as they were required to offer other imports; and even if they "sold" directly to the mint on terms providing that they receive their metal back as coin, they were forbidden after 1306 to export the coin by sea. Exportation to the Levant

[14]See below, chap. 13, sec. i, on silver from the Balkans; chap. 13, sec. iv, on gold from Hungary and the importation of perperi for recoinage; and chap. 17 for the peak in silver imports and on gold from Egypt and central Europe. For the fifteenth century see vol. 2.
[15]See below, chap. 11, sec. iii.

from Venice, whether of merchandise, bullion, or coin, was a privilege of Venetians rarely extended to foreigners. But even foreigners were not as a general rule forbidden to export coin by land, although the rules changed with changing circumstances, as will be explained in later chapters.[16] In gaining rights abroad for its own citizens, Venice often ceded reciprocal rights and sometimes granted privileges to win groups of exiles, such as the Lucchese makers of silk cloth. The Germans were the most important in the bullion trade, but other foreigners participated. When a particular effort was made in 1265 to prevent gold and tin from being carried elsewhere for sale, the special officials elected to deal with the problem were restricted by the stipulation that they must not violate the treaties with the Lombards, Anconitans, and others.[17]

Importation of coin as well as bullion was permitted to foreigners, subject to limitations and taxes which were changed from time to time to favor or discourage such imports. Freedom to ship coin in and out by land was not unlimited for either Venetians or foreigners, but considerable movement of that kind was perfectly legal for both groups.[18]

Under what circumstances, if any, foreigners could legally export uncoined bullion is more doubtful.[19] In 1315 the export of new grossi and of coins that had been cut or defaced in some way so as to be sold as bullion was forbidden to foreigners, although such shipments were still permitted to Venetians provided they went beyond the Gulf by sea and

[16]A decree of the Maggior Consiglio of 7 May 1306 (*PMV*, doc. 69) voiced complaint that many grossi belonging to foreigners were exported on galleys that had just left Venice and provided that just as foreigners were forbidden to export gold and silver bullion by sea, so were they henceforth forbidden to export coin, except 100 soldi di grossi for personal expenses.

[17]*DMC*, 2:311.

[18]On import duties see below, chap. 11; on the circulation in Venice of coins from foreign mints see chap. 13, sec. i.

[19]In 1314 the government seized over 60 marks of gold which Rosso Peruzzi was trying to export, on the grounds that it was "contra statuta et ordinamenta comunis venetorum." The Knights Hospitalers protested that 55 marks of the gold seized was theirs as official collectors in Germany of indulgence money destined for a Crusade and that their contract called for their turning over the money to the Peruzzi firm in Venice for forwarding to Florence. Venice rejected their petition for restitution, but the authorities did not declare such export by the Hospitalers themselves to be illegal; the petition was rejected on the ground that evidence showed all the gold to be the property of Rosso Peruzzi and that it was against him that the Hospitalers were to direct their claim. The record does not indicate whether Peruzzi's export of the bullion was judged illegal because it had not been offered for sale, because it was uncoined, because it had not been registered, or—conceivably—because it was involved in Venice's current strife with Florentine firms operating on the Rialto (ASV, Commemoriali, reg. 1, fol. 216v; Riccardo Predelli, ed., *I libri commemoriali della Repubblica di Venezia—Regesti*, 8 vols., Monumenti storici, 1st ser. [Venice: Deputazione di Storia Patria, 1876–1914], vol. 1, doc. 630 [10 August 1314]. On the status of the Florentine firms in Venice, see below, vol. 2).

under license.[20] Quite unusual was the conditional permission granted to foreigners in 1417 to export silver bullion and coin by both land and sea.[21] Apparently even then the conditions were such as to make it generally profitable for them to sell in Venice.

The Venetians to whom the importers sold were generally free to export the metal as bullion, to have it turned into jewelry by Venetian craftsmen, or to take it to the mint to be coined. To be sure, this general freedom was subject to arbitrary abridgments of the kind that applied to all Venetian trade. Not only specie and bullion but any kind of merchandise from this place or that might be banned from export or import in a particular year or sailing season, and travel by Venetians similarly limited, at the will of Venice's governing councils. Examples of such actions abound in the full record of senatorial decisions which is available after 1333; they were generally designed to secure or increase merchants' profits. The scope and purpose of similar earlier actions is less easily determined.[22] The prohibition of the export of gold or silver bullion to France in 1272 may have been a reflection of general policy, but it was probably an expression not of a general policy of opposition to the export of bullion but of the policy of forcing those Venetians who bought cloth in France to bring the cloth to Venice rather than take it directly to the Levant.[23]

[20]In his introduction to *PMV*, xlix, Cessi refers to this action of the Senate by citing only the rubric of the Senate's deliberazioni published by Giomo and interpreting it as forbidding all export. The rubrics, however, are often misleading. The full text is in the *Capitolare dei Signori di Notte,* ed. Filippo Nani-Mocenigo (Venice, 1877), doc. 171. Another resolution of 1315 called for recommendations on how to adjust to changes recently made "in moneta bizanziorum, turonensium, et unziarum," which suggests competition from miaresi, gros, and carlini (*PMV*, doc. 71).

[21]Papadopoli, 1:359; and see below, vol. 2.

[22]For example, in September 1326 the Senate voted to permit the exportation of ducats and florins to Apulia until the following March (Roberto Cessi, Paolo Sambin, and Mario Brunetti, eds., *Le deliberazioni del Consiglio dei Rogati [Senato], serie "mixtorum,"* 2 vols. Monumenti storici, n.s., 15–16 [Venice: Deputazione di Storia Patria, 1960–61], 1:319 no. 243). In December 1326 a motion to forbid the export of gold and silver was voted down (ibid., 328 no. 46). Since only the rubric is extant, the rationale behind the provision is not clear. By contrast, the full record of special provisions of 1344–48 was preserved and is described below in chap. 17.

[23]See *PMV*, doc. 18; and Roberto Cessi, "Le relazioni commerciali tra Venezia e le Fiandre nel secolo XIV," reprinted from *NAV*, n.s. 27 (1914) in his *Politica ed economia di Venezia nel Trecento* (Rome, 1952), 73, where Cessi presents a different interpretation, although ours is suggested by his own analysis in *Storia della Repubblica di Venezia*, rev. ed., 2 vols. (Milan and Messina, 1968), 1:289. Decrees of 1315 and 1332 against the exportation by foreigners or by Venetians without a license of "grossos novos nec de bolçonis" appear to have been temporary restrictions on the export of coins that had been culled or cut up to be sold for recoinage (for 1315 see above, n. 20; for 1332 see Cessi, Sambin, and Brunetti, eds., *Le deliberazioni dei Rogati*, 1:469 no. 359). Such decrees were imposed at times when full-weight grossi were being driven out of circulation by underweight grossi (see below, chap. 15, sec. i) or by soldini and mezzanini (see below, chap. 15, sec. iii). On seasonal movement of bolzone or scrap see Mueller, "'Chome l'ucciello di passagio'"; and below, vol. 2.

A significant restriction on the freedom of the Venetian buyers to dispose of their silver was the requirement instituted in 1331 or 1332 that 1/5 (a "quinto") of all silver imported be sent to the mint to be coined. This quinto was reduced to 1/10 (a "decimo") during the years 1343–1350, and it was abolished altogether in 1417. Since it applied to all silver imported, the quinto was in effect a kind of import tax, as will be explained more fully below (Chapters 10, section ii, and 11), but it served also as a means of supplying the mint with silver bullion.

In spite of the changing restrictions on their activities, Venetian merchants had exceptionally wide opportunities to export bullion, especially to distant overseas markets. On occasion the government showed more interest in encouraging Venetian shipment of silver bullion to the Levant than in keeping the mint busy. There is a casual reference to one such occasion in July 1290, when for a period the doge and his council had forbidden the mintmasters to buy silver. The Great Council then provided that two men appointed by the Supraconsules mercatorum (a commercial court) refine all imported silver to the fineness of grossi or almost. After its fineness had been certified by the mintmasters, it was to be auctioned off, just as refined gold was auctioned by public officials in order, the decree said, that merchants could find an ample supply ("copia").[24]

New restrictions on the export of gold were enacted in 1269. Thereafter it was not to be exported by either Venetians or foreigners unless it had been refined to a fineness of 23 or 23 1/2 or 23 3/4 carats.[25] Earlier, Venice had sent gold ingots much less refined to Apulia to pay for wheat.[26] The new concern for high refining standards appears to have been the first Venetian reaction to the coinage by Genoa and Florence in 1252 of gold coins 24 carats fine, a preliminary to Venice's coinage in 1284–85 of the ducat of the same fineness as the florin.[27]

This freedom of Venetians to export both bullion and coin is in striking contrast to the situation at that time in many other countries, such as England. In Venice there was no sweeping prohibition of the export or

[24]*PMV*, doc. 54.

[25]The 1269 decree of the Great Council, as printed in Papadopoli, 1:339 and *DMC*, 2:304, gives the degree of fineness required as "XXIII ÷." But in the statutes of the Sovrastanti ai lavori in oro ed argento, as recorded—also in 1269—at the office of the Giustizia Vecchia, in charge of the goldsmiths' guild, it is given as "karatis XXIIII minus quartam vel inde supra" (see Giovanni Monticolo, ed., *I capitolari delle arti veneziane sottoposte alla Giustizia e poi alla Giustizia vecchia [dalle origini al 1330]*, 3 vols. Istituto Storico Italiano, Fonti per la Storia d'Italia, 26–28 [Rome, 1896–1914], 3:292. Monticolo's note on that line states that the records of the Great Council give "XXIII" and omit "minus quartam" and does not mention the "one-half" indicated by Papadopoli and Cessi).

[26]*PMV*, docs. 7–9; see also Rösch, *Venedig und das Reich*, 163–64 and n. 94.

[27]Since the legislative record of the Maggior Consiglio before 1280 is incomplete, it is possible that measures were taken even before 1269 to raise the fineness of gold exported but have left no trace.

import of gold or silver as either bullion or coin, at least not before that of 1379, when the city was practically under seige.[28] In England not until 1663 did it become generally permissible to reexport foreign coin or bullion, registering it at the customs house.[29] In medieval and early modern Europe, export of gold and silver was generally deplored by contemporaries as a loss in national wealth. Even today many medieval historians regard it as a sign of economic decline, that is, of the failure of an economy to produce adequately, as indeed it was in some countries under some circumstances.[30] In medieval Venice, in contrast, the export of bullion and coin was normally regarded as good. The Senate took special measures to facilitate it,[31] and chroniclers boasted of it as a sign of the city's prosperity.[32] Venice's economic policies have frequently been called mercantilistic, but they showed none of the bullionist alarm over the export of precious metals. The income of middlemen benefited from large volume, even if one essential in the turnover was the export of gold or silver.

Certainly the Venetian bullion market was sufficiently free that its role in the international exchange of gold and silver did not depend on smuggling. One can go so far as to say that normally bullion moved into and out of the city in response to changes in supply and demand. Although subject to interruption for brief periods for political reasons, the direction and volume of the flows were determined by the values of the metals in relation one to the other at various other market places and by the needs for balancing the import or export of other commodities, such as grain or pepper. In that sense, Venice can be said to have provided a relatively free market for bullion.

The Rialto became a world-famous market place in part because it provided a locus for exchanging information about the worldwide supply and demand for many commodities. The accuracy of the information was improved by enforced standards of weight and fineness and by public

[28]*PMV*, doc. 164.

[29]For England see above, chap. 2, n. 4; and esp. Munro, "Bullionism," 188–89 and passim. For Milan see E. Motta, "Documenti visconteo-sforzeschi per la storia della zecca di Milano," *RIN* 6 (1893)–9 (1896), e.g. 6, docs. 40 (1391), 116 (1423), 126 (1426), 186 (1456), and 7, doc. 236 (1467).

[30]Robert S. Lopez "Il problema della bilancia dei pagamenti nel commercio di Levante," in Pertusi, ed., *Venezia e il Levante*, vol. 1, pt. 1, pp. 446–52.

[31]Special provisions were made regarding the operations of the mint so that merchants who had put their silver there to have it coined could receive the coin in time to send it overseas by the galleys (E.g., ASV, Avogaria di Comun, Deliberazioni del Maggior Consiglio, Brutus, fol. 84v).

[32]Antonio Morosini, *Cronica*, BMV, Ms. It., cl. VII, cod. 2049–II (8332–II), fol. 154r, describes the cargoes of the outgoing fleets of 1433 as proof of Venice's wealth, in spite of a long war and heavy taxes. See also Marino Sanuto [il giovane], *I diarii*, ed. Rinaldo Fulin et al., 58 vols. (Venice, 1879–1903), 3:1187–88; and below, app. B, sec. iv.

recording of sales by brokers and other officials. The institutions that performed these functions for the bullion trade expanded in the latter part of the thirteenth century. Earlier, various Visdomini had been charged with supervising and collecting taxes from foreigners who came to Venice to trade.[33] Those governing the warehouse-hotel in which the Germans were lodged were directly involved in the bullion trade. All the money and merchandise brought by a German merchant had to be shown to the Visdomini del Fondaco dei Tedeschi.[34] In 1268 the importers were required to show their silver bullion also to the mintmasters ("massari"), and if they could not agree with the mintmaster on a price, the Visdomini put it up for auction.[35]

All importers—Venetians as well as foreigners—were obliged in any case to report immediately any bullion that they imported to a special office for the weighing and assaying of gold and silver established at an early date at the Rialto. Sometimes referred to as two offices, sometimes as a single office, it came to consist in the fifteenth century of four officials for registering and weighing—two for silver and two for gold—and three assayers.[36] While the imports of the Germans were reported through their Visdomini, other imports were reported by other customs officials or, especially in the case of Venetians, by the importer himself. The arrival of both gold and silver bullion by many routes and subject to taxes that varied with the importer facilitated smuggling; but registry of all bullion entering the city, whatever its tax status, was the first and basic step. No silver could be sold before being registered. Subsequent changes of ownership were then to be recorded at this Rialto office (here called the Assay Office) so that the source and destination of each ounce would be

[33]Roberto Cessi and Annibale Alberti, *Rialto: l'isola—il ponte—il mercato* (Bologna, 1934), 233–34; Giorgio Zordan, *I Visdomini di Venezia nel sec. XIII,* Pubblicazioni della Facoltà di Giurisprudenza dell'Università di Padova, 59 (Padua, 1971).

[34]Lupprian, *Il Fondaco dei Tedeschi.* Descriptions dating ca. 1500 of the activities of this office (as well as of all other offices and magistracies) can be found in Sanuto, *De origine* (see pp. 134, 273–74); and in "Traité du gouvernement de la cité et seigneurie de Venise," Bibliothèque nationale, Paris, Fonds français, 5599–5600, (see cap. 53), published in a fragmentary edition by Paul M. Perret, *Histoire des relations de la France avec Venise du XIIIe s. à l'avènement de Charles VIII,* 2 vols. (Paris, 1896), 2:285–86 (a complete edition is being edited by Philippe Braunstein and Reinhold C. Mueller).

[35]*PMV,* doc. 14; Simonsfeld, *Der Fondaco,* 2:18–23; Zordan, *I Visdomini,* 669–71. Zordan regards the obligation of the importer to show his silver to the mintmaster as giving the latter a right of preemption and considers it unlikely that the importer would be offered any different price. But Zordan ignores the large export of uncoined bullion. The mint had no right of preemption, certainly not after 1278 (see below, n. 51), although after 1331 it had a right to coin a portion of all imported silver, a right which imposed an import duty on all silver, as explained below in chaps. 10, sec. iii, and 11.

[36]BMV, Ms. It., cl. VII, cod. 95 (8610), fol. 47.

SCALES FOR WEIGHING COPPER, SILVER, AND GOLD

Depicted are scales of three sizes for weighing the metals in various stages
of refinement, types used at the Silver Office at the Rialto as
well as at the mint.

*From Agricola,* De re metallica *(edition of Basel, 1556, at the BMV), 207. Photograph by Toso.*

accounted for.[37] When any silver was presented to the mint, the supplier
presenting it was asked how he had acquired it.

Regulations drawn up in 1266 specified the fees of the official assayers and weighers, who were salaried officials elected by the governing
councils, and limited their personal participation in the bullion trade. The

---

[37]Cessi and Alberti, *Rialto,* pt. 3, refers to several capitolari of officials supervising the
Rialto market. The Capitolari degli Ufficiali sovra Rialto (ASV, Provveditori al Sal, b. 2,
caps. 1, 116, and 147 and passim), which specify operating regulations for "cambiatores,
stationarii et sartores qui habent stationes ad fictum a comuni in Rivoalto," are in MC,
Capricornus, fol. 43 (18 May 1307). But we have been unable to find a capitolare in which
were collected the regulations concerning the officials referred to in the capitolare of the
mintmasters of 1278 as "illis qui sunt constituti super aurum et argentum" (Papadopoli, 1:328

weight and scales they used were subject to most careful inspection.[38] Assayers were ordered to perform their duties at the "stacione comunis" at the Rialto, or in the mint, or in their own shops, but not in the booths or offices of the moneychangers, where, it was felt, they were likely to make mistakes.[39] Gold had to be cast before it was assayed; selling more than 2 marks of gold dust ("paglola") was forbidden. Assay had to precede sale of any amount above a half-mark.[40] If the metal was too low-grade to be

---

[l. 10]). The nearest to it in title is that "de auro seu folia auri" edited by Monticolo in *I capitolari delle arti*, 3:291–322. It is the statute not of a guild but of officials who inspected the work of goldbeaters. As stated on p. 320, cap. 43, dated 1319, an old capitolare had been destroyed by fire. This new one was compiled apparently from diverse sources. Caps. 1–5 and 30 ff. concern goldbeaters; those in between comprise general rules applying to all such administrative officials. Except for the opening formula, cap. 1 is almost the same as *DMC*, 2:304–5 (but see above, n. 25, on the fineness of gold). These officials were given wide authority over all "purified gold (oro cocto)." They were called Domini in 1269 but were subject to the Giustizia, and in later *capitula* they seem concerned only with the goldbeaters or spinners of gold thread, the prices they paid and charged, and the quality of their material. The Mariegola dei Pesatori del Comun in ASV, Arti, b. 438, is a sixteenth-century compilation specifying which commodities were to be weighed by which weigher, and his fees, but without special mention of gold or silver.

Various series contain many references to the assayers and weighers of gold and silver at the Rialto but do not give a coherent picture of their numbers, salaries, and duties as the structure of the office changed. For an example of the inevitable conflicts of jurisdiction see MC, Presbiter, fol. 98 (1313). In 1354 the official weighers of silver at the Rialto, who had been elected previously by the Quarantia "a scrutinio," were henceforth to be elected by the Great Council (*PMV*, doc. 121). The auctioning of silver by an officialis argenti is mentioned, for example, in 1367 (ibid., doc. 149). The weighing offices for gold and silver were combined according to a senatorial decree of 6 May 1371 (ASV, Senato, Misti, reg. 33, fol. 105v. See also on such officials *PMV*, docs. 26, 121, 164; *DMC*, 2:298–301, 304–5, 311–13; ASV, MC, Leona, fol. 234; Consiglio dei Dieci, Misti, reg. 18, fols. 16, 101–2; and the account below, in vol. 2, of the controversy over reforms in 1414–21). Finally, the magistracy that had authority to investigate for clipped and counterfeit coins, the Officium Grossorum Tonsorum, at times was autonomous and at times coincided with the office or offices of assayers and weighers of bullion, as appears from the many dozens of requests for pardons for infraction of bullion ordinances in ASV, Grazie, regs. 5–11 (1331–46). After mid-century, mention of officiales grossorum tonsorum are very rare, as jurisdictions were combined. For the Pesadori all'arzento see Sanuto, *De Origine*, 134–35, 273.

[38]*DMC*, 2:312–13.

[39]Ibid., 312 (1266).

[40]*PMV*, doc. 13 (1264). The assayers' fee was 8 denari piccoli per mark (about 0.02 percent), according to the merchant's manual or manuals published under the title *Tarifa zoè noticia dy pexi e mexure di luogi e tere che s'adovra marcadantia per el mondo* by the R. Istituto Superiore di Scienze Economiche e Commerciali di Venezia (now the Facoltà di Economia e Commercio, Cà Foscari) to celebrate the eleventh centenary of the University of Pavia (Venice, 1925), 14, 54, 69. This *Tarifa zoè noticia* (so cited hereafter) is a composite of two or three compilations of weights and measures. The first section contains a reference to the treaty made with Egypt in 1345 and renewed in 1355 (31 and n) which indicates that this compilation is of later date than the compilation in Stussi, ed., *Zibaldone da Canal*. Most of the data in the first section are repeated in a second, which begins on p. 41 and includes greater detail about Sarai, Alexandria, and spices. A critical edition of the *Tarifa* is being prepared for the FSV.

assayed by touchstone, it had to be refined and then assayed again before it was auctioned. Assays were recorded in writing, and normally the decision of two out of the three assayers was final.[41] There are fifteenth-century references to a "tochator comunis," who checked the assays of lesser officials.[42] The position of assayer called for long experience as well as exceptional skill and probity. When that was recognized, as it clearly was in 1414, when the Assay Office was called "the foundation and base on which depends our honor and profit,"[43] assayers were elected for life and did not have to rotate in and out of various offices, as did almost all Venetian noble officials.[44] But one wonders what remedy was relied on when eyesight began to fail.

Assaying of gold was done with a touchstone by using "needles" ("toche" or "virgule"), that is, tiny rods containing known, graded amounts of impurity mixed with 24-carat gold.[45] The assayers compared the color of the mark left by these needles on the black touchstone with the color left by the gold being assayed. According to a decree of the Great Council in 1345, a gold bar serving as the standard for 24 carats, with the words "est sazium ducatorum" stamped on one end, was kept in the chancery.[46] At about the same time, it was revealed that the "needles" used by the assayers showed only 1 grain of difference in fineness, and a set that would distinguish half-grains was ordered.[47] Since there were 4 grains to a carat (and 24 carats = 100 percent), assayers were being called on to distinguish by needles and touchstone between gold that was only 0.989 fine (95/96) and gold that was 0.995 fine (191/192), which seems impossible.[48] Assayers were also called on to report whether the impurity was copper or silver.

The assay by eye was supplemented by an assay through the refining process, which, especially for separating gold and silver, is described below in explaining the technique used in the mint in order to obtain absolutely

[41]*PMV,* docs. 66, 70, p. 67 (1314). *Cap. Fontego,* caps. 70, 71. Late examples of recorded assays are in ASV, Zecca, b. 18bis, fol. 1.

[42]ASV, Senato, Terra, reg. 4, fol. 168v (11 April 1461); less clearly in 1416 in Senato, Misti, reg. 51, fol. 143v.

[43]ASV, Senato, Misti, reg. 50, fols. 97–98, in the resolution of two Venetian senators of 28 April 1414: "offitium extimatorum nostrorum auri est fundamentum et principium a quo radix honoris et utilitatis nostre ad hoc bene dependere potest."

[44]ASV, Collegio, Notatorio, reg. 8, fol. 145; MC, Ursa, fol. 112v.

[45]On the touchstone and "needles" and how they were used see Georgius Agricola, *De re metallica,* trans. with notes by Herbert C. Hoover and Lou N. Hoover (London, 1912), 252–60. The Hoovers called the small rods of known mixture "needles" because Agricola called them in Latin "acus." They were called "tochis" and "toche" in *DMC,* 2:313, and ASV, Zecca, b. 6tris, cap. 45. Presumably these needles are what are referred to in Marco da Molin's motion of 18 April 1414 as "virgule" (Senato, Misti, reg. 50, fols. 96–97).

[46]Papadopoli, 1:171, citing ASV, Commemoriali, reg. 4, fol. 88v (3 August 1345).

[47]ASV, Zecca, b. 6tris, caps. 45, 46.

[48]Craig, *The Mint,* 69.

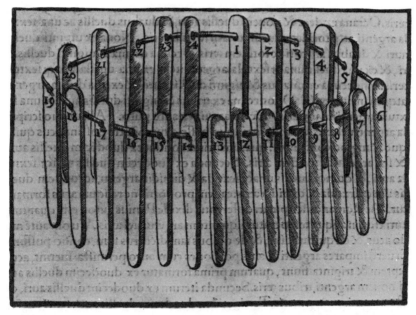

ASSAYERS' NEEDLES

Thin strips of gold graded for purity from 1 to 24 carats were used
with a touchstone in assaying gold.

*From Agricola,* De re metallica *(edition of Basel, 1556, at the BMV), 199.*
*Photograph by Toso.*

pure gold.[49] Our sources leave unclear the distinction and coordination
between the assayers of the Assay Office at the Rialto and the assayers in
the mint at San Marco.

Many other agencies also had a hand in policing the bullion market,
especially in the collection of revenue, and there was a tendency to extend
the authority of the mint. The Assay Office at the Rialto remained of
prime importance in registering, weighing, assaying, and auctioning gold
and silver, but in 1298 the mintmasters were given authority to check up on
the Assay Office. The assayers and weighers were ordered to send the
mintmasters written reports on the amounts sold and to whom. The
mintmasters were then to investigate the records of the buyers of the
bullion to find out whether it had been taken to the mint or what had been
done with it (perhaps just resold to another Venetian before going to the
mint, perhaps used by the jewelers). If they found anyone who had gold

---

[49]Johnson, ed. and trans., *The De moneta,* xl–xli, 83–85, prints a treatise on the process that
was reported to be in use in Venice. The mint's assay is referred to in ASV, Zecca, b. 6tris,
cap. 48; and in *Cap. Fontego,* cap. 71, p. 24.

and silver that had not been assayed and weighed at the designated places, they were to investigate, exacting sworn testimony and inflicting fines which would be collected by the Signori di Notte.[50]

## iv. COMPETING BUYERS

In order to compete as a bullion market with Milan, Bologna, and, indirectly, Genoa and Florence, Venice needed a reputation as a place where gold and silver were in demand and where a dealer would not be taken advantage of through false assaying, weighing, and recording or through collusive bidding and concealment of demand. Venetian regulations obviously protected the buyer in these respects, making the supply fully known through the registration requirements sketched above. To a large extent the regulation of sales protected the seller also and enabled him to learn the extent of the demand.

As early as 1278, purchase of bullion from a foreign importer by a mintmaster directly was forbidden, for, as a general rule,[51] Venetian middlemen came between. The prohibition of purchases by the mintmaster directly from importers seems to have lapsed, however, either by neglect or by interpretation of privileges granted to Germans or other groups of foreigners. Early in the fourteenth century, importers could sell bullion to the mint, provided they delivered it there within five days of arrival and accepted the mint's established price.[52] German importers of gold were encouraged to sell to the mint by special provisions for assuring that they received their payment in less time than it took to turn their bullion into ducats.[53] But most evidence from the fourteenth and fifteenth centuries indicates that the importers sold to Venetian moneychangers and bullion merchants, who were able to make effective payment more quickly than could the mint.

Tables of moneychangers were grouped around the base of the campanile at San Marco, where they were near the mint and were well placed to satisfy the needs of tourists and pilgrims. The Piazza and Piazzetta were the tourist center, even more then than now, not only because of the fame of the saint and his holy relics but also because ship captains offering

---

[50]Papadopoli, 1:337–38, decree of the Quarantia 11 October 1298, apparently the law under which the silver merchant Guglielmo Condulmer was audited by the mintmasters in 1404, as explained below, chap. 11, n. 39. Checking over gold and silver accounts had previously been the responsibility of "illis de super racionibus de foris," of whom Cessi and Alberti (*Rialto*, 238) say that their office was separated from that of the auditors "de intus" in 1281. Successors to these auditing offices had supervisory authority over the mint (see below, chap. 12, sec. iii) after the mintmasters were given this supervisory authority over the bullion office.

[51]That capitolare of 1278 of the massari refers to "aurum vel argentum," even though it was supposedly earlier than the coining of the ducat (*PMV*, doc. 25, cap. 8).

[52]Pegolotti, *Pratica*, 139–40.

[53]See below, chap. 12, sec. iii.

passage to the Holy Land had their booths there. To some general rules, such as that against foreigners exporting specie overseas, there were special exceptions for pilgrims,[54] but a Jew who tried to take advantage of these exceptions when he embarked for Palestine was ruled not a pilgrim, being an infidel, and his funds were sequestered as contraband.[55] In return for the kind of coin that pilgrims needed for their voyages, the moneychangers accepted not only foreign coin but uncoined gold and silver.[56] They were well placed to take it to the mint and to turn in to the mint for recoinage clipped or broken coins that they had purchased cheaply.

Moneychangers who branched out and became regular dealers in bullion were more likely to be found at the Rialto. There moneychangers had developed into deposit bankers as well as bullion merchants, as will be described in volume 2. The handling of both specie and bullion was thus divided between the city's two nuclei. At San Marco were the moneychangers, who were ready to supply tourists with shiny new Venetian coin from the mint next-door. At the Rialto were the bankers' booths, close to the Assay Office, where experts were readily available for evaluating bullion and coin, and to the state treasurer's office, where the bankers kept their cash.[57] The auctions were held there, the workshops of the goldsmiths and silversmiths were nearby in the Ruga dei Orefici,[58] and the warehouse of the German merchants was just across the canal. When speculation in silver by bankers was blamed for bank failures and their investment in silver was limited and in principle forbidden in the period 1374–1482, the place of the bankers was taken by general merchants who became specialists in the bullion trade.[59]

Some of the sales on the Rialto were organized for foreigners by the Visdomini or the Assay Office, auctions announced by the ringing of a bell.[60] Others were organized through the services of brokers assigned to the Fondaco dei Tedeschi and subject to severe penalties, including immediate perpetual loss of their positions, if they gave one Venetian an advantage over others by taking him to a room in the Fondaco where the Germans were lodged. Venetian buyers were penalized if they employed

[54]*PMV*, doc. 26; *DMC*, 2:248–49, 299–300; Nani-Mocenigo, ed., *Capitolare dei Signori di Notte*, cap. 27.

[55]Simonsfeld, *Der Fondaco*, 2:294, doc. 11 (1340, from ASV, Grazie): "Quod Judei non sunt peregrini."

[56]Sales at the tables of the moneychangers there were excluded from a regulation of 29 October 1282 (*DMC*, 3:12) but are mentioned later in Nani-Mocenigo, ed., *Capitolare dei Signori di Notte*, caps. 27, 30, 100.

[57]The fees fixed for the official assayers in 1266 included fees for assaying gold and silver coin as well as bullion (*DMC*, 2:312). Moneychangers were under orders to turn in all clipped grossi (*PMV*, docs. 17, 30).

[58]On the "ruga aurificium" see Monticolo, ed., *I capitolari delle arti*, 1:125 n. 3.

[59]Mueller, "The Role of Bank Money," 61–68; and below, vol. 2.

[60]*DMC*, 2:301, 3:12; *PMV*, docs. 14, 26, 54; Sanuto, *De origine*, 154.

any such subterfuge for getting an advance look at what a seller had to offer. It was the broker's duty to lead the importer around the Rialto to the moneychangers' booths there, hearing bids, so that the importer could sell to the highest bidder. Sale of silver elsewhere than in the area of the Rialto, called "inter duas scalas," was forbidden. In 1344 these provisions against forestalling were explicitly made applicable also to the silver brought by Lombards and Ragusans.[61]

The gold brought by German merchants in the 1260s and 1270s was brought to the Rialto for auctioning each day at mid-morning and at vespers by the Visdomini del Fondaco, according to their statute.[62] Later, when the mint's coinage of gold was well established, it provided a dependable market at a price that naturally varied with the fineness of the gold and became fixed at 108 soldi a oro per mark per carat of fineness. The officials in the Assay Office were instructed to tell the importers that they could either sell at auction at the Rialto to the highest bidder or, if they thought that the bid underestimated the fineness of their gold, reject that bid as too low and take their gold to the mint, where they would be credited with 108 soldi for each carat of fineness recorded for their gold by the Rialto's assayers.[63]

Venetian bullion merchants who bought from the importers did more of the refining of the gold and silver than did the mint, although the procedures varied considerably from one period to another. In 1273, before Venice coined the ducat but shortly after the Florentines and Genoese had begun coining gold and shortly after Venice had in 1269 forbidden the export of any gold not refined up to 23 1/2 carats, the refining of all gold imported was entrusted to two goldsmiths elected, bonded, and salaried as part of the Assay Office.[64] After the coining of the ducat began in 1284–85, the mint concentrated on removing the last traces of impurity from the gold used. It accepted only gold already 23 1/2 carat (except as provided by special privileges of the Germans in some years), and refining gold to that fineness was left to private enterprise. In the fifteenth century, Venetian suppliers tried to offer gold that would pass assay as 23 3/4 carat, having themselves made provision to obtain as much value as possible from the dross, especially from ores containing silver.[65]

For silver also, refining was at one time in the thirteenth century

---

[61]See below, app. G, docs. 3 and 4, taken from ASV, Secreta, Capitolare dei Capi Sestiere, caps. 134 and 192–95, which record lost deliberations of the Quarantia. In 1278 the sale of gold and silver at the Rialto had been restricted to an area described as "inter pedem pontis et scalam Rivoalti" (*PMV*, doc. 26. Cf. Cessi and Alberti, *Rialto*, 29).

[62]*PMV*, docs. 13, 14; *DMC*, 2:301; *Cap. Fontego*, xvi.

[63]*PMV*, doc. 39; *Cap. Fontego*, 26 (1362). Explanation of the seller's option by the assayers is explicitly referred to in the reforms of the gold mint, 1414–21 (see below, chap. 12, sec. iii).

[64]Papadopoli, 1:341 (1273).

[65]See above, n. 14; and below, chap. 10, sec. iv.

assigned to two salaried goldsmiths,[66] but in the following century it was mainly in the hands of the merchants who bought silver from the Germans.[67] They could take it to the mint, which at the end of the thirteenth century was obliged to accept all silver offered for conversion into ingots of certified fineness.[68] Or they themselves could have it refined, perhaps in their own shops, up to the somewhat lower standards required for silverware by the Guild of Jewelers and Goldsmiths. Or, as a third option, apparently much chosen, they themselves could refine it to the mint's highest standard, taking it to the mint only to have it certified, and then sell it to other Venetians for shipment to the Levant or export it themselves.[69] Finally, they had a fourth option, namely, sending it to the mint to be coined at whatever price and coinage fee the mint was then offering. After 1331 all the options were subject to the obligation to have some portion of the silver coined in Venice, an obligation that will be more fully explained below.[70] German importers of silver ores containing gold had the option of selling it in that form or of paying the cost of having the metals separated in order to sell them separately.[71]

Buying from foreign importers, refining the bullion, and either marketing the metal or having it coined were profitable operations for many of Venice's merchant-nobles, although they were by no means reserved for nobles alone. An example of how one moneychanger operated for years— 1389–1408—in spite of restrictions imposed on Rialto bankers (and how his account books were carefully checked by the mint to make sure it received its due in silver) is provided by the estate papers of Guglielmo Condulmer, a distant relative of the later Venetian pope Eugenius IV.[72] Mathematical exercise books used in training Venetian merchants included problems in calculating the value in moneys of account of pieces of silver and gold of various weights and fineness.[73] The successful mer-

---

[66]*PMV*, doc. 54; *DMC*, 2:272.

[67]A merchant's notebook of about 1310 says: "L'inchanbiadori da Venexia conpra l'arçento che vien d'Alemagna e d'Ongaria lo qualle nonn è afinà çerto e puo' lo fasse afinar" (Stussi, ed., *Zibaldone da Canal*, 7. On later situations see below, chap. II, sec. ii).

[68]See below, chap. 10, sec. i.

[69]In 1515 the weighers of silver at the Rialto could also certify ingots (Sanuto, *De origine*, 273; cf. p. 134).

[70]See below, chap. II, sec. ii.

[71]That was the case at least in the early sixteenth century, according to the papers of the Paumgarten firm (see Karl Otto Müller, ed., *Welthandelsbräuche [1480–1540]*, Deutsche Handelsakten des Mittelalters und der Neuzeit, Historische Kommission bei der Bayerischen Akademie der Wissenschaften [Stuttgart and Berlin, 1934], 27, 317, 322). The reference is to silver containing less than 10 percent gold, in contrast to the gold containing a little silver removed by the mint.

[72]See below, vol. 2.

[73]Stussi, ed., *Zibaldone da Canal*, 5. BMV, Ms. It., cl. IV, cod. 497 (5163), fol. 35. A sixteenth-century manuscript in the library of Frederic C. Lane, boxed as Libro di Gasparo, fols. 83–89. Cf. Müller, ed., *Welthandelsbräuche*, 317–18.

chant's skill in such calculations had to be complemented by good judgment or good luck in deciding how to dispose of the refined metal.

Altogether, these buyers of imported bullion represented demand of three different kinds. One arose from the need for coins in Venice itself on the part of the government and local traders. This need was reflected in the prices paid by the mint and, in some periods, in legal requirements that a portion of all silver imported be coined in Venice.

A second element in demand was expressed in bids by merchants desiring to ship either coin or bullion overseas. These exporters represented a demand that in many periods was larger than that of the mint. Much silver in the form of ingots or flat bars stamped with a seal of San Marco to guarantee their fineness went to the Levant and to North Africa to be sold to the mints there.[74] Before Venice offered superior facilities by coining ducats, much uncoined gold went to Apulia and Sicily to buy wheat and other foodstuffs[75] and was probably made into the gold coins used there. The Venetian buyers of silver and gold bullion for export represented an overseas demand for metal to use as coin as well as for adornment or hoarding. Venice's shipping and commercial network gave the Levantine demand especially effective representation at Venice.

Another kind of demand was for consumption in Venice in what is now called industrial uses. In this category the main consumers at Venice were the craftsmen who used gold to gild silver and to make jewelry and religious objects. Use of gold and especially of silver in tableware was then much more important than it is now, since in Venice as elsewhere the use of plates, bowls, and cups of gold and silver served the double purpose of enhancing status and providing a reserve of wealth that could be transformed into coin if necessary. The tableware and jewelry that the women of Venice brought to the mint to be turned into coin was credited with saving Venice during the War of Chioggia when other sources of funds for buying supplies and hiring mercenaries had been cut off.[76] The ladies' patriotism was later memorialized by Andrea Vicentino's painting on the ceiling of the hall of the Great Council in the Ducal Palace. During a later crisis, Paduans taunted Venetians by saying that their money smelt of the wine goblets that had been melted down to pay war costs.[77]

Makers of tableware, jewelry, or coins were attached to the same

[74]See below, chaps. 13, sec. ii, 14, sec. iii; and 17, sec. i.

[75]*PMV*, docs. 7–9.

[76]Marino Sanuto [il giovane], *Vite de' Duchi di Venezia*, Rerum Italicarum Scriptores, 1st ed., 22 (Milan, 1733), col. 723; BMV, Cronaca (pseudo-) Zancaruolo, Ms. It., cl. VII, cod. 50 (9275), fol. 443; *PMV*, doc. 164, p. 158 ff.

[77]Gerolamo Priuli, *I diarii*, ed. Arturo Segre and Roberto Cessi, Rerum Italicarum Scriptores, 2d ed., 24 (Bologna, 1938–41), vol. 4, pt. 3, p. 166. Reinhold C. Mueller, "Effetti della Guerra di Chioggia (1378–1381) sulla vita economica e sociale di Venezia," *Ateneo veneto* 19 (1981). On their compensation see below, chap. 11, n. 37.

## DEHOARDING PLATE AND JEWELRY

Patriotic Venetian ladies bring their plate, chains, and jewelry to
the doge to be melted down by the mint and made into coin during the War of Chioggia.

*Late-sixteenth-century monochrome by Andrea Vicentino on the ceiling of the
Sala del Maggior Consiglio. Palazzo Ducale, Archivio fotografico. Photograph by Cameraphoto.*

guild, that of the goldsmiths (aurifices). Its earliest statutes, dated 1233, were among the oldest Venetian guild statutes. They were much concerned with the fineness and the proportions of the gold and silver used by the goldbeaters in gilding silver. The oath opening their earliest statutes included a promise not to work with gold inferior in quality to the tarí, the Neapolitan coin, nor with silver inferior to sterling, the English standard well known in the Mediterranean after the Crusades.[78] Importers who brought gold or silver refined to those standards must have counted the jewelers among their customers. Members of that guild were certainly experts in assaying gold and silver.[79] To what extent they were active also as buyers of precious metal of lower quality which they themselves refined up to the specified standards is not clear. Whether they obtained their silver or gold from merchant members of their guild or from merchants and moneychangers who were members of no guild but who employed private refiners, the craftsmen in private employ were certainly one element represented on the Venetian market.[80] Works of precious metal such as reliquaries were much in demand also by churchmen, who had substantial funds at their disposal.

Among more mundane uses was the minting by Venetian goldsmiths of imitations of the coins of foreign countries. The elaborate provisions taken to stop the minting of such coins when it was forbidden in 1354 imply that it was being vigorously practiced.[81]

In brief, the demand side of the market for bullion was presented to importers almost entirely through wholesale merchants who were members of the noble class, which was then consolidating its position. Not silversmiths as craftsmen nor manual dealers in coins but merchants and bankers were the principal buyers. German importers at least could present bullion directly to the mint to be converted for them into coin, but the mint generally bought from Venetian middlemen.

The intensity of the competition when the mintmasters were negotiating with the suppliers in making a purchase is suggested by a provision forbidding any other potential buyer to be present in the mint when a

---

[78]Monticolo, ed., *I capitolari delle arti,* 1:115; cf. below, app. E.

[79]The Capitolare degli orefici provided that when an aurifex was chosen "ad extimacionem," he had to serve or pay a fine (Monticolo, ed., *I capitolari delle arti,* 1:121–22 [1262].

[80]The statutes of the jewelers suggest difficulties in drawing lines between the general rights to trade of all Venetian "citizens" ("cives") and the jurisdiction of particular guilds, in this case that of jewelers, over all kinds of gold- and silverware or jewelry (see caps. 46 and 47). A special study is needed to clarify how this differentiation in trading rights of guildsmen and general merchants is related to the social stratification that developed during the next century into a sharp distinction between nobles and guildsmen. For the important role played in the Venetian bullion market of the later fifteenth century by the goldsmith-wholesaler Zorzi "orexe" see below, vol. 2.

[81]*PMV,* doc. 121; ASV, Cataver, b. 1 (capitolare), cap. 148, fol. 81; G. B. Galicciolli, *Delle memorie venete antiche profane ed ecclesiastiche,* 8 vols. (Venice, 1795), 1:370.

mintmaster was examining a possible purchase, a prohibition repeated and rephrased in December 1278 to give the mintmaster explicit authority to order the dealer out and levy a fine against him if he refused to go.[82] The same kind of competition at the auctions at the Rialto was the best assurance the importers had of receiving good prices in Venice. Some of the purchasers were merchants buying silver to send to the Levant in order to receive spices or cotton to sell to the Germans from whom they were buying the silver. Others were buying to make profits from refining and selling the product in Venice. Some were mere speculators hoping to resell at higher prices to exporters or to the mint or perhaps to sell a bit at a time to craftsmen.

The possibility existed that these wealthy operators who dominated the purchasing would rig the bidding. At least as early as 1285 it was felt necessary to forbid combines to buy silver.[83] In 1299 there was complaint that such combines had indeed been formed to buy gold from the Germans. Instead of bidding against each other, the Venetian buyers kept the price down by placing just one bid with deferred payments and later dividing the gold among themselves to resell at a higher price. The Great Council forbade forming any company ("compagnia") to bid at the auctions and made provisions to force all bidders to pay within three days the amounts bid.[84] Similar collusion among buyers was complained of and forbidden again in 1362 and 1367.[85] The presence of many buyers at the auctions was encouraged in 1357 by providing that no more than 100 marks be offered in a single lot ("pro quolibet incantum").[86] The prohibitions against privately negotiated deals between individual Venetians and foreigners—avoiding the auctions or predetermining their outcome—were repeated many times. Overseas, the Venetian government encouraged combines among its merchants to buy cheaply in Syria and Egypt,[87] but at Venice it legislated to enable the Germans to auction their gold and silver in a competitive market so that they would be encouraged to bring bullion to Venice rather than take it elsewhere.

[82]*PMV*, docs. 25, caps. 8 and 38; 27.

[83]Ibid., doc. 43; also in *DMC*, 3:122.

[84]*DMC*, 3:458, where the length of time within which payment was required is left blank, whereas it is given as three days in the capitolare (see Melchiore Roberti, ed., *Le magistrature giudiziarie veneziane e i loro capitolari fino al 1300*, 3 vols., Monumenti storici, 2d ser., 16–18 [Venice: Deputazione di Storia Patria, 1909–11], 3:67). The term was eight days in 1317 (ASV, Zecca, b. 6bis, Capitolare dei massari all'argento, fols. 18v–19v), but three again in the 1330s (Cessi, Sambin, and Brunetti, eds., *Le deliberazioni dei Rogati*, 2:53, 197, 354).

[85]*PMV*, doc. 147; *Cap. Fontego*, 25–26.

[86]Nani-Mocenigo, ed., *Capitolare dei Signori di Notte*, cap. 291 (1338); ASV, Zecca, b. 6bis, fols. 29–31; *Cap. Fontego*, 44, cap. 119 (1357).

[87]Gino Luzzatto, "Sindacati e cartelli nel commercio veneziano dei sec. XIII e XIV," *Rivista di storia economica*, 1943, reprinted in his *Studi*, 165–66; Lane, *Venice: A Maritime Republic*, 144.

Preventing collusion among the buyers was more difficult when the bankers had become so firmly established that the chief means of payment among large dealers on the Rialto was the transfer among themselves of their credits on the bankers' books. Payments in bank money were likely to involve some extension of credit, perhaps in the form of overdrafts. The possibility that buyers would use such loans as a way of constructing temporary cartels is obvious. They could be suppressed if the regulation of the Great Council requiring all buyers to pay in cash within three days was strictly observed. But payment by transfer of credits on a banker's books was much more convenient for the seller, as will be explained in volume 2. Forbidding it proved difficult to enforce, and the law against payment through the banks had to be suspended temporarily in 1379.[88]

In spite of complications in the application of the rules, the purposes of Venetian market regulation are clear. They included not only the collection of taxes, the enforcement of standards, and the sale in Venice of imports but also the maintenance at Venice of a free market in the sense of a competitive market. For centuries silver and gold were attracted by the presence in Venice of competing buyers who had opportunities to export.

[88]Mueller, "The Role of Bank Money," 63.

# 10

## THE MINT'S PRODUCTS,
## PURCHASES, AND PRICES

HE EXTENT TO WHICH the mintmasters were active participants in Venice's bullion market varied from one period to another and more in the silver market than in the gold market. In preparation for the coinage of the first gold ducat and for a few years after 1284, while the government was pushing the use of the new gold coin in payments that previously had been made in silver grossi, the mintmasters went into the market to buy gold bullion with the grossi that the Great Council had appropriated for that purpose. Within a few years that was no longer necessary. Importers or Venetians who purchased from importers brought the bullion to the mint knowing that the mint would coin all gold presented to it at a legally prescribed price, paying them with the product or similar gold coin (see below, sec. iv). In the acquisition of silver bullion, on the other hand, the mintmasters played an active and more varied role during a much longer period. Not until 1353 were the mintmasters ordered to turn into coin all the silver offered to them at prices legally specified. Until that date, the number of coins produced depended not only on decisions by silver merchants but also on governmental decisions that determined how aggressively the mintmasters bid for silver.

### i. THE RELATION OF PRICES TO MINT CHARGES

In the early centuries the price the mint offered for bullion determined the total mint charge. When the mintmaster paid the silver merchant for the bullion supplied, the mintmaster valued the coins at the rate fixed in the law, which specified how many coins were to be made from each mark of metal. The difference between the price paid for the bullion and the value of the coins made from it constituted the mint's charge, which included a seigniorage (a "profit" for the Commune) as well as the cost of manufacture. From the point of view of the mintmaster and his accounting, the mint charge can be described as the difference between the purchase price of bullion and the sale price of coin. From the point of view of the silver merchants, the difference between the price the mint paid for their bullion and the value of the coin made from it was the cost of having their bullion converted into coin.

In the fifteenth century the suppliers' point of view was adopted in new governmental regulations specifying that suppliers be paid back in coin containing the same weight of fine silver as the bullion that they had deposited and be charged a fee calculated as so much per mark. Although after 1353 the mintmasters no longer had any discretion in offering prices for bullion, the entry of silver into the mint for a time still took the form of a sale. The sale had become a mere technicality, so much so that silver or gold that the mint had bought was often referred to, while it was being coined, as silver or gold "of the merchants."[1]

Before 1353, considerable discretion was left to the mintmasters, subject to orders from higher authorities such as the Quarantia. The prices they offered for silver were an influential factor in the market. Normally, however, the amount of silver minted must have depended mainly on how much silver the Venetian merchants who bought from importers decided to have coined and how much they decided to ship overseas as bullion.

## ii. CERTIFIED SILVER INGOTS

Although they were not obliged to accept for coinage all silver offered, the mintmasters became obliged in the thirteenth century to buy at a fixed price all silver offered with the scope of converting it into ingots or bars of certified fineness.

Bars of two slightly different standards of fineness were prepared. In May 1273 the Great Council ordered that all bars cast in the mint be stamped with the design used on grossi coins, with Christ on one side and St. Mark on the other. This clearly implies that these silver bars thus stamped and certified for export were of the very high standard of fineness that had been set for the grosso, 0.965 fine.[2] The following month other

[1]This is most clearly so with reference to the ducat in 1414–21 (see below, app. A, sec. v; see also the capitolare of 1279, cap. 2, *PMV*, doc. 25. On the shift in the way of stating mint charges for silver coins see app. A, sec. vii, on the years 1394–1407).

[2]*PMV*, doc. 19. On Venetian standards of fineness and how they were expressed see below, app. E.

certified bars of lesser fineness, later called sterling, were provided for.[3] They were prepared by adding 32 ounces of copper to 800 ounces of the silver of the fineness of grossi, which made them 0.925 fine, almost exactly the same as the English pennies from which they took the name sterling.[4] These bars stamped and certified as sterling are mentioned in a Venetian merchants' manual ca. 1310 as the kind exported;[5] and Francesco Balducci Pegolotti, a Florentine compiler of commercial information in the early fourteenth century, distinguished between the "verghe della bolla di Vinegia," of which he gave the fineness as the same as that of sterling, and "argento della bolla di Vinegia," of the same fineness as that which he gave for the Venetian grosso.[6] Since all later references to Venice's export of silver bullion seem to refer to silver of the fineness of grossi, the production of sterling bars in the mint seems to have ceased soon after 1340, if not before, perhaps because the chief market for those Venetian sterling ingots had been the mints of the Christian states in the Levant supported by the Crusaders from England and France. Almost the last such mint was that of Lesser Armenia, which was closed with the destruction of that kingdom by the Mamluks in 1347.

The attention paid in the legislation of the 1270s to silver ingots may have been one of the several moves in that decade to reduce the mint's production of coin, particularly of piccoli, of which the coinage had been resumed by Lorenzo Tiepolo on his election to the dogeship in 1268.[7] Export of silver bullion was encouraged later by the Venetian authorities,

[3]*PMV*, pp. 14–15 and 32, where doc. 20 refers to the bars not as sterling but as "legatum istius lege qua hodie ligatur" but doc. 22 of October calls them "argentum de sterlin," as does Romanin, *Storia documentata*, 2:383 n. 4. In the mintmasters' capitolare of 1278 they were obligated to alloy and certify the fineness of sterling bars at the price fixed by the doge and his council (*PMV*, doc. 25, cap. 74; and Papadopoli, 1:324, cap. 73).

[4]*DMC*, 2:245–46; *PMV*, doc. 20 (see app. E). Feavearyear, *The Pound Sterling*, 8, says that the English penny was 0.925 fine.

[5]The oldest relevant merchant's manual, the *Zibaldone da Canal* (Stussi, ed., 5–6), distinguishes between "fin arçento" and "arçento de sterlin," which "li marchadanti de Venexia porta per lo mondo." The entire first part of this *Zibaldone* was composed before 1311.

[6]Pegolotti, *Pratica*, 291. Although Pegolotti completed the compilation of his *Pratica* ca. 1340, it embodies compilations made earlier, as do most merchant manuals. Philip Grierson, "The Coin List of Pegolotti," in *Studi in onore di Armando Sapori* (Milan, 1957), vol. 1, pp. 485–92, concludes that the foundation for the list "was laid in c. 1290," and it was not kept up to date, although some additions were made in the 1320s. Pegolotti's list of "Leghe," 287–92, may be of similar date. Pegolotti's general description of Venetian coinage, pp. 138–40, shows no knowledge of the new silver coinage issued in 1331–32. His valuing Venice's "fiorino d'oro o vero ducato" at 52 solidi a grossi (p. 50) can be interpreted not as proof of composition after the law of 1328 which gave the ducat that legal value (see below, chaps. 13, sec. iv; and 14) but only as proof of composition after 1305, when commercial practice had given the ducat that value.

[7]See above, chap. 8, sec. iii, and below in this chapter, sec. iv.

but in the form of "argento di bolla," that is, ingots of the same fineness as grossi coins. It was shipped in the form of bars called "peze" or sheets called "piatine" often weighing 3–6 kg.[8] Their fineness was lowered from 0.965 to 0.952 in 1369 and to 0.949 about 1422.[9]

Also exported from Venice, at least in the fourteenth century, were smaller ingots—"about the size and shape of a woman's index finger"—of the same fineness but weighing only 200–400 grams each. They were called "verge d'arzento de sumo" and were used as money by the Tartars occupying the Tana and the Crimea. These "sommi" (or "sumi") were made not in the mint but in private shops in Venice.[10]

The price that the mint paid for silver that it accepted to be made into certified bars was set in 1273 at 11 lire 13 soldi a grossi per mark of fine silver. To make comparisons easy using the familiar decimal system, that mint price is here referred to as 233 soldi a grossi.[11]

[8]There are many references to pieces of silver of this size in the letters in the estate papers of Fresco Quirini, 1343–45, in PSM, Misti, b. 100; in the account book of Giacomo Sanudo, 1449–51, in ASV, Misc. carte non appartenenti a nessun archivio, b. 29; and in the accounts of Guglielmo Condulmer, PSM, Misti, b. 182 (see below, chap. 11, n. 39). The assayers at the mint were forbidden in 1461 to assay a "peza de arzento" that did not weigh as much as 25 marks (ca. 6 kg) (*Cap. Broche*, fol. 35).

[9]Assuming that they were of the fineness of the silver coins minted after the minting of grossi of the old standard ceased (cf. below, chap. 14, n. 44, and table A.2).

[10]Robert P. Blake, "The Circulation of Silver in the Moslem East down to the Mongol Epoch," *Harvard Journal of Asiatic Studies* 2 (1937):315 n. 74; Sir Henry Yule, ed. and trans., *The Book of Ser Marco Polo, the Venetian, concerning the Kingdoms and Marvels of the East*, rev. ed. by Henri Cordier, 4 vols. (reprint, New York, 1966), 3:148–49. The size of those made in Venice was limited by a regulation of 23 June 1357 requiring all makers of "summi" to present them to the bullion office at the Rialto ("a extimatoribus auri"), which judged their fineness and placed its seal on them, provided they did not weigh more than 40 sazi each (196.8 grams) (ASV, Zecca, b. 6bis, fols. 32–33). Among the letters in the papers of Fresco Quirini (see above, n. 8) that refer to the shipment on the Venetian galleys of these silver ingots, that of 27 April 1344 sets the same value per mark on "argento di sumo" and "argento di bolla." The way "arzento di sumo" is referred to shows that the names distinguish one kind of bullion from another, although the two kinds had the same value, so that the distinction could not have been based on their fineness. That it was based on the size and form of ingots is suggested by the description of sommi as silver bars "about the size . . . of a woman's index finger" given by R. P. Blake. The "sumo" or "sommo" was also a unit of weight equal to 316.75 grams, and that weight of fine silver served also as a monetary unit in Crimea and Tana. It is referred to in Venetian regulations concerning the payment of freight there (Geo Pistorino, "Banche e banchieri del '300 nei centri genovesi del Mar Nero," *Cronache Finmare* 5/6 [May–June 1974]:8–13; Freddy Thiriet, ed., *Regestes des délibérations du Sénat de Venise concernant la Romanie*, 3 vols., EPHE-6, Documents et recherches, P. Lemerle, ed., 1, 2, 4 [Paris and The Hague, 1958–61], vol. 1, nos. 316, 328, 388). But the individual ingots called sommi varied in weight (Cf. Pegolotti, *Pratica*, 40–41). Instructions for the manufacture of "summo dello ariento che se navichano nella Alexandria" are included in a Florentine treatise on refining dating perhaps from ca. 1500 (BMV, Ms. It., cl. IV, cod. 48 [5365], fol. 107).

[11]The price 233 soldi is clearly linked to silver of grossi fineness in the regulation of 1273 (*PMV*, doc. 20). It is applied in an arithmetical exercise in an early fourteenth-century treatise (see below, app. A, sec. ii) and in the *Zibaldone da Canal* (Stussi, ed., 6) as the price of "fin

When the supplier of bullion for casting into sterling bars was paid, the bars he received were priced at only 11 lire 5 soldi a grossi per mark, or 225 soldi. The lower price was due mainly to the reduction of fineness from 0.965 to 0.925 by adding copper, but partially it was the result of the mint's charge for alloying accurately, for casting, and for certifying the bars with its seal. The mint charge was about 0.8 percent.[12]

Concerning charges for assaying and certifying silver bullion of the fineness of grossi the evidence is less clear. In the fourteenth century the refining was done mainly by merchants, who then presented their peze to be certified by being stamped with the seal of San Marco. Those refined outside the mint in 1416 were required to bear the seal of the craftsman who had refined them. If their fineness was questioned, the expense of assaying was born half by the government and half by the merchant if the silver proved to be up to standard, entirely by the merchant if it proved to be below standard. Even if the silver to be certified was cast in the mint, no charge was made until a charge of 2 grossi per mark was levied in 1442.[13]

The continued importance of ingots certified to be of standard fineness received recognition at the very end of the fourteenth century in new provisions designed to give appropriate "solenitade" to placing the seal of the mint on the ingots. All five of the top officials were to be present, and four of the five were to approve before the seal was applied. Although their weight was not standardized, the ingots sealed with the seal of San Marco were in effect, the Senate declared, coined money ("una moneda chuniada").[14] At the beginning of the sixteenth century, a well-informed French observer, after describing the coins then issued, said that the mint also produced ingots weighing about 25 marks each (6 kg) for export to the Levant to the amount of 800,000 écus (about 800,000 ducats) a year, whereas he put the value of the silver coined in a year at about 400,000 écus.[15]

### iii. COINS OF FINE SILVER

The variable weights of the silver ingots or bars did not greatly decrease their usefulness, since during most of the Middle Ages even when

---

arçento." Pegolotti, *Pratica*, 140, applies it to silver in general. In describing ca. 1280 the alloy for minting piccoli, the capitolare of the mintmasters specified the proportion of "argenti tam boni sicut est grossus" (Papadopoli, 1:326, cap. 80). With 233 soldi as the price of silver of the fineness of grossi, bullion that was 100 percent pure silver should have fetched 241.5 soldi (233/0.965). Some references leave room for doubt whether a silver price applied to bullion of the fineness of grossi or to what bullion would have been worth if 100 percent pure silver, but for a long time after 1273 the price important in minting regulations was 233 soldi a grossi.

[12]See below, app. A.
[13]See *Cap. Broche*, fols. 18, 29v; and below, chap. 12, sec. ii.
[14]ASV, Senato, Misti, reg. 45, fols. 39–41 (16 November 1400).
[15]"Traité du gouvernement de Venise," 5599, fols. 118v–119.

coins were used in international trade they too were weighed, at least in the Levant, to make sure that they were up to standard. Coins, however, were needed for smaller payments, since the bars cast in the mint were worth hundreds or thousands of grossi each.[16] Coins had an additional advantage when they were made sufficiently uniform so that they could be counted instead of weighed. Payment by tale instead of by weight became more general once mints developed the capability to give the same weight to all of an issue bearing a single design. The popularity of the Venetian grosso initiated by Enrico Dandolo may well have owed much to their relative uniformity. In its effort to make grossi all of the same weight, the Venetian mint employed a group of craftsmen distinguished from the others by their name—"mendadores" or "mendatori" ("mendadori" in Venetian)—whose function it was to check and correct the weight of the blanks before they were struck. The work of these weight adjusters (sizers) was one feature that distinguished the manufacture of grossi from that of piccoli and black money of lower denominations.[17]

During the century and a half when the mint coined Enrico Dandolo's grosso, the number minted depended on how much silver was acquired by the Commune through purchases by the mintmasters or other means. The contrast with the situation during the same period in Genoa and Florence is striking. In those cities the mints merely performed a service for bullion merchants by coining their metal for a service charge.[18] In Venice the mintmasters were a major factor in the silver market, indeed the dominating factor during most of the thirteenth century. This contrast between the active role of the communal mint in the Venetian bullion market and the complete domination of the bullion market in Genoa and Florence by private enterprise is in accord with the generally contrasting roles of government in the three republics.

In purchasing silver to be made into grossi, the mintmasters were enjoined to buy as advantageously as they could under the general direction of the doge and his council and to keep the payments for craftsmen and other expenses and the amount paid for the bullion low enough so as to make a profit for the Commune of 2 soldi per mark. If they did not achieve that profit of 2 soldi per mark, a seigniorage of 0.86 percent (2/233), they were legally responsible for making up the difference personally.[19] Their statutes also forbade their having personal financial interests

[16]If they weighed as much as 25 marks (ca. 6 kg [see above n. 8]) and were sterling silver, which was valued at 223 soldi per mark, even sterling ingots were worth 5,575 soldi a grossi, which is more than 2,500 times the value of a grosso (25 × 223 × [12/26.111] = 2,562 grossi).

[17]See below, chap. 12, sec. iii and table 7.

[18]At least in the fourteenth century (see Giuseppe Felloni, "Ricavi e costi della zecca di Genova dal 1341 al 1450," in *Studi in memoria di Federigo Melis,* 5 vols. [Naples, 1978], 3:143 n. 8. On Florence see below, chap. 19, sec. iv).

[19]Papadopoli, 1:116; *PMV,* doc. 25, the capitolare, cap. 1, and in cap. 4 "ostendere racionem

in any transaction in bullion or specie.[20] Buying as cheaply as possible was not only their duty; it was to their political interest to do so while keeping the mint busy so as to make a good reputation during their term of office.

They were bound by their capitolare of 1278 to cut 109 1/2 to 109 1/3 grossi (109.4 used here in calculations) from a mark (of 238.5 grams).[21] Since each coin was valued at 26 1/9 denari a grossi, the 109.4 coins were worth 238 soldi a grossi. If mintmasters paid the same price for bullion that they paid for the silver cast into certified bars—233 soldi—they had to cut their expenses, mainly the wages of craftsmen and supervisors, down to 3 soldi per mark in order to balance their account, thus:

| | |
|---|---|
| Cost of silver | 233 soldi |
| Expenses | 3 soldi |
| Profit (seigniorage) | 2 soldi |
| | 238 soldi |
| Value of product (109.4 × 26.111/12) | 238 soldi |

These figures show a total mint charge of only 2.15 percent,[22] which is low for such coins but not below the mint charges on similar coins at Florence.[23]

One source of metal for coinage into either grossi or piccoli was the collection by customs offices of foreign coins, which they turned in for recoinage. The receipts of the Ternaria, which collected taxes on oil, hides, and other products that came mainly from both shores of the southern Adriatic, were important in this connection.[24] The price at which the mint credited the Ternaria for silver thus received was probably 233 soldi, since that price came to be referred to as traditional.

In some years, could the mintmasters make more profit for the Commune by paying less for silver to be made into grossi than for silver that was returned in certified silver bars? Some possessors of bullion may have been willing to sell for less than 233 soldi for the sake of receiving grossi coins in return. In some markets, payment in that well-known coin was probably preferred. An interruption of voyages might give merchants

---

de argento non rendente soldos duos pro marcha qualibet et plus si plus lucrabitur; et si accideret quod deficeret eis ad soldos duos pro marcha, teneantur refundere Comuni de suis denariis."

[20]*PMV*, doc. 25, cap. 18.

[21]*Ibid.*, cap. 1, last sentence; Papadopoli, vol. 1, doc. 4.

[22]See below, app. A, sec. iv. The total mint charge was divided by the Venetians into (1) "expensis et calo," here generally rendered as "expenses"; and (2) "lucro Comuni nostro," here rendered as "seigniorage." On the relation to English terminology see below, app. A, n. 1.

[23]See below, app. A. See also Feavearyear, *The Pound Sterling*, 346; Usher, *The Early History*, 198, 224–25; Craig, *The Mint*, app. 2; and Bernocchi, 3:38–39.

[24]See below, chap. 13, sec. i.

slight desire to have bars for export, while they still wanted grossi coins to make purchases within the city or within Italy.

The guaranteed price on silver to be cast into bars for export supplied a kind of floor under the market. If there was a sudden flood of imports, perhaps from new Tyrolese, Bohemian, or Balkan mines, and the supply drove the price offered in Venice for silver bullion very low, merchants could chose to export ingots rather than sell to the mint for coin. In such cases, the Venetian government might be said to be subsidizing the preparation of bullion in a form suitable for export and thus moderating the effects of large and sudden imports of silver on monetary circulation within Venice.

On the other hand, when imports of silver were slight for an extended period, market forces might tend to correct the situation. Suppose the price for silver bullion became so high that the mintmasters could not buy profitably and no grossi were minted. Add the assumption that some grossi were exported meanwhile to settle trade imbalances and some wore out or were lost. As a result, the number of grossi in circulation in Venice would decrease and the demand for grossi would exceed the supply, even if hoarding remained unchanged, although it probably would increase. The extent to which silver as coin was worth more than silver in the form of bullion depended partly on the cost of coinage but partly also on the demand for coin, or as some economists might now say, for liquidity. In a trade center such as Venice the cessation of coinage would tend to raise the value of coins compared with that of bullion. The continuation of such a trend might give the mintmasters a chance to buy silver bullion for less than 233 soldi per mark.

Actually, the market price of silver bullion expressed in soldi a grossi rose and was at about 300 soldi early in the fourteenth century.[25] The price of bullion could not have been bid up to that level by the mintmasters operating under their statutes of 1278. It must have been bid up by merchants exporting bullion. In the Levant, the value of silver compared with that of gold was indeed higher than in Venice.

The result was a rise not only in the price of silver bullion but also in the value of full-weight grossi.[26] There were two possible ways for the mint to continue to issue grossi without sustaining a loss. One was to credit the supplier with 233 soldi a grossi for each mark of bullion received and debit him with 26 1/9 denari a grossi for each grosso paid him, always paying him at that rate and in that coin, even though the market value of the grosso had risen from 32 piccoli to 36 or even 44.[27] This practice is

---

[25]ASV, Grazie, regs. 5, fol. 57 and 8, fol. 62; below, app. C, sec. i.

[26]See below, chap. 15, sec. iii.

[27]PMV, doc. 103; DQ, 2:15–16, doc. 55. That the mint had been using monetary denominations of a special kind before 1348 is evident from the order then given to the mintmasters by the Quarantia not to write in their books (in the same account) "libras grossorum de ducatis

indicated for a period in the 1320s when full-weight grossi had not yet risen much above 36 and when most grossi in circulation were clipped, sweated, or worn so as to be underweight. Pegolotti, a Florentine who ignored the fractions created by Venetian regulations, stated that a mark of silver yielded 109 coins each worth 26 denari a grossi; and in spite of the higher market price of silver bullion, he stated that the mint price was 233 soldi a grossi.[28] Those figures indicate a total mint charge of 1.7 percent. The preamble to a motion made in the Senate in 1362, while urging senators to follow the example of their ancestors, who did not try to make great profits from the mint, gave figures indicating that the seigniorage on the grosso used to be only 0.7–0.9 percent.[29] Thus scattered sources agree in indicating that the total mint charge on grossi was about 2 percent, of which about 0.8 percent was seigniorage.

After 1330 the price of silver kept on rising, as will be described in analyzing Venice's various efforts to unify a bimetallic standard. The grosso was valued as high as 44 piccoli, perhaps even 48, by 1370. To continue its minting of grossi, the mint may have adopted a second possible method of coining them without a loss, namely, paying the market price for silver bullion and reckoning also at market value the price of the grossi with which the supplier was paid.[30] By some method, in spite of complications, the mint continued to issue grossi of the old standard until 1356.[31]

The Venetian monetary system underwent a revolution between 1328 and 1356. One feature of this revolution was the issuance of two new silver coins intermediate in value between the piccolo and the grosso: a mezzanino worth 16 piccoli and a soldino worth 12 piccoli. The more important in the long run was the soldino, the first Venetian coin to be imprinted with the lion of San Marco. The characteristics and the reasons for minting these two coins will be explained below in the account of

---

et medianinis cum libris grossorum de cecha in introitu et exitu nostri Comunis," because that was causing losses to the Commune, but to keep records in such a way that "introitus et exitus nostri Comunis que sunt libre grossorum de ducatis et medianinis stent in suo statu et ille que sunt libre de cecha scribantur ad libras grossorum de cecha." Before this decree, prices the mint paid for silver were referred to in lire a grossi; thereafter they were referred to in lire di grossi a monete (which will be explained below, in chap. 16 and app. C), but that change may be coincidence, for the decree says nothing about lire a grossi.

[28]Pegolotti, *Pratica*, 140. The "*Pratica della mercatura*" *datiniana* (Ciano, ed.), 66, also gives the price of silver as 233 soldi "di piccioli a grossi." Cf. below, app. A.

[29]That the "lucrum" used to be 20 denari a grossi and most recently was 25 denari a grossi per mark was asserted by Carlo Capello in a motion of 1362 containing a number of passages that seem contradictory or difficult to interpret (*PMV*, doc. 139).

[30]On the price of grossi in mid-century see below, chap. 15, nn. 61, 63, and 64. On the lira di grossi a monete see chap. 16, sec. ii. On prices of silver see app. C.

[31]Papadopoli, 1:189–91, indicates that the last grosso of the standard established by Enrico Dandolo was coined under Giovanni Gradenigo (1355–56).

Venetian difficulties with bimetallism. Here it suffices to note the accompanying change in the way the mint acquired silver. The silver for the new issues was obtained by ordering that 1/5 of all silver imported be delivered to the mint. For this "quinto" the mint paid only 233 soldi a grossi per mark. The new coins were given values and silver content that enabled the mint, while paying that low price for the bullion, to collect high mint charges, some as high as 25–30 percent of the value of the coins minted. That was about 20 percent higher than mint charges on other silver coins. The high charges cannot properly be attributed to seigniorage, however, since the quinto was taken from all silver imported, including silver turned into artwork by craftsmen and silver destined for export in uncoined form. Exacting an extra mint charge of about 20 percent on 1/5 of all silver imported was equivalent to exacting 4 percent on the total amount imported. Thus the quinto was in effect an import tax of about 4 percent.[32]

Why Venice was able to impose such an import tax on silver and still attract a large supply to its bullion market and mint, as it did even before cutting the tax in half between 1343 and 1353, will be explained in chapter 19, section v. Why that import duty took the form of requiring the minting at a very high mint charge of a portion of all silver imported can only be surmised. Records of the legislation governing the first issues of the new coins, as well as any record of debates over policy, have been lost. Compulsory minting of 1/5 of all imports had several advantages from the point of view of the mintmasters. They were relieved of bidding competitively for silver for the new coins, as they had had to do in obtaining silver for the grossi. They could put the new type of coin into circulation by paying the importers and yet have about 1/5 of them left for the Communal treasury. Not all silver imported would be at once shipped on eastward either as ingots or as grossi; some would be put into circulation in Venice. The quinto channeled silver bullion directly into the new types of coin and assured employment and income for the craftsmen and officials of the mint.

The institution of the quinto did not change entirely the market position of the mintmasters. They still had discretionary powers in offering prices for silver bullion to be coined into grossi or piccoli, although occasionally they were authorized to use for that purpose some of the silver obtained through the quinto.[33] Their activity in the bullion and coin market of Venice was still subordinate, however, to that of the silver merchants, who bought from importers and decided whether the 4/5 of their silver that was "freed" by the consignment of 1/5 to the mint at its lowest price should be shipped abroad in certified ingots, sold to crafts-

---

[32]On the quinto see below, chap. 11, sec. ii; and table A.5. On the new issues see chap. 15, sec. iii; and app. A, sec. vi.

[33]*RES*, doc. 217; *DQ*, vol. 1, doc. 139; below, chap. 15, sec. iii.

men, or coined at the lower mint charge applied to free silver. Even most of the coins made from the "servile silver" of the quinto passed through the hands of these dealers as bullion and coin. Out of the 372 soldini produced from a mark of silver, 86.5 soldini were kept by the mint. Of that amount only about 20 percent was needed to cover the costs of coinage; the balance was in essence revenue from the import tax. Four-fifths of the 86.5 soldini could be used for various governmental expenses, notably for the war that began in 1336 against the Scaliger ruler of Verona, Venice's first mainland war in which large cash payments were made to mercenaries.

The capacity of mintmasters to influence the silver market was almost completely eliminated in 1353, when the mintmasters were required to accept for coinage all silver offered at a price stipulated by the Senate. The mintmasters were instructed to pay the equivalent of 325 soldi a grossi per mark to all offering "free silver." The free silver was to be coined into soldini. The regulation caused the mintmasters to lose any flexibility in setting the mint's prices.

How much silver was coined beyond that provided by the quinto then depended entirely on the decisions of the silver merchants. The amount of such coinage of free silver was probably not large as long as the mint charge remained at the high rate provided by the law of 1353. The law set the value and content of the soldino in such a way that the mint charge for coining "free silver" was 7.4 percent of the value of the amount coined. It was set even higher—at 13.8 percent—when the rules in regard to the quinto were changed for fiscal reasons in 1369 so as to reduce the mint charge on servile silver to 15.5 percent.[34] Not until the need arose to encourage imports during the War of Chioggia (1378–81) (as will be more fully described below) were the mint's prices for bullion and the content of the silver coins so adjusted as to bring the mint charge on free silver down to the level that had applied to the old grossi coined before 1356, that is, down to about 2–2.5 percent. After the war, mint charges were again raised, and the system of two mint prices—one for the quinto, the other for free silver—was continued until the quinto was abolished in 1417.

When the quinto was abolished, employment for the staff of the mint was assured by a requirement that 1/4 of all silver imported be sent to the mint for coinage. Unlike the quinto, the "quarto" was not a tax in disguise.[35] The mint charge for coining the quarto was the same as that for coining silver freely offered, only 2.7 percent. The quarto did not, therefore, add much to the government's revenue. The requirement to coin 1/4 of the silver imported was sweetened for foreigners by enlarging their

[34]*PMV*, doc. 117; below, chap. 16 and app. A.
[35]To be sure, a sort of disguised tax was enacted at the same time through the institution administratively of a new governmental refinery, as explained below in chap. 12, sec. iii.

All six different kinds of coins—gold, fine silver, and billon—shown here in their actual size, were minted under Doge Francesco Dandolo (1329–39).

*a*. Gold ducat.

*Obv.:* **FRADANDVLO DVX SMVENETI** St. Mark, facing three-quarters right, presents the banner to the kneeling doge.
*Rev.:* **.SIT.T.XPE.DAT.Q.TV REGIS.ISTE.DVCAT.** (Sit tibi Christe datus qui tu regis iste Ducatus). Christ in the act of blessing, in a mandorla with nine stars in the field.

*AV, 19.7 mm, 3.511 gr. Museo Bottacin, inv. no. 131 (Papadopoli, 1: 162, no. 1).*

*b*. Grosso, type I.

*Obv.:* **FRADANDVLO.DVX .SMVENETI.** St. Mark hands the banner to the doge; both face front.
*Rev.:* Christ enthroned, flanked by $\overline{\text{IC}}$ $\overline{\text{XC}}$.

*AR, 20.1 mm, 2.141 gr. Museo Bottacin, inv. no. 133 (Papadopoli, 1: 162, no. 5).*

*c*. Mezzanino, type I.

*Obv.:* **.FRA.DAN. .DVLO.DVX** The doge, standing facing left, holds the banner in both hands.
*Rev.:* **.SMARC/. .VENETI.** Bust of St. Mark, facing front, holding the gospel in his left hand, his right hand raised in blessing.

*AR, 17.3 mm, 1.260 gr, Museo Bottacin, inv. no. 136 (Papadopoli, 1: 163, no. 7).*

*d.* Soldino, type 1.

*Obv.:* **+FRADAN DVLODVX** The doge, kneeling facing left, holds the banner in both hands.

*Rev.:* **+.S.MARCVS.VENETI.** Lion rampant left, holding the banner, in a circle.

*AR, 17.5 mm, 0.953 gr. Museo Bottacin, inv. no. 137 (Papadopoli, 1: 164, no. 12).*

*e.* Piccolo.

*Obv.:* **+FRA.DA.DVX** Cross patée in a circle.

*Rev.:* **+.S.MARCVS** Cross patée in a circle.

*B, 12.7 mm, 0.257 gr, Museo Bottacin, inv. no. 132 (Papadopoli, 1: 164 no. 13).*

*f.* Mezzodenaro or bianco (specimen minted under the previous doge, Pietro Gradenigo).

*Obv.:* **+.PE.GRADONIC.DVX** Within a double circle, a cross with wedge points in each quadrant.

*Rev.:* **+.S.MARCVS.V.N.** Rudimentary bust of St. Mark in a double circle.

*B, 13.1 mm, 0.347 gr, Museo Bottacin, inv. no. 102 (Papadopoli, 1: 145 no. 4).*

freedom to export the other 3/4 of the silver they owned.[36] These measures were all part of an effort in the fifteenth century to strengthen Venice's position as a bullion market (described in detail in volume 2).

Meanwhile the grosso, which had not been coined since 1356, underwent a degenerate kind of reincarnation. Coins called grossi, and resembling the old grossi in their design and fineness, again became the best-known products of Venice's silver mint. The new grossi were authorized in 1379 and were minted in large numbers in the last decades of the fourteenth century and in the early fifteenth. Although in weight and fineness only slightly inferior to the old grossi and visually distinguishable from the latter chiefly by the addition of a star on the reverse side, they differed completely from the old grossi in their relation to the Venetian moneys of account. Each new grosso was declared to be worth 4 soldini, and its weight was specified as 4 times that of the soldino; it had the same fineness.[37] The cost of their manufacture per mark or per lira was of course lower than that of soldini, since the number of coins struck per mark or lira was 4 times less. The new grossi constituted a large part of the 800,000 ducats' worth of silver money being minted annually when Doge Tommaso Mocenigo in 1423 delivered his often quoted "Death Bed Oration." By the time he became doge, additional varieties of silver coin were being minted in Venice for use in provinces that came under Venetian dominion during the expansion of its empire at the beginning of the fifteenth century: a mezzanino for Verona in 1406 and a soldo for Zara in 1410, followed by a grossone and a mezzo grosso for Brescia and Bergamo in 1429.[38] (These and other changes in Venetian silver coinage later in the fifteenth century will be described in volume 2.)

## iv. GOLD DUCATS

When the first Venetian gold ducat was struck in March 1285, the event was dated and memorialized by an inscription carefully noted two hundred years later by the diarist and antiquarian Marino Sanuto.[39] As soon as the minting of the ducat had been authorized the year before, the masters (massari) of the newly created gold mint had become buyers of gold. Previously Venetian goldsmiths or general merchants had been buying imported gold and refining it as much as necessary to raise it to the fineness required for export.[40] Of course even after 1285 these Venetian

[36]Papadopoli, 1:359–61.
[37]See below, chaps. 16, sec. iv, and 18, sec. iii.
[38]See below, app. B, sec. iii; and Mueller, "L'imperialismo monetario," 282–84.
[39]Sanuto, *Vite de' Duchi,* cols. 574–75. The inscription was still displayed in 1493, but by 1515 it had been removed (idem, *De origine,* 132, 264).
[40]See above, in chap. 9.

buyers remained important customers of importers but were limited by the extensive role assumed by the mint, which, in cooperation with the Assay Office at the Rialto, regulated and may be said to have dominated the gold market. The mint accepted from Venetians only gold that had been refined to 23 1/2 carats, although gold less pure was accepted from foreign importers. The latter could sell either to Venetian bullion dealers at the auctions at the Rialto or to the mint at its price. Germans who sold to the mint were assured of quick payment according to the assay made at the Realtine Assay Office; about 1338 a special fund was established to assure the Germans of payment in ducats within three days.[41]

The mint charges on gold originally were high, but they were quickly much reduced, not because of any change in the content of the coin but because of changes in its valuation in moneys of account and changes in the prices paid for gold bullion. The content remained as fixed by the Great Council on 11 October 1284, when it was ordered that 67 be made from a mark. That gave the ducat a weight of 3.559 grams, practically the same as that of the florin.[42] Seven months later the price at which the mint bought gold bullion was specified in two ways.[43] For gold that had already been refined up to the standard set by the government and so certified by the officials at the Rialto, the mint would pay 130 lire (2,600 soldi) per mark. For gold not necessarily refined to the same degree but weighed and estimated by the proper officials, the mint would pay 108 soldi per carat out of the 24 carats of fineness, so that the price for 1 mark that was 24 carats fine (100 percent pure) would be 2,592 soldi (24 ×

[41]ASV, Zecca, b. 6bis, fol. 26, and b. 6tris, fol. 20v. Cf. *PMV*, docs. 113, 166; below, app. A. n. 29; and on the difference between assays at the Rialto and in the mint chap. 12, sec. iii.

[42]*DMC*, 3:88; Papadopoli, 1:137, where the weight is given as 3.559 grams. Bernocchi gives the weight of the florin as 3.5368. Philip Grierson gives 3.536 grams for the florin (see "The Weight of the Gold Florin in the Fifteenth Century," in *Quaderni ticinesi di numismatica e antichità classiche* [Lugano] 10 [1981]). Merchant manuals, account books, and contracts attest that at least before 1340 the florin and the ducat had practically identical values, except for costs of exchange at particular times and places. Pegolotti considered them of identical value (*Pratica*, 97, 152, 248). For calculating bimetallic ratios (as below, in chaps. 14, sec. iii; and 18–19), it would be misleading to consider different the gold content of the two coins, and they are thus both considered here to have a gold content of 3.55 grams. Generally, extending figures to the third decimal place implies a measure of accuracy that is unrealistic; it merely serves to identify the arithmetical derivation of the figures. Consistency in rounding off figures would have converted Papadopoli's figure of 3.559 to 3.56, but continual reference to a ducat of 3.56 grams and a florin of 3.54 grams might imply a greater difference between them than actually existed in the first century of their competition. On later changes in the florin, see Mario Bernocchi, "Le monete di conto e il fiorino di suggello della Repubblica fiorentina," in Barbagli Bagnoli, ed., *La moneta nell'economia europea*; and Bernocchi, 3:61–63, 66, 274–88.

[43]*PMV*, doc. 40; Papadopoli, 1:126, 342; *DMC*, 3:109, dated 30 May 1285 in the first edition, 2 June in the other two.

108).[44] The difference in the two prices represents a differential in favor of gold already refined and certified.[45] At these prices the mintmasters were required to accept all gold offered.

The practice actually adopted by the Venetian mint, on the other hand, shows that the first way of calculating, that is, the price of 2,600 soldi per mark, was abandoned. Instead, at the beginning of the fourteenth century the mint used the price offered in the law of 1285, namely, 108 soldi per carat of fineness. Thus, the mint paid 2,592 soldi per mark for pure gold.[46]

Mint charges were determined by the relation between the price of the bullion and the price of the coin, both stated in lire and soldi a grossi. In 1285 the value specified for the ducat was 40 soldi a grossi. When the mint paid 2,600 soldi per mark for gold by repaying the supplier with ducats at that value, he received only 65 ducats (2,600/40).[47] The 2 ducats retained by the mint was a high mint charge for such a coin—3 percent (2/67).[48] Actually the mint began almost at once to charge less. While valuing 24-carat gold at 2,592 soldi, it set at less than 40 soldi the value of the ducats it paid suppliers, who consequently received more ducats for the number of soldi due them. For gold that came from "within the Gulf," the mint valued the ducats at 39 1/2 soldi as it paid them out. Paying at that rate made the mint charge 2 percent. For gold that came from "outside the Gulf," the mintmasters valued the ducats they paid out in return for the gold at 39 soldi. Paying at that rate reduced the mint charge to 0.8 percent, since the mint had to pay the supplier 66.46 ducats per mark for the bullion for which it owed 2,592 soldi (2592/39 = 66.46). It could keep only 0.54 ducats per mark, 0.8 percent (0.54/67 = 0.008). The mint could calculate the same result if it valued all the 67 ducats produced at 39 soldi, for a total value of 2,613 soldi (67 × 39). Since it paid the supplier only 2,592 soldi, the mint's gain was 21 soldi (2,613 − 2,592), also about 0.8 percent (21/2,592). About half of the 0.8 percent went for the cost of manufacture, so that the government's profit or seigniorage was only

[44]In the Capitolare dei Massari della Moneta d'Oro, *PMV*, doc. 37, cap. 2, the rate of 108 soldi per carat is specifically applied to purchases made from Germans. That the statement "a raxion de libra V et soldi VIII" meant 108 soldi per carat of fineness per mark is evident, furthermore, from *PMV*, doc. 8, which records gold payments in 1227 in which gold is valued lower, at 99 soldi per carat of fineness; and from the explanation in Pegolotti, *Pratica*, 138, and all other published merchant manuals of the fourteenth and fifteenth centuries.

[45]If gold previously refined and certified by the massari of gold at Rialto had been only 23 1/2 carats fine, and if it had been purchased at 108 soldi per carat, it would have cost only 2,558 (23 1/2 × 108) soldi per mark instead of the 2,600 otherwise offered. Perhaps the difference was partly covered by fees for casting and estimating.

[46]*PMV*, doc. 37 (capitolare), cap. 2; Stussi, ed., *Zibaldone da Canal*, 71.

[47]This seems to have been part of the intent of the law of 1285, even though it makes no reference to mint charges as such.

[48]See below, app. A, sec. v.

about 0.4 percent. In the 1340s the gold brought from "within the Gulf" by German merchants was also coined at this low rate.[49]

In the fifteenth century the ducat had become the basis of a money of account used in pricing gold. In this money of account, 1 ducat equaled 24 grossi a oro (as will be explained below, in chapter 16); and the mint price of 24-carat gold was stated as 66 ducats 11 grossi (or 66.46) per mark. Consequently the value of the gold retained from each mark by the mint was calculated to be 13 grossi, also 0.8 percent of 67 ducats. When the Council of Ten took charge in 1473, it set the price of gold bullion at 67 ducats, thus abolishing seigniorage and indeed all mint charges on the coinage of gold.[50]

Both the gold bullion presumably already 23 1/2 carats fine presented to the mint by Venetians and the bullion of lower fineness accepted from German importers were subject to further refining in the mint so as to bring the bullion up to the 24-carat fineness required before it could be turned into ducats. The disposal of the impurities removed became important as an element in the mint charge when the dross consisted very largely of silver, as was true in the early fifteenth century. If the mint paid the supplier even before the gold had been turned into ducats, as it did the Germans, who were assured of payment in three days and were paid the number of carats of fineness determined by the assayers at the Rialto, the mint kept the dross after it was removed. Since its removal caused a drop in the weight of the bullion, the dross was called the "calo" or "callum." When the dross was kept by the mint, the refining was said to have been done "a calo di comun." The alternative procedure, called "a calo di mercanti," returned the dross to the supplier. Generally he was then paid only for the weight of the 24-carat gold that remained after his assignment of bullion had been separated from the flux ("cimento") used to remove the impurities.

When refining was done "a calo di comun," the mint might be said to be taking from the supplier as part of its mint charge the value of the dross it retained, as well as the 21 soldi of difference between 2,592 soldi

[49]The two rates, 39 1/2 for ducats made from gold from "dentro da lo colfo" and 39 for ducats made from gold arriving "de fuora da lo colfo," are clearly distinguished in a paragraph of the capitolare of the mintmasters for gold dated 1338, in *PMV*, doc. 93, confirmed by reading the original, now in ASV, Zecca, b. 6tris, cap. 38, fol. 13v; the rates are referred to as being customary. Clearly a rate of 39 1/2 was in use before 1296, when a resolution was passed ordering the mintmasters not to give ducats at 39 1/2 soldi ad aurum but at 40 soldi ad grossos (*PMV*, doc. 65; *DMC*, 3:402 [14 July 1296]). On the failure of that resolution to halt the mint's use of a "soldo a oro" and low mint charges see below, chap. 14, sec. i. On the reduction in the rate for Germans see below, chap. 17, n. 55. In the 1340s the rates were manipulated as follows: *DQ*, vol. 1, doc. 17: 39 soldi (= *PMV*, doc. 95), October 1342; doc. 120: 38 soldi, 3 March 1343; doc. 275: 39 soldi, October 1343. The rate is given as 39 soldi in all published merchant manuals of the fourteenth and fifteenth centuries except the *"Pratica della mercatura" datiniana* (Ciano, ed.), 66, which gives 39 1/2.

[50]See below, app. A, sec. v.

(the price of the bullion) and the 2,613 soldi that represented the value of the 67 ducats made from a mark (67 × 39). The additional charge might be insignificant in the case of some bullion but of considerable importance when the bullion came from ores containing a mixture of gold and silver.

When the refining was done "a calo di mercanti," the supplier could be sure that he would not be paying any additional mint charge by letting the mint retain the dross, but he might receive payment for a smaller amount of pure gold than he had been led to expect by the assay made at the Rialto. If he claimed that some of his gold had been absorbed in the flux and was in the dross, it was up to him to recover it from the dross which had been returned to him. The problem became a subject of intense controversy about 1414–22 (as is described in volume 2).[51]

Regulations required that all ducats be of precisely equal weight. Originally Venetian ducats were allowed to vary from the standard by as much as 1 grain (0.0517 grams). In 1317 the mint was charged with not issuing any that varied from the standard by as much as a half-grain. In 1330 the divergence was ordered narrowed to a quarter-grain "se far se può."[52] The assayers were instructed to have a specially stamped weight with which to test the weight of new ducats and to test those of anyone who paid a fee of 12 denari per 100 ducats. Bags of ducats that had been tested and sealed with the seal of the assayers—"ducati bullati"—became a common means of making large cash payments.[53] In Florence in 1294 only those florins that were 1 1/2 grains or more underweight (0.074 grams) were ordered out of circulation,[54] but about 1324 sacks of florins of more exact weight, "fiorini di suggello," came into use. The Florentines distinguished between florins that were full-weight under a new standard and those that passed only an older standard. Later, several different issues of

[51]On the refining process see below, chap. 12, sec. iii.

[52]*PMV,* docs. 72, 89.

[53]Ibid., docs. 37, cap. 4; 72, 73. The reference to "bullata" in connection with the work of the Assay Office in Venice in 1317 (doc. 72) seems to apply only to the seal on the weight they were to use in testing the weight of coins, but the creation of an office for such a purpose at that time suggests that very soon thereafter the ducats tested and approved were put into bags closed with a seal showing that they had been tested and approved by the officials. The earliest reference that we have found to such bags is dated 5 October 1328; after reconfirming the use of the weight mentioned in 1317, the provision continues: "Item, quod liceat illi qui recepit ducatos in solucione, venire cum ipsis ducatis ad officium grossorum tonsorum pro faciendo eos cercare et bullare . . ." (ASV, Cinque Savi alla Mercanzia, 1st ser., b. 22bis, fol. 20 [cap. 45]). A law of 1352 orders Communal officials not to accept "ducatos non bullatos" (in Vincenzo Padovan, first in *AV* 14 [1877]: 23 and then in his collection of those many notes and documents from the *AV* published as *Le monete dei veneziani: Sommario,* rev. and expanded ed. [Venice, 1881], 137; Papadopoli, 1:172; *Cap. Fontego,* 57, cap. 140). The permission to have ducats sealed in a sack was a requirement by 1414, and officials were to accept ducats only if "boladi in un borseto e no altramente" (*Cap. Fontego,* 114, cap. 224. See, finally, ASV, Senato, Misti, reg. 54, fol. 76v [4 January 1422/23]).

[54]Text from the provvisione of 1294 in Zanetti, *Nuova raccolta,* 1:425.

florins, some lighter when minted, were distinguished by the seal under which they were bagged.[55] Venice, on the other hand, avoided such subtleties and declared all ducats that passed the weighing test of their assayers to be of equal value.[56]

That in Venice all ducats were of equal legal value and were practically of equal weight and treated as equal regardless of their date of issue may well have been one reason why the ducat proved a more widely accepted international standard of value than the florin in the long run. It was quite overshadowed by the florin for a long time, however. Not only did the florin have a thirty-year head start in gaining international acceptance but for a half-century after the ducat appeared, florins were much more extensively used in international trade, not only in the west but also in the Levant.[57] In the 1340s, however, gold began flowing into Venice both from the north and by sea, and in the fifteenth century Venice was sending gold coin as well as silver to the Levant.[58] In the 1360s in Bologna the ducat was priced higher than the florin.[59] Both Venice and Florence made great efforts to mint coins 24 carats fine, but perhaps Florence's lack of political stability weakened the general reputation of the florin. In the fifteenth century the reputation and the production of the Venetian ducat became outstanding, and it was much imitated.[60]

## v. PICCOLI AND BLACK MONEY

While the Venetian mint provided the media of exchange that Venetians wanted for their international trade, concentrating on the high standards necessary to make its products acceptable in the centers of commerce and government in Italy and the Levant, before the fifteenth century the needs of Venice's immediate hinterland for less valuable coins to be used in local trade were met mainly by other mints. The output of the imperial mint at Verona long dominated the Veneto, just as the output of the imperial mints in Pavia and Lucca at one time dominated Lombardy and Tuscany, respectively.[61] Both pennies and groats from Verona circulated extensively, even in Venice itself. Also a type of groat called the

[55]Bernocchi, "Le monete di conto"; Bernocchi, 3:61–63, 66, 274–88 (esp. 282), where it is indicated that some later florins—esp. those ca. 1402—were 5–6 percent lighter than the original weight. Cf. Grierson, "The Weight of the Gold Florin."

[56]*PMV,* doc. 72.

[57]Philip Grierson, "La moneta veneziana nell'economia mediterranea del '300 e '400," in *La civiltà veneziana del Quattrocento* (Florence, 1957), 82–83.

[58]See below, chaps. 17, sec. ii, and 19, sec. v.

[59]Antonia Borlandi, "Moneta e congiuntura a Bologna, 1360–1369," *Bollettino dell'Istituto Storico Italiano per il Medio Evo e Archivio Muratoriano* 82 (1970):390–478.

[60]Herbert E. Ives and Philip Grierson, *The Venetian Gold Ducat and Its Imitations,* American Numismatic Society, Notes and Monographs, 128 (New York, 1954); see also below, vol. 2.

[61]Cipolla, *Le avventure della lira,* 21; Robbert, "The Venetian Money Market," 8–16.

"friesacher" ("frisacense" or "friacense"), from the name of a city near silver mines in Carinthia, was the first to penetrate the back country north and east of Venice. Freisachers were coined by the Patriarch of Aquileja at Udine as well as at Friesach.[62] Consequently Venetian manufacture of coins of relatively low silver content, namely, of piccoli and fractional black money, was at first largely restricted to the needs of the city and became voluminous only at a relatively late date.

The production of certified ingots, grossi, and ducats went on year after year, fluctuating with the ups and downs of international trade and the output of mines. The level of production of piccoli was even more irregular.[63] A yearly output of relatively low value sufficed to replace what was worn out or lost, although in a city arising from the waves there may well have been, more than elsewhere, an irretrievable loss of small coin. The bridge across the Grand Canal at the Rialto when first built was called the "ponte della moneta o del quartarolo," probably because previously boatmen had charged 1/4 of a piccolo to ferry persons across from the Campo San Bartolomeo to the Rialto.[64] This detail suggests how much more frequently small change passed from hand to hand in a thoroughly commercialized seaport such as Venice than in a rural village. But production of large issues of piccoli, which were on the border line between black money and white money, being only 20–25 percent silver, was sporadic. In contrast to long periods of slight activity, there were years in which the mint was called on to produce large quantities of moneta parva rapidly, (1) to replace coins from a deteriorated old issue that were called in for recoinage, (2) to replace foreign coins that the government wished to drive out of circulation, or (3) in a more or less sophisticated stimulation of inflation.

For a half-century after Doge Enrico Dandolo (1192–1205) stopped the coinage of piccoli, the replenishment of the supply of small coins depended on the issue of half-pennies (mezzo denari or bianchi) and quarter-pennies (quartaroli), which were more than 90 percent copper. The number of such fractional coins must have been considerable, since specimens survive from issues under all doges, at least until the piccoli became so debased that coins worth only a fraction of a piccolo were no longer useful.

When Doge Lorenzo Tiepolo (1268–75) resumed the coinage of piccoli, he probably increased considerably the volume of Venetian coins

[62]David Michael Metcalf, *Coinage in the Balkans, 820–1355,* (Thessalonike, 1965; Chicago, 1966), 63–72, 191–94; idem, *Coinage in Southeastern Europe, 820–1396,* Royal Numismatic Society Special Publications, 11 (London, 1979); G. Bernardi, *Monetazione del Patriarcato di Aquileia* (Trieste, 1975), 9–15, 29, 42–43.

[63]Cf. Bernocchi, 3:143–46.

[64]Pompeo Molmenti, *La storia di Venezia nella vita privata,* 3 vols. (Bergamo, 1927), 1:51. On normal loss by wear and tear see below, chap. 18, sec. i.

circulating within the lagoons. His piccoli (weighing 0.289 grams, 0.250 fine) contained less silver than the previous issues but probably not less than old coins still circulating after sixty years.[65] But his issue of piccoli, the crucial step in the separation of the lira di piccoli from the lira a grossi, may well have had an inflationary effect, especially on local retail prices. It was in general a period of rising prices and of expansion of Venice's long-term public debt. In view of Lorenzo Tiepolo's political association with the guilds and with new families in conflict with old families headed by the Dandolos, one is tempted to regard his dogeship as a period of politically motivated inflation and intense minting activity.[66]

By the time Giovanni Dandolo became doge (1280), the coining of piccoli had been placed under the authority of the same mintmasters who supervised the minting of grossi,[67] and very specific limits had been placed on the volume of production, especially on the output of piccoli and small coins (moneta parva). A relatively low rate of production about 1278 is suggested by regulations of that date. The men in control of Venice's governing councils when the mint's statutes were then codified seem to have wished to restrict the city's money supply. Consistent with such a policy was the encouragement of the export of silver bullion implied in the obligation placed on the mint in the 1270s to accept all silver offered, not for coinage, but for the preparation at low cost of certified ingots of the two kinds then exported, as explained above, in section ii.

Minting of piccoli was also discouraged by a high mint charge. It appears to have been about 24 percent in 1280, which seems relatively high even for small coin of low silver content. At least it was more than their cost of manufacture; for under Lorenzo Tiepolo the mint charge, if calculated on the same basis, had been only 9.2 percent.[68] The high mint charge

[65]See above, chap. 8, sec. iii; and below, app. A, esp. table A.1. Provisions for piccoli are in *DMC*, 2:389 (1268), 393 (1269), 397 (1270), 406 (1271), and 408 (1272); cf. *PMV*, xxix–xxx.

[66]Interpretations of the rivalry between the Tiepolo and Dandolo factions, which do not however analyze monetary measures, are in Giorgio Cracco, *Società e stato nel medioevo veneziano* (Florence, 1967), chap. 2, secs. 1 and 2; and in Lane, *Venice: A Maritime Republic,* 102–8.

[67]That the officials in charge of coining piccoli before 1278 were distinct from those in charge of coining grossi can be inferred from the capitolare approved in March 1278 (printed in Papadopoli, 1; and in *PMV*, doc. 25). While it is quite specific about grossi, it contains no specifications for piccoli. They were in sections added after the approval given the revision of 1278, namely, in caps. 80–82. A reference to combining the two offices appears in a decree of the Quarantia of 1289 (Papadopoli, 1:326–27, cap. 83): ". . . comitatur officium faciendi monetam parvam illis officialibus qui faciunt monetam argenti grossam . . ." and is reflected in the wording of a resolution by the Great Council in 1287: "Capitolari massariorum monete argente, scilicet grossorum et parvorum . . ." (ibid., 332, cap. 100).

[68]See below, app. A. Bernocchi's table of Florentine mint charges on billon coins (3:39) begins in 1315 with the charge at 17.77 percent, but between 1332 and 1350 the charges were 5.74–8.04 percent.

## BLACK MONEY

The quartarolo (1/4 of a denaro) and mezzodenaro or bianco (1/2 of a denaro) were larger than the piccolo (1 denaro), but since they were almost entirely of copper, their intrinsic values were far below their nominal values when compared with the piccolo, which in the mid-fourteenth century was still nearly 20 percent silver.

*a.* Quartarolo of Jacopo Tiepolo (1229–49).

*Obv.:* **+.I.TEOPVL?.DVX** Within the circle, **V.N.C.E.** forming a cross.
*Rev.:* **+.S.MARCVS** Within the circle, a cross, with a lily in each quadrant.

B, *18 mm, 0.958 gr. Museo Bottacin, inv. no. 11 (Papadopoli, 1: 99 no. 6).*

*b.* Mezzodenaro or bianco of Pietro Gradenigo (1289–1311).
*Obv.:* +.PE.GRADONIC.DVX Within a double circle, a cross with wedge points in each quadrant.
*Rev.:* +.S.MARCVS.V.N. Rudimentary bust of St. Mark in a double circle.

B, *13.1 mm, 0.347 gr. Museo Bottacin, inv. no. 102 (Papadopoli, 1: 145 no. 4).*

*c.* Piccolo of Francesco Dandolo (1329–39).
*Obv.:* +FRA.DA.DVX Cross patée in a circle.
*Rev.:* +.S.MARCVS Cross patée in a circle.

B, *12.7 mm, 0.257 gr. Museo Bottacin, inv. no. 132 (Papadopoli, 1: 164 no. 13).*

about 1280 helps to explain the intrusion into Venice shortly thereafter of much coin of foreign mintage.[69]

During the 1280s there was a change of policy, probably because of the excessive intrusion of foreign coins. In 1282, by valuing the grosso at 32 piccoli, the mint charge on piccoli was reduced to about 13 percent.[70] The need to make piccoli available to those wanting coin of that denomination was met more directly in 1287, when the mint was ordered to have a reserve fund of 2,000 lire. In the fund were to be moneta parva worth 1,200 lire and grossi worth 800 lire. The mintmasters were to pay out moneta parva, up to a limit of 50 lire in any one day, to anyone asking for that kind of coin, for which presumably the mint would receive payment in grossi, bullion, or foreign coin valued as bullion.[71] In 1289 mintmasters were ordered to assign 100 lire a month for use in making moneta parva until a fund of 500 lire had been accumulated. On 21 May 1291 the mintmasters were instructed to make as much moneta parva as they could following the rules in their statute and to make at least 250 marks every two months.[72] If they could coin more, they would receive an incentive bonus of 1 piccolo (denarius parvus) per mark for each mark above 250. On New Year's Day 1292 (which was 1 March according to the Venetian calendar) the mint-masters were to report to the Signoria so that it could propose to the Quarantia what to do next. To reach the desired volume of production, special low rates of seigniorage were set. In reminting foreign coin the mintmasters were required to show some profit, but if they made the alloy from copper and silver bullion, the requirement was only that they should show no loss to the Commune.[73] In this campaign against an excessive intrusion of foreign coins in the late thirteenth century, the Venetian government relied partly on banning those coins considered inferior or counterfeit and partly on increasing the availability of its own piccoli.

The next recorded drive to increase production of piccoli was in 1317, when the grossi in circulation had so deteriorated from long use that they were being discounted, as described below in chapter 15, section i. Before banning the use of underweight grossi, the council then in charge, the Quarantia, ordered the coinage of at least 1,000 lire di piccoli per month and raised the appropriation for making moneta parva.[74]

After the introduction of the soldino in 1331–32, there was less need

[69]See below, chap. 13, sec. i.

[70]Papadopoli, 1:120–23; below, app. A, n. 17.

[71]Papadopoli, 1:332; *PMV,* doc. 48.

[72]Papadopoli, 1:326–27; below, app. B, sec. iii.

[73]Papadopoli, 1:327. Cessi's publication of this decree in *PMV,* doc. 32, dates it 21 May 1281, but his source in ASV, ex Misc. cod. 133 (now reclassified as Secreta, Commissioni, Capitolari diversi), fol. 99, shows the date to be 1291, as indeed is indicated by Papadopoli, 1:327. See also below, app. A, sec. iii.

[74]Nani-Mocenigo, ed., *Capitolare dei Signori di Notte,* doc. 180 (19 May 1318, in Quarantia); and below, app. B and chap. 15, sec. i., on deterioration of the grossi.

for piccoli in order to make change for sums below the value of a grosso. That need may also have been met occasionally later in the century by use in Venice of a kind of black money called the "tornesello," which Venice minted for use in its Grecian dependencies and which was valued at 3 piccoli. In general, the importance of the piccolo both as a standard of value and as a means of payment in Venice declined during the fourteenth century.[75]

As an element in the mint's activity in the fifteenth century, however, black money acquired a new importance when Venice was able to impose the use of coins from its mint on its expanding mainland empire. For both the Terraferma and Romania, many millions of coins of very low silver content were issued very profitably. Whereas in the thirteenth century the mint coined black money only for use in the lagoons and concentrated on issuing the fine silver and gold coins needed for international trade, in the fifteenth century Venice was coining both black and white money for use in the large hinterland and the colonial area dominated by her trade, while her gold ducat gained in preeminence as the basis for a dependable standard of value used in the high finance of international market places.

[75] See below, chaps. 16; 18, sec. i; and 19, sec. iii.

# 11

# COMMUNAL REVENUE

IKE OTHER MEDIEVAL GOVERNMENTS, the Venetian republic expected to get revenue from its mint, but its sovereign monopoly of minting and determining the legal value of coins was for many centuries a less important source of revenue than its sovereign right to tax the importation and sale of gold and silver. The contrast between its budget and that of a feudal monarch is extreme. King Philip the Fair (1285–1314), who extracted more monetary revenue from France than any previous ruler, "made enormous profits from his mints, probably more than he made from general taxation."[1] The amount of revenue that the Venetian Commune received from seigniorage even when the mint was very active was a small part of the government's total income.

The Venetian mint was considered a source of revenue, albeit only a potential one, as early as 1187, when it was listed as one of three offices that were to repay in installments a loan made to the Commune, "si redditus de moneta fuerit tantus."[2] Standing financial obligations on the mint's income, extraneous to its own operating expenses, were generally small,

---

[1]Strayer, *The Reign of Philip the Fair*, 392, 394; Miskimin, "L'applicazione della legge di Gresham," 4 and n. 16. In Burgundy in the fourteenth century the mints contributed about 1/5 of total revenues (see Hans van Werveke, "Currency Manipulation in the Middle Ages: The Case of Louis de Male, Count of Flanders," *Transactions of the Royal Historical Society*, 4th ser., 31 [1949], 123; and Spufford, *Monetary Problems and Policies*, chap. 5. Cf. Munro, *Wool, Cloth and Gold*, 22).

[2]*PRV*, doc. 3, pp. 14–15.

however: paying the salaries of the ducal trumpeters and musicians[3] or of the doge himself.[4] Only for a relatively short period around the mid-fifteenth century was the mint in a position to meet heavy obligations out of its profits.[5] Of the rare extant communal budgets, only that of 1490 contains an entry for the mint, for which it lists revenues of only 2,700 ducats.[6] But even in the decades when mint revenues were much higher than that, the Commune drew far more revenue from indirect taxes levied on sales and imports.

As in medieval communes generally, sales taxes on consumption within the city, such as on wine and salt, were Venice's main source of regular revenue before she acquired an empire on the mainland. Even as late as 1469, the date of the earliest itemized list of the revenues of the Serenissima, which at that time totaled about 1 million ducats, only a little more than half came from the empire and direct taxation combined. The sales taxes called the "8 dazi" still formed much the largest item among revenues collected in Venice itself, yielding about 235,000 ducats yearly. Their yield had been as large a half-century earlier also: wine, 76,000 ducats in 1423, 77,000 in 1469; the butcheries, 10,700 ducats in 1424, 22,000 in 1469.

Of comparable importance with such items was one sales tax levied on commercial contracts that yielded 36,000 ducats in 1469.[7] A large part of the revenue from that tax depended on the bullion trade. Indeed, the rough estimates attempted in this chapter indicate that taxes collected on the turnover of gold and silver bullion yielded twice as much as did seigniorage collected on the minting of gold and silver coin. Seigniorage was often high on black money, but the total take was important only on certain coins in certain periods, such as the tornesello for the maritime dominions about 1368–1415 and various coins for the Terraferma dominions in 1442–70.

### i. BROKERAGE FEES

The tax on wholesale transactions took the form of brokerage fees called the "dazi di messetaria." The participation of a broker was required

---

[3]ASV, Senato, Terra, reg. 4, fol. 72 (15 May 1458); *Cap. Broche,* fols. 51v (1481) and 59v (1486).

[4]*Cap. Broche,* fol. 61v (1487).

[5]Ibid., fol. 32 (13 March 1449): of 11,000 ducats to be collected annually to pay crews, 5,000 were to come from the gold and silver mints. In 1455 the mint was to turn over 1,000 ducats per month, earmarked for the office of government bonds (*BG,* vol. 1, doc. 108; and Luzzatto's introduction to *PRV,* p. cclviii. See also below, vol. 2).

[6]*BG,* vol. 1, doc. 129. That figure may correspond to a period of inactivity when the Council of Ten had suspended the production of silver coin (*Cap. Broche,* fol. 63v [28 September 1490]).

[7]For all figures just cited, see *BG,* vol. 1, docs. 82, 84, 122 (1464); extant figures for 1469 and 1500 (docs. 123, 134) are virtually the same.

to complete any deal between merchants, and two groups of brokers were active—one in the Fondaco dei Tedeschi (under the jurisdiction of the Visdomini del Fondaco), another on the Rialto (under the jurisdiction of the Ufficiali alla Messetaria). Special rates often applied to contracts with German merchants in the Fondaco and with certain other groups of foreign merchants covered by ad hoc commercial treaties. Differential rates applied to Venetian merchants and to foreigners. When the brokerage tax was instituted, it was only 0.25 percent (5 soldi per 100 lire), but that percentage was paid by each contracting party, and the number of transactions made the total large. Half went to the broker and half to the Commune.

The rate was raised in 1258 to 0.5 percent (10 soldi per 100 lire, of which the broker kept 3 soldi, the other 7 going to the Communal treasury), except for foreigners who were protected from such raises by treaties, as were many of the Germans in their Fondaco.[8] It was moved back to 5 soldi in 1339,[9] raised to 15 soldi during the financial crisis of the Third Genoese War, 1350–55, and set at the conclusion of that war at 10 soldi for each party to the contract.[10] After further adjustments,[11] the fee was being paid at the rate of 3/4 of a ducat per 100 ducats by each party in 1413 and was then raised to 1 ducat per 100.[12] The total paid was then 2 percent, so that if the brokers were then still retaining half, the Commune's take was 1 percent of the value of the turnover. To summarize roughly, the government's take as a percentage of the turnover was as follows: before 1350, at least 0.25 percent; from 1350 to 1413, at least 0.75 percent; and after 1413, 0.75 percent at the Fondaco and 1.00 percent elsewhere.

The decree raising the rate in 1413 from the 3/4 of a ducat then in force to 1 ducat contained a provision that it would not apply to those Germans and others who were protected from such an increase by their particular commercial treaties. Accordingly, it did not apply to the very

---

[8]Ibid., doc. 36; *DMC*, 2:310. See also Lupprian, *Il Fondaco dei Tedeschi*, 5; and Pegolotti, *Pratica*, 143.

[9]Lupprian, *Il Fondaco dei Tedeschi*, 18.

[10]*RES*, docs. 217, 240 (pp. 162, 197–98). The decree of 1355 setting the rate at 10 soldi specified that that amount was to be paid by both buyer and seller, but it did not specify how the fee was to be divided between the broker and the Commune.

[11]In 1371 the rate was returned to 15 soldi (0.75 percent) each, with the added 5 soldi each [10 soldi = 0.5 percent] going exclusively to the Commune (ibid., doc. 270, p. 241). That rate was called for again in 1378 for the Fourth Genoese War and is mentioned as still in force in 1386 (ASV, Ufficiali alla Messetaria, b. 1, fols. 24v, 31). Sales contracts negotiated directly between foreigners were generally illegal. The rationale for the prohibition from the fisc's point of view is obvious. In 1407, for example, it was ruled that "vendando forestier a forestier, s'habbi da metter un venetian de mezo, acciochè il comun habbi due messetarie" (ibid., fols. 51r–v).

[12]*BG*, vol. 1, doc. 78; the increase was to hold for the next six years. The law is also in *Cap. Fontego*, cap. 223; further increases were passed in 1439 (cap. 264), but they were abolished within eight months (cap. 266).

large part of the sale of bullion that took place in the Fondaco dei
Tedeschi. Even with that exclusion, the increase was expected to add
15,000 ducats per year to the Commune's income and make the total yield
of the brokerage tax 60,000 ducats per year, a figure that implies a yearly
turnover of at least 6 million ducats. The gap between that figure and the
10 million ducats given as the annual turnover in Doge Mocenigo's "Death
Bed Oration," delivered a few years later, is partially bridged by considering the turnover in the Fondaco, to which the increase did not apply.[13]

A turnover of at least 2 million ducats on which the brokerage was
paid within the Fondaco is indicated by calculations based on four independent sources. The earliest is a report of 1442 in which total annual
revenue from the Fondaco was estimated at 20,000 ducats, a figure not at
all out of line with that of 18,000 ducats entered in the "budget" of 1490.[14]
Total revenue, however, included rent for the Fondaco and receipts from
various import taxes, as well as brokerage fees, as is clear from a description of the administrative structure of the Fondaco by Marino Sanuto in
1493. That description provides another source from which to estimate the
size of the turnover. Sanuto says that the total revenue of the Fondaco was
earmarked to pay the salaries of the members of the three Councils of
Forty then operative (the Quarantia Criminal, the Quarantia Civil Nova,
and the Quarantia Civil Novissima). Since the 120 members were paid at
least 130 ducats per year, the Fondaco had to turn over 15,600 ducats each
year to pay those salaries.[15] How much of these totals of 20,000, 18,000,

[13]Gino Luzzatto, in his essay "Sull'attendibilità di alcune statistiche economiche medievali," *Giornale degli economisti*, 1929, signalized the importance of this figure in constructing a
general picture of Venetian finances of that date. In the reprint of his essay in his *Studi*, 282–
83, there are two typographical errors. In the note on p. 283 the references should be, not to
doc. 74, but to doc. 78; and in the passage from the decree quoted on p. 282 the text in *BG*,
1:90, reads, not "1/4 ducat," but "quarti tres ducati." Luzzatto's calculations, however, show
that he used the correct figures as found in the *BG*, there correctly transcribed from ASV,
Senato, Misti, reg. 50, fol. 20v. The law is found in Venetian in *Cap. Fontego*, cap. 223, p. 113.
For the later period see "Traité du gouvernement de Venise," 5599, fol. 96, which indicates
that around the year 1500 the rate of 1 percent per party was still in force. Although it is not
stated, presumably half (or 1 percent) went into the treasury. Receipts from the Messetaria
are recorded as 36,000 ducats at different dates (1464, 1469, 1490, 1500) (see *BG*, vol. 1, docs.
122, 123, 129, 134).

[14]Jacopo d'Albizzotto Guidi, a Florentine long resident in Venice, included the estimate in
his long description (in verse) of Venice, "El sommo della condizione e stato e principio della
città di Vinegia e di suo territorio," Seminario Patriarcale, Venice, Ms. 950, cap. 14 (unnum-
bered folios). The "budget" figure that corroborates this estimate is in *BG*, vol. 1, doc. 129.

[15]Sanuto reports the salary as 8 grossi per half-day attended. Assuming that half the time
they met also in the afternoons, when they earned another 8 grossi, they would have averaged
12 grossi, or 1/2 of a ducat, per day for 260 working days in a year (Sanuto, *De origine*, for the
Quarantie, 113–14, 127–28, 240–41; for the Fondaco, 134, 273–74). The "Traité du gouvernement de Venise" gives practically the same base pay ("environ sept escuz le moys") for a half-
day, an annual total of 10,080 ducats for all members, while indicating that sessions often
continued into the night (Perret, *Histoire des relations*, 2:269. Cf. Brian Pullan, "Service to the

COIN STORAGE AT THE MINT

Next to the offices of the mintmasters on the second story of the
mint were vaults for coins not yet paid out.

*Reproduced from* La Biblioteca Marciana nella sua nuova sede *(Venice, 1906), 86.*
*Photograph by Toso.*

or 15,600 ducats came from the brokerage can be estimated less securely,
for such an estimate depends on statements about the total amount of
silver imported. Such statements, ambiguous or inconclusive as they are,
indicate that brokerage on bullion yielded between 10,000 and 15,000
ducats.[16] If we estimate the revenue from brokerage collected through the
Fondaco as 15,000 ducats, that implies a turnover of 2 million ducats on
which the fee of 0.75 percent was collected from Germans (15,000/0.0075,
or 2,000,000 × 0.0075).

---

Venetian State: Aspects of Myth and Reality in the Early Seventeenth Century," *Studi
secenteschi* 5 [1964]: 122, where salaries in the Quarantie ca. 1582 are given as 130–60 ducats per
year). The second Quarantia was instituted in 1400, the third in 1492. The Fondaco normally
produced revenues surpassing the needs of the Quarantie, and other salaries were added, as
reflected in *Cap. Fontego:* in 1413 for the Quarantie (cap. 222, p. 112); in 1414, 200 ducats per
month for the Signori di Notte, the Capi Sestiere, and their men (caps. 286, p. 114, and 290,
p. 178); in 1449 for prison guards (cap. 286, p. 176); and in 1454 for the Ducal Councillors
(caps. 295–96, pp. 183–86).

[16]See below, sec. iii.

Adding that 2 million to the 6 million estimated by Luzzatto, which did not include the turnover of the privileged Germans in the Fondaco, gives a total that still falls short of the 10 million ducats of which Doge Mocenigo boasted. But Mocenigo's figures, even if not exaggerated, applied to an exceptional peak year. They are not in violent conflict with a figure of 8 million ducats as the total turnover in more normal years such as 1410 or 1490.

In that total turnover, sales of silver and gold formed only a part, to be sure. But in view of the importance of imports of silver and gold in enabling Germans and others to make their purchases of spices, silks, cotton, and so on, the sale of bullion was essential to the completion of a considerable proportion of the transactions on which the brokerage fees were collected.

## ii. TARIFFS ON IMPORTS

Less revenue than that from brokerage fees came from the early import taxes, which distinguished between imports by land or within the Gulf and imports from overseas. On the former, foreign merchants paid 2.5 percent (the "quadragesimo"), and Venetians, half that (the "octuagesimo"), while on imports from beyond the Gulf, foreigners paid 20 percent.[17] This levy of 20 percent on imports from outside the Gulf of Venice constituted a quinto earlier in date and quite distinct from the quinto of "argento servo" described above which importers of silver had to sell to the mint at its price.

The general rates of the ad valorem customs duties were gradually superceded by differing rates paid on specified commodities brought from specified places.[18] The quadragesimo and the quinto ad valorem became penalty duties imposed on those who for political reasons were not granted privileges or those who tried to abuse them.[19]

The earliest commercial treaties—of 1107 with Verona and of 1217 with Hungary—exempted coined and uncoined gold and silver from import duties.[20] In 1237 silver bullion was specifically exempted from the usual duties as long as the importers sold directly to the mint.[21] In that period Venetians as well as foreigners were importing bullion from Hungary, as reflected in a case of highway robbery in 1223 in which three

[17]Fabio Besta, introduction to *BG*, 1:liii–lvi, lixff.; Lupprian, *Il Fondaco dei Tedeschi*, 5; Rösch, *Venedig und das Reich*, 72–73.

[18]*BG*, 1:lix ff. and docs. 38–40 ff.; Zordan, *I Visdomini*, 8–16. The document that Zordan quotes (p. 11, from *DMC*, 1:100) suggests that goods from Dalmatia (Schlavonia) and from within the Gulf may have paid 2.5 percent rather than 20 percent from the beginning.

[19]For the "dazio-pena" see Zordan, *I Visdomini*, 12.

[20]Rösch, *Venedig und das Reich*, 81–82, 91–92.

[21]*DMC*, 2:43–44.

Venetian merchants were victimized.[22] Later, when Venetian middlemen in Venice were the buyers, importers paid duties that varied with their status. By mid-century, merchants from Lucca were exempt from the regular taxes on bullion and coin,[23] and importers from the Veneto were exempted even from the octuagesimo, provided that within four months they exported merchandise equal in value to the amount of the specie that they had brought in with them.[24] The Germans, the most important importers, paid only 0.15 percent ("iii soldi pro centenario librarum") on gold bullion, although they paid much more on gold jewelry or plate,[25] and in most periods they also paid 0.15 percent on silver bullion.[26] To summarize roughly concerning the thirteenth century, one may say that most gold and silver imports were subject to a tariff for revenue of about 0.15 percent.[27]

A much higher rate, 1.4 percent, was the standard set in an extension of the jurisdiction of the mintmasters in 1295, but it was weakened by many exceptions. The mintmasters were to collect that percentage from importers who could not show that they were exempt because of what they had already paid to other offices.[28]

---

[22]Gerhard Rösch, "Die Wirtschaftsbeziehungen der Ostalpenländer zu Venedig am Beginn des 13. Jahrhunderts und ein Raubzug babenbergischer Ministerialen nach Ungarn," *Zeitschrift des historischen Vereines für Steiermark* (Graz), 1979, esp. 78–82. The three were robbed "in terra regis Ungarie" of gold, silver, and jewels worth about 850 marks of silver.

[23]*PMV*, docs. 15, 16; Zordan, *I Visdomini*, 543–55.

[24]*Cap. Fontego*, xxii (1271); *DMC*, 2:274.

[25]*Cap. Fontego*, xxi, xxii, 9–10 (cap. 29), 42 (cap. 117, dated 1338); *PMV*, docs. 16 (1270), 64 (1296), and 33 on the toll stations of the landward side of the lagoons. Zordan, who ignores the *Cap. Fontego*, argues (pp. 677–79) that the Germans paid no duty on bullion before 1277. He states (pp. 552–53) that silver from Hungary in 1270 paid 14 soldi, or 0.7 percent.

[26]See the preceding note. Cap. 134 of the *Cap. Fontego*, contains the following passage: "Oro florini ducati paga per centener de libra a grossi soldi 4 picoli 7. Arzento paga per centener de libra a grossi soldi 5 pizoli 10." These rates, which seem to refer to import duties, were included in a list of "brokerage fees" dated by Lupprian (*Il Fondaco dei Tedeschi*, 19) as 1363. In percentage, the indicated rates are: for gold bullion and coin, 0.225 percent; for silver, 0.29 percent. Half of the 0.29 charge on silver would be 0.15 percent, the same amount indicated in cap. 117 (dated 1338), referred to in the previous note.

[27]Other references to the tax of 3 soldi are: Cessi, Sambin, and Brunetti, eds., *Le deliberazioni dei Rogati*, vol. 1, p. 189, no. 146; p. 210, no. 390 (concerning Ragusan silver, on which see below, n. 47); p. 325, no. 23. ASV, Senato, Misti, regs. 16, fol. 11 (1333); 17, fol. 100 (1338). *RES*, doc. 219, p. 166 (2 September 1350).

[28]*PMV*, doc. 62 (1295); *DMC*, 3:377–78. The mintmasters were told to collect 1.4 percent (28 soldi) on all silver bullion and on coin presented to them to be minted or recoined except for three kinds: (1) Venetian grossi, (2) amounts of 2 marks or less, and (3) silver on which duties had been paid elsewhere, namely, at the Fondaco dei Tedeschi, to the Visdomini Maris in the case of Friulians ("Furlanis, videlicet Venzonascis et Clemonscis"), to the Visdomini Lombardorum, or to the supervisors of the Guild of Jewelers and Goldsmiths. The mintmasters were not to demand the tax from importers who could show that they had satisfied any of these offices. Although the text of the law implies that these offices would

Later, at least in some periods, a still higher rate was in force on imported bullion. In fact, it was the task of the Offitium Extraordinariorum to collect an ad valorem import duty of 2–3 percent on goods arriving in Venice by sea. In 1394, for example, gold and silver arriving from Constantinople and Greece had been paying the tax of 3 percent. At that time, the duty to be collected by the Estraordinari was reduced to 1 percent, first on bullion arriving from Romania and then more generally on all that arriving "de extra Culphum." These measures of the Senate were a response to the complaints of importers whose bullion was not of German-Hungarian origin that they were burdened by "magna datia," since they were also subject to other impositions presently to be discussed.[29] Serious lacunae in the documentation make it impossible to know, however, how long these duties of 3 percent and 1 percent were in force.

In addition to these tariffs levied simply for revenue and to much smaller fees for the officials connected with the registration, assaying, weighing, and auctioning of bullion at the Rialto,[30] there was one instance of what seems to have been a tariff for protection. In 1277 a tax of 5 percent was imposed on Germans who were bringing to Venice "groats, gold florins, Tyrolese coins, and pieces of 20 (denarios grossos, florinos aureos, denarios de Tyrol, denarios de XX)."[31] In regard to the silver coins at least, it was repealed in 1332, reestablished in 1338, and definitively repealed at the request of the emperor and of the city council of Nuremberg in 1355.[32] One can question which was sought more—the protection of the

---

have collected the 1.4 percent, it seems to leave open the possibility that many importers, because they belonged to favored groups, would benefit from lower rates by paying at these offices. Previously some of the bullion imported by sea had been paying 0.7 percent ("xiiii soldi") (see Zordan, *I Visdomini*, 554. See also *Capitulare Visdominorum Ternarie* [which Zordan ignored], fol. 27v, cap. 81; and *PMV*, docs. 16, 33, 61).

There is no reference to a tax as high as 1.4 percent in the capitolare of the Massari al Argento in ASV, Zecca, b. 6bis. On the list in the *Cap. Fontego*, pp. 9–10, cap. 29, the "dacii" the Visdomini were to collect were "soldi xxviii per centener" on "l'oro lavorato" but "soldi iii per centener" on silver.

[29]On the Estraordinari, who also collected freight charges, see their capitolari in ASV, Cinque Savi alla Mercanzia, 1st ser., b. 22bis and 22ter; on the duties of 2–3 percent see for example the latter, fol. 67v, cap. 79 (1423), and the former, fol. 40v (1457). The Senate provisions of 1394–95 are in *PMV*, docs. 189–90.

[30]Pegolotti, *Pratica*, 138–40; *Cap. Fontego*, 26 (cap. 73); MC, Leone, fols. 79, 109 (in 1395). The amounts of all these various fees, not easily distinguished from import duties, prove to be less than 0.2 percent ad valorem when compared with the prices for gold of 67 ducats or for silver as given below, in table C.1. On the refining fee introduced in 1417 and not collected on silver bars, at least not before 1442, see below, app. A, sec. ii.

[31]*DMC*, 2:302; Zordan, *I Visdomini*, 674; Braunstein, "Wirtschaftliche Beziehungen," 381–82. On coins of Tyrol and "de XX" see below, chap. 13, sec. i.

[32]*PMV*, docs. 91, 94, 132; and Simonsfeld, *Der Fondaco*, vol. 1, docs. 91, 97 (dated as 1337 instead of 1338), 179. See also *Cap. Fontego*, cap. 72.

mint and coinage of Venice against the products of competing mints[33] or
protection against German capital that could reduce Venetians to mere
agents. The latter is suggested by the provisions in the decree of 1277
forbidding Venetians to lend their names to facilitate such importation[34]
or to accept loans or commissions from Germans for operations outside of
Venice. After 1355, Germans could import gold and silver coins of high
quality and pay only 0.15 percent, as they did on bullion.[35]

The institution of the quinto in 1331 or 1332 as a means of obtaining
silver to coin mezzanini and soldini imposed in effect a new tax on all silver
imports.[36] Importers of any kind of silver, including those who intended
to use their silver to make jewelry, reliquaries, or tableware or to reexport
it as silver bars or ingots, were required to sell 1/5 of it to the mint at the
mint's traditional lowest price. Venetians who took to the mint silverware
or jewelry to be made into coin had to accept for 1/5 of it that same low
price, unless it could be proven that the silverware was made from silver of
which 1/5 had been turned over to the mint as quinto, that is, of silver that
had been registered as it should have been at the time it was imported. The
rule is illustrated by an exception passed during the emergency of the War
of Chioggia, when Venetian ladies took their jewelry to the mint to be
made into the coin then so badly needed. Their patriotism in agreeing to
unhoard part of their wealth was rewarded by their being given special
exemption from the quinto on such valuables up to 5 marks.[37] More
enlightening still is a ruling of 1343 regarding the importation of a nest egg
of silver coin by the lord of Milan, Luchino Visconti, for deposit at the
Venetian Grain Office, at the time a kind of state bank. The Milanese
envoys disputed the application of the quinto in this case, invoking a
commercial treaty that permitted free import and export of coined bullion
by Milanese citizens. A Senate committee ruled, however, that the treaty
did not extend to foreigners privileges that were more favorable than those
extended to Venetian citizens, who were required by law to consign the

[33]Zordan, *I Visdomini*, 674–80, considers it part of the "defense of the grosso," an effort to
keep out foreign coin.

[34]*DMC*, 2:302. Cf. above, chap. 9, sec. ii. A provision forbidding Venetians to "tansare . . . rectum" is interpreted by Zordan (p. 679) as meaning to pay the tax for the foreigner, ignoring the many instances of about this date in which *tansare* refers to pretended
purchases made by Venetians to enable foreigners to operate under the names of Venetians,
who thus became what we call dummies, stand-ins, or strawmen. See, for examples, *DMC*,
2:28–29; *Cap. Fontego*, 285; Predelli, ed., *I libri commemoriali*, vol. 1, bk. 2, docs. 137, 138;
Papadopoli, 1:351; ASV, Grazie, reg. 5, fol. 29v.

[35]*Cap. Fontego*, 25 (cap. 72); *PMV*, docs. 94, 132.

[36]On the date of the institution of this quinto see below in this chapter, n. 39; and in app.
A, n. 43.

[37]*PMV*, doc. 164, pp. 158–59. Cf. *Cap. Broche*; and above, chap. 9, n. 77. Earlier, even such
an item as a silver crucifix purchased by an importer from the Archbishop of Ravenna had to
be weighed and registered (see ASV, Grazie, reg. 7, fol. 67v [12 October 1337]).

quinto.[38] Such provisions make it clear that the mint's quinto was not really an addition to seigniorage, but a tax on all silver imports.[39]

The amount of the import tax imposed by the requirement to consign the quinto varied with the mint charges. On the requisitioned silver, the mint withheld about 27 percent of the product. On free silver, it withheld about 7 percent. Taking 7 percent as the mint charge that would have been paid if there had been no quinto, the added 20 percent withheld on coins minted from the quinto can be considered in effect a tax of 20 percent on 1/5 of the supplier's total import of silver. For the importer, paying 20–25 percent extra on 1/5 of his imports was equivalent to paying 4–5 percent on the whole.[40] When the mint charge reached 30 percent, it had the effect of an import tax of 5.4 percent.

The import duty embodied in the mint's quinto was cut in half, to about 2.0–2.5 percent, when that quinto was reduced to a "decimo" in 1342 or 1343.[41] Restored as 1/5 in 1350 in the broad increase of duties for the Third Genoese War, the rate of its yield was at its maximum in the period

[38]ASV, Senato, Misti, reg. 21, fol. 13, par. 2 (10 February 1342/43).

[39]The earliest reference to enforcement of the provision is an appeal, dated 14 September 1333, against a fine levied jointly by the mintmasters and the Assay Office because of a bullion merchant's failure to consign the quinto within 15 days of the date of importation, as required by law (ASV, Grazie, reg. 5 [subtitled "Grazie de contrab."], fol. 30v. Many appeals from similar fines are found in reg. 5, e.g., fols. 38v, 41v, and 50 [1334], and in later registers of the same series). Although the quinto was collected by the officials of the mint, they acted—as reflected in the case of the above-mentioned appeal—in close collaboration with the silver office at the Rialto, which supervised the weighing and registering both of imported partially refined silver and of the silver bars produced by refiners, whether inside or outside the mint. Buyers at the first stage ("omnes illi qui consueti sunt emere argentum pro affinando") were the ones required to consign the quinto, even though the 20 percent was to be calculated on the refined or pure product. On these silver merchants as buyers of unrefined silver see also below, app. G, doc. 4 (25 October 1344).

Around 1350 the silver office called in the buyers for a monthly audit of their books, to see that they had consigned the quinto on time (ASV, Grazie, reg. 14, fol. 50v [September 1358]). Around 1400 we find the mint officials themselves auditing the records of the banker and silver buyer Guglielmo Condulmer covering the period 1388–1413. The banker listed what he bought, registered at the Rialto, and brought to the mint for refining ("Chonpre e prezenti per l'ofizio da l'arzento per portar a la zecha a finar"), as well as the net pure product on which he owed the quinto ("Questo è l'arzento che i'ò e trato di fuogo, el qual è tegnudo di meter el quinto"); a separate account contains purchases on which the mint's quinto had already been paid ("Questo è l'arzento ch'i'ò chonprato franco el qual non s'è tegnudo a meter quinto") (PSM, Misti, b. 189, commis. G. Condulmer; quotations are taken from "vacchetta" no. 3, 1398).

[40]See below, app. E, sec. ii.

[41]The wording of the decree of the Quarantia of 28 March 1343 leaves some doubt as to whether the 1/5 had already been reduced to 1/10 in a decree of 6 May 1342 (PMV, doc. 98; DQ, vol. 1, doc. 139, p. 39. Cf. ibid., doc. 288). Such decrees provided for using unfree silver for coining grossi instead of soldini during specified periods. On the continuation of the decimo until the revision of taxes for the Third Genoese War restored the quinto see RES, docs. 217, p. 162 (August 1350); and 240 (1355).

1353–69, but illegal dealings in unregistered silver seem to have increased so much in the latter part of that period as to have reduced the yield.[42] To meet this difficulty in collecting the quinto, authorities raised the price paid for the servile silver. They thereby reduced to only 15.5 percent the mint charge on soldini made from servile silver. At the same time, the mint charge on free silver was raised to 13.8 percent, much higher than mint charges levied elsewhere for coins comparable to the soldini. The net fiscal effect is difficult to estimate.

During the financial and commercial crises of the Fourth Genoese War (1378–82) and the ensuing recovery, the mint charge on free silver was cut to 2.5 percent in an effort to win back German importers. For a few years it was even less than 2 percent, perhaps hardly enough to cover costs. The mint charge that importers had to pay for the coinage of their quinto was also reduced, but gradually the charge on servile silver was raised until it again amounted to an import duty of 2–3 percent, and in 1407–17 to 4 percent. Finally, in 1417 the quinto was abolished altogether, and mint charges on all silver were set at low levels, fluctuating but below 3 percent.[43]

Meanwhile some straightforward import duties levied on the Germans had also responded to pressures. A wartime tariff of 2 grossi per mark on gold (0.12 percent) was decreed in 1350, reconfirmed in 1355, and repealed in 1362.[44] A rate of 17 grossi 4 piccoli per 100 ducats' worth on silver (0.71 percent) was repealed in 1441 following a severe drop in imports.[45] When gold imports from Barbary became important, they were taxed 1 percent.[46]

For the Ragusans, whose importation of silver from the Balkans both as bullion and as silverware became important particularly at the end of the fourteenth century, the levies were complicated and changeable because of Ragusa's ambiguous political position and the damage that its low-cost shipping was inflicting on the Venetian merchant marine.[47]

---

[42]See below, chap. 18, sec. ii.

[43]See below, app. A and chap. 18.

[44]*Cap. Fontego*, 26; *RES*, docs. 219 (p. 166) and 240 (p. 200); *PMV*, doc. 141.

[45]*Cap. Fontego*, 164 (cap. 275).

[46]*BG*, vol. 1, doc. 114, p. 138 (1463).

[47]Susan Mosher Stuard, "The Adriatic Trade in Silver, c. 1300," *Studi veneziani* 17–18 (1975–76):121–23, gives a somewhat confused account of the duties paid by Ragusans. Indeed, the sources are confusing concerning how the special status of the Ragusans affected the payments that they made on their large shipments of silver in the fourteenth and fifteenth centuries. On Venetians' financing of this Ragusan trade see Bariša Krekić, "Italian Creditors in Dubrovnik (Ragusa) and the Balkan Trade, Thirteenth through Fifteenth Centuries," in *DMB*, esp. 242–45; and the general view in idem, *Dubrovnik (Ragusa) et le Levant au Moyen Age*, EPHE-6, Documents et recherches, ed. P. Lemerle, 5 (Paris, 1961), 77–78.

## iii. SEIGNIORAGE COMPARED WITH OTHER REVENUES

The preceding account of brokerage fees and tariffs is inadequate for many purposes, but it definitely indicates that the Commune's receipts from taxing the bullion trade were larger than its receipts from seigniorage on gold and silver coin. Receipts from black money will be discussed separately later. The following four comparisons—for 1423, ca. 1400, ca. 1345, and ca. 1280—include many questionable figures, but even when the questions are resolved by making assumptions that enlarge the receipts from seigniorage and belittle receipts from taxing the turnover of precious metal, the taxes on the turnover still seem to be about twice as important as seigniorage.

### According to Doge Mocenigo, 1423

The most comprehensive starting point for such a comparison is provided by the figures in the above-mentioned oration attributed to Doge Mocenigo in 1423. Activity in that year was not typical, but it nevertheless provides a starting point. While boasting that the Venetians invested 10 million ducats of capital in foreign trade each year, he gave the value of coin minted as 1.2 million ducats in gold and 800,000 ducats' worth of silver. Since his figures are credible only as a report of a year of peak production, which included a recoinage, old silver turned in for new may well have been worth about 500,000 ducats, but at least 300,000 ducats' worth can be considered imports.[48] Mocenigo's figures imply that in the years of which he was speaking, about 1/6 of the turnover in Venice's international trade (1.5 million ducats out of 10 million) was an exchange of other commodities for the bullion imported and coined. The amount of revenue produced by activity on that scale is estimated below:

| | | |
|---|---|---|
| 1. Seigniorage on gold coin | 4,800 ducats | (1,200,000 × 0.004) |
| 2. Seigniorage on silver coin | 2,010 | (300,000 × 0.0067) |
| Subtotal | 6,810 ducats | |
| 3. Old import tax on gold | 1,800 ducats | (1,200,000 × 0.0015) |
| Old import tax on silver | 450 | (300,000 × 0.0015) |
| 4. Brokerage fees | 12,250 | (1,000 + [1,500,000 × 0.0075]) |
| Subtotal | 14,500 ducats | |
| Total | 21,310 ducats | |

[48]On its credibility and interpretation see below, app. B, sec. iii. On the commercial situation in 1420–30 see vol. 2.

The explanation of the estimates is as follows:

1. The total mint charge for the coinage of gold ducats remained stable at 0.8 percent until 1473. Since evidence that only 1/2 of that was used up in the costs of minting is found in documents of the thirteenth century, the seigniorage is estimated as 0.4 percent. At the same time, it must be kept in mind that the complications of refining bullion containing both gold and silver into 24-carat gold may well have increased the costs and thus reduced the amount of seigniorage.[49] The situation changed in 1473, when the Council of Ten eliminated any charge on coining ducats. In order to meet production costs, the "dazio," or refinery fee, on silver consigned to the mint was raised from 2 grossi to 3, with the added grosso per mark going to the gold mint.[50]

2. When the quinto was abolished in 1417, the mint was ordered to coin all silver offered for a fee that amounted to only 1.34 percent of the value of the product—much less, the decree specified, than the actual cost of minting. The rest of the cost (6 soldi out of listed expenses totaling 14 soldi) was to be contributed by the Commune. But at the same time, a refinery fee was instituted which at first was 4 1/4 grossi per mark and in 1420 was reduced to 2 grossi. The refinery fee was used to meet the Commune's contribution to the costs of manufacture. Indeed, the amounts were nearly the same: 6 soldi = 72 piccoli (6 × 12) and 2 1/4 grossi = 72 piccoli (2.25 × 32). When the refinery fee was lowered to 2 grossi, legislators called it a "dazio." How much of the 2 grossi was really spent on refining is questionable.[51] Assuming that the refinery fee—even after it was reduced to 2 grossi—still yielded some profit, the latter is here estimated as 1 grosso per mark of silver. Since 149 grossi were struck from 1 mark in the period 1421–29,[52] the seigniorage on 300,000 marks of silver coined is figured as 0.67 percent (1/149 = 0.0067).

3. The old import tax on gold and silver is estimated at the rate of 0.15 percent paid by the Germans. Although a higher rate was paid by some other importers, the figure is most uncertain and probably would not change the general picture.

4. If the Commune's share of brokerage fees on all transactions involving imported gold and silver had been collected at the rate of 1 percent, the rate to which the fees had been raised in 1413 by the decree discussed

[49]See above, chap. 10, sec. iv; below, app. A, sec. v.

[50]*Cap. Broche*, fols. 43 (9 December 1473), 49v (20 November 1478). The fee of 3 grossi was cut in half in 1506 (fol. 81), eliminated in 1509–11 (fols. 83r–v), in force on gold, silver, and bolzone in 1541 (fol. 128).

[51]See below, chap. 12, sec. iii and nn. 53 and 54; and app. A, sec. vii.

[52]See below, app. A, sec. vii. The number of coins per mark was increased in 1421 to 149 (£29 16 *s.* = [580 + 16]/4 = 149).

above, the yield on the turnover indicated in Mocenigo's oration would have been 15,000 ducats. Since that decree implied that the increase did not apply to Germans, who were the chief importers of precious metals, it seems preferable to apply the lower figure of 3/4 of a ducat per 100 ducats; that would have produced a yield of 11,250 ducats. At the same time, so as not to ignore the imports by Ragusans and others, the estimate has been arbitrarily raised by 1,000 to 12,250 ducats.

### 1399–1407

The years to which Doge Mocenigo's figures seem to apply were boom years following the conclusion of Venice's trade war with Emperor Sigismund in 1422. Before and during that contest, both total turnover and coinage were almost certainly at much-reduced levels. (Note the complaint in 1417 that production at the mint had ground to a halt.) The relative importance, however, of various sources of revenue at an earlier date can be indicated roughly by applying the rates that had been in effect before the beginning of that trade war and before the abolition of the quinto, namely, those in effect between 1399 and 1407, to the turnover estimated by Mocenigo. The resulting figures for 1399–1407 are:

| | | |
|---|---|---|
| 1. Seigniorage on gold coin | 4,800 ducats | (1,200,000 × 0.004) |
| 2. Seigniorage on silver coin | 0 | (300,000 × 0) |
| Subtotal | 4,800 ducats | |
| 3. Import tax collected through the quinto | 8,820 ducats | (300,000 × 0.0294) |
| Old import tax on silver | 450 | (300,000 × 0.0015) |
| Old import tax on gold | 1,800 | (1,200,000 × 0.0015) |
| 4. Brokerage fees | 11,250 | (1,500,000 × 0.0075) |
| Subtotal | 22,320 ducats | |
| Total | 27,120 ducats | |

Explanation of the estimates follows:

1. In that period the seigniorage on gold coin was the same as in 1423.
2. On silver the amount of seigniorage has to be entered as zero because free silver was turned into soldini and grossi for a fee. That fee was only 1.8 percent of the value of the product, so that it probably did not include much padding.[53]
3. The largest import tax was collected through the quinto. From unfree silver the mint kept 16.5 percent of the yield (the gain resulting from the relatively low price for a mark of bullion, the same price in force since 1386, and from the value of the coins cut from a mark under regulations of 1399). Deducting 1.8 percent as the cost of manufacture leaves 14.7

[53]See below, app. A, sec. vii.

percent as profit.[54] Since that rate was retained on 1/5 of all silver imported, it was equivalent to 2.94 percent on total imports and yielded 8,820 ducats (300,000 × 0.0294), as on item 3 in the above list. It will be assumed in these estimates that the old import duties of 0.15 percent had not changed between 1399 and 1423 on the bulk of imports, even though bullion arriving by sea was probably still paying 1 percent.

4. The amount collected from the brokerage fees before the increase voted in 1413 is estimated as having been 3/4 of a ducat per 100 ducats, as indicated in the law of 1413, although it must be admitted that the figure is questionable because of the uncertainty about the amount of bullion imported by foreigners whose treaties gave them different rates.

The figures are to be considered unrealistically hypothetical. There is no evidence that importation and coinage attained any such large volume between 1399 and 1407. A best guess for that period would lower all the figures. But size of the items relative one to the other is significant. It shows the importance of gold ducats before 1407 and of the quinto.

### 1340–70

Gold rose to comparable prominence at Venice only about 1340, as will be explained in later chapters, and in the decade beginning in 1340 large quantities were minted. In peak years—in 1343–45 and 1369–70—gold was minted at the rate of 600,000 ducats per year,[55] about half the rate of which Doge Mocenigo boasted during the wave of imports at the end of Emperor Sigismund's boycott. The seigniorage on 600,000 ducats was 2,400 ducats (600,000 × 0.004), the brokerage 4,200 ducats (600,000 × 0.007).

While those sums are not trifling, the income from the quinto must have been much larger. In the boom years for the Venetian bullion trade, when German, Bohemian, and Balkan silver mines were near peak production, the silver bullion imported may well have equaled the imports in Doge Mocenigo's day or may have been even higher.[56] On the soldini coined from the servile silver in 1331–53 the mint charge was 23–29 percent, on mezzanini and on the new soldini of 1353 a little higher. Deduction for manufacturing costs takes off 1.37–7.4 percent. Rounding off gives 20–25 percent as the profit on coins made from unfree silver. Taking 25 percent on 1/5 of the import was equivalent to taking 5 percent from the total. If during the boom of the 1340s the total silver imports reached the minimal figure indicated by Mocenigo's statistics—300,000 ducats' worth—the quinto yielded about 15,000 ducats per year (300,000 × 0.05). Even when

[54]See below, table A.5.
[55]See below, app. B, sec. iii.
[56]See below, chap. 17, sec. i.

the quinto was cut to a decimo, in 1343–50, at the peak of the boom, the yield of 7,500 ducats was much the largest item in the government's revenue connected with precious metals, larger about 1350 than the 4,200 ducats collected in brokerage fees.

### About 1280

An estimate for an earlier period, before the first gold ducat was coined and when grossi were the only coins of fine silver minted, can best be made in lire di grossi. If the mint operated a whole year at "full capacity" (as defined and explained below, in chapter 12 and appendix B) about 1280, it produced 445,000 grossi coins per year, worth 1,854 lire di grossi (445,000/240). Such steady production at full capacity was no doubt quite improbable, but the figure provides a starting point. A comparable amount of silver may well have been prepared in the form of certified ingots of sterling silver or silver of the fineness of grossi. On those two assumptions, the value of silver from which customs and brokerage were collected can be calculated as 3,754 lire di grossi. That revenue compares with the seigniorage on grossi worth 1,854 lire as follows:

| | | |
|---|---|---|
| Seigniorage on grossi | 15.57 | $(1,854 \times 0.0084)$ |
| Seigniorage on ingots certified | 3.71 | $(1,854 \times 0.002)^{57}$ |
| Import tax on silver | 5.63 | $(3,754 \times 0.0015)$ |
| Brokerage at 0.7 percent, not allowing for special exemptions by treaty | 26.28 | $(3,754 \times 0.007)^{58}$ |

Although again the totals are hypothetical and unrealistic, the proportions are significant. Income from seigniorage could not have been very much more than the 19.28 lire di grossi indicated (15.57 + 3.71), but revenue from taxes on the silver flowing through Venice would have been much higher than estimated if the value of the silver ingots exported had exceeded the value of the grossi coined, as seems likely.

### iv. BLACK MONEY

Venice began to make very large profits on black money before the end of the fourteenth century, but previously income from that source must have been moderate. As decreed by the mint statutes of about 1280, the maximum production of piccoli (presumably including fractional bianchi and quartaroli) was limited to about 1 million piccoli coins per year, even when the mint operated at full capacity. The million coins had a

---

[57]See below, app. A, secs. ii and iv. On certified bars the mint charge was only 0.8 percent. Whether that was more than the cost of refining and assaying seems doubtful, but to be on the safe side, seigniorage has been assumed and calculated at 0.2 percent.

[58]The rates are explained above, in secs. i and ii.

value of only about 130 lire di grossi.[59] For a few years around 1280 the mint charge seems to have been very high, about 24 percent, but by the revaluation of the grosso at 32 piccoli in 1282 it was cut to 13 percent, a rate at which it remained until the mid-fourteenth century.[60] There is no direct evidence from Venice in that period concerning how much of the 13 percent was cost and how much was profit, that is, seigniorage. Costs elsewhere on coins of about the size and value of the piccoli varied from 5 percent to 10 percent, whereas costs of making smaller, blacker fractional coinage ranged from 15 percent to 25 percent.[61] If in Venice about 1280 the cost of making piccoli, including the cost of the copper, was 10 percent, leaving 3 percent as seigniorage, the income from coining piccoli worth 130 lire di grossi was 3.9 lire di grossi. Since in 1282 piccoli were only about 20 percent silver, the revenue from import and brokerage taxes on the silver imported for the purpose was not very much. Although the seigniorage on black money generally constituted a larger part of the mint charge, revenue from either seigniorage or the turnover of silver used in black money was so small as to reinforce later statements that Venetians had not looked to the mint as an important source of income in the thirteenth century. So long as the fine silver content of 240 piccoli was about equal to that of 20 soldini and the production of piccoli was restrained, no great profit was to be made from coining piccoli.

The situation changed drastically when Venice began minting black money for use in its empire. Particularly heavy production of torneselli for the Greek dominions from 1368 to 1415 was followed by similarly heavy production of various black coins for the Terraferma provinces between 1442 and 1465. For about a half-century at least, revenue from minting such coins acquired an importance in Venice somewhat comparable to the importance it had long occupied in the budgets of feudal princes.[62]

The above account of Venetian taxes on specie is far from complete. In view of the gaps in the records of the Quarantia, compiling a full record may well be impossible. Although inadequate for many purposes, this survey seems sufficient to demonstrate the contrasting fiscal situations in Venice and in feudal monarchies. To feudal monarchs their mints were a main source of income; taxes collected on the sale or importation of precious metals were not. In Venice taxes on the bullion trade yielded much more than did seigniorage rights. As one of the senators active in the debates in the 1360s on monetary policies asserted, earlier generations had not considered the mint a main source of revenues.[63] The income derived

---

[59]The output permitted is estimated in table B.2 as worth 3,404.8 lire a grossi, the equivalent of 130.4 lire di grossi (3,404.8/26.111).

[60]See below, app. A, sec. iii.

[61]Usher, *The Early History,* 222–23; and above, chap. 5, n. 10.

[62]Mueller, "L'imperialismo monetario."

[63]*PMV,* doc. 139; and above, sec. iii.

through the mint from the quinto was really an import tax collected on all silver imported. The strategic location of Venice between regions that supplied and regions that demanded gold and silver made her activity as a bullion market an essential element in the city's prosperity and therefore indirectly in the health of the Commune's finances. That consideration dominated the regulation of the market place and of the mint, as well as Venice's monetary policy in general.

# 12

# WITHIN THE MINT

HE ATTRACTION OF VENICE as a bullion market depended primarily on the competitiveness of prospective buyers, but it was enhanced by the ability of the Venetian mint to turn bullion into coin at a reasonable cost. By the fifteenth century the number and varied kinds of coins it was producing for circulation in Venice's expanding empire, and beyond in its economic hinterland, created a concentration of workers of diverse skills that was large enough, by medieval standards, to require special administrative and industrial organization. Coinage was, as Philip Grierson has said, the one true example in the centuries before the industrial revolution of the mass production of a manufactured object.[1]

In contrast to that later complexity in output and organization, Venice's first mints were probably temporary affairs devoted to the production of particular coins. Mints are mentioned in several locations before 1200, the best authenticated being close to the Rialto bridge but on the other side of the canal at San Bartolomeo, near the later location of the Fondaco dei Tedeschi.[2] In the next century minting was concentrated at the other center of Venetian life, at the Piazzetta, across from the Ducal Palace. In the sixteenth century the mint was rebuilt into the structure that has

[1]Philip Grierson, "Note on Stamping of Coins and Other Objects," in *History of Technology*, ed. Charles Singer, 5 vols. (Oxford, 1954–78), 2:485.

[2]It is mentioned on that site in 1237 (Federico Berchet, "Contributo alla storia dell'edificio della veneta zecca prima della sua destinazione a sede della Biblioteca Nazionale Marciana," *Atti dell'Istituto Veneto di Scienze, Lettere ed Arti* 69, pt. 2 [1910]:339–41; Molmenti, *Storia*, 1:50–51, 267).

become the main part of the Marciana Library.[3] In 1319 the building then in use was considered too small and too crowded. A part of the shipyard adjoining the mint and extending over the present location of the Giardinetto was taken to enlarge it.[4] During ensuing centuries, coinage for Venice and all its expanding empire was concentrated in that building, while much of the refining was done elsewhere, some as far away as the Giudecca because of the evil-smelling smoke.[5]

## i. THE SCALE OF OPERATIONS

The growth over centuries in the output of the mint at San Marco can be indicated only in general terms. No surviving records of the mint have been found from which to construct a series tracing the amounts of bullion received or coins issued.[6] At best we can make only rough estimates for a few dates of the number of workers employed and the number, weight, and value of the coins issued.

The earliest date for which there is any basis for a numerical estimate is about 1280. In the regulations compiled shortly before that year, limitations were placed on the number of craftsmen to be employed and the amount of silver or billon to be distributed to them per day. These permit an estimate of output at "full capacity" about 1280, giving that term a conventional meaning. Its meaning in modern usage is also conventional. A modern steel mill generally operates at less than "full capacity," but it can, as in wartime, produce much more than "full capacity." Being an estimate here based on regulations, "full capacity" is not to be taken literally. At most times the mint produced much less, and it could, if ordered to do so, produce well beyond its "full capacity."

About 1280–1300 the work force of the mint at "full capacity" so understood was about 100. The breakdown of that round figure, explained in greater detail in appendix B, may be summarized as follows:

| | |
|---|---|
| Supervisory staff, from the mintmasters to their pages | 5–6 |
| Refinery workers | 5–12 |
| Other master craftsmen | 70–100 |
| Apprentices | 10–30 |
| Total | 90–148 |

[3]Deborah Howard, *Jacopo Sansovino: Architecture and Patronage in Renaissance Venice* (New Haven, 1975), 40–44.

[4]*PMV*, doc. 76; MC, Fronesis, fol. 13. The cost was to be met "de introitu monete." In most of the intervening centuries the former shipyard was occupied by the grain warehouses shown in the third of the pictures of the mint shown here.

[5]ASV, Zecca, b. 6tris, fol. 32; and below.

[6]ASV, Zecca, b. 16, "Catastico di Giornali e Quaderni, 1731," indicates that such records existed then.

## THE MINT AND PIAZZETTA BEFORE SANSOVINO

One side of the mint was obscured by shops; at the base of the
campanile were the booths of moneychangers.

*Detail of an engraving by E. Reuwich in Breydenbach's* Peregrinationes *(1486).*
*BMV, Incun. no. 391. Photograph by Toso.*

Particularly dubious are the estimates of the number of apprentices and of
the number of refinery workers.[7]

Since the striking of the coins by the moneyers was the last step in the
process of production, the number they struck in a day gives a measure of
the mint's output. By limiting the number to be employed and the amount
of metal given them, regulations in effect about 1280 limited production of
piccoli and grossi, particularly of piccoli. The limits varied with the different
lengths of the working day in winter and summer. It is indicative of the
arbitrary meaning of "full capacity," and the distinctiveness of the rules
defining it in Venice, that the summer season, in which the permitted daily
production was largest, was longer for grossi than for piccoli. Whereas the
summer rate of production of piccoli ended in August, that for grossi
extended to the end of September, in order to permit more coinage at "full
capacity" of coins of the type loaded onto the fleets leaving for the Levant in
the fall.

Thus delimited, annual production at "full capacity" about 1280 may

[7]See below, app. B, sec. i.

206

SANSOVINO'S MINT

The facade of the mint, only two stories high, faced the waterfront.
The entrance was from the Piazzetta, where shops occupy the space
where Sansovino's library, here not yet completed, would stand.

*Detail from an anonymous woodcut, "Il volo del Turco," of about 1550. BMCV,*
*Archivio fotografico. Photograph by Toso.*

be estimated very approximately as follows: 445,000 grossi coins weighing 4,000 marks (about 950 kg); and 1 million piccoli coins weighing 1,270 marks (about 300 kg).[8] These estimates seem low when compared with records of production at other mints, such as that of London, or at Venice at other dates. A much higher rate of production probably had been reached at Venice earlier in the century when Doge Enrico Dandolo had collected more than 40,000 marks (about 9,500 kg) of silver from the Crusaders.[9] Although that was not all they owed, it was enough silver to coin more than 4 million grossi. Several million must have been minted in 1202 and 1203 while the fleet for the Fourth Crusade was being provisioned and accounts were being settled within the Adriatic. The "full capacity" about 1280 was not a reflection of the technical possibilities but a level of production limited for social ends. As explained in the discussions elsewhere of the coinage policies of Doge Lorenzo Tiepolo (1268–75) and his immediate successors, the restrictions in force in 1278–80 are best interpreted as a reaction against an expansion of the money supply about 1270.[10]

Those severe restrictions on the coinage of piccoli were relaxed in the decades following 1280. Production of 250,000 piccoli per month for at least three months, a rate of output three times as large as the capacity prescribed in 1280, was called for in 1318, and the building housing the mint was then enlarged. After the coinage of grossi diminished and then was discontinued in 1356, the silver mint was kept busy by the production of mezzanini and soldini, for which the needed bullion was supplied by the levy known as the quinto.

Meanwhile, the gold mint had grown from its small beginnings in 1285. As late as 1342 it employed only 10 craftsmen in the shaping and striking of coins, but in the 1340s, when Venetian production of gold coin was expanded and the number of furnaces in the gold mint was doubled,[11] the number of employees also must have more than doubled.

Before the Black Death struck in 1348–49, the mint may well have seemed crowded again. The plague, which cut the city's population by about a third, no doubt relieved the crowding. During the commercial and political upheavals of the latter part of the century, the minting of billon coins for Greek lands—torneselli—expanded. On the other hand, Venetian coinage of silver for export to the Levant probably dropped with the discontinuance of production of the old grosso and the success of the carlino minted by the Angevin rulers of Naples. It revived with the production of many of Venice's lighter, new grossi in the 1380s.[12] But no

---

[8]See ibid., sec. ii.
[9]See above, chap. 8, n. 31.
[10]See above, chaps. 8, sec. iii, and 10, sec. v; and below, app. B, sec. iii.
[11]See below, app. B, sec. iii.

## THE MINT AFTER SANSOVINO

The third story, authorized in 1558, was completed about 1566, and the
extension of Sansovino's library was completed. Between the
facade (here shown bricked up) and the waterfront was a fish market.

*Detail from an early eighteenth-century print in Luca Carlevaris,* Le fabriche.
*By permission of the Houghton Library, Harvard University.*

yearly records survive that might enable us to quantify the extent of
these shifts.

The statistics on the mint's operations in Doge Mocenigo's speech of
1423, although they do not include black money nor reflect a typical year,

[12]See the numismatic evidence referred to below, in chap. 13, sec. ii; and E. Ashtor,
"Observations on Venetian Trade in the Levant in the Fourteenth Century," *JEEcH* 5 (1976):
565.

209

indicate that the mint's operations in his day were on a scale entirely different from that in 1280. Besides the 1.2 million ducats coined, he indicated a yearly coining for export of just about 20 million pieces of fine silver in the form of soldini and grossi. His figures allow also for the coinage of a similar or even greater number of such coins for use in Venice and its mainland possessions. The production for domestic use in that year was especially far above a typical level, a situation explained by the recoinage ordered in 1422, the first in many decades. Even the figures on gold and silver coin exported must be considered far above average, reached only in a peak year, as is true also of Mocenigo's figures on the Venetian fleets. Mocenigo's figures seem to have been rounded off optimistically upward and also to reflect a prosperous interlude of relief from the plague and from war after the recovery of Dalmatia, the conquest of the Veneto, and Venice's successful defense against Emperor Sigismund's counterattack.[13]

The black money minted could not compare in value with the gold and silver coin of which Mocenigo boasted, but the manufacture of the torneselli introduced under Andrea Dandolo also reached figures that might be called mass production. Contemporary documents and die studies give firm ground for estimating that the output of torneselli rose to 5.5 million coins per year under Doge Antonio Venier (1382–1400).[14] Later in the fifteenth century, while the output of torneselli was not maintained, comparable millions of largely copper coins were produced for use in Venice itself and in the subject cities of the mainland.[15]

The only figure for the number of employees in this period comes from direct testimony concerning the extraordinary spring of 1472. The Council of Ten, then responsible for the mint, ordered the demonetization and immediate recoinage of practically all of the silver coins circulating in Venice and her dominions. Production at full capacity was declared essential to the survival of the economy; it was ordered that 30,000 ducats' worth of soldi pieces, called "marchetti," for a total of 3,720,000 pieces, be produced immediately. In those weeks of crisis the envoy Giovanni de Strigis, an expert on mints, wrote from Venice to the marquis of Mantua that the Venetian mint was working day and night with all the master artisans ("maistri") the officials could find—60 men.[16] Regrettably, the

---

[13]See below, app. B, sec. iii.

[14]Alan M. Stahl, *The Venetian Tornesello: A Medieval Colonial Coinage*, American Numismatic Society, Numismatic Notes and Monographs, 161 (New York, forthcoming), sec. 7.

[15]Mueller, "L'imperialismo monetario"; and below, vol. 2.

[16]Archivio di Stato di Mantova, Carteggio Estero, Carteggio da Inviati, b. 1431bis (on microfilm at the Fondazione G. Cini, Venice), letter of 22 May 1472: ". . . e de questi [marchetti] se lavora a furia cum quanti maestri i àno poduto havere, che son più de 60." See

writer does not say how many workers of lower category were on the job at the same time.

Production of several different coins on such a scale suggests that the number of persons employed had grown much beyond the 100 estimated above for periods of "full capacity" about 1280–1300, although it is hard to believe that the number of workers in the mint rose in proportion to the increase in the number of coins minted, since there is no record of comparable expansion of the space in which they worked. Expansion of production without expansion of the space needed may have been achieved by contracting out operations previously performed within the mint. Certainly, much of the refining was sometimes done elsewhere, and the discussion of the industrial organization below will reveal possibilities of "putting out" to craftsmen of work normally done within the mint.

## ii. TOP MANAGEMENT AND STAFF

Administrative and industrial organization seem to have changed little to provide for the increased production. Fuller records of early accounting and technical practices might give a different picture. For later centuries more voluminous records invite descriptions of techniques, industrial discipline, and administrative arrangements more complete than what can be attempted in this sketch. Here we can hope merely to indicate the nature of the problems that arose but not all the solutions attempted.

There is early evidence of some growth of a supervisory staff, some elaboration of the accounting, and some spreading of supervisory tasks by more subcontracting, but only a little. Piecework so dominated labor relations that transitions were relatively easily made to inside contracting or to putting out work for which the mint lacked space. A proposal to farm the whole gold mint to an entrepreneur who would operate it to make a profit, as was the general practice under feudal monarchs, was made during a discussion of reforms in 1416, but it was decisively rejected.[17] While some aspects of the subcontracting done by the mintmasters are clear, many others escape us. And any description of the organization of the mint has to depend heavily on the formal regulation. As a result, the description is dominated by the structure formed in the thirteenth century and permits only a partial analysis of how that structure was modified later.

Like all offices and magistracies in the republic, the mint was governed by a committee of nobles, strictly speaking by two committees.

---

also Reinhold C. Mueller, "Guerra monetaria tra Venezia e Milano nel Quattrocento" (Paper presented at the international congress "La Zecca di Milano," Milan, May 1983); and below, vol. 2.

[17]ASV, Senato, Misti, reg. 51, fol. 142v.

After 1284 there was one for the silver mint and one for the gold mint. Decrees often referred to the two mints as separate institutions, although their mintmasters acted jointly in some matters and they were located in the same building.[18] Unification did not come until 1522, when the Provveditori in Zecca were created by the Council of Ten.[19]

The number of mintmasters, their salaries, and their terms of office varied from time to time. They were elected first by the Ducal Council, then by the Quarantia, in some years by the Great Council, and after 1416 by the Senate.[20] In 1279 the three mintmasters for silver were paid 100 lire per year each and served for two years. None could be a member of the Great Council during his term as mintmaster, a provision presumably inspired by fear lest the mintmasters absent themselves from the mint in order to attend meetings of that council. Their trips outside Venice were also restricted. But all three were not expected to be at the mint every day during all their term of office; instead they rotated in one- or two-month assignments as managing mintmaster ("massaro della quindena"), associate mintmaster ("massaro associato"), and then backup ("l'altro") or reserve ("il terzo").[21]

The massaro della quindena may be called the managing mintmaster, because it was his responsibility to be present every day at every step, from the purchase of bullion and the consigning of it to refiners or casters through its transfer from one craftsman to another until coinage was complete, inspecting for quality at each stage and seeing that it was weighed and precisely recorded at each transfer. His hours were as precisely specified as those of his subordinates, hours governed by the bells of the campanile; and he was subject to fines if he did not arrive before the designated bell had ceased sounding.[22] He was under orders to complete during his quindena the coining of the bullion that he received. After 40 days of receiving bullion from merchants wanting coin, he was to settle his accounts and pay them in the next 20 days, and then he had a few weeks more in which to settle his account with the Communal auditors and turn over to the Communal treasurer all the profits that he had made for the Commune during his operation of the mint.[23] In many decisions, es-

---

[18]The union of these two mints was discussed in October 1349 (perhaps because of the devastation wrought by the Black Death) and rejected because two mints could operate more expeditiously (*PMV*, doc. 108).

[19]Da Mosto, *L'Archivio di Stato*, 1:149–52.

[20]The names of the mintmasters are listed in Papadopoli, vol. 1, app. 2, with much detail about their number, salaries, and terms of office. See also Padovan, *Le monete dei veneziani*; and Giovannina Majer, "L'officina monetaria della Repubblica di Venezia," *AV*, 5th ser., 52–53 (1954).

[21]*PMV*, doc. 25; and below, app. F.

[22]Papadopoli, 1:316, 333. Cf. references to the bells in *Cap. Fontego*, 6–7, but see esp. Sanuto, *De origine*, 25.

[23]*PMV*, doc. 107.

pecially in approving the fineness of workmanship, the managing mint-master had to have the agreement of the associate mintmaster. If they disagreed, the backup master was called on. If he failed to come when told he was needed, he was subject to a loss of salary.[24] A similar system of rotation was applied in the gold mint.

In both mints the assignments and the length of the "quindena" was changed from time to time. In the silver mint in 1417 one mintmaster was in charge of refining, another was in charge of coining soldini and grossi, and the third was in charge of coining piccoli and torneselli.[25]

In giving out the precious metals to one workman after another, the mintmaster was accompanied by the weigher ("pesador"), whose authority was much broader than his title implied, for the weigher participated in many decisions, for example, regarding hiring, firing, or fining workmen. In the regulations of the silver mint in 1279 the weigher appears much inferior in status to the mintmasters, but in the gold mint a century later weighers seem to be of much the same status as the mintmaster.[26] Although paid less, they were also, at least in some cases, members of noble families and moved up later to become mintmasters.[27] Weighers and mintmasters could in some periods be reelected to successive terms, unlike most Venetian noble officials. One weigher served twenty years, and another, Alvise Giustiniani, became the dominant personality in the mint in the first half of the fifteenth century.[28]

An administrative staff of a half-dozen served this governing committee's general functions. Most influential and highest paid was a "lay scribe," or accountant.[29] In the early statutes the mintmasters were personally enjoined to keep account of all transactions and all movement of the metal, and the scribe was to record in his book everything that the mintmaster wrote in his and to show the profits for the Commune, but one can doubt whether the two records were made independently.

One objective of the mint's accounting was calculation of the ex-

[24]Papadopoli, 1:323.

[25]Ibid., 245, 246, 357.

[26]A decree of ca. 1290 reduced the number of weighers from 4 to 3 and authorized the massari to assign them to either the silver mint or the gold mint as needed (ibid., 327). In 1349 they were chosen in the same way as the massari and were considered eligible to become massari (*DQ*, 2:297–99, 306; also in *PMV*, doc. 108).

[27]*DQ*, 2:10–11; ASV, Zecca, b. 6bis, fol. 55v; Papadopoli, 1:243. When the pay of the mintmasters for gold was raised in 1363 to 8 lire di grossi, that of the weighers was raised to 6 (*RES*, doc. 263).

[28]ASV, Grazie, reg. 16, fol. 111 (1369/70); Papadopoli, 1:317, 320; and on Alvise Giustiniani, below, app. F.

[29]The specification of a "scribanus laycus" in Papadopoli, 1:317 (1278), contrasts with the reference in ibid., 336 (1295), to "Frater Franciscus olim fuit ad officium monete." On the clerics as clerks and notaries at Venice until a relatively late date see Giorgio Cracco, "Relinquere laicis que laicorum sunt. Un intervento di Eugenio IV contro preti notai di Venezia," *Bollettino dell'Istituto di Storia della Società e dello Stato Veneziano* 3 (1961):179–89.

pense and the profit or loss to the Commune for each kind of coin. A very elementary form of cost accounting was embodied in a "fattura," a listing similar in name and in content to the invoice or list of expenses that a commission agent sent to his principal itemizing the costs charged to the principal for the ware shipped to him.[30] The earliest examples—of 1394, 1405–6, and 1417—included little more than the costs of labor, which were indicated as so much per mark for each category of craftsman employed (see table 6). Out of the total of 10 1/2 soldi in the fatture for grossi, 5 2/3 soldi went to moneyers, shearers, or sizers.[31] The charge for the found-ryman, who cast the silver into bars or sheets after it was refined, was linked to the expense involved in the loss of materials in the removal of the dross (the calo); the combined charge amounted to 3 soldi. The charges listed for the mintmaster, weigher, and scribe were additional to their regular salaries, an additional "cut" or "take" per mark, commonly referred to as their "utilità."[32] For charcoal and utensils no charge appears on the fatture for 1417, although there is such an item in 1394 and more elabo-rately in the more detailed, more complete fattura of which there are many examples for the sixteenth century.[33] The mint's early fatture were basical-ly only compilations of labor costs.

They did indicate fairly accurately, however, the relative costs of manufacture of different coins, and they were used in conjunction with prices for silver bullion in determining the relations to be established between the weight of silver coins and their legal value on the one hand, and the resulting amount of gain or loss for the mint, on the other. This was spelled out in regulations of 1417, when the quinto was abolished and Venice made an effort to attract silver by appearing to offer to coin it at less than the cost of minting. The reform decree stated that the price of silver was 5 3/4 ducats and that soldini should circulate at 100 to a ducat. That made the cost of the silver 575 soldi di piccoli per mark. The fattura, combining those for soldini and grossi, was said to average 14 soldi "more or less" ("soto sovra"). Adding that expense gave 589 as the value of the coin to be made from a mark and the number; that is, from each mark, 589

[30]Many examples of "fatture" are to be found as loose sheets in merchants' account books, for example, in the ledger of Niccolò Barbarigo, in ASV, Raccolta Grimani-Barbarigo, b. 43, reg. 6.

[31]*PMV*, doc. 187; *Cap. Broche*, fol. 14v; Papadopoli, 1:362. See also below, table B.1. "Shearing" and "sizing" are terms used by Charles Johnson, ed., in *The De Moneta*, xxxv, 76; Cf. Craig, *The Mint*, 42, 44.

[32]Collections by mintmasters beyond their salaries are referred to in the description in "Traité du gouvernement de Venise," 5599, fol. 120. The income of the mintmasters for gold is referred to in ASV, Zecca, b. 6tris, fol. 37 (1415), as 120 gold ducats to each, in addition to their "cuts" on the turnover ("con le altre utilitade che àno a presente") of about 60 ducats a year. In ibid., fol. 38, there is reference to similar "utilitade" of the pesadori.

[33]Examples of later date are in ASV, Zecca, b. 18bis.

TABLE 6.

Labor Costs of Manufacturing Grossi and Soldini, 1417

| Type of Labor | Costs ("spexe di fatura") in Soldi di Piccoli per Mark of Alloy | |
|---|---|---|
| | Grossi | Soldini |
| Mintmasters (massari) | 1 | 1 |
| Weigher (pesador) | 1/4 | 1/4 |
| Bookkeeper (scrivano) | 1/4 | 1/4 |
| Inspectors (gastaldi) | 1/3 | 1/3 |
| Shearers (ovrieri) | 3 | 5 |
| Sizers (mendadori) | 1 1/3 | 3 |
| Moneyers (stampidori, monetari) | 1 1/3 | 3 |
| Casters (fondatori) | 1/2 | 1/2 |
| Loss in casting ("cali del fondador e altri cali uxadi," "per callo de argento") | 2 1/2 | 2 1/2 |
| Total | 10 1/2 | 15 5/6 |

NOTE: The costs are as listed in Papadopoli, 1:362; and *Cap. Broche*, fol. 20v. Relevant for comparison are (1) the costs of manufacturing torneselli in Clarentza early in the fourteenth century, as given in Pegolotti, *Pratica*, 118: refining, 1/2 sterlino per libbra; loss in casting, 3 sterlini per libbra; ovrieri, 2 1/2 sterlini per libbra; moneyers, 1 1/2 sterlini per libbra; engraver of the dies, 150 "soldi di viniziani grossi" per year; ironsmith, 100 perperi per year; weigher, 100 perperi per year; and mintmasters, 300 perperi per year. (2) Labor costs per pound at Florence in 1332 as given in Bernocchi, 3:25 (see below, n. 71). (3) At Genoa a breakdown of expenses on craftsmen among fondatori, operai, and monetari (with no mendadori mentioned) shows the cost of operai (which presumably included the work of the Venetian mendadori) as generally three times that of the monetari (Felloni, "Ricavi e costi," table 2).

soldini or 147 1/4 grossi.[34] The supplier received back—half in soldini, half in grossi—the same weight of fine silver that he had furnished. He was charged only 8 soldi di piccoli per mark, the other 6 soldi being paid by the Commune in order, as it said, to cause more silver to be brought to Venice. But the government did not really intend to coin at less than cost and without collecting any seigniorage, for it ordered the mint to collect the Commune's contribution of 6 soldi per mark out of the receipts of a new refinery tax (explained below, in section iii).

The accounts kept by the scribe were important not only in formulating minting specifications but also, and primarily, in checking up on the mintmasters. At the end of his term, each managing mintmaster turned in a booklet itemizing all receipts and expenditures and specifying who

[34]Papadopoli, 1:360–61.

SEAL OF THE MINT OF ORVIETO

This drawing of a small and rare seal shows an operaio or ovriero
flattening metal sheets (*left*) and a moneyer striking coins (*right*).
The seal reads:

**+·S.LABORENTI:E:MONETARI:D'VRBIS:VETERI**

(Sigillum laborentium et monetariorum de Urbis Veteri).

*Reproduced from E. Babelon,* Traité des monnaies grecques et romaines
*(Paris, 1901), vol. 1, col. 816 (Museo Bottacin).*

was responsible at each stage of manufacture.[35] The scribe's independence
in keeping or checking these records was affirmed by the government's
declaring that he could not be removed except by action of the Signoria,
to which he reported.[36] Obviously the honesty of this accountant was
important in assuring the honesty of the mintmasters.

Trustworthiness was important also in the pages or orderlies assigned to each mintmaster and especially in the guardians who slept in the
mint all night or were posted at the door during the day to keep out
intruders. In the 1270s they were bonded for 100 lire; the mintmasters were

---

[35]A surviving example from the gold mint is the "Quaderno de mi Zuan Trivisan della
quindexena de mazo e zugno 1485, fatta per misser Piero Quirini fo de Misser Biasio," in
ASV, Zecca, serie seconda o finale, b. 3.

[36]ASV, Zecca, b. 6tris, fol. 31v; Notatorio di Collegio, reg. 5, fols. 86 and 87, which records
the choice among several applicants, almost all cives originarii and some campsores; Consiglio dei Dieci, Misti, reg. 18, fol. 108v.

bonded for 1,000 lire.[37] Although referred to as "pueri" and "fanti," they may well have been—in the thirteenth century, as they were later—men of very mature years who had proved their reliability during decades of service in the mint either as craftsmen or in less skilled labor.[38]

No technical expert steadily employed as part of the central staff is mentioned in the thirteenth-century regulations. The "gastaldo," who inspected the work of the craftsmen and was expected to identify those craftsmen who had produced products found defective was probably a guild officer. On days when silver was being coined, he was to come each morning and stay as long as the mintmasters told him to. Only at the end of the fourteenth century does the gastaldo appear as a full-time employee at the mint. A century earlier the managing mintmaster was ordered personally to inspect the blanks prepared for striking.[39]

While skill in execution was certainly the exclusive domain of the craftsmen, mintmasters were certainly expected to be qualified to judge the quality of the product and must have had considerable understanding of the methods used.[40] Being responsible for providing the rooms and apparatus the craftsmen, they needed to know the kinds of furnaces and implements the craftsmen needed for various purposes and to understand different ways of casting and of shaping the blanks. A mintmaster named Marco Sanuto proposed in 1391 a money-saving way of preparing blanks for torneselli.[41] It involved casting the metal into sheets ("tolle") instead of rods or bars ("verge"), probably a method resembling that described in the treatise on metalwork by Biringuccio. Although written by a Sienese noble about a hundred years later, it indicates the wide range of knowledge useful to the men of means who contracted with princes to operate their mints. Biringuccio, metallurgist and once a mintmaster himself, described various ways of casting into bars or sheets, which were cut into strips, and the strips cut into small squares comparable to dice, which, if copper, were then heated by charcoal and flattened by heavy blows to the

[37]Papadopoli, 1:322, 334, 321; *Cap. Broche,* fol. 73; ASV, Zecca, b. 6tris, fol. 32v; Consiglio dei Dieci, Misti, reg. 18, fol. 103.

[38]ASV, Zecca, b. 1309, fols. 9v, 10v; and on fanti, below, nn. 146–49.

[39]The capitolare of 1278 mentions an "inquisitor" to inquire whether the "magistri artis" know their craft (Papadopoli, 1:316, cap. 12), but there is no further mention of this "inquisitor," unless he is the same as the gastaldo referred to in caps. 40 and 43. Cf. below, nn. 173–74.

[40]The judgment of the mintmasters in assaying was subject to being overruled by the assayers of the bullion office at the Rialto, some of whom were nobles and some not. In the silver mint in 1278, assayers were called in as needed (Papadopoli, 1:316, cap. 25). In the regulation of the gold mint there are references to assayers, but it is not clear when and to what extent they were distinct from the assayers of the bullion office at the Rialto (see ASV, Zecca, b. 6bis, fol. 64; and in the new regulations of 1414–21, described below).

[41]*Cap. Broche,* fol. 7.

desired thinness.[42] Marco Sanuto's innovation must have been some variation of this process for which he calculated such items as the saving in charcoal and additional expense for apprentices ("fanti").

Venetian nobles are sometimes contrasted with upper-class Florentines, who in spite of wealth and political power still paid attention to their cloth-producing businesses. The most-cited evidence for the contrast is from the sixteenth century, however, and perhaps too much has been made of the difference, especially for earlier centuries. To the extent that rich Venetian nobles spent time and energy on industrial production, they did so in those industries that earlier were more important at Venice than textiles, namely, the building industry, including shipbuilding, and the chemical industries, including the refining of precious metals. Certainly the nobles who were mintmasters or assayers were called on to apply a high level of technical knowledge.

## iii. THE MANUFACTURING PROCESS

Although a managing mintmaster was responsible for distinguishing good work from bad, that was quite different from being able to do the work himself. Trained fingers and biceps were properties of craftsmen. The mintmasters were most involved in the beginning and end of the production process—in the acceptance and refining of bullion, in the design and distribution of dies, and in the inspection and paying out of the final product.

In the silver mint most of the bullion came from Venetian merchants who bought silver from the German importers at the auctions on the Rialto. Some traders bought intending to sell the bullion in the same condition in which they had purchased it, but many Venetian bullion merchants had their purchases refined, either up to the standard required by the jewelers' guild so that they could sell it later to craftsmen who made jewelry or tableware or up to the standard required by the mint.[43] In the

---

[42]Vannuccio Biringuccio, *De la pirotechnia libri X* (Venice, 1550), bk. 10, cap. 3, fol. 133v. This edition, which was consulted at the Houghton Library, Harvard University, is cited below also. Carmello Trasselli considered the Venetian edition of 1540 (at the BMV) to be the best (see his *Zecche e monete*, pt. 1 [published as a separate volume] of his *Note per la storia dei banchi in Sicilia nel XV secolo*, Banco di Sicilia, Fondazione "I. Mormino," n.s., Quaderno no. 2 [Palermo, 1959], n. 230). On the biography of Biringuccio see *The Pirotechnia of Vannuccio Biringuccio*, ed. and trans. from the Italian with introduction and notes by Cyril Stanley Smith and Martha Trach Gnudi (New York, 1942); most recently, Adriano Carugo's introduction to the facsimile reprint of Biringuccio's treatise (Milan, 1977), and Franco Brunello, "La Pyrotechnia di Vannuccio Biringuccio," in *L'editoria scientifica a Venezia nel '500* (Venice: Università Internazionale dell'Arte, forthcoming). The treatise was used extensively by Agricola for his better-known *De re metallica*.

[43]Stussi, ed., *Zibaldone da Canal*, 7; *DQ*, 2:140; ASV, Grazie, reg. 14, fol. 50v. See also below, sec. iv.

latter case, they might merely take it to the mint to be certified as argento di bolla.[44] If they wished coin, they went through the form, at least before 1394, of selling the bullion to the mint. In addition to the bullion being coined at the initiative of merchants, there was some really communally owned bullion, which the mint purchased with funds appropriated explicitly for that purpose by the governing councils or acquired by transfers to it from other government offices of clipped or defaced coins or of forbidden foreign coins that they had confiscated. Bullion not supplied by a merchant was referred to as "di comun."[45]

The extent to which the silver bullion supplied by merchants was refined within the mint or outside the mint, even if under the direction of the mintmasters, is difficult to determine. The thirteenth-century regulations imply that refining was ordinarily done within the mint.[46] There is mention in 1393–94 and 1435–40 of some 6–15 refiners among the craftsmen whom the mints employed.[47] But fifteenth-century rules imply that most refining was done outside the mint.[48] Certainly some of the silver received needed to be refined, and the mint contained facilities for refining silver as well as gold, but the quantity processed within the mint varied from one period to another.

When the mint refined the silver, both the managing mintmaster and the associate mintmaster were under orders to be present so that they would note carefully how much weight had been lost by the removal of impurities. This loss of weight, which together with the dross containing the impurities removed was called the calo or callum, was carefully recorded by the scribe. Since some silver might remain in the crucibles and the flux along with the impurities, the dross was set apart under lock and key until all three mintmasters acting together decided how to recover the silver for the Commune.[49] When silver merchants had their bullion thoroughly refined before submitting it, they could make their own provisions for recovering anything of value in the dross. That seems a sufficient reason for them to have had their silver refined as near to the standard for grossi as was practical before taking it to the mint.

The craftsmen whom merchants hired to do the refining were

[44]See above, chap. 10, sec. ii.

[45]ASV, Senato, Misti, reg. 51, fols. 142–43. On the use of the term "virgis comunis" as distinct from "virgis mercatorum" see *PMV*, doc. 25, cap. 2.

[46]The capitolare of 1278 (*PMV*, doc. 25); and the provision regarding certified ingots cited above, in chap. 10, sec. i.

[47]ASV, Grazie, reg. 18, fol. 77v; *Cap. Broche*, fols. 36–37; ASV, Zecca, b. 6bis, fols. 43, 44.

[48]Papadopoli, 1:248, 363; increased refining outside the mint during the fourteenth century also is suggested by references to it in ASV, Grazie, reg. 14, fol. 50v; ASV, Senato, Misti, reg. 45, fols. 39–41; *DQ*, vol. 2, no. 294 (1349).

[49]Papadopoli, 1:320–23, caps. 55–56, 66–67. His note on p. 322 dates the law from which cap. 55 was derived as of 1276, and cap. 56 implies that previously there had not been a furnace in the mint for use in recovery of metal from the dross or ashes.

among a varied group of metalworkers who had shops outside the mint and probably worked both in the mint and in their own shops. Within the mint they contracted as groups at piece rates and for a time pooled their receipts. When in 1383 they began working each man for himself, the merchants and the government objected, probably because when pay depended on piece rates and on an individual's productivity, the craftsmen worked more hastily and produced a less trustworthy product.[50] Difficulties over the quality of the refining and indeed over the quality of the silver coins generally increased at the end of the fourteenth century. Measures were taken to tighten inspection and personal responsibility and also to replenish through apprentices a declining number of refiners.[51] About 1400, when many senators considered the silver currency to be in deplorable condition, most of the refining was being done at private foundries.[52]

In 1417 an effort was made to have all the refining of silver done by the mint. As soon as silver was weighed and registered at the Rialto, it was supposed to be taken to a "refinery" supervised by one of the mintmasters and a newly authorized scribe experienced in these matters. When refined and sealed to certify its fineness, it was to be turned over to the mintmaster in charge of coining grossi and soldini. He was then to collect from the merchant owning the silver 4 1/4 grossi a oro per mark, about 3 percent of its value.[53] The practical effect of this regulation, however, was not to transfer all silver refining from private foundries into the mint. Later procedures imply that the mintmaster in charge of the refinery merely contracted out the refining for considerably less than 4 1/4 grossi. But he collected that relatively high charge from the merchants who supplied the silver, and they felt that they were paying a tax. Such a tax was more than offset by the abolition of the quinto in that same year. Until this refinery fee was lowered in 1420 to 2 grossi, or about 1.4 percent, it was certainly expected to be a source of revenue. The fee was probably the most effective part of the legislation, except that it created an administrative mechanism to prevent any refining of silver being begun by craftsmen without a mintmaster and scribe having a full record of the process.[54]

[50]*Cap. Broche,* fol. 5v. On private shops outside the mint see below, n. 131.

[51]*Cap. Broche,* fols. 9, 11r–v; ASV, Zecca, b. 6bis, fols. 38, 43, 44, and passim; and below, vol. 2.

[52]See below, chap. 18, sec. ii.

[53]The refining fee set on 11 November 1417 (Papadopoli, 1:357) was stated as "grossi quattro et un quarto a oro per marcha che vien ducati tre e grossi do a oro per cento." In the same decree the value of the silver was said to be 5 3/4 ducats per mark (i.e., 138 grossi a oro, of which 3.1 percent was also 4 1/4 grossi).

[54]ASV, Senato, Misti, reg. 53, fol. 19v (4 January 1419/20), in a special "collegio." When reduced from 4 grossi 8 piccoli per mark to 2 grossi, the charge was called a dazio. The vote was close (19 to 12 with 1 abstention), whereas the immediately preceding action on the same day, permitting the sale of silver otherwise than at auction, was passed unanimously. The decree of 1417 specified a fine for any "affinador metesse in fuogo ad affinar senza parola del

Shaping the metal into pieces of the desired weight and size involved casting and then cutting into strips or squares. It involved also flattening the sheets, strips, or squares by hammering them to the desired thinness. The hammering occurred at different stages in the making of the small squares. According to early descriptions, its place in the procedure differed according to the kind of metal (whether gold, silver, or copper alloy) and at various times and places.[55] Silver and billon alloy was commonly cast into rods, not sheets, at Venice, to judge from the repeated references to "verge" in the early regulation,[56] at least before 1391, when, as described above, the mintmaster Marco Sanuto introduced a new method of casting the copper alloy for torneselli into sheets or plates.[57] Very likely, Venetians had previously used a method described as new and revolutionary in England in 1279. Instead of being cast into ribbons, as had been done earlier in the English mint, the molten metal was cast "in sand molds . . . into little square rods."[58] But in the earliest Venetian capitolare there is mention of casting silver into plates ("plate argenti") as well as rods ("verge").[59] In the gold mint, ingots were pounded into sheets of the desired thickness before being cut into squares.[60]

Whichever method was used, the caster of the sheets or bars could exercise an intermediate organizational function. He was responsible for casting metal in such form that the designated workmen could cut and shape it into blanks. In the silver mint his responsibility for the quantity of silver passing through his hands was recognized in the early capitolare by special provisions for recording it in the presence of the mint's scribe and of the apprentices of the casting smith.[61] If the silver was alloyed with copper to make billon coin, that was done under the immediate supervision of the managing mintmaster.[62]

After the metal was cast into rods or sheets, it was assayed anew. Even if the caster ("fondador") was not considered responsible for the quality of the work done by the refining workmen, he might be suspected of having adulterated the metal given him, as in a case that perplexed the managing mintmaster in 1381. The mintmaster had given a fondador 60 marks of silver belonging to the Commune. When they were cast into

massaro e del scrivano" and on any "mercadante che metesse o fesse metter contro l'ordene predito" (Papadopoli, 1:358). Another clause (ibid.) provided that the returns from the fee be used for expenses and that the surplus be turned over to the mintmaster in charge of torneselli and piccoli (on later developments see below, nn. 64, 65).

[55]Biringuccio, *De la pirotechnia libri X,* fol. 133; see also below, nn. 56–60.

[56]Papadopoli, 1:311–12, 315, 326 (caps. 1, 2, 23, 80).

[57]*Cap. Broche,* fol. 7; and above, n. 41.

[58]Craig, *The Mint,* 41–42.

[59]Papadopoli, 1:322, cap. 60.

[60]*PMV,* doc. 37, cap. 4. Cf. Biringuccio, *De la pirotechnia libri X,* fol. 133r.

[61]Papadopoli, 1:315, cap. 22.

[62]Ibid., 326, cap. 80.

rods, the weigher, Gian Sagredo, took from them three samples. On assaying them, he found that all three were below the fineness for grossi. Acting according to regulations, he had the whole batch refined over again and was astonished at the amount of weight lost (the calo). The craftsmen who had done the refining said that copper had been added. The mintmasters and weighers were split as to whether to penalize the caster. Finally, they voted, 3 out of 4, that thereafter none of those involved—the refiners and the caster—should ever be in charge of casting in the mint.[63]

After the attempt at creating a monopolistic silver "refinery" in the mint by the reform of 1417 had proved a sham (or at best an administrative device designed to pin on one mintmaster the responsibility for seeing that all refining was done properly), the casting foundryman became an intermediary between the merchants and the managing mintmaster. The Council of Ten intervened in the mint's affairs in 1425, ordering the election of a second caster in the silver mint, since one was not considered to be enough.[64] After the Council of Ten had taken full charge of the mint, it specified in the general reform of mint regulations in 1475 that no silver should be recorded as received by the managing mintmaster (so that he would be held responsible for it) until after it had been cast and then assayed. While it was in the possession of the caster, the silver was to be considered still the property of the merchant for whom it had been refined. If the casting and assaying process was interrupted, the unassayed silver or alloy was to be put in a safe place, one of the keys to which was to be given to the merchant. How the calo was to be figured, paid for, or recovered was to be negotiated between the merchant and the caster, but not in such a way as to make the caster the debtor of the merchant beyond a specified amount for more than four months. The managing mintmasters were also forbidden to extend credit to the caster for more than four months or for more than a limited percentage of the calo on the silver that they gave him for recasting.[65] These provisions left room for the two foundrymen in charge of casting silver to gain not only a regular fee on each mark cast but also some profit from their handling of the dross by making arrangements with other foundrymen about refining it. The caster could become a kind of subcontractor in the combined process of refining and casting.

Once the metal had been refined, cast, and reassayed, turning it into blanks ready to be struck by a moneyer was the task of a group of masters who worked together sharing a common furnace and responsibility for their product. If the blanks were not well prepared, all the masters at the

[63]*Cap. Broche*, fol. 4.

[64]ASV, Zecca, b. 6bis, fol. 64v. Before the Black Death there nad been two or three (*DQ*, vol. 2, doc. 384; *PMV*, doc. 113 [May 1350]).

[65]ASV, *Consiglio dei Dieci*, Misti, reg. 18, fols. 100–101.

THREE STEPS IN COIN MAKING

*Center:* beating a sheet of metal to the desired thinness;
*left:* rounding the blanks by clipping; *right:* the moneyer, with an
apprentice—very likely his son—who placed the blanks between
the upper and lower dies before they were struck by the master moneyer.

*From an eighteenth-century edition of Emperor Maximilian's* Weisskunig, *at the
Houghton Library, Harvard University.*

shop that had prepared them were fined.[66] There were 8–12—later 16—
such shops, each under a "capo di bottega" or "capo di ovrieri."[67] But a
separate status and pay scale was enjoyed by those who were responsible
for making the weight of the silver coins correct and uniform. These

[66]Papadopoli, 1:318–19, cap. 41.
[67]*Cap. Broche,* fol. 24, indicates that there were 8 in 1425. A regulation for the silver mint of

weight adjusters, here called sizers, were called mendadori or mendatori to
distinguish them from the others, here called shearers, who were referred
to by the more general terms "operari" or "ovrieri."[68] Sizers are not
mentioned in regulations for the manufacture of piccoli, but they were
clearly distinguished in the regulations concerning grossi and in itemizing
labor costs for soldini.[69] As early as 1278 and probably earlier, the concern
with making all grossi of equal weight led to orders to select two of the
sizers at each furnace to check the weight of the blanks being prepared by
other sizers.[70]

The work of these craftsmen—distinguished by the specialized function of making equal in weight all coins of the same denomination—
absorbed much more of the cost of manufacturing silver coin at Venice
than in mints elsewhere. There was, for example, no comparable labor
expense at Florence.[71] At Venice the sizers accounted for about as much of

---

1498 refers to 12 botteghe under 12 ovrieri (ibid., fols. 71v–73). Majer, "L'officina monetaria,"
38, describes the operation of ovrieri, of which she says there were 16 assigned to 16 shops,
where each was assisted by 3 lavoranti and a "garzone." Her details are not specifically dated
or documented but seem to be based on archival material from the late sixteenth or the
seventeenth century, such as are found in ASV, Zecca, b. 1309 and 1310.

The three steps in coin production pictured in Maximilian's *Weisskunig* were not completed in the same room or shop, at least not at Venice. The woodcut was designed by a
distinguished artist on orders from Emperor Maximilian I ca. A.D. 1500 to display his life and
achievements, including how much he had learned of arts and crafts (Arthur Burkhard,
"Hans Burgkmaier," *Speculum* 7 [1932]:236; and in much more detail, H. Th. Musper, "Hans
Burgkmaier und der Weisskunig," in *Kaiser Maximilians Weisskunig*, ed. H. Th. Musper, vol.
1, *Textband* (Stuttgart, 1956), 35–39. The woodcut is not one of those that Musper (p. 46)
attributes to Burgkmaier himself. The caption underneath it reads, "Il apprend l'art de batter
monnaie" (*Weisskunig. Tableaux des principaux evenemens de la vie et du regne de l'Empereur
Maximilian I en une suite de deux cent trente sept planches gravees en bois sur les dessins et sous la
conduite de Hans Burgkmaier* [Vienna and London, 1799], no. 32). On the location of the
shops see below, n. 110.

[68]On the varied terms used in early Venetian documents see below, sec. iv; and Papadopoli, 1:318–20, caps. 41–45, and 362. See also below, app. B.

[69]The sizers are conspicuous by their absence from the paragraphs about piccoli in caps.
80–83 of the early capitolare (Papadopoli, 1:326) and from the lists of labor costs for piccoli in
1442 in *Cap. Broche*, fol. 29 (also in Papadopoli, 1:367, n. 1). The mendadori are mentioned in
the lists of craftsmen paid for work on soldi, grossi, and tornesceli in *Cap. Broche*, fols. 24
(1424), 25 (1429), and 29 (1442/43).

[70]Papdopoli, 1:320, cap. 45. This may be interpreted as creating a division of labor between
two groups of sizers.

[71]Bernocchi, 3:14, 25, 37–43, gives breakdowns of the labor costs at Florence into payments
to four crafts: uvrieri, paid 23 denari per pound; addrizzatori, paid 4 denari; monetari, 8 1/2
denari; and fonditori, 2 denari. Although the addrizzatori seem in some ways to correspond
to the mendadori at Venice, the name suggests straightening or some aspect of shaping
rather than weighing. Whatever their function, their pay was a smaller factor in total costs
than were payments to mendadori in Venice (see tables 6 and 7). In the mint at Messina,
according to Trasselli (*Zecche e monete*, 121), one group among the ovrieri, a group whose
distinctive name, "affilatori," suggests that they worked mainly with files, had the tasks "di

the labor cost of making traditional silver coin as did the moneyers who struck the coin (see table 7).

The intended weight of each type of coin was generally stipulated by specifying the number to be made from a mark of metal. For the grossi minted from 1194 to 1356 it never changed: it remained 109 1/3 to 109 1/2 coins per mark.[72] For the soldini and the new grossi minted after 1379 it changed frequently. On 20 May 1391 the number of soldini per mark was fixed as 496–504.[73]

Preventing the total number of coins in a mark from being above or below the stipulated number was not the difficult part of the sizers' labor. They were called on also to prevent any individual coin from being much above or below the standard, the average weight that would make the specified number weigh 1 mark. The procedure they used was specified in provisions concerning soldini made on 30 May 1391 by a special committee of nobles who proposed new methods in an early experiment in quality control.

In the method of quality control previously used, the sizers had relied on a heavier weight and a lighter weight to indicate the amount of permitted variation. Thereafter the sizers were to use only one weight ("sagium"). The testing weight was to be 1/62 of an ounce (0.481 grams). None of the blanks or squares ("quarelas") they approved were to be heavier. A second gastaldo was to be added to the one already employed, and the two gastaldi were to check or cull ("trabucare") about 1/4 of all the blanks in a batch prepared by sizers. If they found none that were overweight, they were to put together and weigh as many blanks out of that batch as would tip the scales at 1 mark. If the number was between 496 and 504, the batch was to be accepted and given to the shearers, who prepared the blanks ("flaones") for striking. But if the inspector found 1 square that

---

rendere i pezzi quanto più fosse possibile simili al cerchio e del peso previsto" with shears and balances, but the cost of their labor compared with that of other "operai" is not specified (cf. below, app. B, n. 12; or in this chapter, below, n. 143. Cf. also Craig, *The Mint*, 42). On labor costs by crafts see the notes to table 6; and the valuable, much more complete list for Venice in Giorgetta Bonfiglio-Dosio, "Lavoro e lavoratori nella Zecca veneziana attraverso il 'Capitolar dalle broche' (XIV–XVI sec)," in *Viridarium floridum: Studi in onore di Paolo Sambin*, ed. Giorgio Cracco, Maria Chiara Billanovich, and Antonio Rigon (Padua, forthcoming).

[72] Although the earliest text specifying that weight is of relatively late date, in the capitolare of 1278, Papadopoli reports the same weight and fineness for the earliest grossi, of Enrico Dandolo and Pietro Ziani (1:86, 93).

[73] ASV, Senato, Misti, reg. 41, fol. 141v. The instructions for soldini in 1353 had specified exactly the number of soldini by saying 36 dozen (see below, app. A; and *PMV*, doc. 117). For piccoli the numbers to be struck—1,104 in 1390 and 1,440 in 1394—were stated in the same manner (*PMV*, docs. 158, 182). On the tolerances in the fineness of the silver used for grossi of type 1 and after 1353 for soldini, mezzanini, and later grossi with star see below, app. E. The standard declined from 0.965 to 0.952 in 1379 and to 0.949 in 1421–29 (see below, tables A.2 and A.3).

was overweight or found 1 mark that contained more than 504 coins, then the whole batch was to be given back to the sizers to be corrected ("emendare") at their expense and loss. To control the inspectors in this system of quality control, the gastaldi were to be fined 1 denaro for each soldo found to have left the mint ("de dicta domo exibunt") heavier than the prescribed weight. To pinpoint the gastaldo responsible, a point ("punctus") was to be added on each soldo die so as to identify the batch inspected by each of the gastaldi. Imposing the fine, and keeping part of it, was assigned to the Silver Office at the Rialto, although the mintmasters were of course to check the number of coins per mark and keep their share of other fines, such as those for not reporting for work before the bell had stopped sounding.[74]

That program proved too ambitious. The craftsmen had apparently promised that they would attain a higher degree of standardization in return for a raise in piece rates from 22 piccoli per mark to 24, but they found the accuracy required of them impossible and refused to work under those terms. During the next six months the formulation of the accuracy required was modified at least twice to meet their demands. The added inspector and the penalties were not changed, nor was the range of variation in the number of coins in a mark, but the individual coins were allowed to have a variation of between 1/61 and 1/66 of an ounce, a provision that implies the continued use of two weights to indicate the limits of the tolerance. Even when the standard was thus relaxed, the senators felt it necessary to force the craftsmen to accept it by the threat that anyone who did not agree to work on soldi on those terms would be excluded from working on any other kind of coin and deprived of an assignment to a shop for at least six months.[75]

After this relaxation of the standard initially set, the quality control demanded of the gastaldi allowed the coin, the weight of which was less than a half-gram, to depart from the mean standard only by less than 2/100 of a gram.[76] There is reason to doubt that such accuracy was achieved in practice. In fact, the currency deteriorated through the intense, immediate culling, which left only the lightest of new coins in circulation.[77]

How the sizers and shearers arranged their cooperation working in the same shops is not clear, but it would seem that the weighing must have

---

[74]*Cap. Broche,* fol. 7v.

[75]Ibid., fol. 8, recorded changes that were voted by the Senate on 11 and 20 July 1391, and a third formulation is implied by the confusing departure of the text in that capitolare from the text in Senato, Misti, given in the footnote to the law of 11 July (also Papadopoli, 1:225–26).

[76]The mean standard was 63.5 coins cut from an ounce (29.812 grams), or 0.469 grams per coin; the maximum deviation was between 0.4887 (29.812/61) and 0.4517 (29.812/66), or a difference of 0.0370; the deviation from the mean was therefore $+/-$ 0.0185 (0.0370/2), which is $+/-$ 3.94 percent (0.0185/0.469). Trasselli (*Zecche e monete,* 123) figured that the mint at Messina used balances capable of weighing 0.009 of a gram.

[77]See below, chap. 18, sec. ii.

## A MUCH-USED UPPER DIE

The upper die, called the punch die or torsello, became "bearded" from
repeated striking. The die pictured here was used for making
the "carrarino da 2 soldi," under Francesco il Vecchio da Carrara,
lord of Padua (1355–88).
*Obv.:* **.FRANCISCI.DE.CARARIA.** [retrograde] A cart, flanked
on each side by an **F**, cut in intaglio. (The die is slightly enlarged;
the die face, actual size, is about 20 mm).

*Museo Bottacin, inv. no. 871.*

been done after the blanks had been shaped. The shearers, clearly, were
responsible for their being well rounded. The shearers were also responsible for having the blanks washed in an acid, by apprentices, a process
called blanching, to prepare their surfaces for striking.[78]

The hammermen who struck the coins, the "minters" or "moneyers"
("monetari" or "stampadori"), were supplied with the needed dies by the
mintmasters. The blanks to be struck were placed between an anvil die and
a punch die. All three were held firmly in position by a collar or by pegs
and sockets which fitted snugly together so as to align the images on the
two faces of the coin.[79] The anvil die below ended in a sharp point so that

[78]Papadopoli, 1:319, cap. 43.
[79]Grierson, *Numismatics,* 101; on the whole process see pp. 101–11. See also idem, "Pegged
Venetian Coin Dies," *Numismatic Chronicle,* 6th ser. 12 (1952):103–4.

it could be driven into a block of wood but was splayed outward halfway up so that it would stay in position without being driven further in when struck. The obverse of the coin, the side with the more complicated image and the inscription identifying the authority minting the coin, was generally cut intaglio into the upper end of the anvil die. The design for the reverse side was cut into the upper die, called the "trussell." The repeated blows received by the trussell die gradually cracked and flattened its upper end, spreading it out in a kind of beard and making trussell dies wear out faster than anvil dies. By the regulations of 1278, the managing mintmaster was instructed to have made immediately at the beginning of his term 24 trussell dies and 16 anvil dies.[80] To make sure that the work of the moneyers would not be held up, mintmasters were under orders always to keep a reserve of 12 pairs of dies, and each moneyer had an extra set at hand. In both the gold mint and the silver mint an important duty of the mintmaster as he made his daily rounds was to inspect the dies of these hammermen and replace any that were deficient.[81]

In the gold mint the stages of manufacture were much the same as in the silver mint, although there was need throughout for more rigorous inspection and for more exact measurement. "Compare your weights often in order to satisfy your own mind if for no other reason," wrote Biringuccio, "for it is clear that even mice and birds carry away gold."[82]

Attaining the desired exactitude was particularly important and difficult in assaying gold and in refining it to the purity of 24 carats. In this regard as in many others, the technical skill attained in such medieval mints as those of Venice and Florence was high enough to deserve our admiration, but their technical ambitions and pretensions were even higher. An impossible degree of accuracy seems to have been expected from the experts who used touchstones and needles to assay the gold by eye before it was assayed by chemical methods—one of which, called the "lasagna," will be explained shortly.[83] In two cases we have a clear and precise record of the fineness assigned by assaying with touchstone and needles before impurities were extracted from the gold being coined into ducats, followed by a precise statement of the amount of 24-carat gold yielded after refinement by the mint's chemical process. Both batches of bullion had been assayed as 23 1/2 carat (0.979 fine). If that assay had been correct, and if precisely the same refining process had been successfully applied to both lots so as to remove only the impurities and remove them completely, the

---

[80]Papadopoli, 1:321, cap. 53, a clause probably superceded later when the supply of dies had been built up. The way the dies were used is clearly pictured in the woodcut described above in n. 67.

[81]Papadopoli, 1:321, 331, 335; ASV, Zecca, b. 6tris, cap. 32.

[82]Biringuccio, *The Pirotechnia,* ed. and trans. Smith and Gnudi, 360.

[83]On assay by touchstone see above, chap. 9, sec. iii; on assay by "lasagna" see below, n. 88.

loss of weight would have been the same for both batches—2.08 percent (0.5/24) or (2/96). Actually, the weight of pure gold obtained and returned to the merchants who supplied the bullion was 5.19 percent less than the weight of the bullion received in one case, 3.42 percent less in the other. Since the process used actually took away some gold with the flux and dross, one of the two batches seems to have been quite accurately assayed by touchstone, but the other should have been assayed at nearer 23 carats than 23 1/2.[84]

Whether the chemical process used in the mint really succeeded in making gold of 24 carats has been questioned, but recent tests confirm Papadopoli's judgment that ducats were better than 23 3/4 carat, that is, better than 99 percent pure gold.[85]

Even if there were doubts about the adequacy of the refining technique in removing a last half-grain of impurity, there would be no doubt that mintmasters thought their craftsmen had the ability to do so. Merchants and officials assumed that the measurements determined important profits or losses for either the merchants or the Commune, as appears clearly in lengthy debates early in the fifteenth century over the accounting connected with the final refining of gold that contained traces of silver.

Regarding the situation in Venice early in the fourteenth century, Pegolotti wrote that the separation of gold from silver was the specialty of the nephews or grandsons of Francesco da Bologna, most of whom lived in Venice and charged 4 grossi per mark "or more or less as they wished."[86] After the initial separation, each metal was further refined separately.[87]

Before the middle of the century, if not earlier, a process for completely removing silver from gold was well known. Alternate layers of the gold to be refined and a flux (cimento) composed of sea salt and crushed red tile (essentially silicon) were placed in a crucible. Comparing the spreading of the cimento on the layers of gold to the sprinkling of cheese in a lasagna, the Italians gave the combination that appetizing name. The lasagna was heated for two to three days. The cimento absorbed the silver,

[84]See below, app. A, sec. v.

[85]Papadopoli, 1:124; and a forthcoming note by Philip Grierson about tests carried out at the British Museum of which he has generously given us the benefit. J. L. Bacharach, "The Dinar versus the Ducat," *International Journal of Middle East Studies* 4 (1973):93–95, reported that no ducats in the Horowits collection in Geneva came up to that standard. Perhaps that hoard which was found in Egypt represented inferior coins, perhaps selected to export further east. On the fineness of the florin, comparable at least before 1420 to the fineness of the ducat, see Bernocchi, 3:109–20.

[86]Pegolotti, *Pratica*, 140.

[87]Beginning in 1336, Venetian regulations imply that the initial separation was done outside the mint and were concerned with having the mixed metals and separated metals both reported to the bullion office at the Rialto (ASV, Zecca, b. 6bis, fols. 27–29; ASV, Senato, Misti, reg. 17, fol. 58v).

and perhaps some of the gold too if the salt solution was very strong, but what remained when the dross was removed was 24-carat gold.[88]

A somewhat similar process was used to test gold supposed to be 24-carat in order to determine whether it really was free of impurities. Its purity was accepted as confirmed if the metal and an appropriate flux were heated together for an appropriate length of time without the metal's losing any weight.

When the lasagna method was used with a strongly salty flux to extract silver as an impurity from gold, metal of considerable value was retained in the dross, called the calo. If the calo was kept by the mint, the supplier might feel that he deserved compensation. In a renewal and revision of the privileges for German importers in 1362, a compensation was provided if the gold that they supplied the mint was less than 23-carat, but there was none if the gold was more than 23-carat—presumably on the assumption that in the latter case the amount of precious metal in the cimento would be little more than enough to pay the expense of extracting it.[89] Recovering precious metals from the dross presented special problems; to meet them the mintmasters were instructed to build a special furnace for that purpose and locate it at the Giudecca because of its especially obnoxious fumes (a foretaste of Porto Marghera).[90]

While guaranteeing the Germans a market by accepting directly their imports of gold at the value set on it by the Assay Office at the Rialto, the mint received much more gold, at least in some periods, from Venetian bullion merchants who had bought either from the Germans or from importers from the Balkans, Africa, or Asia. Although they were required to have their gold already refined to the purity of only 23 1/2 carats,[91] in the early fifteenth century it was said often to be refined to 23 3/4 carats. The more they refined it themselves—that is, in establishments that they completely controlled—the more chance the merchants had of recovering for

---

[88]A description of the process, which continued in use in the Venetian mint until the nineteenth century, is in the Red Book of the English exchequer in the text published and translated by Johnson in *The De Moneta*, 84. The mixture was left in the fire three days and nights, and the amount of salt depended on the amount of the impurities (See also ibid., xl–xli, and on its use in Venice, xiii). Pegolotti, in his long description (*Practica*, 331–38) of both the removal of the silver and the recovery of gold from the cimento with quicksilver, describes placing a layer of cimento next to one of gold as "come gittase formaggio grattugiato sopra lasagne" (p. 331). A couple of centuries later, Biringuccio, (*De la pirotechnia libri X*, bk. 4, cap. 7) and Agricola (*De re metallica*, 453–57) describe a similar process with alternate layers of gold leaf but do not use the appetizing name. Agricola emphasizes the importance of slow heat and the kind of furnace needed (with illustration, p. 455).

[89]*PMV*, doc. 141.

[90]At San Zuan di Giudecca, at the east end of the island (ASV, Zecca, b. 6tris, fol. 32). Biringuccio and Agricola both mention the need of a blast furnace for the recovery of the silver.

[91]Stussi, ed., *Zibaldone da Canal*, 71; ASV, Senato Terra, reg. 4, fol. 168v (11 April 1461).

themselves all that could be recovered from the dross or from any ashes or crucibles used in any part of the process of refining.

The kinds of lasagna to be used in this test and in removing impurities became important in controversies in the early fifteenth century over efforts to make ducats really of 24-carat gold. In determining the composition of the refining lasagna and the length of time it should be heated, the mint had used the simple rule that gold would lose 6 carats of weight for each half-grain of impurity removed (these carats being the units of weight of which 1,152 constituted a mark, and the grains being each 1/4 of the 24 carats in which the fineness was calculated). That was mathematically correct in that 1,152/6 = 192 and 2 × 4 × 24 = 192. But it was found that removing 6 carats of weight per mark did not in fact assure 24-carat gold, because the flux used extracted not only silver but also some gold as well. It was decided in 1414 and reaffirmed in 1421 that the flux should remove 9 carats of weight per mark for each half-grain of impurity. That had the disadvantage of removing some gold as well as the silver, but removing some gold in the dross was regarded as necessary in order to remove all the silver and attain the gold purity that gave Venetian ducats their high reputation.[92]

When the craftsmen doing the refining had finished their work, the gold passed to a caster to be cast into ingots and have its purity again checked by assayers. As in the silver mint, the caster of gold ingots became an intermediary between the managing mintmaster and the refining craftsmen. The caster reported on and was credited for the pay due the refiners, whereas the mintmaster reported directly in his account the pay of other craftsmen. But there is no hint that the caster in the gold mint could make separate arrangements with the bullion merchants, as did the caster in the silver mint.[93]

After he had received the 24-carat gold from the caster, the managing mintmaster was enjoined to oversee personally and, with the weigher, to keep a written record both by weight and by tale of each of the following transfers: (1) from the caster to the craftsmen (lavoranti or ovrieri) who beat the gold into sheets and cut it into squares (quarelli); (2) from those lavoranti to mendadori; (3) from mendadori to lavoranti who finished the blanks ("flaoni complidi"); (4) from them to apprentices (fanti) for washing ("sblanchizar"); (5) from those apprentices to the weigher, who checked weights both by a sampling of individual blanks

---

[92]See below, app. A, sec. v.

[93]The fondadori are referred to in the early capitolare (*PMV,* doc. 30, cap. 21). They were forbidden to cast gold coin for reminting except after sending for an assayer (ASV, Zecca, b. 6bis, fol. 33). But their role between the managing mintmaster and the craftsmen doing the refining appears only in the surviving "account rendered" above cited of a managing mintmaster, dated 1485 (in ibid., serie finale, b. 3. On fol. 4v is the account, kept in marks, of ovrieri as refiners; on fol. 7v is the account of ovrieri as shearers, paid for blanks [*flaoni*]).

and by the number per mark;[94] (6) from the weigher to the moneyers, who struck the coins; and (7) from the moneyers to a chest in the mintmaster's office.[95]

In addition to all that inspection within the mint, there were several kinds of inspection from outside for both gold coins and silver coins. The accounting and auditing officials of the republic ("Raxon nuova") who went over the accounts of the mintmasters were also given the right to inspect the mint at any time, as well as to make regular weekly visits.[96] A ceremonial weekly inspection of both grossi and ducats by three members of the Quarantia to see that they were "beautiful, clean, and round" was begun in the thirteenth century.[97]

In both the silver mint and the gold mint special provisions were made to pin responsibility on the managing mintmaster. From an early date, silver grossi had small dots which were differently placed on the dies used by different mintmasters.[98] A pair of dies might strike about 10,000 coins,[99] and each managing mintmaster turned over to his successor the reserve of dies which he had been keeping under lock and key.[100] There was no need then of making all new dies, for it was relatively easy to change the privy marks so as to show which coins had been struck under which mintmaster.

There were no such privy mint marks on gold ducats. Instead, samples of all the gold ducats made during a mintmaster's tenure were kept until his term was ended and were then recast so that they could be reassayed before his account was cleared.[101]

In determining the design of the coins struck through their control of the dies, the mintmasters were supposed to be merely executing the decisions of higher authorities. The decree authorizing the coinage of the

[94]In inspecting the weight of the blanks with the tolerance of 1/4 grain referred to above, the weigher (pesador) was instructed to take a sample of the blanks in the proportion of 5 marks out of 20 and weigh each coin individually. In the earliest capitolare, any blank that weighed 1 grain less than it should was to be cut in two, and if four were found underweight, then the weights of all the blanks in the batch were to be checked individually and all that were underweight were to be cut in two. The weigher, the mintmaster, or both of them then mixed the whole batch together and took out 67 to see if they weighed within 2 carats of 1 mark. Only if they passed that check were the blanks to be given by the mintmaster to the moneyers (*PMV*, doc. 37, cap. 4). On restriction of the tolerance later to a half-grain and then to a quarter-grain see above, chap. 10, sec. iv.

[95]*PMV*, doc. 37, cap. 4.

[96]ASV, Zecca, b. 6tris, fol. 43v, cap. 107; Papadopoli, 1:360.

[97]Papadopoli, 1:321, cap. 54; *PMV*, doc. 37, cap. 24.

[98]Papadopoli, 1:98, 101, 117, 137, 301; Metcalf, *Coinage in the Balkans*, 206–7.

[99]Grierson, *Numismatics*, 109.

[100]ASV, Consiglio dei Dieci, Misti, reg. 18, fol. 18v (1473).

[101]ASV, Zecca, b. 6tris, fol. 43, cap. 106.

ducat specified that the design ("stampa") be determined by the Signoria.[102] Since each doge had at least his initials on the coins, he had reason to try to make his preferences felt and could use for that purpose his power as presiding officer of his small council which usually decided on the details of designs.

When the weight of the soldini was changed in 1369 and the desirability of a new design to distinguish them was recognized, not only the doge, his councillors, and the Chiefs of the Quarantia but also the Savii decided by majority vote to change the leone rampante to a leone seduto.[103] More controversial was the design of the new grosso authorized in 1379. After voting down a motion that would have left that question entirely to the Collegio, the Senate approved a motion stipulating that the new kind of grosso, which, like the new kind of soldino then issued, contained less silver than the old, should be distinguished by a star or some other feature.[104] When the new, big silver lira and new auxiliary copper coins were first issued under Doge Niccolò Tron, the controversies raised (which will be described in volume 2) were settled at the highest level.

## iv. CRAFTSMEN IN A CENTRALIZED WORKSHOP

Viewed as an industrial organization, the Venetian mint was an example of a centralized workshop, one of several types intermediate between independent handicraft and the factory. Prior to the industrial revolution, while retailing handicraftsmen dominated most manufacturing, the lives of many industrial workers were shaped by centralized workshops, which possessed one essential characteristic of the factory, "the assemblage of large bodies of workers in one place there to accomplish their tasks under supervision and discipline."[105] So assembled, workers who had been individually selling products of their labor became employees paid for labor services, even when they were highly paid skilled labor. In centralized workshops methods were developed and personnel were trained for the enforcement of discipline and of technical standards, prerequisites

[102]*PMV,* doc. 36.
[103]Ibid., doc. 157. Comparable decrees concerning silver coins presumably were in records now lost.
[104]Ibid., docs. 163; 164, p. 158.
[105]David Landes, "Technological Change and Development in Western Europe, 1750–1914," in *The Cambridge Economic History of Europe,* vol. 6, pt. 1 (Cambridge, 1965), 343–44, also in idem, *The Unbound Prometheus* (Cambridge, 1969), 114. In his next paragraphs, Landes emphasized the contrasting social contexts of the mechanized textile factories and earlier temporary mobilizations of many workers, for example, in naval arsenals.

for the introduction of the power-driven machinery that transformed centralized workshops into factories.[106]

In the evolution of the factory the line of ancestry best studied leads from peasant households producing under a putting-out system in regions where the textile industry had spread to the countryside, as in parts of England and Silesia, through the formation of capitalistic machineless manufactories.[107] The Venetian mint, in contrast, represents a different line of ancestry, one that leads from family workshops of specialized artisans loosely regulated by self-governing urban guilds to larger, more elaborately equipped workshops. Some were organized by merchants or master craftsmen who in spite of guild restrictions were able to become employers of numerous other masters or of a body of apprentices (so-called) and journeymen who would never become masters. Others were organized under princes, mainly for the supply of their armies or the artistic luxuries of their courts, and some were organized by guilds or city

[106]This aspect is emphasized by Herman Freudenberger in "Die Struktur der frühindustriellen Fabrik in Umriss (mit besonderer Berüchsichtigung Böhmens)," reprinted in *Wirtschafts- und Sozialgeschichtliche Probleme der frühen Industrialisierung,* ed. Wolfram Fischer (West Berlin, 1968). Emphasis on this aspect was considered a bourgeois ("bürgerlichen") distortion by Rudolf Forberger, "Zur Auseinandersetzung über das Problem des Übergangs von der Manufaktur zur Fabrik," in *Beiträge zur deutschen Wirtschafts- und Sozialgeschichte des 18. und 19. Jahrhunderts,* ed. Deutsche Akademie der Wissenschaften, Schriften des Institut für Geschichte, 1st ser., 10 (East Berlin, 1962), 177–79.

[107]Peter Kriedte, *Spätfeudalismus und Handelskapital* (Göttingen, 1980), 166–71; Jurgen Schlumbohm's chapter ("Relations of Production: Production Forces—Crises in Proto-industrialization") in Peter Kriedte, Hans Medick, and Jürgen Schlumbohm, *Industrialization before Industrialization: Rural Industry in the Genesis of Capitalism,* trans. Beate Schempp (Cambridge, 1981), 107–11. The classic descriptions of the large centralized workshops called manufactories are Adam Smith, *The Wealth of Nations* (New York, 1930), bk. 1, chap. 1; and Marx, *Capital,* vol. 1, chaps. 13 and 14. The classic analysis of processes of evolution leading to the factory was Karl Bucher, *Entstehung der Volkswirtschaft,* translated into English by S. Morley Wickett as *Industrial Organization* (New York, 1901; reprint 1968), chap. 4. Of his fifth stage, "factory work" (p. 154), he says (p. 175): "The machine is not the essential feature of the factory." He found that its essential was its way of organizing the division of labor. Luigi Dal Pane, *Storia del lavoro in Italia dagli inizi del secolo XVIII al 1815,* Storia del lavoro in Italia, ed. Amintore Fanfani, 4 (Milan, 1958), 55–58, summarizes Bucher's scheme. Amintore Fanfani, *Storia del lavoro in Italia dalla fine del secolo XV agli inizi del XVIII,* Storia del lavoro in Italia, ed. Amintore Fanfani, 3, 2d ed. (Milan, 1959), does not consider stages or the centralized workshops as such but gives data (pp. 106–12) on the large numbers of workers employed in some private shops in his discussion of "Concentrazione aziendale del lavoro." Many kinds of central workshops were described in Werner Sombart, *Der Moderne Kapitalismus* (Munich and Leipzig, 1924), vol. 2, chap. 46; and N. S. B. Gras, *Industrial Evolution* (Cambridge, Mass., 1930), chap. 7, where he described "the central workshop" as the first phase of "centralized manufactory," of which he considers the factory with power-driven machines a later phase. The traditional stage theories were thoroughly criticized, and the history of their nomenclature analyzed, in Herman Freudenberger and Fritz Redlich, "The Industrial Development of Europe: Reality, Symbols, Images," *Kyklos* 17 (1964):375–403.

governments to meet public needs. In both princely and communal work-shops guild functions atrophied.

At Venice there were three communal centralized workshops: the mint, the arsenal, and the separately managed rope factory, called the Tana. Some other Venetian industries—for example, glassmaking, tan-ning, and candlemaking—were also carried on in centralized workshops, but these privately owned workshops were smaller. It was in the commu-nal workshops that as many as 100 persons were brought together under one management, and the problems of discipline and control were faced on that scale.[108]

Communal and princely centralized workshops were created mostly in order to ensure the safeguarding and the high quality of the materials used and the products. In contrast, private entrepreneurs enlarged their workshops to cut costs, and in so doing they changed more or less the process of production. In the Venetian communal workshops the gather-ing of many workers together in one place did not necessarily bring any immediate substantial change in their work. Although under one roof, many of the craftsmen in the mint worked much as they had in scattered, separate workshops and were similarly paid. Piece rates and subcontract-ing left the masters some room for economic maneuver. A change in status came only gradually. Nevertheless, as early as the fourteenth century one can see the beginning of their transformation into salaried employees or day laborers as mint officials began taking over such traditional guild functions as upholding technical standards and controlling an individual's progress to the rank of master and shop foreman.

From the architectural point of view, Venice's mint was mostly a series of separate shops ("botteghe"). Sansovino's rebuilding of the mint in the sixteenth century probably provided much the same facilities as had the earlier structure, since he was replacing the existing building piecemeal over a ten-year period, while minting continued. His plan provided for the coinage of silver on the ground floor and of gold on the floor above. The entrance was from the east, from the Piazzetta (via a corridor through his as yet unfinished library). Within, to the right was a large open courtyard (now the main reading room of the Marciana Library).[109] On each side of the courtyard on the ground level were five vaulted rooms ("stantie over volte"), each of which was subdivided into two shops. The twenty shops were to be assigned to twenty craftsmen as follows: 12 to the ovrieri (sizers and shearers), 4 to the stampadori, 2 to those who cleaned the blanks, and two to the diemakers. The spacial divisions created by the vaulting were

---

[108]Lane, *Venice: A Maritime Republic,* chaps. 12 and 22 and sources cited in the bibliogra-phies to those chapters.

[109]Howard, *Sansovino,* 40–41. Sansovino's plan, as approved by the Council of Ten, was published by V. Lazari (see ibid., 169 n. 7); it is also in *Cap. Broche,* fols. 94v ff. See also Berchet, "Contributo," 341 ff.

### THE COURTYARD WITHIN THE MINT

The courtyard was thus restored shortly before it was converted to its present use as the main reading room of the Biblioteca Nazionale Marciana.

*Soprintendenza per i beni ambientali e architettonici di Venezia, Gabinetto fotografico.*

not initially subdivided on his plan. Most were dedicated to the production of gold coins; of the three situated at the end (towards the Piazza), one was to hold 12 mendadori of small coin, another the makers of dies for small coin. In short, the division of labor envisioned was the traditional one: each bottega in the silver mint was the responsibility of an individual master craftsman who had persons under him. The situation envisioned by Sansovino for the gold mint was seemingly more flexible, that for petty coin distinctly crowded.[110]

To the left of the entrance corridor were the staircase and then the offices and coin-storage rooms of the mintmasters and a room for refining and casting, those for silver below and for gold above. A top floor was added later, but it could not be used in summer because of heat from the sun on the low roof and heat from furnaces on floors below. For the lower floors the large, central courtyard (which was not covered over as it is now) provided air in summer and light in winter for the craftsmen whose shops were grouped around it. A well stood in the middle.[111]

The craftsmen whose working conditions and life style were changed least by their employment in the mint were the most skilled, the diemakers. Even more than most of the other craftsmen, they found a market for their skills outside the mint as well as inside and worked in the mint irregularly. Dies could be made quickly—those for a simply marked penny in perhaps fifteen minutes, those for a more complicated design like that on the grossi in very few hours. Steel dies did not have to be replaced very frequently; a moneyer could use the same die for several days.[112] But although diemakers received a monthly salary, they were not always available when wanted. More than once they were told that if they did not come whenever they were sent for, they would be discharged, fined, or both.[113] Few of them seem to have been diemakers only; most were

[110]On earlier expansion of the mint see above, n. 4. On the shops see above, n. 67; and the plan in *Cap. Broche*, fols. 95v–96. For the silver mint, the capitolare of 1278 ordered that the blanks from each furnace were to be handled separately so that the makers could be held responsible (Papadopoli, 1:318–20). The account of the managing mintmaster for gold of 1485 (ASV, Zecca, serie finale, b. 3) records payments made to a few masters named personally and to their unnamed "compagni."

[111]Howard, *Sansovino*, 41–44; Manfredo Tafuri, *Jacopo Sansovino e l'architettura del '500 a Venezia* (Padua, 1972), 82–94.

[112]Estimates of the number of coins that could be struck from the same obverse die vary from 1,800 to 10,000, with more evidence for the latter figure. The number varied with the kind of metal or alloy (Philip Grierson, "Byzantine Coinage As Source Material," in *Proceedings of the XIIIth International Congress of Byzantine Studies, Oxford, 5–10 September, 1966*, ed. J. M. Hussey et al. [Oxford, 1967], 322–23; idem, *Numismatics*, 104, 109; D. G. Sellwood, "Medieval Monetary Technique," *British Numismatic Journal* 31 [1962]:59–64).

[113]Papadopoli, 1:335, cap. 116; *PMV*, doc. 100; ASV, Zecca, b. 6tris, caps. 32, 42. In 1475 the Council of Ten required that they come to the mint every morning and afternoon (ASV, Consiglio dei Dieci, Misti, reg. 18, fol. 103).

CRAFTSMEN AT WORK IN SHOPS AROUND THE COURTYARD

A smoke-filled courtyard is pictured in the illuminated frontispiece of a register enrolling some mint workers in a mutal aid association dedicated to their patron, St. Eligius (late eighteenth century).

*BMCV, cl. IV, mariegola no. 128. Photograph by Toso.*

skilled in other kinds of metalwork.[114] In the capitolare of 1278 they are referred to sometimes as ironsmiths ("fabbri") and sometimes as engravers ("incisores" or "intagliatori"), but a regulation of about 1287 clearly implies a distinction and the employment of both.[115] At late dates there are references to ironsmiths, one of whom provided not so much dies as locks, most of which required three keys.[116] Keeping precious metals in different stages of production under lock and key in separate rooms and chests must indeed have provided many calls for a locksmith.

As engravers and metalworkers, the diemakers were part of that segment of the artisan class that was to be transformed during the sixteenth century from manual laborers into artists.[117] Through their art they became leaders in setting intellectual styles, as is illustrated by the careers of the stonecutter Michelangelo and the mason Palladio. The beginning of that process can be observed among versatile diemakers active in the Venetian mint at the end of the fifteenth century, especially in the career of Alessandro dei Leopardi, better known as Leonardo del Cavallo because of his success in casting Verrocchio's equestrian statue of Colleoni and erecting it on a worthy pedestal. He began as a diemaker in the mint in 1483, and after brilliant successes in casting his own bronze sculpture, was in later life most highly esteemed by the Venetian government for his services as a military engineer, probably in casting cannon. He was only the most talented of a group of diemakers who transformed their art during the fifteenth century. From such artist-craftsmen came the production of portrait-bearing coins of the type called "testoni," large silver pieces with the head ("testa") of the prince on their obverse. The lira Tron, issued by Doge Niccolò Tron in 1472, was the first of that type. (The first in gold was the Milanese ducat of Francesco Sforza in the 1450s.) The diemakers of that period and the artistic aspects of Doge Tron's monetary changes, together with their economic and political aspects, will be more thoroughly discussed in volume 2.

Long before diemaking had thus moved into the realm of the fine arts, a diemaker who was especially highly esteemed received special rewards. As early as 1301, Giannino Albizzi di Castello was assured of employment for four years at 100 lire per year (about 40 ducats).[118] The same

---

[114]In 1440 an Antonio Sisto (father of the Luca Sesto mentioned below?), who was described as an "aurifex" as well as the "fondator" of the bullion office at the Rialto, was granted permission to go to Austria, where he was working on a cross and other silver ornaments (ASV, Collegio, Notatorio, reg. 7, fol. 19v).

[115]In Papadopoli, 1:228, 321, 332–33, 335.

[116]ASV, Zecca, b. 1309, fol. 33 (1578).

[117]C. H. U. Sutherland, *The Art of Coinage* (London, 1955). For a fine explanation of the techniques employed in striking and casting medals, as well as excellent reproductions, see Ulrich Middeldorf and Dagmar Stiebral, *Renaissance Medals and Plaquettes* (Florence, 1983).

[118]Assuming that lire a grossi were meant (the kind of lire is not specified). (Favaro, ed., *Cassiere della bolla ducale*, docs. 51, 173.)

diemakers worked for both the silver mint and the gold mint, but of course the most precious coins received most attention. The inferior quality of some of the grossi coined under Doge Giovanni Soranzo (1312–28) may have been due to Giannino Albizzi's death, as Papadopoli suggested.[119] Usually the diemakers were chosen by the joint action of the two groups of mintmasters, and in the fifteenth century all had to be chosen from among native-born citizens or persons granted that status (cittadini originarii).[120] Family dynasties became established in the mint as in the arsenal. In 1394 two brothers named Sesto were given a raise in pay from 20 ducats per year to 30.[121] In 1457 another Sesto, Luca Sesto, petitioned successfully to be treated as a salaried official and not have deductions made from his pay because of holidays.[122] In 1483 his son was appointed to his post, but by that time the new group of artist-craftsmen were pushing the Sesto family out of center stage. In the 1470s Luca Sesto had had his salary cut by the Council of Ten because, it said, he was serving "inutilmente."[123]

The transformation of craftsmen into highly appreciated, socially important artists owed much to the existence in the Italian Quattrocento of a highly refined, varied, and well-paying demand for their products and to the direct contact between these consumers and the craftsmen. The personal, even intimate relations between craftsmen and the men and women who bought and used their products stimulated the originality and independence of the artist-craftsman. Among the makers of coins, only the diemakers could benefit even to a limited extent from that influence. Craftsmen employed in central workshops, whether in embryonic manufactories or in communal central establishments, were not stimulated by such contacts.

While the techniques of the craftsmen were little changed by their employment in the mint, their economic activities were much changed, their choices much restricted. While working in the mint they had no opportunity or need to devote time and thought to seeking customers, to obtaining supplies, to building or renting furnaces, or to sharing work with other craftsmen.

[119]Papadopoli, 1:153, citing MC, Capricornus, fol. 69, according to which on 7 May 1308 Giannino was again granted an advance on his salary, as he seems to have been earlier for his sister's wedding.

[120]Papadopoli, vol. 1, docs. 21 and 30 (1447). That they be cittadini originarii was specified in 1447 (ibid., p. 226 and doc. 30).

[121]Papadopoli, 1:228; Roberto Weiss, "La medaglia veneziana del Rinascimento e l'umanesimo," in *Umanesimo europeo e umanesimo veneziano*, ed. Vittore Branca (Florence, 1963), 339.

[122]ASV, Collegio, Notatorio, reg. 9, fol. 112. He had been exempted a few years before from a special burden placed on all "salariati" on the grounds "quod exercitium fabri et magistri stamparum erat manufactura."

[123]Papadopoli, 2:5.

SMALL MEDAL DESIGNED BY MARCO SESTO

This imitation of the style of Roman antiquity by a Venetian diemaker active at the mint about 1393–1417 is an example both of the close relationship between artist and craftsman and of the early Renaissance interest in antiquity. Here it is shown twice its actual size.

*Obv.:* +MARCVS*SESTO*ME*FECIT:V Bust of the Roman emperor Galba in profile, facing left.
*Rev.:* PAX.TIBI*-VENETIA Female personification of Venice, holding a banner in the left hand and standing on the Wheel of Fortune.

*AE, 33 mm, Museo Nazionale del Bargello, Florence, inv. no. 5882 (G. De Lorenzi, ed., Medaglie di Pisanello e della sua cerchia [Florence, 1983], no. 1). Photograph by Museo Nazionale del Bargello.*

The strikers of coins—the moneyers or minters—at Venice in the thirteenth and later centuries had none of the special rights and status that men of that craft had enjoyed earlier.[124] Even outside of Venice, Venetian moneyers were much more restricted than were the Tuscan moneyers, who operated mints for many princes. Venetians had done so in some Crusader states[125] and in Friuli for the Patriarch of Aquileia in 1255,[126] but in 1328 they were forbidden under severe penalties to farm any mint outside Venetian domains[127] (within which the mint at Venice was to become the only mint), and in 1343 they were forbidden to take employment in any foreign mint.[128] These prohibitions were reiterated in 1437 with reference especially to Turkish territory.[129] In Venice moneyers worked in assigned rooms at the mint with dies supplied to them and on blanks provided by the managing mintmaster. Each moneyer was usually assigned to either grossi or piccoli, but those who usually worked on piccoli could be assigned to grossi if there was no work for them on piccoli or other "monete parve." They were paid weekly. If the mintmaster found the work inferior—not well-centered or not clearly imprinted—he reduced by half the amount given the offending craftsman until his product improved. Each moneyer was individually bonded and individually responsible; he could not hire another to work on the blanks assigned him when he had too many nor work on those of a fellow moneyer when he had too few.[130]

Similar in their economic status to the moneyers were the other master craftsmen who formed the bulk of the workers within the mint, namely, the shearers, sizers, and refiners. Within the mint they all lost

[124]Robert S. Lopez, "An Aristocracy of Money in the Early Middle Ages," *Speculum* 28 (1953):1–43; idem, "Continuità e addattamento nel medio evo: Un millennio di storia delle associazioni di monetieri nell'Europa meridionale," in *Studi in onore di Gino Luzzatto*, vol. 2 (Milan, 1949), pp. 74–117; Cinzio Violante, *La società milanese nell'età precomunale* (Rome, 1953; reprint Bari, 1974), chap. 2; Grierson, *Numismatics*, 96–100.

[125]G. Schlumberger, *Numismatique de l'orient latin* (Paris, 1878), 470; L. Blancard, "Le besant d'or sarracinas pendant les Croisades," *Memoires de l'Académie des Sciences, Lettres et Beaux Arts de Marseilles*, 1879–80, 155.

[126]Bernardi, *Monetazione*, 29; *Cap. Broche*, fols. 32, 71–73; ASV, Consiglio dei Dieci, Misti, reg. 18, fol. 103 (1475). The writer on Friulian money in Argelati's collection refers to an "orefice veneziano dimorante in Aquileia, Gabriele di Pietro incisore dei coni e custodi della zecca," who assayed money given out by Florentine contractors operating the Aquileian mint (F. Argelati, ed., *De monetis Italiae variorum illustrium virorum dissertationes*, 6 vols. [Milan, 1750–59], 2:100, see also p. 104).

[127]ASV, Senato, Misti, reg. 60, fol. 21, refers to the law of ca. 1328, which is given in ASV, Zecca, b. 6bis, fol. 22. Enforcement, which had been left to the Avogaria, was transferred to the mintmasters. Heavy penalties were provided for operating a mint without their permission.

[128]*DQ*, vol. 1, no. 306.

[129]ASV, Senato, Misti, reg. 60, fol. 21.

[130]Papadopoli, 1:320–33, caps. 46, 48, 50, 85, 97, 107.

entrepreneurial functions, but many worked outside the mint as well as inside, either as employees of other masters or as managers of their own shops. Skills of various kinds in working precious metals enabled not only diemakers and moneyers but also refiners and other craftsmen to earn their livelihood at the mint when it was busy and to find employment in the many private workshops in the city at other times.[131] Or they could leave the city to seek work elsewhere. Moneyers of the mint could go away on leave provided they did not stay away for more than three months.[132] The extent to which the master craftsmen had shops of their own outside the mint is evident from the need to forbid their taking home work given to them in the mint.[133]

But assignment to a shop in the mint was a definite asset, so much so that moneyers could sell their positions to substitutes. As early as 1279 they were forbidden to do so;[134] and as late as 1498 such abuses were a main theme of a general reform decree of the Council of Ten. Both master shearers and moneyers were said to be too often absentees who got others to do the work assigned to them. To prevent it, mintmasters were ordered to provide silver to work on only to masters who had personally been assigned one of the twelve shops and to give them only restricted amounts.[135]

General procedures and trends of development in this communal central workshop were different from those in a capitalistic central workshop, because decisions were made, not by a private entrepreneur, but by public officials. The engagement, fining, and dismissal of master craftsmen as well as of clerks and guardians was by formal ballot by the mintmasters and weighers. All except the refiners had to be Venetians. Already in the thirteenth century, regulations tried to prevent patronage bargains on the principle baldly formulated as "accipe meum et ego accipiam tuum."[136] Positions in the mint were occasionally granted by higher councils to

---

[131]A prosperous enterprise in separating gold and silver run by the half-brothers de Martellis is mentioned in ASV, Petizion, Sentenze a Giustizia, reg. 60, fols. 75–6 (4 February 1431/32). A contract between two goldsmiths of whom one provided the silver and the work place ("stacionem") at the Rialto and the other only labor is in Tiepolo, ed., *Domenico Prete di S. Maurizio*, doc. 351, pp. 245–47. Goldsmiths were forbidden to have their shops elsewhere than in "insula Rivoalti" (ASV, Avogaria di Comun, Deliberazioni del Maggior Consiglio, Brutus, fol. 126 [23 March 1331]).

[132]They needed formal permission from the mintmasters. If they left the city without permission for more than four days, they could not resume their post in the mint during the term of those mintmasters (Papadopoli, 1:320–21, caps. 48, 51; 334, cap. 115).

[133]*Cap. Broche*, fols. 32, 71–73; ASV, Consiglio dei Dieci, Misti, reg. 18, fol. 103v. The important reform of the mint in 1475 says that mendadori had gotten into "the bad and dangerous habit of taking silver outside the mint to 'mendar'"; they were enjoined not to take silver out of the mint under the penalties for counterfeiting (*Cap. Broche*, fol. 47).

[134]Papadopoli, 1:331, cap. 97.

[135]*Cap. Broche*, fols. 72–73.

[136]Papadopoli, 1:317, caps. 31, 32.

deserving citizens even if the mint did not need them.[137] In Venice, as in European states generally, there was a growth of bureaucracy in the fourteenth and fifteenth centuries. In Venice it strengthened the dominance of the aristocracy by making more and more of the lower middle class humble petitioners for favors conferred by governing councils composed of hereditary nobles. Increasingly Venice's communal central workshops were welded into that general bureaucratic pattern.

Although not energized by a profit-seeking drive for efficiency, a communal central workshop presented some of the same difficulties and opportunities as did a capitalistic manufactory. Both fostered division of labor, the cost-cutting feature of the central workshop emphasized by Adam Smith and other economists. In contrast, when industrial production was carried on in separate craft shops each of which sold at retail, specialization, like competition, was less concerned with cutting costs than with perfection of the product. It was consumer-oriented.[138] It was reflected in the organization of separate guilds or of separate branches within a guild of craftsmen specializing in different end-products although they were users of the same kind of material. Thus first the workers in wood divided into house carpenters and ship carpenters, and then within each guild separate branches were formed for such specialized crafts as the making of rococo furniture or the building and repair of gondolas.

Similarly, among craftsmen distinguished by skill and experience with precious metals there developed within the goldsmiths' guild separate organizations for setters of precious stones and for ringmakers.[139] Silversmiths were part of that same guild, but how its specialized branches developed is obscure because of the loss of the guild's statute books.[140]

---

[137]Giorgetta Bonfiglio-Dosio furnishes many examples of special grants made by various councils and stresses the emphasis of the petitioners on their poverty, loyal service, etc. (see her "Lavoro e lavoratori." See also ASV, Grazie, reg. 6, fol. 65v; and Papadopoli, 1:337).

[138]Bronislaw Geremek, *Le salariat dans l'artisanat parisien aux XIII–XV siècles* (The Hague, 1969).

[139]Cessi and Alberti, *Rialto,* 245, mentions as "colonelli" of the jewelers' guild silversmiths and also engravers of gold and silver. Research starting with the more plentiful eighteenth-century sources might be able to trace some of the development of these and other branches.

[140]The thirteenth-century capitolare is printed in Monticolo, ed., *I capitolari delle arti,* vol. I. The most important compilations of their statutes and regulations were probably in volumes adorned with jewel-studded metalwork, which assured their quick disappearance in the plundering of the guilds' possessions at the fall of the republic. The "Capitolare di Auro seu Folia Auri," of about 1327, which Monticolo edited and which was published posthumously in his vol. 3, pp. 291–322, contains no bylaws for a guild; indeed it mentions no guild. It is a compilation of regulations controlling the activities of officials appointed to enforce rules made by the government concerning the preparation of gold leaf. The "Capitolare del Soprastante dell'Arte della folia d'oro," 1409–1583, contains regulations concerning not only the preparers of gold leaf but also the spinners of gold thread, as well as regulations concerning the relation of such craftsmen (or craftswomen) to merchants. There

Although one of the first to be organized, the goldsmiths' guild seems to have lacked the solidity of associations of the ship carpenters or the caulkers. It probably contained at its formation some very rich dealers in gems, jewelry, gold, and silver, but guildsmen certainly had no monopoly in those activities. They were open to all Venetian citizens with full trading rights. The trade in precious metals was dominated, as explained above, by general merchants or by moneychangers who were turning into bankers. The case of Zorzi Orese, one of the foremost bullion dealers of the later fifteenth century, is exceptional in that he was practically surnamed "goldsmith."[141] At the other extreme within the guild were goldbeaters and the spinners of gold thread, who were subject to special regulation. Women are mentioned in early guild statutes as makers of jewelry as well as of gold thread but not as members of the coinmaking crafts.[142]

Evidence is too scanty to indicate whether the guild organization reflected the same craft divisions as those recognized by the mint. Official regulations distinguished among engravers (diemakers), refiners, casters, shearers, sizers, and strikers (moneyers), but the overlapping and varying use of the names ovrieri, lavoranti, affinatori, and mendadori implies that these categories were not well recognized as separate crafts in any guild organization.[143]

The one specialization that clearly depended on the gathering of many workers inside one building was that between shearers and sizers. It was not a result of an effort to cut costs but, as described above, appears as

---

is no reference to the mint before the requirement in 1518 that all these workers register at the mint (cap. 18), a rule that explains why this capitolare is in the archive of the mint (ASV, Zecca, b. 7). A parchment-bound booklet in ASV, Zecca, b. 1318, entitled "Mariegola . . . dell'Arte di Batte o Tira Oro," on which are written the dates 1419–1583 seems to be a later copy or version. Of little value in this context except for the quality of the gold and silver used in gilded tableware are seventeenth- and eighteenth-century copies of a fourteenth-century mariegola in the BMCV, cl. IV, nos. 139 and 205.

[141] See vol. 2.

[142] Monticolo, ed., I capitolari delle arti, 1:122, caps. 21, 22, 46, 47.

[143] See below, app. B, sec. i. In the capitolare of 1278 and most clearly in the long reforming regulation of 1417 "ovrieri" is the term used for the shearers who rounded off the blanks (Papadopoli, 1:362). "Ovrieri" is also the term most used for those who refined the metal before giving it to the fondador, but in a few places these craftsmen are more precisely specified as "affinadori" Biringuccio, De la pirotechnia libri X, fol. 132v, refers to the following "ministri" employed by a mintmaster: "coniatori" (equivalent to the Venetian monetari), "giustatori del peso" (referred to only by this descriptive phase), "ouerieri," "fondatori," and "stampanini." These "little hammermen" flattened the strips or squares to the desired thinness (ibid., fol. 133v). Their counterparts in Venice presumably were the apprentices (fanti) of fondadori or ovrieri. Both Trasselli, regarding the Sicilian mints, and Spufford, regarding those of Burgundy, found all craftsmen except the moneyers commonly lumped together as "operai" or "ouvriers" (Trasselli, Zecche e monete, 121–31; Peter Spufford, "Mint Organisation in the Burgundian Netherlands in the Fifteenth Century," in Studies in Numismatic Method Presented to Philip Grierson, ed. C. N. L. Brooke et al. [Cambridge, 1983], 242).

### ST. ELIGIUS STRIKING COINS

This stained-glass window was offered to the Cathedral of Milan
by the local goldsmiths' guild. It depicts their patron, St. Eligius,
at work in the mint of the king of France. Work of the artist
Nicolò da Varallo, dated between 1480 and 1488.

*Fabbrica del Duomo, Milan; Archivio-Fototeca.*

an effort to attain a high standard in making equal in weight all coins of the same denomination.[144]

Aside from the craftsmen and their apprentices, the mint's employees seem to have numbered hardly more than a dozen who might be considered part of the central staff, such as the bookkeepers and the servants of the mintmasters, and another half-dozen or more who were unskilled laborers.[145] Many of the latter are referred to as apprentices (fanti), and among the underlings in the refinery were certainly some young men learning the secrets of that craft. Through a vote of the mintmasters and other officials, an apprentice was promoted to "mezo maistro" in 1432.[146] When yearly salaries were voted for three master refiners in 1460, the salaries were made subject to the condition that they take, support, and train apprentices approved by the mintmasters.[147] In contrast, a group of eight who petitioned for and obtained a raise in pay for themselves from 8 to 9 soldi in 1402 described themselves as "famuli" in the silver mint who had twice as much work as the famuli in the gold mint, burning their clothes in work in the foundry during the day and standing guard at night.[148] More than a century later a group of four workers in the silver mint called "fanti" and paid 9 lire per month described their work as carrying bags of coin and charcoal up and down stairs, building fires for the shearers, and washing silver and copper coins, as well as working in the foundry—in short, being available day and night for all kinds of heavy but unskilled labor.[149] In addition to these general-purpose "apprentices," there presumably were many others who were real apprentices, perhaps sons, of skilled master shearers, sizers, and moneyers who supported or paid them.

The pay of apprentices, like that of top management, was fixed by month or by year, but the pay of the master craftsmen depended primarily on how much was produced.

A comparison of piece rates paid moneyers, sizers, and shearers is presented in table 7. What these rates yielded as daily or monthly earnings depended not only on the speed with which the men worked but also on the amount and kinds of materials distributed to them.

Shearers felt that they were being underpaid when in 1424 they were getting 4 soldi per mark for preparing blanks of piccoli or torneselli. At that rate, they said in petitioning for a raise, they could not make more than 8 soldi a day, and 8 soldi a day was not enough to live on, thus clearly

[144]Papadopoli, 1:320, cap. 45.
[145]ASV, Zecca, b. 6tris, fols. 32v, 45; *Cap. Broche,* fol. 73; *PMV,* docs. 37, 107; Papadopoli, 1:322, cap. 60, and 334, cap. 114; ASV, Consiglio dei Dieci, Misti, reg. 18, fol. 103.
[146]*Cap. Broche,* fol. 38v.
[147]Ibid., fol. 34v.
[148]Bonfiglio-Dosio, "Lavoro e lavoratori," n. 25.
[149]Ibid., n. 26.

TABLE 7.

Some Piece Rates Paid in the Venetian Mint, 1406–42
(In Denari Piccoli per Mark Processed)

| Coins and Year(s) | Piece Rate Paid to: | | |
| --- | --- | --- | --- |
| | Moneyers | Sizers | Shearers |
| Grossi for Venice, 1417–24 | 16 | 16 | 36 |
| Soldi for Venice, 1417–24 | 36 | 36 | 60 |
| Piccoli, 1412–24 or 1442 | 32 | 0 | 48 |
| Soldi for Zara, 1410 | 30 | 24 | 48 |
| Soldi for Verona, 1406 | 32 | 24 | 52 |
| Grossoni for Brescia, 1429 | 19 | 12 | 36 |
| Torneselli, before 1424 | ? | 16 | 48 |

SOURCES:
For grossi and soldi for Venice, 1417, see Papadopoli, 1:362, and *Cap. Broche,* fol. 20v. The entry on fol. 24 gives the same rates as those also being paid in 1424, when, however, the pay of the sizers was raised from 36 piccoli per mark to 54 when working on soldi and from 16 piccoli per mark to 18 when working on grossi. The rate for shearers working on soldi was raised from 60 piccoli to 66. In 1391 the rate for sizers on soldi had been 22–24 piccoli per mark (*Cap. Broche,* fol. 7v). In 1384 for work on grossi the rate for shearers had been raised from 24 piccoli to 36, that of sizers from 8 piccoli to 12 (ibid., fol. 4v).

For piccoli in 1442 see Papadopoli 1:367; and *Cap. Broche,* fol. 29. The rate for shearers rose from 48 piccoli to 60 in 1424 (*Cap Broche,* fol. 24).

For soldi for Zara in 1410 see ibid., fol. 16v. The pay of the minters is given as 16 soldi per sack (sacco) weighing 6 marks 3 ounces. It is entered as 30 piccoli because 16 × 12/6.325 = 30.36. The shearers also received 3 marks per 100 for calo.

For soldi for Verona in 1404 see ibid., fol. 14v.

For "grossi grandi," or grossoni, for Brescia in 1429 see ibid., fol. 25, where the pay for the minters is given as 10 soldi per sack. If the sack weighed 6 marks 3 ounces as stipulated regarding coins for Zara, the rate per mark was 19 piccoli, since 120/6.325 = 18.97.

For torneselli in 1424 see ibid., fol. 24, which records the rise in the rate for sizers in December of that year from 16 piccoli per mark to 18 and for shearers from 48 piccoli per mark on both torneselli and piccoli to 60 piccoli. In 1377 the rate for shearers on torneselli had been raised from 40 to 48 (ibid., fol. 2).

On labor costs by crafts in other mints see the note to table 6 and the valuable, much more complete, list for Venice in Bonfiglio-Dosio, "Lavoro e lavoratori," table 1. The Quaderno de la Quindexena, which concerns the gold mint in 1485, records specific payments made to a few craftsmen, identified by name, and their work group ("e compagni") rather than individual payments to a list of all craftsmen. ASV, Zecca, serie finale, b. 3.

implying that the individual shearer when working on piccoli and torneselli, which were largely copper, could not process more than 2 marks a day. Their protest was successful, and the piece rate was raised to 5 soldi per mark, so that they could make 10 soldi a day when working on piccoli or torneselli.[150] The 10 soldi per day was what they could have made

[150]The petition was considered on 18 November 1424 by the Senate, which passed the matter on to the Collegio; the latter authorized a raise on the same day and, together with a

before 1424 by processing 2 marks per day while preparing the blanks for soldini.[151]

The favorable response to the petition of the shearers was part of a general raising of piece rates in 1424 (see notes to tables 6 and 7). It is likely that the raise was felt to be necessary in order to attract workmen. In fact, the new rates were set at a doubly important juncture. First, in the previous year Venice, in the most serious outbreak of plague since the Black Death, had lost perhaps as much as 20 percent of the population. Surely workers at the mint were not spared, and a certain number probably had to be replaced from a sharply reduced number of potential candidates.[152] Second, this was a time when the mint was very active during a recoinage at the end of the trade war with Emperor Sigismund, which had reduced bullion imports in the previous decade. It was the period of high output reflected (and probably somewhat exaggerated) in Doge Mocenigo's "Death Bed Oration."

A daily wage of 10 soldi di piccoli seems very low for skilled labor, at least when compared with 32 soldi per day for stonecutters,[153] 22 soldi in winter and 32 soldi in summer for caulkers,[154] 20 soldi as compensation for silk weavers who lost a day's work,[155] 10 soldi for the unskilled laborers in the arsenal,[156] or 8–9 soldi for the mint's own "apprentices."[157] Ten soldi per day was roughly equivalent to 24 gold ducats a year if they

---

special committee, worked out details on 20 December (ASV, Collegio, Notatorio, reg. 6, fol. 3v; *Cap. Broche*, fol. 24).

[151]Before 1424, shearers had been able to make 10 soldi per day by shaping 2 marks of soldini at the piece rate of 60 piccoli per mark (cf. above, table 7). Since it took more soldini than torneselli to weigh 1 mark (see below, app. A, sec. vii), the rates were not out of proportion to the size of the coins, but the relative difficulty of shaping the silver soldini and the largely copper torneselli may have been a factor. More difficult to explain is paying the same rate for both piccoli and torneselli. Although of similar alloy, 962 piccoli but only about 400 torneselli were produced from a mark (see ibid., secs. viii and ix). It may have been connected with the lack of any sizers in the preparation of piccoli and as a result with less careful work by the shearers in their cutting of the blanks for piccoli. Earlier, in 1391, sizers had preferred work on torneselli to work on soldi under the new quality-control regulations then introduced (see above, sec. iii).

[152]See Reinhold C. Mueller, "Aspetti sociali ed economici della peste a Venezia nel Medioevo" and successive contributions in *Venezia e la peste, 1348–1797* (Venice, 1979), 84, 93. The previous very serious outbreak, in 1400, had led to an increase in builders' wages in Venice as elsewhere (ibid., 74; and below, vol. 2).

[153]Wirobisz, "L'attività edilizia a Venezia," 334.

[154]Lane, *Navires et constructeurs*, 74.

[155]Romolo Broglio d'Ajano, "L'industria della seta a Venezia," in *Storia dell'economia italiana*, ed. Carlo M. Cipolla, vol. 1 (Turin, 1959), p. 250.

[156]Lane, *Navires et constructeurs*, 153–54; Luzzatto, *Storia*, 234; and idem, *Studi*, 297, in general on the cost of living.

[157]Bonfiglio-Dosio, "Lavoro e lavoratori," table 2. Marco Sanuto, in calculating the costs of changes that he proposed in methods of casting (as described above, in sec. ii), calculated the cost of two additional fanti at 8 lire per month each.

worked 20 days a month, since at that time a ducat sold for about 100 soldi di piccoli (10 soldi per day = ca. 10 lire per month = 10 × 12 = 120 lire per year = 2,400 soldi/100 = 24 ducats). These comparisons make 10 soldi per day seem like an absolute minimum for skilled craftsmen.

Because of the nature of their crafts, the moneyers who struck the coins probably earned more per month or year than did shearers. Since the piece rate paid them for processing grossi was less than half as many piccoli per mark as the rate paid the shearers, more than two shearers were required to prepare enough blanks to keep a moneyer sufficiently employed so that he could earn even as much as a shearer (see below, appendix B).

From one week to another, earnings probably varied erratically and seasonally both in the mint and in the building trades. Building trades were more directly affected by the weather, to be sure, but the seasonal nature of Venice's import and export of gold and silver, dependent on ships and Alpine passes, created contrasting periods of feast and famine also for shearers and moneyers. Illness and lack of will added to the irregular pattern. Richard Goldthwaite concluded from his study of the Florentine building industry that "the worker himself did not have the hope, if even the desire, for regular employment."[158] On the other hand, the workers needed a minimal yearly income, and the managers of the mint needed a core of dependable employees.

As a result, there developed a system of combining fixed yearly salaries and payments varying with the amount produced. That combination had been applied very early to the highest officials, the mintmasters and the weighers.[159] At first their yearly salary was more important than the variable element called their "utilitates." A weigher with a salary of 80 ducats per year was said in 1404 to receive as his "utilitates" about 8 ducats.[160] But when the volume of production was high, the total "take," especially of the mintmasters, was considerable.[161] The combination was also applied at a relatively early date to other members of the central staff and to supervisory or special services. The bookkeeper's 3 piccoli per mark (see table 6) was in addition to his regular yearly salary of 40 ducats.[162]

[158]*The Building of Renaissance Florence*, 330.

[159]In her analysis of the *Capitolare dalle broche*, Bonfiglio-Dosio ("Lavoro e lavoratori") describes the combination of salary and "utilitates" as if it were applied to all employees. It did indeed become general, but we can find no evidence that it was applied to the main body of craftsmen—the shearers, sizers, and moneyers—before 1468. In his "Ricavi e costi," table 1, Felloni distinguished in the Genoese mint "salari a cottimo" from "salari a tempo," but in his table 4, all those paid "a tempo" appear to have been supervisors.

[160]*Cap. Broche*, fol. 14.

[161]"Traité du gouvernement de Venise," fol. 120; Bonfiglio-Dosio, "Lavoro e lavoratori," table 2.

[162]*Cap. Broche*, fol. 14. When an additional bookkeeper for special duties at the refinery was authorized in 1417, his salary was set at 80 ducats per year (Papadopoli, 1:357; on his "utilitates" see ASV, Consiglio dei Dieci, Misti, reg. 18, fol. 103v).

The two gastaldi, whose duties in inspecting the work of the sizers in 1391 have been described above, were rewarded then for their increased responsibility by an increase in pay from 2 piccoli for each mark of soldi produced to 4 (or 3 if torneselli). When they were voted 30 ducats per year in 1417, the decree specified that they would have also perquisites ("le sue regalie").[163] Regular salaries were paid to one or two assayers,[164] to a maker of shears,[165] and to the diemakers,[166] although the latter may perhaps be said to have received "retainers" obligating them to come when called but leaving them free to sell their skills in engraving and metalwork to other customers as well.

For the main body of master craftsmen the first provision of a minimal regular income was taken in 1468 because less silver than usual was then being coined as a result of the cutoff in the production of grossi. The hardships that that imposed on the ten shearers ("operarii") who were shop foremen ("capita apothecharum") led the Senate to vote them 2 ducats per month for a year, although making it conditional on their taking and teaching apprentices.[167] In 1471 the Council of Ten extended the 2 ducats per month to eleven masters to assure those workers enough to live on. The permanence of this minimal salary was sufficiently in doubt that the managing mintmaster in 1476 decided against paying it. The shearers appealed successfully to the Council of Ten in terms that implied that they would not have been asking it if they had had enough work to earn it by piece rates. The Council of Ten ordered that they should receive 1 1/2 ducats per month provided that they worked personally and diligently.[168] The 1 1/2 ducats per month was probably a minimum to be paid when not enough coins were being minted to enable the shearers to earn more. Or it may have been initially—as it was later—a supplement to what they were earning at piece rates. In 1479 the amount was raised to 2 ducats per month.[169]

Monthly salaries for coinmakers thus began as measures to maintain a desired labor force during slack times, measures comparable to those taken in the fifteenth century to guarantee employment in the arsenal to ship carpenters and caulkers so as to maintain the supply of that strategic

---

[163]Papadopoli, 1:360.

[164]Bonfiglio-Dosio, "Lavoro e lavoratori," table 2.

[165]*Cap. Broche,* fol. 16v. The craft of Antonio de le Forfede is inferred from his name (the Venetian *forfe* means "scissors" or "shears").

[166]See above, n. 39, and below, n. 174; and Bonfiglio-Dosio, "Lavoro e lavoratori," table 2.

[167]ASV, Senato Terra, reg. 6, fol. 40v (8 November 1468).

[168]*Cap. Broche,* fol. 48. There was little or no production of silver coin in Venice in 1468–72, a plight experienced also by the mint of Milan (see Mueller, "Guerra monetaria tra Venezia e Milano nel Quattrocento"; and below, vol. 2).

[169]*Cap. Broche,* fol. 49v. At that date the quotation of the ducat in lire di piccoli was stabilized at 124, so that the raise that the Council of Ten voted in 1478 from 1 1/2 to 2 ducats per month was equivalent to a raise from 8.9 soldi to 11.9 soldi per day.

labor force. Actual earnings of the mint's craftsmen probably averaged much above 10 soldi per day, which was close to the subsistence level. To match the pay of skilled arsenalotti, the master craftsmen in the Commune's other big industrial establishment, master craftsmen in the mint had to earn about 24 soldi per day, or about 50 ducats per year. The base salary of the top foremen in the arsenal was 100 ducats a year. The most energetic and highly esteemed shipwrights could get even higher rates when they were selected for special tasks by private employers,[170] and that was probably true also of some mint workers who also worked on the outside as goldsmiths and silversmiths.

After the system of combining regular salaries and piece rates was applied to the shearers, it was extended to other craftsmen, although only to a limited number. Salaried employees must have been a minority among the silversmiths and goldsmiths employed during the monetary expansion of the sixteenth century, for a list of salaried employees compiled in 1606 included in a total of 72 only the following: of shearers, 4 for silver, 2 for gold, at 2 ducats per month; of sizers, 6 for silver, none for gold, at 1 ducat 10 grossi per month; of moneyers, none for silver, 3 for gold, at 2 ducats per month. The supervisory and central administrative staff numbered 34, including the mintmasters and many bookkeeping and financial officials needed for the role that the mint had by then acquired in managing the public debt. Included under the category of apprentices, in addition to some with specific functions, were 4 "all'arzento" and 4 "all'oro," each paid 4–5 ducats per month.[171] That the "salaries" of the "fanti" were higher than "salaries" of the master craftsmen shows that the earnings of the latter depended mainly on what they earned at piece rates. And the many craftsmen who must have been added when the demand for coinage was high presumably received only piece rates.

As substitute for or as supplement to salaries, piece rates were judged necessary to assure that the craftsmen did not spend their time in the mint loafing. With no machinery dictating speed, there was little except piece rates to keep men at work. Only the most elementary aspects of factory discipline were stressed, namely, attendance at regular hours and control of who entered.[172] Not maximum output but work of high quality was

---

[170]Lane, *Navires et constructeurs*, 118–19, 172.

[171]BMCV, Arch. Donà dalle Rose, b. 161, fol. 80. Under the heading "1606, Salariadi della Ceccha" are listed the personal names of seventy-two individuals with their position and monthly salary, which are added up and multiplied by 12 to give a total of 5,280 ducats. Included are one or two in such specialized categories of craftsmen as ironsmiths, assayers, and diemakers (two maestri delle stampe for silver at 10 ducats per month and none for gold). The proportionally very small number of shearers, sizers, and moneyers shows that most craftsmen in those categories did not receive monthly salaries from the mint.

[172]*Cap. Broche*, fol. 7v; Papadopoli, 1, capitolare of 1278, passim.

the objective that the mintmasters were instructed to strive for. It was also the concern of guild officials in their inspection of the work of masters, whether outside or inside the mint. Before they created a supervisory staff of their own, the mintmasters could appeal to guild officials for aid in spotting and penalizing poor workmanship. The capitolare of 1278 provided that when a sizer was turning out blanks that were not of proper weight, the gastaldo of the sizers should be summoned and asked to identify the craftsman responsible. If he could not or would not, the gastaldo had to pay the cost of remaking the blanks.[173]

Before the end of the fourteenth century, however, the duty of checking the quality of workmanship was taken over by inspectors appointed and paid by the mintmasters. The single inspector on duty in 1391 was supplemented by a second with the introduction then of the program described above to standardize more accurately the weight of soldini. In 1417 the Senate ordered that the selection of these two "gastaldi da puovolo" be made jointly by the mintmasters and the Signoria, that they be paid a regular salary of 30 ducats per year, that they be present whenever money was being sheared and sized, and that they have no other task in the mint other than inspection.[174] When the Council of Ten took over a half-century later, it felt that because these gastaldi shared in the emoluments, they should do some of the work, and issued orders accordingly. It also ordered the appointment of an additional inspector, whose assignment was to see that the design on the new, big silver coin then being issued, the tron, was clear and well centered. If he let 3 bad coins pass, he was to be fired. The job went to one of the incumbent gastaldi.[175]

Long after the guild lost technical control of the craftsmen who were employed in the mint, some guild social customs persisted. One was the obligation of an apprentice or journeyman to give a dinner to celebrate his admission as a master—at least that seems the likely origin of the expectation of all the officials and moneyers already employed that they would be entertained at such a feast given by any newly engaged moneyer. Protesting that poor men were being ruined by having to spend 4–5 ducats at

---

[173]"Gastaldo" was a common title for the head of a guild. It was also the title of executive officers of the courts, but in the capitolare of the mintmasters (Papadopoli, 1:319, cap. 43) a "gastaldio mendatorum" is mentioned, and the preceding provision in cap. 40 requiring only his limited attendance at the mint implied that he was not primarily a mint employee as were the gastaldi appointed in the fifteenth century. The position of the gastaldi in the guilds was sometimes ambiguous, to be sure, since they did not originate out of the voluntary religious association of men of the same occupation ("scuola") but were initially officials responsible to the doge for enforcing on the men of the craft their obligations (Monticolo, ed., *I capitolari delle arti*, vol. 2, pt. 1, pp. xxiv–xv, lxvi, cvii; Molmenti, *Storia*, vol. 1, chap. 5, on the general relation between scuole and arti).

[174]Papadopoli, 1:360, on the appointment ordered in 1417 of two gastaldi.

[175]ASV, Consiglio dei Dieci, Misti, reg. 18, fols. 18, 103.

such parties, where drinking led to fighting, the Quarantia forbade such dinners twice in the 1350s.[176]

In contrast to the arsenalotti, the goldsmiths or silversmiths of the mint did not have the social-security benefits offered by such strong guilds as those of the ship carpenters and the caulkers. Efforts in the sixteenth century to provide the kind of health or accident insurance furnished by many other guilds show that the craftsmen in the mint lacked that kind of guild assistance and felt the need for it. The preamble to an association formed in 1560 by 52 members of the Guild of Goldsmiths and Jewelers expressed their desire for the kind of benefits in times of illness that were enjoyed by the shipwrights, caulkers, sawyers, and house carpenters. Two distinct, apparently rival mutual-aid societies had been formed some years earlier by craftsmen employed in the mint.[177] The existence of these special fraternities suggests the weakness of the inherited guild organization. Not only did it fail to control piece rates, speed of production, working conditions, or even technical competence in the mint but it failed also to provide as much social security as did strong Venetian guilds. The trend towards a bureaucratic structure adulterated by aristocratic patronage was not balanced by any organization among the work force.

[176]*DQ*, vol. 2, docs. 115, 383.

[177]Fervent expression of admiration for the support given the "poveri infermi" by other guilds is in the mariegole of the scuola founded in 1560 (BMCV, cl. IV, Mariegole, no. 140). Two similar fraternities among workers in the mint both seem to have been founded earlier, on 10 October 1540, for there are in the BMCV two mariegole quite different in content bearing that date (cl. IV, nos. 62 and 128). One was entitled "Mariegola dei Stampadori di Zecca." As late as 1806, after the fall of the republic, that "fraterna" was trying to collect 2,704 ducats that it claimed were owed it by the mint.

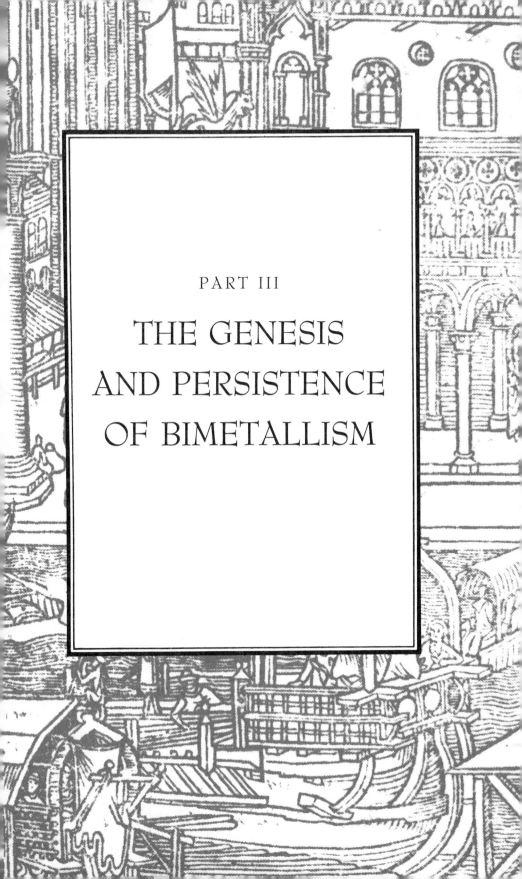

PART III

# THE GENESIS
# AND PERSISTENCE
# OF BIMETALLISM

# 13

## COMPETING MONEYS AND VENICE'S FIRST BIMETALLIC STANDARD

FTER BEING ON A SILVER STANDARD for centuries, Venice shifted to a bimetallic standard, or rather to a series of bimetallic standards, as the use of gold increased. Some shifts occurred in usage independently of their legal formulation, just as in England the shift from a silver to a gold standard during the eighteenth century occurred in practice before it was recognized in legislation.[1] In Venice, however, as in Florence, the simultaneous use of several different monetary standards— reflected in the simultaneous use of several moneys of account, each linked to a different coin—interfered with any complete transition from a silver to a gold standard during the fourteenth century. At the same time, efforts to unify Venice's monetary system with a bimetallic standard were complicated by Venice's position as a central bullion market.

### i. SILVER AND BILLON COINS CIRCULATING WITHIN VENICE

Back before Venice began minting gold, it had a different kind of bimetallic problem, a problem arising from treating as legal tender both the grosso which was 96 percent silver and the piccolo which was 75 percent copper and only 25 percent silver as coined by Doge Lorenzo Tiepolo (1268–75). In his day, Venice may for a time have had two standards of exchange value, one based on the billon piccolo, the other on the silver grosso, but they were tied together into a single standard after 1282,

---

[1]See above, chap. 4.

when the exchange was maintained at the rate of 32 lire di piccoli for 1 lira di grossi.[2]

That standard was bimetallic in that it was based on the use of the two metals copper and silver, and like any bimetallic standard, it was potentially unstable. Its stability was threatened by any substantial variation in the market value of the two coins. The market value was determined mainly by the metal they contained but partly by the labor they embodied and by the level of demand relative to the quantity minted.

The metallic content of both coins remained substantially unchanged for many decades after 1282. According to the minting regulations, a freshly coined grosso contained 36 times as much silver as a piccolo, even though the piccolo was accepted in exchange at its legal value, which was 1/32 that of the grosso. About half of the difference between the legal and metallic values (between 1/36 and 1/32) can be attributed to the higher cost of manufacturing piccoli. For grossi the cost of manufacture was roughly 2 percent of the value of the product, while for piccoli it was roughly 8 percent. The 6 percentage points of difference were enough to raise from 1/32 to 1/34 the comparative value of the piccolo. As explained in our introductory discussion of metallic equivalents of moneys of account, 1/34 can be called the relative "cost value" of the piccolo—a valuation including not only its silver value but also the value of the added labor required to manufacture the smaller coin.[3]

The other half of the difference between the silver value and the legal value can be attributed to seigniorage, or potential seigniorage. It was a

---

[2]See above, chaps. 8, sec. iii, and 10, sec. v.

[3]On the piccolo of Lorenzo Tiepolo of ca. 1270 the total mint charge was 9.2 percent, and from 1282 to 1343 it was 13 percent on free silver (see below, app. A, secs. iii and iv and table A.5). At Florence in that period the mint charge varied between 5 percent and 18 percent (Bernocchi, 3:169). The expenses incurred in coinage, exclusive of seigniorage or any profit for the Commune, were, to be sure, much less than the total mint charge. For Venice the earliest documented figure of expenses for piccoli, dated 1369, was 6.2 percent (see below, app. A, sec. viii). These indications support a rough estimate of 8 percent as the manufacturing cost of the piccolo. On fine silver coins, in contrast, the total mint charge was 2.1 percent on the old grossi, and usually 2.5 percent on the new grossi issued after 1379 (See ibid., secs. iv and vii). Since the seigniorage on the old grosso was moderate and that on the new grosso was kept low by Venice's monetary wars with mainland neighbors ca. 1400, an average estimated labor cost can be put at 2 percent. When in 1414 the mint's charges on fine silver were first specified as a fee calculated from an itemized list of expenses of manufacture, mostly labor, the costs were 1.8 percent for grossi and 2.6 percent for soldini (see below, table A.5 and app. A, sec. vii). In short, manufacture added about 8 percent to the intrinsic value of billon coins and only about 2 percent to the intrinsic value of fine silver coins; there was a 6 percent difference in the cost of minting. Since the silver value of the piccolo (0.058 grams) was 1/36 that of the grosso (2.1 grams), adding the 6 percent additional cost of manufacture made the cost value of the piccolo equivalent to the value of 0.06148 grams of silver (0.06148 is 1/34.16 of 2.1).

profit that the government could collect so long as it used its monopoly of coinage to restrict the amount available to such an extent that the coins had scarcity value. The utility of having small coins for small purchases and making change gave the piccoli an exchange value higher than their cost value so long as the supply of piccoli was limited. If great quantities of piccoli had been minted, they would no longer have been accepted as worth 1/32 of a grosso. Grossi would have commanded a premium, or piccoli would have functioned as "bad money" according to Gresham's law. Grossi as "good money" would have been driven into hoards or into export. In 1282, any such undermining of the circulation of the grosso in Venice and its dominance as the standard of value had been prevented by the restrictions placed on the coinage of piccoli under the successor to Lorenzo Tiepolo and continued under Giovanni Dandolo (1280–89).[4] Thereafter, as long as the number of piccoli in circulation did not exceed the need for coins of that denomination, the utility-scarcity value of the piccoli, added to their full cost value, gave them an exchange value equal to their legal value, and Venice's billon coinage acted jointly with its fine silver coinage in supporting a single monetary standard.

Venice's main monetary problem under Giovanni Dandolo was well characterized by Roberto Cessi as "the defense of the grosso."[5] A unified stable monetary standard depended on maintaining the use and prestige of the grosso against two threats. One came from the increased use of the new type of gold coin minted by Florence and Genoa, an innovation that was accompanied by a fall in the value of silver compared with that of gold. Under Giovanni Dandolo, Venice tried to parry that threat by issuing its gold ducat in 1284–85 on terms that would enhance the relative value of the silver grosso, as will be explained below, in section iv.

A second threat came from the other side, from the circulation of billon or silver coins containing much less silver than the grosso but winning acceptance within Venice at more than their intrinsic value. The restrictions placed on the minting of piccoli by the mint statutes of about 1278, reinforced probably by the reluctance of both craftsmen and officials of the mint to turn out the small coin of low value which required more work for less return, led to the production of even fewer than were needed. Before the end of the dogeship of Giovanni Dandolo, special instructions were given to the mintmasters to produce more piccoli, and in 1291 the restrictions were treated as obsolete. By that date, a shortage of piccoli had opened the way for an influx of billon and silver coins of foreign manufacture which was causing alarm.

The lack of any general prohibition against the use of foreign coin

4See above, chap. 10, sec. v.
5*PMV*, xxxvi–xxxix.

GROAT OF TYROL, TYPE I

Coined at Merano by Count Mainardo II (1259–ca. 1274), these
groats were valued at Venice legally at 20 or 22 piccoli.
*Obv.:* **+:COMES:TIROL:** Eagle with wings spread, facing right.
*Rev.:* **.DE. MA RA NO** Long cross.

*AR, 20.8 mm, 1.33 gr. Museo Bottacin, inv. no. 2 (CNI, 6:98, no. 50.)*

favored this influx. Products of the imperial mint at Verona were still generally accepted in Venice even by government officials,[6] and other nearby mints increased their output in the last quarter of the thirteenth century. Silver mines in the upper valley of the Adige became very productive, and both pennies and groats from the mint of the count of Tyrol at Merano were widely diffused in Italy between 1270 and 1306. Many bore the imperial eagle and were sometimes referred to as aquilini. Weighing 1.6 grams and, if they were like earlier issues at Verona, 0.956 fine, these groats were intermediate in value between Venetian piccoli and Venetian grossi. The Tyrolese issues were called "Kreuzer" in German-speaking lands, where they also circulated widely, and sometimes "de croce" in Italy. From their values in money of account both Tyrolese and Veronese groats were named "pieces of xx" or "pieces of xxii" ("vigintiarii" or "denarii a vigintiduobus").[7] Among coins being imported by Germans in 1277, along with florins and groats in general, pennies from Tyrol and pieces of xx ("Zwanziger") are mentioned specifically. They were subjected to a tax of 5 percent (revised in 1332). The tax may have been meant to discourage the importation of coin instead of bullion but certainly did not forbid it.[8] In the 1320s a Venetian notary recorded that many payments

---

[6]The action of the Maggior Consiglio in 1282 setting the value of the grosso at 32 piccoli included a prohibition of the acceptance by government offices in Venice of any pennies (denarios) except those of Venice and "grossatos de Verona." But that prohibition implies their acceptance in the city for other payments (Monticolo, ed., *I capitolari delle arti*, 3:309, cap. 29. That clause does not appear in the versions of that resolution in the Deliberazioni del Maggior Consiglio, but Monticolo says that the record from which he took it is of earlier date than the surviving record of the Deliberazioni [see his n. 4, p. 309]). Some specific coins were banned at various times, or subject to a tax that may well have had the same effect (for the tax on large silver and gold coins imported by Germans see below, chap. 15; and *DMC*, 2:302 [1277], but note the defeat of a proposal in 1358 to ban pieces of xx originating in Tyrol [*PMV*, doc. 132]).

[7]Aldo Stella, *Politica ed economia nel territorio trentino-tirolese dal XIII al XVII secolo* (Padua, 1958), 10–15, 32, and 51, table 1, for weights and fineness at various dates. Roberto Cessi calls the pieces of xx "grossi veronesi" in "Studi sulla moneta veneziana: II. La coniazione del ducato aureo," *Economia. Rassegna mensile di politica economica* (Trieste) 2 (1924):42–52 (p. 1 of the offprint). "Aquilini" might refer to any coin with the imperial eagle which was common on the groats minted on the Terraferma, but the association of the pieces of xx and of xxii with German merchants suggests Tyrol. Edoardo Martinori, *La moneta: Vocabolario generale* (Rome, 1915; reprint 1977), 13–14, 528, calls them "tirolini," coined at Merano since 1267, weighing 1 to 1.55 grams, 0.900 fine. Bloch, "Le problème de l'or," in *Mélanges historiques*, 2:860 and in *Land and Work*, 211, refers to their importance. In ASV, Avogaria di Comun, Raspe, reg. 3641, fol. 32 (1326), there is reference to "aquilini a xx et xxii et non bene ac juste lige." The inventory of cash on hand in the estate of Paolo Signolo at his death in 1348 (ASV, PSM, Ultra, b. 88) included "monete a xxii," also called "aquilini," as well as ducats, florins, grossi, mezzanini, soldini, and "parvi falsi." A new issue in 1330 by Verona of a "moneta di 20 piccoli" is mentioned in Zanetti, *Nuova raccolta*, 4:166–67.

[8]Stella, *Politica ed economia*, 30 n. 107; *PMV*, xxxi and the repeal in docs. 94, 132. See also *DMC*, 2:302; and above, chap. 11, sec. ii.

of lire di grossi were made in "pieces of xx,"[9] although they could not be used to pay debts to the Commune.[10]

Less-esteemed silver coins came to Venice from the other direction when new silver mines were opened in the Balkans. Saxon miners driven from Transylvania by Mongol raids in the 1240s developed a rich find at Brescoa (Brskovo), east of Ragusa. Much of its product was brought to Venice, mainly by Ragusans. Some came as tableware or jewelry, and some was welcomed as bullion, but when it came as coin, it took forms that were not welcomed. A mint at Brescoa of the king of Rascia (Serbia) by 1276 was turning out groats that so closely resembled Venetian grossi that the Venetians called them counterfeits. Although they bore the name of the Serbian king, their design and weight made it easy to confuse them with the issues of the Venetian mint. Serbian groats and similar coins from Bosnian mines and mints penetrated other cities of northern Italy, as well as Venice, Dalmatia, parts of Greece, and many interior Balkan valleys where little money had previously circulated.[11] By 1282 they were circulating in Venice to an alarming extent, and the Great Council forbade their use. All Venetian officials, including those overseas, except the counts in Ragusa, where they continued to circulate, were ordered to be on the lookout for them, to cut them up, and to turn the scrap coin in to the mint. All moneychangers and their "boys over twelve years of age" were required to take an oath to do the same. But the penalty on Venetians for possessing the Rascian groats was relatively light: only 1/10 of the forbidden coin would be taken without compensation; the rest would be paid for as bullion.[12] Probably as effective in reducing their importation was the reduction in that same year of the mint charges on the coinage of piccoli from 24 percent to 13 percent, a reduction that gave some encouragement to importing bullion rather than coin, although the low mint charge on grossi, about 2.1 percent, was more important for that purpose.[13] But the intrusion of groats from Serbia and Bosnia continued,

[9]In 1320–22, records of payments in "libre . . . denariorum venecialium grossorum in denariis a viginti" are found in several private contracts, such as docs. 144, 146, 226, 565 in the cartulary of *Felice de Merlis* (Bondi Sebellico, ed.), 95, 96, 131, 262.

[10]In the *Capitulare Visdominorum Ternarie,* fol. 48; Nani-Mocenigo, ed., *Capitolare dei Signori di Notte,* no. 114; and in the capitolare of the Officiali sovra Rialto, ASV, Sal, b. 2 (ex-Sala Margherita 62), cap. 78. Printed from the Deliberazioni del Maggior Consiglio in *PMV,* doc. 67 (1302).

[11]Metcalf, *Coinage in the Balkans,* chaps. 8, 9, 10, and esp. pp. 68, 197–200, 203–5. The silver mine at Brskovo began production in 1254, and four to seven others further inland came into production between 1290 and 1326 (according to Desanka Kovačević "Dans la Serbie et la Bosnie médiévales: Les mines d'or et d'argent," *Annales, ESC,* 15 [1960]:249 ff., with map and diagram).

[12]Mosher Stuard, "Adriatic Trade in Silver," 108–20; *DMC,* 2:293–94, 3:12; Papadopoli, 1:330, cap. 88.

[13]See below, table A.5.

GROAT OF TYROL, TYPE 2

Issued in great quantity by Count Mainardo and his sons (1274–1310), these aquilini, so called because of the eagle pictured on the reverse, circulated very extensively at Venice.

*Obv.*: **ME IN AR DV** Long cross with a short cross superimposed.
*Rev.*: + **COMES TIROL** Eagle with wings spread, facing left.

*AR, 21.8 mm, 1.543 gr. Museo Bottacin, inv. no. 6. (CNI. 6: 102, no. 12.)*

and the ban on their use was reiterated by the Great Council in 1290 with more severe penalties, including confiscation of 50 percent of any that had been bought by a moneychanger.[14] The doge, the Ducal Council, and the Quarantia followed this up in 1291 with orders that four tables be set up at the Rialto where everyone who had imported such money should turn it in to be paid for as bullion.[15]

A more tolerant attitude was adopted a few years later. A decree of 1294 stipulated that the Serbian groats would be paid for at the rate previously established in valuing certified sterling bars—225 soldi per mark.[16] Doing so implied that the Serbian groats were also 0.925 fine. Although they were supposed to be turned in within fifteen days, they might be accepted after fifteen days as a means of payment, provided they were valued at only 28 denari. Whoever accepted them was ordered to take them to the mint within eight days; if he did not—and was caught—he lost only 3 piccoli per groat. In effect that permitted them to circulate at 25 piccoli. In 1299, when their circulation was similarly made legal, but at 24 piccoli, mintmasters were instructed to check every month to see whether their intrinsic value had diminished. The change was made, the law declared, perhaps having in mind the teenage boys referred to earlier, so that fewer souls would be endangered by perjury.[17] In short, the Great Council became reconciled to letting these groats circulate at their intrinsic value, which was about 25 percent less than that of the grossi, while still requiring customs officials to send all they received to the mint for recoinage.

The extent to which the Serbian groats resembled the Venetian grossi without maintaining the same standard gained for king Stefan Uros II Milutin (1282–1321) the reputation—held also by his contemporary Philip the Fair of France—of being a counterfeiter, as reflected in Dante's lines:

> "quel di Rascia
> Che male ha visto il conio di Vinegia."
> *(Paradiso*, XIX.140–41)

If the king of Rascia (Serbia) deserved Dante's condemnation, it was not simply because the groats he coined resembled those of Venice. In fact, his coins bore letters and features that deliberately distinguished them from the Venetian coins.[18] The Venetian decree of 1282 referred to them as

[14]*DMC*, 3:283, pars. 125, 126; *PMV*, doc. 56, where paragraph 126 is omitted.

[15]Reference to the four tables at the Rialto is in the somewhat longer version, without dates, of the decrees of 1290 and 1291 recorded in the *Capitulare Visdominorum Ternarie*, fol. 18, cap. xlv, and fols. 42v–43.

[16]*PMV*, doc. 60; see also above, chap. 10, sec. ii.

[17]*PMV*, docs. 57, 60; *DMC*, 2:360, 453; Papadopoli, 1:330, 335, 336.

[18]Metcalf, *Coinage in the Balkans*, pls. 13, 14.

"contrafactos," to be sure, but that is not the only case in which competing coins were given that bad name simply because of their resemblance and ability to compete with a previously established home product.[19] Such competitors should be distinguished from real counterfeits, that is, coins that pretended by false insignia to contain far more fine metal than they really did. The first issues of the king of Rascia were of about the same weight as the Venetian grossi and had a high silver content. They are an example of the kind of coin used in the well-studied monetary wars of the Netherlands, similar enough to those of the country into which they were introduced to be accepted but inferior enough to make profits for the mint from which they came. Presumably it was later issues, lighter and with a higher percentage of copper, that earned for the Serbian king his fame as a counterfeiter.[20]

The situation in Bologna in 1305 shows the extent to which the Rascian coinage had driven out Venetian grossi and could at about that date have inspired Dante's lines. Bologna itself minted groats smaller than the Venetian, but the Venetian grossi were so well known in Bologna that when the Serbian groats of the same size as the Venetian first began to be used, the Bolognese called the Serbian coins "veneziani di Rassi." By 1305 they were the most common coin in use. Their deterioration led to a motion to reduce immediately their legal value from 20 Bolognese denari piccoli to 19 and, after two months, to a motion to ban them completely. That motion was defeated; apparently the city councillors had too many old Rascian groats on hand to be willing to vote a reduction in their value. Instead they voted to distinguish between the new Rascian groats, some of which, the resolution said, were worth only 12, 16, or 18 denarii bononini, and the old issue, which should still be accepted as worth 20 denarii.

[19]Giovanni Villani, *Cronica,* ed. F. G. Dragomanni, 4 vols. (Florence, 1844–45), bk. 12, cap. 107.

[20]Metcalf, *Coinage in the Balkans,* 192, says of the Ragusan grossi mentioned in 1301 that their weight standard, ca. 1.84 grams, corresponded to the reduced Serbian weight standard of 1282, but he explains at length about the Serbian coins (pp. 207–8): "The very early Serbian coins are of about the same weight as the Venetian . . . ; later coins are appreciably lighter and were exchanged against the Venetian ones according to the records of 1294, 1302, and 1303 at various ratios such as 8:7, 9:8, 10:9. It seems reasonable to suppose that the Venetian embargo of 1282 was in response to the reduction in the weight standard of the Serbian grossi early in that year or in 1281." But he is not more specific about the reduction in weight presumed to have occurred in 1281 or 1282. He describes wide variation in the weights of later issues: for 60 specimens, the average was 1.807 grams, but 10 were over 2 grams. He says nothing about the fineness. Vuk Vinaver, "Der venezianische Goldzechin in der Republik Ragusa," *Bollettino dell'Istituto di Storia della Società e dello Stato Veneziano* 4 (1962):113, cites an article by Dinic to indicate that in 1303 the weight of the Serbian groat called a dinar was 9/10 of a Venetian grosso, that is, 1.96 grams (2.178 × 0.9). Mosher Stuard, "Adriatic Trade in Silver," 98, gives the weight of the Serbian groat as 1.807 grams. At that weight and sterling fineness, their silver content was 1.67 grams (1.8 × 0.925), 80 percent of the 2.1 grams in the Venetian grossi, as implied by the Venetian law of 1294 (*PMV,* doc. 60).

GROSSO OF RASCIA

One of the imitations of the Venetian grosso issued by the king of Rascia (Serbia) Uros II Milutin (1274–1321).

*Obv.*: **VROSIVS REX SSTEFANVS** St. Stephen hands the banner to the king; both face front.

*Rev.*: Christ enthroned, flanked by **IC XC**.

*AR, 19.9 mm, 1.991 gr. Museo Bottacin, inv. dupl. no. 429.*

Vigorous inquests then identified and obtained from a handful of moneychangers—half of them foreigners—confessions that they had indeed imported and passed off as worth 30 to a florin Rascian groats that they had obtained at more than 41 for a florin. But on a promise from Bolognese moneychangers that within the next four months they would have coined 60,000 lire of good Bolognese groats, inquests and prosecutions stopped.[21]

While concern with invasion by Serbian groats was at its height in Bologna, it was waning in Venice. The office that had been created to suppress the Rascian grossi was charged in 1304 with inspecting the loading and armament of privately owned merchant galleys, an assignment that suggests that that office was no longer sufficiently occupied by its earlier assignment.[22] But Communal offices were still under orders to melt down all the Rascian groats they received, and the Ternaria, the customs office that handled hides, cheeses, and other products imported largely from or through Dalmatia, came into the possession of so many that it itself was authorized to melt down the coins that it confiscated or collected.[23] Such destruction of foreign coins was unusual; generally coins from foreign mints were allowed to circulate at their market value, although efforts were made to limit their use.[24]

In the effort to meet the competition of foreign coins within Venice, any reduction in the silver content of the Venetian grosso is noteworthy by its absence. The foreign groats would not have had Gresham's law operating in their favor if the Venetian grossi had been debased to be as "bad" as their competitors. That would have helped to maintain the circulation within Venice of its own grossi, but it would have hurt the use of the grossi in Venice's eastern markets, where the grosso had become a sort of international standard of value. Its acceptability facilitated Venetian purchases of raw materials and of eastern products for sale to western

[21]Giovanni Battista Salvioni, "Il valore della lira bolognese, dalla sua origine alla fine del secolo XV," *Atti e memorie della Deputazione di Storia Patria per la Romagna* 14–18 (1896–1900), here 16 (1898):313–22, or in the 1961 reprint (Turin) of the revised offprint of 1902 (Bologna), 15 ff. The situation at Bologna is mentioned by Charles S. Singleton, ed. and trans., in Dante Alighieri, *The Divine Comedy*, 6 pts. in 3 vols., Bollingen Series, 80 (Princeton, 1980), vol. 1 (*Inferno*), pt. 2, pp. 328–29.

[22]The inspection was assigned to "officialibus de super denariis Brescoe" (Avogaria di Comun, Maggior Consiglio, Deliberazione, Magnus, fol. 41). Many regulations governing the combined office are in the capitolare, formerly Brera 263, described in Frederic C. Lane, *Venice and History: The Collected Papers of Frederic C. Lane* (Baltimore, 1966), 248 n. 86, or in idem, "Venetian Maritime Law and Administration, 1250–1350," in *Studi in onore di Amintore Fanfani*, 6 vols. (Milan, 1962), 3:45–46 n. 84.

[23]*Capitulare Visdominorum Ternarie*, fol. 59.

[24]In 1306, confiscation or export was ordered of certain pennies coined in Lombardy ("moneta parva crosata") that had been allowed to circulate at 40 to the grosso, but on the ground that in fact they were circulating at 32 to the grosso, as were Venetian piccoli, not by invoking a general rule against foreign coin (*PMV*, doc. 68).

Europe and gave the Venetians good reason to keep high the reputation of the grosso by keeping its fineness and weight unchanged. When groats of less intrinsic value began coming in from Balkan mints, any temptation to drive out this "bad money" by lowering the silver content of the grosso, and thus making it no longer so vulnerably "good," must have been checked by the desire to keep the grosso at a high rate of exchange.

## ii. BIMETALLISM IN OVERSEAS TRADE

Although some usages apply the term "bimetallism" to any monetary system in which two metals are legal tender, according to strict definitions it is a contradiction in terms to speak of international bimetallism. Webster's definition assumes a single standard of value, not a number of independent standards such as those of different nations. But an international monetary system may be said to have had a single standard approximately when one money was widely used in settling trade balances and evaluating reserves (as was the English pound before World War I or the American dollar after World War II). If the coin that in this way served as an international standard equaled both a fixed amount of gold and a fixed amount of silver, or if two national currencies, one based on gold and the other on silver, maintained the same relative value for a considerable period of time, one may say that there was for that period and that area a kind of international bimetallic system.

In the Mediterranean world in which Venice's trade developed, the Byzantine nomisma (earlier called the solidus and later the hyperpyron or perpero) came closest to dominating an international monetary system. Although the original nomismata were almost pure gold, the later perperi were a varying mixture of gold and silver, as explained above, in chapter 8. It may be viewed as being for a time an example of what is called symmetallism, that is, a standard of value based on a combination of both gold and silver in one coin or one ingot in fixed proportions. Once the Byzantine emperors had begun increasing the amount of silver, the proportions of the two metals did not stay fixed. Moreover, the value of the gold in a perpero was far greater that the value of the silver, so that changes in its value depended mainly on the changes in its gold content.

During the twelfth and thirteenth centuries silver coins circulated increasingly not only in the Byzantine Empire but in the Moslem states that had been issuing coins imitating those of the Byzantine emperors. Silver coins were used to pay prices and settle contracts that had been stated in the moneys of account based on perperi or other gold coins. In the course of time, moneys of account that had originally been identified with gold coins shifted their base to silver coins or became payable in coins that were partly gold and partly silver. During the transition, much of the international trade of the eastern Mediterranean may be said to have used a nebulous kind of bimetallism.

A crucial role in the transition from gold to silver was played by the Venetian grosso, especially by its relations to the perpero during the thirteenth century. In the whole area that Venice came to dominate as a result of the Fourth Crusade, the coins issued by the Comneni had been in general use and had determined existing standards of value. The Comneni hyperpyron, or perpero, was of the traditional weight, 4.4 grams, but contained enough silver and copper mixed with its gold that its value was about 7/8 that of the traditional gold coin. This Comnenian perpero became the basis of the most-used Byzantine money of account, the perpero, divided into 12 milieresia or 24 carats as units of account. When Enrico Dandolo coined the grosso and it was accepted as worth 26 denarii ven., 18 1/2 grossi sufficed to pay 1 perpero at the traditional rate of exchange in Venice, according to which 1 perpero was worth 40 soldi ven. At that rate of exchange, 1 gram of coined gold was considered to be worth a little more than 10 grams of coined silver.[25]

From 10 to 1 about 1200, the bimetallic ratio fell, and the value of the perpero fell accordingly. In Genoa and Florence at the time of the coinage of the gold genovino and florin in 1252, gold was considered little more than 8.5 times as valuable as silver,[26] and there is some reason to believe that gold fell to an even lower value in some places in the Levant in that decade.[27]

The valuation set on perperi was affected by the overthrow of the Byzantine Empire through the Fourth Crusade, which the coinage of the Venetian grosso had helped to finance, and by the subsequent political confusion. One result was the contemporaneous existence of many kinds of perperi. Whether the Latin emperors at Constantinople coined perperi is debated. No specimens have been found; yet surviving documents contain passages that seem to refer to them.[28] Perperi certainly were coined by the Greek rulers at Nicaea, who claimed to be the legitimate successors of the Byzantine emperors. Those issued when the Nicaean Greek emperors regained Constantinople, which continued to be minted by the triumphant Michael Palaeologus, contained only about 16 carats of gold.[29]

Meanwhile, in many regions that had once been part of the Byzantine Empire, the perpero as a money of account became based on the Venetian grosso rather than on the coins issued by Byzantine emperors. In this connection two different perperi can be clearly distinguished as mon-

[25]See above, chap. 8, sec. ii.
[26]See below, app. E, sec. iii.
[27]Ashtor, *Les métaux précieux,* 37, 31, 52; Watson, "Back to Gold," 27.
[28]Bertelè, "Moneta veneziana," 31–38 and apps. 1, 2; Grierson, *Byzantine Coins,* 269.
[29]Bertelè, "Moneta veneziana," 17–18; Hendy, *Coinage,* 247–50.

eys of account. That based on the Comnenian perpero became known as the "good old perpero." Since it had been worth 40 soldi at Venice, a perpero paid in grossi was worth 18 1/2 grossi. Even after 1204, good old perperi are often quoted at 40 soldi.[30] Some lower quotations may also refer to Comnenian gold perperi coins or a money of account based on them. Such perperi declined in value when gold became worth less than 10 times as much as silver,[31] but good old perperi were mainly equated with 40 soldi a grossi and with 18 1/2 silver grossi.

A second kind of perpero important as a money of account was the "current perpero," worth about 26 soldi a grossi or 12 grossi coins.[32] It was derived from perperi coins issued by Michael Palaeologus. Since these coins were only 16/24 gold, there was just about 8.6 times as much silver in 12 grossi as there was gold in 1 Palaeologian perpero ($12 \times 2.1 = [16/24] \times 4.4 \times 8.6$). After allowing for the silver in these perperi which were 2/3 gold, the equating of 1 Palaeologian perpero with 12 grossi implies a bimetallic ratio as low as 8.16,[33] but some Palaeologian perperi contained less than 16 carats of gold.[34] Since in money of account 12 grossi coins equaled 26 soldi, the current perpero was rated in exchange at about 26 soldi.[35]

The subdivision of the perpero in Byzantine money of account was the miliaresion, of which 12 equaled 1 perpero; it could be considered materialized in the grosso when the perpero equaled 12 grossi.[36] The

[30]Bertelè, "Moneta veneziana," 35 (a bequest made in 1207), 35–36 (exchange on Venice in 1210), 36 (exchange on Venice in 1210 and 1224); DMC, 3:78, or PMV, doc. 35 (1284, official rates overseas). Cf. below, sec. iv.

[31]In 1228, repayment at 35 soldi in Modon and Coron or 38 soldi in Venice was ordered for each perpero expended by officials (BG, vol. 1, doc. 27).

[32]Bertelè, "Moneta veneziana," 108–10. References to "yperpera in Creta currentia" are the standard form in Mario Chiaudano and Antonino Lombardo, eds., Leonardo Marcello, notaio in Candia (1278–1281), FSV (Venice, 1960), docs. 155, 339, 347; and in Antonino Lombardo, ed., Documenti della colonia veneziana di Creta, I: Imbreviature di Pietro Scardon (1271), Documenti e studi per la storia del commercio e del diritto commerciale italiano, ed. F. Patetta and Mario Chiaudano, 21 (Turin, 1942), e.g., nos. 3, 187, 280.

[33]Assuming that 1 carat in the 24 was copper for hardening, approximately as in the Comnenian perpero, leaves as silver 7/24 of 4.4 grams, or 1.283 grams. Subtracting that from the 25.2 grams of silver in 12 grossi ($12 \times 2.1$) leaves 23.917 grams of silver equated in value with 2.93 ($4.4 \times [16/24]$) grams of gold, a bimetallic ratio of 8.16 to 1 (23.917/2.93).

[34]Hendy, Coinage, 247–50. On the variation from city to city see Lopez and Raymond, Medieval Trade, 15.

[35]Earlier exchanges of perperi at about 26 soldi are reported by Bertelè, "Moneta veneziana," as follows: 1205—at 25 soldi di denari, to be repaid in Constantinople (p. 35); 1206—at 28 and 30 soldi di denari, to be repaid in Constantinople (p. 35); 1213—at 26 in exchange on Coron and Modon. Bertelè's compilation does not include any quotations between 1241 (p. 37) and 1315 (p. 40). Desimoni, "La moneta e il rapporto dell'oro all'argento," 35–39. Morozzo della Rocca and Lombardo, eds., Documenti del commercio veneziano, 2:354, doc. 827, refers in 1255 to paying 13 grossi in Venice for 1 perpero received in Crete.

[36]Lopez and Raymond, Medieval Trade, 14, and the document printed (p. 170) from Marseilles, 1227, referring to "135 bezants of good miliaresia."

equivalence of 1 perpero with 12 grossi seems indeed to have become firmly established in Crete about 1250, when Venetian power in Romania was at its height and before Genoa and Florence had spread the use of their new gold coins. That was the period in which the grosso was a prevalent means of payment, and gold reached its low near 8.5 to 1. With that bimetallic ratio, the "current perpero" as a money of account could be based on both the Palaeologian perpero coin and 12 Venetian grossi coins.

In Syria and other parts of Islam, the Arab conquerors had issued gold or electrum coins called "dinars," which were similar in weight and equal in fineness to the gold coins of the Byzantine emperors. In the kingdoms established by the Christian Crusaders—regions called "Oltremare" in Venice, just as in England they were referred to as "Beyond-the-Sea"—the rulers also issued silver or billon pennies and groats of the type with which the French nobles were familiar, but their gold coins were similar to the Arab dinars. They became known at Venice as "saracen bezants" ("bisanti saracenati") or simply "saracenati." Many of these bezants came from the mints at Tyre and Acre, which were managed for local princes by Venetian entrepreneurs. Their gold content, like that of the perperi, was diminished. Those minted at Acre at the time of St. Louis were of 18 carats.[37] After the fall of Acre, the last Christian stronghold in Palestine, saracenati circulated extensively in Cyprus, which was still ruled by the French nobles established there during the Third Crusade. The saracenati were reckoned as equal to 3 1/2 of a later Cypriot type of bezant called a "white bezant" ("bezante biancho"), which was more than 1/2 silver, a little less than 1/6 gold, the rest copper. The saracenati were also equated with 7 groats of a type derived from those coined in France and called "tornesi grossi."[38] While saracenati as coins were generally considered gold, saracenati as units of account were beginning to be paid at established rates in coins that were largely or entirely silver.

Thus both in Romania and in the Crusader states, the basic money of account was derived from a gold coin but was coming to be used more and more for accounts settled in silver coins at traditional rates. Even the gold coins were about 1/3 silver. As a whole, the Levantine moneys embodied a nebulous kind of bimetallism with unstable relations between coins and moneys of account.

A comparison of the value of Venetian money with the values of the moneys of some of its important overseas trading partners is made possible by a clause in the Venetian Maritime Code of 1255 of Doge Renier Zeno. It made provisions regarding four moneys of account in which freight rates were set overseas for wares shipped to Venice: perperi of Romania, bezants of Oltremare, bezants of Barbary, and oncie of Sicily and Apulia.

[37]Blancard, "Le besant d'or," 155, 167, 181–83.
[38]Schlumberger, *Numismatique de l'orient latin*, 176–78; Stussi, ed., *Zibaldone da Canal*, 63–64. Cf. Watson, "Back to Gold," 8–9.

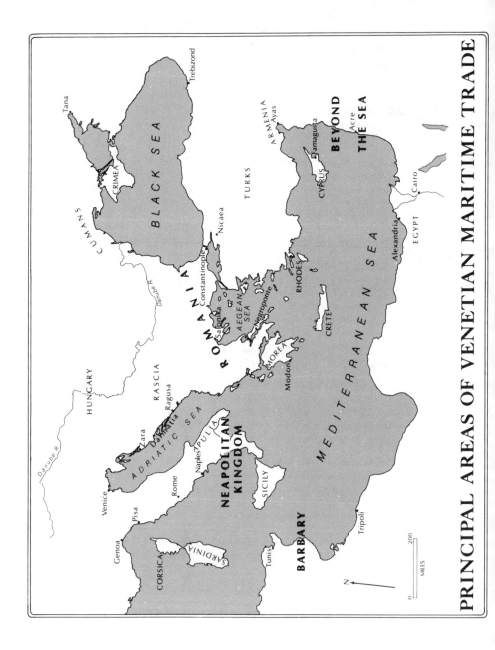

PRINCIPAL AREAS OF VENETIAN MARITIME TRADE

Trebizond

Tana

BLACK SEA

CRIMEA

ARMENIA
Ayas

BEYOND
THE SEA

Famagusta

CUMANS

TURKS

CYPRUS

Acre

ROMANIA

Nicaea

Cairo

Constantinople

Alexandria

EGYPT

Danube R.

AEGEAN
SEA

RHODES

Salonika

MEDITERRANEAN SEA

Negroponte

HUNGARY

RASCIA

CRETE

Ragusa

MOREA

Modon

ADRIATIC SEA

Zara

Dalmatia

APULIA

NEAPOLITAN
KINGDOM

Naples

Venice

Rome

SICILY

Pisa

Tripoli

Genoa

CORSICA

SARDINIA

BARBARY

Tunis

200

0        MILES

N

272

For each it specified the number of soldi to be collected in Venice from shipowners for penalties that had been imposed by Venetian consuls or other officials overseas. Because the amount of penalty was double the freight rate, the penalties were stated in the moneys of account used overseas in setting freight rates.[39] The exchange rate probably included a surcharge levied on the shipowners, because they had paid the penalties, not at the time they were incurred, but at the conclusion of the voyage. A century or so later, shippers who paid in Constantinople or in Tana freights on wares shipped from Venice were required to pay an added 25 percent.[40] The amount of the surcharge in 1255 is uncertain. It is here estimated to have been about 20 percent, with a margin of error making between 10 percent and 30 percent probable. Our comparisons investigate the extent to which the foreign moneys of account were based on gold or on silver and what the prevailing bimetallic ratios were about 1255.

For each perpero of penalty imposed in Romania (mainly in Constantinople) the shipowners were to pay 32 soldi in Venice. Estimates of how that figure was reached may be made in either of two ways. If we assume that the Byzantine perpero was then based on the grosso and valued at 12 grossi, which was about the equivalent of 26 soldi, exchange at 32 soldi contained a surcharge of 6 soldi, which is 23 percent. If we assume that the Byzantine perpero was then based on a coin weighing 4.4 grams, 2/3 gold and 1/3 silver, then if the bimetallic ratio was 8.5 to 1, there was a surcharge of 18 percent.[41] The difference between 18 percent and 23 percent is not so great as to discredit the above-formulated conclusion that at that date the perpero of Romania as a money of account had about the same value whether it was considered linked to the Byzantine coins called perperi or to the Venetian coins called grossi.

For each bezant of penalty incurred in Acre or other ports of the Crusader states, the shipowners were to pay 28 soldi. If the bezants referred to were "saracenati" that were 3/4 gold, 1/4 silver, no surcharge was included so long as the bimetallic ratio was 7.9 to 1 or more. This calcula-

---

[39]Riccardo Predelli and Adolfo Sacerdoti, eds., *Gli statuti marittimi veneziani fino al 1255* (Venice, 1903), cap. 45. The soldi are those of the lib. ven. before it split into the lira a grossi and the lira di piccoli and when the value of 1 soldo was 12/26 grosso, almost the same as the value later of the soldo a grossi (12/26.111 grosso), as explained above, in chap. 8, sec. iii.

[40]Bertelè, "Moneta veneziana," 27, 52n. For the galleys of Flanders, 1/5 more had to be paid at the port of unloading (ASV, Senato, Misti, reg. 53, fol. 208v).

[41]Thirty-two soldi equaled 31.01 grams (32 × 12 × [2.1/26]) of silver. The perpero contained 2.93 grams (4.4 × 0.667) of gold plus 1.46 grams (4.4 × 0.333) grams of silver. Equating 29.55 grams of silver (31.01 − 1.46) with 2.93 grams of gold gave a bimetallic ratio of 10.08 to 1. But if the bimetallic ratio was 8.5 to 1, then 2.93 grams of gold equaled in value only 24.90 grams (2.93 × 8.5) of silver, so that there was a surcharge of 4.6 grams (29.55 − 24.90) of silver, or 18 percent (4.6/24.9).

tion suggests that the saracen bezants were then, as later, based on white bezants or other largely silver coin.[42]

For each bezant of Barbary the shipowners were to pay 18 soldi. There was then no coin in western North Africa called a bezant. The bezant was a money of account equal to 10 silver coins called by Arabs "dirhems" and by Europeans "migliaresi" or, in Venice, "miarexi." Before 1262 or thereabouts, the link coin of the bezant was a dirhem weighing about 1.5 grams, which was called the "old dirhem" to distinguish it from a "new dirhem," of the same weight but 0.937 fine and worth 20 percent more. It seems likely that the new dirhem was created between 1262 and 1272, shortly after the old dirhem had been debased so as to lose 20 percent of its value. The debasement may have had the purpose, as Robert Brunschvig has suggested, of lightening the burden of the tribute that Charles of Anjou as king of Naples-Sicily had imposed on Tunis.[43] Being of the same weight but worth 20 percent less, the old dirhems must have been only 0.749 fine (0.937 × 0.80) after debasement, containing 1.12 grams of silver. Before debasement they probably had been 0.937 fine, as were the new dirhems, according to Pegolotti. In that case, the silver equivalent of the bezant of Tunis at the time of the Venetian Maritime Code of 1255 was 14.05 grams (0.937 × 1.5 × 10). In comparison, 18 Venetian soldi of that date represented 17.37 grams (18 × [19.3/20]) (cf. above, table 4). However, deducting a 20 percent estimated surcharge for late payment of the penalty leaves only 13.9 grams, sufficiently close to the silver value of the bezant of Tunis.

The long Byzantine and Moslem rule of Apulia and Sicily had established gold coin as the standard of value there, and that habit continued under the Norman rulers who united Sicily with southern Italy. The gold coin they minted was not the dinar, however, but the quarter of a dinar which Moslems called a "ruba'i" and the Italians called a "tarì." Before the

[42]Twenty-eight soldi equaled 27.14 grams (28 × 12 × [2.1/26]) of silver. The saracenato at one time contained 3.3 grams (4.4 × 0.75) of gold plus 1.1 grams (4.4 × 0.25) of silver. Subtracting 1.1 grams from 27.14 leaves 26.04 grams of silver. Equating in value 26.04 grams of silver with 3.3 grams of gold gives a bimetallic ratio of 7.89 to 1. If the bimetallic ratio was 8.5 to 1, then the 3.3 grams of gold equaled in value 28.05 grams (3.3 × 8.5) of silver, which is 2.01 grams more than 26.04 grams.

[43]Robert Brunschvig, "Esquisse d'histoire monétaire Almohado-Hafside," in *Mélanges William Marçais* (Paris, 1950), 68–74. Before 1200 the coin most mentioned in Genoese contracts regarding payment in North Africa was the Sicilian tarì. Then occurred a shift to silver coin (see Henry L. Misbach, "Genoese Trade and the Role of Sicilian Coinage in the Mediterranean Economy, 1154–1253," *Revue internationale de l'histoire de la banque* 5 [1972]:305). Presumably, the "silver" Misbach refers to were the migliaresi, also called grossi, which were minted in Genoa and Tuscany (referred to by Lopez in *Settecento anni fa*, 32n, 35). A value for the bezant of Tunis as high as that given in Zeno's code is implied by the contracts printed in Morozzo della Rocca and Lombardo, *Documenti del commercio veneziano*, docs. 776, 777 (dated 1245). On the fineness of silver migliaresi see Pegolotti, *Pratica*, 291. On later values of the bezant see below, chap. 14, sec. iii.

Swabian emperors succeeded the Norman kings, in 1194, the tarì had degenerated so that an improvement over earlier issues was required when the Swabian rulers declared the official fineness of the gold to be 18 1/3 carats. The weight of tarì coins was so extremely variable, from 0.23 grams to 1.89 grams, that they were accepted only by weight, and the basic money of account came to be an ounce of tarì. This money of account, the oncia of 26.4 grams, was divided into 30 tarì of account each figured as 0.88 grams, as accounting units, while tarì coins continued to vary. Emperor Frederick II issued a new style of large gold coin, the augustale, which weighed 1/5 of an oncia. He set its value at 1/4 of an oncia of account, since it contained 20–21 carats of gold, compared with the 16 1/3 carats in the tarì.[44] Although not all coins issued were up to standard, as a money of account the oncia represented either 17.95 grams of pure gold, figuring from the tarì (0.88 × 30 × 0.68), or 18.48 grams (26.4 × [4/5] × 0.875), figuring from the augustale—roughly speaking, 18 grams of gold— and some silver mixed with the gold. For a penalty imposed in Apulia, Calabria, or Sicily, the payment per oncia required in Venice was 9 lire.[45]

Comparing the silver content of 9 lib. ven. (173.7 grams) with the gold content of an oncia gives a bimetallic ratio of 9.5 to 1;[46] but if we allow for a 20 percent surcharge, the bimetallic ratio is reduced to 8 to 1, a not impossible ratio for 1255, since a contract concluded in Genoa in 1253 indicates a ratio of 8.16 to 1.[47]

This analysis of the exchange rates indicated by the Venetian Maritime Code of 1255 lends support to the conclusion that the bimetallic ratio was at that time as low as 8.5 in many parts of the Mediterranean. It indicates also that of the four areas mentioned as important for Venetian shipping, only the Neapolitan-Sicilian kingdom used a money of account based entirely on gold, and its gold was of uncertain quality. In the other three areas, silver coins were becoming important as means of payment and as determinants of the comparative values of the moneys of account, just as at Venice silver coins determined the value of Venetian moneys of account.

[44]Lopez, *Settecento anni fa*, 7–13, 17–18; Carmelo Trasselli, "Le aree monetarie," 54–55, 60–62.

[45]Predelli and Sacerdoti, eds., *Statuti marittimi*, cap. 45.

[46]Since 1 lira a grossi = 9.19 grossi, then 9 lire = 9 × 9.19 × 2.1 grams of silver = 173.7 grams. There were 2 1/2 carats of silver in the 4 augustali, each of which weighed 1/5 of an oncia, so that 2.2 grams of silver ([2.5/24] × 4 × [26.4/5]) were paid back in that form, leaving only 171.5 (173.7 − 2.2) grams of silver to be paid for by the 18 grams of gold in the oncia, a bimetallic ratio of 9.5 to 1 (171.5/18).

[47]Robert S. Lopez, "Back to Gold, 1252," *EcHR*, 2d ser., 9 (1956):234; cf. idem, *Settecento anni fa*, 36–37. Adding 20 percent for late payment to 8.16 would give a ratio of 9.79 to 1 (8.16 + 1.63). On the extensive circulation of Venetian grossi in Apulia see Giovanni Cassandro, "I porti pugliesi nel medio evo," in idem, *Saggi di storia del diritto commerciale* (Rome, 1974), 378.

## iii. THE NEW GOLD COINS OF WESTERN RIVALS

In the nebulous bimetallic and symmetallic systems of the eastern Mediterranean about 1250, the mixture of gold and silver in the same coin obscured the exact relation between their relative market values as metals and their monetary value as legal tender. Consequently, governmental authority and tradition had a wider range of influence in determining the values at which the coins were accepted. Rational calculation of the metallic value of coins became easier when the coins in use were of pure silver or pure gold.

Coins that were more purely gold than any then in general circulation in the Mediterranean were issued by Genoa and Florence in 1252. Their initiative in coining gold was rooted in their commercial situation, especially that of Genoa, which probably issued its genovino before Florence issued its gold florin. They both depended heavily on trade with areas where gold coins had long been the main standard of value, namely, Naples, Sicily, North Africa, and Spain. The gold coins being minted in the Kingdom of the Two Sicilies in 1252 were not of consistent, dependable fineness. But the Genoese and Florentines needed gold coins in order to buy grain in Sicily. Their trade with North Africa and Spain supplied the needed gold. Both the genovino and the florin were given the gold content and the value in Sicilian money of account that seemed most likely to make them acceptable in Sicily.[48]

Within a few decades Florence had succeeded in having its gold coins accepted not only in all Italy but at the fairs of Champagne also, then in England and the Netherlands as well as in France.[49] By the end of the century florins were so much used in the Levant that in a collection seized

[48]Robert S. Lopez, in his "Prima del ritorno all'oro nell'occidente duecentesco: I primi denari grossi d'argento," *Rivista storica italiana* 79 (1967):174–81, reprinted in his *Su e giù per la storia di Genova* (Genoa, 1975), rebuts objections to his thesis, stated in *Settecento anni fa*, that Florence imitated Genoa in coining gold, and not vice versa and rejects the argument that the first gold genovino was coined at the beginning of the century. The analysis of Sicilian gold coinage and its importance for the trade of Genoa by Trasselli, "Le aree monetarie," and by Misbach, "Genoese Trade," strengthens Lopez's case for Genoese priority, although there is no doubt that within a decade the florin gained wider circulation and international prestige. Grierson, in "The Origins of the Grosso," 43, accepts Lopez's arguments for the priority of the genovino over the florin, while rejecting the argument others make for gold coinage at Genoa before 1252. Giuseppe Felloni, in his introductory "Profilo economico delle monete genovesi dal 1139 al 1814," in *Le monete genovesi—Storia, arte ed economia delle monete dal 1139 al 1814*, by G. Pesce and Giuseppe Felloni (Genoa, 1975), 246–50, presents the argument for Genoese coinage of gold considerably earlier, as Astengo had maintained. See also the rest of the volume, Pesce and Felloni, *Le monete genovesi*; and the recent rebuttal by Lopez in "The Dawn of Medieval Banking," 18 n. 11.

[49]Bloch, "Le problème de l'or," in *Mélanges historiques*, 2:842; Feavearyear, *The Pound Sterling*, 23–25; Fournial, *Histoire monétaire*, 81–82; Robert Davidsohn, *Geschichte von Florenz*, 4 vols. (Berlin, 1896–1927), vol. 2, pt. 1, p. 413; Day, "La circulation monétaire en Toscane."

by the Mamluks in 1291 when they captured the last Crusader foothold in Palestine, about 600 out of 630 gold coins were florins.[50]

When they coined the florin of 24-carat gold, or at least as nearly pure gold as was technically possible, the Florentines created a bimetallic standard and at the same time made the maintenance of such a standard more difficult. Previously, Florence, like Venice, might be said to have had a bimetallic monetary system but not a bimetallic standard, for the standard was provided by silver coins only. Gold coins—Byzantine, Spanish, or Neapolitan—did not have a value guaranteed by the state. The new florin, on the other hand, was officially declared worth 1 lira in the current Florentine and Pisan moneys of account, which were based on silver.[51] Thus in 1252 Florence established a single bimetallic standard based on two kinds of coins, one containing all gold and no silver, the other containing silver and no gold.

Within a few years, Florentine rationalistic calculation destroyed this bimetallic standard. Gold rose in value far above the bimetallic ratio set by equating 1 gold florin with 1 lira composed of 20 Florentine silver groats or 240 billon pennies.[52] The traditional Florentine lira then split into several moneys of account by processes not unlike those that separated the lira a grossi from the lira di piccoli at Venice. As gold rose in value, the Florentines rated their gold coin at more than 20 soldi of silver coins. Between 1272 and 1296 they used three moneys of account and spoke of three different kinds of soldi: (1) a soldo a oro, a denomination of account equal to 1/20 of a gold florin; (2) a soldo a fiorini, equal to the silver coin called a fiorino or its equivalent in similar silver coin; (3) a soldo di piccioli, equal to 12 of the billon coins called piccioli.

By 1279 the gold fiorino coin was quoted as worth 29 of the current silver florin coins. The gold florin was still equated with 1 lira, but that lira became distinguished by being called a lira a oro or fiorino a oro, and its subdivisions were called soldi and denari a oro. Accounts were still being kept largely in the more traditional money of account that had been based on the silver coin also called a florin. Its lira was distinguished by being called a lira a fiorini, and its subdivisions were called lire, soldi, and denari a fiorini. After 1279, in the leading merchant guild, the Calimala, in accounts kept in lire and soldi a fiorini, 1 gold florin was by law regularly counted as worth 29 silver florins. Accordingly they reckoned:

[50]Grierson, "La moneta veneziana," 83.

[51]de Roover, *Rise and Decline of the Medici Bank,* 51; Bernocchi, 3:76, 78, 263, 4:v–vi; Bruno Casini, "Il corso dei cambi fra il fiorino e la moneta di piccioli a Pisa dal 1252 al 1500," in *Studi sugli strumenti di cambio a Pisa nel medioevo,* by G. Garzella et al. (Pisa, 1979), 137.

[52]In spite of difficulty in determining the bimetallic ratio at Florence in 1252, as explained in app. E, sec. iii, there is general agreement that gold was more valuable, compared with silver, in 1280 than in 1252 and kept on rising. At Pisa the florin was at 24 1/2 soldi in 1268 and up to 36 1/2 in 1278 (Casini, "Il corso dei cambi," 137).

## THE FLORENTINE GOLD FLORIN

The essentials of the design of the first florin issued in 1252 were preserved thereafter. This specimen was struck in the second semester of 1324, under the mint official Tano di Baroncello.

*Obv.*: **.+FLOR..ENTIA** Lily.

*Rev.*: **.S.IOHA NNES.B** St. John the Baptist, facing front. In his left hand he holds a cross, while with his right hand he is in the act of blessing; to the left of the nimbus is a hatchet.

*AV, 20.4 mm, 3.448 gr. Museo Bottacin, inv. no. 11 (Bernocchi, 2: 145 nos. 1312–13).*

1 gold florin = 1 lira a oro = 20 soldi a oro = 29 soldi a fiorini; and 1 soldo a oro = 29/20 soldi a fiorini.

Subsequently Florentine silver coins, as well as Florentine billon coins, declined in value—clearly so after 1296. These equations were still used,[53] but "soldo a fiorini" no longer referred to silver coin. Instead, Florentine silver groats became linked to the Florentine lira di piccioli.[54] The "soldo a fiorini" remained linked to gold; it was constantly worth 1/29 of a gold florin. It became a mere fractional denomination of account.[55]

As a result, after 1296 the gold florin coin had three different values in money of account: (1) 20 soldi a oro; (2) 29 soldi a fiorini; and (3) a number of soldi di piccioli which varied from year to year. In 1279 it was 33 soldi di piccioli; in 1302, 51 soldi di piccioli.[56] These variations depended partly on changes in the bimetallic ratio, partly on changes in the quantity, weight, and fineness of the silver and billon coins. The widening gap between the values of the florin in soldi a oro and in soldi di piccioli showed that Florence no longer had a single bimetallic standard.

Possibly Florence abandoned any attempt at a single bimetallic standard almost immediately, and the gold florin was quoted at 25, not 20, soldi a fiorini as early as 1260. But there is also evidence that from 1279 to 1296 a gold florin was invariably quoted at 29 soldi a fiorini, which indicates that the lira a fiorini was based equally on the gold florin and the silver florin.[57] In that case, the lira a fiorini expressed a bimetallic standard

[53]Bernocchi, 3:78, 263–66; 4:v–vi.

[54]When other new silver coins—the guelfo and the popolino—were issued after 1279, they were valued in soldi di piccioli; they did not become the basic coins for the lira, soldo, and denaro a fiorini (Bernocchi, 3:156–65).

[55]de Roover, *Rise and Decline of the Medici Bank*, 31–34. De Roover describes the Florentine moneys of account of the fifteenth century (although without describing the role of the silver fiorini, recently described by Bernocchi) and the genesis of those moneys of account between 1250 and 1296. De Roover explains also (p. 33) the lira affiorino (equal to 20 soldi affiorino) as distinct from the fiorino a fiorino (equal to 29 soldi a fiorino), which Bernocchi (3:266–67) says developed later.

[56]Bernocchi, 3:78.

[57]Bernocchi (3:78, 264) gives the quotation of the gold florin as 25 soldi a fiorini in 1260 and 29 soldi a fiorini invariably from 1270 to 1296. However, the silver coin that Bernocchi considers the base of the soldo or fiorino a fiorini from 1279 to 1296 was called the "fiorino nuovo di denari 12." It was minted only from 1267 to 1279 (3:152–54). Its weight when first coined implies, he says (3:154), a bimetallic ratio of 10.84 to 1, but later issues were lighter. For 1279 Bernocchi (3:158) gives a bimetallic ratio of 11.64 to 1, for 1296 a ratio of 11.55 to 1 (3:163). The invariability of the rating 1 gold florin = 29 soldi a fiorini in 1279–96, while no new silver fiorini di denari 12 were being coined, is taken as an indication that the bimetallic ratio was stabilized in that period at about 11.6 to 1. After 1296 the fiorino d'argento nuovo disappeared from circulation, he says (3:265), and only then did the gold florin coin cease to be quoted at 29 soldi "in fiorini d'argento da s. 1" (see also Bernocchi, 4:iv–vi). But the evidence that 29 fiorini d'argento nuovi were in fact accepted in payment for 1 gold florin, or for a debt recorded as 1 fiorino, is not crystal clear, so that the case for the stabilization of the bimetallic ratio during those years is weak. In general, Bernocchi does not determine bimetallic ratios

in those years by being equal to both 20 silver florins and 20/29 of a gold florin.

This attempt at resurgence of a Florentine bimetallic standard is the more interesting because it overlaps the Venetian attempt at bimetallism, 1284–1296, described below as part of the "defense of the grosso."

The short-lived, silver-based lira a fiorini, as recently described by Mario Bernocchi, had a role at Florence between 1260 and 1296 that was parallel in many respects to that of the lira a grossi in Venice. Both diverged in value from the lira di piccoli of their respective cities, continuing in different ways a traditional lira and giving the traditional money of account a new base in silver coin that was more than 90 percent fine. Since Florence was coining gold at the same time, however, whereas Venice coined gold only later, Florence had less need then for a money of account based on fine silver to serve as a standard of value. Its lira a fiorini was based on both gold and silver only very briefly.[58] After 1296 it clung to the gold connection. All the accounts of the Bardi and Peruzzi, great Florentine firms of international merchant-bankers of the fourteenth century, were kept in lire, soldi, and denari a fiorini, with regular conversions of fiorini d'oro into lire, soldi, and denari a fiorini by use of the equation 1 fiorino d'oro = 29/20 lire a fiorini.[59]

No further effort was made by Florentines to maintain a bimetallic basis for a money of account. Thereafter they used two quite separate monetary standards, one based on gold, the other on silver. The lira di piccioli expressed the silver standard, while the gold standard was expressed by the lira a fiorini as well as by the lira a oro, usually named the fiorino d'oro.

## iv. THE DUCAT AND VENICE'S FIRST BIMETALLIC STANDARD

In the face of the developments just described, the coinage of the ducat in 1284–85 can be considered part of the "defense of the grosso."

---

from the study of the coins but applies ratios given elsewhere as one element in estimating the content of coins (3:140–43). But it may be significant that the two decades in question are the decades when the Venetian "defense of the grosso" was trying to hold the ducat down to 18 1/2 Venetian grossi and indeed may have held it down to 20 grossi, which implies a bimetallic ratio of 11.8 to 1 (see below, chap. 14, sec. i).

[58]Such a bimetallic lira was called a "fiorino" more often than a "lira," according to Bernocchi's description. He calls the lira a fiorini a fourth money of account developed from the fiorino a fiorini (Bernocchi, 3:266–68).

[59]In Armando Sapori, ed., *I libri degli Alberti del Giudice* (Milan, 1952), in many cases where payment in the gold coin is indicated by the notation "in sua mano," e.g., pp. 115, 132, and in many cases of transfers of book entries, e.g., pp. 85, 268, and others in which the form of payment is not indicated, e.g., in payments of rent for real estate, pp. 74, 101, 85; also in idem, ed., *I libri di commercio dei Peruzzi*, e.g., p. 29. In a few entries, to be sure, the fiorino a oro was reckoned at 30 soldi a fiorini (ibid., 8) or 30 soldi 6 denari a fiorini (ibid., 29), but all such cases seem to involve payments in gold florins outside of Florence. On the Covoni books see below, chap. 14, sec. iii.

Within the city, foreign silver coins, more or less similar to Venetian grossi but of inferior value, were circulating increasingly. Overseas, especially in the Levant, more and more mints were issuing silver coins of good quality, and silver coins were increasingly determining the value of the moneys of account used in international trade and shipping. The golden perperi and bezants minted in the Levant were becoming ever more diverse and unreliable. Coins of practically pure gold, however, had been issued by Genoa and Florence, and for decades gold had been rising in value. Compared with silver coins or with obligations based on silver, gold coins and moneys of account based on gold were proving more reliable for storing away exchange value for future use.

The availability side by side of coins of pure gold and coins of almost pure silver raised the possibility of bimetallic standards more clearly defined than the nebulous bimetallic standards that had been in use in the Levant and were based on loosely defined relations between silver coins such as the Venetian grossi and coins containing both gold and silver, such as the Byzantine perperi. When in coining gold Venice imitated what Genoa and Florence had done thirty years earlier, Venice attempted to tie her gold coin to her existing moneys of account so as to create a bimetallic monetary standard. As we have just seen, the Florentines had quickly abandoned the bimetallic standard created when they first coined the florin. Subsequently they gave up any effort to maintain a single unified monetary standard. While continuing the use of a money of account based on silver or billon in local trade, they were content to use gold as the basis for the moneys of account that they employed in their international business. Venice, on the other hand, would not so easily give up using silver as a standard of value in international trade, especially for purchases in the Levant, which were more important to Venetian merchants than to Florentine merchants and for which the Venetians used silver received from the Germans.

The ratio that Venice established in its first bimetallic standard shows an effort to stop the rise of gold. To make its Levantine purchases on traditional and favorable terms, the Venetians needed to maintain the relative value of silver. When they voted in October 1284 to mint the ducat, they voted to make it of exactly the same weight and fineness as the florin, although with a distinctively Venetian design. The following spring, when the coin was actually minted, it was made legal tender for 40 soldi a grossi, the equivalent of 18.38 (480/26.111) silver grossi.[60] When the ducat was valued at 40 soldi a grossi, coined gold was being valued only 10.9 (18.38 × [2.1/3.55]) times as much as coined silver, although in that decade the bimetallic ratio between coined gold and silver at Florence was about 11.6 to 1.[61]

[60]Papadopoli, 1:342; see also above, chap. 10, sec. iv and n. 42.
[61]Bernocchi, 3:158.

THE VENETIAN GOLD DUCAT

An example of the first issue, struck under Doge Giovanni
Dandolo (1280–89).

*Obv.*: .IODANDVL. DVX .S.M.VENETI. St. Mark, facing three-quarters right,
presents the banner to the kneeling doge.

*Rev.*: .SIT.T.XPE.DAT.Q.TV REGIS.ISTE.DVCAT. Christ in the act of blessing,
in a mandorla with nine stars in the field.

*AV, 20.3 mm, 3.548 gr. Museo Bottacin, inv. no. 81 (Papadopoli, 1: 137 no. 1).*

282

An opportunity to check the rising value of gold and at the same time to obtain from the bullion trade more profits for Venetian merchants and more earnings for its craftsmen was being presented to the Venetians because German miners were exploiting the gold veins in the mines located in the Kingdom of Hungary. Florentines managed the Hungarian mints and turned much of that gold into Hungarian florins resembling those of Florence, but much gold bullion was brought to Venice by German merchants. Genoa and Florence had better commercial networks through which to obtain the gold from North Africa or Spain, but Venice was the Italian city best placed to offer a market for gold bullion mined in Hungary and Transylvania.[62] The auction of the Germans' gold by the Visdomini of the Fondaco dei Tedeschi is mentioned as early as 1272.[63] Increased production of the Hungarian gold mines in the latter part of the century may well have given Venetians reason to hope that they could arrest the rising price of gold.

Concern with keeping down the price of gold is apparent in the provisions made when the ducat was first coined. In 1284 the mint was instructed to buy gold at such a price that the ducats would not cost more than 18 grossi each.[64] It is doubtful that gold bullion could have been obtained with that ceiling on its price, for that price implied a bimetallic ratio of 10.6 to 1, distinctly less than the 11.3 to 1 generally estimated as the ratio at that time[65] and even less than the ratio of 10.9 to 1 between coined gold and coined silver implied by the official value of 40 soldi a grossi given the ducat the following year.[66] An appropriation of 8,000 lire a grossi was then put at the disposal of the mintmasters for buying gold.[67] Later in that same year, on 28 August 1285, they were authorized to borrow money at 8 percent with which to buy gold for minting in order to put the gold coins in circulation ("ut moneta auri currat"). The loans were to be repaid the following 8 June.[68] In August 1286 the mintmasters were authorized to borrow up to 10,000 lire from the fund that had been accumulated at the office of the Procurators of San Marco, almost certainly in the form

<hr/>

[62]Bálint Hóman, *Geschichte des ungarischen Mittelalters,* trans. for the Ungarische Institut of the University of Berlin by Hildegard von Roosz and Max Pfotenhauer, 2 vols. (Berlin, 1940–43), 2:338, 353–55. Arthur Pohl, *Ungarische Goldgulden des Mittelalters (1325–1540)* (Graz, 1974), 8–9.

[63]*DMC,* 2:301.

[64]Ibid., 3:88.

[65]Desimoni, "La moneta e il rapporto dell'oro all'argento," 37–41, presents evidence of a general rising trend in Italy in the last two decades of the thirteenth century and says (p. 39) that 11.285 to 1 was the commercial ratio in 1284, when the Venetians set a ratio of 10.648 to 1 by equating 1 ducat and 18 grossi.

[66]Since 26.111 denari a grossi equaled 1 grosso, 40 soldi a grossi equaled 480/26.111, or 18.38 grossi. And $18.38 \times 2.1/3.55 = 10.9$.

[67]Papadopoli, 1:342.

[68]*DMC,* 3:120; *PMV,* doc. 42.

of grossi, assigned for payments on the public debt, and were required to pay the Procurators back in gold ducats within three days after their minting.[69] With this provision, the government suggested that bond-holders would soon have to accept payments on the public debt in the form of ducats instead of grossi.

Concern with keeping down the price of gold while encouraging acceptance of the new coin is evident also in the inducements offered for importing gold coins from overseas. In December 1286 the mint was or-dered to recoin into ducats 24,000 perperi just arrived from Constantino-ple and to do it with such charges that the government neither lost nor gained.[70] In March 1287 it was provided that thereafter, those bringing perperi or tarì or other gold coin for reminting should receive 132 1/2 lire (2,650 soldi) a grosso for each mark instead of the 2,600 soldi paid for bullion certified by the officials of the Rialto.[71]

This special concern with attracting gold from overseas was later expressed in the lower mint charges on gold from "outside the gulf," which meant in practice Africa and the Levant, compared with the mint charge on gold imported from "within the gulf," meaning gold that the Germans brought by land or across the head of the Adriatic.[72] Not until the 1340s was the lower seigniorage of only about 0.4 percent, represented by the mint's paying out ducats at 39 soldi, extended to the Germans.[73] Recoinage of gold coins from the Levant, such as high-quality Egyptian dinars and any very old perperi that contained more than the 3.55 grams of gold in the ducat (that is, perperi that were of more than 20 carats gold), was encouraged by forbidding rectors to accept in payment of taxes any bezants as worth more than 40 soldi, the minimal value set on the ducat. "Current" perperi and saracenati were to be valued at no more than 20 soldi (1/2 a ducat).[74] Being thus made worth less as legal tender than as bullion, old good Levantine issues of gold or electrum coins were more likely to be brought to the mint to be converted into ducats.

Since for centuries trading to and through Constantinople had been the chief activity of Venice's leading merchants, many of them may have thought of gold as "real money," the "true" standard of value, and reck-oned their fortunes in perperi traditionally worth 40 soldi in Venetian money of account. After 1285 the good old perperi, even in the form of

[69]DMC, 3:153–54. PMV, doc. 44, gives the same text, except that the limit of the borrowing there reads "XII^M libras," while it is "X^M" in the DMC and in PRV, doc. 45.

[70]DMC, 3:160–61; PMV, doc. 45 (where the sum involved reads 23,000!).

[71]DMC, 3:167. In PMV, doc. 46, the figure reads "libras CXXXII." Consulting the original records shows that 132 1/2 is correct (MC, Zaneta, fol. 24v). Since 67 ducats were made from a mark, this price was equivalent to 39.55 soldi (2,650/67) per mark.

[72]See above, chap. 10, sec. iv; and below, app. A, sec. v.

[73]See below, chap. 17, n. 55; and app. A.

[74]PMV, doc. 35 (1284); DMC, 3:78.

Comnenian coins, were disappearing or had disappeared. But those who thought of gold as the "true" standard of value could find their standard resurrected materially in the ducat when it—like the old perpero—was thus valued at 40 soldi a grossi. If so, there is here some similarity to the development at Genoa earlier as interpreted by Robert Lopez. He suggests that the genovino, the first of the new type of gold coins weighing 3.5 grams, embodied a defunct unit in the Moslem-Sicilian system of gold coinage much used in the Genoese trading area.[75] At Venice the ducat gave golden reembodiment to the value of 40 soldi that earlier had its physical basis in the somewhat larger gold coin of the Byzantine Empire.

[75] Lopez, *Settecento anni fa*, 12, 13–14, 31; Trasselli, "Le aree monetarie," 63, n. 25. The defunct unit was the ghost of the dinar from 1/4 of which was derived the tarì, of which the legal weight was 0.88 grams, so that the weight of 4 tarì (4 × 0.88) was not far from the weight of the genovino (3.55 grams). See also Misbach, "Genoese Trade." Of course, the genovini coined in the 1250s were more nearly pure gold than the tarì coined then, but earlier Moslem dinars had been of finer gold than the later tarì.

# 14

# THE RISE OF GOLD

## i. CHANGING BIMETALLIC RATIOS

ENETIAN EFFORTS TO CHECK the rise of gold met only partial and temporary success. In the 1280s and 1290s, ducats and florins were quoted at 20 grossi as well as at 18 1/2, which reflects bimetallic ratios of 11.8 to 1 and 10.9 to 1, respectively, between the coined metals.[1] After 1296 the bimetallic ratio shot up. The ducat and the florin were by 1305 apparently, by 1310 surely, quoted generally at 24 grossi,[2]

[1]See below, table D.2. See also GianRinaldo Carli, *Delle monete e dell'istituzione delle zecche d'Italia*, vols. 2–8 of his *Opere* (Milan, 1784), 5:308–9; Bernocchi, 3:158, 163. Our calculations are as follows: 20 × (2.1/3.55) = 11.8; and 18.5 × (2.1/3.55) = 10.9. The ratios of 12.9 to 1 and 13.1 to 1 given by Watson, "Back to Gold," 24, may be derived from the same sources as those indicating a ratio that high before 1300 found in Cipolla, *I movimenti*, 45. Cipolla compiled the figures from the old works of Argelati and Padovan, which contain some confusions concerning the lira a grossi, as explained in the note to table 1 in Lane, "Le vecchie monete di conto." At Zara the ducat rose immediately to 20 grossi and stayed at that value, according to Antonio Teja, *Aspetti della vita economica di Zara dal 1289 al 1409*, vol. 1, *La pratica bancaria* (Zara, 1936), 16–17. But the evidence that he gives for the ducat's being worth 20 grossi as late as 1386 must refer not to grossi coins but to accounting units probably similar in origin to the Venetian grosso a oro, explained below, in chap. 16.

[2]See below, table D.2. Cf. Desimoni, "La moneta e il rapporto dell'oro all'argento," 39; Casini, "Il corso dei cambi," 137–38; Watson, "Back to Gold," 24; K. H. Schäfer, ed., *Die Ausgaben der Apostolischen Kammer unter Johann XXII. nebst dem Jahresbilanzen von 1316–1317*, vol. 2 of *Vatikanische Quellen zur Geschichte der Päpstlichen Hof- und Finanzverwaltung, 1316–1378* (Paderborn: Görres-Gesellschaft, 1911), "Einleitung," 51*, 126*–27*. Charles M. de La Roncière, *Un changeur florentin*, 53–54, in describing how Lippo brought grossi coins to

indicating a bimetallic ratio of 14.2 to 1. Carlo M. Cipolla in describing the rise of gold coins in Italy as a whole gives the average bimetallic ratio in the period 1315–25 as 13.5 to 1,[3] and it went higher in Venice in some years. The gold used by goldsmiths in gilding silverware and jewelry was reported in 1314 to have been bought at a rate equivalent to 24 grossi plus 12 piccoli per ducat, and earlier at 28 grossi. Gold's rise had begun in the 1290s. It was up from the 108 soldi a grossi per carat of 1285 to 112 soldi a grossi already before 1297, and it went up to 120 soldi in September of that year and to 132 soldi in 1298.[4]

High prices are commonly associated with scarcity; it may be misleading, therefore, to call 24 grossi a high price for ducats or florins. Not scarcity of gold but increased supplies of silver were the principal cause of the rise in the bimetallic ratio between 1250 and 1320. So far as is known, prices of goods in general were rising, not falling, in that period.[5] What was falling was the value of silver compared with that of either wheat or gold. This chapter, instead of being entitled "The Rise of Gold," could more accurately have been entitled "The Fall of Silver."

The increase in the amount of silver available for coinage is inferred

---

Venice in 1310, 1315, and 1323 to buy ducats or florins, which he then remitted to Florence, gives the rate of exchange as 10 florins to 1 lira di grossi, which is in accord with the rate of 1 florin or ducat to 24 grossi; but de la Roncière still seems to accept Luzzatto's assumption that the ducat was worth only 18 or 18 1/2 grossi even that late. Roberto Cessi, in "Studi sulla moneta veneziana: II," p. 6 of the offprint, recognized that the ducat rose from 18 1/2 to 24 grossi soon after 1296. Those "Studi" stressed a difference between "valore legale" and "valore di zecca," that is, between what we would call value as legal tender and market value. But Cessi did not clarify his conception of "valore di zecca." He seemed to consider it equivalent to market value when he said that the law of 1328 that gave a ducat the value as legal tender of 24 grossi, "non faceva che sanzionare una condizione di fatto" (p. 6). But in trying to explain in his "Studi sulla moneta veneziana: I. Il denaro *piccolo* ed il denaro *grosso* fino alla coniazione del ducato," *Economia. Rassegna mensile di politica economica* (Trieste), 1 (1923), pp. 10–11 of the offprint, how the grosso equaled 26 or 26 1/9 piccoli, he considered this exchange as the "valore di zecca." In these articles, Cessi treated as references to soldi a grossi all those mentions of 39, 39 1/2, and 40 soldi here interpreted as soldi a oro, as explained in Lane, "Le vecchie monete di conto" and in n. 10 below. In later studies, Cessi seemed less willing to believe that the ducat had been at 24 grossi two or three decades before 1328, probably because he could not reconcile that with his interpretation of how the mint kept its accounts. Revision of his interpretation was suggested by discovery of the *Zibaldone da Canal* and confirmed by the accounts of the estate of Leone Morosini (PSM, Misti, b. 127), which record sales ca. 1343 to the mint that were paid for in ducats valued at 39 soldi.

[3]*Le avventure della lira,* app. 3, table A.1. On ratios elsewhere in Europe, see below, sec. iii in this chapter, and chap. 19, sec. iii.

[4]Monticolo, ed., *I capitolari delle arti,* 3:320. These prices must be in the soldi a grossi based on silver, whereas the mint's price remained 108 soldi only by creating the soldo a oro, that is, by valuing the ducats it paid out at 39 of the same kind of soldi in which it valued the gold received.

[5]Michael M. Postan, "The Trade of Medieval Europe: The North," in *The Cambridge Economic History of Europe,* vol. 2 (Cambridge, 1952), pp. 165–66; Ruggiero Romano, ed., *I prezzi in Europa dal XIII secolo a oggi* (Turin, 1967), 18, 104, 119, 147.

from the extensive evidence of the opening of many new silver mines in central and eastern Europe. The most productive were those at Kutna Hora (Kuttenberg), in the Kingdom of Bohemia.[6] Much came also from older mining districts in Germany; those in Tyrol in the upper valley of the Adige were especially important to Venice.[7] To the traditional sources of supply handled by German merchants were added the outputs of the new mines in Serbia and Bosnia.[8]

The rise of gold made it impossible for Venice to maintain the bimetallic standard clearly envisaged in 1284, when the minting of its ducat was planned. The very rapid rise in the value of gold coin after 1295 destroyed all hope of maintaining or recreating that standard. Venice thus ceased to have a bimetallic standard for some years. For about a decade after 1295, Venice reverted to its traditional silver standard based on the silver grosso.

Mint practices also were adjusted accordingly. After the bimetallic ratio rose, Venetian mintmasters could not hope to buy with 18 1/2 grossi the gold needed to mint 1 ducat. They had never been under obligation to pay in silver grossi for all the gold they minted. Instead they adopted the practice of paying for gold with the gold coined, just as they paid for silver with the silver coined. The law of 1285 on the coinage of the ducat specifically provided that the mintmasters might pay for the gold with the ducats into which it was minted ("de denariis auri supradictis").[9] In doing so, the mintmasters developed a special accounting unit, a mint soldo a oro, which was distinct from the older soldo a grossi, although historically derived from it. The mint still valued the gold it received at the price of 108 soldi per carat set in 1285 and therefore paid 2,592 soldi for 24-carat gold, but the soldo referred to was the special accounting unit of the mint, a soldo a oro, not the traditional soldo a grossi linked to the grosso coin. The mint used this same special accounting unit, the soldo a oro, in setting the values of 39 or 39 1/2 soldi on the ducats it paid out.[10] In short, the

[6]Josef Janáček, "L'argent tchèque et la Méditerranée (XIVe et XVe siècles)," in *Mélanges en l'honneur de Fernand Braudel* (Toulouse, 1973), vol. 1, pp. 245–51; F. Graus, "La crise monétaire du XIV siècle," *Revue belge de philologie et d'histoire* 29 (1951):446–52.

[7]Stella, *Politica ed economia*, 14, and works there cited. Arnold Luschin von Ebengreuth, "Goldgeschäfte Meinhards II., Grafen von Tirol und seine Söhne: Ein Beitrag zur Geschichte der Edelmetalle (1289–1303)," *Veröffentlichungen des Museum Ferdinandeum in Innsbruck* 8 (1928):441–58, shows the other side of the coin: how in 1289–1303 the count of Tyrol accumulated gold stocks which he then sold off in Venice and the Veneto in return for coined silver at substantial profits.

[8]Kovačeviè, "Dans la Serbie et la Bosnie médiévales," 250–57.

[9]*DMC*, 3:109 (1285); also in *PMV*, doc. 40.

[10]The complicated analysis of evidence in Lane, "Le vecchie monete di conto," 61–72, may seem superfluous in view of the clear, simple statement of the practice of the mintmasters for gold in making payments for the gold they received in "deneri d'oro" in their capitolare in *PMV*, doc. 37, p. 42. But the date of the vernacular language used in that capitolare (now

mint did not accept and give out gold and silver one for the other at legally determined prices and thus maintain a single bimetallic standard. It permitted the separation of two standards: one standard, which was unofficial, based on gold; the other, the official standard, based on silver.

Thus within 10–15 years after the coinage of its first ducat, Venice, like Florence, gave up temporarily its attempt at maintaining a bimetallic standard, although Venice resumed the effort later.

Whether the temporary abandonment of the effort for a bimetallic standard was deliberate is questionable. Probably the mintmasters who executed it had the approval of the strong-minded Doge Pietro Gradenigo (1289–1311) and his inner circle, especially of the Quarantia, which in that period was rising to the peak of its power and was the council most concerned with the mint. But many members of the Great Council did not approve and may not have understood the mint's practices. A law that the Great Council passed in 1296 stated that whereas the mintmasters were giving out ducats at 39 1/2 "solidi ad aurum," they should give them out at 40 "solidi ad grossos."[11] One can wonder what those who voted for it had in mind. Perhaps they were thinking only of reaffirming a traditional statement of value. It seems unlikely that they meant to order the mint, at a time when ducats could be sold to a moneychanger for 20 grossi, to pay ducats to anyone who offered 18 1/2 grossi. If the mint had valued ducats at 40 soldi after paying 2,592 soldi per mark for the gold, it would have been collecting a mint charge of about 3 percent.[12] Perhaps some member of the Great Council hoped that the high mint charge would make the value of the silver coin higher compared with that of gold than it would otherwise have been. But at Florence the mint charge on gold had been only 1.25 percent since 1252 and was lowered to 0.625 percent in 1294.[13] A high mint charge at Venice would have encouraged bullion merchants to take their gold to Florence. Probably the action in the Great Council in 1296 ex-

---

ASV, Zecca, b. 6tris) is uncertain, and some passages in pertinent laws and treaties are ambiguous, so that it seemed worthwhile emphasizing that this method of accounting was authorized as early as 1285. In some passages Cessi seems to imply that the mint paid out ducats in return for 40 soldi a grossi in legal tender, that is, in return for 18 1/2 grossi. If the mint had done so, it would have prevented the rise of the ducat to 24 grossi. The evidence that the ducat went to 24 grossi, not in 1328, when it was made legal tender for that amount, but at least twenty years earlier, necessitates the conclusion that the mint valued the ducat, not in the usual soldi a grossi, but in soldi a oro. Allan Evans, in n. 4, p. 140, of his edition of Pegolotti's *Pratica,* says that the mint used soldi a grossi at "the old valuation," recognizing that this was a special kind of soldo still used by the mint when the current value of the ducat was 52 soldi a grossi; but we have preferred to call it the soldo a oro to make clear that it was *not* the kind of soldo in which the ducat was valued outside the mint. Perhaps it should be called the "soldo a grossi in oro di zecca." On this soldo see also below, sec. iii.

[11]*PMV*, doc. 65; *DMC*, 3:402.
[12]See below, app. A, sec. v.
[13]Bernocchi, 3:40.

pressed a frustrated desire to have a single standard of value in which both 1 ducat and 18 1/2 grossi were worth 40 soldi a grossi. Later resolutions give reason to believe that some Venetians thought wistfully of a single, bimetallic standard but that the motion that passed the Great Council in 1296 in fact had no effect.

The two standards of value, even though only that based on silver was official, had the advantage of enabling the mint to continue to operate while the bimetallic ratio rose after 1296, and the ducat was accepted as the equivalent of 24 grossi.

## ii. VENICE'S SECOND BIMETALLIC STANDARD

Soon after the ducat touched 24 grossi, the rate of change in the bimetallic ratio moderated. The values of gold and silver coins then began to come together at Venice into a new bimetallic standard in which 1 gold ducat equaled 24 silver grossi, a bimetallic ratio of 14.2 to 1. Plentiful supplies of silver kept the bimetallic ratio high in Europe generally until about 1330. Consequently, silver remained at the low price it had reached by 1305 long enough for the equating of 1 ducat with 24 grossi to become established in usage as Venice's second bimetallic standard even before it received legal formulation; that came only in 1328, under circumstances that will be described in chapter 15.

Since the lira a grossi, the money of account used in most big business operations and governmental affairs, had remained tightly tied to the silver grosso coin, and since 24 grossi had traditionally been valued at 52 soldi a grossi, 1 ducat was valued also at 52 soldi a grossi. The law of 1285 had specified that no one could refuse to accept a ducat in payment of 40 soldi a grossi. For that amount it was legal tender. But that law did not forbid accepting ducats at more than 40 soldi a grossi, which thus constituted a floor.[14]

Not only the lira a grossi but also Venice's two other moneys of account, the lira di grossi and the lira di piccoli, continued to be tied to silver coins for years after the coinage of the ducat. Since the lira di grossi equaled 240 grossi, when 1 ducat came to be valued at 24 grossi it was valued also at 1/10 of a lira di grossi and 2 soldi di grossi. Its value in lira di piccoli was derived from the legal relation of the grosso to the piccolo, namely, 1 grosso = 32 piccoli; thus 1 ducat = 24 × 32 piccoli = 768 piccoli, commonly expressed as 64 soldi (768/12) or 3 lire 4 soldi.[15] In short, after

---

[14]The emphasis in the law of 1285 was all on making the ducat legal tender for at least 40 soldi. It reads: "omnis persona . . . debeat ipsum ducatum aureum pro suo pagamento accipere per xl solidis ad grossos . . ." (*PMV*, doc. 40).

[15]Papadopoli, 1:120–21; see also above, chap. 8, sec. iii.

the rise of gold, keepers of accounts made conversions at the following rates:

1 ducat = 24 grossi = 2 soldi di grossi   = 1/10 lira di grossi
                    = 768 piccoli        = 64 soldi di piccoli (768/12)
                    = 624 denari a grossi = 52 soldi a grossi

These conversions reflected a bimetallic ratio of 14.2:1.[16]

Between the rise of the bimetallic ratio in 1296–1305 and the elevation of the value of the ducat as legal tender to 24 grossi in 1328, the above equivalences seem to have been well established in practice. At least evaluations very similar to the above must have been in use, although at some times gold coin was worth even more. The moneychangers who had developed into bankers (as described below, in volume 2) kept their books in lire a grossi or lire di grossi. When they accepted ducats as deposits in current accounts, they had to credit depositors for the current value of the ducat in these lire. Otherwise, it can be assumed, merchants would not have made such deposits. Taxes were of course stated in lire and soldi, based on silver coins, and laws required that import duties be paid in good grossi, but gold coin was specified as a satisfactory form of security. It was accepted instead of grossi when offered by those eager to get their wares out of customs. In the calculation of international exchange rates the ducat, like the florin, was considered equal to 24 grossi.[17]

Gradually the lira di grossi came to be used more and more, and the lira a grossi less and less, because it was easier to express the relation of coins to the former than to the latter. In fixing the salaries of officials and the terms of commercial contracts, the lira di grossi was used increasingly. The lira a grossi, however, continued to be used in some established series of accounts such as those of the Loan Office (Camera degli Imprestiti) and in some commercial transactions. Rates of exchange with Levantine moneys were still recorded in lire and soldi a grossi; those with London and Bruges were recorded in lira di grossi.

A significant recognition of this bimetallic standard prevailing at Venice, and particularly in Venice's relation with the Levant, is contained in the merchants' manual compiled by Francesco Pegolotti. The section on Venice must refer to the period about 1320–30. Pegolotti provided a table for converting from ducats into Byzantine perperi and from perperi into soldi a grossi with a statement of the value, in lire, soldi, and denari a

---

[16]On complications connected with the lira di grossi manca see below, chap. 16, nn. 16, 17. The ratio between coined metals is calculated as follows: 1 ducat = 24 grossi; 3.55 grams gold = 50.4 grams silver (24 × 2.1); 50.4/3.55 = 14.197:1.

[17]Schäfer, *Die Ausgaben*, vol. 2, "Einleitung," p. 51*. See also below, table D.2; and chap. 15, n. 10.

grossi, of both the gold ducat and the silver grosso. He specified that 52 soldi a grossi of Venice equaled 1 ducat and that 26 denari a grossi equaled 1 grosso.[18] Pegolotti thus explicitly linked the value of the denominations of that Venetian money of account, the lira a grossi, to both a gold coin and a silver coin.

### iii. EFFECTS ON EXCHANGE RATES, COLONIAL AND FOREIGN

The rise in the bimetallic ratio changed the relations of coins to moneys of account also of Venice's trading partners. Although the two phases of the rise—before and after 1296—in many cases cannot be clearly distinguished, in both phases there was increased use of silver in the east and of gold in the west, both as means of payment and as standards of value. The use of coins composed entirely or more largely of silver, and the reckoning in money of account based on such coins, continued to increase in the Levant and to affect Venetian trade and monetary policies.

Evidence about the value of foreign monetary units compared with those of Venice becomes more varied in the later thirteenth and early fourteenth century. As in analyzing domestic exchange, that is, when comparing the value of Venice's own monetary units one with another, so also in foreign exchange an obvious starting point for examination is the metallic content of coins; but to compare coins of different metals or of different mixtures of metals, or units based on coins with such diversities, knowledge of their value in moneys of account is essential.

Official values are among the earliest recorded and must be distinguished, if possible, from the market value and real exchange values. Generally the legal tender value of a state's own issues was a minimal value. In contrast, the legal tender value of foreign coin was intended to be a maximum, that is, the value above which it should not be accepted, at least not by government officials. For example, the Venetian laws of 1285–86 declared that the gold ducat was worth 40 soldi a grossi and that no gold perpero was to be valued at more than 40 soldi.[19] These laws did not

---

[18]Pegolotti, *Pratica*, 50. In giving exchange on Genoa, in contrast, he links the relevant Genoese money of account only to the gold "florin" (ibid., 48). Pegolotti describes exchange of Venice with London, Naples, and Bruges in lire di grossi (151–52, 171–73, 247–49). Since various parts of Pegolotti's *Pratica* were composed at various dates, there is a temptation to interpret the passage on p. 50 as evidence that the section on Venice was composed after the passage of the law of 1328. But Pegolotti makes no mention whatever of the new coins issued in 1331–32—the mezzanino and the soldino—so that his information must have been collected before that date. To date the passage within those specific three to four years is questionable, however. It seems likely that whether it was written shortly before 1328 or immediately after, Pegolotti would not have referred to the ducat as being worth 52 soldi in the way that he did unless that had already been its value in commercial practice for some time.

[19]See above, chap. 13, sec. iv.

## GERMAN MINING

A cross-section view of a mine designed
to show the use of many shafts.

*From Agricola,* De re metallica *(edition of 1556, at the BMV), 73.
Photograph by Toso.*

prevent the ducat from being valued by moneychangers a few years later at more than 40 soldi a grossi, nor did they prevent moneychangers from paying much less than 40 soldi a grossi for inferior varieties of perperi and saracenati.

Apart from decrees setting legal values on coins, many official documents indicate the comparative values applied in practice, with allowances for either penalties or premiums. Examples are the exchange rates derived from Zeno's Maritime Code of 1255, analyzed above in chap. 13, sec. ii, which included a penalty for late payments. Many other payments to or from Romania included either discounts or premiums because of the terms on which payments made in the one place were to be repaid in the other.[20] Official rates given in such sources were presumably influenced by the market rates.

More completely independent of the official legal tender values are those found in merchants' accounts and letters. To determine whether these rates were market quotations or rates bargained for on a particular transaction in which an extension of credit was involved, they have to be examined case by case.[21] In merchant manuals, which became important sources during the first half of the fourteenth century, some exchange rates are indicative of market rates, some of rates used in transactions with officials.[22] The foreign exchange value of various moneys in the second half of the century is definitely indicated by the bills of exchange which by then had become widely used in standardized form and were being bought and sold every day in such money markets as Venice, Bruges, and Florence.[23] For earlier periods we have to depend heavily on the exchange

[20]Bertelè, "Moneta veneziana," 31–38; and below, n. 29.

[21]For examples see below, chap. 19.

[22]Besides the manuals already cited (Stussi, ed., *Zibaldone da Canal;* *Tarifa zoè noticia;* Pegolotti, *Pratica;* Ciano, ed., *"Pratica della mercatura"* datiniana), there are some other manuals and fragments both earlier and later that are particularly worthy of note here. Perhaps the earliest is the "Racione de Alexandria," BMV, Mss. It., cl. XI, cod. 87 (7353). Dated about 1270 by David Jacoby, who has prepared the six small folios for publication, it contains bullion prices and exchange rates between Acre, Constantinople, and other centers in the Levant. Also very early is the *Memoria de tucte le mercantie,* compiled by a Pisan in 1278 and recently published by Roberto S. Lopez and Gabriella Airaldi (*Miscellanea di studi storici* [Genoa, 1983]) which also contains Levantine exchanges. (For a description of the manuscript see Robert S. Lopez, "Stars and Spices: The Earliest Italian Manual of Commercial Practice," in Herlihy, Lopez, and Slessarev, eds., *Economy, Society, and Government,* 35–42; and idem, "Un texte inédit: Le plus ancien manuel italien de technique commerciale," *Revue historique* 94 [1970]:67–76). See also Antonia Borlandi, ed., *Il manuale di mercatura di Saminiato de' Ricci,* Università di Genova, Istituto di Storia Medievale e Moderna, Fonti e studi, 4 (Genoa, 1963); and Bruno Dini, ed., *Una pratica di mercatura in formazione (1394–1395),* Pubblicazioni dell'Istituto Internazionale di Storia Economica "Francesco Datini," 1st ser., 2 (Florence, 1980).

[23]See below, vol. 2. It should be kept in mind that rates of foreign exchange generally included interest at rates that fluctuated according to supply and demand.

TABLE 8.

Some Exchange Rates in Overseas Trade, 1255–1330:
Values of Foreign Moneys of Account in Venetian Soldi a Grossi

| Foreign Money of Account | 1255 (Zeno's Code) | 1268–93 (Ternaria) | 1311 (*Zibaldone*) | 1310–30 (Pegolotti) |
|---|---|---|---|---|
| *Based on Gold Coin* | | | | |
| Oncia of Apulia | | | | |
| Bezant of Alexandria | | 200 | 60 | 60 |
| Bezant of Barbary | 180 | 55–60 | (13.6) | 13.9 |
| *Symmetallic Base (Partly Gold)* | | | | |
| Perpero of Constantinople | 32 | 33 | 28 or 32 | 26–32.8 |
| Saracenato | 28 | 32 | | 30.33–45.5 |
| *Based on Silver Coin* | | | | |
| Perpero of Crete | (26) | 30 | (26) | (26) |
| Perpero of Slavonia | (26) | 30 | (26) | (26) |
| Perpero of Clarentza and Morea | | 26 | | |
| Perpero of 20 aspri of Crimea[a] | | 33 | 32.7 | (35.6) |
| Perperi of 11 Cuman aspri[b] | | | | |
| Perperi of 10.5 Turkish aspri | | 33 | | |
| Bezant of Armenia | | 32 | | 21.67 soldi a grossi |
| Bezant of Barbary | 18 | 13 | | (10.8) |
| Oncia of Apulia[c] | | | | 238–312 |

NOTE: Numbers in parentheses were calculated from values given in other units, mostly from values given in grossi.

[a]See below, n. 44.

[b]In the Ternaria list but not valued.

[c]See below, sec. iii; and chap. 19, nn. 94, 95.

rates specified in contracts, such as the notarized exchange contracts in use before the development of the bill of exchange. Rates from such contracts, like those from letters and accounts of merchants or of such international financial officials as papal collectors,[24] cannot support conclusions as precise as those that can be derived for later dates from bills of exchange; but they provide rough indications of shifts, as do those in official administrative records.

The earliest extensive listing of the values in Venetian money of account to be given to foreign moneys is embodied in the regulations of the Ternaria, a customs office that collected many import duties ad va-

[24]For examples see the sources cited below in this section. On exchange contracts in general see Lopez and Raymond, *Medieval Trade*, chaps. 7 and 8.

lorem. When the values of which they collected a percentage were declared or recorded in foreign moneys of account, the values of those moneys in Venetian lire and soldi a grossi were reckoned using the rates indicated in table 8.

The Ternaria list shows the extent to which the use in the Levant of moneys of account based on silver coins had increased during the thirteenth century and how much gold had risen in value after 1250. The rates were certainly in effect before 1293 and were possibly in the main fixed as early as 1268.[25] They probably represent exchange values after the bimetallic ratio had risen from the nadir of about 8.5 to 1 of 1250 and reached about 11.8 to 1 by the 1280s. They provide a framework for a survey before the rapid additional rise in the value of gold between 1295 and 1305.

### Romania

Among the moneys most important for Venice's overseas trade were the four kinds of perpero in use in regions that had been parts of the Byzantine Empire before 1204. The perpero of Crete, the largest territory directly under Venetian rule, was specifically identified by the Ternaria as the money of account worth 12 grossi. In mid-century, when the bimetallic ratio had been 8.5 to 1 or 9 to 1, the metallic value of 12 grossi had been about the same as that of the perpero coins then being minted.[26] When the value of gold rose,[27] it became much cheaper to pay a debt of 1 perpero with 12 grossi than with a perpero that was 2/3 gold. In Crete and in some other portions of the Byzantine Empire that came under Venetian rule, the perpero became a money of account based on the Venetian grosso. (As early as the 1270s, equating 1 perpero with 12 grossi was a regular practice.)[28] Since 12 grossi were equal to about 26 soldi a grossi, the rate of

[25]The Ternaria's list (cap. 17 of its capitolare) is printed below, app. G, doc. 1. The opening paragraph resembles *DMC*, 2:284 (cf. 3:78), which suggests a date of 1261; but the valuations of foreign moneys probably are those referred to in the rubric of 20 September 1268 (ibid., 2:390), which may be translated as follows: "How, on merchandise that comes to Venice from Beyond-the-Sea and other regions, bezants, etc., ought to be valued."

[26]See above, chap. 13, sec. ii.

[27]Desimoni, "La moneta e il rapporto dell'oro all'argento," 35–39.

[28]Freddy Thiriet's account in *La Romanie vénitienne au Moyen Age: Le développement et l'exploration du domaine colonial vénitien (XII–XV siècles)*, Bibliothèque des Ecoles Françaises d'Athènes et de Rome, 193 (Paris, 1959), 307, fails to distinguish between coins and moneys of account or between the perperi of Crete and those of Constantinople. While recognizing the lack of any evidence for the existence of a mint in Crete, he apparently failed to realize that the perperi often referred to in Cretan documents were not equivalent in value to any coin of that name but were accounting units equal to 12 Venetian-coined grossi. Such are the perperi referred to in the notarial register of *Leonardo Marcello* (Chiaudano and Lombardo, eds.), docs. 79, 155, 339, 341, 344, and passim. See also Lombardo, ed., *Documenti della colonia veneziana di Creta, I;* doc. 50 quotes the perpero as 28 soldi, but thereafter, in doc. 71 and in others, it is consistently equated with 12 grossi.

exchange between the Cretan perpero and the Venetian soldo a grossi fluctuated around 26. It was higher when there was a demand in Venice for funds in Crete and when a draft on Venice drawn in Crete involved an extension of credit.[29] It was not affected by the rise in the value of gold because both the Cretan perpero and the Venetian soldo a grossi were based on silver. But when the gold ducat rose from 40 soldi a grossi to 52, the ducat became worth no longer 40/26 perperi but 52/26, or 2 perperi.

In addition to the perpero used in Crete, the Ternaria list of exchange rates includes three other kinds of perperi, of which the most important was the money of account used in Constantinople, Salonica, and "toto imperio," that is, the restricted territory still ruled by the Byzantine Greek emperors. There the good old perperi of the Comneni had practically disappeared from circulation and been replaced during the second half of the thirteenth century by issues of the Palaeologian emperors, which at first contained 2.93 grams of gold. They were about equal in metallic value to 12 Venetian grossi if the bimetallic ratio was then, in the 1260s, at 8.6 to 1, as seems likely.[30]

The subsequent rise of gold would have raised the value of perpero coins far above 12 grossi if the gold content of the Byzantine perpero, like the silver content of the Venetian grosso, had remained unchanged. But during the second half of the thirteenth century the percentage of gold in the Byzantine perpero was reduced so much that it became worth only 1/2 a Venetian gold ducat and as a money of account was about equal to the perpero in use in Crete.[31]

The debasement of the Byzantine perpero (that is, the diminution of its gold content) lagged, however, behind the rise of gold in Italy. That is to say, it lagged behind the fall of silver in the west. That lag is another indication that the change in the bimetallic ratio was caused mainly by the large increase of silver production in the west. The lag in the debasement of the perpero of Constantinople explains why it was rated as high on the Ternaria list—at 33 soldi—as it had been in Zeno's Maritime Code, in fact a soldo higher. In the earliest extensive merchant's manual of Venetian origin, the *Zibaldone da Canal* of 1311, two kinds of perpero are valued: the

---

[29]In 1286 the Venetian official called the duke of Crete ("duca di Candia") was authorized to draw on Venice for 14,000 perperi but not to pay more than 30 soldi per perpero (*DMC*, 3:153). In Scardon's notarial register (Lombardo, ed., *Documenti della colonia veneziana di Creta, I*) docs. 50, 58, 65, 243, rates of 28–30 soldi per perpero are explicitly stated to mean "solidi ad denarios grossos."

[30]Bertelè, "Moneta veneziana," 66; Hendy, *Coinage*, 247–48, 250; above, chap. 13, sec. ii. Some exchange rates that specify perperi d'oro probably refer, not to current perperi nor to a standard good old perpero, but to specific perpero coins of different and varying fineness.

[31]Bertelè's exposition ("Moneta veneziana," 17–21) implies that the traditional relationship of 1 perpero as equal to 12 grossi was maintained but does not give direct evidence relative to the period between 1260 and 1314.

"old" at 32 soldi, the Palaeologian at 28.[32] In the 1320s some of the later types of perpero coins circulating in Constantinople and Pera contained 11 carats of gold, 6 carats of silver, and 7 carats of copper.[33] If such a coin could have been bought with 12 Venetian grossi, the exchange would have valued coined gold as only 11.9 times as valuable as coined silver.[34] In fact, Pegolotti, describing the situation probably sometime around 1330, reported perperi selling at 12 1/2 to 13, the rate varying according to the cheapness of silver. If such a price applied to perpero coins of the same fineness, it reflected bimetallic ratios of 12.45 to 1 and 12.97 to 1.[35]

Exchange rates with foreign cities fluctuated widely, as Pegolotti suggests by his table for converting the moneys of account of Venice and Constantinople. He allows for a variation of about 12 percent above and below the median. The tables for Constantinople are the first of several that he provides for calculating exchange rates between the three north Italian exchange centers (Venice, Florence, and Genoa), two Levantine centers (Constantinople and Famagosta), two or three cities in southern Italy (Messina and Barletta or Naples), and two in the west (Bruges and London). The way he uses fractional denominations of account in his tables is at first slightly confusing. His tables are most easily explained by comparing them with a modern equivalent, which would be a table with such listings as: "When 1 dollar equals 800 lire, then 100 lire equal 12 1/2 cents"; and "When 1 dollar equals 600 lire, then 100 lire equal 16 2/3 cents." Correspondingly, the last entry in Pegolotti's table for exchange between Constantinople and Venice means: "When 1 ducat equals 48 carats, then 1 perpero equals 26 soldi a grossi."; or substituting 1 perpero for 24 of its subdivisions, the carats: "When 1 ducat equals 2 perperi, then 1 perpero equals 26 soldi a grossi."

Pegolotti gives such equivalents for the perpero from a low of 26 soldi a grossi to a high of 32 soldi 10 denari a grossi, so that the median was 29 5/12 soldi a grossi. That was the equivalent of 13.52 grossi coins, so that the median in his table is higher than his earlier statement of the perpero's price. It suggests a bimetallic ratio around 13.51 to 1,[36] only a little lower

---

[32]Stussi, ed., *Zibaldone da Canal*, 67.

[33]Bertelè, "Moneta veneziana," 47 n; Pegolotti, *Pratica*, 40.

[34]The 6 carats of silver may be calculated as 1.1 grams (6/24 of the 4.4 grams in a full-weight perpero). Deducting that amount from the 25.2 grams of fine silver in 12 grossi (12 × 2.1) leaves 24.1 grams of silver to be compared in value with 2.02 grams of gold (11/24 of 4.4), giving a bimetallic ratio of 11.9 to 1 (24.1/2.02).

[35]Pegolotti, *Pratica* 40. Calculating as in the preceding note: 12.5 × 2.1 = 26.25 grams of silver; deducting 1.1 grams for the silver in the perpero leaves 25.15, which divided by the 2.02 grams of gold in the perpero equals 12.45. Similarly, 13 × 2.1 = 27.3, 27.3 − 1.1 = 26.2, and 26.2/2.02 = 12.97.

[36]Ibid., 50–57. The 29.42 soldi a grossi = 13.52 grossi (29.42 × [12/26.111]). Since each grosso contained 2.1 grams of silver, 1 perpero corresponded to 28.932 grams in grossi (13.52 × 2.1). Deducting 1.1 grams for the silver contained in a perpero, as explained in n. 8 above,

than the ratio of 14.2 to 1 embodied in the Venetian decree of 1328, which gave the ducat a legal value of 24 grossi. But the range clearly allows for fluctuations which would sometimes make it profitable to make payments in Venice in gold and payments in Constantinople in silver.[37]

One reason for the debasement of the Byzantine perpero may have been a desire to keep viable in domestic use the traditional relation between the semigolden perpero and the Byzantine silver coins. The Byzantine emperors were coining an increasing proportion of silver coins. Shortly after 1295, if not before, Andronicus II issued silver coins called "basilica," of which 12 equaled 1 perpero, as had 12 of the traditional Byzantine miliaresia. These new coins resembled the Venetian grosso and were of almost the same degree of fineness. Because the Venetian grossi had been issued by a duke, not an emperor, the Byzantines had called them ducats—silver ducats; and the Venetians in Constantinople called the Byzantine imitations "ducatelli" or "duchatopuli."[38] But the Byzantine emperors themselves, as well as merchants, preferred to be paid a perpero in 12 Venetian grossi rather than in coins of their own mintage. The obvious explanation of this attitude is that the weight and fineness of Byzantine silver coins had often changed, while Venetian grossi had remained unchanged in weight and fineness since first issued.[39]

Two other kinds of perperi of account distinguished in the Ternaria list are the perpero of Slavonia (Dalmatia) and the perpero of Clarentza, both based on silver. The former was specified as a perpero of 12 grossi. Its use was restricted in 1293 to areas of Venetian influence situated beyond Ragusa.[40] Much more important was the perpero of Clarentza because it was also used in Coron and Modon and at a later date in all Morea[41] and

---

assuming the perpero of account was based on that kind of perpero, leaves 27.29 grams of silver to be compared with 2.02 grams of gold in that perpero, giving a bimetallic ratio of 13.51 to 1 (27.29/2.02).

[37]See below, chap. 15, sec. iii, on Venetian export of grossi. Use of Pegolotti's tables is made in what follows, realizing the problems involved. The figures that he gives are for foreign exchange (he says "for payment of merchandise and exchange" or for "cambiora") and thus normally include some form of premium over and above the par or metallic exchange value. The medians derived from the tables often find confirmation in other sources, however, and seem, therefore, to be usefully indicative.

[38]Bertelè, "Moneta veneziana," 24–25; Grierson, Byzantine Coins, 278–80, 295–96. On the generally increasing use of silver in the fourteenth century see idem, "Byzantium and the Christian Levant," in Coins: An Illustrated Survey, 650 B.C. to the Present Day, ed. Martin J. Price (New York and London, 1980), 131, 140.

[39]Bertelè, "Moneta veneziana," 16–21 and "Allegato 2"; idem, "L'iperpero bizantino dal 1261 al 1453," offprint from RIN, 5th ser., 5, no. 59 (1957):5–6.

[40]DMC, 3:331. This law of 1293, which fixed a perpero at 30 soldi, says that lire and soldi were by then being used in calculations in Dalmatia as far as Ragusa and thus helps to date the Ternaria list.

[41]Stussi, ed., Zibaldone da Canal, 54; Pegolotti, Pratica, 116. As early as 1274, payments for Clarentza, Coron, and Modon were ordered at 26 soldi per perpero (DMC, 2:65).

in Negroponte.[42] Moreover, this perpero was based neither on perperi coins being issued at Constantinople nor on grossi being coined in Venice. It was identified as worth 20 sterlings ("asterlini"), a kind of "ghost" or money of account derived from types of silver or billon coins introduced by the French princes who had occupied Greece. The varying value of these coins and the varying number of sterlings in a perpero will be examined in connection with the role they played later in Venice's issues of coins called tornéselli for use in Greece.[43] For present purposes it suffices to note that the value of perperi of Morea and Negroponte, like the value of the perperi of Crete, was determined, not by the partly golden perperi, but by coins containing silver.

Silver provided also the basic coins for the standards of value used in the Black Sea ports where the Venetians as well as the Genoese were multiplying their commercial activities in the latter part of the thirteenth century. Perperi served there as a denomination of account for various kinds of silver aspri. A perpero based on 20 aspri of the kind used in Crimea was valued the same as a perpero of Constantinople by the Ternaria. Since a perpero of Constantinople at that time could be paid with 12 grossi, the aspro of Crimea must then have been worth 12/20 of a grosso. A series of equivalences given in the *Zibaldone da Canal* indicates that it was worth 3/4 of a grosso, and aspri of nearby Tana (Azov) are reported worth about 1/2 of a grosso, but differences of date as well as location make the relevance of the comparisons dubious.[44] The Cuman aspro, of which 11

[42]The Ternaria list treats the perpero of Negroponte as identical with that of Crete, and the *Zibaldone da Canal* (p. 54) and Pegolotti, *Pratica* (p. 119) agree in equating it with 12 grossi, but Pegolotti also says (p. 149) that the perpero of Negroponte was composed of 25 sterlini, and on p. 119 he gives 23 1/2 sterlini. In 1291 officials in Negroponte were ordered not to go above 30 soldi in drawing on Venice (*DMC*, 3:303), although Pegolotti (p. 149) gives it as 20 soldi!

[43]See below, chap. 19, sec. ii.

[44]Aspri were made from small silver ingots called sommi, which were of the same fineness as Venetian grossi (see above, chap. 10, n. 9). The sommo was also a unit of weight; Stussi, ed., *Zibaldone da Canal*, 69, indicates that that weight of silver was worth 90 Venetian grossi or 120 aspri. Hence, 1 aspro equaled 3/4 grosso. Since a grosso contained 2.1 grams of fine silver, the weight of fine silver in an aspro would have been about 1.58 grams (3/4 × 2.1) and a perpero of 20 aspri would represent a silver content of 31.6 grams (20 × 1.58). Cf. above, chap. 10, n. 9. Those figures may have been more pertinent some decades earlier, for the *Zibaldone da Canal*'s figures concern Soldaia (Sudak), in southern Crimea, which was the center of Venetian trade in the Black Sea between 1204 and 1260. Later in the century, the Genoese made Kaffa the most important market in Crimea, and the Venetians rivaled the Genoese in making Tana (Azov), at the other end of the Sea of Azov, an important trading center. Pegolotti (*Pratica*, 22, 25) reported in the 1330s that the mint at Tana paid 190 aspri for a sommo of silver ingots, from which it made 202 aspri, keeping the difference for expenses and seigniorage. He valued the sommo as 5 gold florins (p. 22) and as 96 Venetian grossi (p. 150). That would indicate that the sommo was a weight equal to 209.3 grams (96 × 2.18). If 202 aspri were made from a sommo, the weight of the aspro must have been only about 1.04 grams (209.3/202). A Venetian decree of 1322 confirms Pegolotti's figures for the relation of

equaled a perpero, according to the Ternaria, was probably that used in ports on the eastern side of the Black Sea, whence Constantinople received much of its food. Perhaps they were the same as the aspri that Pegolotti said were used in Pera and Constantinople in selling wheat and barley and other grains and vegetables.[45] Or that reference, like his reference to the aspri used in Rhodes, may refer to the third kind of aspro on the Ternaria list, that of the Turkish sultans, who were already occupying most of Anatolia.[46] This third type of aspro was also a silver coin and was worth about half as much as the grosso, for only about 10 1/2 were required to constitute a perpero worth 33 soldi.

A fourth kind of aspro became important later to Venetian merchants, that minted at Trebizond or in the Iranian khanate, to which Trebizond was a northern gateway. Like the others important in the trade of the Black Sea, this aspro was of silver.[47]

### Beyond-the-Sea

In the lands Beyond-the-Sea (Oltremare) the largely gold coins is sued by the kingdoms of the Crusaders, known as saracen bezants, had risen in value with the rise of the bimetallic ratio in the second half of the thirteenth century and were valued at the Ternaria at 32 soldi.[48] Actual payments were increasingly made in silver coins, however. At Limossol, in southern Cyprus, a saracenato was paid with 7 tornesi grossi,[49] elsewhere generally with 10 "deremi" or "dirhems," local silver coins 10 of which—according to the Arab tradition—equaled an Arab dinar (of which the saracenati were distant imitations). The use of these silver coins is reported in the early merchants' notebooks or manuals.

---

the aspri of Tana to the sommo but values the sommo at 11 1/2 lire. If lire a grossi were meant, that indicates that 1 aspro equaled 0.56 grossi (11.5 × [240/190] / 26.111) (ASV, Cinque Savi alla Mercanzia, ser. 1, b. 22bis [ex Misc. cod. 131], fol. 11r–v [cap. 26]; b. 22ter [ex Misc. cod. 132], fol. 6r–v [cap. 9]). A similar value is indicated in Bondi Sebellico, ed., *Felice de Merlis,* doc. 197. See also the rubric in Cessi, Sambin, and Brunetti, eds., *Le deliberazioni dei Rogati,* 1:225, no. 50. The perpero of 20 aspri would then be worth 38.333 soldi ([230/120] × 20). For other values of the sommo and the aspro see Stussi, ed., *Zibaldone da Canal,* 70; Pegolotti, *Pratica,* 22, 150; ASV, Cinque Savi alla Mercanzia, ser. 1, b. 22ter, fols. 7–9; below, app. G, doc. 2 (1333); and for 1357 and later dates, see Thiriet, ed., *Regestes du Sénat,* vol. 1, nos. 316, 328, 388, 458. Official rates set in Venice indicate that the sommo fell somewhat while remaining close to its value of 11 lire a grossi; that is, the rates stayed relatively close to the value a sommo had had in lire a grossi before 1311.

[45]Pegolotti, *Pratica,* 39. The decree of 1322, cited in n. 44, says that on the Trebizond side of the Black Sea, 1 aspro equaled 25 denari a grossi.

[46]Pegolotti, *Pratica,* 103.

[47]Ibid., 29.

[48]In 1288 a rate of 33 soldi per bezant was the highest that the "bailo" in Acre was authorized to pay in borrowing 5,000 bezants to complete the city's walls (*PMV,* docs. 49, 53). According to Blancard, "Le besant d'or," 182, the saracenati were 18-carat gold.

[49]Stussi, ed., *Zibaldone da Canal,* 63 (carta 38v, lines 20–21).

The differences between the exchange rates given in these manuals about 1310–30 and those in the Ternaria list reflect changes resulting from the fall of Acre, the last Crusader stronghold in Palestine, to the Mamluks in 1291. Its loss enhanced the importance for the Italians of the Christian Armenian kingdom, which served as an alternative gateway to the Mongol khanate in Iran, since the Armenian kingdom touched the Mediterranean at Ayas (Lajazzo or Laius). The Ternaria list, compiled before 1291, valued at 32 soldi the bezants of both Armenia and Cyprus and ignored the existence of a separate Armenian money of account headed by an Armenian bezant worth only about 3/4 of a saracen bezant. In Ayas about 1310 it took 13 Armenian bezants to equal 1 saracenato, and an Armenian bezant could be paid with 8 1/3 "deremi novi" or with 10 of the distinctive coins of Armenian coinage called "tacholini."[50]

Commercial contacts between Ayas and Famagosta on the more securely Christian territory of Cyprus were very close. A group of contracts made in Ayas in 1317–18 specifies the variable amounts to be paid in Cyprus for money received in Ayas. The Armenian monetary units designated in these exchange contracts were "deremi novi." The Cypriot money to be paid was specified in "white bezants (bicenciis albis)."[51] The Cypriot white bezants, which contained 3 3/4 carats of gold, were by that time no longer minted. As coin they had been displaced by silver grossi under King Henry II (1285–1324).[52] Currency exchange between Ayas and Cyprus was therefore an exchange between two moneys each of which was based on silver coin.

Within Cyprus itself, the saracen bezant was still widely used in pricing and in stating obligations, but there is room for doubt as to when its metallic value was determined by the gold coin of the same name and when by the number and alloy of the silver coins with which it was equated in making payments. According to Pegolotti, the gold content of the coin was 15 carats, which represents a decline of 1/6 from the 18 carats reported for the saracenato of St. Louis's time. Both the *Zibaldone da*

[50] The passages in ibid., 62, are difficult to interpret, but the clear statement in lines 26–27 of carta 37v that 13 taccolini equaled 10 deremi seems to justify interpreting the "dir" in lines 14–15 of carta 38r as a reference to taccolini valued at 13 per 10 deremi when paying for merchandise although at 14 in exchange. See also Pegolotti, *Pratica,* 59–60, on the taccolino. He gives the Armenian mint price for sterling as 109 taccolini, 5 denari. According to Stussi, ed., *Zibaldone da Canal,* 108, the price at the mint at Sissa in Armenia was 9 1/2 bezants of Armenia (only 95 taccolini), a price fixed by a treaty.

[51] Bondi Sebellico, ed., *Felice de Merlis,* nos. 81, 82, 86, 87, 89, 97. Since Stussi, ed., *Zibaldone da Canal,* 62, says that 3 Armenian bezants were worth 8 white bezants, moneychangers in Ayas may have considered 100 deremi novi (3 × 8 1/3 × 4) worth 32 white bezants (8 × 4), but the contracts indicate that 100 deremi paid in Ayas commanded only 26–28 white bezants to be paid later in Cyprus (Famagosta).

[52] Grierson, "The Coin List of Pegolotti," 489, confirming Evans's note in Pegolotti, *Pratica,* 82.

*Canal* and Pegolotti give its value in silver coin as 7 tornesi grossi, the kind of large groats issued by the French nobles in imitation of the French groats. Whereas the *Zibaldone* says that 3 white bezants equaled a saracenato (at least at Limossol), Pegolotti says that 3 1/2 white bezants equaled 1 saracenato, thus equating each white bezant with 2 tornesi grossi.[53] In his table for converting exchange rates between Venice and Famagosta, Pegolotti used bizanti bianchi as a subdivision of the saracenato just as he used Venetian soldi a grossi as subdivisions of the ducat or florin, while valuing the ducat at 52 soldi a grossi. His table provided for a variation in exchange rates between Venice and Famagosta from 30 soldi 4 denari to 45 soldi 6 denari a grossi for 1 saracenato.[54] Since Famagosta was Pegolotti's last foreign assignment,[55] his information about Cyprus probably represents the situation in the early 1330s, at the peak of the rise of the largely gold saracenato. As early as 1323 a saracenato paid in Cyprus commanded 37 3/4 soldi in Venice,[56] almost exactly the median of the rates indicated by Pegolotti. At about that date and for decades thereafter, freights contracted for in Venice were to be paid in Cyprus as follows: if the charge was set in soldi a grossi and payment was made in saracenati, the saracenati were to be valued at 40 soldi, if the payment was set in grossi and the payment was made in white bezants, the white bezants were to be valued at 2 1/2 bezants for each 12 grossi.[57] The value of saracenati in white grossi derived from these figures is 3.8 white bezants to a saracenato. Provision was made for payments in comparable rates in the other silver coins: the aspri of Tana and the Black Sea, the aspri of Trebizond, and the taccolini of Armenia. Only for payment in Constantinople was provision made for payment in other than silver coin, namely, for payment in perperi at the rate of 1 perpero for each 13 1/2 grossi, about the same value indicated by Pegolotti.

Taken as a whole, Pegolotti's description of money and exchange in Cyprus gives the impression that in those years Cyprus, like Venice, had a bimetallic standard, that the saracenato was based on both the tornese grosso made of silver and the saracen bezant, which was more than 1/2 gold.

---

[53] Stussi, ed., *Zibaldone da Canal,* 63–64; Pegolotti, *Pratica,* 77–80, 97–98.

[54] *Pratica,* 97–98.

[55] Ibid., xx–xxi.

[56] Bondi Sebellico, ed., *Felice de Merlis,* doc. 672.

[57] ASV, Cinque Savi alla Mercanzia, ser. 1, b. 22ter, fol. 10, cap. 24 (4 August 1347): ASV, Senato, Misti, regs. 22, fol. 23v (1344), and 23, fol. 13v; *L'armeno-veneto. Compendio storico e documenti delle relazioni degli armeni coi veneziani. Primo periodo: secoli XIII–XIV* (Venice, 1893), 102–3. These decrees give the following equations: 1 saracenato = 40 soldi = 18.4 grossi (40 × [12/26.111]), and 1 white bezant = 2/5 × 12 grossi = 4.8 grossi, so that 1 saracenato = 3.8 white bezants (18.4/4.8), which is credibly close to Pegolotti's equation: 1 saracenato = 3.5 white bezants.

## Africa

In regard to the bezant of Alexandria listed at 55 soldi by the Ternaria, there are no such complications. It was the equivalent of the coin known in Venice by the same name and known to the Arabs as the dinar. It contained 4.13 or 4.25 grams of gold, which was 20 percent more than the Venetian ducat contained.[58] The Ternaria's valuation of 55 soldi was 40 percent more than the official value of 40 soldi a grossi given the bezant of Alexandria in 1285, and 26 percent more than the ducat's commercial value of 20 soldi a grossi soon after that date.[59] Already in 1290 the Alexandrian bezant was valued at 60 soldi in payments in Venice of official obligations contracted in Alexandria.[60] It was valued at 60 soldi also in the *Zibaldone da Canal* and by Pegolotti.[61] Apparently, the value of the Alexandrian bezant at Venice had risen with the rise in the bimetallic ratio between 1250 and 1290 but had been little affected by gold's sharp rise at Venice after 1296.[62]

The bezant of western North Africa (known as Magrib to the Arabs, Barbaria to the Venetians) was valued at 13 soldi on the Ternaria list. It was a money of account for which there was no coin of the same name and of which the metallic value in the thirteenth century depended on its link to the silver coins called dirhems or migliaresi (or in Venice "miaresi").[63] The difference between the 18 soldi mentioned in Zeno's Maritime Code of 1255 and the 13 soldi on the Ternaria list (about 1280) can be accounted for by two elements: the surcharge, probably about 20 percent, included in the figure in the Maritime Code and the debasement of 20 percent that occurred about 1268 of the "old dirhem," which was then the link coin of the bezant. Also to be explained by that same debasement of about 1268 is

---

[58]The canonical weight was 4.25 grams (see Eliyahu Ashtor, *Histoire des prix et des salaires dans l'orient médiéval*, EPHE-6, Monnaie, prix, conjoncture, 8 [Paris, 1969], 39–40, 274). Stussi, ed., *Zibaldone da Canal*, 68, describes the fineness of the "bexanto veio" of Alexandria as 23 carats 3.5 grains and the weight as 55 cut from a Venetian mark, which indicates a gold content of 4.31 grams (238.5 × [0.994/55]).

[59]Twenty grossi equaled 43.5 soldi a grossi, which is 79 percent of 55.

[60]*PMV*, docs. 55, 58.

[61]Stussi, ed., *Zibaldone da Canal*, 65; Pegolotti, *Pratica*, 75.

[62]Prices of the Alexandrian golden dinar in silver dirhems for many years during the period 1289–1344 have been collected by Ashtor (*Histoire des prix*, 275–76, and *Les métaux précieux*, 47–48), but they cannot really be used to judge changes in the bimetallic ratio in Egypt, because the extent of changes in the silver content of the dirhems in those years is not known. The fluctuation of prices was violent and erratic in a way that suggests that they were probably due more to changes in the metallic content of coins than to changes in the relative values of gold and silver.

[63]See above, chap. 13, sec. ii. The Ternaria rate (13 soldi per bezant) was probably set about 1268, as explained above, n. 25. In 1270 a rate of 10 soldi was set for those going to Tunis (*DMC*, 2:65; and *BG*, vol. 1, doc. 51).

TABLE 9.

Moneys of Tunis and Venice ca. 1311

| Monetary Unit | Number Made from a Mark of 238.5 Grams | Content in Grams of Gold | | Value in Soldi a Oro at 108 Soldi per Carat: 1 Mark = **2,540** ([108 × 23.5] + 2) | Value in Venetian Bimetallic Soldi a Grossi of 1311 | Value in "Grossi" of the Venetian Mint's Gold Money of Account | Value in Silver Grossi Coins ca. 1311 |
| | | **23.5** Carats Fine | **24** Carats Fine | | | | |
|---|---|---|---|---|---|---|---|
| Doplla | **50** | 4.77 (238.5/50) | | 50.8 (**2,540**/50) | 68.1 (50.8 × 1.34) | **50.83** | 31.33 (68.1 × 0.46) |
| Bezant | **250** | 0.95 (238.5/250) | | 10.16 (**2,540**/250) | 13.6 (10.16 × 1.34) | **10.17** | 6.26 (13.6 × 0.46) |
| Venetian ducat | 67 | | 3.55 (238.5/67) | 38.7 (2,592/67) | 52 | | 24 |
| Mint Soldo a oro | | | | 1 | 1.34 (52/38.7) | 1 | |
| Soldo a grosso | | | | | 1 | | 0.46 (24/52) |

SOURCES: Figures in boldface type are from Stussi, ed., *Zibaldone da Canal*. Figures in italics are from above, chap. 13, sec. iv; from this chap., secs. i, iii; and from below, table A.2. All other figures are from the calculations indicated within parentheses.

the rise in value of the gold coin of Barbary, its dinar, from 30 dirhems in 1268 to 37 1/2 dirhems in 1280.[64]

But an additional rise of the dinar later to 50 dirhems can be attributed to a rise in the bimetallic ratio from 9.25 to 1 to 12.3 to 1. There are indications of such a rise in 1285–90 in Catalonian-Tunisian treaties which refer to a dinar of 50 dirhems. That figure is given also in Tunis in 1311.[65] A bezant was then equated with 1/5 of a dinar, as well as with 10 old dirhems, and there are several other indications that the bezant as the money of account of Magrib could be tied to the dinar, as well as or instead of being tied to the dirhem, and thus have either a bimetallic or a purely gold base.

One indication that "bezant" could refer to a money of account tied to gold is in the compilation of weights and measures dated 1311 incorporated in the *Zibaldone da Canal*. This Venetian merchant's notebook pays special attention to Barbary, describing the relation of its "doplle" (gold dinars) to its new and old "miarexi" (silver dirhems) and to its bezants. The author reiterates a constant relation between the bezant and the doplla but reports variations from one city to another of the value of doplle in new and/or old miarexi.[66] When he turns to describing their value in Venetian money, he thinks in terms of weights and compares the prices paid for a mark at the Venetian mint with the number of doplle produced from the same quantity of gold at the mint of Tunis.[67] Following that

[64]Brunschvig, "Esquisse," 72–73.

[65]Ibid., 74. For the gold content of the dinar or "dobla," Brunschvig (p. 69) gives 4.72 grams; H. W. Hazard, *The Numismatic History of Late Medieval North Africa*, Numismatic Studies, 8 (New York, 1952), 48, gives a gold content of 4.55 grams. Pegolotti, *Pratica*, 13, 291; and Stussi, ed., *Zibaldone da Canal*, 42, give it as 23 1/2 carats fine. If the quotations are all for Tunis, and if all were in "old dirhems," as Brunschvig says was the practice, then the rise of the dinar from 37 1/2 to 50 dirhems between 1268 and 1290 or 1311 equaled a rise of the bimetallic ratio from 9.26 to 1 (37 1/2 × 1.5 × [0.749/4.55]) to 12.3 to 1 (50 × 1.5 × [0.749/4.55]).

[66]The "new" miarexi contained 1/5 more silver than the "old" (Stussi, ed., *Zibaldone da Canal*, 41–51). In the more western cities of Barbary a doplla could be obtained with fewer migliaresi, for example, in Bougie (Bucia) with 35 miaresi novi (ibid., 49). The "dupla," or "doblla," was so called because it was twice the weight of an earlier gold coin. In the *Zibaldone da Canal* the half-doplla is called a "masamutina," and its values are calculated.

[67]In his comparison of the prices and products of the Venetian and Tunisian mints he uses "dople" and "miaresi," equivalents of "dinar" and "dirhem," as names of weights as well as of coins. The Venetian mark (238.5 grams) was equal, he said (carta 27, lines 26–29), to 165 miarexi or 7 1/2 oncie of the Tunisian "rotolo," which was composed of 16 oncie each composed of 22 miaresi. (In a slightly different calculation, carta 27v, lines 9–14, he gives the Venetian mark of silver as weighing the same as 50 dople, which also made the mark the same weight as 165 miaresi and made the oncia weigh 22 5/8 miaresi.) These calculations give very nearly the weights (the dopla 4.72 grams and the miareso 1.53 grams) indicated by the Arab sources cited by Brunschvig, "Esquisse," 69, 72: for the dopla (dinar), 238.5/50 = 4.77 grams; for the miareso (dirhem), 238.5/165 = 1.44 grams. To indicate monetary equivalents, the *Zibaldone* starts (carta 27r, line 12) with the price that the Venetian mint paid for gold according to the law of 1285—108 soldi per carat (*PMV*, doc. 40). Since the mint at Tunis accepted gold of 23 1/2 carats, the gold minted was worth 2,538 soldi per mark (carta 27r, lines

method, he gives the values of the Tunisian money, not in the lire, soldi, and denari a grossi of Venice's second bimetallic standard, but in the special mint soldo a grossi a oro, which the Venetian mint used in valuing the gold bullion it received, as described above in section i. Weights and values derived from the *Zibaldone,* compared with the weight and value of the ducat, are shown in table 9.

Although the *Zibaldone da Canal* computed the value of a bezant based on gold, Pegolotti, writing twenty to thirty years later, linked the bezant of Tunis to silver, namely, to 8 new "miglioresi," which he declared were minted 360 to a Tunisian measure of weight, the "ruotolo." This silver-based bezant contained, therefore, 10.4 grams of silver and was worth only 10.7 of the Venetian soldi a grossi of 1311, considerably less than the bezant based on gold.[68] Most later references are to this bezant based on silver, notably the specification in the Venice-Tripoli treaty of 1356 that a doplla was worth 6 bezants.[69]

## The West

Before the general acceptance of the florin and ducat, silver coins alone determined the value of Venetian moneys compared with those of England, France, and northern Italy. A moneychanger would give approximately 1 1/2 English pennies for a Venetian grosso, since the former contained about 2/3 as much fine silver as the latter (2.1/1.33). He would give a French groat such as the gros tournois of Louis IX at the rate of

---

5–6, 14–17), to which the anonymous author added 2 soldi paid "a la entrada del fontego," presumably an import tax, so that his total for a mark came to 127 lire (2,540 soldi). For gold of that value, the Tunisian mint gave 50 dople, worth 250 bezants, so that each bezant was worth 10 1/6 soldi (2,540/250). He calls them "soldi a grossi," but obviously they were not soldi based on the silver coin that the Venetians called the grosso but were the units of account in which the mint valued gold at 108 soldi per carat, which in the *Zibaldone* is also called a soldo a grossi but which, as is explained above, was a mint soldo a grossi a oro. In van Werveke's classification of moneys of account (see below, chap. 20, n. 3) this Venetian mint soldo a grossi a oro is an example of type A.

After giving the values of Tunisian coins in these gold soldi, the compiler of the *Zibaldone* (p. 43) gives them also in grossi, converting at the rate of 1 grosso for each 26.1 denari a grossi, as follows:

1 bezant = 10 soldi 2 denari = 4 grossi 22 piccoli
1 dopla = 50 soldi 10 denari = 23 grossi 13 piccoli
1 maxamutina = 11 grossi 23 piccoli

But these "grossi" are not coins but units of account linked—by the old, legally established formula cited above—to the mark of gold. The next paragraph in the *Zibaldone* calculated the cost after paying customs duties as 10 soldi 11 denari per bezant and 54 soldi 10 1/2 denari per dopla.

[68]Pegolotti, *Pratica,* 135.
[69]Brunschvig, "Esquisse," 78 ff.

about 1 for 2 grossi, since the gros contained about 4 grams of fine silver, the grosso 2.1 grams. In each case a moneychanger would of course raise or lower the rate according to his supply of the coin asked for and the eagerness with which it was demanded. While this kind of manual exchange of coins could meet the needs of pilgrims, merchants dealing in large sums used exchange contracts, later simplified into bills of exchange, which specified the amount to be paid in a designated money of account, usually in a different place, at a future time. When both moneys of account were based on silver coin, rates of exchange were affected by devaluations but not by changes in the bimetallic ratio. The rise in the value of gold which was accentuated in 1295 affected all Venice's neighbors in northern Italy. In Florence the florin rose, so that the bimetallic ratio reached 13.73 to 1 about 1320.[70] In Milan and Lombardy generally, before the Milanese mint began coining gold, the florin was extensively used and rose as the bimetallic ratio rose. Between 1252 and 1330 the florin rose from 10 soldi imperiali to 32, even more than the rise in the bimetallic ratio, because the fineness of the silver coins on which the lira imperiale of Milan was based was reduced in the meantime.[71] Even when that factor is allowed for, the bimetallic ratio is calculated as more than 16 to 1 in Milan about 1315,[72] even higher than in Florence and Venice.

With both Venice and Florence issuing gold coin, the rate of exchange between them was not affected by changes in the bimetallic ratio. In the transmission of funds from one to the other by means of bills of exchange, rates based on those gold coins were used, and they varied only slightly, according to market conditions, from counting 1 ducat as equal to 1 florin. By no means so simple, however, was the expression of their relative value in the moneys of account of the two cities! In bills of exchange, both cities used the moneys of account that had developed out of their earlier coinage systems. The payments made in Venice were stated in lire di grossi, but—until almost 1350—in the lire di grossi manca of only 239 grossi described above, in chapter 8, section iii. At the other end, the payment in Florence was specified in lire a fiorini. In the Florentine lira a oro the florin was worth 20 soldi, but in the lira a fiorini the florin was

[70]Bernocchi, 3:178.

[71]Cipolla, *I movimenti*, 27–34; idem, *Le avventure della lira*, 32, 33, 54; Zerbi, *Moneta effettiva*, 48.

[72]Soldi Rondinini, "Politica e teoria monetarie," 291–92, calculates the ratio as 17 to 1 by comparing the prices of an ounce of gold and an ounce of silver. For reasons explained below, in app. C, between coined gold and coined silver the ratio was lower. The silver content of the coins on which the soldo imperiale was based can be calculated from the value Soldi Rondinini gives for the Venetian grosso and the French gros tournois in soldi imperiali. When 1 grosso (containing 2.1 grams of silver) was worth 14 denari imperiali and the florin was worth 32 soldi imperiali, the ratio was as follows:

$$1.8 \ (2.1 \times [12/14]) \text{ grams silver} = 0.1109 \ (3.55/32) \text{ grams gold}$$
$$10.23 \text{ units of silver} = 1 \text{ unit of gold}$$

worth 29 soldi a fiorini (as explained above, in chapter 13, section iii). Each of the moneys of account had a firmly fixed value in the gold coin of its own city: the lira di grossi manca at 9 23/24 ducats; the lira a fiorini at 20/29 florins.[73] The gold content of 9 23/24 ducats was 14.4 times as much as the gold content of 20/29 of a florin. Metallic content justified giving the Venetian lira di grossi manca a corresponding value in Florentine money of account of 14 lire 8 soldi 9 denari a fiorini.[74] Compared with that figure, the rates actually paid in 1337–38 fluctuated between 14 lire 10 soldi 10 denari a fiorini and 15 lire 3 soldi a fiorini for each lira di grossi manca, that is, from 0.4 percent above the metallic equivalents to 4.9 percent above.[75] The actual rates were always above that indicated by the gold equivalent, because the time between the two payments involved an extension of credit, as explained in volume 2.

Later, when the lira di grossi manca went out of use, parity between the moneys of the two cities was expressed more simply by equating 1 lira di grossi a oro (10 ducats) with 14 lire 10 soldi a fiorini (10 florins).

Within a very few years after the coinage of the florin, the Florentines were able to use it to make payments at the fairs of Champagne, which in the thirteenth century were the meeting place of merchants from northern and southern Europe. These gold florins served to pay debts that had been contracted in the silver-based French money of account, the livre tournois. Thereafter the prices set on the florin—and the ducat when it also gained acceptance—reflected changes in the bimetallic ratio. In the 1260s a member of a Sienese firm reported quotations of the florin at 8 soldi 1 denaro and 8 soldi 9 denari.[76] The rate of 8 1/2 soldi per florin or ducat reflected a bimetallic ratio of 9.6 to 1 ([8.5 × 4 grams silver]/3.55 grams gold).

After 1295, exchange rates between Italy and France were radically altered by two developments: the general rise in the value of gold in 1296–1306 and the debasement, devaluation, and restoration or revaluation of French moneys by Philip IV during exactly that same period. The connection between those two major developments has not been clearly analyzed, although the existence of some basic connection is suggested by the fact that they occurred in the same decade. They were accompanied by a change in trade routes, resulting in a decline of the Champagne fairs, a decline to which Philip's policies contributed, and the rise of Bruges as the

---

[73]Mandich, "Per una ricostruzione," clii.

[74]9.9583 ducats/0.6897 lire a fiorini = 14.44; and 14.44 × 20 = 288.8 soldi = 1 lira 8 soldi 9 denari a fiorini.

[75]Mandich, "Per una ricostruzione," cliii, rates in the Covoni accounts. The Alberti in 1334–35 also reckoned the Venetian lira di grossi manca in foreign exchange at 14 lire 17 soldi and at 15 lire a fiorini (Sapori, ed., *Libri degli Alberti*, 8, 12).

[76]Adolf Schaube, "Ein italienischer Coursbericht von der Messe von Troyes aus dem 13. Jahrhundert," *Zeitschrift für Sozial- und Wirtschaftsgeschichte* 5 (1897):250–52, 300.

preeminent exchange center of the northwest. Specie shipments were also much affected by the shift of the papacy from Rome to Avignon, on the southeastern edge of the French kingdom, and the skyrocketing of papal collections under John XXII (1316–34). But for the settlement of commercial balances by merchants, Avignon was much less important than the Flemish city of Bruges, on the opposite border of the French kingdom. Flanders was a fief of the king of France, but the king had practically lost control even before an independent Flemish monetary system was established legally in 1319, practically in 1337.[77]

Pegolotti describes foreign exchange rates at Bruges shortly before 1320. In his tabulation of the rates between Bruges on the one hand and Italian cities on the other, he considers the gros tournois, the coin worth one sou tournois in the most used French money of account, as the link coin of the money used in Bruges.[78] The French gros of good weight contained about 4 grams of silver.[79] Pegolotti's table covers a wide range of prices, from 12–16 of these gros ("grossi tornesi" he calls them) to a ducat or florin. That indicates a high bimetallic ratio: from 14.2 to 1 to 18.9 to 1, with a median of 16.56 to 1.[80] Lower ratios—14.66 to 1 and 14.85 to 1— are indicated by the official values of French gold and silver coins issued in 1322–28.[81] Higher are the bimetallic ratios derived from the rates of conversion used in 1315 in an account book of the Florentine firm of Alberti del Giudice—18.45 to 1 and 17.48 to 1[82] —and from French royal accounts— 18.8 to 1.[83] Pegolotti's information probably dates from about 1317, when his employers, the huge Florentine international banking firm of the Bardi family, sent him from the Netherlands to manage their branch in Lon-

---

[77]de Roover, *Money, Banking and Credit*, 266; data concerning 1319 kindly supplied by John Munro.

[78]Pegolotti used the "grosso tornese" as a subdivision of the "reale," which was a money of account derived from a French gold coin but no longer linked to that gold coin (*Pratica*, 247, 248). See also Peter Spufford and Wendy Wilkinson, *Interim Listing of the Exchange Rates of Medieval Europe* (Keele, 1977), 262–63.

[79]van Werveke, "Monnaie di compte et monnaie réelle," 129–31. The timing of its debasements from that weight and fineness is not clear, but many exchanges seem to have been figured on the basis of that old standard, some with explicit reference to "tornesi buoni."

[80]*Pratica*, 221, 247–49. On the method of calculating bimetallic ratios from Pegolotti's tables see above, sec. iii.

[81]Fournial, *Histoire monétaire*, 93.

[82]Sapori, ed., *Libri degli Alberti*, 52, converts "lbr. 2 s. 4 d. 9 tornesi" into "lbr. 4 a fior." Consequently, since 1 lira tornese = 20 soldi tornesi, each containing about 4 grams fine silver, then 2 lire 4 soldi 9 denari tornesi (i.e., 2.24 lire tornesi) = 179.2 grams silver (2.24 × 80 grams). And since 1 lira a fiorini = 2.45 grams gold, so that 4 lire a fiorini = 9.8 grams gold (4 × 2.45), then the bimetallic ratio is: 179.2 silver/9.8 gold, or 18.3 to 1. Similar calculations for the conversion from the "soldo di parigini" to denari a fiorini are in ibid., 99.

[83]Those accounts equated 1 gold florin with 16 soldi 8 denari tornesi, i.e., with 66.68 grams silver (16.67 × 4 grams). Then, 66.68 grams silver/3.55 grams gold = 18.8/1 (Renouard, *Les relations des papes d'Avignon*, 36 n. 156).

don.[84] That was just about the time when in Venice also the bimetallic ratio reached its peak.

Very likely the bimetallic ratio never rose quite as high in Bruges as is suggested by the above calculations, for we cannot be sure that the grossi tornesi to which Pegolotti referred at that date contained that much fine silver. The Flemish groats minted in 1331 contained only 3.60 grams silver, so that the bimetallic ratio of Flemish coinage in 1331 was 14.5 to 1.[85]

The price of florins or ducats in London gives indications concerning the bimetallic ratio that do not involve the same uncertainty, since English pennies kept the same fineness and the same legal weight—1.33 grams silver—until 1335.[86] Pegolotti tabulated equivalents for London prices of from 33 to 42 English pennies per florin or ducat,[87] quotations that represent bimetallic ratios of 12.36 to 1 and 15.73 to 1, with the median at 14.05 to 1, almost exactly the same as the ratio in Venice at that time[88] but considerably below the rates that Pegolotti's figures seem to indicate for Bruges. The difference may have been due to deterioration or debasement of the silver actually in use in Bruges, or perhaps gold really was less highly valued in England. In fact, the English kings began coining gold only in 1344.

### The Neapolitan Kingdom

The money of account for the Kingdom of Naples, the oncia, listed by the Ternaria as worth 10 lire a grossi, was clearly based on gold, just as it had been at the time of the Venetian Maritime Code of 1255.[89] At the earlier date the oncia was rated at only 9 lire, even adding a surcharge. The rise between 1255 and 1296 to 10 lire is less than one might expect from a rise in the bimetallic ratio elsewhere—from about 8.5 to 1 to 11.8 to 1—in that interval.

Later, silver coinage became more important in the kingdom. The rise in the value of gold after 1296 in southern Italy is reflected only indirectly in the exchange rates between Venice and Naples reported by Pegolotti, because the Neapolitan moneys of account ceased to be based on gold. An "oncia" composed of 30 "tarì" was still the denomination

---

[84]Evans's introduction to Pegolotti, *Pratica*, xiv–xxi.

[85]Munro, "Mint Policies," 110.

[86]Feavearyear, *The Pound Sterling*, 9, 350; Craig, *The Mint*, 64; 22.2 grains = 1.44 grams which were 0.925 fine; and 1.44 × 0.925 = 1.33.

[87]Pegolotti, *Pratica*, 152, 202–3. On rates in Spufford and Wilkinson, *Interim Listing*, see below, chap. 19, sec. iii.

[88]Calculating:

33 × 1.33 = 43.89 grams silver; 43.89 silver/3.55 gold = 12.36
42 × 1.33 = 55.86 grams silver; 55.86 silver/3.55 gold = 15.73
37.5 × 1.33 = 49.87 grams silver; 49.87 silver/3.55 gold = 14.05

[89]See above, chap. 13, sec. ii.

used in tabulating rates of exchange between Venice and Barletta, the Apulian city where the Venetians were most active.[90] But the oncia and tarì to which Pegolotti referred no longer depended for their value on the weight of gold they represented but on the relations they had acquired with silver coins issued after the Hohenstaufens had been overthrown by the Angevin dynasty. The bullion for the earlier gold coinage had been obtained from the Genoese, Pisans, or Florentines in return for their export of wheat from Sicily to Spain and North Africa. After Charles of Anjou, the brother of King Louis IX of France, displaced the Swabian rulers, he began in 1271 or 1278 to issue silver coins called "carlini." They were also called "gigliati" because they bore in their design the lillies associated with the French royal house. The silver was obtained mainly through Apulia from the Venetians or Dalmatians, who paid there for much of their grain and oil. Charles was not only king of the Two Sicilies but also claimant to the Byzantine throne as heir of the Latin emperors of Constantinople. He needed silver coins to man and provision his fleets operating off Greece and for that purpose began issuing his own silver coins, as well as using Venetian grossi.[91] The first silver carlini were worth about 1 1/2 Venetian grossi, being 3.341 grams, 0.934 fine.[92] Being of that fineness, they could serve in making payments outside the Neapolitan kingdom. After 1309, when they were slightly heavier (4.009 grams) and minted in large quantities,[93] they rivaled the Venetian grossi in their acceptability in the Levant,[94] and became the dominant currency in the Kingdom of Naples.

Pegolotti's tables of exchange rates between Barletta or Naples and Venice or Florence considers constant the rate of 60 carlini (gigliati) as equal to 1 oncia, just as they consider constant for Venice 24 denari grossi as equal to 1 ducat, although he refers to Venetian ducats as florins, as in many other passages. Since Pegolotti gives the value of the oncia, not in Venetian soldi a grossi, but in soldi di grossi, a comparison between his exchange rates and those of the Ternaria requires conversion of his median figure, 10.616 soldi di grossi, into 277.19 soldi a grossi (10.616 × 26.111), that is, 13.85 lire a grossi (277.19/20).[95] The rise to 13.85 lire from the 10 lire a grossi given in the Ternaria list is about the same as the rise in the bimetallic ratio indicated by other sources. The oncia's value compared with

[90]Pegolotti, *Pratica*, 162, 171–74, 182–87.

[91]Francesco Carabellese, *Carlo d'Angiò nei rapporti politici e commerciali con Venezia e l'Oriente* (Bari, 1911), 151–52.

[92]Cipolla, *I movimenti*, 71. Cf. Trasselli, "Le aree monetarie," 64–65 (where the fineness is given as 0.959).

[93]Grierson, "La moneta veneziana," 83–84; idem, *Monnaies*, 186, 220–24.

[94]Grierson, *Monnaies*, 220–24; J. Yvon, "Deux trésors médiévaux de la Méditerranée orientale." Congresso Internazionale di Numismatica, Rome, 1961, *Atti*, 2:638.

[95]Pegolotti, *Pratica*, 171–73.

THE RISE OF GOLD

that of the Venetian silver grosso had probably risen when the oncia was based on gold, just as had the value of the Venetian gold ducat.

The range of fluctuation in the exchange rate between the ducat and the oncia was very large. Pegolotti allowed for bimetallic ratios that varied from 10.3 to 1 up to 13.4 to 1, if one assumes that the oncia was then based on the silver carlino and that the Venetian soldo a grossi was then based on the gold ducat.[96]

For unexplained reasons, Pegolotti provides conversions for the same range of variations in value between the Genoese "florin" and the oncia as between the Venetian ducat and the oncia; but between Florence itself and Naples or Apulia he provides for only a slight variation, rates representing bimetallic ratios of 10.5 to 1 to 11.2 to 1.[97] They are so low as to suggest that he composed that section after the price of gold had peaked and plummetted. In the 1340s, in his last years, he was in Florence, concerned with liquidating the large Bardi debts in Naples after the firm had gone bankrupt while gold fell,[98] a drop which contributed to the collapse of the biggest Florentine international banks (as will be described below, in chapter 19, section iv).

From this survey of the exchange rates between Venice and its trading partners it appears that during the period when gold was rising in value, silver coins became more important in lands eastward, gold coins more important in the west. To an increasing extent, silver coins were the bases of the moneys of account in the regions to which Venetians exported bullion and specie to pay for merchandise. It would be an exaggeration to say that markets to the west of Venice had previously been on a silver standard, those to the south and east on a gold standard, and that during the rise in the value of gold those to the west moved towards a gold standard, those to the east to a silver standard. Although that was not true of official standards, in the monetary standards used in international trade there were strong trends in those directions.

[96]His lowest price for the ducat in Barletta is 50 gigliati for 5 ducats, his highest, 65 gigliati for 5 ducats. Assuming that the gigliato contained 3.65 grams of fine silver (Grierson, *Monnaies,* 220–24), then 50 × 3.65 grams silver = 5 × 3.55 grams gold, and 182.5 silver/17.75 gold = 10.28 to 1. And 65 × 3.65 grams silver = 5 × 3.55 grams gold, and 237.25 silver/17.75 gold = 13.36 to 1.

[97]Pegolotti, *Pratica,* 173–75; cf. 115–216. His quotations of florins in gigliati vary from 10 to 10 2/5 per florin. On the rates given in account books in the 1330s see below, chap. 19. With 3.65 grams of silver in each gigliato, 10 gigliati = 36.5 grams silver, and 36.5 silver/3.55 gold = 10.28 to 1.

[98]Evans's introduction to ibid., xxiii–xxvi.

# 15

## THE RESTRUCTURING OF VENICE'S MONETARY SYSTEM

FTER VENICE HAD ADJUSTED to the rise of gold by adopting her second bimetallic standard, the republic's monetary system was disrupted once again and after only a brief respite. Some contemporaries described the difficulties as simply the lack of good silver coin. That was the symptom, however, of two distinct and independent developments. One was the deterioration of the grossi coins in circulation. The other was the beginning of a dramatic drop in the value of gold, a drop caused both by large supplies of gold and by larger demands for silver.

### i. THE DETERIORATION AND REVALUATION OF THE GROSSO

During the century that had elapsed since the dogeship of Enrico Dandolo (1192–1205), grossi had been coined in large quantities, and there had been no recoinage, that is, no calling in of old coins, as in the seven recoinages that occurred in England between 1100 and 1300.[1] There is no record of any demonetizing of grossi bearing the names of earlier doges in order to force their exchange for grossi bearing the name or initials of a later doge. There were many laws, not only against counterfeiting but also against clipping and sweating; the mintmasters had been instructed since 1279 to destroy all clipped coins and to pay for them according to their weight in new grossi. Mintmasters were also under instructions to ex-

---

[1] Feavearyear, *The Pound Sterling*, 10–11.

change new coins for old for merchants going to Albania, Apulia, or Romania, provided that the old coins had not been clipped or were not less good than they should be ("minus boni quam esse debent").[2] Such instructions indicate the interest in making grossi acceptable in payments by tale, without need of weighing. It supplemented the efforts made in the mint through the employ of specialized craftsmen to standardize the product. But where did the mintmasters draw the line? Exchanging dull, old coins for bright, new ones would be very expensive unless the mintmasters demanded that all the old coins be of full weight. In practice, coins that were underweight from wear and tear continued to circulate, even if discounted according to their weight.

In addition to worn-down grossi, many coins of similar size minted outside Venice were in circulation (as explained above, in chapter 13, section i), namely, groats resembling the Venetian coins but minted in Rascia and groats from the mainland, especially from Tyrol and Verona. The diversity of the silver or partially silver coins that were in circulation in the opening decades of the fourteenth century gave their users reason to examine coins closely and to ask for payment by weight.[3] Shopkeepers and workmen who had no choice but to accept inferior pieces in order to get paid would pass them on as quickly as possible; the best specimens were hoarded or exported.

In seventeenth-century England similar processes drastically reduced the average weight of silver coin in circulation. Experts estimated that with no recoinage since 1601, in 1652 the average silver coins in circulation were only 70–80 percent of the mint standard, and in 1695 "mixed silver . . . received in the ordinary course at the Exchequer over a period of three months weighed 51 percent of the standard weight."[4] Vivid contemporary complaints of the deteriorated condition of England's silver coinage and the chaos it caused are reflected in Macaulay's description quoted above, in chapter 3, section i. There are no similar details nor extant sources of that kind for thirteenth- and fourteenth-century Venice. But a hundred years without recoinage probably had had somewhat similar, if less severe, effects in Venice by the beginning of the fourteenth century. Culling for export, the process by which good, new money was driven out by bad, old money, must have been more intense in medieval Venice than in seventeenth-century England, because in Venice the export of silver normally was not only permitted but encouraged. A major difference between the

---

[2]Papadopoli, 1:318, cap. 39; 323, cap. 64. See also, *PMV*, 24, 31.

[3]The distinction between good grossi and underweight grossi is referred to in a notarized receipt, dated July 1312, of a payment that was to be made "in denarios novos de la çecha vel in tornesiis secundum valorem grossorum novorum da la çecha, si denarii novi de la çecha non invenirentur, salvos ibi Corono vel Mothono sine omni pericolo . . . " Tiepolo, ed., *Domenico prete di S. Maurizio*, doc. 224.

[4]Feavearyear, *The Pound Sterling*, 84 110–34.

English and the Venetian situations was that Venice, being a good market for the products of German mining enterprises, received continually new, large inflows of silver bullion.

Correction of this century-long deterioration of Venetian silver coinage was undertaken during the early 1320s by the leaders who directed Venice's recovery from the strains of the war with the pope over Ferrara and from the Tiepolo-Querini conspiracy. Constitutionally, they were hardening the rule of the aristocracy by using the procedures formulated during the enlargement of the Great Council in 1297–1302 to define nobility clearly and to make it hereditary.[5] The admission of members of new families was made increasingly difficult. Economically, their policy has been characterized by Roberto Cessi as that of hard-money, budget-balancing protectionists.[6]

The first step towards monetary reorganization was the order given in 1317, and reiterated in 1318, that the mintmasters coin as many piccoli as they could and turn out at least 200,000 pennies per month.[7] This required the enlargement of the mint in 1319–20.[8] A plentiful supply of pennies could help drive out foreign coins of small denominations, but being only about 1/5 fine silver, piccoli could not take the place of grossi in international affairs or the related wholesale trades. At the same time, the needs of the prominent merchants of the Rialto were not ignored. The increasing importance of bank credits as their means of payment was recognized in 1318 when an increase in the bonds required from moneychangers turned bankers was ordered.[9]

After these preliminaries, in October and November 1321 the ruling councils took measures that perhaps inadvertently, perhaps deliberately, precipitated a squeeze. On 19 October 1321 customs officials and other government agencies were forbidden to accept payments in any form except in good grossi. They could accept other silver or gold coin as security that payments would be made, but only if the security was worth 10 percent more than the amount due.[10] This did not result in simply placing a 10 percent premium on good grossi. Since debtors of the government had solid claims to receive back the coin or jewelry deposited as security, the government bureaus and the central treasury could not freely

---

[5]Lane, *Venice: A Maritime Republic*, 112–14, 184–85.

[6]Cessi, in *PMV*, li–liii.

[7]Nani-Mocenigo, ed., *Capitolare dei Signori di Notte*, no. 180; and below, app. B.

[8]*PMV*, doc. 76; MC, Fronesis, fol. 13 (7 January 1318/19). As mentioned above, the expansion was to be financed "de introitu monete."

[9]*PMV*, doc. 75 (1318); and below, vol. 2.

[10]This decree of the Quarantia is recorded as cap. xxvii in the Capitolare degli Estraordinarii, ASV, Cinque Savi alla Mercanzia, b. 22bis, (ex. Misc. cod. 131), fol. 11v. It is not published in *PMV*, although that collection includes the decree of the Maggior Consiglio of 27 October 1321 referring to it (doc. 77).

transfer or spend the coin deposited with them. As a result, they could not meet their own obligations or turn in their accounts for auditing at the times legally specified. The state treasurers and other officials were granted more time.[11]

Moreover, because the merchants importing wares on the state-owned galleys lacked grossi with which to pay freights so as to get their wares unloaded, the Great Council voted on 24 November 1321 that they be permitted to unload as soon as customs officials received adequate security of future payment. This new law did not repeat the earlier require-ment that security had to be in the form of coin or that it had to be valued at 10 percent more than the freight due.[12] That opened the way, either immediately or sometime later, for bankers to provide the "security" under arrangements that were, in effect, a form of paying by transfer of bank credits.[13]

The state and other shipowners might be satisfied by payment in bank credits, but crews demanded wages in coin. To meet their demands, the treasurers were ordered to transfer enough of what they had received as security, which totaled more than 24,000 lire, to the Procurators of San Marco in order to receive in return—from the funds in the hands of the Procurators—the coins needed to pay the crews.[14]

The order that customs duties be paid in good grossi was only a first step towards banning underweight grossi entirely from circulation. On 26 November 1321 the Great Council declared to be illegal the practice of circulating grossi at values determined by their weight,[15] clearly implying at the same time that many inferior grossi had been circulating at values below 32 piccoli although a freshly minted grosso contained, according to minting regulations, more than 36 times as much silver as a piccolo.[16] There is record of one large payment as early as 1307 in which grossi coins were valued at an average of 30 piccoli instead of 32.[17] The decree of 1321 ordered the destruction of grossi that had been clipped or sweated "cum ferro vel aqua vel aliter malo modo." It permitted grossi well worn by use to circulate at a discount, but any moneychanger who bought grossi for

[11]MC, Fronesis, fols. 81v, 82v, 83.

[12]Ibid., fol. 83v; and ASV, Avogaria di Comun, Deliberazioni del Maggior Consiglio, Neptunus, fol. 166v.

[13]Mueller, "The Role of Bank Money," 68–73; and below, vol. 2.

[14]ASV, Avogaria di Comun, Deliberazioni del Maggior Consiglio, Neptunus, fol. 166v; MC, Fronesis, fol. 83.

[15]PMV, doc. 79.

[16]See below, table A.2.

[17]Predelli, ed., I libri commemoriali, vol. 1, bk. 1, items 341, 342; ASV, Libri commemoriali, reg. 1, fol. 121v, which implies that in order to pay a balance due of 1,341 lire 8 1/2 soldi di piccoli, it was necessary to turn over grossi coins that, if counted at 32 piccoli each, amounted to 1,430 lire 17 soldi. In 1309 the grosso was rated at 30 piccoli in paying salaries in Istria (PMV, xlv).

less than 32 piccoli was immediately to destroy those grossi. In effect, the circulation at par or by weight of grossi that were within 10 percent of the mint standard was permitted, and the large issue of new piccoli ordered in 1318 was given a crucial role in setting the standard. Grossi below that standard were to be turned in for recoinage.[18] To enforce that decree, an office of shorn grossi (Officium de Grossis Tonsis) was created. That its operations were expected to be unpopular is implied by the permission given to its officials to carry arms.[19]

These provisions against the circulation of grossi that were more than 10 percent below standard constricted the money supply severely. It was felt necessary to renew the earlier permission to accept pledges in lieu of payment in acceptable grossi.[20] Since there were not enough grossi in circulation to meet demand, other means of payment were used but met with official opposition. The need for some kind of coin to replace the grossi that were being forced out of circulation is better appreciated when it is realized that except for the vanishing grossi, the Venetian mint was not issuing and had not issued any coins intermediate in value between the piccolo and the ducat, which was worth 768 times as much as the piccolo. The gap left a real need for such coins as the pieces of xx and xxii from Verona and Tyrol and the groats from Dalmatia, which were tolerated provided they were valued at only 24 denari piccoli. But new restrictions were placed on the use of smaller foreign coins;[21] and the use of bank credit as a means of payment was restricted by forbidding drafts by one banker on another.[22]

## ii. THE SUPPORT OF THE DUCAT

In the same decade in which the silver base of Venice's second bimetallic standard was being undermined by the deterioration of the grossi circulating within Venice, the gold base was shaken by a drop in the relative value of gold. For more than a half-century before 1320, the bimetallic ratio had been moving up. It reached a peak of about 14.2 to 1 in the 1320s, but during the next decade it began to fall. The downward

[18]*PMV*, doc. 79. A grosso that was 10 percent underweight contained 1.89 grams of silver; 32 piccoli of that date contained 1.86 grams.

[19]MC, Fronesis, copia, fols. 168, 189 (May, July, November 1323).

[20]Cessi, Sambin, and Brunetti, eds., *Le deliberazioni dei Rogati*, 1:254, no. 92 (June 1322).

[21]Nani-Mocenigo, ed., *Capitolare dei Signori di Notte*, no. 204, 26 February 1321/22 (in Quarantia), ordering destruction of "omnes parvi qui sunt de alia çecha quam de nostra, exceptis meçanis et incrosatis veteribus." For an earlier measure against "moneta parva crosata" see *PMV*, doc. 68.

[22]*PMV*, doc. 80 (30 October 1322); Mueller, "The Role of Bank Money," 74; and below, vol. 2.

movement occurred in three or four dips. The first, which was relatively slight and may have affected only a few centers, came late in the 1320s, the second came in the 1330s, and the third and deepest occurred in the 1340s. After gold made a slight recovery in the 1360s, the bimetallic ratio began sagging again in the 1370s. The most obvious explanation of the fall is the arrival in the Mediterranean of more gold, either from eastern central Europe, Africa, or the Black Sea or from several of these sources simultaneously. The lack of statistics makes problematical any effort to quantify the relative importance of various factors that may have caused either the dips or the longer-term trends in the bimetallic ratio. But clearly the value of gold peaked in the 1320s and was falling during the 1330s and 1340s.[23]

The first dip seems to have begun with the fall of gold in Egypt in 1324 from 11.7 to only 8.1 times the value of silver.[24] The importance of the arrival then of Sudanese gold in Egypt has been dramatized by its association with the passage through Egypt in 1324 of the sultan of Mali, who was making a pilgrimage from West Africa to Mecca and was bringing with him large quantities of his country's gold to pay expenses and make magnificent gifts.[25] This flooding of Egypt with gold did not prevent the gold "genovino," equivalent to the florin and the ducat, from rising at Genoa in 1326 to a high of 27 soldi of the Genoese money of account based on silver coins. But the following year the genovino dropped to only 21 soldi 4 denari.[26]

In Florence and Siena the gold florin peaked at 67 soldi in 1327 and then fell to 60 in 1332; it declined similarly at Pisa and Bologna.[27] A drop in the bimetallic ratio in Egypt was likely to affect more especially Genoa

---

[23]See below, chap. 17, sec. ii. Watson, "Back to Gold," 24, 26, emphasizes the persistence of a high ratio in northern Europe. His figures for Venice in 1342 and 1350 seem based on a misunderstanding, and that for 1328 seems based on the assumption that 1 ducat would really buy 24 full-weight grossi coins, whereas, as shown in the following section, the full-weight grossi coins were at a premium, at least soon after 1328.

[24]Ashtor, Les métaux précieux, 48 (table). In the text, pp. 37–41, Ashtor emphasizes the preceding rise of gold, that is, the fall of silver, because of large supplies of silver.

[25]Bovill, The Golden Trade of the Moors, 87; Ashtor, Les métaux précieux, 18; Bloch, Esquisse, 55.

[26]Cipolla, I movimenti, 42.

[27]Bernocchi, 3:78–79. Drops from a ratio of 13.668:1 to 12.834:1 and then to 12.356:1 are indicated by new silver coinages in Savoy-Piedmont in 1327 and 1335, according to Desimoni, "La moneta e il rapporto dell'oro all'argento," 42. In Pisa there was a short, sharp drop in 1326, according to the graph in Casini, "Il corso dei cambi," 142, but the rates listed on p. 150 blur that picture. The sharpest drop indicated by Casini's rates, pp. 150–51, was from a high of 62 1/2 in 1330 to a low of 54 in 1332. Casini does not analyze the content of Pisan silver coins in those years. For Bologna and Siena see Cipolla, I movimenti, 50 and app. 2. In Perugia the florin peaked in 1334 and dropped in 1335 (Romano Pierotti, "La circolazione monetaria nel territorio perugino nei secoli XII–XIV," Bollettino della Deputazione di Storia Patria per l'Umbria 78 [1981]:115).

and Venice. Although direct Venetian trade with Egypt was in defiance of a ban imposed by the pope, indirect trade through Crete, Cyprus, and Lesser Armenia flourished;[28] and Tunis, where Venetians were very active in the early fourteenth century, provided not only a roundabout way of trading with Egypt but also direct access to supplies of gold from across the Sahara.[29]

Although the record of market fluctuations in the price of ducats in Venice during the 1320s is spotty and less reliable, it seems likely that Venice, as well as Genoa and Tuscany, experienced some drop in the amount of silver coin demanded in exchange for a gold ducat, genovino, or florin. It then became questionable whether a gold ducat would satisfy a debt of as much as 52 soldi a grossi or 64 soldi di piccoli, although it had been worth that much or more for a couple of decades. Even if the ducat did not go below those figures, a drop of any such magnitude as the 15–20 percent recorded for Egypt and Genoa must have scared bankers who during the rapid rise of gold had outgrown mere moneychanging and turned their "tables" into real "banks" accepting deposits and permitting transfers among their depositors. In the 1320s they were having trouble paying depositors promptly.[30] Doubts about the soundness of banks may well have arisen in Venice from discovery of a conspiracy involving members of the Barozzi and Querini clans, families connected with the earlier, more dangerous Tiepolo conspiracy, which expressed discontent with the way the membership of the Great Council had been enlarged and then made hereditary. The banker Giovanni Stornato needed special action by the Council of Ten to enable him to collect what he was owed by Jacopo Quirini, whose investments in pepper he had financed.[31]

Two diplomatic events of 1327 were of the kind likely to stimulate the fears of bankers and others that the ducat, because it was a gold coin, was about to lose value. One was an effort by the Venetian government to

[28]Wilhelm Heyd, *Storia del commercio di Levante nel Medioevo,* Biblioteca dell'Economista, 5th ser., 10 (Turin, 1913), 613–15, 651–53; George F. Hill, *A History of Cyprus,* 4 vols. (Cambridge, 1948), 2:195–97; Ashtor, "Observations on Venetian Trade in the Levant," 534–38.

[29]On the rulers of Tunis in this period and Venice's relations with them see Alberto Sacerdoti, "Venezia e il regno hafsida di Tunisi: Trattati e relazioni diplomatiche (1231–1534)," *Studi veneziani* 8 (1966):309–17. On Venice's role compared with Pisa's see David Herlihy, *Pisa in the Early Renaissance* (New Haven, 1958), 171–73. Tunis, its mint, and its money have the most prominent place in the merchant's manual embodied in Stussi, ed., *Zibaldone da Canal,* 42–46.

[30]*PMV,* doc. 79, p. 73.

[31]Ferruccio Zago, ed., *Consiglio dei Dieci—Deliberazioni Miste—Registri III–IV (1325–1335),* FSV (Venice, 1968), reg. 3, docs. 393, 396. Stornato, at the same time, was fined for marrying a Querini (see docs. 340, 341, 388–91).

## A GOLD DUCAT CA. 1330

Although the content and the basic design of the gold ducats of Francesco Dandolo (1329–39) and Giovanni Dandolo (1280–89) were the same, and the silver content of their grossi was also the same, the large silver production of German miners had reduced the value of silver so much that Francesco's ducats were worth 24 grossi, whereas Giovanni's had been worth only 18–20.

*Obv.*: **FRADANDVLO DVX SMVENETI** St. Mark, facing three-quarters right, presents the banner to the kneeling doge.

*Rev.*: **SIT.T.XPE.DAT.Q.TV REGIS.ISTE.DVCAT.** Christ in the act of blessing, in a mandorla with nine stars in the field.

*AV, 19.7 mm, 3.511 gr. Museo Bottacin, inv. no. 131 (Papadopoli, 1: 162 no. 1).*

resume the direct trade with Egypt that had been banned since 1323.[32] The other was the agreement in that year between the kings of Hungary and Bohemia, an agreement that could be considered likely to stimulate gold production in Hungary, as it did.[33] Such news may have made bankers feel keenly the need of reassurance that the ducat could be used in repaying deposits recorded in soldi a grossi at the rate of 52 soldi a grossi per ducat.

From the point of view of the Communal Loan Office also, such assurance was welcome. The public debt was still swollen by borrowing for the War of Ferrara and the resulting indemnity owed to the pope. The debt was recorded in soldi a grossi. Its reduction, and even the payment of interest, would have been more difficult had ducats not been accepted as worth as much as 52 soldi a grossi.

These difficulties or fears were met when it was decreed in 1328 that the ducat should circulate at 24 grossi and "should be accepted by everyone in sales and payments both in commerce and in everything else, and that the Commune should also pay and receive them at that rate."[34] This was ordered by the Quarantia, which just the year before had been given full charge of monetary matters for the next two years; its authority was later extended indefinitely.[35] Anyone refusing to accept payment in ducats at that rate was subject to a penalty of 12 denari piccoli per lira.

Making the ducat legal tender for 24 grossi made it legal tender also for 768 piccoli, since the law of 1321 banning underweight grossi had reaffirmed the grosso's legal value of 32 piccoli ($32 \times 24 = 768$). Thus the ducat's values as legal tender for 64 soldi (768/12) di piccoli, for 52 soldi a grossi, and for 2 soldi di grossi were consolidated and legally reaffirmed. The ducat could not be refused when offered in payment at those rates. But its values could rise higher, as they sometimes had earlier and soon did again.

In giving legal status to the bimetallic standard that had been used in commercial and official practice for about twenty years, the law of 1328 accepted a bimetallic ratio of 14.2 to 1 (see above, chapter 14). Changes in supply and demand would make the relative value of the two metals vary, however, from time to time. If the relative value of gold rose above that

[32]Heyd, *Storia del commercio*, 614, citing the rubrics of Senato Misti published in *AV* 19, p. 313; and "Tafel and Thomas, eds., IV, 208 et seq." The latter garbled reference is apparently to Georg Martin Thomas, ed., *Diplomatarium Veneto-Levantinum, sive acta et diplomata res Venetas Graecas atque Levantis illustrantis, a. 1300–1350*, Monumenti storici, 1st ser. (Documenti), 5 (Venice, 1880), pt. 1, doc. 105, namely, the doge's appeal to the pope, dated 1327.

[33]Hóman, *Geschichte*, 2:348–55; see also below, chap. 19, sec. iii.

[34]The records of the Quarantia for these years are lost, but copies of this decree are in ASV, Cinque Savi alla Mercanzia, b. 22bis (ex Misc. cod. 131), cap. 44; Nani-Mocenigo, ed., *Capitolare dei Signori di Notte* (from which it was printed by Papadopoli, 1:380n), cap. 44; and in A. Nagl, "Die Goldwährung und die handelsmässige Geldrechnung im Mittelalter," *Numismatische Zeitschrift* 26(1895):168 f. (12 September 1328).

[35]*PMV*, doc. 86.

ratio, those who had silver grossi available had reason to prefer to pay in grossi, and goldsmiths would have to pay a premium to buy gold. If the relative value of gold on the international market fell, as it did, those who had both gold ducats and silver grossi available would have reason to prefer to pay their obligations in Venice in gold and export the grossi, at least the full-weight grossi. On the other hand, grossi worn down by long use and yet acceptable under the law of 1321 as worth 32 piccoli would not be put aside for export, while domestic payments were made in gold or in piccoli, unless the ratio established by the international market fell to 12.5. Even at that ratio, piccoli were unlikely to be hoarded for export because of their high utility value in Venice for making small payments.

The immediate effect of assuring the acceptance of ducats as worth at least 24 grossi (the equivalent of 2 soldi di grossi and 52 soldi a grossi) was to check inflation. Giving the ducat that value as legal tender was only one of several steps taken after 1325 favorable to an expansion of money and credit. The control of Venetian economic policies had slipped out of the hands of the "protectionists." They had pushed their restrictive policies to the extreme the year before by creating an Officium de Navigantibus, of which the obvious purpose was to exclude all foreign capital from Venice's eastern trade but which could also be used to curb small traders for the benefit of those of established wealth. The abolition of that office in 1325 signaled a change in policy.[36] An expansion of bank credit was made possible in 1326 by the repeal of the prohibition against drafts by one banker on another.[37] Several measures in 1326–28 show concern for the money supply, and while they suggest conflicting policies, on the whole they relaxed earlier restrictions.[38] Making the ducat legal tender at what had become its accepted market value fits into that general pattern. The combined effect of the laws of 1321 and 1328 was to assure the ducat's continued use at what had become its traditional value in banks, customs houses, the Loan Office, and in wholesale transactions generally. To that

[36]Roberto Cessi in his introductions to La regolazione (RES, lxiv) and to PMV, lv, and esp. "L'Officium de Navigantibus e i sistemi della politica commerciale veneziana nel sec. XIV," NAV, n.s., 32 (1916), reprinted in his Politica ed economia. The policy and the office were reinstated 1331–38 and 1361–63.

[37]PMV, doc. 87 (2 December 1326), from MC, Spiritus. See also Mueller, "The Role of Bank Money," 52.

[38]The export of florins and ducats to Apulia and Romania (presumably to buy grain) was permitted in 1326 and reaffirmed two years later (Cessi, Sambin, and Brunetti, eds., Le deliberazioni dei Rogati, 1:319, no. 243; 328, no. 46). When two special galleys were sent to Romania in 1326, they were ordered to load only Flemish and Venetian cloth, and passengers were forbidden to take with them any gold and silver, except 5 lire di grossi each for traveling expenses; but in 1328 the export of silver on the galleys was facilitated by extending the assignment of a mintmaster so as to have silver ready in time for sailing (ASV, Avogaria di Comun, Deliberazioni del Maggior Consiglio, Brutus, fols. 45 and 84v; also MC, Spiritus, Copia, fol. 95). On the galley voyages of 1326 and 1328 see Lane, Venice and History, 214.

extent, the financial squeeze that had begun in 1321, when the Commune demanded that all payments to it be made in good grossi, was relieved. The effect of the laws was to increase the means of payment in circulation as measured in money of account, or at least to prevent a decrease. That was probably its purpose.

Since the nineteenth century it has been assumed that gold has always been the "hard money" and that the overvaluing of silver was inflationary. But in Venice in the 1320s and 1330s, silver grossi represented hard money, and the overvaluing of gold was inflationary; at least overvaluing gold tended to check deflationary effects of the fall in gold's value compared with that of silver.

The range of variation in bimetallic ratio tolerated by Venice's second bimetallic standard might have served to moderate the instability inherent in any bimetallic standard, but it did not remove that instability. To the extent that it overvalued gold, the ratio of 14.2 to 1 encouraged the export of grossi. In terms of Gresham's law, ducats were made the "bad money" and drove out full-weight grossi, which were "good money" in that the silver they contained was undervalued at Venice compared with the price it could command in gold elsewhere. Even if silver became scarcer and gold more plentiful, the 50.4 grams of fine silver in 24 full-weight grossi had no more value as legal tender in Venice than did the 3.55 grams of gold in a ducat. Possessors of silver bullion were likely, therefore, to send it elsewhere to be coined or to export heavy, full-weight grossi received from the Venetian mint.

In many places in the Levant, gold could be had for much less than 14 times its weight in silver. At Constantinople, for example, the gold in perperi coins could be bought for less. A Venetian with grossi could increase his wealth by shipping grossi to Constantinople to buy perperi, selling the perperi as bullion to the mint in Venice and using the ducats the mint paid him to buy grossi at 24 to the ducat. For example, if an enterprising young Venetian inherited a chest full of full-weight grossi from a miserly parent and took some to a moneychanger, the moneychanger might take 24 and say he owed only 1 ducat, citing to prove it the text of the law of 1328. If the heir then took a bag of 100 grossi to Constantinople to exchange them there for perperi or for gold bullion to bring back to Venice, he would have to reckon that the freight charges out and back on galleys would total 2 1/4 percent[39] and the charge for recoinage or coinage

---

[39] In 1321 the freight on silver to Constantinople, which had been 1 percent, was lowered to "15 s. pro centenario [librarum]," or 0.75 percent (ASV, Cinque Savi alla Mercanzia, 1st ser., b. 22bis [ex Misc. cod. 131], cap. 29, and b. 22ter [ex Misc. cod. 132], fol. 6v, cap. 10, whence noted by Giuseppe Giomo, "Regesto di alcune deliberazioni del Senato Misti già esistenti nei primi 14 volumi distrutti [1290–1332]. . . ." *AV* 31 [1886]:179–200, no. 330). In March 1330, gold brought from Romania, which used to pay 1 1/2 percent, was henceforth to pay 1 percent

into ducats would be at most 1 percent.[40] After deducting for these expenses, paid or foreseeable, he would be left with 96 3/4 grossi containing 203.18 grams of silver (96.75 × 2.1). At Constantinople perperi would cost him 12 1/2–13 grossi, "according to whether silver was dear or cheap."[41] Even if he paid the relatively high price for perperi of 13 grossi, his 96.75 grossi would get him 7.44 perperi (96.75/13). Each perpero would contain 11 carats of gold, 6 carats of silver, and 7 carats of copper.[42] Ignoring the copper, he could calculate that he had received in silver 8.18 grams (7.44 × [6/24] × 4.4) and in gold 15.00 grams (7.44 × [11/24] × 4.4). Deducting the 8.18 grams of silver from the 203.18 grams of silver in his 96.75 grossi, he could figure that the remainder—195.0 grams of silver—was the cost of the 15 grams of gold. That reflected a bimetallic ratio of 13 to 1 (195.0/15). The 15 grams of gold could be coined into 4.23 ducats (15/3.55), which under the law of 1328 were worth 101.41 grossi (4.23 × 24), and the 8.18 grams of silver could be coined into 3.89 grossi (8.18/2.1), making a total of 105.3 grossi (101.4 + 3.89), a net gain of 5.3 percent.

In general, as the above calculations show, a profit of at least 5 percent could be made when the exchange rate in Constantinople reflected a bimetallic ratio of 13 to 1. In the 1320s the bimetallic ratio was lower— much lower in some parts of the Levant[43]—and in the 1330s the price of silver was unusually high (and the bimetallic ratio unusually low) on the northern shore of the Black Sea.[44] Silver was in demand in the mints of Cyprus, Armenia, and Syria.[45] The more the demand for silver drove down the price of gold and the bimetallic ratio, the higher the profits the Venetians could make by shipping bullion or coin eastward. According to Pegolotti's figures, they could make a profit of about 11 percent when the price of Levantine gold coin represented a bimetallic ratio of about 12.3 to 1.[46] While such profits could be made by shipping coin, most merchants

---

(ASV, Cinque Savi alla Mercanzia, 1st ser., b. 22bis, fol. 21, cap. 52, and b. 22ter, fol. 7v; and Giomo, "Regesto di alcune deliberazioni," no. 132).

[40]See below, app. A, sec. v.

[41]Pegolotti, *Pratica*, 40.

[42]Ibid.

[43]Watson, "Back to Gold," 27–29.

[44]ASV, Senato, Misti, reg. 17, fol. 48 (20 February 1335/36); and below, chap. 17.

[45]The mints and their handling of silver are mentioned in Stussi, ed., *Zibaldone da Canal*, 42, 62, 67, 70, 108. Pegolotti, *Pratica*, mentions grades of Venetian bullion (60, 291) and the Levantine mints (25, 27, 60).

[46]In the hypothetical example analyzed above, if gold perperi cost 12 1/3 grossi at Constantinople, the young Venetian's 96.75 grossi would get him 7.85 perperi (96.75/12.33). He could calculate that he had received in silver 8.64 grams (7.85 × [6/24] × 4.4) and in gold 15.83 grams (7.85 × [11/24] × 4.4). Deducting the 8.64 grams of silver from the 203.17 grams of silver in his 96.75 grossi, he could figure that the remainder, 194.53 grams of silver, was the cost of the 15.83 grams of gold. That reflected a bimetallic ratio of 12.3 to 1 (194.53/15.83). The 15.83 grams of gold could be coined into 4.46 ducats (15.83/3.55), which under the law of 1328

gained more by dealing in commodities. When their shipments of merchandise left them with a debt in Constantinople, it was obviously much to their advantage to settle it by sending grossi, not ducats, eastward.

If this eastward flow of all the best silver coins was to be checked, Venice had either to lower the bimetallic ratio embodied in its legal bimetallic standard or to give up any attempt at maintaining a single, bimetallic standard. Wishing to maintain a single standard, its rulers could have lowered the top bimetallic ratio embodied in that standard either by diminishing the amount of silver in the grosso coin or by raising the value of the grosso coin in money of account. They did neither. They did not tamper with the grosso; instead, in 1331–32 they issued new kinds of silver coins, the mezzanino and the soldino.[47]

The new coins changed the bases of Venice's moneys of account to such an extent that thereafter Venice did not have any money of account that expressed a single, bimetallic standard of value.

## iii. NEW SILVER COINS AND SCARCE GROSSI

The relations between the fine silver content and the legal value of the new coins minted between July 1331 and November 1332 made them "bad moneys," able to drive out other silver coins. They were made of alloys containing a much higher percentage of silver than the piccolo but not nearly as high a percentage as the grosso. The larger of the two new coins, the mezzanino, was about 0.78 fine; the smaller, the soldino, about 0.67 fine. The mezzanino, sometimes called the mezzo grosso, by its name invited comparison with the grosso and weighed more than half as much, 1.24 grams. Its official value was what its name implies, half a grosso, or 16 piccoli, although it contained less than half as much silver. Being only 78 percent fine, its 1.24 grams of weight contained only 0.960 grams of pure silver, compared with the 2.1 grams in the grosso.

Although both the mezzanino and the soldino contained enough silver to be classed as white money, not black money, the soldino was only

---

were worth 107.02 grossi (4.46 × 24), and the 8.63 grams of silver could be coined into 4.11 grossi (8.64/2.1), making a total of 111.13 grossi (107.02 + 4.11), representing a net gain of more than 11 percent.

[47]As Papadopoli lamented (1:158), the incomplete survival of the records of the Quarantia and the Senate make incomplete our knowledge of just when or with what avowed intent the new coinage was ordered. Full powers in the matter were shifted from the Quarantia alone to the Quarantia and Senate jointly on 18 July 1331 (*PMV*, doc. 31). The Senate took action on 23 July apparently approving the proposals of specially appointed sapientes (Cessi, Sambin, and Brunetti, eds., *Le deliberazioni dei Rogati*, 1:454, no. 172). That the coins were circulating in November 1332 is proved by the letter of the podestà of Treviso in Zanetti, *Nuova raccolta*, 4:189. See also below, n. 49; and above, chap. 11, n. 39, on the institution of the quinto at the same time.

about 2/3 silver. Weighing 0.957 grams, it contained only 0.64 grams of pure silver.[48] Since it was declared worth 1 soldo di piccoli, the precious metal it contained was less, compared with its value as legal tender, than the content in precious metal of any other Venetian coin—even less than the silver content of the piccoli in circulation.

Not surprisingly, the new coins were greeted with some skepticism. In 1332 the podestà in charge of Treviso wrote to his Scaliger overlord in Verona questioning their worth, and the council of anziani voted that in the meantime the new Venetian issues should be assayed and their worth compared with that of other coin in circulation.[49] To justify valuing the mezzanino at 16 piccoli, the Venetians could point out that the 0.968 grams of fine silver it contained was more than the 0.925 grams of silver in 16 piccoli (16 × 0.198 × 0.292 = 0.925). The silver content of the mezzanino was probably based on the assumption that a full-weight grosso was really worth about 35 piccoli, so that the mezzanino was correctly given about 16/35 of the silver of a grosso (16/35 × 2.1 = 0.96).[50]

Suspicion of the new coins was certainly justified, however, if efforts were made to pass off 2 mezzanini as the equal of 1 full-weight grosso in paying lire a grossi, for 2 mezzanini contained 8 percent less silver than 1 grosso. The name given them implies that they were intended to circulate at 2 to a grosso, but the decrees governing their issuance in 1331–38 have not survived. Evidence that they became the basic coin for the lire a grossi is lacking. They had a transitional, ambiguous status; and after a few years they were no longer issued.

The soldino, which was destined to play a more basic role in Venice's monetary system, became legal tender in Venice's overseas possessions, as well as within the city.[51] It circulated extensively in Dalmatia and Greece and was much counterfeited in those regions, as grossi had been.[52] (Its role there will be more thoroughly explored in connection with that of the black money called torneselli in chapter 19, section ii.) The relatively low

[48]Papadopoli, 1:160, 163; see also above, chap. 10, sec. iii.

[49]Zanetti, *Nuova raccolta*, 4:166–67, 189. Papadopoli, 1:160, says that this evidence caused him to have his specimens assayed, with the results indicated in 1:163. The Trevisans had, he says, some cause for complaint. Another reason for doubts about the new coins was the issue of many counterfeits by the Frangipani counts of Veglia and Segna (ibid., 1:160–61; ASV, Catamer, b. 1, reg. 1, caps. 130–31).

[50]This is the essence of Cessi's argument (in *PMV,* lxii–lxiii) in acquitting Venice of having practiced deception, as Papadopoli had implied.

[51]Officials in Venetian possessions such as Crete were instructed to push the circulation of soldini and mezzanini (ASV, Senato, Misti, reg. 15, fol. 66v). Many soldini circulated widely in Greece (see Stahl, *The Venetian Tornesello,* secs. 1 and 2; and below, chap. 19, sec. ii).

[52]David Michael Metcalf, "The Currency of Deniers Tournois in Frankish Greece," *Annual of the British School at Athens* (London) 55 (1960):57–58; ASV, Cattaver, b. 1, cap. 128; Papadopoli, 1:160–61.

fineness of the soldini, however, prevented their playing the role in the Levant that the grosso had played earlier. Especially beyond the seas, where the Crusaders had ruled, the finer silver coins issued by the Angevin rulers of the Kingdom of Naples were more acceptable. In fact, the popularity of the carlino made it impossible for the soldino to assume the dominant role once played in the Levant generally by the old Venetian grosso.[53]

Within Venice the issuance of the new coins successfully met the need for more silver coins. The need must have increased, since there was much hiring of mercenaries during the Scaliger War, 1336–39, in which Venice gained Treviso from the lord of Verona. Indeed, the issuance of the mezzanini and soldini may have been planned as part of the Venetian attack on the Scaliger domination of the Veneto. But silver ceased to be scarce within the lagoons. A resolution of the Great Council in 1337 declared that silver coin was by then so abundant that it would be well to reimpose the tax on the importation of pieces of xx and xxii, repealing an exemption therefrom that had been granted German merchants in 1332.[54] Meanwhile, the debased silver coins had accelerated the disappearance of good grossi, but probably grossi were already so scarce when the new types were issued that one purpose in introducing them was to displace the foreign coins that had to a large extent already ousted the grossi, namely, the pieces of xx and xxii from the mainland and the groats from Bosnia and Serbia.[55] Freshly minted grossi were commanding a premium over their legal value.[56] Efforts to prevent it had appeared as early as 1324 and 1326 in connection with the rise in the price of building materials. The operators of kilns were then forbidden to give a premium, a "lazio," for

[53]See above, chap. 14, sec. iii.

[54]*PMV*, doc. 94 (incorrectly dated 1338); the exemption (doc. 91) had been granted in November 1332. Cf. Simonsfeld, *Der Fondaco*, vol. 1, docs. 91, 97 and 798.

[55]After 1331, mentions of "libre grossorum in monetis" refer to a money of account based on the new silver coinage, as explained below, in chap. 16. In notarial contracts, references to "libre ad grossos" and "libre grossorum in monetis" appear already in 1323, however! (Bondi Sebellico, ed., *Felice de Merlis*, docs. 288, 297, 303, 357, and of later date, docs. 974, 983). Cf. the reference in doc. 969 to "libre grossorum in ducatis auri." Following the banning of underweight grossi by just two years, this usage implies that already before 1331 a distinction was being made between payments made in grossi or ducats and those made in coins of lesser value, namely, foreign coins and perhaps Venetian piccoli. A distinction also between payment "in monetis" or "ad monetas" and in piccoli coin is implied in the regulations of prices of building materials in 1327 which used such expressions as "soldos X et denarios VIII parvorum ad monetas" (Monticolo, ed., *I capitolari delle arti*, 1:221). The addition of "ad monetas" after "parvorum" clearly implies that payments were being made in coins other than piccoli or grossi. The meaning is more clearly expressed in a resolution raising the salary of the podestà of Pirano in 1342, in which part of his salary was referred to as "libr. VI^c denariorum parv. ad monetam que ibi currit" (*RES*, doc. 151).

[56]Cessi's introduction to *PMV*, lxii; and Mandich, "Per una ricostruzione," cvi.

preferred coins or to take a discount on others. They were ordered to accept all usual coins ("omnem monetam usualem in Venetiis").[57]

Paying a premium for preferred coins became an accepted practice after the minting of the new types in 1331–32. Both grossi and ducats were generally accepted at prices above their legal values.

In regard to the ducat, the lazio, or "aggio," was clearly formulated. It was the difference between the market value and the legal value. The legal value was 64 soldini, as a result of making the ducat legal tender for 24 grossi each of which was worth 32 piccoli ($24 \times 32 = 12 \times 64$). When the soldino was first coined, the market value of the ducat was above 64 soldini. The silver content of 64 soldini was 41 grams of silver ($64 \times 0.641 = 41.02$). Valuing the ducat at 64 soldini meant giving equal value to 41 grams of silver in soldini and 3.55 grams of gold in a ducat, a bimetallic ratio of 11.5 to 1. A ducat worth 24 grossi had expressed a bimetallic ratio of 14.2 to 1. From 14.2 down to 11.5 was an even bigger drop than was justified by the change in the bullion market. Although the relative value of gold had indeed plummeted, it had not fallen that low, a fact evidenced by the market price quoted for the ducat. In 1331 the ducat was priced at 70 soldi, the equivalent of 70 soldini. Since the lazio was the difference between the market price and the legal value, the lazio was then 6 soldi.[58] It was 6 soldi again in 1353–54, for the ducat again touched 70 soldi, although between 1333 and 1350 it was generally below 68.

Use of the lazio represented a recognition of the fact that Venice's second bimetallic standard was collapsing. The collapse had two aspects: the abandonment of the previously approved bimetallic ratio; and the change in Venice's moneys of account. A bimetallic ratio of 14.2 to 1 had been embodied in Venice's bimetallic standard. By minting the soldino and maintaining at the same time the legal value of the ducat at 64 soldi di piccoli, a much lower bimetallic ratio—11.5 to 1—was approved. That ratio was embodied in what may in a certain sense be called Venice's third bimetallic standard, in which 1 soldo di piccoli was equated with both 1 soldino, a silver coin, and 1/64 of a ducat, a gold coin. But that equation was not maintained in practice. Variations from it were recorded and measured by the lazio until, as is described in the next chapter, the variations became so great as to lead to the differentiation of new moneys of account. The legal status of the "third bimetallic standard" then became uncertain, but it served as a point of reference for two or three decades.[59]

Meanwhile, the old grosso had been rising in value compared with

[57]Monticolo, ed., *I capitolari delle arti,* 1:93. Compare various prices in 1:81–92, 215–29.
[58]Examples of the early calculation of the lazio are in the accounts cited below, in chap. 16, sec. iv.
[59]See below, app. D and chaps. 16 and 18, sec. ii.

both the ducat and the soldino. The rise of the grosso was expressed by its price in denari piccoli. Its fluctuations cannot be traced year by year as well as can those of the ducat, but the grosso was valued at 36 piccoli already in 1331 and 1332.[60] In 1344 and 1352 the grosso was valued at 41 piccoli,[61] later at 48.[62]

Such high prices meant that grossi coins were being valued at more than 1/24 of a ducat coin. When the ducat was valued at 70 soldi di piccoli and the grosso was valued at 36 piccoli, as was the case in 1331, only 23.3 grossi were needed to buy a ducat (70 × [12/36]). When the ducat was valued at 64 soldi di piccoli and the grosso was valued at 41 piccoli, as was true about 1344, only 18.7 grossi were needed.[63]

In order to coin grossi without great loss to the mint after grossi had risen so much in value, the mint must have paid a conventional low price to suppliers of silver or else raised the price it set on the grossi it paid out.[64] That the mint was in fact turning out grossi as late as 1350, when

[60]Cessi, in *PMV*, lxii–lxiii, lxxxii; Papadopoli, 1:174, 209–10; Mandich, "Per una ricostruzione," cvi. The decree of 1282 setting the value of the grosso at 32 piccoli was canceled in the records of the Maggior Consiglio, 10 July 1349 (see Monticolo, ed., *I capitolari delle arti*, 3:309 n. 4), a belated recognition of the inapplicability of the old law to the coins then circulating.

[61]A receipt for various forms of silver being shipped to Cyprus in 1344 said that 122 lire 3 soldi 4 denari "de grossi de zecha" were worth 156 lire 15 soldi 7 denari di grossi con piccoli 10, that is: 1 grosso = (32 × 156.8)/122.167 = 41 piccoli (see PSM, Misti, b. 100, estate of F. Quirini, 27 April 1344).

[62]Papadopoli, 1:174; Cessi, in *PMV*, lxxxii.

[63]The decree requiring 1 ducat to be accepted as legal tender for 24 grossi could not have meant that over the next decade owners of grossi were required to give 24 grossi in order to acquire 1 ducat. To do so would have been to give more than 14 grams or grains of silver for 1 gram or grain of gold. They were unlikely to do that when they could acquire 1 ducat by giving either 768 piccoli or 64 soldini. If they could acquire 1 ducat by paying 768 piccoli, they were acquiring 3.55 grams of gold by giving coins that contained only 44.54 grams of silver (768 × 0.058).

Before the soldino was coined, the ducat was quoted in Venice at 70 soldi di piccoli, or 840 piccoli (70 × 12). Since each piccolo at that time contained 0.058 grams of fine silver, the quotation of 70 soldi equated 3.55 grams of gold coined into ducats with 48.72 grams (840 × 0.058) of silver coined into piccoli, a ratio of 13.7 to 1. If that same bimetallic ratio had been used in setting the relative value of ducats and grossi, 1 ducat would have been worth 23.16 grossi. After the coinage of the soldino containing 0.641 grams of fine silver, there were many quotations of the ducat at only 64 soldi or between 63 and 67 soldi between 1333 and 1340. The figure 64 reflects acceptance of the official rate, but the rates used in actual commercial transactions cluster around that figure. At 64, 1 ducat containing 3.55 grams of gold was being equated in value with 41.02 grams of coined silver (64 × 0.641 = 41.024), a bimetallic ratio of only 11.6 to 1. If that same bimetallic ratio prevailed in the exchange of ducats and grossi, 1 ducat was worth 19.6 grossi ([3.55 × 11.6]/2.1). Taking into account the different manufacturing costs of the different coins, one may say roughly that the ducat was worth 23 1/2 grossi when it was quoted at 70 soldi and 20 grossi when it was quoted at 64 soldi di piccoli. Cf. below, tables 18, 19, and 20.

[64]If moneychangers were buying grossi at 42 denari di piccoli by counting out 3 1/2 soldino coins for each grosso coin (3.5 × 12 = 42), the mint could charge the accounts of the

their value was well above 32 piccoli, is clearly documented. A decree of that year applied specifically to the mint the principle applied to other officials since 1335, namely, that they could not use the grossi that passed through their hands to pay their own salaries. The officials in the mint were said to be paying themselves in grossi, because their salaries had been set in lire a grossi, and they were accused of not valuing the grossi they paid to themselves at their current high price. The Quarantia ordered that thereafter the mintmasters should pay all expenses of manufacture (presumably mainly the payroll) in a recent type of silver coin, a new issue of mezzanini, and sell the grossi so as to be able to pay the Communal treasurers the excess in value of 1 grosso over 2 mezzanini.[65]

Whether by charging their full market value for the grossi they paid out or by the use of artificial conventional prices for both bullion and coin, the mint continued to coin grossi until 1356.[66] Most of its production of silver coins was in the form of mezzanini or soldini, however, for which the silver was provided by the requirement that 1/5 of all silver imported to Venice be sold to the mint at its traditional lowest price. The equivalence of this quinto to an import tax of 4–5 percent, as explained above,[67] raises the question, How could Venice attract silver imports in spite of such a tax? Attract silver it certainly did between 1332 and 1338, as indicated by the evidence just cited and by the silver exports described in chapter 17. An explanation can be found in the high Venetian price for silver reflected in the bimetallic ratio that results from equating 64 soldini of 1331–32 with 1 ducat (see below, table 19). The international significance of that move will be explored in chapter 19. To understand its significance for Venice's own monetary system, it must be recognized that already in 1330 the grosso was at a premium and in the 1330s it was disappearing. It was being displaced before 1331 by foreign groats. By 1334 the Venetian grosso was so scarce that its rarity was recognized in an adjustment of shipping regulations. Transport of specie on "unarmed" ships had been limited to the amounts that a shipmaster or a merchant might take with him for his expenses, the limit being fixed in grossi. In February 1334 these limits were more loosely and broadly defined because, the law stated, "grossi are hard

---

merchants who supplied them with silver bullion with an equivalent amount. Forty-two denari piccoli equaled 34.3 denari a grossi in the money of account used at the mint in soldi or denari a grossi. If the mint charged the supplier that much for each grosso when paying him the grossi made from his silver, it could pay the supplier as much as 300 soldi a grossi for a mark of silver and still keep 5 coins out of every mark, since it manufactured 109.4 grossi coins from each mark and needed only 105 coins at 34.3 denari each to pay 300 soldi a grossi (300 × [12/34.3] = 104.96). By retaining 5 grossi out of the 109.4 made from a mark of silver, the mint would be collecting a mint charge of 4.6 percent.

[65]DQ, 2:105, doc. 348; PMV, doc. 110, p. 98. Cf. below, n. 69.

[66]Papadopoli, 1:189–91; CNI, 7:69–94.

[67]See above, chap. 11, sec. ii.

to come by."[68] It was at about the same time that Communal officials generally, and the Communal treasurers specifically, were forbidden to pay themselves in grossi and were ordered to sell instead for the profit of the Commune any grossi they received, paying themselves with "money commonly circulating, namely ducats and soldini."[69]

All this evidence indicates that the grosso had ceased to be a common means of payment in Venice by 1335. It was no longer able to serve as one of the two link coins of a money of account expressing a single, bimetallic standard. The word *grossi* still appeared in the names of moneys of account, but the word referred not to coins called grossi but to subdivisions of a lira, a money of account based on other coins. The lira di grossi split into a lira a oro and a lira a moneta, as will be explained in chapter 16, section i. Venice was left without any money of account embodying a bimetallic standard. Instead it had several moneys of account expressing different monetary standards.

[68]ASV, Senato, Misti, reg. 16, fol. 48: "grossi male possint habere."

[69]ASV, Avogaria di Comun, Deliberazioni del Maggior Consiglio, Philippicus, fol. 7. The significance of this decree, in showing that grossi were no longer circulating in Venice at their value as legal tender but could be sold at a premium, was appropriately stressed by Gino Luzzatto in "L'oro e l'argento nella politica monetaria veneziana dei sec. XIII–XIV," as reprinted in his *Studi,* 269. An alternative way of making sure that the Commune, and not moneychangers or officials personally, gained the lazio was provided in 1342 by ordering the Grain Office to accept ducats from other agencies but to pay them in silver coins "sine lazio" (*RES,* doc. 149 [11 April 1342]).

# 16

# THE MULTIPLICATION OF MONEYS OF ACCOUNT

### i. THE SEPARATION OF "A ORO" FROM "A MONETE"

OUBTS AS TO WHETHER the basic coin of the lira di grossi was the silver grosso or the gold ducat may have occurred to some merchants and administrators even before 1328; but as long as their relative value was constant at about 24 grossi to a ducat, as it was for about two decades, accountants had no serious problems. They could keep the value of both coins constant in their books, recording both 1 ducat and 24 grossi coins as worth 2 soldi di grossi.

The disappearance of grossi coins from common use and their replacement by mezzanini and soldini necessitated a change. Bookkeepers had to decide whether they would consider gold coin or the new silver coins as the basis of the money of account they were using. Many merchants and administrators who handled gold coins daily thought of the ducat as the basic coin. They continued to record payments or receipts of ducats as 2 soldi di grossi given or received and varied the values they set on silver coins such as the soldini in accord with the fluctuating rates being given by moneychangers. To make clear that the lire, soldi, and denari that they were using were linked to the ducat, they called them lire, soldi, denari "a oro." Other merchants and administrators may have decided for a silver base, either because their business gave them more reason to handle silver coins or because their official position made it more essential that they follow the legal regulations concerning the values of silver coins. Since the new silver coins were collectively referred to as "monete," they called the money of account they were using lire, soldi, and denari "a monete" to make clear that their lire, soldi, and denari were linked to the silver or partly silver coin. They recorded mezzanini and soldini at constant values and varied the value they recorded for ducats paid or received, adding the amount of lazio being allowed by the moneychangers and bankers.[1]

In this way, two moneys of account came to be clearly distinguished:

1. A lira di grossi a oro was tied to the ducat by considering 1 denaro grosso of account as 1/24 of a ducat. One lira di grossi a oro accordingly equaled 10 ducats, 1 soldo di grossi a oro equaled 1/2 of a ducat, and 24 denari grossi a oro equaled 1 ducat.

2. A lira di grossi a monete, in contrast, became tied to the soldino, which had the legal value of 12 piccoli (1 soldo), by considering 1 "grosso" of the lira di grossi a monete as 2.67 (32/12) soldini, since 1 grosso was here valued at 32 piccoli. One soldo di grossi a monete thus equaled 32 soldini coins (12 × [32/12]), and 1 lira di grossi a monete equaled 640 soldini (240 × [32/12]).

As units of account, piccoli had become the smallest subdivision of the lira di grossi, and thus with 32 piccoli still reckoned as 1 denaro grosso for accounting purposes, the lira di grossi contained 7,680 (240 × 32) of these piccoli. In value these piccoli were identical with the piccoli of the lira di piccoli, so that 1 soldo di grossi a monete equaled 32 soldi di piccoli.[2] When the soldino was issued with the legal tender value of 1 soldo di piccoli, it was thereby made equal to 12 of the piccoli of account of which 7,680 constituted a lira di grossi.

The ducat, meanwhile, besides being used as a means of payment, became a standard of value and gave its name to a money of account. Soon that money of account split just as the lira di grossi had. When the ducat of account was equated with the gold coin, it was called a ducato a oro or ducato d'oro and was divided for accounting purposes into 24 grossi a oro. Thus, the value of 1 of these grossi a oro was 1/24 of a gold ducat. When the ducat of account was equated with silver coin, it was called the ducato a monete and was equated with 64 soldi di piccoli, worth 64 soldini coins (that is, 1 lira di grossi a monete equaled 640 soldini or 10

[1]Cessi's interpretation was similar in that he wrote in *PMV,* lxxxi: "nell'ambito della lira di grossi si era verificato una differenza di valore tra quello argenteo rappresentato dal mezzanino e dal soldino, fermo al rapporto 1:32 [lire di grossi a monete] e quello aureo aderente al ducato, giusta la posizione di duc. = gr. 24, anche quando il grosso effettivo si era scostato di tale parità." We differ in emphasizing the divorce immediately after 1331 of the old grossi coins from the grossi of account, that is, from both the grosso a oro and the grosso a monete.
[2]Piccoli appear as the smallest units of account of the lira di grossi in documents of 1311, 1312, and 1318 in Tiepolo, ed., *Domenico prete di S. Maurizio,* docs. 55, 199, 543 (p. 356); they are used in the fourteenth-century mathematical treatise *Trattato di Aritmetica,* at the BMV, Ms. It., cl. IV, cod. 497 (5163). On the identity of the "piccoli" of the lire di piccoli and the "piccoli" of the lire di grossi a monete see below, n. 15.

ducats; thus 1 ducat equaled 64 soldini, or 64 soldi of the lira di piccoli, or 24 denari grossi). The ducato d'oro was equal to 2 soldi di grossi a oro. The ducato a monete was equal to 2 soldi di grossi a monete, that is, to 24 denari grossi a monete, and to 768 (24 × 32) piccoli a monete. The 768 piccoli a monete were of course equal to 64 soldi di piccoli (768/12), since the piccoli of the lira di grossi a monete and the piccoli of the lira di piccoli were the same.

Although "ducato a oro" may make a reader think first of all of the gold coin, to a Venetian merchant working on his books it meant 24 grossi a oro. The grosso a oro was a money of account in the narrow sense; that is, it was a denomination of account for which there was no corresponding coin. The ducato a oro of the accountant was also a money of account, but in the broad sense explained in our opening chapter—that is, a denomination of account for which there was a corresponding coin and which was used as a standard of value.

Accounts clearly referring to the ducato a monete are mostly relatively late, as in a will of 1365,[3] in the Talenti accounts of the 1380s analyzed below,[4] in a list of retail prices of 1381,[5] and in regulations about seamen's wages at the beginning of the fifteenth century.[6] Florentines sometimes referred to it as the Venetian "ducat of 64 soldi" and calculated with a soldo that was 1/64 of the "ducat of 64 soldi," a reflection perhaps of the practice of considering 1 soldo a fiorini to be 1/29 of a fiorino a oro.[7] Some

[3]The legacies in a will dated 2 December 1363—except for a small sum in lire di piccoli—are all specified in "ducati in monede," "ducati di monede," or "ducati a monede," without any apparent difference in meaning between these terms (Antonino Lombardo, ed., *Nicola de Boateriis, notaio in Famagosta e Venezia* [*1355–1365*], FSV [Venice, 1973], 214–15).

[4]See below, n. 15.

[5]The list of sensationally high prices printed in Papadopoli, 1:209n, confirmed in BMV, Ms. It., cl. IV, cod. 342. There is a similar list in the "Cronaca di Venezia sino al 1385," in BMV, Ms. It., cl. VII, cod. 324 which also gives the ducat as 3 lire 4 soldi (64 soldi) per ducat. Papadopoli, not recognizing that the lira di grossi had split and that the ducato a monete had also separated from the ducato a oro, for which he gives higher quotations (1:210–11), interprets the low quotation on the price list as evidence that the ducat coin had kept the value of 64 soldi until 1381. For evidence of the earlier rise of the coin and the ducato a oro see below, table D.3.

[6]In the listing of the pay provided for men of various ranks on the merchant galleys ca. 1400, the pay for bowmen, for example, is given as 6 ducats "in monetis," although for many ranks it is given in lire di piccoli (see ASV, Senato, Commissioni, Formulari, reg. 4, fol. 51, cap. 4). That the ducati referred to were the money of account divided into 64 soldi is indicated by comparison with the treatise on navigational matters by Pietro de Versi, BMV, Ms. It., cl. IV, cod. 170, fols. 79v and 85v (of ca. 1440). He gives the same rate of pay for bowmen but quotes it as 19 lire and 5 soldi di piccoli, which is 385 soldi, whereas 64 times 6 is similarly 384 soldi.

[7]Pietro Sella and Giuseppe Vale, eds., *Rationes Decimarum Italiae nei secoli XIII e XIV, Venetiae-Histria-Dalmatia*, Studi e testi, 96 (Vatican City, 1941), contains accounts of papal tax collectors kept in the years 1349 and 1351 in florins equated with ducats each composed of 64 soldi (371, 459), as well as in lire di piccoli ("lib. bag." on 366–70) and in florins equated

earlier references to "ducati . . . in monetis" and "ducati auri" may refer to the kind of coin in a particular shipment or payment, but in mid-century already the distinction between the worth of a gold ducat coin and that of a ducat "in monetis" was recognized officially.[8]

Very much later, after two generations of stability, from 1456 to about 1517, the ducat again split off as a money of account (worth in that period 124 soldi), and it then clung to the name ducat so tightly that a new name, "zecchino," was needed to designate the gold coin.[9] In fourteenth-century Venice, in contrast, the gold coins were called simply "ducati a oro" or "ducati d'oro"; no other name was applied to distinguish the gold ducat from the ducat of account based on silver and called "a monete." More often than not, "ducati" without other appellation meant simply gold ducats.

## ii. LINK COINS AFTER THE SEPARATION

For both the lira di grossi a oro and the ducato a oro the metallic base was unchanging and clearly defined (35.5 and 3.55 grams of gold, respectively), and that was not true for the lira and ducato a monete. The silver content of the soldino was changed several times, and in some periods other coins helped determine the metallic equivalents of the silver-based moneys of account. It is useful initially to distinguish three periods: 1331–53, in which piccoli and mezzanini as well as soldini were important; 1353–79, when the soldino's determining role was most clear; and after 1379, when a new grosso received a new role.

In all three periods the metallic value of the lira di grossi a monete was meshed with that of the lira di piccoli. The base of that ancient money of account was also changed by the new issues of silver coins, and the same three periods are to be distinguished in determining the metallic value of the lira di piccoli after 1331.

Before 1331 the silver equivalent of the lira di piccoli had been determined by the silver content of 240 of the piccoli coins of which the

---

with ducats composed of 24 grossi (376 ff.). On the use in Florence of florins reckoned at variable numbers of soldi see above, chap. 13, sec. iv. There is reference to a ducat of 64 soldi also in a passage written in 1396 in A. Borlandi, ed., *Manuale de' Ricci,* 126.

[8]In 1363 the Avogaria di Comun was authorized to spend on travel allowances "ducatos quattuor in monetis in die" (ASV, Avogaria di Comun, reg. 2, Capitolare, fol. 95v, cap. 270 [30 March]). There are references to "grossi in monetis" in 1342 (in MC, Spiritus, copia, fols. 298, 299) and in 1327 and 1329, even before the coinage of the new silver coins in 1331, "soldos parvorum ad monetas" and "grossos ad monetas" appear in Monticolo, ed., *I capitolari delle arti,* 1:221, where "monetas" probably refers to foreign coins then circulating. Cf. below, n. 18; and above, chap. 15, n. 55.

[9]Nicolò Papadopoli-Aldobrandini, "Le monete trovate nelle rovine del Campanile di San Marco," *Atti dell'Istituto Veneto di Scienze, Lettere ed Arti,* 20 March 1904 (Reprint, Venice, 1905); idem, *Le monete di Venezia,* vol. 2.

TABLE 10.

Silver Equivalents of the Lira di Piccoli, 1282–1391:
Grams of Fine Silver in Piccoli, Soldini, and Mezzanini

| Dates of Issue | Piccoli | | Soldini[a] | | Mezzanini[b] | |
|---|---|---|---|---|---|---|
| | In 1 Coin | In 240 Coins | In 1 Coin | In 20 Coins | In 1 Coin | In 15 Coins |
| 1282–1331 | 0.058 | 13.92 | — | — | — | — |
| 1331–46 | 0.058 | 13.92 | 0.641 | 12.82 | 0.969 | 14.54 |
| 1346–53 | 0.063 | 15.12 | — | — | 0.744 | 11.61 |
| 1353–69 | 0.054 | 12.96 | 0.533 | 10.66 | — | — |
| 1369–79 | 0.041[c] | 9.84[c] | 0.488 | 9.76 | — | — |
| 1379–85 | 0.027[d] | 6.48[d] | 0.472 | 9.44 | — | — |
| 1385–91 | 0.027 | 6.48 | 0.472 | 9.44 | — | — |

SOURCES: See below, app. A, esp. tables A.1 and A.2.
[a]No soldini were coined before 1331. The extent to which soldini were coined in 1346–53 is doubtful.
[b]No mezzanini were coined before 1331 or after 1353.
[c]Authorized but no specimen in Papadopoli or CNI; all piccoli recalled in 1379.
[d]Authorized but not issued.

production was accelerated in 1318.[10] With only 0.058 grams of silver in each, 240 piccoli gave 1 lira di piccoli the silver value of 13.92 grams.[11]

When soldini worth 12 piccoli were minted in large numbers, as they were in 1331–35, a lira di piccoli could be paid with 20 soldini each containing only 0.64 grams of fine silver, a total of 12.8 grams, less than the amount in 240 piccoli (see table 10). The comparison shows that the soldino was the coin with the lowest metallic value compared with its value as legal tender. It held that position relative to the piccolo for many decades. The mezzanino was even more legally overvalued in some years, but only a few. It was the soldino that remained—for about a half-century—the link coin of the lira di piccoli.[12]

Not only its silver content but also the attention focused on the soldino in the monetary legislation of the mid-fourteenth century indicates that the soldino became the basic coin of the lira di piccoli. Reductions in the silver content of the soldino, rather than changes in the piccolo, com-

[10]See above, chap. 10, sec. v. To judge from the number of surviving specimens, there was also extensive coinage of piccoli under Doge Pietro Gradenigo (1289–1311). For decades thereafter, there are more surviving examples of coins of lower denominations made entirely or almost entirely of copper—bianchi, quartaroli, and torneselli (CNI, 7:54–110. See also below, app. B; and above, chap. 10).

[11]Papadopoli, 1:155.

[12]See below, chap. 18, sec. 1, on the quantity of soldini minted; see also app. A. On identifying link coins see above, chap. 5, sec. 1.

bine with the variations in the bimetallic ratio to explain the variations in the price of a ducat.[13] The soldino became so identified with the soldo di piccoli that the name soldino disappeared from decrees and the coin was called simply a soldo.[14]

When it became the basic coin of the lira di piccoli, the soldino became also the basic coin that determined the metallic value of the lira di grossi a monete, because the piccoli that were the lowest common denominator of both the lira di piccoli and the lira di grossi a monete had the same value. The piccoli of which 240 equaled a lira di piccoli and 7,680 equaled a lira di grossi a monete each had the metallic value of 1/12 of a soldino.[15]

The above explanation of the separation of "a oro" from "a monete" ignores the lira a grossi, while focusing on the lira di piccoli and the lira di grossi. Awkward fractions (fractions explained above, in chapter 8, section

[13]Tables 10, 12, 14–22, and D.3. Between 1320 and 1369 the fine silver content of the piccolo was lowered only from 0.058 to 0.054 grams. Because there was a general fall in the bimetallic ratio in that period of about 30 percent, the value of the ducat in soldi di piccoli would have fallen by a somewhat similar amount if the value of the soldo di piccoli had been based on the silver content of the piccolo coin. But despite the considerable change in the bimetallic ratio, the ducat fell only from 70 soldi to 64 (about 9 percent) because the lira di piccoli was based on soldini coins and the fine silver content of those coins was lowered by the mint from 0.641 to 0.533, a drop of 16.8 percent. Between 1369 and 1390 the silver content of 240 piccoli dropped to half of what it had been, while the silver content of 20 soldini dropped by only 10 percent. The rise of the ducat in that period was approximately proportional to the drop in the silver content of the soldino, not to that of the piccolo.

[14]"Soldino" is used in the documents in Papadopoli, 1:347, 348, and "soldo" in those on pp. 350, 352, and 362.

[15]The identity of these piccoli of account is demonstrated conclusively in an entry of 1380 in the account book in which Petrarch's "friend" Tommaso Talenti and his brother Zaccaria kept the accounts of their grain business (PSM, Citra, b. 141, fol. 20r, below in app. G, doc. 6). The account with the Provveditori alle Biave, reads: "E de' avere dicto dì £ 78 di grossi a monete le qual me fe' prometere a ser Gabriele Sovranzo, posti a suo conto a c. 21 che debia dar, val a s. 64 per ducato in summa di piccoli, £ IIᴹIIIIᶜLXXXXVI." His reference to "s. 64 per ducato" suggests that his way of figuring was as follows:

$$1 \text{ lira di grossi a monete} = 10 \text{ ducati a monete}$$
$$1 \text{ ducato a monete} = 64 \text{ soldi di piccoli}$$
$$78 \text{ lire di grossi a monete} = 78 \times 10 \times 64 \text{ soldi di piccoli}$$
$$= 78 \times 32 \, (640/20) \text{ lire di piccoli}$$
$$= 2{,}496 \text{ lire di piccoli}$$

The identity of the piccoli of the lira di piccoli with the piccoli of the lira di grossi a monete is confirmed by the conformity of the following equations to his calculations:

$$78 \text{ lire di grossi (each of 7,680 piccoli)} = 599{,}040 \text{ piccoli}$$
$$2{,}496 \text{ lire di piccoli (each of 240 piccoli)} = 599{,}040 \text{ piccoli}$$

In a passage written around the time of the above account book, the *Manuale de' Ricci* (A. Borlandi, ed., 99–100) distinguishes between a "lira di moneta di soldi 64 il fiorino" and a "lira di baghatini di s. 80 il fiorino."

iii) impede stating accurately the relation of the lira a grossi to the lira di piccoli. The split between "a oro" and "a monete" occurred also in the lira a grossi, but that money of account, although in many ways the most important, came to be used less and less as its relation to the new coins involved more and more fractional computations. Many accounts and prices previously recorded in lire a grossi were converted in the late fourteenth century to lire di grossi. For such conversions the lira a grossi was generally divided by 26.[16]

The tendency to drop the awkward fraction 1/9 in the conversion 1 lira di grossi = 26 1/9 lire a grossi reduced the significance of the earlier distinction between the lira di grossi complida (240 grossi) and the lira di grossi manca, representing 239 grossi or 26 lire a grossi. This must have hastened the demise of the lira manca. Born about 1254, the lira manca was used around 1300, as we know from the arithmetical exercises in the *Zibaldone da Canal*. Sometime later it was adopted probably as a gold-based money of account by the foreign exchange market in quoting exchange rates between Florence and Venice. In that role it was widely used in the late 1330s, as evidenced by the *Libro giallo dei Covoni* and as explicated by Giulio Mandich. The lira manca seems to have dropped out of use by about 1350, partly because of the accounting problems involved and partly because the lira di grossi became anchored to the gold ducat, most definitely so when the grosso was no longer minted, beginning in 1356.[17]

In the second of the three periods distinguished above—1353–79—the silver content of the soldino was clearly decisive in determining the silver equivalent of the lira di piccoli and the lira a monete. Before 1353 the situation was not so simple. In some years during that earlier period other coins may have been of equal or even greater importance in determining the metallic equivalent of the lire based on silver (see table 21). "Monete" was a generic term for silver coins less valuable than the grosso. It certainly included mezzanini and almost certainly included also the foreign silver coins that the soldini and mezzanini were intended to replace. Lire di grossi a monete were referred to in notarial documents even before the coinage of soldini or mezzanini. Both before and after 1331, lire a monete

---

[16]The lira di grossi complida, equated with 10 ducats, was worth 26 1/9 lire (or 26 lire 2 soldi 2 denari) a grossi. The lira a grossi may not have been well understood by many foreigners who came to the Venetian market. In ordering conversions in 1390, the change was supported by the statement that when foreigners paid 10 ducats and this amount was written down as 26 lire 2 soldi 2 denari, they suspected trickery (*PMV*, doc. 183).

[17]See above, chap. 8, sec. iii; and Lane, "Le vecchie monete di conto," 53–57. The accounts of the Covoni partnership, which dealt extensively in exchange between Venice and Florence, specified carefully that the lira di grossi in which they recorded payments and receipts in Venice was the lira di grossi manca and equated it not with 10 ducats but with 9 ducats 23 grossi ([9 × 24] + 23 = 239 grossi) (Mandich, "Per una ricostruzione," cvii, cix, cxii; and below, chap. 19, sec. iv).

are referred to in Latin as "libre" (or "solidi") parvorum "ad monetas." They are mentioned in contexts implying that "monete" meant some other kind of coin than piccoli, probably foreign groats.[18] These usages of "ad monetas" indicate that the lira di grossi was showing signs of splitting even before 1331. Or to say the same thing differently, even before 1331 not all the lire di grossi referred to in contracts were assumed to be based on the grosso coin, even if based on silver. The metallic base of the lira di grossi was already in doubt before 1331. After 1331 the metallic base of the lira di grossi a monete may well have been even more in doubt for a couple of decades, there being some question both as to which were its link coins and what their fine silver content was.

To be sure, the piccolo and its fractions, the biancho and the quartarolo, which together constituted Venice's black money, were issued in amounts sufficiently small that there was no danger in the fourteenth century that they would displace the more purely silver coins in the payment of prices and obligations recorded in lire di piccoli or in lire di grossi a monete. Moreover, until the silver content of the piccolo was drastically reduced after 1379, piccoli contained enough intrinsic value that they supported rather than weakened the value of the lira di piccoli compared with that of the other moneys of account. On the other hand, piccoli worn down by use were likely to be more than 8 percent underweight, so that the coining of the soldino probably did not occasion an extensive culling out of piccoli for hoarding or export.

The relative values of the moneys of account were clouded between 1331 and 1353 by the varied finenesses of the coins issued. The mezzanino of 1331 was only 0.78 fine, so that although it weighed more than half as much as the grosso (which was 0.965 fine), it contained less than half as much silver.[19] On the other hand, the soldino was at best 0.67 fine, and the

---

[18]Bondi Sebellico, ed., *Felice de Merlis,* docs. 288, 297, 303, 357; see also above, chap. 15, n. 55.

[19]The actual or intended role of the first mezzanino as a basic coin is doubtful. When first coined in 1331 or 1332, the mezzanino contained 0.969 grams of silver and was valued at 16 piccoli, so that the 15 mezzanini required to equal in value 240 piccoli contained 14.5 grams of silver, more silver than 240 piccoli of that date. But if, as its name implies (it was also called the mezzo grosso), it was intended to be a basic coin of the lira di grossi, it would have lowered the silver equivalent of that money of account, for the 480 mezzanini required to pay the equivalent of 240 grossi (a lira di grossi) contained only 465.1 grams (0.969 × 480) of silver, whereas 240 grossi contained 504 grams (2.1 × 240). When a smaller, finer mezzanino was coined in 1346, it probably functioned for a few years as the basic coin of the lira di piccoli, for it too was given the official value of 16 piccoli, and it contained only 0.774 grams of silver, so that 15 mezzanini contained not only somewhat less silver than 240 piccoli of that time but less silver than 20 of the soldini then functioning as the basic coin of the lira di piccoli (table 10). If any effort was made to have the mezzanino accepted as worth 1/2 of an old grosso so that 480 would pay a debt of 240 grossi, the creditor could have objected. He would have been receiving only 371.5 grams of silver (0.774 × 480), whereas he was due 504 grams (2.1 × 240).

piccolo 0.2 or 0.19 fine.[20] With so much variation in fineness and with individual coins varying in weight as a result both of the imperfect techniques used in minting and of wear and tear, sweating and clipping, moneychangers could profit while Venice's reputation suffered.

In general it may be said that never during the Middle Ages did Venice debase its coinage, not in the narrow sense of the term "debase." That is, it did not lower the percentage of precious metal by increasing the amount of copper or lead used as alloy while maintaining the former legal value of the coin and even its weight and general appearance. The new issues that came from the Venetian mint in 1331 or 1332 did not constitute debasement in that sense, for neither the mezzanino nor the soldino had a sufficiently close resemblance to any previous Venetian coin or any coin issuing from a neighboring mint. But neither the mezzanino nor the soldino was close to the standard of fineness that had previously characterized silver coin bearing the insignia of Venice, even though each contained a percentage of silver sufficiently high to make it clearly distinguishable from black money. Their issuance lowered the metallic equivalents of the Venetian moneys of account to which they were linked, and they may have been presented as worth more than their silver content justified.[21] In that sense the new Venetian coinage of 1331–32 had some of the characteristics of a debasement.

### iii. COINAGE UNDER ANDREA DANDOLO

With the circulating currency in this dubious condition and the good old grossi disappearing because they were officially undervalued, it must have been gauling to some Venetians proud of their country's monetary tradition to realize that Venice lacked silver coins of the old Venetian standard. It was at that juncture that the Venetians chose as their doge a noble remembered for legal and historical studies which reflected just that kind of pride. Andrea Dandolo (1343–54) was esteemed not for military victories, but for the chronicle that Venetians accepted as the authoritative account of their past.[22] As doge he added a sixth book to the five in which Venetian statutory law had been codified a century before. He had personal family—or clan—reasons to be especially interested in the operations of the mint, for all the principal innovations in Venetian coinage bore the imprint of doges named Dandolo: the grosso that of Enrico Dandolo (1192–1205); the gold ducat that of Giovanni Dandolo (1280–89); and the first mezzanini and soldini that of Francesco Dandolo (1329–39).

[20]A soldino with a fine silver content of 0.625 is mentioned in 1353 (*PMV*, doc. 115). On the others see below, table A.2.

[21]See above, chap. 15, sec. iii; and below, in chap. 19, sec. ii. For comparisons with Florence see ibid., sec. iv.

[22]See above, chap. 8, n. 33.

## MEZZANINO, TYPE I

On the mezzanino introduced by Francesco Dandolo (1329–39) the doge is shown holding a banner, the symbol of military command.

*Obv.*: .FRA.DAN. .DVLO.DVX The doge, facing left, holds the banner in both hands.

*Rev.*: .SMARC/. . VENETI. Bust of St. Mark, facing front, holding the gospel in his left hand, his right hand raised in blessing.

*AR, 17.3 mm, 1.260 gr. Museo Bottacin, inv. no. 136 (Papadopoli, 1: 164, no. 7).*

## MEZZANINO, TYPE 2

On the new type of mezzanino, smaller but of finer silver, issued under Andrea Dandolo (1343–54) the doge is shown receiving a candle from St. Mark.

*Obv.*: **ANDADVL .SMVENE. DVX.** St. Mark, facing three-quarters right, presents a candle to the doge, who, facing left, receives it with both hands; **M** below the candle.

*Rev.*: **XPERES VRESIT.** Christ with nimbus rising from the tomb; in the right hand a banner, in the left a cross.

*AR, 16.7 mm, 0.765 gr. Museo Bottacin, inv. no. 164 (Papadopoli, 1: 181 no. 3).*

Conditions during the dogeship of Andrea Dandolo (1343–54) gave him exceptional opportunities to use his office to shape the development of Venetian coinage. Those years almost coincided with the period 1342–50, during which the amount of "servile silver," the 1/5 of all silver imported that merchants were obliged to sell to the mint at the mint's traditional low price, was reduced to 1/10. Partly for that reason and partly because of changes in trade routes, those were years of intense minting and large shipments of gold and silver through Venice, as will be described in the next chapter. Chronicles ascribe to Andrea Dandolo the merit for introducing the new coins issued during his dogeship.[23] That by itself would be poor evidence for his having had a personal influence, since chroniclers customarily attribute to an incumbent doge actions taken by the governing councils during his reign. But the attendant circumstances indicate his personal interest.

Under his predecessor no mezzanini had been coined. Within a few years of Andrea's election, the Quarantia voted on a proposal for a new issue of mezzanini which were to be of the same fineness as the traditional grosso; 27 members voted for the purer silver, 7 for the mixture that had been used under Francesco Dandolo.[24] Although little more than half the size of the old grosso, Andrea's mezzanino was a handsomer coin and of equally fine silver (0.965), although it weighed much less than half as much (0.802 grams compared with 2.178).[25] Officially valued at 16 denari di piccoli, the new issue reduced the silver content of the lira di piccoli by 9 percent (from 12.82 grams of pure silver to 11.61).

The design of Andrea Dandolo's mezzanino was strikingly distinct from that of other Venetian coins. The obverse bore the doge's name and a scene resembling that on Venetian ducats and grossi, yet significantly different. The doge, not kneeling as on the ducat, but standing, is receiving from St. Mark, not the flag, symbolizing military authority, but a candle, a symbol of moral, spiritual, or ecclesiastical bonds. The symbolism of the candle is not easily defined precisely, but a candle must have

---

[23]BMCV, Ms. Cicogna 2831, fols. 49v–50. Two chronicles report that soldini were made less easy to clip than the previous silver coins or "monete" (BMV, Ms. It., cl. VII, cods. 1275 and 50 [9275]). For other chronicle accounts see ibid., cod. 38, fol. 35; London, British Library, Kings 148, Giustiniani Chronicle, fol. 99v; Roberto Cessi and Fanny Bennato, eds., *Venetiarum historia vulgo Petro Iustiniano Iustiniani filio adiudicata*, Monumenti storici, n.s., 18 (Venice: Deputazione di Storia Patria, 1964), 231; Lorenzo de Monacis, *Chronicon de rebus venetis* . . . (Venice, 1758), 310–11 (written in the 1420s); and Sanuto, *Vite de' Duchi*, col. 616.

[24]Marino Sanuto's notes (ASV, Quarantia Criminal, b. 14bis, fol. 14) preserve the decision of 24 January 1345/46 to name eleven experts to deal with "ista negotia . . . de mutatione monete," and that of 9 February: "Cum diferentie que hic ponuntur in construtione monetarum sit solum in faciendo monetam puram de argento grosso vel mista cum ramine," on which the voting was as follows: "Quod sit pura de argento," 27; "Quod sit mista cum ramine," 7; "non," 3; "non sinceri," 0.

[25]Papadopoli, 1:173–82; *CNI*, 7:69–77.

seemed—to his friend Petrarch, for example, who praised Andrea's humane qualities—more appropriate for Andrea than a banner of military command.[26] For a half-dozen years these mezzanini were minted in large numbers and at high profit, competing successfully with the new "guelfo" which Florence had issued in 1345.[27]

During those same years, soldini were still being minted with the much inferior fineness of 62–67 percent. In 1353, in the midst of Venice's Third Genoese War, proposals were made to reduce the silver content of the soldino in a way that would have reduced further still the silver equivalent of the lira di piccoli. Opinion was divided in the Quarantia as to how to do it. A drafting committee was appointed, and each of its three members had a different opinion. Andrea Gabriel, probably the former banker of that name, wished to achieve the reduction by minting soldini that would be only about 5/8 silver, like those previously coined, and of lighter weight. The other two members of the drafting committee, Donato Honorado and Michele Duodo, although they differed on the price to be paid for free silver, both proposed giving the new issue of soldini the same fineness as the old grosso and the new mezzanino. On the first balloting on 29 March, Gabriel's motion received the most votes, but the doge himself and one of his councillors intervened successfully to move postponement. When a vote was taken on 8 April, after Honorado and Duodo had agreed on the price for free silver bullion, their unified motion passed, 26 to 9.[28] All servile silver was henceforth to be used for soldini.[29] Thus in the last year of Andrea Dandolo's dogeship the minting of his distinctive mezzanini ceased and a soldino of fine silver was left as the basic coin of the lira di piccoli.

The refinement of the soldino reestablished the sharp distinction that had prevailed in Venetian coinage before 1331 between coins of less than 1/5 silver and those that were of almost pure silver. The piccoli coined

---

[26]According to Papadopoli's description (1:181–82) the saint is receiving the candle from the doge, but the similarity of the obverse of this mezzanino to the obverse of the ducat suggests that the saint is giving and the doge receiving, as in the miniature of about the same date pictured in Agostino Pertusi, "Quedam regalia insignia," St:udi veneziani 7 (1965), on p. xxxvii and identified on p. 56. On the frequent use of the candle in Venetian ceremonies as a symbol of a moral, religious bond see Edward Muir, Civic Ritual in Renaissance Venice (Princeton, 1981), s.v. "candles." The presentation of a white candle by the pope to the doge had acquired a firm place in the legend of Venice's defense of the pope and reconciliation of pope and emperor in 1177. In Andrea's own chronicle, the white candle, presented as soon as the pope reached Venice, seems a symbol of gratitude for Venice's offer of protection (Dandolo, Andreae Danduli Chronica, vol. 12, pt. 1, p. 263). On the coin, the candle, presented not of course by a pope but by St. Mark, may have symbolized the doge's authority as protector of the body of the saint and of the Venetian Church.

[27]See below, app. A, sec. vi; and chap. 19, sec. iv.

[28]PMV, docs. 106, 114, 115, 117; DQ, vol. 3, docs. 30, 31, 33.

[29]PMV, doc. 118.

under Andrea Dandolo, although somewhat heavier than those coined under his predecessors, contained a slightly higher proportion of copper.[30] Also of a relatively low grade of billon—in fact more than 85 percent copper—was a new type of coin first coined in the last years of Andrea's dogeship, the tornesello. Since torneselli were intended for use in the Venetian dependencies in Greece, not within Venice, their characteristics and function will be described in connection with Levantine monetary exchange rates.[31]

The sharp distinction thus reestablished in the output of the Venetian mint between silver coins, more than 95 percent fine, and billon coins, less than 20 percent fine, did not apply to all the coins used within Venice. Several kinds of foreign groats of intermediate fineness were allowed to circulate legally, but an effort was made to ban pieces that were below the standards established at the places where they were minted ("in locis ubi consuetum est cuni et laborari dictas monetas"). Thus, all pieces of xxii that were less than 7/8 silver or weighed less than 204 coins to the mark were made subject to confiscation in 1354. If they were found in the hands of a moneychanger, he received no compensation for the coins confiscated and was fined 50–55 percent of their face value. If they were found in the hands of someone who was not a moneychanger, the fine was only 25 percent of the face value, in addition to confiscation, and even that penalty could be waived if he not only was not a moneychanger nor connected with a moneychanger but also was judged by the inspecting official not to be a "persona suspecta." But in any case, the coins of inferior fineness or weight were to be cut up and melted down. Similar decrees were issued concerning Paduan carrarini that were not of the fineness of grossi and concerning friesachers that did not contain 50 percent fine silver.[32] The explicitness with which the standards for these foreign coins were specified makes clear the legality and wide use of those that could meet the standard.

The reforms made under Andrea Dandolo set the pattern of Venetian coinage for several decades. The three separate types—gold, fine silver, and low-grade billon—continued to be sharply distinguished. Of greater importance in future years than in his own time was the provision introduced in 1353 requiring mintmasters to coin into soldini at a price specified by law all the silver offered. Although since the previous century the mintmasters had been required to accept for casting into certified bars all silver offered, the regulation concerning soldini in 1353 is the first surviving record of an order to the mintmasters to accept for coinage, at a specified price and charge, all silver offered. The silver thus voluntarily

---

[30] Papadopoli, 1:183; *CNI,* 7:69–75.

[31] See below, chap. 19, sec. ii.

[32] ASV, Commissioni, Capitulare Officii de Levante (ex Brera 263), fols. 19–21.

offered was called free silver to distinguish it from the servile silver of the quinto or the decimo. The mint charge set on free silver in 1353 was high— 7.4 percent—although not nearly as high as the charge on servile silver. It was soon set even higher—at 13.8 percent—so that the free silver attracted immediately was probably slight, but it was lowered in later years to 2.5 percent, so that the charge barely covered the costs.[33] The provision for unlimited coinage of silver contained in the law of 1353 proved an important step towards letting the initiative of silver merchants determine the amount of silver coined. It limited the discretion of the mintmasters in acquiring silver and increased the extent to which private enterprise determined the amount of coinage.

Taken as a whole, the monetary policies pursued under Andrea Dandolo seem well designed to expand and make profitable the operations of Venetian dealers in bullion. The import tax on silver was lowered by reducing the quinto to a decimo. The role of market conditions in determining the amount of coinage was strengthened by providing for the unlimited coinage of silver. The three kinds of coin—gold, silver, and billon—were again sharply distinguished, and in a way likely to enhance or at least restore the reputation of Venetian silver coins. The voyages of the merchant galleys, which will be described in chapter 17, were adjusted precisely in order to meet the needs of the bullion trade. The reductions in weight of the silver coins, to be analyzed more thoroughly in chapter 18, were consistent with the flexible, resilient bimetallic standard that had been introduced in 1331–32. According to that standard, 1 lira di grossi was supposed to equal both 10 gold ducats and 640 silver soldini, but the ducat was allowed to fluctuate freely. It did so at prices a little above 64 soldini. No effort was made to impose the exchange of gold and silver at a rate determined by the government.

## iv. COMPLICATIONS ARISING FROM MULTIPLE STANDARDS

Andrea Dandolo was the last doge to issue an appreciable number of the old Venetian grossi. None survive bearing the name of his ill-fated successor, Marino Falier; the last of the old grossi was issued by the latter's successor, Giovanni Gradenigo, 1355–56.[34] No doubt some grossi minted under earlier doges continued to circulate and many more lay in treasure chests within Venetian palaces, in spite of the large numbers that had been exported. But during twenty-odd years, 1356–79, no grossi of any kind issued from the Venetian mint.

Their discontinuance marks the end of the first of the three periods mentioned above (1332–53; 1353–79; and after 1379), periods which coin-

---

[33]*PMV*, doc. 117; and below, app. A, table A.5.
[34]Papadopoli, 1:181, 187–90 ff.; *CNI*, 7:69–75, 77–79, 82.

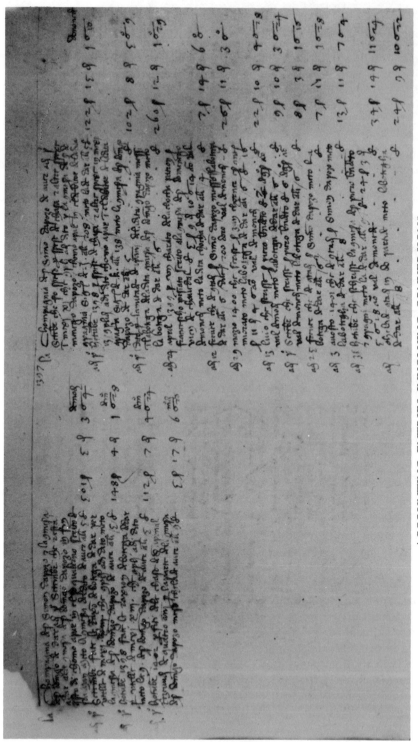

ACCOUNTING ENTRIES INVOLVING CONVERSIONS

Examples from 1397–1400 in the ledger consigned by the executors of the estate of Domenego da Pozzo to the Procuratori di San Marco for their administration of the estate of Domenego's son Andrea. The entries involve converting lire a oro into lire a monete.

ASV, PSM, Misti, b. 84, Commissaria Andrea da Pozo. By permission of the ASV, Sezione di Musei, Venice.

cided with three stages in the process by which Venetian money of account bifurcated into lire a oro and lire a monete. In 1331 the ducat was quoted at 70, and again in 1345 it was nearly that high, but in the years between it dipped, and in 1349–51 it was back down to 64 soldi di piccoli.[35] So long as fluctuations were within that range, probably many accounts were kept on the assumption that there was a single bimetallic monetary standard in which 1 gold ducat equaled 64 silver soldini.[36] Adjustment to commercial reality was made by allowing for the extent to which the ducat was priced above 64 soldi di piccoli through the addition of the lazio.[37] Use of such a variable lazio treated the silver coins, called "monete," as the basic coins of the traditional lira di grossi and lira a grossi.

After 1353, in the second period, the lazio increased as the ducat again rose. When its price reached 74, it stabilized at about that level, so that the lazio remained at about 8–10 soldi from 1362 to 1374. If in spite of the large lazio a ledger was still kept in lire di grossi a monete, the accounting became cumbersome, as is illustrated by an explanation of the entries in a small ledger of the Da Pozzo family reproduced here.

The first entry in the lefthand column, while crediting the estate of Domenego, debits a company in which he had been a partner for a sum taken from the ledger which Domenego had kept "in his own hand" in which debits and credits had been recorded in lire di grossi a monete, as are most of the debits and credits in this ledger. It reads:

La Chompagnia de ser Simon da Pozo e la
commessaria de ser Domenego de dar a dì
primo Setembre che resta a dar a la
commessaria de ser Domenego da Pozo in
fin questo dì, chomo apar in el
quaderno scrito de soa man; meto                de monede
la commessaria del dito de aver a k. 5     £ 501 s. 5 d. 3 p. 4

In the righthand column, the fourth entry, while debiting a "ship account," credits that same partnership for transferring to the estate one share in the ownership of a cog, a share that had been valued in lire di grossi a oro. The entry reads:

[35]Below, table D.3; Zanetti, *Nuova raccolta*, 4:169–76; *PMV*, lxxxi; Papadopoli, 1:210; Mandich, "Per una ricostruzione," cvii n. 1.
[36]Mandich, "Per una ricostruzione," cv, concluded that the transactions in Venice of the Covoni were usually recorded (1336–40) in "la lira 'di grossi manchi' (o lira 'manca') senza mai precisare [*expressis verbis*] a quale effettiva moneta veneziana essa la riferisce, se al grosso d'argento, o al ducato d'oro."
[37]On the lazio on the ducat see above, chap. 15, sec. iii.

a dì 24 april 1399 per un charato
de la chocha patron ser Francescho
Pesiato scrito a la commissaria
de ser Domenego, vien de chavedal
£ 5 s. 9 d. 10 pic. 14 a oro, val
de monede, meto la dita chocha
de dar a k. 4                                     £ 7 s. 14 d. 6 p. 0

The accountant had converted from lire a oro in order to make his entry in lire a monete. He had converted by adding to the gold value the difference between the legal value of the ducat (64 soldi) and the day's market valuation. We can find the latter (namely, 90 soldi per ducat) by reducing both figures to piccoli, then dividing the amount "de monete" by the amount "a oro" and multiplying the result by 64 ([59,328/42,190] × 64 = 89.997).

The fifth righthand entry records an investment of 200 ducats in cash. Using the same procedure reveals that the market rate of the ducat on 12 February 1400 was 85 soldi. The entry reads:

a dì 12 frever che de contadi
ser Simon da Pozo, messo la
botega de dar a k. 6, ducati
200 d'oro val de monede                          £ 26 s. 11 d. 3 p. 0

The accountant who made the conversions took off from a knowledge of the current price of the ducat. But he also had to calculate by reducing figures in lire to figures in piccoli, since piccoli were the lowest common denominator of both the lire a oro and the soldi di piccoli in which ducats were priced. For the entry of 12 February 1400, when the ducat was quoted at 85, its price equaled 1,020 piccoli (85 × 12). Since each denaro grosso of the lire di grossi a monete contained 32 of these piccoli, the 1,020 piccoli equaled 31.875 denari grossi a monete (1,020/32). Two hundred gold ducat coins, valued at 31.875 denari grossi each, gave a total of 6,375 denari grossi a monete (200 × 31.875), which he recorded as 26 lire 11 soldi 3 denari a monete, having calculated that 26 × 240 denari = 6,240 denari, which leaves 135 denari; and 11 × 12 = 132 denari, which leaves 3 denari for the total of 6,375 denari.

A shortcut is difficult to imagine. The procedure of conversion must have consumed time and energy and added to a businessman's transaction costs!

Increasingly, merchants and officials who handled ducats kept their books in lire di grossi a oro.[38] They avoided use of the lazio by treating the

---

[38] The accounts of the estate of Tommaso Querini, kept by the Procurators of San Marco

ducat as the basic coin, always valuing it at 2 soldi di grossi, that is, 24 denari grossi, or 768 piccoli a oro. They then varied the valuation of silver coins. For example, if the moneychangers gave 85 soldi for a ducat, when a merchant who kept his books in lire a oro received a cash payment of 17 soldini, he would value each soldino as 1/85 of a ducat. Since 2 soldi di grossi a oro always equaled 1 ducat, each soldino would be valued as 2/85 soldi di grossi a oro, so that the 17 soldini coins were worth 2/5 (17 × [2/85]) of a soldo di grossi a oro, which was the same as 2/5 of 12 grossi a oro and also the same as 2/5 of 384 piccoli a oro, that is, 153.6 piccoli a oro (384 × [2/5]). He would record that valuation as 4 denari 25 or 26 piccoli a oro, having calculated that 32 × 4 grossi = 128 piccoli, which leaves 25.6 piccoli of the total of 153.6 piccoli.

With the development of these two contrasting ways of keeping accounts, the lira di grossi a oro became clearly distinct from the lira di grossi a monete during the second period (1353–79).

It is possible that while those lire, which were both clearly detached from the grosso coin, were bifurcating, a third kind of lira di grossi, called a "lira di grossi di zecca," remained tied to the old grosso of 2.1 grams fine. Among the assets recorded in the estate of Giovanni Stornado in 1353 were "libras xii grossorum di zecha." Did that merely mean that the estate administrators had found 2,880 freshly minted grossi coins (12 × 240) in the deceased's treasure chest? Or does it mean that alongside the lira di grossi a oro and the lira di grossi a monete should be placed a third kind of lira di grossi also used as a standard of exchange value? If so, this lira would deserve being called "una vera lira di grossi." The appellation has been applied to the lira di grossi a oro, perhaps because its comparative value rose when the amount of silver in the soldino and other "monete" was reduced and the lira a monete fell.[39] But since grossi coins were always silver, never gold, calling a lira di grossi based on gold a "true lira di grossi" carries the anachronistic implication that gold was the only "real money."

During the mid-fourteenth century, silver was rising in value and gold was falling, so that the old grosso rose in value compared not only with the soldino but also with the ducat. A "true lira di grossi" worth 240 old, full-weight grossi coins would have represented 504 grams of silver (240 × 2.1). That was not only much more than the 410 grams of silver (640 × 0.641) then represented by the 640 soldini in a lire di grossi a

---

(PSM, Citra, b. 260), before 1341 convert sums entered originally in libre parvorum or libre grossorum into libre ad grossos. Beginning in 1341 all sums are converted into libre grossorum in monetis. Only in the 1350s are there signs that sums recorded in lire di grossi a monete were later converted into lire di grossi a oro. The accounts of the estate of Jacobello Gabriel (ibid., Misti, b. 67) from 1361 on clearly convert sums initially recorded in other lire into lire di grossi a oro.

[39]Mandich, "Per una ricostruzione," cviii.

monete. It was also worth much more in 1353 than the 35.5 grams of gold which were the metallic equivalent of the lira di grossi a oro, the bimetallic ratio being at that date only about 11 to 1. Indeed, Stornado's estate managers evaluated the 12 lire di grossi di zecca as 15 lire 8 soldi di grossi a oro, allowing a lazio, they said, of 5 soldi 8 denari (28 percent).[40] In that case the "lazio" was in fact a premium allowed for old, full-weight silver grossi by an accountant keeping books in lira di grossi a oro!

While one may not exclude the possibility of the use of a third lira di grossi linked to the old grosso, the kinds of lire di grossi clearly distinguished in common use were two: the lira a oro (equal to 10 ducati a oro) and the lira a monete (equal to 10 ducati a monete). As a subdivision, the grosso a oro was similarly quite distinct from the grosso a monete, which was more explicitly called a denaro of the lira di grossi a monete, for 24 grossi a oro was understood to mean 1 gold ducat, whereas 24 grossi a monete was understood to mean 64 silver soldini. The market value of the denominations of the lira and ducato a monete varied in gold coin, perhaps as often as week to week. In contrast, the value in silver coin of the denomination of account of the lira and ducato a monete remained invariable as follows:

$$1 \text{ lira di grossi a monete} = 640 \text{ soldini}$$
$$1 \text{ ducat a monete} = 64 \text{ soldini}$$
$$1 \text{ grosso a monete} = 2 \ 2/3 \text{ soldini}$$
$$1 \text{ piccolo a monete} = 1/12 \text{ soldino}$$

During this second period, 1353–79, the soldino was the basic coin tying together three moneys of account: the lira di piccoli, the lira di grossi a monete, and the ducato a monete.

In the third period—after 1379—the three were similarly tied together by both the soldino and a new grosso. This new grosso, in contrast to the old grosso, when issued was made—by law—a link coin of the lira di piccoli. Its coinage was physical, numismatic recognition of the way the moneys of account had been transformed since 1331.

The new grosso was distinguishable visually from the old grosso chiefly by the star added beside the figure of Christ risen and was only slightly (about 2/10 of a gram) lighter, but it had an entirely different relation to Venice's money of account. In spite of their name, the new grossi had a legal value stated not in lire di grossi but in lire di piccoli. The

---

[40]PSM, Misti, b. 62A, estate of Giovanni Stornado, register for 1348–1428, fol. 3. The lazio of 5 soldi 8 denari means that for each 240 grossi di zecca the administrators added 5 soldi 8 denari to the 20 soldi in a lira a oro, since 15 lire 8 soldi = 308 soldi = 240 + 68 = (12 × 20) + (12 × 5 2/3) soldi. On new grossi di zecca see above, chap. 15, sec. i. On the speculation in silver by the administrators of the Stornado estate see Mueller, "The Procurators of San Marco," 151–52.

law governing their coinage specified that they were to be worth 4 soldini and also specified that each soldino was worth 12 piccoli.[41] Thus the new grosso was given the value of 48 piccoli as legal tender. Since these piccoli were the lowest denomination of account of the lira di piccoli, the lira di grossi a monete, and the ducato a monete,[42] the new grosso was able to function as a basic coin of all three of these moneys of account.

(The fiscal and commercial situation leading up to the coinage of this new type of grosso with a changed weight and slightly changed design but with a relation to Venice's moneys of account entirely different from that of the old grosso will be explained below, in chapter 18, section ii.)

The coining of a grosso having four times the legal and metallic value of the soldino accentuated the artificial, antiquated, or abstract meanings of all the denominations of account in use. As a denomination of account, the piccolo of which 240 made 1 lira di piccoli had long been distinct from the piccolo coin.[43] When the soldino had become the basic coin of the lira di piccoli, a "piccolo" as a denomination of account equaled in value, not a piccolo coin nor an average of piccolo coins, but 1/12 of a soldino.[44] A similar contrast between the tangible metallic coin and the denomination of account with the same name was extreme in the case of "grosso." The new grosso was not a physical embodiment of the "denaro grosso" of either of the two lire di grossi; that is, it did not have the same value as either. It was not of the same value as the denaro grosso of the lira di grossi a oro, for the metallic value of the latter depended on its being 1/24 of a gold ducat. The new coins were not of the same value as the denaro grosso of which 240 constituted a lira di grossi a monete, for the latter denaro grosso was merely an accounting unit equal to 32 piccoli and derived its metallic value from the equivalence of 12 piccoli with 1 soldino. The new grosso coin authorized in 1379 (type 2) with the legal tender value of 48 piccoli was accordingly worth 1.5 denari grossi (48/32) of the lira di grossi a monete.

[41] The decree (in *PMV*, doc. 163, p. 157) reads: "Qui vero grossi esse debeant ponderis soldorum quatuor et eiusdem fineçe et currere debeant ad dictum precium soldorum quatuor et soldini predicti pro parvis duodecim pro quolibet; et predicte monete currere debeant in Veneciis et in omnibus terris et locis subditis Comuni Veneciarum, nec refutari possint per aliquem." The weight was 1.987 grams, the fineness 0.952. The mint charge was the same percentage in 1379 for grossi as for soldini (see below, app. A, sec. vii).

[42] See above, n. 15.

[43] Mandich has emphasized that when the old grosso still determined the value of the lira di grossi, the full-weight grosso coin was worth 36, not 32, piccoli coins. At that time the piccoli referred to in accounts kept in lire di grossi were not of the same value as real piccoli coins ("Per una ricostruzione," cvii).

[44] Mandich did not analyze the effects of the new silver coins of 1331 and the displacement of the piccolo coin by the soldino coin as the basic coin of the lira di piccoli. Whether that shift occurred in the 1330s or 1340s is indeed doubtful, but it seems certainly to have occurred before 1353. Papadopoli records no piccoli minted between 1368 and 1382.

One can summarize as follows the relations after 1379 of the denominations "a monete" to the silver soldini and to the new type of silver grossi coins:

| | | |
|---|---|---|
| 1 lira di grossi a monete | = 640 soldini | = 160 grossi |
| 1 ducato a monete | | |
| (1/10 of a lira a monete) | = 64 soldini | = 16 grossi |
| 1 denaro grosso a monete | | |
| (1/24 of a ducato a monete) | = 2 2/3 soldini | = 2/3 grosso |
| 1 denaro a monete | | |
| (32 piccoli a monete) | = 1/12 soldino | = 1/48 grosso |

Inverting the picture shows the relation of the new grosso coin to the moneys of account in the 1380s as follows: 1 silver grosso coin, type 2 = 48 of the denari piccoli of the lira di piccoli = 1.5 denari grossi of the lira di grossi a monete = 1.2 grossi a oro when 1 gold ducat was priced at 80 soldi di piccoli (24 × [4/80] = 1.2) < 1.2 grossi a oro when the gold ducat was priced at more than 80 soldi di piccoli.

## v. CHOICES AMONG MONEYS OF ACCOUNT

With so many different moneys of account linked some to one coin, some to another, it is often difficult for a modern reader of old Venetian records to know which lira or soldo is meant in a particular document. The Venetians who used those moneys of account every day also had difficulties unless the kind of lira or soldo was specified or unless, as was the case in most official governmental accounts, the kind of lira meant could be assumed because of the long established practice of a particular office.

When doubt arose regarding private contracts, the courts of civil justice could be called on to decide on the correct interpretation. Even if the kind of lira or soldo was not in question, a dispute was possible over whether coins offered in payment should be valued as they were at the time the contract was made or at the rate prevailing at the time the payment was due.[45] In the long run the latter interpretation may be said to have favored debtors. Generally if coins kept their full weight, in the course of time they acquired values higher in money of account than they had had when first issued. As a result, fewer coins would be needed to pay a sum stated, for example, in lire di piccoli. Paying a debt of 640 soldi di piccoli in ducats in 1383 would have required 10 ducats if the coins were valued at the old rate of 64 soldi but only 8 ducats if the coins were valued

[45]Martino Garrati of Lodi, *Tractatus de Monetis*, fully cited and described in Soldi Rondinini, "Politica e teoria monetarie," 315–27.

at their market price in 1383, which was 80 soldi. In the sixteenth century and earlier the Venetian courts were more likely to decide in favor of the creditors and require payment at the rate that was legally established at the time the contract was made.[46]

Long after the ducato a monete was separated from the ducato a oro, and long after the ducat coin and the ducato a oro had risen far above 64 soldi, a court could still rule that an obligation that had been formulated in lire di piccoli and was being paid in ducat coins required paying 1 ducat for each 64 soldi due. An example of such a decision is a case of 1396 concerning an annual legacy of 50 lire di piccoli made in 1338 by Marsilio of Carrara to three Venetian monasteries. The administrators of the estate, the Procuratori of San Marco, wished to pay by valuing ducats at 84 soldi di piccoli, that is, at the market rate in 1396. The judges declared that as a general rule when a will read "50 lire" without further specification, 50 lire a grossi was to be understood. But since lire di piccoli had been specified in this case, the bequest should be paid by giving ducats the value they had in lire di piccoli at the time of the bequest. That meant a difference of almost 4 ducats (24 percent of the annual bequest) for each of the beneficiaries.[47] The case exemplifies one of the many disadvantages of a monetary system with multiple monetary standards expressed in several moneys of account linked now to one coin, now to another, with changing metallic contents.

While courts decided in doubtful cases about payments due between private parties, administrative officials or higher councils decided what moneys would be used in various aspects of Communal affairs. For example, the special police court concerned mainly with the illicit carrying of weapons, the Cinque alla Pace, imposed fines stated in lire di piccoli but then collected part of the fines "ad aurum" and part "ad monetam." They had different rules for men fined less than 5 lire and men fined 5 lire and more. The latter paid the first 64 soldi they owed by paying 1 ducat, but they were allowed before 1403 to pay all the rest of the fine in monete. The Ducal Councillors changed the rules in 1403 to require that all fines larger than 3 lire be paid entirely in ducats, valuing them at only 64 soldi. Only fines of less than 3 lire could be paid in silver coin. The Ducal Councillors made the change, they said, in order to increase Communal revenue.[48]

Increasing Communal revenue was also the reason given in 1361 for changing the kind of coin in which naval officials paid themselves their

[46]Tucci, "Le monete in Italia," 527.

[47]Below, app. G, doc. 7, from ASV, Santa Maria Gloriosa dei Frari, b. 128 (formerly b. 129), fasc. Marsilio da Carrara, sentence of the Curia del Procurator, 17 May 1396. Fifty lire × [20 soldi/64 soldi] = 15.625 ducats, whereas 50 lire × [20 soldi/84 soldi] = 11.9 ducats.

[48]ASV, Collegio, Notatorio, reg. 3, fol. 100 (16 May 1403). The same rule held as late as 1438 (see ASV, Petizion, Sentenze a Giustizia, reg. 82, fol. 6v).

share of the fines they imposed on seamen or ship operators. The officials had at one time been paid "ad monetas," but just before 1361 they began to receive payment partly in ducats. Since the ducat had reached a new high of 73 soldi in mid-1361, after some years at about 64, the loss to the Commune was noteworthy, and the Avogadori ruled in December of 1361 that because of the "magnis laziis," the officials were to get their share in ducats only if the penalty had been paid in ducats, in silver if it had been paid in silver coin.[49]

As late as 1348 a sweeping conversion of import duties from ad valorem to ad pondus specified rates in lire a grossi,[50] but the lira a grossi, which in the thirteenth century had been used more than the lira di grossi, became much less popular during the course of the fourteenth century. In 1386 the brokerage fees were being calculated on some deals in lire di piccoli, on others in lire a grossi. It was then ordered that thereafter they all be calculated in lire di piccoli counting 64 soldi to a ducat.[51] The disuse of the lira a grossi is quite understandable in view of the arithmetically difficult relation of the lira a grossi to the new silver coins. On the other hand, the difficulties of converting regulations, debts, penalties, and balances recorded in lire a grossi into lire di grossi delayed the change even after it had become public policy.

One customs office, the Tabula Maris, which collected the freights on most costly merchandise, the kind brought by galleys, undertook the conversion of its accounts from lire a grossi to lire di grossi under orders from the Senate at some date prior to December 1390. On 12 December of that year, the Senate expressed its satisfaction with the results of the conversion, which had perhaps been undertaken as an experiment, and ordered all other "tabule" and revenue-collecting offices still using the old money of account to convert similarly but to proceed in such a manner that no customs duties ("datii") would be either raised or lowered. The proponents of the measure asserted that keeping accounts in lire a grossi "inducit confusionem et intacamentum" in those bureaus and implied that the conversion, which would expedite matters, would also make superfluous a certain number of employees (scribani, ratiocinati, massarii, et famuli), who could as a result be dropped from the payroll.[52]

In 1409 another customs bureau, the Tabula Ternarie, still had not carried out the order; it continued to keep its accounts "in lire a grossi and in various kinds of perperi." The old system was probably more conve-

---

[49]ASV, Avogaria di Comun, reg. 2, fol. 96, cap. 271.

[50]*BG*, 1:61–62; and the decree raising taxes in 1350 in *RES*, docs. 217–20.

[51]This is probably the first official change from lire a grossi to ducati a monete (ASV, Senato, Misti, reg. 40, fol. 15 [25 January 1385/86]).

[52]Ibid., reg. 41, fol. 120.

TABLE II.

Moneys of Account and Measures Used in Quotations
of Wholesale Prices before 1404

| Commodity | Money of Account | Unit of Measure |
|---|---|---|
| Pepper | Lire a grossi | Carica ("cargo") = 400 libbre sottili |
| Refined silver | Lire a grossi | Mark |
| Silk | Lire a grossi | Libbra sottile |
| Sugar, ginger, wax, etc. | Ducati | 100 libbre sottili |
| Cloves, nutmeg, saffron, etc. | Grossi "of 24 per ducat" | Libbra sottile |
| Cotton | Lire di grossi | Migliaio sottile (1,000 libbre sottili) |
| Wool, metals (copper, tin, etc.) | Lire di grossi | Migliaio grosso (1,000 libbre grosse) |
| Wheat | Lire di piccoli | Staio |

NOTE: All the accounting units are a oro except for the lire di piccoli used for wheat. Letters that circulated through the Datini agencies were accompanied by price lists called "valute." They specified that the lira a grossi was "di s. 52 al duchato," showing that this money of account is also a oro. Market operators regularly made conversions using the equation: 26 lire a grossi = 1 lira di grossi = 10 ducats; that is, dropping the awkward fraction 1/9. There is one exception, a valuta of 1396 (ASP, Datini, b. 1171). The price of pepper is there given as "lire 183, di s. 52, d. 2 ducato." This appears to be an attempt to recuperate the 1/9, although it undershoots the mark slightly. In this case, 26.111 lire a grossi = 10 ducats; 2.6111 lire a grossi = 52.222 soldi = 1 ducat; and 0.222 × 12 denari = 2.667 denari, so that 1 ducat = 52 soldi 2.667 denari, whereas here they figured 52 soldi 2 denari (or 52.167 soldi) per ducat. This method seems to have been an exception, however, and it is likely that most calculations were made without the fraction, a convenience that involved a difference of only 0.43 percent (0.222/52).

nient for these customs officials, who had jurisdiction over fats, salted meats, and so on, and, as the inference to perperi suggests, imports of olive oil from Corfu and other Greek islands. On 4 June the office was ordered by the Great Council to convert all accounts to lire di grossi.[53]

The freight rates charged by the galley masters who chartered galleys for a season's operation were set by the charter contracts in lire a grossi, at least on galleys for Romania, until 1420. Then new rates were set in lire di grossi a oro.[54]

In the market place the lira a grossi continued to be used for some time in the quotations of wholesale prices for several important commodities. The customary system of quoting wholesale prices in Venice in

[53]MC, Leone, fol. 184.
[54]ASV, Senato, Misti, reg. 53, fol. 48 (1 June 1420). That the new rates were ad aurum was specifically stated. The freight rates were specified also in 1424 (ibid., reg. 55, fols. 26–27).

the period around 1400 can be reconstructed with help from Venetian private account books and from letters sent from Venice to a rich merchant of Prato, Francesco di Marco Datini, and to his factors in various cities.[55] Table 11 presents selected commodities prominent in long-distance trade.

Finally, in 1404 the lira a grossi was officially replaced in quoting the prices of pepper, silver, and (presumably) silk. No trace of an order to change the practice has remained in the deliberations of the major Venetian governing bodies,[56] but a letter written in Venice on 22 March 1404 informed the Florentine branch of the Datini firm of the change, in a manner clearly indicating approval: "It has been arranged here that pepper no longer be quoted in lire a grossi but be priced in ducats, which is better and more expeditious. Accordingly henceforth the quotation will be so many ducats per load."[57] The change is reflected in the market quotations. In the price series gathered from the same correspondence, the last quotation of pepper in lire a grossi dates from 15 March, the first in ducats from 12 April. The change is clear also in the accounts for refined silver kept by the banker and bullion merchant Guglielmo Condulmer: the last occasion on which silver is quoted in lire a grossi dates from 20 February; the first in ducats from 11 April.[58] No relapse to the old system has been found, which indicates that the abandonment of the lire a grossi was welcomed, as it had probably been prompted, by all operators on the Rialto, foreign and Venetian alike.

One of the last important government bureaus to remove all traces of the lira a grossi was the Loan Office (Camera degli Imprestiti). In 1380 it received specific orders to change from using lire a grossi to using lire di grossi. But it continued until after 1403 at least to keep the record of the

---

[55] A useful example of a "valuta" (1393) is in Melis, *Documenti per la storia economica,* doc. 86. The valuta of 1396 is mentioned by Jacques Heers in "Il commercio nel Mediterraneo alla fine del secolo XIV e nei primi anni del XV secolo," *Archivio storico italiano* 113 (1955): 184, and 202, where Heers, however, mistook the lira of 52 soldi 2 denari as a lira di piccoli. In this he is followed by Spufford and Wilkinson, *Interim Listing,* 141. For silver, finally, see the accounts of Guglielmo Condulmer in PSM, Misti, b. 189.

[56] It is not in the "deliberazioni" of the Great Council, the Senate, or the Collegio. It is possible that the regulation was lost in the archive of the Collegio, whose register for 1403–4 is very confused. More likely, the order was issued by a lesser office such as the Provveditori di Comun or the Consoli dei Mercanti, whose records are not extant.

[57] "È si fatto qui che di pepe non si ragiona più a lire a grossi, ma facisi el pregio a ducati, ch'è meglio e più spaciativo; sicchè ogimai si dirà tanti ducati el charicho" (ASP, Datini, b. 714, Commissaria Gaddi to Florence, misdated 22 April 1403 for 22 March 1403 [1404 modern]: in fact, the letter arrived in Florence on 28 March 1404, after the Florentine new year [25 March]).

[58] PSM, Misti, b. 189, for silver. ASP, Datini, all letters from Venice, including b. 929, Paoluccio to Barcelona.

assessments, the basis for its collection of forced loans, in lire a grossi, although it made its record of payments in lire di grossi. Changing the record of assessment was particularly difficult because part of the assessments were made by applying fixed relations between artificial valuations, stated in lire a grossi, and estimated real income, stated in ducats.[59] Payments of interest by the Loan Office were made partly in gold, partly in silver. Considering it unfair that some bondholders received gold and others silver, the Senate in 1434 ordered that all payments of 5 ducats or more be made 3/4 in gold, 1/4 "ad monetas."[60] But the proportion to be observed was changed from time to time, as was the way the silver money was to be valued. The Loan Office, in fact, usually paid 2–4 soldi less per ducat than the market rate, thus applying a kind of withholding tax.[61]

Elsewhere the lira a grossi lived on only in the old statutes and in routinely repeated formulae. One legal situation where it seems to have remained was that of the "augmentum doctis" of 12 1/2 lira a grossi for mourning garb ("pro suis indumentis vidualibus"), to which a widow had rights on the estate of her deceased husband on the basis of the statutes of the early thirteenth century.[62] Other examples appear in the Promissioni Ducali, such as the paragraph that assigns to the newly elected doge 3,000 lire a grossi for the expenses of taking office.[63] Finally, the nominal salaries for positions of prestige, such as that of the Procurators of San Marco, in this case 200 lire a grossi per year, were fixed and continued to be quoted in the money of account used when the office was established.[64]

All the conversions described above were conversions into lire di grossi a oro. The one important governmental use of the lira di grossi a monete was by the grain magistracies. There were two grain magistracies: the Provveditori alle Biave, directly involved in buying and selling wheat and flour, and the Camera del Frumento, which specialized in the financial side and acted in many ways like a public bank. Although wheat prices were quoted in lire di piccoli, it seems that around 1400 both offices kept their accounts in lire di grossi, the former a monete, the latter a oro.

One can conclude that the Provveditori alle Biave kept their accounts

[59]Luzzatto, *Il debito pubblico,* 146–49, 150n; cf. *PRV,* lxxix, cxxxviii, cxl, cxlv–viii, docs. 176, 184.

[60]*PRV,* doc. 233.

[61]Luzzatto, *Storia,* 216, 218; *PRV,* docs. 265, 270; MC, Ursa, fols. 91, 109. In 1455 all payments "in monetis" were ordered made at 124 soldi per ducat, by then the current rate (*BG,* vol. 1, doc. 109 and p. xlvii).

[62]Mueller, "The Procurators of San Marco," 176; ASV, Giudici di petizion, Sentenze a Giustizia, reg. 27, fol. 1 (13 October 1406).

[63]ASV, Senato, Terra, reg. 4, fol. 57v (23 November 1457).

[64]See the salary cuts of 11 January 1411/12 in ASV, Senato, Misti, reg. 49, fol. 71; see also PSM, late capitolari of the sixteenth century.

in lire di grossi a monete, that is, in terms of a ducat of account worth 64 soldi, on the basis of the account opened in their name by the merchant Tommaso Talenti in 1380.[65] That the Camera del Frumento kept its accounts in gold appears in a regulation of 1408 ordering the office to change its accounts from gold to silver. The order probably aimed at improved coordination of accounts between the two offices. In fact, the officials of the Camera del Frumento at the Rialto honored the orders to pay ("polize") sent them from the warehouse at San Marco by the Provveditori. Furthermore, it happened, especially in times of crisis, that grain importers could not be paid in cash; instead, they would agree to be credited with the amount due on the books of the Grain Office's depository, where it earned interest at 3–5 percent, as will be explained below, in volume 2.

An important general reform of the accounting procedures of the Camera del Frumento, prepared by a special commission and approved by the Collegio on 1 March 1408, contained specific monetary provisions. They stated that one source of the existing "confuxion" would be eliminated by keeping cash accounts in silver rather than in gold: "che le soe chasse se tegna a monede e non mentoava plui oro." All deposit accounts were to be checked and converted "a monede" at 96 soldi per ducat, the then current rate, or close to it, such that 2 lire di grossi (a oro) were equal to 3 lire di grossi a monete ($[2 \times 96]/64 = 3$). In the course of the conversion, however, reference to the gold value was to be retained in the body of the entry, in this way: "Ser Tal die aver per j° depossito ducati M d'oro, val a monede lire 150 de grossi" ($[1,000 \times 96]/64 = 1,500$ ducati a monete = 150 lire di grossi a monete).

Current income and expenditures, however, were to distinguish gold from silver. Accounts payable were to be rendered half in silver and half in gold, as was then generally the case regarding the interest paid out by the Bond Office. The example given is this: if a person is owed 100 lire di piccoli, he should be paid with 52 1/2 lire di piccoli, that is, in silver, and with 10 ducats, which at 95 soldi per ducat comes in fact to 47 1/2 lire di piccoli, the balance. The ducats were to be valued in the body of the accounting entry at the day's market quotation and then debited to cash ("la cassa de' aver") in lire di grossi a monete at that rate. At the same time, the account was to be balanced to the separate ducat account ("raxon de ducati"). Finally, the ducats to be paid out as interest on the deposits were to be calculated at 96 soldi for accounting purposes, "even though it was ducats that were both received and expended." In this way, it was affirmed, the Commune gained 1 soldo per ducat, "e più quanto el lazo chalasse."[66] Just how long this regulation remained in effect is not known.

---

[65]See below, app. G, doc. 6.

[66]The commission was formed in 1407 as the "tres sapientes super quinque officiis" (MC,

## vi. SOME TEMPORARY SIMPLIFICATION

Once the adjustment to the new silver coinage of the fourteenth century was completed, the complexity arising from the moneys of account "a monete" gradually subsided. Just two moneys of account were in very general use throughout the fifteenth century—the lira di piccoli and the lira di grossi a oro, of which the ducato a oro was in effect a subdivision. The ducato a monete of 64 soldi di piccoli was overshadowed and then pushed out of use altogether by these simpler moneys of account.

The government made no attempt to impose the old official value of the ducat at 64 soldi. In the early fifteenth century it occasionally applied to the gold ducat for specific purposes values very different from the 64 soldi and 24 grossi decreed in 1328. The specific values sometimes corresponded to current market quotations but other times were lower or higher, reflecting a desire to impose a kind of withholding tax on some or perhaps to give the benefit of a premium. Such an official value for the ducato a oro—96 soldi di piccoli—appears clearly in the regulation of 1408 regarding the accounts of the Camera del Frumento. In 1417 an official price of 100 soldi for a gold ducat was envisaged in planning a reform in the silver coinage.[67] In the next year the Bond Office announced that it would make its payments of interest on the public debt at that rate. On protest from the Avogadori that the current value of the ducat was 104 soldi, the Signoria ordered payment at the higher rate.[68] In setting wages

Leona, fol. 165). Examples are from (and assumptions based upon) ASV, Collegio, Notatorio, reg. 4, fols. 29v–30r, esp. pars. 3–6. The essential text follows:

> Quarto, per redure a chiareza questi chonti el plui che se porà, volemo che tuti i depositi che sono a la chamera che i se inscontrano chon I libri e che tute siano redute a monede a soldi 96 per ducato e per fare la chossa pui stricta, perchè lire 2 de grossi a soldi 96 per duchato fa lire 3 de grossi a monede. Ma dentro de la posta scriva, 'Ser Tal die aver per j⁰ depossito ducati M d'oro, val a monede lire 150 de grossi.'
>
> Quinto, per i ducati che fosse ricevuti per i diti signori, se chaxo serà che uno debia dare lire C de piccoli, el ge dia lire 52 1/2 de piccoli e ducati 10 d'oro, che valeria a soldi 95 [sic] per ducato lire 47, s. 10 piccoli, Volemo che dentro de la posta el scriva j⁰ ducato al priexio ch'à in qual dì lo averà abudi, ma subito el scriva al'incontro che la cassa de' aver per tanti ducati al priexio lo j averà abudi, E portar quelli in raxon de ducati e de questi tegnir conto separato.
>
> Sesto, quando j vignerà a pagar algun pro', che j conta j diti ducati s. 96 l'uno, E questo non monta niente perchè debiando aver ducati e pagandoli de queli, la raxon sta ben; El chomun avanza in questo chonto s. 1 per ducato, e più quanto el lazo chalasse.

[67]Papadopoli, 1:360–61.
[68]ASV, Collegio, Notatorio, reg. 5, fol. 192v.

and salaries for seamen on war galleys in 1422–27, the Collegio specified some of them in lire di piccoli and some in ducats. It ordered the use of an exchange rate of 106 soldi to the ducat in 1422, 105 soldi in 1425–27.[69] While those rates were slightly above the market rate, in 1428 it was decided to pay out the salaries of Venetian rectors and provincial administrators at 100 soldi when the market rate was 104 soldi.[70]

Such divergences were largely eliminated in mid-century, for the ducat stabilized at 124 soldi (6 lire 4 soldi di piccoli) in 1456 and remained at that rate until about 1510. During the monetary crisis of 1472 the tron, representing one lira or 20 soldi di piccoli, and the soldo, or marchetto, were coined in such a way as to maintain the exchange at 124 soldi per ducat. After 1518 the gold ducat coin, renamed the "zecchino," resumed its rise to 130 soldi and beyond.[71] A ducato valued at the long-maintained rate of 124 soldi developed as a much-used money of account. The term "ducato d'oro," says Papadopoli, sometimes referred to this silver-based money of account worth 124 soldi. To indicate the gold coin it became necessary to say "zecchino" or "ducato d'oro in oro."[72] In 1562 a silver ducat worth 124 soldi was coined, giving real form to that ducat of account. In time, still another ducat of account, called the "ducato a monete" and worth 120 soldi, was born and materialized as a silver coin, the "ducato mozzo," minted under Doge Marino Grimani (1591–1605), with its value indicated by the figure 120 incorporated in its design.[73]

But the fifteenth century was spared these developments. The term "ducato" meant the gold coin or the money of account based on gold, which was used for wholesale and international trade and some salaries, while the lira di piccoli, based on silver, was used for wages and retail

---

[69]Ibid., regs. 5, fol. 169v, and 6, fols. 17–19, 23v, 38; Freddy Thiriet, ed., *Délibérations des assemblées vénitiennes concernant la Romanie*, 2 vols., EPHE-6, Documents et recherches, ed. P. Lemerle, 8, 11 (Paris, 1966–71), vol. 2, nos. 584, 1250. These domestic exchange rates contrast with the valuing of a ducat at 64 soldi in traditional formulae used in earlier commissions for commanders of galley fleets mentioned above, in n. 5. If the ducats used in that case had meant a unit worth nearly 100 soldi, as the gold ducat was in those decades, the 6 ducats per month given as the pay of bowmen would have been equal to 30 lire di piccoli a month (6 × [100/20]), very much more than any recorded rate for bowmen in those decades.

[70]Francesco Semi, *Capris, Iustinopolis, Capodistria* (Trieste, 1975), 165.

[71]Papadopoli, 2:91, 100.

[72]Ibid., 211: "ducato, grossi, e piccoli, che continuarono a chiamarsi ducato d'oro, grossi a oro, piccoli a oro anche quando non correspondevano più alla moneta d'oro effettiva ma al ducato ideale di 124 soldi."

[73]Nicolo Papadopoli-Aldobrandini, "Sul valore della moneta veneziana," *Atti del R. Istituto Veneto di Scienze, Lettere ed Arti*, 6th ser., 3 (1884–85):690; idem, *Le monete di Venezia*, vol. 2.

trade. Paradoxically, the lira di grossi, being based on gold, had no connection with the grossi coins that passed from hand to hand. Paradoxically also, the silver grossi coins that were minted after 1379 supplemented the soldini in determining the metallic equivalent of the lira di piccoli, which did not depend for its value on the piccolo coin.

# 17

# THE FALL OF GOLD

HE CHANGES IN MONEYS of account described in chapter 16 were adjustments to unusually rapid changes in the relative value of gold and silver. Not even the large influx of gold and silver following the oceanic discoveries of the fifteenth and sixteenth centuries produced changes in the bimetallic ratio in western Europe as drastic as those that occurred during the hundred years between 1250 and 1350. Within that earlier century the ratio rose (as described above, in chapter 14) from a low of about 8.5 to 1 to a high of 14.2 to 1. It then fell back to below 10 to 1.[1] The extremes were not reached everywhere, to be sure; more typical of Italy as a whole was a rise from about 10 to 1 to 13 to 1, followed

---

[1]On Europe generally see Robert-Henri Bautier, "Les rélations économiques des pays occidentaux avec les pays d'Orient au Moyen Age: Points de vue et documents," in *Sociétés et compagnies du commerce en Orient et dans l'Ocean Indien, Actes du 8e Colloque Internationale d'Histoire Maritime,* ed. Michel Mollat (Beirut, 1966; Paris, 1970), 307–8; Watson, "Back to Gold," 24–26; and most recently, with copious bibliography, Hermann Kellenbenz, "Final Remarks: Production and Trade of Gold, Silver, and Lead from 1450 to 1750," in Hermann Kellenbenz, ed., *Precious Metals in the Age of Expansion: Papers of the XIVth International Congress of the Historical Sciences. Introduced and Edited on behalf of the International Economic History Association,* Beiträge zur Wirtschaftsgeschichte, ed. Hermann Kellenbenz and Jürgen Schneider, 2 (Stuttgart, 1981), which includes much on production before 1450. On changing supplies and ratios in Venice see above, chaps. 13 and 14, and below, chap. 19, where we date the general fall in bimetallic ratios a decade or two earlier than does Kellenbenz in "Final Remarks," 334–35.

364

by a fall to 10.5 to 1.[2] But even that degree of change—first a rise and then a fall of about 30 percent, both within the first half of the fourteenth century—was more rapid than the rate of change in the bimetallic ratio in the sixteenth and seventeenth centuries.[3] Venice in particular experienced extremes between 1250 and 1360—up from 8.5 to 1 to above 14.2 to 1 and then down by the latter date to 9.9 to 1 or 9.6 to 1 (see table 12).

Such changes obviously created opportunities for brilliant gains and crushing losses for merchants who dealt in either bullion or coin. The opportunities and dangers were especially large for the Venetians because of their central position as a bullion market. Although the violent fluctuations in the relative values of gold and silver caused headaches for accountants and for policymakers desiring monetary stability, they were a potential source of prosperity for the city, provided it kept its position as a bullion market by adjusting its commercial and monetary policies so as to attract to the Rialto the acceleration of buying and selling stimulated by the changing prices of the two precious metals.

The nature of the opportunities and dangers is clearer when we examine the reasons for the fall in the value of gold. Its causes cannot be explored by comparative analysis of statistical series on bullion shipments and price movements, as is done for the nineteenth century and, albeit less successfully, for the sixteenth century; medieval records of bullion flows are too scattered and unreliable. But Venetian sources indicate in general terms that supplies of both silver and gold were increasing. Even during the sharp rise in the relative value of silver, there is no indication of a decline in the amount of silver coming to the Rialto. But the demand for silver rose more rapidly than the supply, and while the demand for gold was also increasing, the supply of gold seems to have risen much more rapidly than did the supply of silver.

## i. SILVER SUPPLY AND DEMAND

The existence of an unusually large supply of silver in Venice at the very time that silver was rising in value is indicated by several bits of

---

[2]Cipolla, *Le avventure della lira*, 134, contrasts average bimetallic ratios in Italy in significant decades. The rise from 11 to 1 to 15 to 1 occurred over about 150 years, the ratio in the decade of 1690–1700 being about 1/3 higher than the ratio in 1545–55.

[3]In western Europe generally the rise during the century from 1550 to 1650 was from about 11 to 1 to 14.3 to 1, with the most rapid change in the years between 1600 and 1650 (see Braudel and Spooner, "Prices in Europe from 1450 to 1750," 459, fig. 5). At Venice the amounts of silver and gold of equal legal value in the gold zecchino and the silver scudo were in the proportion of 1 to 10.8 in 1525; 1 to 12.3 in 1593; 1 to 10.3 in 1608 (by decree of that year); 1 to 13.9 in 1635; 1 to 13.3 in 1704 (Papadopoli, 2:752, 3:1005). Illegal prices of zecchini recorded privately in lire indicate somewhat higher ratios. The zecchino was privately priced at 16 lire in 1635,

TABLE 12.

Bimetallic Ratios at Venice, 1285–1398

| Date | Silver Value of the Gold Ducat[a] | | | Ratio (Grams of Silver/ 3.55 Grams of Gold) |
| | In Money of Account | In Coin | In Grams of Silver | |
| --- | --- | --- | --- | --- |
| 1285 | 40 soldi a grossi | 18.38 grossi, type 1 (40 × [12/26.111]) | 38.598 (18.38 × 2.1) | 10.9 |
| 1295 | 1.667 soldi di grossi | 20 grossi, type 1 (1.667 × 12) | 42.000 (20 × 2.1) | 11.8 |
| 1305–28 | 52 soldi a grossi | 24 grossi, type 1 | 50.400 (24 × 2.1) | 14.2 |
| 1331 | 70 soldi di piccoli | 840 piccoli | 48.720 (840 × 0.058) | 13.7 |
| 1333 | 64 soldi di piccoli | 64 soldini, type 1 | 41.024 (64 × 0.641) | 11.5 |
| 1349 | 64 soldi di piccoli | 48 mezzanini, type 2 (64 × [12/16]) | 37.152 (48 × 0.774) | 10.5 |
| 1353 | 64.5 soldi di piccoli | 48.4 mezzanini, type 2 (64.5 × [12/16]) | 37.46 (48.4 × 0.774) | 10.5 |
| 1354–69* | 64 soldi di piccoli* | 64 soldini, type 2* | 34.112* (64 × 0.533) | 9.6* |
| 1358 | 70 soldi di piccoli | 70 soldini, type 2 | 37.31 (70 × 0.533) | 10.5 |
| 1374 | 72 soldi di piccoli | 72 soldini, type 3 | 35.136 (72 × 0.488) | 9.9 |
| 1382 | 80 soldi di piccoli | 20 grossi, type 2 (80 × [12/48]) | 37.84 (20 × 1.892) | 10.7 |
| 1398 | 90 soldi di piccoli | 22.5 grossi, type 3 (90 × [12/48]) | 38.993 (22.5 × 1.733) | 11.0 |

NOTE: Comparing bimetallic ratios derived from mint prices for gold and silver bullion is impractical for Venice because so much of the silver minted in 1331–1417 was requisitioned at an artificial price through the quinto; but a comparison of the silver and gold content of coins, combined with a comparison of their values in money of account, reveals the extent and timing of the changes at Venice in the relative value of the two metals (see below, app. C). Ratios calculated from prices of bullion would have been higher, because the cost of minting, as a percentage of the value of the product, was higher for silver than for gold, and the seigniorage was also generally higher.

[a]Market value unless followed by an asterisk, in which case the legal value.

evidence. Most definite is the assertion in a decree of 1338 that the supply of small silver coin was then adequate. The assertion was contained in a decree that reimposed on German merchants a tax on Tyrolese pieces of xx

---

when the official price did not exceed 15 lire (Giulio Mandich, "Formule monetarie veneziane del periodo 1619–1650," *Il risparmio* 5 [1957]:681–82).

and xxii or Veronese groats which had been repealed when the supply of Venetian silver coins was judged inadequate.[4] The newly introduced soldini were so plentiful by 1338 that they were driving the grossi out of circulation within Venice. The disappearance of full-weight grossi had begun before 1330, however, and had been quickened by arrivals of gold which caused the bimetallic ratio on the market place to fall from the ratio of 14.2 to 1 expressed by pricing the ducat at 24 grossi. For a few years about 1330 the bimetallic ratio provided incentive to export silver coin in settling trade deficits, but the new silver currency of 1331–32 lowered the official ratio from 14.2 to 1 to 11.5 to 1 in such a way that the new silver coins became plentiful at the same time that silver continued to be sent east in large quantities in the form of ingots or grossi. Importation of silver was further encouraged in 1342 by the reduction from a "quinto" to a "decimo" of the amount of silver that importers were required to sell to the mint at its traditional, relatively low price.[5] What was for all practical purposes a tax was not restored to 1/5 until 1350, when more revenue and more coins were wanted for the war with Genoa then beginning.[6] At the same time, administrative records refer to coinage of silver in such quantities that the work of the mintmasters had to be rearranged to provide for it.[7]

Even more impressive evidence of the large amounts of silver on the Venetian market in the 1340s are the unusual provisions made for shipping silver to the Levant. Venice's position as the most active, best supplied of bullion markets had been strengthened over the years both by the extension of its commercial connections through the mountains of central and eastern Europe and by skillful management of sea lanes in the Mediterranean and especially those leading to supplies and markets in the Levant. Quasi-military governmental control of all the Commune's shipping had been used to organize new types of ships and new methods of navigation into an integrated system of shipping lines that was especially suitable for the transport of precious metals. The security and flexibility of the resulting Senate-directed fleets of merchant galleys proved particularly useful during an intensification of the international exchange of gold and silver in the 1340s.

As a general rule, shipping gold and silver to and from the Levant in amounts beyond the traveling needs of merchants, crewmen, and ship captains was restricted by law to merchant galleys for the sake of security. During the 1320s and 1330s a pattern was established of sending two convoys of merchant galleys east each year: one to Cyprus and Ayas, the port

---

[4]*PMV,* doc. 94; the exemption, doc. 91, had been granted in November 1332. Cf. Simonsfeld, *Der Fondaco,* vol. 1, docs. 97, 798; and above, chap. 15, sec. iii.

[5]*DQ,* vol. 1, docs. 139, 274; *PMV,* doc. 98. The decree of 1343 seems to refer to the quinto as having been changed to a decimo already in May 1342.

[6]*RES,* doc. 217.

[7]Ibid., docs. 94, 111 (1350), 112; *DQ,* 2:365.

of Lesser Armenia, or simply to Cyprus; the other, called the galleys of Romania, to Constantinople and the Black Sea.[8]

In 1342, six merchant galleys were sent to the Black Sea and seven to Cyprus. Large amounts of silver were shipped to Constantinople and to the Black Sea, where it was used especially at Tana in buying slaves, salted fish, and furs.[9]

In 1343 the amounts of silver destined for that market were so great that in addition to the usual transport by merchant galleys—nine going to the Black Sea and seven to Cyprus—the export of silver on "unarmed ships" to Constantinople was also permitted. Technically the term "unarmed" was defined by the size of the crew, but practically speaking, "unarmed" vessels were round sailing ships.[10] As a general rule, only the largest round ships, those of more than 300 tons, were allowed legally to pass the Dardanelles, and round ships of that size were by no means defenseless.[11] To ensure greater security for the round ships carrying silver to Constantinople, the commander of Venice's patrolling fleet of light war galleys was ordered to accompany them and make sure that the silver was delivered to Constantinople.[12]

In that year, 1343, both round ships and galleys also took silver to Cyprus, the intermediary in trade with Syria and Egypt. The expectations of one of the exporters are illustrated by a letter that Fresco Quirini wrote in July to an agent to whom he sent 13 certified silver ingots (de bolla) weighing 231 marks (for which he had paid 3,407 lire 5 soldi a grossi) with instructions that the proceeds be invested in gold to be sent to Venice by the return voyage of that year's galleys, provided it could be done with a net profit of 8 percent or better. If he could not buy gold at that price, the agent was to invest in either cotton or spices.[13] Eight percent seems a moderate profit, but the proceeds could be expected back in Venice before Christmas, that is, within six months.

In planning ahead for 1344, special provision was made to send more silver out of Venice to eastern markets. Continuance of export on "unarmed" ships was voted down, but special departures of additional galleys were ordered. In addition to the fifteen to sixteen that would be auctioned

[8]Frederic C. Lane, "Venetian Merchant Galleys, 1300–1334: Private and Communal Operation," *Speculum* 38 (1963), and in *Venice and History,* 213–14.

[9]ASV, Senato, Misti, reg. 20, fols. 49–51; reg. 20, copia, fols. 143, 155, 158; reg. 21, copia, fols. 61–63, 96. M. Berindei and C. Veinstein, "La Tana-Azaq, de la présence italienne à l'empire ottomane," *Turcica: Revue d'études turques* 8, no. 2 (1976):134–36.

[10]ASV, Senato, Misti, reg. 21, copia, fols. 69, 92. Only galleys with as many as 60 oarsmen were considered "armed ships" (Lane, "Venetian Maritime Law and Administration," in *Venice and History,* 234–35 nn. 20–21).

[11]After 1340 only ships of 600 milliaria or more were authorized for that voyage (MC, Spiritus, copia, fol. 253; Cf. Lane, *Navires et constructeurs,* 249).

[12]ASV, Senato, Misti, reg. 21, copia, fol. 79 (15 May 1343).

[13]PSM, Misti, b. 100, commis. Fresco Quirini.

as usual for a fall voyage, two were ordered to go to Tana and two to Cyprus, leaving in March under commanders appointed by the government and with strict orders to load only merchants with their baggage and their silver.[14]

The plans for 1344 were completely upset by a fight at Tana during the stay there of the Venetian galleys in the fall of 1342. The hostility of its Tatar ruler prevented any galleys from visiting Tana in 1344 and for several years thereafter.[15] The two special communally operated galleys that had been ordered to leave in March 1344 were told to stop at Constantinople and hold a council to decide whether to go to Trebizond or to take their silver and merchants to Cyprus. No galleys were auctioned in May 1344 for the usual privately operated fall convoy to Tana: the only galleys of Romania in 1344 were two to Constantinople and two to Trebizond. On the other hand, more merchant galleys than usual were sent to Cyprus: not only the two operated communally especially to carry out silver but also eleven for the usual privately operated voyages in the fall.[16] By those galleys Fresco Quirini's agent in Famagosta received two bags of grossi "de zecha," 130 of the small silver ingots called sommi, and ten of the large ingots "de bolla," with the considerable value altogether of just about 3,260 ducats.[17]

Cyprus was an intermediary in trade with Egypt. Looking ahead to the voyages that could be made in 1345 and later, the Senate tried to repair relations with the Tatars of Tana and at the same time to compensate for the blocking of that market for silver by enlarging the Mamluk market through direct trade with Egypt. Licenses from the pope were sought successfully, new and larger galleys were especially built for the voyage, and a special envoy was sent to Egypt to obtain commercial privileges.[18] The envoy was instructed to ask for specified low tariffs on both gold and silver, but especially on silver, "because that is most important for our situation and we are more interested in a reduction of the tariff on silver

[14]ASV, Senato, Misti, reg. 21, copia, fols. 92–95, 168v–69.

[15]Ibid., reg. 21, copia, fols. 143–46; reg. 22, copia, fols. 20, 37. Cf. Heyd, *Storia del commercio,* 756–57.

[16]ASV, Senato, Misti, reg. 21, copia, fols. 157, 169; reg. 22, copia, fols. 24–25, 42–44; or reg. 22, originale, fols. 23v–24v, 85 (12 January 1343/44). The two special silver-carrying galleys to Cyprus are also mentioned, along with the two going to Constantinople, in April and June 1344 in ibid., reg. 22, copia, fols. 25, 26, 49v, 59v; see also Frederic C. Lane, "The Venetian Galleys to Alexandria, 1344," in *Wirtschaftskräfte und Wirtschaftswege: Festschrift für Hermann Kellenbenz,* ed. Jürgen Schneider, Beiträge zur Wirtschaftsgeschichte, 4–8 (Stuttgart, 1978), vol. 1, *Mittelmeer und Kontinent,* 431–40.

[17]PSM, Misti, b. 100, commis. Fresco Quirini, receipt from Mandallin Contarini.

[18]Ibid. Kenneth M. Setton, *The Papacy and the Levant (1204–1571),* vol. 1, *The Thirteenth and Fourteenth Centuries* (Philadelphia, 1976), 182–90. Heyd, *Storia del commercio,* 508–9, 555-57. ASV, Senato, Misti, reg. 21, originale, fol. 83v; reg. 22, copia, fols. 63, 94, 97; reg. 23, copia, fol. 90. The papal license was dated 27 April 1344 (see Setton, *The Papacy,* 1:197 n. 24).

than on any other merchandise." The ambassador was instructed specifically to ask that the mint in Alexandria be reestablished and that Moslem silver coins (deremi) be made legal tender as payment for merchandise.[19] In the charter of privileges that he brought back, the very first clause provided that silver or gold imported or exported should pay a duty of only two percent, while merchandise paid ten percent; and the fourth and fifth of its thirty-six clauses provided that purchasers of bullion must pay for it immediately and that the Soldan's mint would pay the customary prices with only customary charges.[20]

Legitimized by the papal permission and the commercial treaty with Egypt, the two newly built extra-large galleys made the voyage in the fall of 1345.[21] They were so successful that the government had no difficulty in auctioning three galleys for private operation in 1346[22] and similar fleets thereafter.

At the same time, a galley fleet of the usual size sailed annually to Cyprus and Lajazzo, and another sailed to Constantinople.[23] Although direct commercial relations with Tana were not resumed for some years,[24] the other usual Levantine markets for Venetian silver continued to be important, probably more important than the newly opened market in Egypt. Silver coins did not gain wide circulation in Egypt; most of the silver sent there either was used for conspicuous ornamentation, as on the saddles of the Mamluk soldiery, or was sent on eastward to India to pay for spices. The demand for silver coinage was much larger in Syria.[25]

Venice's large shipments of silver eastward were in response to a demand for the metal originating partly in the Middle East, partly in the Far East. For a century at least, the minting and use of silver had been increasing around the eastern end of the Mediterranean, both within the Byzantine Empire and in the surviving Christian states. A notable example is the mint operated at Sissa by the king of Lesser Armenia until his kingdom was destroyed by the Mamluks in 1349.[26] Silver that Venetian galleys unloaded at Trebizond could be shipped inland either to Lesser Armenia or to Tabriz, the capital of the Mongol khan ruling in Iran. Fresco Quirini's son left some silver ingots with an agent in Trebizond in

[19]ASV, Senato, Misti, reg. 22, copia, fols. 83v–85; originale, fol. 45v.

[20]Thomas, ed., *Diplomatarium Veneto-Levantinum*, 292–93.

[21]ASV, Senato, Misti, reg. 22, copia, fols. 140–55; reg. 23, copia, fols. 19, 43v–44, 58; reg. 24, copia, fol. 31. The call of the galleys at Crete in November 1345 on their return from Alexandria is mentioned in Raimondo Morozzo della Rocca, ed., *Lettere di Mercanti a Pignol Zucchello (1336–1350)*, FSV (Venice, 1957), 46–47.

[22]ASV, Senato, Misti, reg. 23, copia, fols. 107, 110v–11, 117.

[23]Ibid., reg. 23, copia, fols. 21–22, 49, 107–17; reg. 24, copia, fols. 41 ff.

[24]Berindei and Veinstein, "La Tana-Azaq," 122–23.

[25]Ashtor, *Les métaux précieux*, 21–22, 25–28, 42–43.

[26]Stussi, ed., *Zibaldone da Canal*, 108–9; Lane, "Le vecchie monete di conto," 51–52.

1345.[27] On the northern shores of the Black Sea, where the demand for
silver had grown particularly strong in the 1330s,[28] so as to make the
interruption in 1343 particularly serious, Venetian silver was not destined
for sale to mints. Small ingots (sommi) "about the size of a woman's
finger" and of varying weights were used as the common medium of
exchange among the Mongol and Tatar khanates along the routes through
inner Asia.[29] The demand for silver in the Far East was increasing, particularly in the opening decades of the fourteenth century. The demand in
China seems to have been connected with the discontinuance of the use of
paper money after 1311.[30] In India, Hindu principalities that had coined
gold were losing ground to Moslem rulers who preferred to coin silver and
exported gold to the northwest in order to buy horses and slaves.[31]
Whether it originated much further east or nearer the Mediterranean, the
increased demand for silver was evident in the Levantine ports and enabled the Venetians to raise its price in Venice in spite of the existence of
record quantities.[32]

In the west also—in Venice itself and in Italy generally—the demand for silver increased during the first half of the fourteenth century.
The employment of professional mercenary soldiers instead of citizen mili-
tia required putting more silver coin into circulation.[33] Venice's first extensive employment of the mercenary soldiers was in its war with the
Scaliger lord of Verona in 1336–39. When governments paid out more
coin, there was a corresponding growth in their demand for cash payments as taxes. At the same time, churchmen, especially at the papal court,
were increasing their cash revenue. While the demand for silver as a circulating medium burgeoned, so did the use of more and more silver in
various forms of conspicuous consumption—large silver belts, for example.[34] Among the upper feudal and commercial classes, silver tableware,

[27]PSM, Misti, b. 100, commis. Fresco Quirini, receipt given on 28 September 1345 in
Trebizond by Nicholetto Quirin Boccio.

[28]ASV, Senato, Misti, reg. 17, fol. 48.

[29]See above, chap. 10, sec. ii. Sale of silver by weight also in Damascus and Alexandria is
mentioned in the Tarifa zoè noticia, 26, 30.

[30]Cipolla, Il fiorino, 27–28. Yang Lien-shing, Money and Credit in China (Cambridge,
Mass., 1961), indicates the rise in the demand for silver in a list of bimetallic ratios with a drop
from 10 to 1 in 1309 to 4 to 1 in 1375.

[31]John F. Richards, "Introduction," in Richards, ed., Precious Metals, 14; and John Deyell,
"The China Connection: Problems of Silver Supply in Medieval Bengal," in ibid., 207–13.
See also Richards's as yet unpublished article "Precious Metals and the Pattern of Commerce
in the Late Medieval World Economy, 1200–1500 A.D." We are much indebted to Professor
Richards for placing proofs and typescripts at our disposal.

[32]On silver bullion prices in Venice see below, app. C.

[33]Luzzatto, Studi, 268.

[34]See the summary of Susan Mosher Stuard's paper "The Consumption of Silver after
the 'Defense of the Grosso' in the Fourteenth Century" (Delivered at the Economic History

candlesticks, jewelry, and reliquaries were not only status symbols but a prudent form of hoarding, since they could be melted down for coining if the need arose.

Hoarding silver in tableware, jewelry, and sacred vessels instead of in money chests may have become more attractive also because of the extent to which governments generally were debasing their silver coinage. Many governments demonetized old issues or "cried down" their value in the money of account in which the government reckoned its debts. Once silver began to rise, its rising value became one reason for devaluations, which made hoarding bullion more attractive than hoarding coin. Hoarding drove the price of silver yet higher.[35]

Milan was Venice's nearby competitor as a market place for silver from central Europe, for it was in Milan that the Genoese bought silver for their mint.[36] But in the 1340s the demand at Venice for silver was so strong that it drew silver bullion from Milan. In 1343 Luchino Visconti, lord of Milan, had shipped silver bullion to Venice to make a deposit with the Grain Office. When Venice demanded 1/5 of that bullion for its mint at the mint price of the qunito, his agents objected that that was contrary to the treaty rights of Milanese merchants who could import and export gold and silver money. His claim was rejected on the ground that the treaty gave Milanese only the same rights as Venetians, and Venetians were obliged to consign 1/5 to the mint.[37]

The general movement of prices is consistent with silver's being plentiful. According to the quantity theory of money, prices would have been falling, *ceteris paribus*, if the supply of silver was decreasing to such an extent that the combined total of silver and gold coins in circulation was less than before. In fact, the later 1340s were years of high prices in Italy, high prices caused by events exogenous to the monetary system. Crop failures made 1346–47 years of famine. In 1348–49 the Black Death reduced the population in Venice, Florence, and many other cities by a third or a half. It diminished the amount of trade and the production of goods and services but not the volume of coins and bullion on hand. Rising prices followed, especially during the years following the first attack of the plague, when production was most disrupted. Contemporary descriptions of reckless expenditure suggest accelerated velocity of circulation.[38] These

---

Association Annual Meeting, Baltimore, September 1982), in John H. Munro, "Medieval Monetary Problems: Bimetallism and Bullionism," *JEcH* 43 (1983):294–95.

[35]Munro, "Monetary Contraction," 100–103.

[36]Carlo M. Cipolla, "Argento tedesco e monete genovesi alla fine del Quattrocento," *RIN*, 5th ser., 4, no. 58 (1956):2.

[37]ASV, Senato, Misti, reg. 21, fol. 13 (spring 1343).

[38]On high prices in Venice see *PMV*, lxxvi and doc. 109; Mario Brunetti, "Venezia durante la peste del 1348," *Ateneo veneto* 32, no. 1, fasc. 3, and no. 2, fasc. 1 (1909), p. 20n (citing MC, Spiritus, fol. 165v); and Mueller, "Aspetti sociali ed economici della peste," 74.

factors, not changes in the supply of precious metals, were probably the main determinants of price movements in the 1340s, but at least the behavior of prices gives no reason to believe that there was a shortage of silver.

The contrast between England and Venice regarding silver supplies is striking. Receipts of silver for coinage in England fell from about £90,000 in 1300–1309 to little more than £1,000 in the 1330s, and there were loud complaints about the lack of silver.[39] But from the point of view of the Venetian bullion market, there was no lack of silver at all in the 1330s. The contrast between the positions of England and Venice suggests that there had been a change in the direction in which newly mined silver flowed to market. Solid evidence for a decline in the production of European silver mines comes only later. Diversion from the northwest is explicable by the situation at the outset of the Hundred Years' War, and Venice's attractiveness is explicable by its access to eastern markets. The Levantine demand was sufficiently strong to keep the price of silver rising sharply during the 1340s, even though Bohemian production did not seriously lessen until after 1350.[40] By that time several new mines had been opened in Serbia and Bosnia.[41]

Since there was no scarcity of silver to explain its rise in value in Venice, its rise compared with gold must be attributed either to an increased demand for silver or to an increased supply of gold, or both. A flood of gold was particularly evident in Venice.

## ii. THE GOLD GLUT

Certainly gold was reaching Italy in sharply increased quantity. As during the first dip in the price of gold, about 1327, imports or rumors of large supplies came from two sides, namely, from Hungary and from Egypt.[42] But neither in 1327 nor during the second dip in price, in the 1330s, was the increase in the coinage of gold in Italian mints comparable to what occurred in the 1340s. Not only at Venice but also at Florence the output of gold coin expanded. Nearly every year during the period 1344–51 the number of florins minted exceeded 200,000.[43] There is no comparable series for the contemporary output of ducats in Venice, but scattered references and administrative measures indicate that the Venetian gold mint was also at peak production in those years and very likely outproduced the Florentine mint.

---

[39]Munro, "Bullionism," 180; Michael Prestwich, "Currency and the Economy of Early Fourteenth Century England," in Mayhew, ed., *Edwardian Monetary Affairs,* 45–58; idem, *The Three Edwards,* 234–38, 248–50; Mayhew, "Numismatic Evidence."

[40]Jaňáček, "L'argent tchèque," 255.

[41]Kovačević, "Dans la Serbie et la Bosnie médiévales," 250, 253.

[42]See above, chap. 15, sec. ii.

[43]Bernocchi, 3:66–71; and below, chap. 19, sec. iv, and app. B, sec. iii.

Four sources of gold must be considered in analyzing Venice's increased supplies: (1) African gold; (2) gold brought by Germans to the Fondaco dei Tedeschi, (3) gold obtained from silver ores, only some of which came from the Germans; and (4) gold from the northeastern Mediterranean and the Black Sea.

African supplies have generally been considered the most important. Their source was near the headwaters of the Niger and Senegal rivers, and most of this gold normally crossed the western Sahara to Tripoli, Tunis, or ports further west and thence to Spain, Sicily, Genoa, and Florence. Venetians also were very active in Tunis in the first decades of the fourteenth century, but there is no evidence that the export of gold from Barbary increased in the 1340s or that facilities were improved in a way likely to lead to such an increase.[44]

During part of the fourteenth century, much of the African gold found its way to Egypt, however, in exchange for textiles. While direct trade between Venice and Egypt was interrupted in 1323–44 by the pope's ban on all trade with lands ruled by the Mamluks, Armenia, Cyprus, and Crete served as intermediaries.[45] Some African gold found its way to Venice through Cyprus. Before his death in 1344, Leone Morosini, a Venetian nobleman, had accumulated in Cyprus 7,000 ducats worth of gold, some of it Alexandrian bezants, which his executors sent to Venice for sale.[46] The reopening of direct galley voyages to Egypt in 1345 replaced illicit trade through such way stations as Cyprus. It provided safer, faster transportation and must have reduced considerably the transaction costs in the exchange of European silver for African gold. For a century and a half thereafter, galleys leaving in the late summer or fall for Alexandria were the most stable element in the pattern of Venetian shipping lines, although even these voyages were occasionally thrown off schedule or interrupted, as by the Third Genoese War, which began in 1350.[47] The galley voyage to

[44]Stussi, ed., *Zibaldone da Canal,* gives particularly full information on trade with North Africa, on weighing of gold and silver, and on mint practices, particularly in Venice and Tunis (see pp. 5–7, 17–24, 42–44). A reference to Nicoletus de Canali, son of Andrea (perhaps of the same family as the owner of the *Zibaldone*) is in ASV, Grazie, reg. 3, fol. 92. He was being held prisoner in Tunis by the "saraceni" because he had pledged himself for another Venetian's debt of 8,000 bezants. Le conte de Mas Latrie, in his *Rélations et commerce de l'Afrique Septentrionale ou Magreb avec les nations chrétiennes au Moyen Age* (Paris, 1886), says that much Sudanese gold was exported in the tenth, eleventh, and twelfth centuries and mentions such exports from Magrib in 1461 (pp. 380–81), but he gives more emphasis to the constant importation of gold and silver from Europe (pp. 365–66), because treaties make more mention of the latter.

[45]Ashtor, *Les métaux précieux,* 18–27; Bovill, *The Golden Trade of the Moors,* 87, 89, 241; Heyd, *Storia del commercio,* 613–15, 661.

[46]PSM, Misti, b. 127; and see below, n. 65.

[47]Ashtor, "Observations on Venetian Trade in the Levant," 541–43; Alberto Tenenti and Corrado Vivanti, "Le film d'un grand système de navigation: Les galères vénitiennes, XIVe–XVIe siècles," *Annales, ESC,* 16 (1961):83–86; Ashtor, *Les métaux précieux,* 21–22, 25–28.

Alexandria of 1345 has therefore been hailed as a turning point in Europe's monetary history.[48]

Even so, chronology suggests that Africa was not the main source of the flood of gold into Italy in the 1340s. Supplies from mines in Hungary and Transylvania may well have been of more immediate importance. Their output, which probably had supplied much of the gold that had enabled the Venetians to coin their first ducats, had declined at the beginning of the fourteenth century as a result of the political disorders following the termination of the Arpad dynasty in 1301 and the lack of protection for miners' rights. Then it was kept low for a couple of decades by efforts to operate a "royal monopoly." Under the Anjou dynasty, production expanded after 1327, and much gold that had been accumulated in royal hoards was dissipated in the 1340s in connection with that dynasty's claims to the Kingdom of Naples.[49]

Gold from this source came to market as early as 1342 or 1343. Some of the treasure collected by Charles I of Hungary, who died in August 1342, was carried to Italy by his widow when she learned of the death of King Robert of Naples. His death, which occurred in January 1343, gave her children claim to that throne. Taking much gold with her, she promptly set out for Naples to establish a younger son as king of Naples. He and his Neapolitan queen, both teenagers, rapidly dissipated what she brought, as well as the wealth that King Robert of Naples had accumulated, especially after the Hungarian queen mother was duped into entrusting her son to the Neapolitan nobles, by whom he was murdered in September 1345.[50] Her oldest son, Louis, the new king of Hungary, at once vowed vengeance but did not reach Naples to inflict it until late in 1347, after traversing the length of the Italian peninsula with a large army. To pay its expenses he minted—especially for that journey—gold coins that were so similar to Florence's own florins that Giovanni Villani called them counterfeits, although they were inscribed with Louis's name and

[48]Referring to the fall in the bimetallic ratio from 15 to 1 or even 20 to 1 which had existed in France under Philip the Fair, Fernand Braudel wrote, "Le retour des galères vénitiennes à Alexandrie en 1344 . . . est le signal de ce renversement dramatique, catastrophique" (Fernand Braudel and Frank C. Spooner, "Les métaux monétaires et l'économie du XVIe siècle," in Relazioni del X° Congresso Internazionale di Scienze Storiche, vol. 4, Storia moderna [Rome, 1960], 261). Actually the decision was made in 1344, while the galleys sailed in 1345.

[49]Hóman, Geschichte, 2:335–59; idem, "La circolazione delle monete d'oro in Ungheria dal X al XIV secolo e la crisi europea dell'oro nel secolo XIV," RIN, 2d ser., 5, no. 1 (1922):149–52. See also above, chap. 10, sec. iii.

[50]Villani, Cronica, 4:14, bk. 102, cap. 10; Dominicus de Gravina, Chronica de rebus in Apulia gestis, ed. Albano Sorbelli, Rerum Italicarum Scriptores, 2d ed., 12 (Città di Castello, 1903), pt. 3, pp. vii, 8–9. The Hungarian queen's arrival in Naples is dated June–July 1343 by Émile G. Léonard, Histoire de Jeanne I, reine de Naples, comtesse de Provence (1343–1382): La jeunesse de Jeanne I, 2 vols. (Monaco and Paris, 1932–37), 1:262. The murder was in September (see Setton, The Papacy, 1:199 n. 33). Carlo Cipolla (Il fiorino, 27 n. 49) minimizes the importance of these events and of Hungarian gold.

title.[51] Thus the five years 1343–47 saw extensive disbursement in Italy of royal hoards containing Hungarian gold, as well as newly mined gold from Hungary.

Signs of increasing arrivals of gold at Venice had appeared even earlier, and much of the gold may have originated in other parts of central Europe. Gold was being found in innumerable streams in Bohemia, Silesia, and Franconia.[52]

Gold contained in silver ores had become important in Venice as early as 1336, when provisions were made to ensure full registration of both the gold and the silver obtained from partially refined bullion. These arrivals continued, so that the provisions were reaffirmed in 1344 and 1356.[53] In 1338 gold imports by German merchants were encouraged by special provisions to ensure that when they presented their metal to the mint, they would receive ducats within three days (Venetians had to wait longer for payment).[54] It was at just about this time that the reduction of the minting charge on ducats to 0.8 percent was well established for all kinds of gold, for that imported from "within the Gulf" (which meant mainly eastern central Europe) as well as that from "beyond the Gulf."[55] Late in 1341 the mintmasters of the gold mint reported that the mint was extremely busy and that weighing, recording, and refining all the gold

[51]Villani, *Cronica*, 4:83–84, 107–11, 129, 159–60, and bk. 12, cap. 107; de Gravina, *Chronica*, 33 and n. King Louis also paid partly with silver, however, for in May 1347 Hungarian ambassadors at Venice obtained exemption from the decimo for 230 marks of silver (Sanuto's notes on the lost records, in ASV, Quarantia Criminal, reg. 14bis, fol. 14v). Probably Doge Andrea Dandolo was interested in having good relations with Hungary and willing to pay the market price for silver with which to coin his new, handsome issue of mezzanini (see above, chap. 16, sec. iii. On profits from mezzanini made from the quinto see below, app. A).

[52]Kellenbenz, *Deutsche Wirtschaftsgeschichte*, 1:108–9, 164.

[53]ASV, Senato, Misti, reg. 17, fol. 58v (1336); and ASV, Zecca, b. 6bis, fols. 25, 26, 27–29. Silver ore from Novo Brdo containing gold is mentioned in Ragusan documents of the 1330s (in Mosher Stuard, "Adriatic Trade in Silver," 126, 130, 140).

[54]Decrees of the Quarantia, 9 March 1338, recorded in the capitolare in ASV, Zecca, b. 6 bis, fol. 26.

[55]On the amounts of seigniorage see below, app. A. The *Zibaldone da Canal* (Stussi, ed.), like nearly all the other merchant manuals, which are of later date, says simply (p. 71) that the mint paid out at 39 soldi. But the *Zibaldone* refers mostly to overseas trade, as do most of the others. They indicate the early general use of that rate, but the provisions made in 1336 to encourage import of gold by the Germans and the explicit statement in the old capitolare of the massari al oro in ASV, Zecca, b. 6tris, indicate that the Germans were paid at 39 1/2 soldi until the 1330s. In that decade the Quarantia, which was then in charge of the mint and only a part of whose minutes survive, gave temporary permission to use the rate of 39 soldi in paying the Germans (ASV, Zecca, b. 6bis, fol. 26). The permission was extended again and again and without specification that it was limited to the Germans (*DQ*, vol. 1, docs. 17 [October 1342] and 275 [October 1343]; in some copies made after 1340, the provision dated 1336 or 1338 is given with the 1/2 omitted, probably by a clerical error, ignored because no longer relevant, as in the copy of the capitolare of the mintmasters for silver made in the eighteenth century by copying an earlier one [in ASV, Zecca, b. 6bis, fol. 27]).

brought to the mint both from the galleys and by German merchants required overtime work and night duty. Checking for accuracy the weight of the ducats struck, "que est magna quantitas," also involved extra effort. On the basis of the report, it was decided that the officials, the weighers, and the scribes merited a raise in pay.[56] In the years following, there was no letup in the amount of gold brought from various sources. So much was waiting to be coined that in December 1342 the number of craftsmen working on ducats had to be increased, and in June 1343 the number of supervisory personnel was likewise increased.[57]

The most concrete evidence of the burgeoning production of ducats dates from June 1343. The expectation then of large imports of gold was given as the reason for ordering an enlargement of both the staff and the equipment of the mint. The number of mintmasters for gold was increased from three to four, and the number of supervisory weighers from two to four. They were instructed to work in two teams whenever there were more than 600 marks of gold in the mint.[58]

The bulk of the arrivals of gold were expected by sea and indeed were already coming by sea in May 1343. "By sea" did not necessarily mean from the Levant, because gold from Hungary may have come via Trieste or Segna (Senj),[59] but in this case it probably did mean from the Levant. The gold that was coming "by sea" was said to be arriving all at once, so that the mint had difficulty applying its rule of first come, first served. Some Venetian importers went to Istria to get their gold to Venice ahead of others, a forestalling tactic involving risks that the Senate specifically condemned. The concern expressed by the Senate suggests that gold was arriving on the merchant galleys that normally stopped in Istria for pilots and waited there until wind and tide were right for crossing and entering the lagoons. To meet the difficulty, the mint was ordered to register all arrivals by sea within three days and then to draw lots to determine the order of payment.[60]

The references to a large importation of gold by sea in the spring of 1343—before the galley voyages to Egypt, even before the interruption of trade at Tana—suggests the possibility that substantial supplies came from Constantinople, the Black Sea, and perhaps Asia. Certainly gold was sometimes exported from Trebizond to Venice.[61] Probably some of this

[56]ASV, Grazie, reg. 9, fol. 31.

[57]PMV, docs. 96, 97, 99, 100.

[58]DQ, vol. I, docs. 173–77. See also below, app. B.

[59]ASV, Senato, Misti, reg. 21, fol. 33 (10 May 1343); PMV, doc. 99. Routes later used by the Fuggers reached Venice by water either from Trieste or from Segna (Léon Schick, Un grand homme d'affaires au début du XVIe siècle, Jacob Fugger, EPHE-6, Affaires et gens d'affaires, II [Paris, 1957], 238–39, 280).

[60]ASV, Senato, Misti, reg. 21, fol. 33.

[61]Gold is mentioned as possible freight from Trebizond in ibid., reg. 22, copia, fols. 24v–25; reg. 23, fol. 12.

gold originated in the Caucasus, and some in the Armenian highlands. Gold from the latter source may have found its way through Lesser Armenia to Cyprus.[62] Most of the gold shipped out of the Black Sea probably came from its western and northern shores. References to "oro cumano" suggest the possibility that some gold from Transylvania went east to Constantinople, since the Cumans for some time ruled in much of what is now Rumania, as well as in part of the Ukraine.[63] Certainly the main flow of gold came from the north, especially from Tana. In return for the silver that their galleys took to Tana, the Venetians collected not only slaves, furs, and fish but also gold. "Oro di tanga" came down from Sarai, the capital on the Volga of the khan of the Golden Horde; its origin was probably in the Urals.[64] Venetian sources mention at least a half-dozen different kinds of gold being traded among different parts of the Levant and between the eastern Mediterranean and Venice.[65] Later, in the 1360s, gold was clearly being purchased by Venetians in Tana as well as in Romania in general for import to Venice.[66]

Although merchant manuals and other Venetian sources give no figures on the quantity of metal involved, they give the impression that the Black Sea ports were a major area of exchange of gold for silver in the

[62]On the gold mines in Armenia and the Pontic shore see Spero Vryonis, "The Question of the Byzantine Mines," *Speculum,* 37 (1962), esp. 4–5, 10. See also Bautier, "Les relations économiques," 305–6.

[63]*Tarifa zoè noticia,* 53–54, 45–46; ASV, Senato, Misti, reg. 21, fol. 85 (12 January 1343/44); and Vryonis, "The Question of the Byzantine Mines," 14, who in discussing supplies of Byzantine mints mentions gold mining at Baia-Mara in Transylvania in the eleventh century.

[64]"Oro di tanga" was identified by Allan Evans in Pegolotti, *Pratica,* 424, as gold of the fineness of the Armenian coin called in Arabic "rangah ortangah"; but the Venetian *Tarifa zoè noticia,* 18, 19, 42, 45, 49, 54 (composed apparently after the destruction of the Armenian kingdom), described its use not only in connection with Cyprus and Constantinople but more extensively in connection with Tana and especially Sarai, where, the *Tarifa* says explicitly, sales were paid for in "beli tangi" (19; cf. F. Borlandi, ed., *El libro di mercantie et usanze de' paesi,* Documenti e studi per la storia del commercio e del diritto commerciale italiano, ed. F. Patetta and M. Chiaudano, 7 [Turin, 1936; reprint 1970], 62). The close association of oro di tanga with Sarai is the main reason for suspecting that it came from the Urals. See also John Day, "The Great Bullion Famine in the Fifteenth Century," *Past and Present,* no. 79 (May 1978): 5n. on gold and silver ingots ("tangi") certified by the khan.

[65]Six names for gold in the eastern Mediterranean can be distinguished. Three are in records of the Morosini shipments from Cyprus (PSM, Misti, b. 127), namely: (1) "Auri mosori," "horo musari," or "mesari" in the *Tarifa zoè noticia,* which identified it with gold bezants of Alexandria; (2) "auro scarmeio" or "scarmioro," probably meaning "fragments in a sack"; and (3) "auri chasani," "oro casanin" in the *Tarifa zoè noticia* (54), which says it is gold "che no suol chazer." The other three are: (4) "oro di tanga"; (5) "oro cumano," mentioned above; and (6) "oro nasari," identified in the *Tarifa zoè noticia* (54) "che è bexanti d'oro se stima de fineza de carati 23 grane 2 1/2."

[66]PSM, Misti, b. 73, commis. Pietro Soranzo, reg. 2, fol. 1, and especially fasc. 2 ("note di conto"), account dated 1367 and probably written in Tana, and the last page of the fasc., which reads "oro della Tana e de Romania . . . ave' ser Piero," mentioned by Luzzatto in his *Studi,* 158.

middle decades of the fourteenth century.[67] In this respect the Black Sea seems to have been in those decades what western North Africa had been in the thirteenth century and became again during the fifteenth. The focus on the Black Sea of Venetian-Genoese rivalry in the mid-fourteenth century can be explained by the Black Sea's importance in this exchange of silver for gold. Whatever its source of supply, the Venetian gold mint was planning to increase its output of ducats by 50–100 percent even *before* the institution of the direct galley voyages to Egypt.

Perhaps prospects, not actual arrivals, determined the rates of exchange offered by moneychangers and the flows of bullion to the mint. The mere prospect that gold would be arriving soon at lower cost or in larger volume may well have induced possessors of gold bullion to have it coined and to spend the ducats on merchandise that could be sent east, especially on silver ingots. Similarly, gold coin hoarded in the treasure chests of the rich may have been spent when their owners thought gold would be falling and silver rising. Before the appeal to the pope to lift his ban on trade with Egypt was formulated in December 1343, expectations of large imports from central Europe by German merchants or arrivals from Cyprus or the Black Sea seem to have had more impact on the Venetian market than did African gold.

After 1344, however, the Alexandria voyage contributed importantly to the continued decline in the value of gold. About 1360–70 the bimetallic ratio in Venice and Florence fell below 10 to 1.

Later in the century, as gold was more in demand in both west and east, the bimetallic ratio stabilized at about 11 to 1.[68] A sort of "bullion famine" developed in the last quarter of the fourteenth century in Europe, so high then was the demand for both precious metals compared with the supplies being offered for minting.[69] But before the relative value of gold and silver had leveled off around the mid-fourteenth century, the value of gold had fallen by almost a third. That bimetallic revolution had repercussions in the devaluation of currencies in many European countries and in disturbing changes in the rates of foreign exchange.

[67]Both the first and second parts of the *Tarifa zoè noticia* give that impression strongly, as do the records of the auctioned galley voyages (Cf. Luzzatto, *Studi*, 268n).

[68]Cipolla, *Le avventure della lira*, 57–58, 132; Watson, "Back to Gold," 23; Ashtor, *Les métaux précieux*, 48. Extensive coinage of gold in 1369 is indicated in ASV, Zecca, b. 6tris, cap. 68.

[69]Day, "The Great Bullion Famine."

# 18

# DEVALUATIONS
# OF THE SILVER MONEY

### i. THE GENERAL PATTERN, 1331–1472

EBASEMENTS OCCURRED nearly everywhere in fourteenth-century Europe. It was a century full of catastrophes—famines, plagues, revolutions, and wars that tore at the intestines of states. Corruption of the coinage is usually attributed to these conspicuous calamities. The obvious cause of many debasements was certainly the fiscal desperation of shaky governments, but in Venice devaluations were relatively moderate and more closely connected with the rising price of silver than with debasements in the strict sense.

In Venice—as in England in this period but in contrast to France and the Netherlands—there was no crying down of coins in circulation. The reductions in silver content of successive issues of the silver coins reduced the silver content of the lira di piccoli and then of the lira and ducato a monete, but there was no change in the values in money of account of the old issues.

### Reasons for Devaluation

The extent of the devaluations is shown in table 13 and graph 1. The silver equivalent of the lira di piccoli, which had been stable for about fifty years, fell during the next forty-odd years—1331 to 1369 and 1374—by about 30 percent. During the same forty years, there was a decline in the value of gold compared with that of silver. The bimetallic ratio went from 14.2 to 1 down to about 10 to 1, also about 30 percent (see tables 12, 14, and

TABLE 13.

Silver Equivalents of 1 Lira di Piccoli, 1330–99

| Dates | Grams of Silver | Index (1331 = 100) |
|---|---|---|
| Before 1331 | 13.92 | 100.0 |
| 1331 −46 | 12.82 | 92.1 |
| 1346−53 | 11.61 | 83.4 |
| 1353 −69 | 10.66 | 76.6 |
| 1369−79 | 9.76 | 70.1 |
| 1379 −91 | 9.44 | 67.8 |
| 1391 −99 | 8.92 | 64.1 |

SOURCES: Equivalents calculated from the silver content of link coins at the date of changes in mint standard, as shown above, in table 10, and below, in table 22.

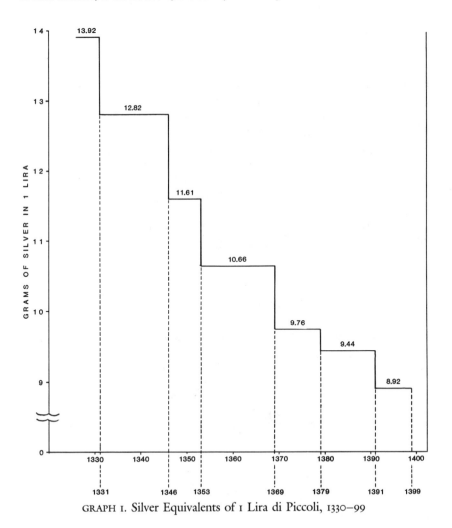

GRAPH 1. Silver Equivalents of 1 Lira di Piccoli, 1330–99

381

TABLE 14.

Market Prices of the Gold Ducat in Silver-Based Soldi di Piccoli
at Selected Dates, 1330–99

| Date | Price | Index (1331 = 100) |
|------|-------|--------------------|
| 1331 | 70    | 100.0 |
| 1349 | 64    | 91.4 |
| 1353 | 64.5  | 92.1 |
| 1372 | 72    | 102.9 |
| 1382 | 80    | 114.3 |
| 1391 | 84    | 120.0 |
| 1398 | 90    | 128.6 |

SOURCE: Below, app. D.

15). The similarity suggests that the devaluations as a whole were an adjustment of Venice's bimetallic monetary system to the rise in the value of
silver compared with that of gold. Venetian attachment to bimetallism
called for keeping both gold and silver coins in circulation. To prevent
silver coins from being exported as the market value of silver rose, less
silver was put in the coin traditionally valued as 1 soldo di piccoli.

But such a statement oversimplifies. Other factors must be considered in order to explain the changes depicted comparatively in graph 2.
Analyzing the motivation for Venice's monetary policies requires considering not only (1) the effort to maintain bimetallism but also (2) fiscal
needs, (3) the deterioration of silver coinage by culling and wear and tear,
and (4) the desire to attract bullion to the Venetian market.

TABLE 15.

Bimetallic Ratios at Selected Dates, 1330–99

| Date | Link Coin | Ratio | Index (1331 = 100) |
|------|-----------|-------|--------------------|
| 1328 | Grosso, type 1 | 14.2 | 103.6 |
| 1331 | Piccolo | 13.7 | 100.0 |
| 1335 | Soldino, type 1 | 11.5 | 83.9 |
| 1349 | Mezzanino, type 2 | 10.5 | 76.6 |
| 1353 | Soldino, type 2 | 9.6 | 70.1 |
| 1374 | Soldino, type 3 | 9.9 | 72.3 |
| 1382 | Grosso, type 2 | 10.7 | 78.1 |
| 1398 | Grosso, type 3 | 11.0 | 80.3 |

SOURCES: Ratios calculated from market values of the gold ducat and legal contents of the
link coins of the lira di piccoli, as shown above, in table 12.

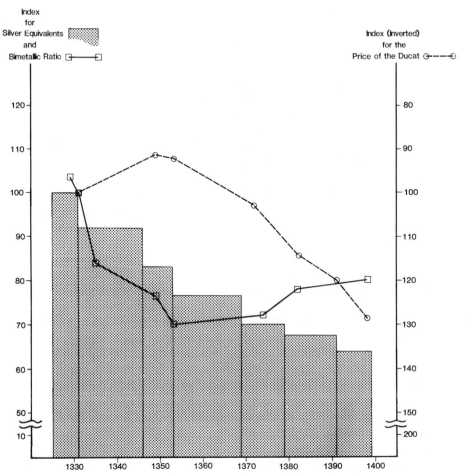

GRAPH 2. Changes in the Price of the Ducat, in the Silver Equivalent of the Lira di Piccoli, and in Bimetallic Ratios, 1330–99 (Index: 1331 = 100)

Fiscal motives explain many devaluations by feudal princes, who looked upon their mints mainly as a source of revenue. They often sought to increase their income by putting less silver into new coins than was contained in issues that they had demonetized and called in in order to obtain metal for the new coinage. Desire for revenue from the mint became a prominent consideration also in a merchants' republic such as Venice when overseas empires and local rivalries involved it in wars requiring large employment of mercenaries. At Venice, that kind of fiscal pressure on the mint became intense with the Cretan Revolt of 1363–64 and the Fourth Genoese War—the War of Chioggia—in 1378–81, as will become apparent in our discussions below of the steps taken in those years.

## Rates of Devaluation and Deterioration

Deterioration of coins from usage by clipping, sweating, and intense culling gave a reason for devaluation not confined to any particular period nor to Venice. Studies of various times and places have led to estimates that deterioration reduced the weight of the coins in circulation at a rate of somewhere between 0.1 percent and 1 percent per year.[1] New coins were likely to disappear, being culled for export or hoarding, if they were minted at a standard set 10–20 years earlier. According to Gresham's law, the new coins would be "good money" and would be driven out by the older coins that had deteriorated so as to become "bad money," unless, that is, the old issues were cried down or demonetized or the amount of silver in new coins were reduced to below the old standard.

One factor in this deterioration was immediate, intense culling of imperfectly made coins. Indeed, deterioration equivalent to 0.3 percent per year sometimes occurred within months of the minting, without either abrasion from use or reduction of weight by clipping and sweating. That conclusion may be drawn from the effort in 1391 to reduce the variation in the weight of soldini leaving the Venetian mint. The standard of weight had previously been expressed in regulations setting the number to be cut from a mark. It was enforced by counting the number placed on a scale to balance a 1-mark weight. The number required to make a mark had been 480. In 1391 it was allowed to vary between 494 and 504. But a new procedure was proposed to prevent individual coins from being too far above or below the average, as has been explained in describing the technical processes of coinage, above in chapter 12. The new procedure was declared necessary because when some coins were heavier and some lighter, culling would immediately reduce the average weight of the coins in circulation below the average weight of those leaving the mint.[2] Under the new rule, the average weight of coins leaving the mint would be 0.477 grams. The new procedure provided for checking on the weight of individual coins and penalizing workers for any coin made heavier than 1/62 of an ounce (0.481 grams). Then to prevent a craftsman, a mendador, from making too many coins too light in efforts to be on the safe side, he was also penalized if more than 504 were required to balance 1 mark. The standard and penalties thus set were rejected by the craftsmen, who refused to work on soldini. The rules were modified on 11 July, but the workers continued to balk until rules were modified so as to permit individual coins to vary between 0.452 and 0.489 gram (1/61–1/66 of an ounce).

[1] See above, chap. 3, n. 1.
[2] *Cap. Broche*, fol. 7v: "coruptio maxima sit in civitate nostra in trabucando monetas novas, in consumando graves et permitendo leves, quod est in grave dannum et infamiam Dominii nostri."

Under that rule, the average weight of the coins minted according to specification was to be 0.469 grams (the weight used by Papadopoli).[3] But if the mint paid the coins to moneychangers, and the moneychangers carefully culled out all but the lightest coins, the new coins in circulation would weigh only 0.452 grams. That would constitute an almost instantaneous deterioration of 0.017 grams (0.469 − 0.452), 3.6 percent. Coins did in fact mainly go first from the mint to moneychangers, who had extended credit in bank money to purveyors and were repaid directly from the mint with fresh coin.[4]

The deterioration of the currency as a result of the combination of deficient minting techniques, clipping, ordinary abrasion, and careful culling by moneychangers was probably most important between 1353 and 1444, a period in which the changes in the bimetallic ratio were less abrupt than in the previous century. During that period a reduction in the legally specified silver equivalent of the soldo di piccoli was made about every eight to ten years. In most cases, the amount of those reductions equaled the weight that would have been lost by cumulative deterioration at a rate of 0.3–0.5 percent per year (see table 16). Devaluation by that amount could perhaps be explained as a sensible reaction by Venice's governing councils to the effects of deterioration and their clear recognition of the effects of Gresham's law.

In contrast to an annual rate of reduction of 0.3–0.5 percent, which in this particular context may be considered normal, were the rates calculated from the reductions in the silver content of the lira di piccoli stipulated by the coinage regulations of 1331, 1353, 1417, 1444, 1472. (Those occurring after 1400 will be discussed in more detail in volume 2, in connection with the developments there described, namely, the trade war with Emperor Sigismund in 1409–24 and the Milanese wars before and after 1444.)

Here our immediate concern is the complications of the two earliest devaluations, in 1331–1353. In spite of the difficulties in making any estimates, we will find reasons to believe that 5 percent out of the total reduction of 7.9 percent in 1331 shown in table 16 can be considered in excess of the reduction needed to allow for deterioration. The devaluation effected by the coinage of the second type of soldino, in 1353, was also more than was needed to allow for deterioration. Out of the total reduction of 24.7 percent from before 1331 to just after 1353, close to 13.6 percent—over half—can be considered adjustment to the rise in the value of silver compared with that of gold.

---

[3]Ibid., fols. 6–7; *PMV*, docs. 180, 185, 186; Papadopoli, 1:243, 354, 356, and esp. 360.
[4]See Mueller, "The Role of Bank Money"; and below, vol. 2.

TABLE 16.

## Devaluations of the Soldo di Piccoli, with Annual Rates, 1331–1472: Reductions in the Legal Standard of Silver Content

| Dates | Number of Years Between Reductions | Fine Silver Content of 1 Soldino or 1 Soldo di Piccoli (in grams) | Loss of Weight under the New Standard | | Compound Annual Rate of Loss |
| | | | In Grams | As Percentage of Previous Content | |
|---|---|---|---|---|---|
| Ca. 1320–1330[a] | — | 0.696 | — | — | — |
| After 1331[b] | ca. 10 | 0.641 | 0.055 | 7.9% | ca. 0.7% |
| After 1353[b] | 22 | 0.533 | 0.108 | 16.8 | 0.8 |
| After 1369 | 16 | 0.488 | 0.045 | 8.4 | 0.5 |
| After 1379 | 10 | 0.472 | 0.016 | 3.3 | 0.3 |
| After 1391 | 12 | 0.446 | 0.026 | 5.5 | 0.4 |
| After 1399 | 8 | 0.432 | 0.014 | 3.1 | 0.4 |
| After 1407 | 8 | 0.417 | 0.015 | 3.4 | 0.4 |
| After 1417[c] | 10 | 0.385 | 0.032 | 7.7 | 0.7 |
| After 1421 | 4 | 0.380 | 0.005 | 1.3 | 0.3 |
| After 1429 | 8 | 0.364 | 0.016 | 4.2 | 0.5 |
| After 1444[c] | 15 | 0.332 | 0.032 | 8.8 | 0.6 |
| After 1472[c] | 28 | 0.310 | 0.22 | 6.6 | 0.2 |

NOTE: The annual rates of reduction have been computed using the compound interest rate formula $P = A/(1 + r)^n$, in which $P$ = the value at the earlier date, $A$ = the value at the later date, $n$ = the number of years in between, and $r$ = the rate of change, a *negative* number. For example, for the period 1331–53, $P = 0.641$, $A = 0.533$, and $n = 22$, so that $r = -0.008$.

Since this analysis focuses on devaluation, the comparisons have been made in terms of the silver content of the coins, although comparison of the total weights of the coins would be more useful if the physical process of deterioration were the central concern.
[a]Before the soldino was coined.
[b]The reduction for these years indicates an abnormal annual rate of loss, the reasons for which are explained in this section.
[c]The reduction for these years indicates an abnormal annual rate of loss, the reasons for which are explained in volume 2.

## Estimates for before 1331

The most baffling difficulties in making estimates relevant to 1331 arise from the uncertain timing of an extralegal devaluation by deterioration before 1331 of the coins then in circulation.

For about a decade before and after 1331, the silver content of the lira and the soldo di piccoli was determined, not by any one coin, but by several coins circulating simultaneously. The two coins with the most influence before 1331 were the grosso and the piccolo. They had jointly supported a single monetary standard ever since their relative value had been stabilized about 1282 as 1 grosso = 32 piccoli.

The piccolo by its name appeared to be the basic or link coin of the lira di piccoli before 1331, but the exchange value of the piccolo did not depend on its silver content alone. For two generations it was accepted as worth 1/32 of a grosso, even though the silver content stipulated by the minting regulations was only 1/36 as much as that of a grosso. Its market value was higher than its silver value because of its "cost value" and a scarcity value derived from its utility, as explained above, in chapter 5, section i. As long as a grosso coin was treated as if it were worth no more than 32 piccoli coins, the lira di piccoli might be said to have had two silver equivalents. Before 1331 it could be paid with 7 1/2 grossi coins or with 240 piccoli coins. If it was paid with 7 1/2 grossi coins, the lira di piccoli had a silver equivalent of 15.75 grams (7.5 × 2.1), whereas if it was paid with 240 piccoli, it had a silver equivalent of 13.92 grams (240 × 0.058).

The above calculation applies to full-weight coins. Grossi, however, were different from gold coins that were kept mainly in treasure chests or carefully sealed bags. Many grossi passed frequently from hand to hand. Even grossi that were not clipped and sweated, as many were, deteriorated from use sufficiently that new grossi minted according to the standard set more than a hundred years earlier constituted vulnerable "good money," likely to be driven out of circulation by earlier issues worn down so as to have become "bad money." The process of culling for export must have been particularly intense at Venice, because the export of grossi was not opposed. On the contrary, it was facilitated by the government, while new arrivals of silver bullion kept the mint busy and the city provided with silver currency. Weighing the coins and discounting those that were underweight enabled both new full-weight grossi and old worn-down grossi to circulate side by side until about 1321. As explained above, in chapter 15, section i, discounting underweight coins was then forbidden, and all grossi were declared legal tender for 32 piccoli—all grossi, that is, except those that were so bad that a moneychanger would not pay that much for them. If they were that much underweight, they were to be demonetized, that is, treated as bullion and cut up for recoinage (see table 17).

The law of 1321 permitted the continued circulation within the city of grossi that contained little more silver than did 32 piccoli—1.85 grams. But in order to induce a moneychanger to pay 32 piccoli for a grosso, the grosso had to contain at least a little more than those 1.85 grams to compensate for the extra cost of manufacturing the smaller coins. The effective silver equivalent of the lira di piccoli, after valuing grossi by weight was prohibited in 1321, must be considered ill-defined within the range of 13.92–15.75 grams.

Deterioration of the piccolo, however, probably widened that range downward, perhaps making the lower limit 13.5 grams. The legal content of the piccolo remained unchanged for a half-century or more after the reforms of Doge Giovanni Dandolo, and considerable deterioration must

TABLE 17.

Highlights of Monetary Changes, 1312–39

| Date | Event |
|---|---|
| 1312 | Ducat's market value already at 24 grossi |
| 1317–20 | Extensive coinage of piccoli |
| 1321 | Underweight grossi banned |
| 1328 | Ducat made legal tender for 24 grossi and 64 soldi di piccoli |
| 1331 | Mezzanini and soldini authorized |
| 1335 | Only ducats and soldini plentiful in Venice |

NOTE: Under Doge Giovanni Soranzo (1312–28) and Doge Francesco Dandolo (1329–39). For details see above, chap. 15.

have occurred before the increased minting of new piccoli was ordered in 1317 and carried out with the enlargement of the mint under Doge Giovanni Soranzo (1312–28).[5] His piccoli were of the old standard and yet were not driven out of circulation by old "bad money," probably because of the scarcity of pennies. Moreover, greater profits were to be made by culling grossi for export than by culling piccoli. Lower transactions costs and smelting costs per mark would make the exporting of grossi much more profitable, as long as the mint kept turning them out. But about 1330, when grossi were scarce and piccoli minted under Giovanni Soranzo had suffered at least ten years' deterioration, the real silver equivalent of the lira di piccoli may have gone below 13.92 grams. Allowance should therefore be made for deterioration of the average piccolo in circulation between about 1321 and 1331. If the rate was at 0.35 percent per year, about the lowest of the rates derived from the later changes in the soldino, then the weight of the average piccolo coin in circulation was so reduced by 1331 that the amount of silver in 240 piccoli was about 13.5 grams. That figure seems a reasonable estimate of the real silver content of the coins used to pay a lira di piccoli just before the coinage of the soldini and mezzanini. It contrasts with the legally prescribed content of 13.92 grams (table 10).

### Estimate for 1331–38

To estimate for comparison the silver equivalent of the lira di piccoli in 1331–38, after the soldino and the mezzanino had been coined, the values and silver content of those two coins when freshly minted must also be taken into account. As many as five different categories of billon or silver coin were in general circulation for a few years after the reforms of 1331–32.

Could several kinds of coin in which the relations between legal

[5]See below, app. B, sec. iii.

values and silver content differed continue to circulate for many years side by side in competition? In fact the soldino's characteristics enabled it to function as the "bad money," and it gradually drove out the other silver coins. It had the lowest silver content compared with its legal value even when freshly minted, and its exchange value was not increased either by scarcity or high manufacturing cost.[6] The extensive production of soldini, although not quantifiable in secure figures,[7] can be inferred from their shipment to Crete[8] and to Dalmatia, where they were so extensively used that they were much copied by counterfeiters.[9] Compared with their value, their manufacturing cost was higher than that of grossi, but it was not enough higher to give soldini an exchange value, such as piccoli had, that was much above their silver value.

When the soldino was firmly established as the link coin of the lira di piccoli, the silver equivalent of that lira was reduced to 12.82 grams (as entered in table 10). Compared with the previous official standard of 13.92, the reduction of 1.1 grams (13.92 − 12.82) per lira—that is, of 0.055 grams per soldo (0.696 − 0.641)—was 7.9 percent (0.055/0.696 = 0.079). But if before 1331 the deterioration of piccoli had lowered the real silver equivalent of the lira di piccoli, as distinct from its legal equivalent, down to 13.5 grams, then the displacement of the piccolo as the link coin of the lira di piccoli and its replacement by the soldino constituted a reduction of only 0.7 grams (13.5 − 12.8), a reduction of only 5.0 percent (0.7/13.5). That 5 percent, however, can be considered an amount of devaluation effected beyond what was needed to allow merely for normal deterioration of the piccolo between 1321 and 1331.

---

[6]The manufacturing cost of the soldino cannot be estimated directly from the mint charges, because it was made from the "unfree silver" of the quinto. A rough comparison of the cost can be made, however, by comparing what was involved in its manufacture. In minting piccoli worth 1 lira di grossi, 32 times as many blanks had to be cut, shaped, checked for weight, and then struck with dies than when minting grossi. In minting soldini, the number of blanks was only 2.5 times as many as were needed when minting grossi. That comparison indicates that the cost value of the soldino did not exceed that of the grosso by nearly as much as the cost value of the piccolo exceeded the cost value of the grosso.

The relative cost can be roughly estimated also from the mint charges in 1414, when the new grosso was exactly four times the weight and value of the soldino then coined. The charges on free silver were then set at 10 soldi a mark for grossi, 14 soldi for soldini. Although the charge for soldini was 40 percent higher, the difference—4 soldi—was only 0.7 percent (4/544) of the value of a mark's weight of the coins.

[7]Lodovico Brunetti, "Del quantitativo coniato di soldini di Francesco Dandolo" *RIN*, 5th ser., 6, no. 60 (1958):63–68, estimated that Doge Francesco Dandolo struck 30 million soldini, but Brunetti's method of calculation from the slight variations showing the number of dies used is questionable.

[8]Stahl, *The Venetian Tornesello;* and below, in chap. 19, sec. ii.

[9]Ibid.; and Papadopoli, 1:160–61.

## Estimate for 1353

After the soldino had begun effectively determining the silver equivalent of the lira di piccoli, the next devaluation of that lira was effected by
the coinage of the second type of mezzanino, the mezzanino of Andrea
Dandolo. Valued at 16 piccoli although it contained only 0.774 grams of
fine silver, it had a higher value compared with its silver content than did
the soldino. It displaced the soldino temporarily as link coin, and it reduced the legal silver equivalent of the lira di piccoli from 12.82 grams to
11.61 grams, a reduction of 9.4 percent.[10]

When the second type of soldino was issued and the coinage of
mezzanini ceased, the soldino, after the additional reduction in its silver
content, again became the link coin of the lira di piccoli. It contained even
less fine silver compared with its value than the mezzanino coined in 1346,
and its coinage in 1353 lowered the silver equivalent of the lira di piccoli
from 11.61 grams to 10.66. The total reduction, between the soldino of 1331
and the second type, issued twenty-two years later, was from 12.82 to 10.66,
a drop of 2.16 grams, or 16.8 percent.

These devaluations of 1346 and 1353 were not tied to the physical
deterioration of the coinage. The three coins—the first type of soldino,
Andrea Dandolo's mezzanino, and the second type of soldino—were so
different in design, fineness, and size that most users of the coins would
have had difficulty telling whether a much used soldino that had been
issued in 1331 was "bad money" or "good money" compared with a
mezzanino or soldino of more recent mintage.

Moreover, the total devaluation of the 22 years 1331–53 was too great
to be explained simply by physical deterioration. If soldini minted in 1331
and still circulating in 1353 had deteriorated so as to lose weight at the rate
of 0.35 percent per year, they would have lost only 7.8 percent of their
weight. If such soldini had determined the metallic equivalent of the lira di
piccoli, that metallic equivalent would have been 11.82 grams. If they had
deteriorated during the 22 years at the annual rate of 0.5 percent, they
would have lost 10.9 percent of their weight, down to 11.42 grams.[11]
Actually, as mentioned, the introduction of the second type of soldino in
1353 reduced the silver equivalent of the lira di piccoli to 10.66 grams,
indicating a much lower rate.

## Summary: From before 1331 to after 1353

To summarize the whole period from before the coinage of the first
soldino to after the coinage of the second type, we must take as our

[10]Using the formula explained in the note to table 16. On Andrea Dandolo's coinage see
above, chap. 16, sec. iii.
[11]A loss of weight of 24.7 percent (7.9 + 16.8) is shown in table 16 because the table uses
legal standard weights for freshly minted coins.

starting point the silver content of a soldo di piccoli when that money of account was based on the piccolo, as it was before 1331. Even if we consider that the silver equivalent was then determined by deteriorated piccoli, it could not have been much less than 13.5 grams if the deterioration during 1321–30 was at the compound annual rate of 0.35 percent, a hypothetical but likely estimate. The difference between 13.5 and 10.66—2.84 grams— was 21 percent. Out of that 21 percent, more than a third, or 7.8 percent (assuming the 0.35 percent annual deterioration), may be considered adjustment for physical deterioration in those much-used coins. Perhaps part of the remaining 13.2 percent devaluation also should be considered appropriate adjustment for physical deterioration, but most of the 13.2 percent devaluation seems likely to have constituted an adjustment to the rise in the value of silver compared with that of gold.

In spite of the range of error likely in the above calculations due to the lack of solid figures in the extant documentation, they seem to justify the conclusion that physical deterioration at an annual rate of 0.3–0.5 percent may well have been a fairly constant factor in the cumulative devaluation. But that deterioration was not the only factor. In examining the successive steps in the devaluation, we will consider the varying importance of the three other factors: desire to maintain a unified, bimetallic monetary standard, desire for revenue, and concern for the prosperity of the bullion market.

## ii. STEPS IN DEVALUATION

### Bimetallism, 1331–69

Concern with the most elementary feature of a bimetallic system— keeping both silver and gold coins in circulation—clearly motivated the first step in the devaluation. The export of grossi to the east, described in chapter 15, was creating a lamented lack of any silver coins available to serve as a medium of exchange. The coinage of the "monete" issued under Doge Francesco Dandolo (1329–39) achieved the desired result: silver coin became plentiful again. Because they were made of less pure silver than the grosso and because of the relation between their silver content and their legal value, the soldini were immune to the lure of the Levantine markets which were attracting grossi. At the same time, the foreign silver coins, such as the groats from Tyrol and Dalmatia, that had been displacing Venetian grossi in the city's currency were made less desirable. The high legal value placed on the silver incorporated in soldini enabled them to act as "bad money" in the sense of Gresham's law and to drive out some undesired coins from foreign mints or at least to hold their own.

The soldino also very soon acquired an essential role in the establishment of a new monetary standard which gave the Venetian monetary system its unity. A single unifying, bimetallic standard had been proclaimed when the ducat was first coined in 1285. When that first bimetallic standard had not proved durable, a second standard, equating 1 ducat with 24 grossi, had become established in practice early in the fourteenth century and had been made legal in 1328, just as it was beginning to fall apart. The new bimetallic standard of which the soldino became an essential part may be called Venice's third. This third bimetallic standard was based on equating in value 1 gold ducat and 64 soldini, an equation corresponding to a bimetallic ratio of 11.5 to 1.[12] It provided a truly unified, single standard only if or when the ducat really could be bought for 64 soldini.

Actually, ducats could not be bought that cheaply on the free market until some years after 1331. When the soldino was first coined, ducats sold for more than 64 soldi di piccoli, although that was the legal value that had been established about 10 years earlier, when the lira di piccoli was based on piccolo coins. If silver had not been falling in market value in 1331–32, the coinage of soldini would have driven the price of ducats higher. In giving the soldino a high value compared with its silver content, the Venetian authorities in 1331 were anticipating the future. They were preparing for a continuing fall in the value of gold compared with that of silver.

As long as gold remained worth more than 11.5 times as much as silver, the ducat was generally priced in commercial transactions at more than 64 soldi di piccoli. The difference was recorded as the lazio or agio described in chapter 15. But as gold fell in value, the lazio disappeared. From time to time, ducats were valued commercially at 64 soldi di piccoli, and the monetary standard became bimetallic in practice as well as in law.[13]

An analysis of the process by which the soldino became the basic coin of a third Venetian bimetallic standard is facilitated by tables 18–21. They are designed to permit comparison of coin content, coin values, and bimetallic ratio, coin by coin, between the soldino and its competitors. Silver coins were in competition not only with each other but with gold ducats. During the transition to a third monetary standard, the lira di piccoli may be said to have had not only six potential silver equivalents but also a gold equivalent. Ducats also could be used to pay debts and prices set in lire di piccoli. The gold equivalent of the lira di piccoli was 1.11 grams when a gold ducat was received in payment at its legal value of 64 soldi di piccoli. The gold equivalent was 1.04–1.01 grams when a ducat was accepted at a higher market value, about 68–70 soldi, in 1331.

This bimetallic element in the values of the lira di piccoli shaped the

[12]See above, chap. 15, sec. iii.
[13]See below, app. D; and above, chap. 15, sec. ii on the ducat's value as legal tender for 64 soldi di piccoli and sec. iii on the lazio.

392

TABLE 18.

Silver and Gold Coin as Legal Tender, ca. 1333–35:
Amount of Silver and Gold Exchanged in Paying for 1 Lira di Piccoli
with Coins in Circulation

| Coins | Content in Grams |
|---|---|
| *Silver and Billon Coins* | (grams silver) |
| 240 full-weight piccoli | 13.92 |
| 240 deteriorated piccoli | 13.50 |
| 20 freshly minted, full-weight soldini | 12.82 |
| 15 freshly minted mezzanini, type 1 | 14.54 |
| 7.5 grossi, type 1, so deteriorated as to contain little more silver than | |
| 240 full-weight piccoli | 14.00 |
| 7.5 full-weight grossi, type 1 | 15.77 |
| *Gold Coins* | (grams gold) |
| Ducats at legal value of 64 soldi (3.55 × [20/64]) | 1.11 |
| Ducats at market value of 68 soldi (3.55 × [20/68]) | 1.04 |

NOTE: For content and legal values of full-weight coins see above, tables 10 and 12. For estimates of deterioration see above, sec. 1.

process by which the soldino became the basic silver coin of that money of account. When gold had been 14.2 times as valuable as silver, the payee had received metal of almost the same value whether 64 lire di piccoli were paid with 20 ducats or with 7 1/2 full-weight grossi (for 64 × 1.1 = 70.4 grams gold, 64 × 15.75 = 1,008 grams silver, and 1,008/70.4 = 14.3 to 1). When silver rose in value so as to make the bimetallic ratio only 13 to 1, the merchant who had a choice between using grossi or ducats in paying lire di piccoli would find profit in paying with the gold coin. In fact, as we have seen, grossi were used less and less in Venice as the bimetallic ratio fell from 14 to 1 to 12 to 1. Silver grossi went east, while gold came to Venice.

The further fall of the bimetallic ratio affected the circulation of other coins in ways that can be inferred from the ratios shown in tables 19–21. When the price of coins on such an international market as Constantinople considered gold less than 13 times as valuable as silver, that not only stimulated the export of grossi from Venice, but it made questionable the wisdom of coining mezzanini. In fact, no mezzanini of type 1 were coined after the death of Francesco Dandolo. When the ratio on the international market fell to as low as 12 to 1, only soldini and piccoli remained immune to attraction by the higher Levantine prices for silver. The result of this process was described in the law passed by the Great Council in 1335 naming only ducats and soldini as coins in common circulation.[14]

[14]See above, chap. 15, n. 69.

TABLE 19.

Bimetallic Ratios with the Ducat Priced at 64 Soldi

| (1)<br>Type of Silver Coin | (2)<br>Number of Coins<br>Worth 1 Ducat<br>of 3.55 Grams Gold | (3)<br>Silver Content<br>of Number of Coins<br>in Col. 2 (in grams) | (4)<br>Ratio of Silver<br>to Gold (col. 3<br>divided by 3.55) |
|---|---|---|---|
| *Coins in Circulation before 1346* | | | |
| Grosso, type 1 | 24 | 50.4 | 14.2:1 |
| (valued at 32 piccoli) | | (24 × 2.102) | |
| Mezzanino, type 1 | 48 | 46.5 | 13.1:1 |
| (valued at 16 piccoli) | | (48 × 0.969) | |
| Soldino, type 1 | 64 | 41.0 | 11.5:1 |
| (valued at 12 piccoli) | | (64 × 0.641) | |
| Piccolo, until 1343 | 768 | 44.5 | 12.5:1 |
| (valued at 1 piccolo) | | (768 × 0.058) | |
| Mezzo denaro | 1,536 | 21.5 | 6.1:1 |
| (valued at 1/2 of a<br>piccolo) | | (1,536 × 0.014) | |
| *New Silver Coins Minted in and after 1346* | | | |
| Mezzanino, type 2 | 48 | 37.2 | 10.5:1 |
| (valued at 16 piccoli) | | (48 × 0.774) | |
| Soldino, type 2 | 64 | 34.1 | 9.6:1 |
| (valued at 12 piccoli) | | (64 × 0.533) | |

NOTE: Ratios calculated from silver coins also valued in soldi di piccoli with values and content as in apps. A and D.

Between 1335 and Andrea Dandolo's election as doge in 1343, the price of ducats in several years was almost as low as the legal rate of 64 soldi di piccoli. His reforms, the next steps in the devaluation, seem to have been designed to prevent it from going lower. His coinage of the mezzanino, type 2, in 1346, by lowering the legally approved bimetallic ratio from 11.5 to 1 to 10.5 to 1, ensured that the flood of gold imports then at its peak would not drive the commercial value of the gold coin below its legal value. It also ensured that silver brought to Venice could be coined there on favorable terms. At Florence scarcity of silver was being met by issuing a new coin of fine silver called the guelfo. Andrea's handsome mezzanino authorized in February 1346 may be considered a Venetian answer to Florence's new guelfo, coined during the previous autumn.[15]

In spite of the reduction in the silver equivalent of the lira di piccoli effected by Andrea's mezzanino, the ducat rose hardly at all above 64 between 1346 and 1353, a sign that the relative value of gold was still falling.

[15]See below, chap. 19, sec. iv.

TABLE 20.

Bimetallic Ratios with the Ducat Priced at 68 Soldi

| (1)<br>Type of Silver Coin | (2)<br>Number of Coins<br>Worth 1 Ducat<br>of 3.55 Grams Gold | (3)<br>Silver Content<br>of Number of Coins<br>in Col. 2 (in grams) | (4)<br>Ratio of Silver<br>to Gold (col. 3<br>divided by 3.55) |
|---|---|---|---|
| *Coins Minted before 1346* | | | |
| Grosso, type 1<br>(at legal value of 32<br>piccoli [68 × (12/32)]) | 25.5 | 53.55<br>(25.5 × 2.102) | 15.1 |
| Grosso, type 1<br>(if at market value of<br>40 piccoli<br>[68 × (12/40)]) | 20.4 | 42.88<br>(20.4 × 2.102) | 12.1 |
| Mezzanino, type 1<br>(valued at 16 piccoli<br>[68 × (12/16)]) | 51 | 49.42<br>(51 × 0.969) | 13.9 |
| Soldino, type 1<br>(valued at 12 piccolo) | 68 | 43.59<br>(68 × 0.641) | 12.3 |
| Piccolo, before 1343<br>(valued at 1 piccolo) | 816 | 47.33<br>(816 × 0.058) | 13.3 |
| *New Silver Coins Minted in and after 1346* | | | |
| Mezzanino, type 2<br>(valued at 16 piccoli) | 51 | 39.47<br>(51 × 0.774) | 11.1 |
| Soldino, type 2<br>(valued at 12 piccoli) | 68 | 36.24<br>(68 × 0.533) | 10.2 |

NOTE: Ratios calculated from silver coins also valued in soldi di piccoli with values and content as in apps. A and D.

Only after the further reduction of the silver equivalent of the lira di piccoli by the issuance of Andrea Dandolo's soldino of 1353 did the ducat rise significantly. It reached 70 in 1358 and 72 in 1361 and remained between 72 and 74 during most of the 1360s and 1370s. With the ducat at 72 and the silver content of the soldino reduced to 0.488, the bimetallic ratio was 9.9 to 1 (see table 12).

That ratio and the valuing of the ducat at 72 soldi might be called Venice's fourth bimetallic standard. But it was a standard very uncertainly supported. When the ducat began rising above 70 in the 1360s, some leading nobles became concerned to prevent it from rising above 72. A hankering for the "good old days" when there had been (at least comparatively speaking) a stable relation between the ducat and the old grosso is implied in a sweeping proposal presented in 1362 by Pietro Steno, a Ducal Councillor and a member of several special committees appointed to make recommendations to the Quarantia and to the Senate for reforms

TABLE 21.

Bimetallic Ratios with the Ducat Priced at 72 Soldi

| (1) Type of Silver Coin | (2) Number of Coins Worth 1 Ducat of 3.55 Grams Gold | (3) Silver Content of Number of Coins in Col. 2 (in grams) | (4) Ratio of Silver to Gold (col. 3 divided by 3.55) |
|---|---|---|---|
| Grosso, type 1 | 18 | 37.8 | 10.6 |
| (if valued at 48 piccoli) | | (18 × 2.102) | |
| Mezzanino, type 2 | 54 | 41.8 | 11.8 |
| (valued at 16 piccoli) | | (54 × 0.774) | |
| Soldino, type 1 | 72 | 46.2 | 13.0 |
| (valued at 12 piccoli) | | (72 × 0.641) | |
| Soldino, type 2 | 72 | 38.4 | 10.8 |
| (valued at 12 piccoli) | | (72 × 0.533) | |
| Soldino, type 3 | 72 | 35.1 | 9.9 |
| (valued at 12 piccoli) | | (72 × 0.488) | |
| Piccolo, 1355–69 | 864 | 46.7 | 13.2 |
| (valued at 1 piccolo) | | (864 × 0.054) | |

NOTE: Ratios calculated from silver coins also valued in soldi di piccoli with contents and values as in apps. A and D.

of the coinage. Although his proposal was defeated, it reflects the thinking of what might be called a pro-silver wing of the nobility.[16]

When Steno made his proposal, no grossi had been coined under the last three doges. Prominent in his plan was the coinage of a new kind of grosso. He proposed a new type a trifle heavier than the old grosso. It was to be worth 48 piccoli so that the lira di piccoli would have a value of 10.8 grams of fine silver. He also provided that 18 of these grossi should be legal tender for 1 ducat. With the 18 grossi equaling 72 soldi di piccoli ([18 × 48]/12), the ducat would not rise above 72 soldi, because debts recorded in ducats could be paid with 18 of the new grossi.

In addition to proposing to put a ceiling on the price of ducats by making the new silver grosso legal tender for payments due in ducats, Steno proposed to make a mark of silver bullion legal tender for 138 grossi a oro in all commercial transactions but not in paying taxes. This provision would have ensured that a mark of silver bullion could be sold for 5.75 ducats (138/24). The 238.5 grams of silver in a mark would then have had the same exchange value as the 20.4 grams (5.75 × 3.55) of gold in 5.75 ducats.

Steno's proposals in effect would have established two bimetallic ratios: a ratio between silver bullion in certified ingots and gold in coin of 11.3 to 1 (0.965 × [238.5/20.4] = 11.3) and a ratio of 10.9 to 1 between silver

[16]PMV, doc. 140.

coined into the proposed new grossi and gold coined into ducats ([18 × 2.16]/3.55). The ducat in 1362 was valued at 74 soldi, making the market ratio between coined silver and coined gold 11 to 1 (74 × [0.532/3.55]). Steno's proposal would have prevented gold from rising above its current price.

On the other hand, Steno's proposal did not provide any means of preventing a fall in the price of gold; and by 1369 or 1370 there were signs that it might fall below 72. Silver had risen during the later 1360s. In October 1368 there was concern over the disappearance of good silver coins which were being melted down for export at the price of 307 soldi a grossi per mark of silver,[17] which was above the price at which Steno had proposed making silver bullion legal tender (5.75 ducats at 52 soldi a grossi per ducat = only 299 soldi). Steno had been concerned lest silver bullion be worth less than 5.75 ducats per mark. Actually six months later it was worth more than that. As silver rose, gold fell. A couple of quotations of the ducat in 1369 in Treviso indicate that the ducat had fallen back to 67 soldi di piccoli at about the same time that the amount of silver in the soldino was again reduced.[18] The reduction removed any chance that the ducat would go as low as 64 soldi. A new design—a change from the lion rampant to the lion crouched on the reverse—distinguished the lighter soldino issued after 1369.[19] The ducat then rose to 70 and above and stayed high thereafter.

The legal rate of 64 soldi became less and less important as the commercial rate rose. When the third type of soldino, containing only 0.488 grams of silver, pushed the price of a ducat up to 72 soldi, that price reflected a bimetallic ratio of only 9.9 to 1. With those two prices for the ducat—the legal rate of 64 soldi and the commercial rate of 72 lighter soldi—the bimetallic ratio scraped bottom at Venice in the decade of the 1360s (see table 12).

### Revenue, 1369–79

The changes in monetary regulation in 1369 may have been dominated by fiscal considerations, which became an increasingly important factor in monetary policy. In mid-century the Commune was having difficulty meeting expenses. After the War of Ferrara the long-term public debt had been gradually reduced from 2.8 million lire a grossi in 1313 down to 1.1 million lire a grossi in 1343, but in the decade following 1343 the government's debt nearly tripled, and in later decades it continued to rise.[20]

---

[17]Ibid., docs. 151, 153.
[18]See below, app. D.
[19]Papadopoli, 1:207; *PMV*, doc. 157.
[20]Luzzatto, *Il debito pubblico*, 71–106; 283; on the pressure of the wars, 113, 125.

THE FOUR TYPES OF SOLDINO, 1331–91

*a.* Soldino, type 1, issued under Andrea Dandolo between 1343 and 1346.

*Obv.:* + **ANDR.DAN DVLO DVX** The doge, kneeling facing left, holds the banner in both hands.

*Rev.:* + **.S.MARCVS.VENETI.** Lion rampant left, holding the banner, in circle.

*AR, 18 mm, 0.955 gr. Museo Bottacin, inv. no. 153 (Papadopoli, 1: 182 no. 4).*

*b.* Soldino, type 2, the smaller, finer type of which the issue began in the last year of Andrea Dandolo's dogeship, 1353/54.

*Obv.:* same as type 1.

*Rev.:* + .S.MAR.CVS VENETI. The rest as in type 1, bur with an S in the left field.

*AR, 15.4 mm, 0.529 gr. Museo Bottacin, inv. no. 157 (Papadopoli, 1: 182 no. 5).*

*c.* Soldino, type 3. The change in design that accompanied the change in silver content made in 1369 is illustrated by issues of Andrea Contarini (1368–82) before the year 1379.

*Obv.:* +**ANDR'9. TAR'DVX** The doge, standing facing left, holds the banner in both hands.
*Rev.:* +**.S.MARCVS.VENETI.** Winged lion crouching, facing front, holds the gospel in his front paws.

*AR, 15.6 mm, 0.523 gr. Museo Bottacin, inv. no. 215 (Papadopoli, 1: 216 no. 5).*

*d.* Soldino, type 4. The slight change in content ordered in 1379 was shown (as in the case of grossi minted after 1379) by the addition of a star on the obverse. This is an example of Andrea Contarini's later issues.

*Obv.:* + ANDR°9 TARDVX The rest as in type 3, but with a star in the left field, F in the right field.

*Rev.:* +.S.MARCVS+VENETI+ The rest as in type 3.

*AR, 15.2 mm, 0.491 gr. Museo Bottacin, inv. no. 223 (Papadopoli, 1: 216 no. 6).*

Income from the mint was needed to meet large interest payments and such military emergencies as the Cretan rebellion of 1363–64.

Profits at the mint came almost entirely from the quinto, for which the mint paid a price far below the market price. After the reduction of the amount requisitioned to a decimo in 1342–43, it had been raised to a quinto again in 1350. Since the burden fell on all dealers in silver, as explained above, even those who did not deal in coins but turned all their free silver into jewelry or into ingots which they exported, the quinto had the effect of an import tax.[21] The form of collection made the rate of the tax rise as the price of silver increased. When a market price was 307 soldi, as reported in 1368, silver merchants who had to turn over to the mint 1/5 of their silver at 233 soldi a grossi instead of exporting to sell it at 307 soldi were paying a tax of 74 soldi per mark on that 1/5 of their turnover.[22] Enforcing the collection of the quinto became extremely difficult. Much bullion passed through Venice or into silverware without leaving any unfree silver ("argento servo") in the mint. The number of pardons for persons who had been found guilty of not depositing silver that they owed as quinto is evidence both of the amount of evasion and of sufficiently vigorous enforcement to give the mint charges fiscal significance.[23] In the 1360s there were many complaints, many drafting committees appointed, and many proposals that were not accepted. The common cause of dissatisfaction seems to have been an apparent lack of silver in Venice, either as good coin in circulation or available for export.[24]

After rejecting several proposals, in December 1369 the Senate finally accepted the formulation presented by an influential ducal councillor, Lorenzo Zane. Besides reducing the amount of silver in the soldino, as just described, it raised the price paid for the quinto. It also raised the mint charge on the coinage of soldini from free silver. From 1369 to 1379, free silver and unfree silver were subject to mint charges that differed little (13.8 percent and 15.5 percent, respectively).[25] Smuggling imports thus became less profitable.

The most controversial clause in Zane's motion was the exemption of those who registered silver from having to declare where they had obtained it. An alternative motion, with different provisions about inquiries into past dealings in silver, was defeated definitely only on the sixth balloting, when Zane's motion passed with 31 in favor, 23 for the alter-

[21]See above, chap. 11, sec. ii.
[22]Equal to 14.8 soldi per mark on their total turnover, a rate of about 5 percent (*PMV*, docs. 151, 153).
[23]Many pardons from penalties inflicted in connection with violations concerning registration of silver and paying the quinto or decimo are in ASV, Senato, Misti, e.g., reg. 16, fols. 29, 85; and in ASV, Grazie, e.g., reg. 5, fols. 53, 69, reg. 8, fols. 28v, 62v, 101v, reg. 11, fol. 11v.
[24]*PMV*, docs. 144–56.
[25]See below, app. A, sec. vi, Soldini of 1369.

native, 4 nos, and 5 "undecided," as 11 had been on the first ballot. Prohibitions of furtive sales and furtive export of unregistered silver were reaffirmed, but the willingness not to press inquiries about unregistered sales that had occurred in the past was apparently accepted as one way of getting silver to come out of hiding.[26] On 13 December 1371 the law was reaffirmed for two more years or until repealed.[27]

## Bimetallism and the New Grossi, 1370–1400

After the reforms at the end of 1369, the market price of ducats stayed within the range 72–74 until 1378 except for dips to 71 and 70 in 1370–71 and brief dips in August 1373 and September 1374. Meanwhile there were more violent changes in the quotation on gold coins in other Italian cities in the 1370s, as well as reports of violent changes in the price of silver bullion in Venice. The 1370s were years of bank failures, high prices, bad harvests, and interruptions of Venice's trade through Austria and Tyrol.[28] But changes in mint regulations—and they were major changes—came only in 1379, after the beginning of a new war with Genoa, commonly called the Fourth Genoese War, or the War of Chioggia.

Aside from fiscal aspects—to be treated shortly—the key feature of the changes voted in 1379 was the resurrection of the grosso, or, rather, the creation of a new grosso that resembled in appearance and fineness the coin first struck almost two centuries earlier by Enrico Dandolo but contained slightly less silver, only 1.89 grams (see tables 4 and 22). Henceforth half of the silver from the quinto was to be used for producing grossi, and half for producing soldini, unless the Signoria decided otherwise. The new grosso resembled the grosso that had been proposed by Pietro Steno seventeen years earlier in that it had the legal value of 4 soldi di piccoli.

The regulations of 1379 did not contain any clauses comparable to those in Steno's proposals that would have made silver grossi legal tender for a specified number of ducats. They contained no legal barriers to a rise of the ducat above 74. But some of those who voted for the reform of 1379 may have desired, as Steno obviously had, to stop the rise of the ducat.

The Senate refused to approve the new grosso when it was first proposed in May 1379. It was approved only at a second meeting, at which the drafting committee accepted an amendment providing that the new grosso, as well as the soldino then issued with a reduced silver content, should have in their design a star, which would make it possible to distinguish them from older issues containing more silver.[29] The opposition

---

[26]*PMV*, doc. 157 (19 December 1369).

[27]ASV, Senato, Misti, reg. 33, fol. 144v.

[28]*PMV*, docs. 159, 161; *RES*, cclv n. 6. The bank failures and changes in Venice's regulation of banking will be described in volume 2.

[29]*PMV*, docs. 163–64.

TABLE 22.

## Silver Equivalents of the Lira di Piccoli, 1379–1429

| | Grams of Fine Silver in: | | | | | |
| | Piccoli | | Soldini | | Grossi | |
| Dates | 1 Coin | 240 Coins | 1 Coin | 20 Coins | 1 Coin | 5 Coins |
|---|---|---|---|---|---|---|
| 1379–85[a] | — | — | 0.472 | 9.44 | 1.892 | 9.46 |
| 1385–91 | 0.027 | 6.48 | 0.472 | 9.44 | 1.892 | 9.46 |
| 1391–94 | 0.027 | 6.48 | 0.446 | 8.92 | 1.892 | 9.46 |
| 1394–97 | 0.027 | 6.48 | 0.446 | 8.92 | 1.787 | 8.94 |
| 1397–99 | 0.027 | 6.48 | 0.446 | 8.92 | 1.733 | 8.67 |
| 1399–1407 | 0.027 | 6.48 | 0.432 | 8.64 | 1.733 | 8.67 |
| 1407–17 | 0.027 | 6.48 | 0.417 | 8.34 | 1.668 | 8.34 |
| 1417–21 | 0.027 | 6.48 | 0.385 | 7.70 | 1.541 | 7.71 |
| 1421–29 | 0.027 | 6.48 | 0.380 | 7.60 | 1.521 | 7.61 |

[a]No piccoli coined.

to changing the silver content of the grosso is understandable both because the grosso had been kept unchanged for almost two centuries and because it was the silver coin that upheld the reputation of Venetian silver in the east. The silver content of the soldino had been changed twice within the last fifty years, to be sure, but each change in the soldino's silver content had been accompanied by a conspicuous change in the size or design of the coin. The reduction in the weight of the new grosso compared with that of the old was somewhat more than the probable loss of weight by wear and tear in such old grossi as were still circulating. The reduction in weight of 0.191 grams (2.178 − 1.987) seems more than enough to allow for deterioration by culling and wear and tear during the twenty-three years since Doge Giovanni Gradenigo (1355–56) had coined the last grossi of the standard of Enrico Dandolo. A loss of 8.769 percent (0.191/2.178) in twenty-three years would result from deterioration at a compound annual rate of about 0.4 percent, but the rate of deterioration of grossi presumably averaged less than that of soldini. Some grossi were likely to lie undisturbed in treasure chests. The danger that old grossi that had been minted more then twenty-three years earlier would act as "bad money" and drive the new issue out of circulation if it was issued at the old standard probably had less influence in the decision to lower the weight of the new grossi than did the desire to make the grosso worth exactly 4 soldini and to align the value of the grosso with that of recent Byzantine coins.

Indeed, the change in Byzantine coinage initiated a few years before 1379 may well have been the main reason for resuming the coinage of grossi. As explained in more detail below, in chapter 19, section i, the emperors at Constantinople suspended the minting of a perpero that was largely gold and inaugurated instead a "silver perpero." It was based on a series of new silver coins of which the largest, called a "stavraton," was worth 1/2 of a perpero and the smallest, which the Venetians called a "ducatello," was worth 1/16 of a perpero. After the coinage of the stavraton and of Venice's new grosso, the new silver coins supported the equation of 1 gold ducat with 2 Byzantine perperi when the gold ducat was at 74, as follows: 1 gold ducat = 74 soldi di piccoli; 74/4 = 18.5 new grossi; 18.5 × 1.89 grams silver = 34.97 grams silver; 1 silver perpero = 16 ducatelli; 16 × 1.1 grams silver = 17.6 grams silver; 17.6 × 2 = 35.2 grams silver. If the new grosso had had the same fine silver content as the old grosso, the silver content of 18.5 grossi would have been more than twice that of the new "silver perpero"; it would have been 38.9 grams of silver. As coined, 18.5 of the new grossi with the star contained 34.97 grams, very close but a little less than the silver equivalent of 2 of Constantinople's new silver perperi.[30]

Elsewhere in the Levant, as well as at Constantinople, the new Venetian grossi found readier acceptance than had the soldini. Two large coin hoards found at Hamath in Syria and dating from the last years of the fourteenth century contain many Venetian grossi and an especially large number of those minted under Antonio Venier (1382–1400).[31]

The issuance of the new grosso also served the useful function within Venice itself of providing a means of payment intermediate in value between the soldino, worth only 12 piccoli, and the gold ducat, which at 72 soldi was worth 864 piccoli coins. A coin of intermediate value became all the more useful as the ducat rose higher and higher.

Any hopes of stabilizing the relationships between gold-based and silver-based moneys of account proved quite vain. Within two years the ducat rose to 86 soldi di piccoli. That was a rate determined by wartime conditions, to be sure. After Venice recovered from the war, the ducat fell back, but not below 80 (except for some official rates at Padua). Then it remained relatively stable at about 80 soldi for almost five years. During this short period of stability of the ducat, 1382–87, the bimetallic ratio, which was reflected in the price of the ducat, was also relatively stable, at about 10.6 to 1 to 10.9 to 1.

Between 1390 and 1400 the reductions in the weights of the soldini and grossi, and accordingly of the silver equivalent of the lire di piccoli, occurred in a series of small steps too complex to be displayed fully in the tabulation of the devaluations. They seem to have been still connected with intensive culling of freshly minted coins. Certainly the mint regulations of those years show much concern with a deterioration of the coins

---

[30]See below, chap. 19, sec. i.
[31]Ashtor, "Observations on Venetian Trade in the Levant," 565.

THE THREE TYPES OF GROSSO, 1194–1394

*a.* Grosso, type 1. Only the doge's name distinguished a grosso minted under Enrico Dandolo and this grosso minted under Giovanni Gradenigo (1355–56), the last of type 1.

*Obv.:* IOGRADOICO. DVX .S.MVENETI St. Mark to the right, handing the banner to the doge, both facing front.

*Rev.:* Christ enthroned, flanked by $\overline{\text{IC}}$ $\overline{\text{XC}}$.

AR, 23 mm, 2.279 gr. Museo Bottacin, inv. no. 177 (Papadopoli, 1: 191 no. 2).

*b.* Grosso, type 2. On the reverse a star distinguished the new issue, with the slightly changed content authorized under Andrea Contarini in 1379, from the old grosso.

*Obv.:* **ANDR.** ⌐ **TARENO DVX .S.M.VENETI** St. Mark, on the right facing front, hands the banner to the bearded doge, in profile.

*Rev.:* Christ enthroned, flanked by I̅C̅ X̅C̅, a star in the left field, **F** in the right field.

*AR, 21.4 mm, 1.867 gr. Museo Bottacin, inv. no. 208 (Papadopoli, 1: 215 no. 2).*

THE THREE TYPES OF GROSSO, 1194–1394 *(cont.)*

*c.* Grosso, type 3. The weights and designs of the new issues of grossi were slightly but frequently changed, as illustrated by this specimen issued after 1394 by Antonio Venier (1382–1400).

By this time grossi were completely detached from the lira di grossi and were tied instead to the soldini as basic coins for the lira di piccoli.

*Obv.:* ANTOV.ENERIO DVX .S.M.VENETI Figures as in type 2, except for the addition of two stars in the left and right fields.

*Rev.:* .+.TIBI.LAVS. .7.GLORIA Christ enthroned, but without his name in Greek.

*AR, 20.9 mm, 1.784 gr. Museo Bottacin, inv. no. 240 (Papadopoli, I: 227 no. 3).*

in circulation such that their content was well below the legal standard. The attempt made in 1391 to have all the soldini leaving the mint more exactly equal in weight, an avowed effort to prevent an excessive deterioration that was not due to abrasion or clipping but occurred as soon as the coins passed through the hands of the first moneychanger, banker, or paymaster who received them, was clearly unsuccessful.[32]

Since the soldini and the new grossi were almost pure silver, culling them was worthwhile even though the differences in weight were not large. Inability to manufacture small silver coins with weights more precisely equal could in itself have become a cause of successive devaluations. When in 1399 the legal average weight of the soldino was reduced from 0.469 grams to 0.454, intensive culling of the imprecisely weighed coins produced by the craftsmen under the compromise rules adopted at their insistence in 1391 may well have reduced the average weight of that issue of coins to 0.430. Thus the standard may have been lowered by the craftsmen concerned, even if it is not officially registered among the mint's regulations. Meanwhile, in 1397 the weight of the grosso had been lowered, also without formal senatorial approval, perhaps because all the silver from the quinto (except for a little used in black money) was being devoted to soldini. Increasing the number of grossi made from a mark was felt to be necessary in order to attract the free silver needed for making grossi.[33] Certainly Venetian senators continued to complain about the bad minting of silver and the condition of the currency, which deteriorated, not only because of the culling of freshly minted coins but also because of the use of clipped and foreign coins and of many counterfeits, especially when Venice was engaged in both military and monetary wars with Padua and when Venice's supplies of silver bullion were reduced during a trade war in 1409–22, with the emperor.[34] When the quinto was abolished in 1417, the reforming resolution expatiated on the deplorable condition of the mint and of its products, concluding: "The silver coinage now being manufactured is made with so little thought and planning, reason and organization that it greatly dishonors our Signoria and discontents our subjects not a little."[35]

In general, the devaluations of 1391–1421 (table 16) can be attributed more to concern about the deterioration of the currency than to concern about maintaining the price of the ducat. In those years there was no threat that the ducat would go below the level of 80–84 soldi. On the

[32]See above, sec. i.

[33]See below, app. A, sec. vii.

[34]On the circulation of clipped and counterfeit coin see *Cap. Broche,* fol. 6v (also in *PMV,* doc. 180) for 1389, and ibid., fol. 7 (also in *PMV,* doc. 185) for 1391. On Venice's banning of coins minted by Padua during her bitter wars with Venice see *Cap. Broche,* fol. 2v (1379); and Mueller, "L'imperialismo monetario," 282–83 (1405).

[35]Papadopoli, 1:356.

contrary, the devaluation of the silver coinage of 1397–99 coincided roughly with the ducat's rise to about 90 soldi. It rose above 95 soldi after 1407 and then to 100 in 1411.[36] In those years, changes in the bimetallic ratio were of less concern than were fiscal problems.

### Revenue and Bullion Supplies, 1379–1417

The fiscal aspects of the changes made in 1379 were closely connected with the immediate problem, the need for money to fight the war. The new regulations were voted at almost precisely the time when the Venetian war fleet was suffering the catastrophic defeat off Pola which enabled the Genoese to attack within the lagoons.[37] Backed by Padua and the king of Hungary, who then ruled Dalmatia, the Genoese were almost, but not quite, able to subject Venice to a tight blockade. Silver coin was desperately needed to pay for the supplies that still came through from Ferrara, as well as to pay the soldiers that Venice hired to supplement its citizen-manned ships. Some of the provisions passed in May 1379 seem to have been designed to increase revenue, but borrowing was the government's main source of funds, and the pressing practical problem was making silver coin available so that forced loans could be collected.

More revenue was planned by assigning to the new soldini and grossi, with star, weights and legal values that raised the mint charges. The number of soldini to be made from a mark was raised from 464 to 480—the number of grossi was fixed at exactly 1/4 as many—while the price paid for unfree silver was left unchanged, so that the mint charge was raised from 15.5 percent to 18.3 percent. Increasing revenue from the mint was probably the aim also of provisions forbidding thenceforth the circulation of foreign silver or billon coins in Venice and obliging importers of such coin to give 1/5 to the mint, just as if it were unfree bullion.

For making more silver coin available immediately the most effective reform was raising the price that the mint offered for free silver already in Venice and in the possession of Venetians and naturalized citizens ("qui navigare possunt"). The new price reduced the mint charges to only 2.5 percent, whereas previously the price offered for free silver had imposed a mint charge of 13.8 percent.[38] The melting down of silverware and its refinement into argentum de bulla was encouraged by providing that only

[36]See below, app. D.

[37]The decree is dated 4 May in *PMV*, doc. 164. The crushing defeat of Brioni off Pola was on 5 May, according to Heinrich Kretschmayr, *Geschichte von Venedig*, 3 vols. (vols. 1 and 2, Gotha, 1905 and 1920; vol. 3, Stuttgart, 1934), 2:232. According to Daniele di Chinazzo, *Cronica de la guerra da Veniciani a Zenovesi*, ed. Vittorio Lazzarini, Monumenti storici, n.s., 11 (Venice: Deputazione di Storia Patria, 1958), 43, it was on May 6; and according to Raimondo Morozzo della Roçca, "Cronologia veneziana del '300," *La civiltà veneziana del Trecento* (Florence, 1956), 258, it was on May 7.

[38]App. A, sec. vii and table A.5; *PMV*, docs. 163–64.

the low mint fee of 2.5 percent would be charged to those presenting not more than 5 marks, unless they were bankers or moneychangers, and that they be paid immediately. Amounts larger than 5 marks were to be paid for at the usual price. The highly favorable terms applied only to Venetian-made silverware. Large offers of silverware were to be inspected by the gastaldi of the Guild of Jewelers and Goldsmiths, and if they were found to be of foreign manufacture, they were immediately to be melted, and 1/5 was to be taken as unfree silver.[39] Venetians who had accumulated silver in the form of tableware and jewelry were under no legal obligation to take it to the mint, but possessors of already highly refined silver ("de bulla"), whether merchants, moneychangers, or anyone else, were ordered to place half of it in the mint to be coined. They were promised that the coin made from their silver would be paid to them, not anyone else. They could arrange to make the delivery of their bullion to the mint in installments but were to register their holdings at once. The mintmasters were to take an oath not to make public the names of those who thus registered nor their holdings. No similar legal obligation to take silver to the mint was imposed on those who had accumulated it in the form of tableware or jewelry, but the combination of patriotism and the high price for the bullion moved so many to do so that tradition attributed the ability of Venice to hold out during three years of war when no commercial convoys sailed to "the great quantity of silver that the women in that period sent to the mint to be made into coin."[40]

Once the tide of war had turned and the Genoese who had taken Chioggia were closely besieged within that town, new monetary regulations focused on reanimating the importation of silver and gold by the German merchants. During the winter of 1379–80, while Venice was under siege, Bologna tried to take Venice's place as the depot and refining center for the Germans, who, as the Bolognese stated it, "were accustomed to having their warehouse serving mints with gold and silver and other metals in other cities now cut off because of the war." Two Florentines received a contract under which they were to coin each month 1.2 million Bolognese groats (by weight 1,608 kg) and much gold;[41] but by summer it was evident that they were having difficulty obtaining the necessary silver.[42] Even before the Genoese at Chioggia surrendered in July 1380, the Venetian Senate in April had appointed a special, five-man committee to propose measures to prevent the Germans from going elsewhere.[43] In

---

[39]*PMV*, doc. 164, p. 159.

[40]Cronaca Dolfin, BMV, Ms. It., cl. VII, cod. 794, fol. 257. Marino Sanuto also mentions great quantities of silver being taken to the mint, while no fleets sailed, but attributes it to the taxes (*Vite de' Duchi*, col. 742. See also above, chap. 9, nn. 76–77).

[41]Salvioni, "Il valore della lira bolognese," in *Atti e memorie*, 16, pp. 331, 340–43.

[42]Ibid., 343, 353.

[43]*PMV*, doc. 165.

August, Venice lightened the burden that the quinto had imposed on silver imports. In order to undercut the Bolognese mint charge of 3.4 percent on groats,[44] Venice offered a price for "free silver" that reduced the mint charge to 2.5 percent. As a temporary measure, all silver presented to the mint for coinage within 15 days after it had been duly registered and refined was exempted from the quinto. On any silver not offered to the mint, importers had to turn over the quinto of servile silver, but the price they were paid for it was raised from 12 soldi 3 grossi to 14 soldi, so that even on unfree silver the mint charge was only 6.7 percent. As further encouragement, the importers of silver were given more freedom in selling and were allowed to accept payment in bank money. German importers of gold were encouraged by the renewal—in more practical form—of the special fund that had been created earlier to assure them prompt payment in ducat coins.[45]

After peace was restored and trade revived, mint charges were gradually raised to their prewar level by increasing the number of coins struck from a mark of silver and by lowering the price that the mint paid for unfree silver. On coins struck from the quinto the mint charge was raised to 10 percent in 1382, 11.7 percent in 1386, and so on until it reached 16.5 percent in 1399 and 19.6 percent in 1407. For free silver, on the other hand, mint charges stood at only 1.8 percent in 1399.[46]

None of the changes in the silver coinage just described constituted debasement in the strict sense of the word; that is, the fineness of silver in the mezzanino, the soldino, and the grosso did not change after 1353, except for the slight decline from 0.965 and 0.952 which occurred in both soldini and grossi when the star was added to their design. The declining silver equivalent of the lira di piccoli between 1331 and 1379 was a result of making soldini smaller. By 1379 they were so thin and light that one reason for resuming the coinage of grossi may have been the convenience of having in circulation a silver coin that was easier to handle than the small soldino.

The piccoli, in contrast, had indeed been debased. Already in 1331 they were less than 1/5 silver. Even so, the fine silver content of 240 piccoli—assuming that the chemical analysis made for Papadopoli is correct—would have amounted to more silver than did 20 of the soldini minted by Andrea Dandolo in 1353 (15.12, then 12.96 grams compared with 10.66 grams [table 10]). For that reason it was the soldino, not the piccolo, that determined the value in silver of a lira di piccoli. By 1371 piccoli that contained so little silver that 240 of them contained almost the same

<hr/>

[44]The mint retained 9 out of 268 groats cut from a mark (Salvioni, "Il valore della lira bolognese," in *Atti e memorie,* 16, p. 351). The seigniorage included was only 0.37 percent.

[45]See below, app. A, sec. vii and table A.5. See also *PMV,* doc. 166.

[46]See below, app. A, sec. vii and table A.5.

amount as 20 soldini of that date were authorized. They were probably never coined, however. Among the reforms ordered at the beginning of the war in 1379 was the recall of all piccoli, a ban on their use and that of similar foreign coins after a specified date, and the issuance of new piccoli that would be even more largely copper, as well as being smaller than previous issues. Only after recovery from the war were the new piccoli issued, in 1385. Since the piccoli then issued each contained only 0.027 grams of silver, 240 of them contained only about 2/3 as much silver as 20 soldini or 5 grossi.[47] Had the lira and the soldo di piccoli been based on the piccolo, the price of 81 soldi di piccoli for a ducat would have represented a bimetallic ratio of 7.4 to 1. Instead, the ratio in Venice, as in other cities, was about 10.8 to 1, because the soldo di piccoli was actually based on fine silver coins, the soldino and the new grosso. Piccoli had become practically token coinage. Their value did not depend on their metallic content. Since they were not minted in excessive quantity, they were in demand to make change and were generally accepted at their legal value.

### iii. TRANSITORY BIMETALLIC STANDARDS

Venice's long experience with bimetallism confirms the view of the economists who contend that a single monetary standard of value cannot be truly bimetallic, at least not for any length of time. Like most ideals, it can only be approximated. During the many centuries in which Venetian policymakers pursued that ideal, they succeeded in keeping both gold and silver coins in circulation, but only by leaving a margin of variation or ambiguity in the relative values of the gold and silver coin and by shifting many times from one bimetallic standard to another. Between established standards there were transitional periods during which Venice in effect used two separate monetary standards, one based on silver, the other on gold. Nevertheless, in spite of shortcomings, realization of the ideal was close to attainment in several periods of relative stability.

Five such periods of stability before 1400 can usefully be distinguished.

1. The first bimetallic standard was legally established in 1285, when the first ducats coined were made legal tender for 40 soldi a grossi, equal to just about 18-1/2 silver grossi. Although the value of the ducat in international accounts rose almost immediately to about 20 grossi, this first, unified bimetallic standard did not become obsolete until about 1296.

2. After a rapid rise in the value of gold during a transitional period

---

[47]See below, app. A, sec. viii. While piccoli struck under the doges in office from 1343 to 1368 are extant, the years during which they were actually coined and the quantity coined are doubtful. At the fineness given by Papadopoli (by chemical analysis), the piccoli, especially the heavy variety struck under Andrea Dandolo, would not have remained in circulation long. In fact, production of piccoli was terminated by 1368 at the latest.

from about 1296 to 1305, there was a second period of relative stability, during which the gold ducat was equated with 24 silver grossi (and 52 soldi a grossi). It was established in commercial practice for about two decades before being given legal form in 1328, when it was beginning to disintegrate.

3. With the new silver coins authorized in 1331, separate standards of value, one based on silver, the other on gold, came to be expressed in diversely based moneys of account. The link coin of the moneys of account based on gold was the ducat; the link coins of the moneys of account based on silver were the new types of silver coins referred to in accounting formulae and contracts as "monete." Having a unified bimetallic standard depended on maintaining a dependable relationship between the two kinds of moneys of account. The relationship used as the standard for about thirty years was the gold ducat's legal value of 64 soldi di piccoli, equal to 64 silver soldini, later called simply soldi coins. The market value of the ducat was permitted to rise, but twice the rise was checked by reducing the silver content of the silver coins. Before 1361 it hardly ever rose above 70, and it came close to its legally prescribed value of 64 soldi at times when the value of gold dipped lower. During this third period of relative stability, the bimetallic ratio fell by 20–25 percent as a result of the increased supplies of gold. A decline of the ducat below 64 soldi was prevented only by the reductions in the weights of the soldini and mezzanini.

4. During a fourth period of stability the lower bimetallic ratio reached during the third period was not recognized officially by giving the ducat a new official value, but the ducat's market price stayed between 72 and 74 soldi di piccoli for about sixteen years, 1362–78, and the bimetallic ratio changed less than in the previous period. The difference between the market value of the ducat and its value as legal tender was no longer commonly expressed by figuring with a lazio. Instead, a distinction was made between moneys of account based on gold and moneys of account based on silver, that is, between lire and ducati a oro and lire and ducati a monete. No money of account was based solidly on both gold and silver. Insofar as Venice had a single monetary standard, it was not based on any legally established ratio of value between gold ducats and silver soldini. It was based on the stability of the market's evaluation of the relative values of the money of account based on gold and the money of account based on silver.

5. The fourth relatively stable period was ended by the War of Chioggia. After a few years of transition, the ducat stabilized at a higher level. From 1382 to 1387 there was a fifth, notably short period of relative stability with the ducat at about 80. A rise, beginning to be felt in 1386, carried the ducat well over 90 by 1400.

After a long transitional interlude, which will be examined in volume

2, a new period of stability was achieved following the conclusion of the Milanese wars by the Peace of Lodi in 1454. From 1456 to about 1509 the price of ducats was 124 soldi di piccoli or very close to that, and after the demonetization of the grossi in 1472 and the materialization in the same year of the lira di piccoli in a silver coin, the tron, 124 soldi became the official value of the gold ducat.

Long before that change in the ducat's value as legal tender, its old official value of 64 soldi had become practically irrelevant. It had been made officially moribund already as early as 1410 by senatorial actions setting the values to be given the gold ducat in specified uses—for example, the value of 96 soldi for use by the Grain Office in 1408 and of 100 or 104 soldi for paying interest in the public debt in 1418.[48] Such decrees were an accommodation to the fact that at the end of the fourteenth century Venice had no unifying bimetallic standard.

[48]See above, chap. 16, sec. vi.

# 19

# FOREIGN EXCHANGE
# DURING THE FALL OF GOLD

## i. CONSTANTINOPLE

HE FALL IN THE VALUE of gold compared with that of silver
after 1325 affected the monetary systems of Venice's trading partners in the Levant just as it did that of Venice. Prices, taxes, and
monetary obligations in general were recorded in perperi in all the area
that before the Crusades had been part of the Byzantine Empire. As
explained in chapter 14, section iii, perperi as moneys of account in the
thirteenth century had come to be based largely on silver coins. The rise of
gold between 1250 and 1310 had been accompanied by increased use of
silver coins and the attachment of the moneys of account to those coins. In
Crete, 1 perpero was worth 12 old Venetian grossi. Around the Black Sea,
perperi were paid by using a variable number of various silver coins called
aspri. In the Greek peninsula, sums recorded in perperi were paid in the
silver or billon coins called "esterlins" or "tornesi," issued by the heirs of
crusading princes. In the Byzantine capital the same trends were shrouded
by a fuzzy kind of bimetallism or symmetallism.

The perpero of Constantinople, traditionally an almost purely gold
coin, contained less and less gold and more and more silver.[1] Silver coins
called "basilica," imitations of the Venetian old grossi, had the value of 1/12

---

[1] See above, chap. 13, sec. ii; and Tommaso Bertelè, *Numismatique byzantine, suivie de deux
études inédites sur les monnaies des Paléologues* (Paris, 1978), 84, 89–90.

of a perpero,[2] and being considered inferior imitations of Venetian grossi, they were called "ducatelli" or "ducatopoulos."[3] While gold rose in value, the gold content of the perperi coined at Constantinople decreased. This had prevented the gap between the market value of 1 perpero and of 12 grossi or ducatelli from becoming excessive, although perpero coins had risen to as high as 12 1/2 and 13 old Venetian grossi. In short, the rise of gold early in the fourteenth century had led to a shift towards a silver monetary standard in Constantinople.

The rise in the relative value of silver after 1325 did not lead to a simple shift back towards gold. Instead, it led to a lessening of the amount of silver in the silver coins and to a splitting of the old monetary unit. In Constantinople as in Venice, it led to the use of two increasingly distinct monetary units called perperi, one based on gold, the other on silver.

As a money of account based on gold, the perpero prolonged its life by becoming tied to the gold ducat. In accord with the gold contents of the perpero and the ducat about 1300, 2 perperi equaled 1 ducat. Byzantine perperi of that metallic value were still circulating in the surviving frag-ments of the Byzantine Empire in the 1360s,[4] and in the century when gold perperi of that value were no longer minted in Constantinople, a perpero was still used as a denomination of account having the value of 1/2 of a Venetian gold ducat.[5]

The perpero based on silver coin can, by analogy with Venetian usage, be called a "perpero a monete." As in Venice, the amount of silver in Byzantine silver coins was reduced in the fourteenth century as silver rose in value. The reduction was so great that the perpero a oro became worth more than 12 ducatelli, and the gold ducat worth more than 24 ducatelli.

The contrast in 1366 between these two kinds of perperi of account can be summarized as follows:

> 1 perpero a oro = 1/2 of a gold ducat coin
> = 12 grossi a oro (units of account) or 24 carati
> 1 perpero a monete = 12, then 14, 15, and finally 16 ducatelli coins

Although there is considerable room for doubt as to when this contrast between two kinds of perperi was clearly recognized,[6] the above

---

[2]Grierson, *Byzantine Coins*, 13, 278–80, 291, 293–94; idem, "Byzantium and the Christian Levant," 141; Simon Bendall and P. J. Donald, *The Later Paleologan Coinage, 1282–1453* (London, 1979), 12.

[3]Bertelè, "Moneta veneziana," 24–25.

[4]Ibid., 19–22, 45–46, 126; ASV, Senato, Misti, reg. 18, fol. 66.

[5]See below, nn. 18–20.

[6]Peter Wirth ignores their use as denominations of a money of account. Contrary to Bertelè's interpretation, he considers that references to the hyperpyron or to the ducat in

equations appear to be the most reasonable interpretation of the situation, the inception of which was reflected by the clerk Antonio Barbieri, who recorded the receipts and expenses of the famed Green Count of Savoy during his crusade to the Byzantine capital and Bulgaria in 1366–67. His accounts indicate the circulation of gold perperi coins which he valued at 1/2 of a ducat.[7] On the other hand, when recording payments or receipts in silver coin, he called the ducatelli "ducati argenti monete Constantinopolis." He calculated by applying to them the generic Latin term "denarii" and called 12 of them a "solidus," 240 a "libra," using to denominate the multiples, not the perpero, but the terms with which his western background had made him familiar. To explain how he unified his accounts, he stated how many solidi and denarii of the silver coins were worth 1 ducat. He entered on the same list two different rates of conversion, namely, 2 soldi 6 denarii and 2 solidi 4 denarii to 1 ducat.[8] Valuing the ducat at 30 or 28 ducatelli meant valuing a perpero at 15 or 14 ducatelli.[9] This double valuation suggests a period of uncertainty during which the ties between the Byzantine perpero of account and the coins in use were changing and during which there could be doubt whether the perpero was based on the silver ducatelli as much as on partially gold coin. Since the ducatello of that time contained about 1.2 grams of fine silver,[10] valuing 30 ducatelli as equal to 1 ducat represented a bimetallic ratio of 10.1 to 1 ($30 \times [1.2/3.55]$), very little if any less than the bimetallic ratio in Italy about 1366.[11] The

---

amounts due or paid are evidence of the use of gold coin. It can certainly be argued plausibly in support of his main conclusion—that the Byzantine state shifted definitively from a gold standard to a silver standard only in the years 1414–15—that in imperial accounts the hyperpyron was a denomination in a gold-based money of account, but that that was true in all cases seems doubtful (see Peter Wirth, "Das Ende der römisch-byzantinischen Goldwährung," *Jahrbuch für Numismatik und Geldgeschichte* [Munich] 25 [1975]:113–22). Wirth corroborates, however, the conclusion that there was increased domestic use of silver coin.

[7]F. Bollati di Saint Pierre, *Illustrazioni della spedizione in Oriente di Amadeo VI, il Conte Verde*, Biblioteca storica italiana per cura della Deputazione di Storia Patria, 5, pt. 6 (Turin, 1900), 4, 25–27, and item 604, which records the purchase of several ducats at 2 perperi 1 carat per ducat; Eugene Cox, *The Green Count of Savoy* (Princeton, 1967), 223 n. 49, 227 n. 68, 233–38.

[8]Bollati, *Illustrazioni*, 26, 277. Similarly "den. asperorum argenti" are valued at 2 solidi 8 denarii to the gold ducat. Other silver coins were valued in terms of florins "boni ponderis" which were counted as equivalent to ducats (ibid., item 52 and p. 278; and Bertelè, "Moneta veneziana," 126). Notable is the conversion of silver coins of Bulgaria and Misiuri (Mesembria) into florins, with an equivalent in perperi (Bollati, *Illustrazioni*, 4, 26, 278, 96–105), but these conversions are irrelevant except to show that there were many other perperi auri and "ducati argenti monete" in addition to those of Constantinople. The latter are frequently referred to as "ponderis Pere" (ibid., 141–44), sometimes as "ad pondus Constantinopoli" (ibid., 10, 25, 27, 121, item 452, 278).

[9]Cf. Grierson, *Byzantine Coins*, 280, where a perpero is recorded as worth 15 ducatelli.

[10]Bertelè, "Moneta veneziana," 14, 127, 131; Bendall and Donald, *Later Paleologan Coinage*, 12–13.

[11]Cipolla, *Le avventure della lira*, 132; and above, chap. 18.

traditional lower valuation of gold in the Levant was reflected in the other rate, the valuation of the silver ducatello at 28 to a gold ducat, which represented a bimetallic ratio of 9.5 to 1 ($28 \times [1.2/3.55]$). The exact amount of fine metal in the perperi and ducatelli in circulation in Constantinople may well be questioned, but it seems clear that there was difficulty keeping a single money of account securely tied to both the symmetallic perpero and the silver ducatello.

A third kind of perpero of account, distinct from either that based on gold or that based on coins of fine silver, is mentioned in the records of papal tax collectors in 1351, a perpero with the value of 240 billon pennies.[12] Of the three perperi it had the lowest value; "iperperi," or "lire bagatini," were converted to gold florins at rates between 3 iperperi 3 soldi and 3 iperperi 10 soldi to a florin.[13] This third kind of perpero, a perpero based on black money, seems the least useful for the business of Constantinople, but it fathered a perpero that we will find in use in Venetian Romania.

So long as in the domestic trade of the Byzantine Empire 12 ducatelli were considered worth 1 perpero, perpero coins that contained enough gold to be accepted as worth 1/2 of a gold ducat were likely to be sent abroad for international payments. Perhaps for that reason, the Byzantine emperors decided in 1376, or shortly before, that instead of minting gold they would issue a new series of silver coins, coins that formed the basis for what is called a silver perpero.

The new series did not include any coin worth 1 perpero but was headed by a heavy silver coin, the stavraton, worth 1/2 of a perpero. Half-stavrata and quarter-stavrata were also coined. The smallest coins in the series were the 1/8 stavrata, which took the place of the basilica and were similarly called ducatelli by Venetians. These ducatelli contained only about 1.1 grams of silver, and the larger stavrata contained proportional amounts, so that the new "silver perpero" had a silver value of about 17.6 grams.[14] That is very close to half the value in silver that the Venetian market place had put on the ducat during the previous dozen years, when the price of a ducat at Venice had fluctuated between 72 and 74 soldi di piccoli. In the accounts of the crusade of the Green Count of Savoy the ducat was also valued at 74 Venetian soldi. Each Venetian soldo had a

[12]Giorgio Fedalto, "Rationes decimarum Romanie, sec. XIV," *Studi veneziani* 12 (1970):178, 179: "yperperis . . . currentibus valoris .XX. soldorum bagatinorum. . . ." It refers also to the perpero of Crete, of which 2 equaled 1 florin.

[13]Fedalto, "Rationes," 166 and app. 3.

[14]Bertelè, *Moneta veneziana*, 22–25, 135–39; idem, *Numismatique byzantine*, 86–87; Bendall and Donald, *Later Paleologan Coinage*, 13. Grierson, *Byzantine Coins*, 314, gives the weight of the stavraton as about 8.5 grams, which would have given the silver-based perpero a silver equivalent of 17 grams if the stavraton were 100 percent fine. He does not give its exact fineness.

BYZANTINE DUCATELLO, CA. 1300

Ducatello was the Venetian name for the basilicon, the type of silver coin most minted at Constantinople under Emperor Andronicus III (1328–41).

*Dumbarton Oaks Collection, Washington, D.C. (Grierson, Coins, 278–81, 295–99, pl. 83, no. 1317).*

pure silver content of 0.488 grams if at the official standard. When the ducat was at 72, its silver equivalent was 35.1 grams, (72 × 0.488), almost exactly twice that of 16 ducatelli, 35.2 grams (2 × 16 × 1.1). The comparison suggests describing the Byzantine coinage of 1376 as an effort to create a perpero based on silver coins, a perpero that would equal 1/2 of a ducat, as had the perpero based on the earlier Palaeologian gold coinage.[15]

The Venetian decision to coin the new grosso in 1379, coming so soon after the new Byzantine issues, may well have been a competitive response, an effort at Venice to offer equally attractive terms to bullion merchants. Or it also may have been an effort to stabilize the exchange rate between the two moneys of account in terms of silver at the same ratio as the exchange between the gold ducat of account and the gold perpero of account, at 1 to 2. The price of a gold ducat was rising above 74 soldi di piccoli, so that the silver value of the ducat based on a soldino coin containing 0.488 grams of silver was becoming definitely more than twice the silver equivalent of the Byzantine silver perpero, more even than 36.1 grams (74 × 0.488). But by giving their new grosso of 1379 less silver content than the old grosso and reducing at the same time the silver content of the soldino from 0.488 grams to 0.472 grams, the Venetians in 1379 made the silver value of the ducat at 74 a shade less than twice the silver value of the new silver perpero of 1376. After Venice's new coinage rules of 1379, the ducat quoted at 74 soldi had a silver value of 35 grams (74 × 0.472 = 34.928; or 74/4 × 1.89 = 34.965).[16]

In the following decades the silver equivalent of the silver perpero was reduced, just as was that of the Venetian soldo di piccoli as described above in chapter 18. The silver content of 16 ducatelli fell from 17.6 grams to about 14 grams in 1438 and to about 13 grams in 1453.[17] The gold ducat rose from 2 to 3 silver perperi, while in the same period its value in Venetian soldi di piccoli rose from 72 soldi in 1374 to 93 soldi in 1400 and 110 soldi in 1438.

---

[15]Bollati, *Illustrazioni*, 3, 25, 27, 277. See also above, chap. 18; and below, apps. A and D.

[16]See above, chap. 18, sec. ii; and below, table A.2. The bimetallic ratio after the minting of the new ducatelli and the new grossi was 9.8 to 1 or 9.9 to 1 (35.2/3.55 = 9.92; 34.965/3.55 = 9.85).

[17]In 1438 the silver content of a ducatello must have been about 0.88 grams, for the perpero of 16 ducatelli was worth about 14 grams of silver according to entries in Umberto Dorini and Tommaso Bertelè, eds., *Il libro dei conti di Giacomo Badoer, 1436–1440*, Il Nuovo Ramusio, 3 (Rome, 1956). Badoer gives two starting points. First, 89 overweight perperi weighed 4 livre. Then since 1 livra of Constantinople was equal to 1.33 marks of Venice (*Tarifa zoè noticia*, 15) or 317.2 grams (1.33 × 238.5), then 4 livre equaled 1,268.8 grams; 89 overweight perperi equaled 1,268.8 grams; 1 overweight perpero equaled 14.3 grams; 1 standard-weight perpero equaled less than 14.3 grams; and 1 ducatello equaled less than 0.89 grams (14.3/16). Second, 22.625 perperi was the price of 1 livra of silver (as bullion) or 317.2 grams of silver, so 1.0 perpero was the price of 14.0 grams (317.2/22.625), and 1 ducatello was the price of 0.875 grams (14/16).

STAVRATON OF EMPEROR MANUEL II (1391–1423)

The silver perpero instituted by the Byzantine emperors shortly after 1376 was not embodied in any coin of that name but was based on the stavraton worth 1/2 of a perpero as well as on smaller denominations such as a type of ducatello worth 1/16 of a perpero.

*Dumbarton Oaks Collection, Washington, D.C. (Grierson, Coins, 314–16, 385, pl. 95, no. 1513).*

After the coinage of the silver perpero, the gold-based perpero continued in use occasionally as a money of account. For a few decades there are references to perperi worth 1/2 of a ducat, as well as to perperi worth less. Perperi valued at 1/2 of a ducat are specified in Venetian decrees of 1375 and 1382[18] and are mentioned in the chronicles of Daniele di Chinazzo and Antonio Morosini.[19] But when freight rates on the Venetian galleys, which had been set in gold-based money of account, were converted into perperi, the subdivisions of silver perperi, namely, the carats of which there were 24 to a perpero, were used. For payment of freights for each gold ducat due or overdue the payments specified were: in 1382, 54 carats of the silver perpero; in 1386, 60 carats; in 1386–92, 56–60; in 1395, 72.[20] The corresponding values of the silver perpero in grossi of the ducato a oro would be: before 1382, 12 grossi; in 1382, 11 grossi; in 1386–92, 10 1/3–9 2/3, in 1395, 8.

The equation 1 gold ducat = 3 silver perperi seems to have been established in 1395, but only as a norm; actual transactions were concluded at rates that varied according to circumstances. This is clear from the accounts kept by Giacomo Badoer, a Venetian merchant in Constantinople, from 1436 to 1440. All his ledger entries were in perperi and carats. When he received other coin such as aspri, he converted their value into perperi, noting how many aspri were worth 1 perpero. When the transaction involved Byzantine silver coin or book credits in silver perperi, he made no conversion. For example, when he deposited 850 perperi in cash at the bank kept in Constantinople by another Venetian, Carlo Capello, he debited the bank for 850 perperi.[21] The "chontadi perp. 850" did not necessarily mean 850 coins, however. It meant coins of the series on which the silver perpero of account was based. He called the smallest of the series a "duchatelo" and valued it at 1/16 of a perpero (1 1/2 carats).[22] For Venetian ducats his rates of conversion varied considerably—from 2 perperi 22 carats to 3 perperi 10 carats, that is, from 70 to 82 carats.[23] The variation depended very much on the nature of the transaction, since some were in

[18]Bertelè, "Moneta veneziana," 31, 46–48, 127.

[19]Chinazzo, *Cronica,* 226, Morosini, *Cronica,* cod. 2048 (8331), vol. 1, p. 232.

[20]Bertelè, "Moneta veneziana," 48–50. The above sketch of the development of Byzantine money after 1320 relies heavily on Bertelè but differs from his exposition (1) in often interpreting "grossi" as referring not to the old grossi coins but to the grosso a oro which was purely a denomination of account for which there was no corresponding coin, and (2) in making a contrast between the gold perpero and a perpero based on silver even before 1370 or 1376.

[21]Dorini and Bertelè, eds., *Il libro dei conti di Giacomo Badoer,* 72, carta 36 and also carte 63, 183, 293, 371. To be sure, when he deposited overweight coins, he valued the coins as if they were silver, at 22 perperi 15 carats "la livra" (ibid., carta 180, p. 362; carta 186, p. 375, under 4 June 1438; see also the debit of 21 March on the account of the banker Chostantin Critopolo).

[22]Ibid., 16, 22, carte 8, 11; or abbreviated simply "d," 584–88, carte, 291–93.

[23]Bertelè, "Moneta veneziana," 28–29, 51–58.

bills of exchange involving an extension of credit for a substantial period.[24]

## ii. VENETIAN ROMANIA AND THE TORNESELLO

In Crete as well as in Constantinople, the perpero as a money of account split into a perpero based on gold and a perpero based on silver. The bifurcation in Crete is illuminated by some commercial correspondence of the 1340s. Before 1330 the perpero that dominated the Cretan system of money of account was counted as 12 grossi, and as in Venice, each grosso was considered divisible into 32 piccoli. Between 1250 and 1300 the Venetian grosso had become the basic coin of this Cretan money of account, and the rise of gold that had carried the ducat to 24 grossi made 1 ducat equal to 2 perperi. For a time, about 1305–30, the Cretan perpero may have had a bimetallic base, being tied equally to 12 old silver grossi and to 1/2 of a gold ducat.[25]

In 1333, soon after the issuance of the new silver coins, the soldino and mezzanino, the Senate ordered that they be accepted in Crete and other colonies and that the rectors there be so instructed.[26] When the Senate voted to send money to the Venetian authorities in Crete, it ordered that the sum of over 20,000 perperi be sent "in monetis."[27] The effect was to make the soldino instead of the grosso the basic silver coin of the Cretan money of account headed by the perpero. In 1344 a merchant in Venice, Pignol Zucchello, was informed by his correspondent in Candia that soldini were circulating there and thus it would be more profitable to send them than to send ducats.[28] In reporting collections made in Crete to be paid to creditors in Venice, the correspondent referred to "perperi XXXII a munete" as well as to grossi and piccoli "a munete," adding in at least one case that the repayment should be made in soldini, since the loan had been received in that form.[29] The perpero of Crete and the grosso of Crete thus became denominations of account worth, respectively, 32 soldini ($12 \times [32/12]$) and 2 2/3 soldini ($32/12$). Their metallic value depended on the silver content of the soldino.[30]

At the same time, the gold ducat was valued in Crete above its Venetian legal value of 64 soldini, although only at a slight premium.[31] A

---

[24]Dorini and Bertelè, eds., *Il libro dei conti di Giacomo Badoer,* carte 82, 83, 106, 133, 216, 390.

[25]See above, chaps. 13, sec. ii, and 14, sec. iii.

[26]ASV, Senato, Misti, reg. 15, fol. 66v (13 March 1333), transcribed below in app. G.

[27]Ibid., reg. 21, fols. 17v, 31 (1343). On other governmental shipments of soldini to Romania see Stahl, *The Venetian Tornesello.*

[28]Morozzo della Rocca, ed., *Lettere a Pignol Zucchello,* 27.

[29]Ibid., 27, 45.

[30]Stahl, *The Venetian Tornesello,* sec. 1, on the circulation of soldini.

[31]In a price list dated 19 March 1344, the price of a gold ducat was 64 soldi 4 piccoli; the price of a gold florin was 61–61 1/2 soldi (Morozzo della Rocca, ed., *Lettere a Pignol Zucchello,* 23). A letter of 4 October 1344 values a ducat at 2 perperi 3 piccoli (ibid., 24).

gold coin more frequently mentioned in Pignol Zucchello's correspondence was the "bisanto," the Alexandrian gold dinar of which the standard gold content was 4.2 grams, so that it was commonly reckoned as worth 1 1/6 ducats or florins.[32] In the letters to Pignol it is regularly equated with 2 perperi and usually with 30 grossi,[33] once with 32 1/2 grossi.[34]

There is an apparent contradiction in equating the perpero sometimes with 12 grossi and sometimes with 1/2 of a ducat worth 30 or 32 grossi. The contradiction disappears, however, when the existence of two perperi is recognized: 1 perpero a oro = 1/2 bezant (Alexandrian coin), 12 grossi a oro, or 15 to 16 grossi a monete; while 1 perpero a monete = 32 soldini coins or 12 grossi a monete.

The value of the ducat and the florin as coins compared with the bezant and the perpero a oro seems to have been uncertain, probably because it was changing during the flood of gold westward in those years. There are some indications that the ducat, the florin, and the bezant were all three equated with 2 perperi a oro, but there are other indications that the ducat was rated higher than the florin but equal to the Alexandrian bezant.[35] Such a rating, in spite of the different gold contents of the two coins, is not incredible in view of the Venetian political position and the bullion flows of the 1340s.

The difference between the dinar and the ducat was eliminated in the fifteenth century. In Crete as in Venice, a grosso a oro clearly then meant 1/24 of a gold ducat.[36]

Meanwhile, the lessening of the silver content of the soldino and its replacement by the tornesello, shortly to be explained, reduced the value of Crete's perpero a monete compared with that of the ducat. Giacomo Badoer valued the Cretan perpero based on silver at 2/3 of the perpero of Constantinople,[37] that is, at 2/9 of a gold ducat. Much later the silver-based perpero of Crete went to as low as 1/6 of a ducat.[38]

In addition to the perperi of Constantinople and of Crete, a third kind of perpero on the Ternaria's thirteenth-century list of exchange rates

[32]Ashtor, *Histoire des prix,* 39, 274–75; idem, *Les métaux précieux,* 28; Pegolotti, *Pratica,* 72, 75; Bacharach, "The Dinar versus the Ducat," 82–86.

[33]Morozzo della Rocca, ed., *Lettere a Pignol Zucchello,* 7, 8, 13, 15, 17, 77.

[34]Ibid., 14.

[35]Ibid., preface, where on p. xii Morozzo della Rocca says, "sono calcolati alla pari ducati d'oro, fiorini, e bisanti di Alessandria," ignoring the variations here analyzed (see above, n. 31; and Morozzo della Rocca, ed., *Lettere a Pignol Zucchello,* 117). The gold ducat is equated with 2 perperi in 1347 (Morozzo della Rocca, ed., *Lettere a Pignol Zucchello,* 98, 102).

[36]Grierson, "La moneta veneziana," 90–91; Bacharach, "The Dinar versus the Ducat," 88–89.

[37]Dorini and Bertelè, eds., *Il libro dei conti di Giacomo Badoer,* carte 56, 59.

[38]Hippolyte Noiret, ed., *Documents inédits pour servir à l'histoire de la domination vénitienne en Crète, de 1380 à 1485, tirés des archives de Venise,* Bibliothèque des Ecoles Françaises d'Athènes et de Rome, 21 (Paris, 1892), xvi; Thiriet, ed., *Délibérations des assemblées vénitiennes,* vol. 2, item 1281, which mentions a payment at 4 soldi per ducat; Stahl, *The Venetian Tornesello.*

was important in the fourteenth and fifteenth centuries also, namely, the perpero of Clarentza or of Morea. It was the perpero based on black money mentioned in 1351 in the accounts of the papal tax collectors. On the Ternaria list it was identified as the perpero worth 20 "asterlini" ("ubi currunt asterlini xx pro perpero"), but in Pegolotti's time, as he says explicitly, there were no asterlini, or "sterlini" as he calls them, in circulation.[39] The sterlino was only a denomination of account intermediate between the perpero and billon coins called torneselli.

The term "tornesello" was applied first to pennies (deniers) minted for local use by the French nobles who had taken over central and southern Greece. They were called "torneselli," and sometimes "tornesi piccoli," to distinguish them from the tornesi grossi derived from Louis IX's gros tournois. They were minted by the dukes at Achaia and Athens, at Thebes, and most voluminously at Clarentza (Kyllene) before their dukedom was shattered by the Catalan Company in 1311; thereafter the products of those mints declined in both quality and quantity.[40] The decline presented the Venetians with an opportunity to make handsome profit out of supplying the billon coinage that the region needed. Late in the dogeship of Andrea Dandolo, in 1353, the same year that the first type of soldino, which at best was only 2/3 silver, was replaced by a smaller soldino of the higher fineness, the mint was ordered to coin torneselli in large numbers and to send them to Venetian officials in Romania for use in paying expenses.[41]

The torneselli were to be put into circulation as worth 3 piccoli. At that value, they fitted into the systems of money of account in use in Morea, described by Pegolotti. The torneselli that had been minted in Clarentza had been worth 1/4 of the sterlino and 1/80 of the perpero of Morea. In mid-century the largest denomination in that money of account was still the perpero, but the sterlino as the denomination of 1/20 of a perpero had been largely replaced by the denomination soldo, more familiar to the Italians. Since the soldo was divided into 12 piccoli, a tornesello valued at 3 piccoli was worth 1/80 of a perpero.[42]

[39]See below, app. G, doc. 1; Pegolotti, *Pratica*, 116–17; and Antonio Carile, *La rendita feudale nella Morea latina del XIV secolo* (Bologna, 1974), 73–75, which emphasizes that practically no gold coin circulated in Morea.

[40]Metcalf, "The Currency of Deniers Tournois," 39–53; idem, *Coinage in the Balkans*, 67, 220, 232. The distinction between tornesi grossi of fine silver and tornesi piccoli of billon is clearly made in Pegolotti, *Pratica*, 289, 291, 437, and in Ciano, ed., *"Pratica della mercatura" datiniana*, 90–91; but Venetian sources frequently use simply "tornesi" or "turonenses" instead of "torneselli." It is clear that tornesi piccoli are meant, for no tornesi grossi were minted by Crusader states in Greece (*Cap. Broche*, fol. 24; Stussi, ed., *Zibaldone da Canal*, 54; Thiriet, ed. *Délibérations des assemblées vénitiennes*, 1:314; Stahl, *The Venetian Tornesello*, sec. 1).

[41]The decree, unknown to Papadopoli (1:179–80), is in *PMV*, doc. 119; Thiriet, ed. *Délibérations des assemblées vénitiennes*, 1:314; and *DQ*, 3:28, doc. 93.

[42]Schlumberger, *Numismatique de l'orient latin*, 311; Stahl, *The Venetian Tornesello*, sec. 2. Pegolotti, *Pratica*, 116–17, says that the perpero in "tutta la Morea" was 20 sterlini. Although

In Crete the torneselli were fitted into the money of account based on the soldino[43] and headed by the current perpero. The denominations then in use in Crete were:

$$1 \text{ perpero} = 12 \text{ grossi}$$
$$= 12 \times 32 = 384 \text{ piccoli}$$
$$= 384/12 = 32 \text{ soldi di piccoli} = 32 \text{ soldini}$$
$$= 32 \times 4 = 128 \text{ torneselli}$$

In 1350 only the soldino, in 1400 only the tornesello, was represented by coins actually circulating. In contrast, the denominations used in continental Greece were

$$1 \text{ perpero} = 20 \text{ soldi di piccoli} = 140 \text{ piccoli}$$
$$= 20 \times 4 = 80 \text{ torneselli}$$

and only the tornesello was represented by coins in circulation.

General substitution of "soldo" for "sterlino" in the moneys of account used in Romania had been promoted by the extensive circulation there of the Venetian soldini between 1332 and 1353. Although the soldino then being minted, being less fine than the Venetian grosso, did not win wide acceptance in Constantinople or Syria, it circulated extensively in the Balkans, including Greece, to judge from the number found in hoards and the extent to which it was imitated.[44] After 1353 the large issues of overvalued torneselli left less room for the circulation of soldini.[45]

The Venetian torneselli resembled the earlier deniers in having on the obverse a Greek cross slightly splayed at the ends and the initials of the

he gives for Coron and Modon 24 sterlini to a perpero (p. 153), the equation of a perpero with 20 sterlini may have prevailed at Coron and Modon also (see Stahl, *The Venetian Tornesello,* sec. 2). At least after soldi replaced sterlini as the intermediate denomination of account, sterlini and soldi both were always equal to 12 piccoli, not piccoli coins but piccoli as the smallest accounting units. The passage on the money of Clarentza and Morea in the *Zibaldone da Canal* (p. 54, carta 33v) presents difficulties. After saying in line 13 that the perpero was "s. 6, dir 8 [that is, 80 denari] de tornesi," he says in line 14 that grossi of Venice are worth 8 torneselli, having written *8* by mistake, it would seem, for *80*. On p. 58, carta 35v, the "mane XX" in line 30 must mean 20 sterlini (each worth 4 torneselli), for the number of torneselli in a perpero is again given as 80. According to Peter Topping, "Le régime agraire dans le Péleponnèse latin au XIV siècle," *Hellenisme contemporain,* 2d ser., 10 (1956):259, 284n, payments due to feudal or seigniorial lords were recorded in 1336 in "yperpera, sterlinos, and tornenses"; in 1380 in iperperi and soldi. Papal tax collectors used the soldo as the subdivision of the perpero in the mid-fourteenth century (Fedalto, "Rationes," 166, 178).

43Stahl, *The Venetian Tornesello,* secs. 2 and 8. The use in Crete as well as in Morea of "tornesi" from Clarentza is indicated in Morozzo della Rocca, ed., *Lettere a Pignol Zucchello,* 24, whereas ducats are said to be worth "perperi due e uno tornese l'uno" and 5 ducats are calculated to be worth 10 perperi 15 piccoli.

44Metcalf, "The Currency of Deniers Tournois," 55–58; Bollati, *Illustrazioni,* 159; H. Cox, *The Caporelli Hoard,* Numismatic Notes and Monographs, 43 (New York, 1930); above, n. 27.

45Stahl, *The Venetian Tornesello,* sec. 2, nn. 32, 35.

issuing ruler, duke or doge. On the reverse, instead of the castle from which the coins took their name were Venice's winged lion, symbol of St. Mark, holding a book, and the legend "Vexilifier Venetiarum" ("Standardbearer of the Venetians").[46] They weighed at most only 0.65 grams and averaged about 0.6 grams, less than those minted earlier at Clarentza, and their silver content was much less.[47] Being only 0.111 fine, a Venetian tornesello contained only about 0.07 grams of silver, and later issues contained even less.[48]

The circulation of Venetian torneselli lowered the silver equivalent of the perpero as compared with its value as described in Pegolotti's manual.[49] The devaluation may have occurred between Pegolotti's time and 1353; but it seems clear that the Venetians set the silver content of their coin low enough that there would be no danger that it would suffer the fate of "good money" that could be "driven out" by deteriorated previous issues functioning as "bad money." On the contrary, when circulating side by side with silver currency, torneselli could function as the "bad money" and drive out "good" soldini or grossi. The silver content of 4 torneselli was about 1/2 that of 1 soldino (0.28 grams compared with 0.53 grams). If introduced into Crete and Morea by Venetian merchants buying wine, honey, hides, and other wares exported to Venice, their use would spread by the operation of Gresham's law.

Actually they were put into circulation mainly by the Venetian officials who used them to pay expenses in erecting fortifications, outfitting fleets, paying off crews, and so on. The mint's production of torneselli mushroomed on the eve of the War of Chioggia and after that war under Doge Antonio Venier (1382–1400). In 1386, contemporaries estimated the annual output as 14,000 ducats' worth, which meant about 4.5 million coins. Estimates based largely on die studies indicated that "the rate of minting of torneselli was about two million coins per year in the reign of Andrea Contarini (1368–1382), rose to about five and a half million under

---

[46]Ibid., sec. 3.

[47]Stahl (ibid., sec. 5), after thorough analysis, concludes that the legal standard weight, at least in 1363 and 1368, was 0.65 grams, although the average weight of the coins examined was nearer 0.60, and it fell after 1382 to about 0.55 (see his fig. 3). On the official standards, not followed in practice, see below, app. A, sec. ix.

[48]Stahl, *The Venetian Tornesello*, sec. 6, concludes that the legally prescribed fineness of 0.111 was maintained.

[49]Pegolotti gives the fineness of the torneselli coined in Morea, before the Venetians minted their torneselli, in the Florentine manner as 3 once 12 denari in his list of alloys (*Pratica*, 291), but in two other places he gives it as 2 once 12 denari, or 2 1/2 once (ibid., 116, 118). Probably the higher fineness refers to the period when his coin list was first compiled. He gives the weight as 1/400 of a libbra (presumably the Florentine libbra, for which see Cipolla, *Le avventure della lira*, 127). On the coins used in the Morea see also Carile, *La rendita feudale*, esp. 74 n. 145.

## VENETIAN TORNESELLO

In Crete and much of the Greek peninsula earlier torneselli were replaced by this Venetian type begun in 1353 and minted in large quantities under Antonio Venier (1382–1400).

*Obv.*: **+.ANTO'VENERIO.DVX.** Cross patée in circle.

*Rev.*: **+.VEXILIFER.VENETIA4** Winged lion crouching and facing front, holding the gospel in his front paws.

*B, 16.7 mm, 0.579 gr. Museo Bottacin, inv. no. 248 (Papadopoli, 1: 231 no. 7).*

429

Antonio Venier (1382–1400), and dropped again to about two million a year by the reign of Tommaso Mocenigo (1414–1423)."[50]

The torneselli were shipped from the Venetian mint in bags each weighing 20–40 kilograms and containing 30,000–60,000 coins. Many such heavy bags were sent to the duke of Crete, to the admirals of Venice's patrolling fleets, and to the castellans at such outposts as Coron and Modon. Venetian officials were ordered to use them both to pay their own salaries and to pay all their employees, including of course the craftsmen and unskilled laborers needed to maintain fleets and fortifications.[51]

Although these governmental expenditures were the chief means of pushing (one might say "marketing") torneselli, their use spread far beyond the territories under Venetian rule. Among the coins found at such well-explored sites as Athens and Corinth, 92–97 percent of those minted between 1350 and 1450 are Venetian torneselli. In the hoards discovered in central and southern Greece and also in those from the northern areas of Epirus and Thessaly, lands under Byzantine, Albanian, and Serbian rulers in the fourteenth century and Turkish rulers in the fifteenth, torneselli dominate.[52] Soldini are comparatively scarce. To be sure, this does not prove that no soldini circulated, for, as Alan Stahl has pointed out, the soldini, because of their higher value, may have been removed before the finds were marketed or their contents published. The soldini minted after 1353 were tiny, weighing little more than 1/2 a gram, much less than torneselli. But being 0.965 fine, a soldino contained almost 10 times as much silver as a tornesello.

The wide use of Venetian torneselli resulted partly from the fact that Venice was the main market for the exports of that region. It indicates also the real need there for such a coin, a need not being met by any mint other than that of Venice. The large additions that the minting of torneselli brought to the Venetian treasury were not only the fruits of monetary manipulation; they were also profits from an industrial enterprise that met a substantial need.

By 1400 the only coins commonly circulating in Crete and much of mainland Greece were gold ducats and torneselli. As a consequence, all the silver-based and billon-based moneys of account—the perpero a monete, the soldo, and the denaro piccolo—were based on the tornesello.

The gain of the Venetian treasury from this export of torneselli can be seen from two viewpoints. About 50 percent of the torneselli made from silver used for that purpose were retained by the mint as a mint charge. It can be estimated that out of that 50 percent, 25 percent went into the cost of

---

[50]Stahl, *The Venetian Tornesello*, sec. 7, and, at the end of the section, his conclusion drawn from die studies, quoted above.

[51]Ibid., sec. 3, nn. 51–63.

[52]Ibid., sec. 4.

copper and labor, leaving 25 percent as profit for the Commune.[53] At the same time, the government gained by paying torneselli out in Romania at a value about twice as high as the value justified by their intrinsic content compared with the intrinsic content of the coins that previously had been the link coins of the moneys of account in use in Romania.

Consider first the situation in Crete, where the evidence is clearest. When the Cretan current perpero was based on the soldini coined at Venice between 1332 and 1353, its silver equivalent was about 20 grams (32 × 0.641 = 20.5). If the new finer but smaller soldino coined in the last years of Andrea Dandolo had become the link coin of the Cretan current perpero, its silver equivalent would have been 17 grams (32 × 0.533).[54] The silver content of the 128 torneselli that were legally declared worth 1 current perpero and paid out to crews and laborers at that rate was only about 9 grams, since each tornesello, even those first issued, contained only about 0.07 grams of silver (128 × 0.07 = 8.96). The higher cost of manufacturing the smaller, largely copper coins accounted for only a minor part of the difference.

As long as torneselli were minted only in amounts equal to the need for them, their scarcity value enabled them to circulate at their legal value even though that legal value was almost twice their silver value and much above their intrinsic value, that is, much above even an intrinsic value that included copper and labor. That seems to have been the situation before about 1390, for until then there was little divergence between the values of the two moneys of account—the soldo of Crete, which was 1/32 of the current perpero of Crete, and the soldo of Venice, which was 1/20 of a lira di piccoli. When gold ducats were priced in those moneys of account, both soldi were valued as if they were considered linked to the soldino coin. As the amount of silver in the soldino declined, the ducat rose in parallel fashion in both, until in the early fifteenth century it was valued in Venice at about 90–94 soldi, in Crete at about 96–100 soldi.[55]

Then these values of the ducat began to diverge further. Having been minted in large quantities, the torneselli ceased to have the scarcity and utility value that had enabled them to circulate at far above their intrinsic value for some decades. The large number coined and a decline in their average silver content combined to lessen the relative value of the money of account used in Crete.[56] In the 1420s the price in Crete was 120–40 soldi, whereas in Venice the ducat rose only to 104 soldi in the 1420s

[53]Ibid., sec. 3; and below, app. A, sec. ix.
[54]See above, n. 43; and below, table A.2. If the mezzanino coined by Andrea Dandolo had been a link coin of the Cretan soldo and perpero, the silver equivalent of the Cretan money of account would have been between the two figures, but the circulation of mezzanini in Crete is doubtful.
[55]Stahl, *The Venetian Tornesello*, secs. 8 and 9, figs. 9 and 10; and below, app. D.
[56]Cf. Stahl, *The Venetian Tornesello*, sec. 10.

and to 110 in the 1430s.[57] Venetian officials in Crete complained repeatedly about being paid in torneselli at 96 soldi to the ducat, the rate set at the beginning of the fifteenth century.[58]

Although some effort was made to check the fall of the tornesello below its legal value, by 1424 it was already legal to demand 20 percent more in payment for a ducat if the payment was made in torneselli instead of in soldini or new grossi. Actually, the tornesello was being given an exchange value about 30 percent above its silver value compared with that of the soldini being minted in 1424.[59] In 1444, 4 lire or 80 soldi of torneselli were declared worth only 60 soldi of "good" currency, and in 1464 a new official exchange rate for Crete valued the tornesello at 1/6 of a soldino, a devaluation of 50 percent compared with the official rate of 1/4 of a soldino a century earlier.[60]

In other parts of Romania, as well as Crete, the tornesello became the link coin and determined the relative value of the perpero as a money of account. Because the perpero of Morea was equal to 80 torneselli,[61] it was worth just about 2/3 of the perpero of Crete which was equal to 128 torneselli. The resulting equation of 1 perpero of Crete with 1 1/2 perperi of Morea is almost exactly the valuation used in Badoer's accounting in 1438.[62]

In converting the other perperi into the perperi of Constantinople, in which he kept his accounts, Giacomo Badoer valued the perperi based on torneselli above their silver values, but the overvaluations of the money of account based on torneselli was only 20–30 percent, an amount not entirely out of proportion to the higher cost of production of the smaller, largely copper coins.

The falling exchange value of the tornesello had an effect on the terms of trade between Venice and all the parts of Romania where the tornesello became the basic coin. When buying wax, dyestuffs, nuts, honey, or wine, Venetian merchants had good reason to pay constant attention to the rates of conversion from the perperi and soldi in which their

---

[57]Ibid., figs. 9 and 10 and sec. 9; and below, app. D.

[58]Stahl, *The Venetian Tornesello,* nn. 122, 134.

[59]Since the price of ducats in soldi di piccoli was about 100 soldi (see below, app. D) and the silver content of the soldino minted in 1421–29 was 0.380 grams (see below, table A.2), the silver value of the ducat in Venice was 38 grams at that time. The silver equivalent of 120 "soldi di tornesi" was the silver content of 480 torneselli, or 29 grams (480 × 0.06). Finally, 38/29 = 1.31 (cf. Stahl, *The Venetian Tornesello,* 55–61).

[60]Ibid., sec. 9, nn. 135, 136.

[61]On the perperi of Morea and of Modon see above, n. 42.

[62]Dorini and Bertelè, eds., *Il libro dei conti di Giacomo Badoer,* carta 188, p. 378; and the compilation of the exchange rates used by Badoer (on p. 100) by Edward Peragallo in "Jachomo Badoer, Renaissance Man of Commerce and His Ledger," *Accounting and Business Research* 10, no. 37A, *Special Accounting History Issue* (1980), 100.

purchases were priced in Morea or Crete to the ducats or soldi in which they priced these wares for sale in Italy. They expressed the rate in the same way that it was expressed in governmental regulation, namely, by comparing two different prices for the ducat, a price to be paid in soldini or grossi and a price to be paid in torneselli. Both of these prices were expressed in soldi di piccoli. For example, in December 1424, when the market price for gold ducats when paid in soldini or new grossi was 100 soldi di piccoli, the price—if payment was made in torneselli—was 120–22 soldi, or 480–88 torneselli. The difference between 100 and 120–22 was called the "lazo dei tornesi."[63]

The lazo dei tornesi probably varied considerably not only from decade to decade but according to circumstances. A very high lazio is referred to in a proposal, not passed, to regulate the payment of freights due in "Romania bassa" on wares loaded in Venice. For each ducat due, a payment of "160 soldi de tornesis" was called for, that is 640 torneselli compared with 488 torneselli (122 soldi).[64] But the proposed exchange rate in Romania bassa probably included some penalty for late payment of freight due. And there were probably differences between official allowances for the lazio and commercial rates. Lowering the lazio from 22 to 20 soldi in 1424 was an official act concerning an official rate.[65]

Some of the effects on prices and on real wages in Crete of this drop in the exchange value of the tornesello and of the perpero based on it are indicated in a senatorial decree of 1422 concerning seamen's wages. Declaring that the value of "moneta turneseorum" had declined so much that oarsmen could not live on the current wage, it raised the pay of galeotti recruited in Crete from 6 1/2 perperi per month to 8.[66]

Tracing the effects on the terms of trade of changing exchange rates between Venice's own moneys of account and those in use in Romania would raise many questions about the Venetian economy that cannot be developed here but deserve attention. The exchange rates affected not only the cost of Venetian armaments in its overseas empire; they affected also the cost of many foodstuffs and raw materials consumed in Venice, as well as the costs of many wares exported by Venice. Did the exchange rates give Venetian merchants selling wax and hides or Venetian artisans selling candles and shoes advantages over competitors who depended on competing sources of supply?

[63]See *Cap. Broche*, fol. 24 (20 December 1424).
[64]ASV, Senato, Misti, reg. 53, fol. 49v (1 June 1420, "non capta"), a proposal regarding payments in the area known as "Romania bassa usque Negroponte."
[65]ASV, Collegio, Notatorio, reg. 6, fol. 3v.
[66]ASV, Senato, Misti, reg. 54, fol. 75. Cf. Stahl, *The Venetian Tornesello*, sec. 9, last paragraph.

## iii. BEYOND THE ALPS

In the countries north and west of Venice the fall of gold was not accompanied by any such changes in the moneys of account as occurred in the Levant. The number of European mints regularly issuing gold coins increased markedly between 1320 and 1350, and a few new moneys of account based on gold became important;[67] but the principal moneys of account used in Germany, France, the Netherlands, and England had always been based on silver coins and continued to be.

The relative values of the Venetian gold ducat and the currencies of her western trading partners can be inferred from the quotations on the florin. The Florentines had made their coin widely admired and accepted, while the Venetian ducat was comparatively unknown until the mid-fourteenth century. Since the ducat and the florin had practically the same gold content, the exchange rates quoted for the florin in account books, manuals, contracts, and laws can be used in connection with the mint prices and content of silver coins to indicate the timing of changes in the bimetallic ratio.

Official values were not all in accord with the commercial values of the two metals, to be sure. While some official values were efforts to adjust to the changing supply and demand reflected in market values and others were honest efforts to affect those values, many others appear as less honest efforts to pass off by decree coins of which the metallic value was far lower than pretended. For one reason or another, a lightening or debasement of silver coinage comparable to but generally more extreme than that in Venice occurred in most every country and decreased the silver equivalent of the units of the money of account based on silver. Even when the quotations of the ducat or florin in the national or local money of account remained at former levels, the amount of silver exchanged for a ducat or other gold coin declined as the bimetallic ratio fell from 16 to 1 or 14 to 1 to 10 to 1.

In the west generally the turning point from a rising to a falling bimetallic ratio seems to have come shortly after the meeting of the kings of Bohemia and Hungary in 1327. In the fourteenth century, German miners in those two kingdoms produced more than 1/2 of all the silver and 11/12 of all the gold being mined in Europe, according to an informed guess.[68] During the previous two or three decades the boom of silver

[67]Fournial, *Histoire monétaire,* 81–82, 142–44; Wolff, *Commerce et marchands de Toulouse,* 303–54; and below, n. 78.

[68]Hóman, *Geschichte,* 2:349. Like many other of Hóman's sweeping statements, this estimate cannot be backed or challenged by adequate statistics. But most of Hóman's somewhat more specific estimates about Bohemian and Hungarian output are accepted by Janáček, "L'argent tchèque," pp. 247–54, as explained below, in n. 72, although Janáček raises somewhat Hóman's estimate of the output from Bohemia of what Janáček calls "Czech" silver. Janáček does not cite Hóman's *Geschichte* nor its Hungarian version but Hóman's article "La

production in Bohemia and the disruption of gold mining in Hungary had been a main factor in the comparative fall in the value of silver. The highest bimetallic ratios reported anywhere in medieval or early modern Europe, some over 20 to 1, are from Germany and Hungary.[69] At their meeting in 1327 the two kings agreed to coordinate the coinage of silver groats modeled on the Bohemian "groschen" and that of gold florins or "gulden" (imitations of the Florentine florins in weight, fineness, and design), which the new Angevin dynasty in Hungary had started minting in 1323. In Hungary their values were so fixed as to express a bimetallic ratio of 14.5 to 1.[70]

Even more influential in the next decade were the changes in Hungarian mining law, which made it more like the Bohemian code. Previously in Hungary, landlords had had reason to hide deposits and hamper mining, because mineral rights had gone to miners, who had shared with the king. The new law gave landlords a large enough share and a large enough role in the collection of the king's share from miners that nobles promoted the opening of new mines.[71] Gold mining especially boomed. At peak production in the 1330s, while Bohemia was still producing about

circolazione." The more detailed and convincing description of the expansion of Hungarian gold and silver production after 1327 that Hóman gives in his *Geschichte* is probably less known because published in wartime Nazi Germany. His standing now may suffer from his having been a Hungarian fascist.

[69]Watson, "Back to Gold," 23–25; presumably, Bohemia, as part of the Holy Roman Empire, is included under Germany in his table.

[70]Hóman, *Geschichte*, 2:346–51. The Hungarian florin of prescribed weight and fineness containing 3.52 grams fine was declared equal to 16 Hungarian silver groschen, lighter than the Bohemian groschen which provided the model. Each Hungarian groschen contained 3.19 grams of fine silver (cf. Spufford and Wilkinson, *Interim Listing*, 338–39). Hence, 16 × 3.19 grams silver = 3.52 grams gold; and 51.04 silver/3.52 gold = 14.5/1. In 1337–38 the king declared the groschen no longer legal tender and made gold the only standard of value. He changed to the gold standard because, Hóman says (pp. 351–53), the florin had risen to 18 and then 20, 22, and 24 groschen. Hóman gives no indication that the Hungarian groschen had then been debased, as seems likely, since he says (p. 352) that Hungarian groschen had been driving out Bohemian groschen, which were so debased later that under Wenceslas IV (1378–1400) they weighed only 1.88 grams and were only 0.595 fine (see F. Graus, "La crise monétaire," 446–47).

[71]Hóman, *Geschichte*, 2:355–57. The Neapolitan practice with which the Angevin rulers were familiar also favored the change and gave impetus to the royal monopoly of the bullion trade, but Hóman considers Demetrius Nekcsei, "one of the leading statesmen of the age," as the builder of the new Hungarian mining and minting administration (ibid., 2:334–36). On the location of the mines north of Budapest and the technique and organization of the smelting see Oszkár Paulinyi, "The Crown Monopoly of the Refining Metallurgy of Precious Metals and the Technology of the Cameral Refineries in Hungary and Transylvania in the Period of Advanced and Late Feudalism (1325–1700) with Data and Output," in Kellenbenz, ed., *Precious Metals*, 27–39; and Wolfgang von Stromer, "Die Struktur von Produktion und Verteilung von Bunt- und Edelmetallen an der Wende vom Mittelalter zur Neuzeit und ihre bestimmenden Faktoren," in ibid., 13–26.

20,000 kilograms of silver per year, Hungary was producing about 10,000 kilograms of silver and 1,000–2,000 kilograms of gold.[72]

To maintain the relatively high value set on gold in spite of the high output, the king of Hungary attempted to monopolize not only the minting but the whole processing of gold ore. No private buying and selling or exporting of gold bullion was legal. Minting and ore-refining stations were established near all mining centers. Their operation was farmed out to contractors, who paid the miners the stipulated prices for ore according to its grade, hired silversmiths and goldsmiths to refine and coin according to the royal specifications in their contracts concerning the weight and fineness of the coins, and paid out coins at the values there stipulated. The relation between the prices they paid for metal and labor on the one hand and the prices they charged for the coins on the other enabled them to pay the crown about 35 percent on silver coin and 40 percent on gold.[73]

Legally only the coined silver groschen and gold florins could be exported, but the very high rate of profit sought by the royal monopoly must have inspired smugglers and perhaps corrupted contractors. Certainly bullion as well as coin from Bohemia and Hungary found its way through Regensburg and Vienna over the Alps to Venice.

If we had sufficient evidence about the precious metals exported from the Bohemian and Hungarian kingdoms, we would probably find that during the first three decades of the fourteenth century the flow of silver westward through such cities as Nuremberg, Frankfort, and Strasbourg or Basel into the Netherlands and eastern France rivaled in volume the flow southward over the Alps to Venice. Moreover, a westward flow of gold greater in value than that of silver after 1330 is suggested by the evidence concerning the change in the bimetallic ratio in France. A decline from the height of 16.6 to 1 indicated by Pegolotti's median began at about the same time that gold began to fall in Venice. When the French king issued the "royal d'or" of December 1330, its value in livres tournois,

---

[72]Hóman, *Geschichte,* 2:354. Janáček ("L'argent tchèque," 247–48) accepts Hóman's figure for the annual silver production of all Europe's mints and ups the total for Bohemia from 25,000 to 30,000 kg annually in 1300–1330. He expresses skepticism concerning the role Hóman assigned Hungarian gold. Hóman estimated 1,000 kg of gold from Hungary annually, and a figure twice as large is given in the more recent work of Artur Pohl, *Ungarische Goldgulden,* 8: Silesia, 80–100 kg; Bohemia, 70 kg; Hungary, 2,000 kg. Paulinyi says that the figures from contemporary bookkeeping are very few before 1486 but gives gold production in 1434–35 as 1,599 marks (about 400 kg) from the Garam area, north of Budapest. He considers credible the chronicler's statement that in 1343 King Louis I sent to Naples 21,000 marks of gold and 27,000 marks of silver out of the treasure accumulated by his father in ten years. Although specific figures are lacking for the earlier years, Paulinyi concluded: "In my opinion the production of noble metals in Hungary reached its highest level between 1330 and 1380, when (at least in the case of gold) the upper layers were mined, which were more concentrated due to oxydation" (Paulinyi, "The Crown Monopoly," 37–38).

[73]Hóman, *Geschichte,* 2:358; Paulinyi, "The Crown Monopoly," 34.

the money of account based primarily on the silver gros or sous, made 1 gram of coined gold equal in value to 12–14 grams of coined silver.[74] Exchange rates used in the account books of the big Florentine firm of the Peruzzi for 1335–37 varied in a range indicating bimetallic ratios of about 13 to 1 to 16 to 1.[75] A more decisive drop came in 1337, when the French minted the gold piece called in England the florin de l'écu. It was given a price that expressed the ratio 11.5 to 1,[76] the same as the ratio set in Venice a half-dozen years earlier with the coinage of the soldino, in 1331–32.[77] French coinage then reflected the ratio 11.5 to 1 for the next decade and also in 1360–61. In between, during a disastrous period of the Hundred Years' War, bimetallic ratios below 10 to 1 or 9 to 1 and even below 8 to 1 were

[74]Fournial, *Histoire monétaire,* 93–94, gives 40 livres 10 sous tournois as the commercial price of a mark of gold in 1329, when 48 sous tournois was the price of a mark of silver, a ratio of 16.88 to 1 (810/48). But in crying down newly issued coins, the ratio was made 14.2 to 1. In April 1330 in a new issue of silver coins, the gros was 3.9 grams fine. It was valued at 1 sous tournois, while the new issue of the gold "royal," 4.219 grams fine, was valued at 15 sous tournois. The resulting ratio between coined silver and coined gold was 13.87 to 1, according to the following calculations: $15 \times 3.9$ grams silver = 4.219 grams gold; 58.5 silver/4.219 gold = 13.87 to 1. Fournial (p. 100) gives the ratio as 13.94 to 1, apparently using a slightly different content for the gros, of which the content and legal value underwent many changes in 1329–31 (see ibid., 94).

[75]Sapori, in his notes to his edition of *I libri di commercio dei Peruzzi,* give the values of foreign moneys in lire, soldi, and denari a fiorini as he calculated them (cf. his p. xiii). The entries in the books more often give the value of the lira a fiorini in the foreign currency. We have calculated the bimetallic ratios expressed by considering 1 fiorino a oro to be equal to 3.55 grams gold, and 1 lira a fiorini to be equal to 2.45 grams gold ($3.55 \times [20/29]$), as explained above, in chap. 13, sec. iii; cf. chap. 4, sec. iii.

For the content of French silver coin that was the basis of the French money of account we rounded off figures derived from Fournial, *Histoire monétaire,* 94; and van Werveke, "Monnaie de compte et monnaie réelle," 129–31, to wit: 1 sous tournois = 4 grams silver; 1 livre tournois = 80 grams silver; 1 sous parisis = 5 grams silver; and 1 livre parisis = 100 grams silver. Rounding off seemed justified because the exact dating of the quotations is doubtful in many cases, and references in the Peruzzi books to "buoni tornesi" are in some cases explicit, in others not.

The following is an example of our calculation of bimetallic ratio. On p. 192, under the date 1335, a Peruzzi entry reads "soldi 9 d. 7 parigeni per fior d'oro." Since a gold florin contained 3.55 grams gold, then 9 7/12 soldi parisis $\times$ 5 grams silver = 3.55 grams gold; and 47.9 silver/3.55 gold = 13.4 to 1. Sapori's note reads: "a libr.2 s.10 d.1 a fior 2.508 la libbra." Assuming that his "libbra" was the livre tournois containing 20 sous of 4 grams each, which is 80 grams of silver, and that the libbra a fiorini equaled 2.45 grams of gold, then: $1 \times 80$ grams silver = $2.508 \times 2.45$ grams gold; and 80 silver/6.1446 gold = 13.02 to 1. Passages providing starting points for such calculations are found as follows: for 1324–35, p. 164 (ratios of 24.4 and 28.17); for 1335, pp. 7 (a ratio of 12.9), 29 (13.77), and 192 (13.4 and 13.02); and for 1337, pp. 29 (14.25) and 30 (16.6 or 11.68).

[76]Fournial, *Histoire monétaire,* 100, 103, gives 11.52 to 1 for 1337 and 11.62 to 1 to 11.48 to 1 for 1337–46. By independent calculations John Munro has confirmed (and kindly communicated) the rate of 11.5 to 1 after coinage of the new "gros à la couronne" and the "écu d'or" in January 1337.

[77]See table 12.

expressed in the official values because of the official overvaluing of debased silver or billon coins.[78]

The half-dozen years' lag between the lowering of the bimetallic ratio in the Venetian and in the French mints may be one explanation of the large flow of silver to Venice in the 1330s. On the other hand, it also helps to explain the larger use of gold coins in eastern France.[79] The collections and expenditures of the Avignon papacy worked to the same effect. Later, during the dark days of the Hundred Years' War, new French billon or silver issues with legal values equal to old issues that contained more silver gave reason to export the older, better silver coins from France to Italy. That factor may well have become especially important after 1343, just at the time when Venice was making special efforts to market its large supplies of silver.[80]

The bimetallic ratios in the coinage of Flanders fell in much the same pattern as did those in France. According to the official values in pound groot of the gold and silver coins, in 1331 the ratios were 14.51 to 1, in 1332 only 12.38 to 1, and in 1337, 11.44 to 1.[81] Rates of exchange between the florin and the pound groot and in commercial practice indicate about the same ratio.[82]

After the accession of Louis de Mâle as count of Flanders (1346–84), its coinage became even more chaotic than that of France, and with less excuse. Indeed Louis de Mâle provides the classic example of monetary

---

[78]Fournial, *Histoire monétaire,* 97–125.

[79]Henri Dubois, *Les foires de la Saône à la fin du Moyen Age (vers 1280–vers 1430)* (Paris, 1976), 289–94; idem, "Commerce international, métaux précieux et flux monétaires aux confins orientaux du Royaume de France (XIIIe–XVe siècles)," in Barbagli Bagnoli, ed., *La moneta nell'economia europea,* 688–90; Perroy and Fournial, "Réalités monétaires et réalités économiques," 533–40; Fournial, *Histoire monétaire,* 142–44.

[80]See above, chap. 17, sec. i.

[81]According to the fall in value of a mark of gold bullion as given in van Werveke, "Monnaie de compte et monnaie réelle," 130, namely, from 926 gros in 1318–29 to 833 gros in 1330–37.

[82]This assumes that the groats in circulation on which the pound groot was based and which contained 3.5 or 3.6 grams silver, were the bases of the exchange rates given below (on the pound groot see above, chap. 5, n. 37). The *Libri di commercio dei Peruzzi* (Sapori, ed., p. 7) counted 1 pound groot in July 1335 as equal to 30 lire a fiorini, which represented 73.5 grams of gold (30 × 2.45). With the groat at 3.5 grams, that gives a ratio of 11.4 to 1 (3.5 × 240 = 840 grams silver/73.5 grams gold); with the groat at 3.6, the ratio is 11.8 to 1. (The figure of 3.59 grams is in van Werveke, "Monnaie de compte et monnaie réelle," 139; a corrected figure of 3.484 grams was kindly furnished by John Munro.) Only if the "grossi tornesi" referred to in the Peruzzi accounts were based on the old standard of about 4 grams of silver per groat would the equations be 240 × 4 grams silver = 30 × 2.45 grams gold; and 960 grams silver/73.5 grams gold = 13.06 to 1. In 1338–40 the pound groat was valued at 31 lire a fiorini (Sapori, ed., *I libri di commercio dei Peruzzi,* 163) and at 29 lire 13 soldi 4 denari a fiorini (ibid., 269). Cf. the very low ratios given by Prestwich in "Currency and the Economy," 47. (Spufford and Wilkinson, *Interim Listing,* 263–66, contains rates only for later dates, with the exception of one, for 1317, which is not useful for determining a ratio.)

manipulations inspired by greed, or, if attaching greed to government seems either redundant or naive, by fiscal not economic considerations. He minted an exceptionally large amount of coin and obtained the necessary metal mainly by devaluing previous issues and enticing them to the mint by offering more coins of the same legal value with less silver content. In his operations, changes in the market value of the metals or the deterioration of silver and billon coinage through usage figured only as opportunities for profit.[83]

Given those conditions, it is difficult to establish relations between a bimetallic ratio and an exchange rate. For example, the Venetian Senate in 1357 ordered[84] that in paying freights in Bruges, 36 Venetian grossi be paid for 1 "reale" of Flanders.[85] One reale was worth 22 of the groats that were its link coin. The rate might be interpreted as indicating a very low bimetallic ratio if the groat of account was based on the silver coin issued by Louis de Mâle in 1356.[86] But how much had the count's official valuation of the groat or other silver coin that he issued about 1356 overvalued his new issue in order to get more revenue?

In England the bimetallic ratio fell later than in France and Flanders

[83]van Werveke, "Currency Manipulation."

[84]ASV, Cinque Savi alla Mercanzia, 1st ser., b. 22ter (ex Misc. cod. 132), fols. 10–11, cap. 29 (23 March 1357).

[85]Exchange ca. 1400 between Bruges and London was quoted in pennies sterling per écu of 24 groats; between Bruges and Barcelona, in Barcelonese soldi per écu of 22 groats (de Roover, *Money, Banking, and Credit*, 59; idem, *Bruges Money Market*, 21). Earlier in the century usage varied. The Venetian *Tarifa zoè noticia*, difficult to date although probably from about the middle of the century, gives on p. 37:

> 3 sterlini = 1 groat of Bruges
> 22 groats = 1 scudo
> 3 scudi = 4 ducats of Venice

The "scudo" referred to is presumably the French "florin de l'écu" (or "chaise à l'écu") issued in 1337, for the gold content of that coin, 4.53 grams (Fournial, *Histoire monétaire*, 102) was very little less than 4/3 as much as the gold in a ducat (3.55 × [4/3] = 4.73).

[86]One way to find a bimetallic ratio expressed in the Venetian decree of 1357 is to assume that "reali" refers to money of account based on silver coins of the traditional weight—about 4 grams—referred to in the decree as "reali di bona moneta" and to assume that there were 22 Venetian grossi to this "reale" of account. If we assume also that the grossi were "a oro" (as were freight rates generally), then the phrase "soldorum trium grossorum" in the decree meant 36 grossi a oro, which equaled 1.5 ducats. Then the pertinent equations would be: 22 × 4 grams silver = 1.5 × 3.55 grams gold; and 88 grams silver/5.325 grams gold = 16.53 to 1. But if we assume that the silver content of the reali depended on groats of the kind coined by Louis de Mâle in 1356—1.744 grams per groat (according to de Roover, *Money, Banking, and Credit*, 223)—and that 24 of them constituted a reale (as in Pegolotti, *Pratica*), then the pertinent equations would be: 24 × 1.744 grams silver = 1.5 × 3.55 grams gold; and 41.86 grams silver/5.325 grams gold = 7.86 to 1. In contrast, the bimetallic ratio calculated from the legal value of the silver and gold coined in Flanders in 1357 was 10.8 to 1 (Munro, "Mint Policies," table 8). It seems likely that Venetian shippers were being ordered to pay at a ratio closer to 16 to 1, high enough to include some surcharge for late payment.

and under circumstances dominated by the king's borrowing from the Tuscan firms that were the biggest international financiers of the period. For his opening campaigns in the Hundred Years' War, Edward III pyramided his borrowing from the Bardi and Peruzzi and other bankers, and when those campaigns and the connected wool sales in Flanders were failures, he was unable to give his bankers all that he had promised.[87] Although he exempted the Bardi and Peruzzi from the general stoppage of payment that he decreed for his exchequer in 1339, he instituted an auditing of their accounts to eliminate all questionable items, such as the interest they had had reason to expect as "gifts" and various reimbursable expenditures connected with purchases made for him on the Continent.[88] At the same time, the English sought to avoid paying pounds sterling for florins at the rates that the Florentines demanded. From 1339 to 1344 the Florentines kept that exchange rate pegged at 36 English pennies per florin.[89] That rate valued gold coined into florins at 13.5 times as much as silver coined into sterling pennies. In the same period, the French gold pieces (écus) could be bought with sterling pennies at rates reflecting the bimetallic ratio of 11.5 to 1 or less.[90] With the ratio at this low level, the

[87]Sapori, ed., *La crisi delle compagnie mercantili*, 52–80; idem, "Le compagnie italiane in Inghilterra," in his *Studi di storia economica (sec. XIII, XIV, XV)*, 3d enlarged ed., 3 vols. (Florence, 1955–79), 2:1059–60. Sapori's pioneer studies confirmed the king's insolvency but showed that accusation of the king's bad faith was unjustified and that the bankers' affairs in Italy, quite as much as in England, were responsible for their bankruptcies. See the following articles by Edmund B. Fryde, reprinted in his *Studies:* "Financial Resources of Edward I in the Netherlands, 1294–98: Main Problems and Some Comparisons with Edward III in 1337–1340," from *Revue belge de philologie e d'histoire* 40 (1962); "Loans to the English Crown, 1328–1331," from *English Historical Review* 70 (1955); "Edward III's Wool Monopoly: A Fourteenth-Century Royal Trading Venture," from *History*, n.s., 37 (1952); and "Financial Resources of Edward III in the Netherlands, 1337–40," from *Revue belge de philologie et d'histoire* 45 (1967). See also below, n. 140.

[88]In E. B. Fryde's very extensive and detailed account of the king's debts and how they were repaid, all amounts are recorded, as in the English records, in pounds sterling; but that does not mean that the payments that had been made by the lenders to the king or to his suppliers on the Continent, and to the many allies that he was subsidizing there, were all made in wool or sterling pennies and recorded by the continental recipients in English denominations of account. Payments for the king on the Continent are referred to in Fryde, "Financial Resources of Edward I," 1171; idem, "Loans," 202–3; idem, "Financial Resources of Edward III," 1146, 1153; and Sapori, "Le compagnie," 1050.

[89]Feavearyear, *The Pound Sterling*, 25; Mavis Mate, "The Role of Gold in the English Economy, 1338–1400," *Numismatic Chronicle*, 7th ser., 18 (1978):126–41. Prestwich, "Currency and the Economy," 47.

[90]Before 1335 the English penny contained 1.33 grams. With the florin at 36 pence the ratio was 13.49 to 1 (36 × 1.33 grams silver = 3.55 grams gold; 47.88 grams silver/3.55 grams gold = 13.49 to 1). Assuming that the French "florin de l'écu" contained 4.53 grams (as indicated in Fournial, *Histoire monétaire*, 102, not 4.6 as indicated in Feavearyear, *The Pound Sterling*) but was quoted (as Feavearyear says) at 40 pence or a little above, then: 40 × 1.33 grams silver = 4.53 grams gold; and 53.2 grams silver/4.53 grams gold = 11.74 to 1. The English penny of 1335–44 contained only 1.16 grams, so that the ratio then was 10.2 to 1, according to an as-yet-

English king, in 1343, stopped paying the high exchange rates asked by the Florentine merchant bankers.[91]

The lowering of the bimetallic ratio was not reflected in the practices of the English mint as soon as it might have been because Edward III's assault on the Florentines' monopolistic pegging of their exchange rate at first took the form of imitating the Florentines rather than the French. No gold had been coined in the English mint since 1260. In December 1343—a time of instability in bimetallic ratios—the king ordered the minting of a gold coin with the legal value of 72 sterling pennies, a coin almost double the weight of the florin. This attempt to have his gold coinage accepted at the excessively high bimetallic ratio that the Florentines had been asking was unsuccessful. No one wanted to take the coins at the price he had given them. In August 1344 the king yielded to market valuations and ordered a different kind of gold coin minted, the noble. It was more than twice as heavy as the florin, but with a content and legal value that made the bimetallic ratio between coined silver and coined gold 11.05 to 1. The bimetallic ratios between silver and gold bullion later rebounded and, as expressed in the mints' rules, remained at about 11.2 to 1 during the rest of the century.

No doubt the main cause of the heavy losses sustained by the Florentine bankers from their loans to Edward III was the failure of his campaigns of 1339 and 1340. Those campaigns left him unable to pay gifts and expense accounts with the royal generosity that the bankers had expected. But the fall in the value of gold, taking down the value of the florin, deepened their losses. Their claims for repayments in England of sums advanced on the Continent were not denied, but they were reduced by rigorous auditing and turned into slow-paying claims on the king's sources of revenue in England.[92] They shrank additionally because the exchange rate was reduced. A new English coinage recognized that gold was only about 11 times as valuable as silver, not 13.5 times as valuable. Even when the bankers collected on the royal debts years later, they received only 32 pennies for each florin instead of 36, and the 32 were pennies of reduced silver content.[93] The Florentines got only 11 units of silver instead of the

---

unpublished table entitled "The Alterations of English Coinage, 1279 to 1526," generously furnished by John H. Munro.

[91]Munro, "Mint Policies," table 8. See also Feavearyear, *The Pound Sterling*, 26–29; Lloyd, "Overseas Trade," 111–13; and Prestwich, "Currency and the Economy," 47.

[92]The Bardi remained active trying to collect on claims until in 1391 a partner came from Florence to declare that the king had paid all that had been promised in the summary audit of 4 August 1339 (Sapori, "Le compagnie") in *Studi* II, 1060.

[93]Munro, "Mint Policies," table 8. In 1344 the English penny contained only 1.199 grams, but in August 1344 the silver content was increased to 1.217 grams (Craig, *The Mint*, 64, 70; and Munro's table mentioned above, in n. 90). In Sapori, ed., *Libri degli Alberti*, 295, an entry dated 1347 gives the exchange "a sterlini 32 il fiorino d'oro." Hence: 32 × 1.199 grams silver = 1 × 3.55 grams gold; and 38.368 grams silver/3.55 grams gold = 10.81 to 1.

13.5 units of silver they had expected to get in return for each unit of gold for which they had debited the English crown.[94] The fall of gold, to which the Venetians had contributed much by their vigorous export of silver and import of gold and in which they had found profits, hurt the Florentines. In spite of their being the leaders of international finance—indeed because they had been the leaders of international finance while gold was rising—the Florentines were not in a position, as were the Venetians, to take advantage of the changes that took place between 1325 and 1345 in the supply of and demand for the two precious metals. The international bankers had made large loans in gold when gold was priced high and had to accept partial repayments that valued gold at a lower price.

## iv. ITALY AND THE FLORENTINE CONTRAST

From one part of Italy to another, the effects of the fall of gold on exchange rates with Venice varied greatly. In the Kingdom of Naples similarities to Romania are evident. Even before 1330 the Neapolitan money of account, the oncia, had become based on a silver coinage, namely, the gigliati or carlini introduced by the Angevin rulers. As gold fell in value, the number of gigliati required to equal 1 ducat decreased. In his table of exchanges Pegolotti allowed for a wide variation in the value of Venetian gold ducats at Barletta (Apulia) and Naples—50–65 gigliati to 5 ducats—indicating a bimetallic ratio between 10.3 to 1 and 13.4 to 1. Taking the average, the ratio was only about 12 to 1 even before the fall of gold. In contrast, his table of exchange rates between Florence and Naples, proba-

---

[94]In Sapori, ed., *I libri di commercio dei Peruzzi*, the rates of conversion from pounds sterling into lire a fiorini varied considerably, in the range indicated by the compilation by Edward Ames, "The Sterling Crisis," 497 (but misinterpreted by him, since he mistakenly believed that lire a fiorini referred to a "silver currency"). The first conversion as found in the Peruzzi books of July 1335 (p. 7) is at "lbr. 10, s. 15 a fior. la libbra." Since the lira a fiorini was always 20/29 of the fiorino d'oro, that made 1 pound sterling equal to 7.4 gold florins (10.75 × [20/29]). Then, since 1 pound sterling was equal to 7.4 fiorini d'oro, 1 fiorino d'oro equaled 32.43 sterling pennies (240/7.4). The bimetallic ratio was as follows: 32.43 × 1.157 grams silver = 37.52 grams; and 37.52 silver/3.55 gold = 10.57 to 1. That is the lowest valuation placed on the florin before September 1341 and the highest on the pound sterling. In 1337 the pound sterling was valued as low as 9 lire a fiorini (Sapori, ed., *I libri di commercio dei Peruzzi*, 57), which implied in bimetallic ratios: 240 × 1.157 grams silver = 9 × 2.45 grams gold; and 277.7 grams silver/22.05 grams gold = 12.59 to 1. According to Sapori, ed., *Libri degli Alberti*, 295, in 1347 when the English king paid a debt to the Alberti by assigning them a sum that the king owed to the then bankrupt Bardi, the Alberti converted at the rate of "sterlini 32 il fiorino d'oro." With the sterling penny then containing 1.199 grams fine (see above, n. 93) the bimetallic ratio was 10.81 to 1. The bimetallic ratios derived from the direct comparison of the gold and silver equivalents of the pound sterling gave a bimetallic ratio of 12.4 to 1 in January 1344; 11.05 to 1 in August 1344; 10.96 to 1 in June 1345; 11.57 to 1 from August 1346 to July 1351; and 11.16 to 1 from then until 1409 (Munro, "Mint Policies," table 8).

bly compiled when he was back in Florence and concerned with the liquidation of the bankrupt Bardi firm, provides for a range of exchange rates
indicating bimetallic ratios of from 10.5 to 1 to 11.2 to 1.[95] In 1347 the
Florentine firm of Alberti del Giudice recorded what they were owed by
the bankrupt Bardi. Their entry, registered in Florentine gold-based money of account, indicates that by that date only 45 gigliati were needed to
equal 5 florins, a rate of exchange indicating a bimetallic ratio of 9.4 to 1.[96]
The Kingdom of Naples seems to have resembled the Levant in valuing
silver more highly compared with gold than did ultramontane Europe in
both the 1330s and the 1340s.

In Milan the reaction of the authorities to the fall of gold and the
bimetallic ratios was initially similar to that in Venice. Beginning around
1330, when the florin became fixed at 32 soldi imperiali (equal to 64 soldi
terzuoli), they sought to maintain a bimetallic system at a constant valuation of the gold coin in silver-based money of account. However, while
Venice succeeded in keeping their domestic exchange rate at about 64
soldi only during the middle decades of the fourteenth century, after
which the domestic exchange began to rise, Milan maintained constant its
rate of 32 soldi from 1330 to 1395. It was a rate maintained by the market as
well as officially.[97]

Carlo Cipolla has called the flat curve of Milan's domestic exchange
"immobility" and has contrasted the "relative monetary stability" of Milan
with the constant depreciation of the silver-based money of account in
Venice and Florence.[98] Tommaso Zerbi, on the other hand, has pointed
out that the rate of 32 soldi reflected only a nominal stability: in a period of
generally rising but fluctuating silver prices it was impossible to maintain
real stability, which would have been tantamount to maintaining a bimetallic standard. Acting in accord with the general approbation of stable
domestic exchange, the mint of the Visconti manipulated the silver coins

[95]See above, chap. 14, sec. iii, The Neapolitan Kingdom; and Pegolotti, *Pratica*, 171–75.
[96]Sapori, ed., *Libri degli Alberti*, 295. The entry reads in part: ". . . deono dare oncie 4, teri
24, grani 10 di carlini d'argento di 60 per oncia i quali ragiorono in Firenze i carlini 9 di
Napoli fior. 5 d'oro montarono libr. 38, s. 16 a fiorini." A clerical error of writing "fior. 5
d'oro" instead of "fior. 1 d'oro" seems to be a carryover from Pegolotti's practice of giving the
number of carlini (or gigliati, as he called them) equal to 5 fiorini a oro, that is, 50–53 gigliati
to 5 fiorini d'oro (*Pratica*, 173–74). Correcting the clerical error, the entry indicates the
bimetallic ratio as follows: $9 \times 3.7$ grams silver = 3.55 grams gold; $(9 \times 3.7)/3.55 = 9.38$ to 1.
The accountant's error is also pointed up by the conversion that the entry immediately
adjoining makes, namely, of a little over 4 oncie into a little over 38 fiorini a fiorini; for if 4
oncie = 240 carlini, and 9 carlini = 1 fiorino a oro, then 240 carlini = 240/9 fiorini a oro, and
= $(240/9) \times (29/20)$ fiorini a fiorini = 38.67 fiorini a fiorini.
[97]The stability of the rate at Milan was matched by that at Genoa. See Cipolla, *I movimenti*, 31–32, 42; Spufford and Wilkinson, *Interim Listing*, 106–8, 122–23.
[98]"La svalutazione monetaria nel Ducato di Milano alla fine del Medioevo," *Giornale degli
economisti e annali di economia*, n.s., 6 (1947):545; idem, *I movimenti*, 85–86, 89.

that it issued—mostly by devaluations but occasionally also by revaluation—in order to keep the exchange rate constant. Silver coin was "realigned" with the gold coin in small steps that were accepted by creditors and debtors alike. It seems that throughout the long period of nominal stability, the lira imperiale repeatedly shifted from one base coin ("moneta numeraria") to another, linking up with the coin that represented the least fine silver. This horizontal movement was understood, accepted, and promoted by Milanese merchants and their foreign contacts and colleagues.[99] A Venetian buying a bill on Milan knew that he would receive 32 soldi for a ducat, although that figure represented a changing amount of fine silver. In fact, the manner of quoting foreign exchange in Venice on Milan was to express Venetian gold (lire di grossi a oro) in Milanese silver (lire imperiali).

The period of stability ended in 1395, when the Visconti overlords (who when they became dukes in that year started coining their own "ducats") used manipulation of the currency as one way of financing their costly wars. Tension developed between market prices of the ducat and official prices, which were decreed periodically in attempts to restrain the rise.[100] Then a new money of account was born, a ghost very much like one that haunted Milan's neighbor in the lagoons: a "fiorino di moneta," a silver-based money of account worth a fixed 32 soldi imperiali.[101]

Florence, in contrast, kept its clear separation of two monetary standards, one based on gold, the other on silver and billon. The policies adopted in face of the declining value of gold compared with that of silver had different results from those in Venice but were in many respects parallel. The chronological coincidence of the measures taken to devalue the silver-based moneys of account in 1331–78 is shown in table 23. A comparison of the measures taken and their results sets in relief Venice's international position and the different roles of bullion flows in the economies of the two cities—Florence a landlocked industrial as well as financial center, Venice a seaward-looking "world market" drawing much of her prosperity from the shipment and exchange of gold and silver.

Comparison is facilitated by superficial similarity in the coins minted by the two cities early in the fourteenth century. Each had a coin of pure gold—ducat or florin—weighing about 3.5 grams, a silver grosso better than 0.95 fine weighing about 2 grams, and a billon penny less than 0.2 fine and weighing between 1/4 and 2/3 of a gram. In both cities a lira di piccoli

[99]Zerbi, *Moneta effettiva*, chap. 10, "Mezzo secolo di stabilità nominale tra buona moneta d'argento ed il fiorino d'oro," esp. pp. 52–55. Since most of the documents of the mint of Milan have been lost and the dating of the new issues is nearly impossible, Zerbi's well-reasoned hypothesis cannot be tested with precision.

[100]Soldi Rondinini, "Politica e teoria monetarie."

[101]Cipolla, *Money, Prices, and Civilization*, 46–48; and in idem, *Moneta e civiltà mediterranea*, 60–61.

TABLE 23.

Bimetallic Ratios in Venice and Florence: Parallel Changes, 1322–69

| | Venice | | Florence | |
|---|---|---|---|---|
| Dates | Coin | Ratio | Coin | Ratio |
| 1322–28 | Grosso at 32 denari (Ducat at 24 × 32 denari) | 14.2 | Guelfo del fiore da 30 denari (Florin at 66 soldi = 792 denari) | 14.6 |
| | | | Guelfo del fiore da 32 denari | 13.7 |
| 1331–32 | Mezzanino, type 1 | 13.1 | — | — |
| | Soldino, type 1 | 11.5 | — | — |
| August 1334 | — | — | Quattrino | 10.9 |
| October 1345 | — | — | Guelfo da 4 soldi | 10.0 |
| February 1346 | Mezzanino, type 2 | 10.5 | — | — |
| July 1347 | — | — | Guelfo da 5 soldi | 9.4 |
| 1351 | — | — | Quattrino | 9.4 |
| | | | Guelfo da 5 soldi | 9.8 |
| 1353 | Soldino, type 2 (Ducat at 64.5 soldi) | 9.7 | — | — |
| July 1368 | — | — | Popolino da 2 soldi | 10.1 |
| 1369 | Soldino, type 3 (Ducat at 74 soldi) | 10.2 | Guelfo da 5 soldi | 10.1 |

SOURCES: For Venice see above, table 12; and below, apps. A and D, by calculation. For Florence see Bernocchi, 3:79, 168 (by calculation) for 1322–28; 176–77 for 1334; 180–81 for 1345; 188 for 1347; 196–97 for 1351; and 203–4 for 1368.

NOTE: Ratios calculated from the contents of the indicated coins.

meant 240 of the billon pennies (denari), commonly called piccoli ("piccioli" in Florence); and the relative values of the three kinds of coins were expressed in lire, soldi, and denari di piccoli.

There was a striking contrast, to be sure, in the size and kinds of billon or black moneys coined. Although the Florentine and Venetian denari contained almost the same amount of pure silver (the Florentine picciolo 0.052 grams, the Venetian piccolo 0.058 grams), the Florentine coin weighed 0.63 grams, more than twice the weight of the Venetian, and was less than half as fine, only 0.083. Its high copper content made it really black "black money," and the Florentines minted no coins of less value.[102] The Venetians, in contrast, minted also mezzo denari and quartaroli. The former were somewhat smaller and less fine than the piccoli, but the latter were heavier and almost all copper, only 0.003 fine silver.[103] The minting

[102]Bernocchi, 3:146–47, reports the slight evidence concerning Florentine minting of a mezzo denaro called a "medaglia" in the thirteenth century.

[103]According to Papadopoli's lists (1:135, 183), the last doge to mint quartaroli was Giovanni Soranzo (1312–28), but the minting of the mezzo denaro called the "bianco" continued until as late as Andrea Dandolo (1343–53).

in Venice of those fractional coins worth only 1/2 or 1/4 as much as Florence's smallest coin implies more use of small change in Venice and greater dependence in Florence on its picciolo and, perhaps, on mental arithmetic.

Another contrast was the number of times that Florence changed its silver coin of intermediate value. During the 130 years (roughly 1200–1330) while the Venetians were minting their grosso unchanged, and no other coin of fine silver, Florence changed its fine silver coins at least seven times.[104] They were called silver florins, or in the fourteenth century grossi, and were given also such political names as popolino or guelfo. They all had fixed legal values stated in lire di piccioli. That minted in 1318 was called both guelfo del fiore and grosso da denari 30 (although of course no number appeared on the coin.)

The silver equivalent of the Florentine lira di piccioli was determined by both the grosso of fine silver and the picciolo of low-grade billon, much as in Venice the silver equivalent of the lira di piccoli in the 1320s was determined by the circulation of grossi and piccoli, with 1 grosso always valued at 32 piccoli. To be sure, the amount of silver changing hands when a lira di piccioli was paid in Florentine grossi da 30 denari was substantially more than changed hands when the payment was made in piccioli. Carlo Cipolla has calculated the contrast:

12.576 grams if paid with 240 denari,
       each containing 0.524 grams fine;
15.672 grams if paid with 8 grossi da denari 30,
       each containing 1.9588 grams fine.[105]

In effect, when anyone accepted 30 piccioli in exchange for 1 grosso da 30 piccioli, he was accepting piccioli that contained only 1/37 as much silver as a grosso, as if they were worth 1/30 of a grosso. As in Venice, the higher cost of manufacturing the black money and a limitation of the supply to match the local demand for it enabled the black money to circulate with an exchange value above its metallic value. The divergence was larger at Florence than at Venice but not much larger.[106]

[104]Bernocchi, 3:134–68.
[105]Cipolla, *Il fiorino*, 41–44.
[106]Cipolla explains the existence of the different silver equivalents for the lira di piccioli as the result of different costs of manufacture. The difference in mint charges given in Bernocchi, 3:38–39, explains part of the difference but not all. Comparing directly the content and costs of the picciolo and the grosso, as has been done above for Venice ca. 1330, shows that the silver value of the picciolo was about 1/37 of the silver value of a grosso; the cost value (including seigniorage) of the picciolo was 1/32 of the cost value (including seigniorage) of a grosso; and the legal value of the picciolo was 1/30 of the legal value of a grosso. The divergence between the silver value and the legal value of the coins was greater at Florence than at Venice, largely because of the higher costs of manufacture at Florence, which may have resulted from the Florentine picciolo's being a larger coin containing more copper,

In contrast to the silver florins or grossi, the gold florin had no official values in lire di piccioli. The consequent lack of any bimetallic standard made the market price of florins highly flexible and more fully and officially recorded than the market price of ducats at Venice.[107]

When silver rose on international markets in 1325–35, the florin fell from the 66–67 soldi which had been its price in 1322–28 to 65 in 1329–30, and 60 in 1331, and touched bottom at 59 soldi 8 denari in 1335.[108]

Florence, like Venice, responded to the change in the bimetallic ratio by issuing a new kind of coin. In 1332 Florence began minting quattrini, a move comparable in many respects to the Venetian coinage of the soldino and the mezzanino begun the year before. Quattrini, like soldini, were used to increase the amount of silver coin in circulation, and both were successful in meeting the need for a new kind of coin for everyday use within the city. The quattrino in Florence, like the soldino in Venice, took over the role that the picciolo or piccolo had previously had as link coin in determining the silver equivalent of the lira di piccioli.[109] The percentage of silver in the quattrino, like the percentage of silver in the soldino, was intermediate between the high fineness of the grossi of the two cities and the low silver content of the picciolo or piccolo. In each case the new issue lowered the bimetallic ratio expressed by the relation of the content and legal value of the new coin to the market value of gold coin.[110]

On the other hand, there were highly significant differences (1) in the way the mints acquired the necessary bullion, (2) in the fineness and the range of circulation of the two coins, and (3) in the objectives sought in introducing them:

1. In Florence the mint depended for its bullion entirely on the initiative and interest of merchants in bringing to it uncoined metal and old or foreign coins for reminting. If the terms on which the mint was offering new coins for old coin or for bullion did not provide the suppliers with enough profit, the mint was left without customers, on whom it

---

although no more silver, than the Venetian piccolo. In both city-states piccoli could circulate at legal values 10–20 percent above their metallic values. Therefore, basing the lira di piccioli equally on both the billon coin and the fine silver coin at the legal rate was just as practical in Florence as in Venice.

To explain the extent to which changes in the silver content of the link coins of the lira di piccioli did not affect prices, Charles de la Roncière concludes that the silver equivalent of the lira di piccioli did not depend on the silver content of any particular link coin. If one kind of silver or billon coin was scarce, the kind that was available was used instead. As he phrases it on p. 474, "La monnaie de compte peut rester fixée constamment à une même pièce. Elle peut aussi, et c'est le cas le plus frequent, osciller d'une espèce a l'autre" (de la Roncière, *Prix et salaires*, 473–500).

[107]de la Roncière, *Prix et salaires*, 509.

[108]Ibid., 839–43; Bernocchi, 3:78–91.

[109]de la Roncière, *Prix et salaires*, 479–80 and esp. 489 n. 78; Bernocchi, 3:76.

[110]Bernocchi, 3:178.

depended for supplies. A new issue might be ordered but might never actually be minted, at least not in any appreciable amount.[111]

Quite different was the situation in Venice. There the silver being coined was all technically silver purchased by the Commune. True, suppliers were so largely paid with the coins made from the silver they supplied that the purchase was a mere technical formality in most cases, but not in all cases. Moreover, from 1332 to 1417 the mint was supplied by the requirement that all importers of silver had to "sell" one-fifth (or for a short time one-tenth) of it to the mint at a traditional low price. Having turned over that "quinto," the silver merchant could either have the rest of his silver coined at a lower mint charge or reexport it uncoined. Overseas demand determined to some extent how much was coined in Venice, but the mint was assured in any case of having its fifth (or in 1343–50 its tenth), from which soldini could be made. That assurance depended, of course, on continuing silver imports. The imports came because profitseeking merchants—German, Ragusan, or Venetian—decided that Venice was the best place to sell silver.[112]

No such constant stream of silver bullion flowed through or into Florence. More important than in Venice as supplies for the mint were coins culled from earlier issues by moneychangers, bankers, and other merchants and reminted because they contained more silver compared with their legal value than did the newer silver coin. The frequent changes in Florentine silver coinage—the changes that provoked Dante's scorn— had enabled the Florentine Commune, as well as Florentine moneychangers, to profit from the practice of issuing new types of coins with higher legal values than the old—higher, that is, compared with their metallic content.[113]

Without the preemptive rights of the Venetian mint, the Florentine mint, in order to introduce a new coin, had to offer moneychangers and merchants terms that would make it profitable for them to bring in old coins. Under the first regulations for coining quattrini in 1332 those terms were not sufficiently attractive. Little silver or bullion was offered to be made into quattrini until after the mint charge was lowered from 8.04 percent of the yield to 5.74 percent (15 coins out of 261) in 1334[114] Then the lower mint charge and the continued fall of the florin to below 60 soldi in 1334 were followed by a sufficient offering of old coin or bullion to mint quattrini in large quantities.[115]

2. The circulation of the quattrini, like the source of the metal from

---

[111]Ibid., 1, 176, 197; Cipolla, *Il fiorino*, 55–56.

[112]See above, chap. 9.

[113]Cipolla, *Il fiorino*, 56, 107; Dante Alighieri, *Purgatorio*, VI, 145–47.

[114]The first quattrino was minted in the first semester of 1332 (Bernocchi, 3:175–77). On the uncertain date in 1331–32 of the first soldino see above, chap. 15, sec. ii.

[115]de la Roncière, *Prix et salaires*, 479.

which they were made, was much more local than that of Venice's soldini. The quattrino contained such a small proportion of silver that its use was restricted to the city that issued it. To be sure, the quattrino contained twice as high a percentage of silver as did the picciolo, being 1/6 silver instead of 1/12, but even so, its silver content was so low that it circulated only within Florence.[116] The Venetian soldino was not nearly as fine as a Venetian grosso, but it was 2/3 or 5/8 silver and was accepted in Crete and Dalmatia and other parts of the Balkans.[117] Soldini and quattrini shared the characteristic of having a low silver content compared with the legal value given them by their issuing cities, so that each was in Gresham's sense "bad money" and could drive competing coins out of circulation. The quattrino was limited to that function; the soldino served also an important function in the relations between Venice and the area that was, economically speaking, its colonial hinterland.

3. Similarly, while the Venetian motivations for introducing the new type of coin were rooted in both the local situation and the city's foreign trade, the Florentines seem to have been moved entirely by domestic problems. The reason given officially for coining the quattrino in 1332 was that there was no silver coin available and that making large payments with piccioli took too much time.[118]

That statement implies that as long as silver grossi had been available, they had in fact been used to make many payments calculated in lire, soldi, and denari di piccioli. In spite of the differences in their silver equivalents, piccioli and grossi both had been used at official values. Only when it seemed that silver coin would be lacking altogether was it felt necessary to issue a new coin that was less cumbersome than the picciolo in making large payments.

That was the official explanation. A less superficial explanation is suggested by Florence's famed chronicler Giovanni Villani. In regard to other Florentine monetary changes, he says that the reason for the new issues was to stop declines in the value of the florin.[119] Explicitly he attributed to the selfish interest of capitalistic employers of textile workers the coinage change of 1347, described below. The employers sold their cloth for gold florins and paid their workers in silver or billon.[120] This interpretation of Florentine monetary policy in the 1340s has been widely

[116]Bernocchi, 3:175–77.

[117]See above, sec. ii.

[118]Bernocchi, 1 (*Libro della Zecca*): 49, ". . . magnus defectus argenti e quod solutiones que habent ex mercantiis per solutiones denariorum parvorum magno tempore spatio retarda(n)tur."

[119]Villani, *Cronica*, bk. 12, cap. 53. The text is printed in Bernocchi, 3:178–79, as it appears in the edition of 1848, with an alternate reading which suggests a possibility that quattrini also were becoming scarce. A modern critical edition of Villani is badly needed.

[120]Villani, *Cronica*, bk. 12, cap. 97.

accepted and elaborated.[121] When we look at the period 1330–50 as a whole, it appears that the entrepreneurial interest described by Villani was operational from the time of the introduction of the quattrino in 1332. Falling quotations for the florin were even more marked in 1331 than in 1345 or 1347.[122]

Surprisingly, Villani made no mention in his chronicle of the introduction of the quattrino in 1331, although he recorded other earlier and later coinage changes and had an understanding of monetary matters from his membership in the big merchant banking company of the Peruzzi and from his service in 1317 as one of the supervisors of the mint ("ufficiali alla moneta"). Perhaps in 1332 he was distracted from his chronicle by his job of supervising the construction of Florence's new walls being built to allow continuation of the city's recent rapid growth. Villani was the treasurer in charge of the funds assigned for that purpose.[123] In spite of his silence, the circumstances under which the quattrino was introduced in 1331–35 seem to justify considering relevant to those years the motivations that he connects with changes in 1345 and 1347, even though he himself does not attribute those purposes to the change a decade earlier.

Certainly for some years after 1334 the quattrino served both purposes: it provided a handy means of payment domestically and stopped the fall of the price of the florin in lire di piccioli. The quattrino quickly became the link coin determining the silver equivalent of the lire di piccioli. The amount of silver changing hands when, after the coinage of the quattrino, a lira di piccioli was paid in silver or billon coin has been calculated by Carlo Cipolla as follows:

12.58 grams of fine silver if paid with 240 piccioli;
13.02 grams if paid with 60 quattrini (60 × 0.217);
15.68 grams if paid with 8 grossi da 30 denari.[124]

The comparison shows the very large advantage of paying in quattrini and the consequent benefit that suppliers of the mint gained by asking to have quattrini minted for them instead of grossi. In fact the Florentine mint

[121]Elaborated especially by Niccolò Rodolico in *La democrazia fiorentina nel suo tramonto* (Bologna, 1905) and *I ciompi: Una pagina di storia del proletariato operaio* (Florence, 1945). Cessi's criticism of Rodolico's thesis in Cessi's introduction to *PMV*, lxxii–lxxiii, was based on Cessi's interpretation of Villani's reference to "lanaiuoli e altri artefici" as meaning "classe lavoratrice," whereas Rodolico correctly understood it to refer to employers of labor such as those controlling the Arte della Lana, as does Cipolla, in *Il fiorino*, the most recent elaboration, with amendments, of Villani's interpretation. See Bernocchi, 3:67; and de la Roncière, *Prix et salaires*, 500–502.

[122]Bernocchi, 3:79.

[123]*Enciclopedia italiana* (Rome, 1929–36; reprint, Rome, 1949), s.v. "Villani, Giovanni."

[124]Cipolla, *Il fiorino*, 43; cf. de la Roncière, *Prix et salaires*, 485–89.

records make no mention of any coinage of fine silver between 1326 and 1345.[125]

The comparison also shows that whether payment was made in piccioli or quattrini, there was little difference in the amount of silver changing hands. Between the legal values and the metallic values of the picciolo and quattrino the difference was no more than the added costs of manufacturing the smaller coins.[126] Indeed, when allowance is made for both the utility value and the labor value of the picciolo, it appears that a merchant who took bullion (or old coin) to the mint would receive in return coins of higher exchange value if he had his bullion coined into quattrini than if he had his bullion (or old coin) minted as piccioli. It is not surprising therefore that the minting of piccioli gradually ceased and the quattrino became the base coin of the Florentine lira di piccioli.[127]

After the extensive minting of quattrini, the florin recovered somewhat from its recent decline. In 1341–44 it was at 64–66.[128] When the price of a florin was 66 soldi, the bimetallic ratio in Florence was:

11.69 to 1   if paid in piccioli,
for 66 soldi × (12.58/20) grams = 41.51 grams silver, and 41.51 grams silver/3.55 grams gold = 11.69 to 1;
12.10 to 1   if paid in quattrini,
for 66 soldi × (13.02/20) = 42.97 grams silver, and 42.97 grams silver/3.55 grams gold = 12.10 to 1;
14.58 to 1   if paid in grossi da 30 denari,
for 66 soldi × (15.68/20) = 51.74 grams silver, and 51.74 grams silver/3.55 grams gold = 14.58 to 1.

At Venice the ducat, still officially worth 64 soldi, was valued at 68 or even 70 soldi in some transactions in those years. At 68, the ratio in Venice was

13.3 to 1 when the soldi were paid with 816 piccoli;
12.28 to 1 when the soldi were paid with 68 soldini.[129]

Comparing the ratios in the two cities shows that when payment for a florin was made in Florence in quattrini at the price of 66 soldi, coined silver was being valued in Florence at just about the same ratio as in Venice.

[125]Bernocchi, 1 (*Libro della Zecca*):33–82.

[126]Considering both legal values and silver contents and comparing the quattrino with the picciolo and the guelfo shows that the quattrino had legal values in excess of the values justified by its silver content. The excess was about 10 percent when the quattrino is compared with the picciolo; about 30 percent when it is compared with the guelfo.

[127]de la Roncière, *Prix et salaires,* 479–480; Bernocchi, 3:76.

[128]Bernocchi, 3:78–79, 94–95.

[129]See above, table 20.

However, the finest silver coins continued to disappear from both cities. At Florence, such few grossi ("guelfi del fiore") da 30 denari as were still in circulation commanded 32 denari piccioli, more than their legal value.[130] At Venice, such old grossi as were still minted were either snapped up by officials in a position to get them at their official value, well below their market price, as we have seen,[131] or sent to make payments in the Levant, where they were valued in local moneys in accord with their weight and high reputation.

On the other hand, gold coinage boomed in Florence as well as in Venice. The Florentine mint coined 350,000 florins in April 1344–April 1345, the first year for which a definitely datable output can be compiled from the mint's records.[132] The same figure was included by Giovanni Villani in the description of Florentine prosperity that he inserted in his chronicle after recounting the conclusion of the Scaliger War in 1339.[133] That sum is only about half as high as that for Venetian production about 1343 according to casual references to the Venetian scale of production,[134] but the evidence about the Florentine output is based on much more solid evidence. Some of the activity of the Florentine mint in 1347 and 1348 may well have included recoining the Hungarian imitations of Florentine florins which King Louis of Hungary brought with him when he marched through the peninsula to reestablish Angevin authority in Naples.[135] It continued at a high level also during the general disruption of the Black Death in 1348 and 1349 and fell off precipitously only in the summer of 1351.[136]

Gold used to make florins probably came largely from some of the same overseas sources, as did the gold used to make ducats. Through the Genoese colonies in the Black Sea and Cyprus the Florentines had access to Asiatic and Egyptian gold.[137] And some Florentine-minted gold may have come through western North Africa.

To pay for its huge imports of gold in this period, Florence depended mainly on its export of woolen cloth, about which Villani gives glowing statistics. But Florence paid for gold also by exporting some of its silver coin. The Venetian galleys that went to Romania and Cyprus proba-

---

[130]Bernocchi, 3:167; Pegolotti's general description of coins minted in Florence, *Pratica*, 191–94. Valuing the grosso da 30 denari at 32 gave a bimetallic ratio of 12.87 to 1 (Bernocchi, 3:178).

[131]See above, chap. 15, sec. iii and n. 69.

[132]Bernocchi, 3:66–67.

[133]Villani, *Cronica*, bk. 11, cap. 94.

[134]See below, app. B, sec. iii.

[135]Villani, *Cronica*, bk. 12, caps. 107–11; and see above, chap. 17, sec. ii.

[136]Bernocchi, 3:67; de la Roncière, 500–502.

[137]Michel Balard, *La Romanie génoise (XIIe–début du XVe siècle)*, Bibliothèque des Ecoles Françaises d'Athènes et de Rome, 1st ser., 235, 2 vols. published in collaboration with the Società Ligure di Storia Patria (Rome, 1978), vol. 2.

bly carried some Florentine silver coins, as well as fine Florentine cloths. Whether on Genoese or Venetian vessels, silver from Florence was being drained off to the Levant, as Villani complained.[138]

The flow of silver east in the period 1330–45 was quite satisfactory to the Venetians, whether in the form of silver ingots for Levantine mints and Tartar-Mongol traders, or in the form of the traditional grossi with which to buy at good prices in Syrian markets, or in the form of soldini sent to Venetian governors in Crete and to outposts in Greece to pay for fortifications and other expenses. Opening yet wider markets eastward for silver was the main purpose of the new institution of Venetian galley voyages to Egypt in 1345. But in Florence after 1340 the large outflow of silver was intensifying a ruinous deflation. To moderate the effects of that deflation, Florence, by coining a new guelfo in 1345, initiated the second of parallel Venetian-Florentine moves in the process of devaluation.

In this second set of parallel moves, Florence for the first time raised the legal value of its fine silver coins compared with their silver content and significantly reduced the silver equivalent of the lira di piccioli. The difference between paying in quattrini and paying in grossi was practically eliminated by the issuance of the new guelfo, the "grosso da 4 soldi." And when a gold florin was bought with fine silver grossi, the ratio between the amounts of silver and gold exchanged was only 10.06 to 1.[139] That ratio was lower than prevailed at Venice in 1345, but it was immediately countered by Andrea Dandolo's coinage of his mezzanino, which reduced the ratio of the metal in ducats and mezzanini to 10.5 to 1.

Although the change in Florentine coinage that initiated this second set of parallel moves was part of an effort to relieve Florence's deflationary crisis, bimetallic difficulties were not the main cause—certainly not the most conspicuous cause—of Florence's ruinous deflation. The most conspicuous cause was the failure of the political gambles financed by the international bankers who in the 1330s and early 1340s dominated Florentine policies in alliance with aristocratic Florentine factions and the Arti Maggiori, especially the Arte di Calimala. Their family fortunes and their Europe-wide banking connections enabled them to make the loans without which wars could not be waged on a large scale. If the wars they financed had been successful, their investments would have yielded at least 20 percent compounded annually. But in 1338–43 the wars they financed failed. The bankers could not get paid, except perhaps by loaning more money for new wars or accepting a "restructuring" of their credits which would yield no "usury" or only a 5 percent return paid long after it was due.

Their highest hopes and deepest disappointment were bound up

[138]Villani, *Cronica*, bk. 12, caps. 53, 97.

[139]Bernocchi, 3:181–82, with the florin at 62 soldi; cf. ibid., 185.

with the campaigns with which Edward III of England opened the Hundred Years' War. When his campaigns of 1338–39 left him penniless, he temporarily suspended payments, as we have seen, and ordered a careful audit in preparation for an assignment to creditors of sums that he hoped to collect from his subjects. His Florentine creditors could at best hope for slow payment of credits in pounds sterling without hoped-for "gifts." Particularly hard hit were the Bardi and Giovanni Villani's firm, the Peruzzi.[140]

A very similar "restructuring" of debt by the Commune of Florence afflicted its bankers a few years later. They had financed expensive, unsuccessful wars for Tuscan hegemony which left Florence so deeply in debt that the Commune too stopped all payments. Big banks failed one after the other, in spite of moratoria granted them by the Commune in efforts to slow down the panic. The biggest firm, that of the Bardi, was thus protected until 1346 and then began liquidation.[141]

A paradigm for interpreting the situation is suggested by Carlo Cipolla. He likens the Florentine bankers to those of a modern highly developed country at the core of the world economy and likens England and Naples to modern underdeveloped countries, part of what Immanuel Wallerstein calls the periphery. The banks of the dominant core had made large loans to the government of one underdeveloped country, England, to be assured of supplies of a needed raw material, wool. The government of the underdeveloped country, instead of using the money to finance productive enterprises ("opere di sviluppo"), squandered the funds in wars and went bankrupt. In Naples, another part of Florence's periphery, sales of raw materials such as grain and wool or cotton made the local landlords possessors of surplus funds in the form of deposits with their Florentine bankers. It is easy to name underdeveloped countries of the 1970s or 1980s that vivify the analogy. But as Cipolla fully recognizes, the banking organization at the core of the "world economy" and the nature of the money used, as well as other differences, prevent considering the analogy at all complete.[142]

Although the gold glut cannot be considered the main cause of Florence's financial crisis, the voluminous minting of gold while silver coin was scarce may have made the deflation worse. Although no modern analogy helps explain the conjunction of deepening deflation and increased supplies of gold, monetary conditions of the mid-fourteenth century suggest a connection. The profuse coinage of florins in years when

[140]Sapori, La crisi delle compagnie mercantili; idem, "Le compagnie italiane in Inghilterra." Michael Prestwich ("Italian Merchants," 84–91) and Cipolla (Il fiorino, 16) also call it bankruptcy. Cf. Goldthwaite, "Italian Bankers in Medieval England"; and E. B. Fryde and M. M. Fryde, "Public Credit," 459–61.
[141]Cipolla, Il fiorino, 10–21.
[142]Ibid., 14–15.

silver coins were scarce may have lowered the exchange value of the gold coins. Previously, for almost a century, 1250–1330, gold had been rising in value compared with silver. Those who had accumulated wealth had found that gold was the best stuff to hoard and that credits stated in gold-based money of account, in florins, stood up in contrast to credits recorded in a silver-based money of account, which was likely to be devalued by the minting of lighter silver or debased billon coin. When the banks and the Communal treasury stopped payment, men had to draw on their reserves. Amid the general loss of confidence and the resulting need for liquidity, they turned to their gold, only to find that gold that had been worth more than 14 times as much as silver in 1330 was worth hardly more than 10 times as much in 1350. Their gold did not go as far as they expected in meeting everyday living expenses for goods and services priced in lire di piccioli.

The domestic political and financial position of such bankers as the Bardi became hopeless after a violent uprising in October 1343 took the control of the Florentine government out of the hands of the aristocratic banker-merchants of the Calimala. New men, "novi cives," instituted reforms under which the city's economy began a recovery before it was shaken by the Black Death in 1348–49. One of their essential reforms was the refunding in 1345 of all the short-term loans, on which payment had been suspended, into a long-term debt of negotiable obligations paying 5 percent.[143] Another was the issuance of the new guelfo. That new guelfo, or grosso da 4 soldi, was a larger coin than the guelfo del fiore and of the same fineness. Villani wrote proudly of it and of the extent to which it was accepted throughout Tuscany.[144] But the amount of fine silver in it was not increased in proportion to the increase in its value over the guelfo del fiore, which had been issued as worth 30 piccioli and had risen so as to be commonly accepted at 32 piccioli. The new guelfo, worth 48 piccioli, contained only 2.2904 grams of silver, compared with 1.9588 grams in the grosso da 30 piccioli. The relatively low silver content of the new coin enabled the florin to maintain a price of 62 soldi while the bimetallic ratio was as low as 10.03 to 1.[145] In contrast, the guelfo del fiore, even when priced by custom at 32 soldi, above its original value, had supported valuing gold at 12.87 times as much as silver. With the new issue, Florence was at last minting a coin of fine silver on terms that could discourage the export of silver coin. To stress the point, it explicitly forbade the export of any silver.

In 1346, in the spring after the Florentines put their new guelfo into circulation, Andrea Dandolo's mezzanino appeared. Of elegant design and

---

[143]Marvin B. Becker, *Florence in Transition*, 2 vols. (Baltimore, 1967–68), vol. 1, *The Decline of the Commune*, chaps. 4, 5.

[144]Villani, *Cronica*, bk. 12, cap. 53.

[145]Bernocchi, 3:168, 180, 181.

of a fineness comparable to that of the guelfo, it was much better able to compete with the guelfo than the soldino would have been. Moreover, it gave further recognition of the rising value of silver. With the ducat at its official value of 64 lire di piccoli, the new mezzanino lowered the Venetian ratio to 10.5 to 1, almost as low as the ratio in Florence after its new coinage (see table 23).

Although the timing of the new Florentine and Venetian issues of 1345–46 suggests that Florence was taking the lead in a new devaluation, the guelfo of 1345 may also be regarded as a very belated Florentine response to the Venetian coinage of the soldino more than a decade earlier. The quattrino had been only a partial adjustment to the change in the bimetallic ratio reflected in the minting of the soldino, for the quattrino had the limited circulation of black money. Why Florence devalued in 1345 requires less explanation than does the question, Why had Florence not adjusted earlier its fine silver coinage to the rising value of silver, the value to which the coinage of France as well as that of Venice had been adjusted much earlier, before 1340?

The answer has two sides. On the one hand, the quattrino gave all the needed protection against a draining away of the kind of currency needed for small and local transactions. On the other hand, the profits of the international bankers had come to depend on the exchange rates between florins and various foreign currencies. Where Florentines made loans in florins and collected repayment and interest in a local currency based on silver, they profited from maintaining an exchange rate that set a high value on gold. In England, as the English complained, the Florentines had maintained such a high exchange rate.[146] The vested interest that they as international bankers had acquired in a high bimetallic ratio gave them reason to maintain a high bimetallic ratio also in Florentine coinage.

The new men, who had taken control of Florence in 1343 and who in 1345 adopted the new monetary policy that encouraged the coinage of silver, were not satisfied with the amount of devaluation of the silver-based coinage effected by issuing the guelfo da 4 soldi, for it did not produce any appreciable rise in the price of the gold florin.[147] Perhaps the competition of Venice's new mezzanino prevented Florence from attracting sufficient quantities of silver to its mint. A rise came only after another new coin was ordered in 1347, a guelfo da 5 soldi. Again, the increase in the legal value of the coin was greater than the increase in its silver content, which was 2.78 grams. While the florin's market price still stood at 63, the guelfo da 5 soldi reflected a bimetallic ratio of only 9.4 to 1.[148]

[146]Feavearyear, *The Pound Sterling*, 25; and above, sec. iii.

[147]Although it succeeded in attracting enough silver to feed a renewed coinage of grossi, the first since 1324, extensive coinage of grossi came only after 1347 (de la Roncière, *Prix et salaires*, 484).

[148]Bernocchi, 3:94–95, 188.

This was the devaluation that Villani blamed specifically on the manufacturers of woolen cloth who feared that a fall of the florin would eat up their profits, since they sold their cloth for gold florins and paid their workers in silver or billon.[149] Many middling guildsmen who then controlled the government were also employers of labor who manufactured for export and therefore received payment in florins.[150]

During the next four years slight changes were made in content and mint charges for this guelfo and for the quattrino, partly in hopes of increasing revenue from the mint and partly, at least professedly, in order to keep both billon and fine silver money in circulation, but mainly to prevent a decline in the price of the florin in soldi di piccioli. In summary, one may say that the Florentine changes of 1347–51 devalued their lira di piccioli by 8.4 percent, with a reduction in the bimetallic ratio of from about 10 to 1 to 9.4 to 1.[151]

Those reductions were almost matched by Venice in 1353, when Venice began coining its second type of soldino, a soldino as fine as Dandolo's mezzanino, with so little silver content that the official price of the ducat, 64 soldi, valued gold only 9.6 times as high as silver, about the same ratio as that indicated by the price of florins in Florence at that date.[152] Thereafter the price of silver leveled off. In both cities the new coins issued in 1368–69 made only minor changes in bimetallic ratios.

The many changes that occurred in both Venice and Florence between 1378 and 1390 were not interconnected in the way in which those of mid-century had been. The later changes were responses to regional competition, as from Pisa or Padua, and are to be explained in Florence largely by internal politics and social upheavals and in Venice by her commercial and naval wars with the Genoese.[153]

The later changes had one characteristic in common with those of mid-century, however: over the long run they raised the values of the gold coin—florin or ducat—in domestic exchange. Never again after 1347 was the gold florin quoted in Florence at as low as 60, and never again after 1357 was the market value of the gold ducat quoted in Venice at as low as 64. The wealth stored away in gold coin or in assets valued in money of account based on gold was not threatened again by a devastating rise in the relative value of silver.

The defense of gold values had until then been an important element in determining monetary policy in Venice as well as in Florence. Its impor-

---

[149]Villani, *Cronica*, bk. 12, cap. 97.

[150]Becker, *Florence in Transition*, vol. 2, *Studies in the Rise of the Territorial State*, 115–18; and in vol. 1, *The Decline of the Commune*, pp. 195–96.

[151]From 12.145 grams of silver in 1345–47 to 11.1254 grams in 1351–68, a difference of 1.0209 grams (Bernocchi, 3:181, 198; Cipolla, *Il fiorino*, 52–59).

[152]See above, table 18; cf. de la Roncière, *Prix et salaires*, 491–93.

[153]Bernocchi, 3:203–4; Cipolla, *Il fiorino*, 80–86; above, chap. 18, sec. ii.

tance at Venice appears in the rough correlation described above between successive steps in the devaluation of the silver-based money of account and downward dips in the market price of the ducat. Even clearer is the persistent maintenance of the market price of the ducat at or above 64 soldi di piccoli, its minimal value as legal tender. Without the successive devaluations of the silver-based money of account, the gold in a ducat would not have continued to be worth as much as the silver equivalent of 64 soldi di piccoli.

The interest in keeping high the exchange rate between gold- and silver-based moneys of account appears to be the natural result of the dominance in both Florence and Venice of men who had accumulated wealth and were accustomed to counting their wealth in gold.[154] That attitude seems sufficient to explain the devaluations of the silver-based money of account decreed whenever the rising value of silver threatened to push down the prices of the gold coin, but the specific interests affected were different in the two cities. At Florence the more specific reason mentioned by Villani for keeping the florin high compared with the quattrino was the interest of employers who sold their products for gold and paid their employees in silver or billon. At Venice also that may well have had some importance, because Venice had developed some industries that engaged wage labor and sold products abroad. The owners of the secrets and the equipment for glassmaking at Murano were like Florentine wool cloth manufacturers in selling their output to international markets. But basically the relation of the two cities to the wider economic system of which they were parts made manufacturing with wage labor much less important at Venice.

Cipolla's analysis of the Florentine crisis of 1339–48 broadens the interpretation of Florentine policy suggested by Villani. Cipolla identifies prices based on gold with the prices of exports, prices based on silver or billon with those of imports and domestic production.[155] Bimetallism intensified Florence's crisis in the 1340s because the change in the relative values of the two metals changed the terms of trade between Florence's exports and imports, especially her exports of textiles and her imports of raw material and food supplies. Basic to all Florence's troubles with its coinage was the industrial basis for the city's growth, on which its commercial and financial development built. For Venice's prosperity, in contrast, the commercial exchange between land routes and sea routes was basic, the industrial development being a substantial but ancillary supplement.

The terms of trade most vital in Venice are best analyzed, not as a

---

[154]Including major landowners, large creditors generally, and lawyers and physicians, as Cipolla points out (*Il fiorino*, 35).
[155]Ibid., 31–34.

contrast between export prices of domestic industries and import prices of raw materials and foodstuffs, but as a relation between the prices of imports from the Levant and the prices of what was shipped east to pay for those imports. The merchant-princes who ruled Venice were much more concerned with the prices entering into those trade balances than with paying industrial workers. Much more than the Florentines, the Venetian capitalists were involved in the Levant trade, including, to be sure, the importation of much raw material, such as cotton, alum, dyes, raw silk, wax, and hides, as well as all kinds of foodstuffs, from grain to spices. Many of those imports were priced in silver-based money and paid for in silver, while they were sold in western markets at gold-based prices. And because shipments of both silver and gold were important in balancing its interregional exchange, Venice's rulers were less concerned with profits from industries than with profits from trade between regions that valued gold and silver differently.

## v. THE LEADERSHIP OF THE VENETIAN MARKET

In surveying the effects of the fall of gold on the monetary systems of Venice's trading partners, we have slighted many other factors also affecting monetary systems, for example, changes in population. The bullion trade has been the focus of attention because it was mainly through the bullion trade that the changes elsewhere were influenced by what happened on the Rialto. The intensity of the exchanges of silver for gold in Venice made the Venetian market the leader in registering alterations in the relative values of the two metals. The great change in 1330–50 was recognized in new coinage first at Venice. Venice's lead was then followed in other European countries.

Comparison of the dates of changes described above demonstrates the priority of the Venetian recognition of the new bimetallic ratio (see table 24). To be sure, the impact of the new silver coins introduced by Venice in 1331–32 was cushioned by the reduction of the fineness of 0.96 which had hitherto characterized Venetian silver and distinguished it sharply from the billon pennies. Venice's first mezzanino was only 0.78 fine, the soldino only 0.67 fine. And the Venetian innovation of 1331–32 seems not altogether unique, since Florence responded almost as quickly as Venice to the rising value of silver by introducing its quattrino immediately after Venice began coinage of mezzanini and soldini. But the quattrino was only 0.16 fine; it was suitable for paying wages and for retail purchases within Florence but not for extensive purchases elsewhere. Venetian soldini, on the other hand, were accepted as silver coin and were exported to Crete and parts of the Balkans.

In the soldino the silver content was so low compared with the value of the coin—12 soldi di piccoli—that when a gold ducat could be bought

TABLE 24.

Bimetallic Ratios in European Coinage, 1305–53

| Dates | Moneys Compared | | Ratio |
|---|---|---|---|
| | Gold | Silver | |
| 1305–30 | Venetian ducat | Venetian grosso | 14.2 |
| 1322 | Florin in Florence | Guelfo del fiore da 30 denari | 14.6 |
| 1327 | Hungarian florin | Bohemian groschen | 14.5 |
| 1330 | French royal d'or | Livre tournois | 14.1 |
| 1331–32 | Venetian ducat | Soldino, type 1 | 11.5 |
| 1334–44 | Florin in England | Sterling penny | 13.5 |
| 1337 | French florin de l'écu | Livre tournois | 11.5 |
| 1339–44 | Florin in Florence | Guelfo del fiore da 32 denari | 12.9 |
| 1344 | English noble | Sterling penny | 11.0 |
| 1345 | Florin in Florence | New guelfo (grosso da soldi 4) | 10.0 |
| 1346 | Venetian ducat | Mezzanino, type 2 | 10.5 |
| 1347 | Florin in Florence | Guelfo da soldi 5 | 9.8 |
| 1353 | Venetian ducat | Soldino, type 2 | 9.6 |

NOTE: Ratios calculated from the contents and values of the indicated coins.

on the Rialto for 64–68 soldi di piccoli, the relative value of the two coins expressed a bimetallic ratio of from 11.5 to 1 to 12.3 to 1,[156] ratios strikingly lower than the ratios of 14 to 1 to 16 to 1 which had been common north of the Alps in the 1320s. The first new coins minted beyond the Alps that gave recognition to the lower ratios being accepted in Venice were, as explained above, the gold coins issued by the king of France; but only in 1337, about five years after the appearance of the Venetian soldino, did the king's mint produce the florin de l'écu, of which the value in the silver-based livre tournois expressed a bimetallic ratio as low as that in Venice in 1331–32.

Although the golden French écu was soon accepted in England and in the leading commercial centers of the northwest, such as Bruges, the lower value of gold was not expressed in English coinage until a half-dozen years later. The value of gold coin and gold-based money of account was kept high in England by Florentine bankers as long as they controlled England's foreign exchange, and it was only after the English king, in freeing himself from dependence on foreign bankers, issued the gold noble in 1344 that the increased value of silver was recognized in English coinage. The value of the golden noble in silver pennies reflected the lower bimetallic ratio established in Venice more than ten years earlier (see table 24).

[156]See above, tables 19 and 20.

Venice led in lowering the ratio because it was the main center through which increasing quantities of gold available for coinage in western Europe were being redistributed in the middle decades of the fourteenth century. In addition to the expanding gold production of eastern Europe, gold imports from around the Black Sea and from Egypt were flooding the Venetian market.

Venice's ability to attract that gold from overseas was tightly connected with its ability to export silver, as is apparent in Venice's regulations of the trading voyages of its merchant galleys. The special position that Venice occupied in Europe's commercial system made it necessary for Venice, in order to attract gold, to attract also silver. Of course, the attractions were mutual. Plenty of gold being offered for sale in Venice made it a good place to market silver.

Attractiveness had to be expressed in high prices if it was to induce silver producers in Europe to send their silver to Venice. No exercise of military or political power compelled the German merchants to market in Venice the silver that they bought from princes or miners in eastern-central Europe. The arrival of that silver in Venice strongly suggests that buyers in Venice were offering prices higher than were offered in such competing centers as Milan or Bologna, Nuremberg or Bruges.

In order to compare the prices for bullion offered in competing markets, it is necessary to have prices stated in moneys of account based on gold. Direct evidence of such gold-based prices is difficult to find. Mint prices for silver are generally stated in moneys of account based on silver. The variations in these silver-based moneys of account reflect changes in mint charges or in the silver content of the coins more than they do changes in the relative value of silver in different places.

Since direct statements of gold-based prices for silver are lacking for some key dates, estimates have been made from the changes in the bimetallic ratios revealed by the content and values of coins. Those estimates, combined with the few direct quotations available, indicate that in Venice 1 mark of silver bullion was priced approximately as follows:[157]

| | |
|---|---|
| in 1284–85: | 5.8 gold ducats |
| in 1305–25: | 4.5 |
| in 1333: | 5.6 |
| in 1349: | 6.0 |
| in 1417: | 5.7 |

These prices are based largely on official values. The high prices of 1333 and 1349 functioned most effectively in attracting bullion to the Venetian market only when the market price for a ducat corresponded to its legal value. Only when the market price of ducats was really as low as their

[157]See below, table C.1.

legal value of 64 soldi—in 1333—did the coinage regulations have the effect of offering 5.6 ducats for 1 mark of silver bullion. In many years between 1331 and 1360 the ducat was quoted or exchanged at 68 soldi,[158] so that the gold price being offered for silver bullion was in effect probably about 5.3 ducats. But there were many years when the price of the ducat went as low as 64. Even when the market rate was higher, there were still cases in which the official rate was used, for example, by papal agents collecting the papal levy on church revenues.[159] Under those conditions the price of 5.6 ducats for a mark of silver could be collected, if not directly, then indirectly by using soldini to make payments at 64 soldini to a ducat which otherwise would have had to be made with ducats. The rise to a price of 5.8 ducats shocked Villani when it occurred at Florence as late as 1345. Prices in both cities then continued to rise and reached 6.1 ducats a few years later.[160]

Compared with the difference between the prices of 4.5 and 6.0 ducats per mark, the import tax of 4 percent imposed at Venice through the high charge for minting coins from the quinto was a minor matter. It made a price of 6.0 ducats per mark at Venice no better than a price of 5.8 ducats elsewhere.[161] But even a price of 5.8 ducats was much higher than the 4.5 ducats offered when a ducat was valued at 24 grossi and the bimetallic ratio was 14.2 to 1.

In being the first to raise the gold price for a mark of silver bullion, Venice was fulfilling her role as "world market." The abandonment in China of paper money has been pointed to as one cause for the heightened demand for silver in the east, as has the overthrow of Hindu princes in India by Moslem rulers who preferred to coin silver and who exported the gold obtained by their conquests, sending it to the west to buy slaves or horses and other military equipment.[162] These changes in demand and supply in the Far East were reflected in the prices in the Levantine ports reached by the Venetian galleys. Venice's relatively fast and safe connec-

---

[158]See above, table 20. With the ducat at 68 and the ratio between coined metals at 12.3 to 1, the ratio between coined gold and uncoined silver can then be estimated as 12.8 to 1, as explained below, in app. C.

[159]See the sources indicated below, in app. D.

[160]Cipolla, *Il fiorino*, 26; and Villani, *Cronica*, bk. 12, caps. 53, 97. Calculating from Cipolla's figures, at Florence in 1345, 339.5 grams cost 8.28 florins, so that a Venetian mark of 238.5 grams would have cost 8.28 × (238.5/339.5), or 5.8 florins. At Florence in 1347, 339.5 grams cost 8.79 florins, so that a Venetian mark of 238.5 grams would have cost 8.79 × (238.5/339.5), or 6.1 florins.

[161]As calculated above, in chap. 11, sec. ii, the mint charge for coining soldini from the silver of the quinto was about 20 percent higher than the mint charge on "free silver." Paying 20 percent on 1/5 was for the importer equivalent to paying 4 percent on the whole amount of silver that he imported to Venice (6 − [6 × 0.04] = 5.76).

[162] See above, chap. 17, nn. 30, 31.

### THE MINT IN AN ARTIST'S FANTASY

On the ceiling of the Senate Chamber of the Ducal Palace,
Marco Vecellio depicted a noble mintmaster or commissioner giving orders,
a youth bearing plate to be melted at the mint, a fante carrying fuel,
a shearer producing blanks, and a moneyer with his mallet;
in the background is Sansovino's mint and library. Late sixteenth century.

*Palazzo Ducale, archivio fotografico. Photograph by Cameraphoto.*

tions to the markets of the eastern Mediterranean that reflected such changes in supply and demand made their influence felt in Venice also.

After demand and supply reached a new equilibrium about 1360, so that the bimetallic ratio was comparatively stable at about 11 to 1, Venice solidified her central position as a bullion market. The heavy coinage of gold in Venice in the 1340s was accompanied by wider use of the ducat in both the Levant and the west, so that gradually the ducat became as well known as the florin. The accession of lower classes to power in Florence after the revolt of the Ciompi in 1378, though temporary, may have stirred doubts about the stability of Florentine money, as did the issuance of lighter-weight gold florins early in the fifteenth century.[163] By the end of

[163]On later gold florins see Bernocchi, vol. 3; and Grierson, "The Weight of the Gold Florin."

the fourteenth century the ducat was gaining in its competition with the florin as an international standard of value and a medium of exchange.

As a market for silver also, Venice's attractiveness was increased in the second half of the fourteenth century by commercial and political developments, some aided by Venetian policies, some quite outside her power to influence events. Declining productivity in the Bohemian silver mines and increased output from those in the area now forming Yugoslavia gave geographic advantages to Venice, over Nuremberg for example, or Bruges.[164] When Venice's new grossi, of different content and nominal value, were minted in large numbers in the decades following the War of Chioggia, they regained for Venetian coin the predominant role in the circulation in the Levant that it had lost to the Angevin rulers of Naples at the end of the thirteenth century.[165] That kingdom was weakened by seemingly endless wars between claimants to its throne. In northern Italy the timely death in 1402 of Gian Galeazzo Visconti, who had made Milan the most dangerous mainland neighbor, opened the way for the Venetian expansion on the mainland. The control that she achieved beginning in 1406 enabled her to introduce the products of her mint throughout the Veneto.[166] Thus, political circumstances, as much as planned monetary policies, enabled the Venetian mint to maintain the higher levels of production that it had reached in the 1340s, when large silver imports were more than matched by imports of gold.

In northwest Europe, developments yet more completely beyond the influence of Venetian policies helped Venice to hold the market position that she had gained. After the rulers of England, France, and Burgundy-Flanders (the Netherlands) began issuing gold coins adapted to a ratio as low as 11 to 1, Venice was still more successful than they were in attracting silver from such sources as Bohemia. Devastating wars, repeated outbreaks of the Black Death, and social upheavals interfered with the total productivity of northwestern Europe, but expenditures on luxuries increased as a result of the shift of wealth from country to city, as Harry Miskimin has emphasized.[167] Urban expenditures on luxuries strengthened the flow of precious metals towards Italy because Italy, as John Munro has pointed out, serviced most of the most popular forms of luxurious consumption.[168] Northwest Europe became less able to bid successfully for the output of the mines of eastern-central Europe, especially when the mines there showed signs of exhaustion. The result has been called a "bullion

---

[164]See above, chap. 17; and Kellenbenz's summary of figures on production in Bohemia and the Balkans in his "Final Remarks," 318–21.

[165]See above, chap. 18, sec. ii.

[166]Mueller, "L'imperialismo monetario."

[167]Miskimin, "Monetary Movements," 486–90.

[168]Munro, "Bullion Flows and Monetary Contraction," 104.

famine," enduring from about 1380 to about 1420.[169] During this silver famine in western Europe, Venice continued to receive silver, not only from new mines in the Balkans but also from across the Alps.

While Venice remained a center for the exchange of silver for gold, between 1390 and 1420 the direction of the flows out from Venice changed dramatically. Earlier Venice had sent silver to the east and received gold from the east. By 1420 Venice was sending gold to the east and silver to the west. Some silver being sent west was loaded on the fleet called the galleys of Flanders; some of it in the form of soldini was peddled in England as half-pennies. But part of the silver sent west from Venice found its way into western North Africa. In exchange, by the 1430s, if not earlier, Venice received from the Moslem west, Magrib, some of the gold that she then shipped eastward. But that is another story. The reversal of the bullion flows, along with other fifteenth-century developments, will be explored in volume 2. It suffices here to note that Venice's position as the central bullion market was so strong at the end of the fourteenth century that she could maintain that position during the reversal in the direction of bullion flows.

[169]Day, "The Great Bullion Famine"; idem, "The Question of Monetary Contraction in Late Medieval Europe," *Nordick Numismatick Årsskrift* (Nordik Numismatic Journal [Copenhagen]), (1981):12–29.

# 20

# THE MOBILITY AND UTILITY
# OF EUROPE'S MONEYS
# OF ACCOUNT

HE COMPLEXITY OF the relation between coins and moneys of account in fourteenth-century Venice suggests the need to elaborate on the survey of their relation sketched in our introductory comments appearing in chapter 5.

### i. CONTRASTING APPROACHES

In the 1930s, just as the gold standard was passing into history, two contrasting ways of exploring the problem of the relation between coin and money of account were formulated. What may be called a "hard money" view was championed by Hans van Werveke, a Belgian historian expert in medieval coinage.[1] A more theoretical view was expounded by the Italian economist Luigi Einaudi, the specialist on public finance who later became president of the Republic of Italy, in an article entitled "The Theory of Imaginary Money from Charlemagne to the French Revolution."[2] They came at the problem very differently.

From a study of official and commercial records concerning the coinage of the Low Countries between the thirteenth and seventeenth

---

[1]van Werveke, "Monnaie de compte et monnaie réelle." Van Werveke used the term "monnaie réelle" where in English it would be natural to refer to "coins" rather than to "real money." In English his title would be best rendered as "Money of Account and Coin."

[2]"La teoria della moneta imaginaria nel tempo da Carlomagno alla rivoluzione francese," lead article in the first issue of his *Rivista di storia economica,* 1936.

centuries, van Werveke in 1934 marshaled an attack on some assumptions of other specialists in that field. He defined three conceptions of money of account: type A represented a definite weight of gold or silver (usually previously embodied in a coin); type B was based on a coin in use, whether silver, gold, or billon; and type C was imaginary money, absolutely independent of any "real money" ("monnaie réelle"), that is, of any coin or fixed quantity of precious metal. Type C, he maintained, did not describe any historical reality. He criticized M. H. van Houtte, C. Bigwood, and Barelli de Serres for explicitly or implicitly holding that false conception, and he analyzed the moneys of account of the Netherlands to demonstrate his conclusion that all changes in their value depended on changes in their base coins.[3]

Van Werveke's conclusions were accepted, simplified, and applied to moneys of account in general by Raymond de Roover, whose own Belgian background made him familiar with the historical material from which van Werveke had reached his conclusion. In his description of money and banking in Bruges, de Roover wrote in 1948, "Medieval monetary systems were pegged either directly or indirectly to gold or silver. They were based either on a real coin, such as the groat of Flanders, or on a coin which had ceased to circulate, but which still represented a definite weight of gold or silver." In the same passage, de Roover referred to Luigi Einaudi's ideas as an example of fallacious belief in the existence of "some kind of 'ideal' or 'imaginary' money, which was used as a basis for the valuation of the real coins."[4]

A view similar at least in its acceptance of van Werveke's conclusion has been persuasively expressed by Carlo Cipolla. While elaborating his own distinction between "ghosts" and "real coins," Cipolla emphasized also "that all the systems of account in existence in those days were actually based on and tied to a real coin."[5]

Luigi Einaudi, in his article in the *Rivista di storia economica*, devoted the first half-dozen pages to early attempts to analyze money of account. His explanation of the failure of contemporaries to understand the true nature of the moneys of account of which they all made daily use was cryptic: "Imaginary money—here is my thesis—is not money at all. It is a mere instrument or technical device used to perform some monetary func-

---

[3]van Werveke, "Monnaie de compte et monnaie réelle," 145: "le sort de la monnaie de compte est toujours lié à l'existence d'une monnaie réelle. Il n'y a pas d'example de monnaie de compte absolument indépendant d'une monnaie métallique." That in the above sentences "monnaie réelle" should be translated "coin" is made most explicit on p. 123. "le gros flamand de compte ne cesse jamais de coincider en valeur avec son homonyme sonnant et trébuchant."

[4]*Money, Banking, and Credit,* 220–21.

[5]Cipolla, *Money, Prices, and Civilization,* 50; in the Italian edition, *Moneta e civiltà mediterranea,* p. 64.

tions."[6] It was not, he said, money as money was conceived in Europe after the reforms of the French Revolution. Einaudi described that modern, commodity conception of money as "the monetary unit defined as a real physical quantity of gold, silver, or some other metal, or perhaps even another commodity." "The silver coins or bank notes in circulation are representative money, convertible."[7] But that definition is not applicable before the French Revolution. The key to understanding earlier moneys was, he declared, the distinction between a monetary unit used in contracts and a monetary unit used in payments, that is, the distinction between what may be called money as a standard of value and money as a means of payment.[8]

From that starting point Einaudi's 1936 article analyzed the way the "technical device" performed monetary functions in eighteenth-century Milan. A year later, in an article in English in honor of the monetary theorist Irving Fisher, he suggested how the device might be applied even as the gold standard crumbled. In theoretical style, he sketched an extremely simplified model in which the unit of the money of account is a "dollar" that is imaginary money in that there is no coin or bank note or other means of payment called a "dollar." The coins are gold "pounds," platinum "guineas," and silver "florins." The government fixes the value in "dollars" of any one of these coins. Thereafter the values in "dollars" of the other kinds of coin change freely in accordance with the changes in the market values of the different metals. As a result, coins of all three metals circulate without any need for further governmental action. By its separation from the means of payment, its separation from any coin, the money of account becomes a "device" that permits coins of several different metals to circulate, without any need to change their content when changes occur in the relative values of the metals.[9] Using the model as a springboard, Einaudi extolled the future and past possibilities of "imaginary money" in a way that made it natural for him to be considered the "principal protagonist on the other side," against van Werveke and de Roover. He was so presented in Peter Spufford's reconsideration of the issues in 1970.[10]

In spite of their contrasting approaches, van Werveke and Einaudi did not in fact present irreconcilable contradictions. As Peter Spufford recognized, Marc Bloch in his prompt reviews of their articles and later in

[6]See the translation cited above in chap. 3, n. 23, and cited hereafter as Einaudi in *Enterprise*, 237, par. 12.

[7]Ibid., 234–35, par. 9.

[8]The statement in Italian (p. 1)—"la distinzione fra unità monetaria di contrattazione ed unità di pagamento"—is sharper than in the translation in *Enterprise*, 235.

[9]Luigi Einaudi, "The Medieval Practice of Managed Currency," in *The Lessons of Monetary Experience: Essays in Honor of Irvin Fisher,* ed. A. D. Gayer (New York, 1937), 259–68.

[10]*Monetary Problems and Policies,* 14.

his lectures suggested ways in which their views could be brought into synthesis.

Bloch praised both articles but considered each a fragmentary approach.[11] A well-rounded treatment would trace development. His comments suggest that between Charlemagne and the French Revolution several periods might be distinguished. Before the thirteenth century, when the only coin minted in most of western Europe was the denarius, the habit of calculating in multiples of that monetary unit was firmly implanted, while other means of payment such as labor or wheat or bullion were extensively used. Later the availability of many kinds of coin created the problems with which van Werveke was concerned. Einaudi also did not adequately consider, thought Bloch, the extent to which the essential nature of money of account changed prior to the period on which he concentrated attention.

While seeking a more historical analysis, Marc Bloch skillfully applied the distinction that Einaudi proclaimed to be the key to understanding money of account, namely, the distinction between a monetary unit used as a standard of value or of deferred payments and a monetary unit used as a medium of exchange. In Bloch's words, "En d'autres termes, qu'est-ce que le régime de la monnaie de compte, sinon un système où les deux fonctions essentielles de la monnaie, comme mesure des valeurs et comme moyen de paiement, son détachées l'une de l'autre?"[12]

Our monetary history of medieval Venice has necessarily involved testing more or less explicitly the contrasting approaches of Hans van Werveke and Luigi Einaudi and the possibilities of the kind of synthesis suggested by Marc Bloch. Here we will first consider the accuracy and limitations of van Werveke's formulation and then outline the emergence of a distinct, intermediate period in the evolutionary development which Bloch wished explored. Examination of some of the characteristics of that stage leads to consideration of the usefulness of Einaudi's model building for understanding the monetary problems of medieval and early modern times.

## ii. MOBILITY AND BIFURCATION

Carlo Cipolla's statement that "all systems of account in existence in those days were actually based on and tied to a real coin" invites elaboration. One can agree that at any given point of time each money of account was based on (1) a specific coin, (2) the amount of metal contained in a

---

[11]Bloch's review of van Werveke's article is "La monnaie de compte," *Annales d'histoire économique et sociale* 7 (1935):323–25; his review of Einaudi's is "Le problème de la monnaie de compte," in ibid. 10 (1938):358–60.

[12]Bloch, *Esquisse*, 49; see also idem, "Mutations monétaires," 154.

coin minted exactly according to legal specifications, or (3) a set of coins integrated into a system according to their metallic content (such as the English groats, shillings, and pence). On the other hand, neither Cipolla's concise statement nor van Werveke's more elaborate formulation should be accepted as meaning that the value of a unit of money of account was determined solely by its silver or gold equivalent. The case of billon coins is crucial. Their exchange values varied not only according to their content in precious metal and according to their relatively higher costs of manufacture but also according to the quantity in circulation.[13] Elaborated in this fashion, the validity of Cipolla's statement in particular is confirmed by our study of Venice's system of moneys of account and their metallic equivalents.

As others have discovered in other cases, we have found that at Venice the same money of account was based on different coins at different points of time. In this sense, moneys of account were mobile, shifting their attachments from one base coin or link coin to another. The history of the Venetian lira di piccoli is one clear example of this kind of mobility. The link coin determining its metallic equivalent before 1331 was the billon coin called a piccolo. After the soldino was introduced in 1331–32, the soldino became the link coin that determined the metallic equivalent of the lira di piccoli.[14] During roughly the same period in which this shift was occurring in Venice, in Florence the lira di piccioli shifted its base from the picciolo to the quattrino, under circumstances explained above, in chapter 19, section iv.[15] At Milan the lira imperiale shifted its base from piccoli to larger billon or silver coins well before 1330.[16]

Another example of this mobility is the shift in base of the Venetian lira di grossi. For more than a century before 1331 its link coin had been the silver grosso first minted by Enrico Dandolo, but by 1370 at the latest the metallic equivalent of a "lira di grossi" was no longer determined by a grosso coin. It was determined either by the gold ducat or by the new kinds of silver coins, such as the soldino, issued after 1331.[17]

The change in the attachments of the lira di grossi during the fourteenth century raises the question whether some shifts of base by moneys of account are best described as the splitting of old moneys of account or as the creation of new moneys of account. We have called the change in

---

[13]See above, chap. 5, sec. i, on labor and scarcity values.

[14]See above, chap. 16.

[15]Bernocchi, 3:76, 175–77, 189–93; 4:v–vi. In his *Il fiorino*, 87, Cipolla summarizes that shift in Florence: "d'altra parte, con l'emarginazione del denaro piccolo, il quattrino era divenuto la principale moneta d'appoggio del sistema monetario piccolo su cui si basava tutta la struttura dei prezzi interni."

[16]Cipolla, *Le avventure della lira*, 54–55; Zerbi, *Moneta effettiva*, 27, 32–37. Cf. Soldi Rondinini, "Politica e teoria monetarie."

[17]See above, chap. 16.

## PROCURATORI DI SAN MARCO DISPENSING CASH

The Procuratori and their assistants consulted written records of amounts
due before counting out the coins used in payments.

*Seminario Patriarcale, Venice, Catastico di S. Maffeo di Murano.*
*Photograph by Böhm.*

the lira di grossi a split, but certainly the appearance of new moneys of
account is involved. In explaining his conception of "ghost moneys,"
Cipolla referred to three instances of what we consider the splitting in two
of an established money of account—the first at Milan between 1350 and
1400, the second at Genoa at about the same time, and the third at Venice
after 1517.[18] In all three cases a "ghostly" florin or ducat tied to a silver coin
appeared alongside the florin or ducat tied to the "real," gold coin.

Within the restricted scope of this history, we have focused on two
different instances of "splitting," both at Venice and both before 1400.
The first such bifurcation, described above, in chapter 8, section iii, occurred very early, between about 1250 and 1280, when the lib. ven. (libra
denariorum venetialium), which had been in use for more than a hundred

---

[18]Cipolla, *Money, Prices, and Civilization*, 46–48; idem, *I movimenti*, 34 n. 3. Cf. Zerbi,
*Moneta effettiva*, 43–69.

years, split into the lira di piccoli (libra parvorum) and the lira a grossi (libra ad grossos). The second such bifurcation was like those mentioned by Cipolla in distinguishing a ducat based on silver coin from a ducat based on gold coin, but it occurred two centuries earlier than the Venetian example mentioned by Cipolla. Twice in Venetian monetary history the meaning of "ducat" became ambiguous. First, between 1320 and 1380, at the same time that "florin" was acquiring a double meaning at Milan and Genoa, "ducat" came to mean at Venice both the gold coin and a unit of account worth 64 soldi in silver coin. When its meaning became ambiguous a second time, between 1510 and 1580, as described by Niccolò Papadopoli, its silver attachment led to the minting in 1562 of a silver "ducat" worth 124 soldi. Meanwhile the gold coin previously called the "ducat" became known as the zecchino.[19] In the earlier splitting of the ducat, described above, the coin did not change its name; and the account based on the gold coin was distinguished about 1400 only by being labeled "a oro" in contrast to the denominations labeled "a monete."

Calling these developments a splitting of the previously used money of account invites inquiry into how prices, salaries, debts, and promises were carried over from the old money of account into one of the new moneys of account. In the 1270s, retail prices and daily wages in Venice, which had been stated in libre, solidi, and denarii, were thereafter set in lire di piccoli (libre parvorum), while government bonds and salaries of high officials, which had been stated in lib. ven., were thereafter stated in lire a grossi (libre ad grossos).[20]

After that bifurcation had separated lire a grossi from lire di piccoli sometime before 1270, the grosso-based moneys of account underwent new splits between 1330 and 1360 as a result of the coinage of new types of silver coin. Moneys of account called "a monete," tied to the new, less valuable silver coins, were used in much domestic business and in setting some wages (including this time, as we have seen, those of seamen), while big business deals and high salaries were generally stated in the money of account tied to the gold ducat. There were dubious or ambiguous categories, however. Interest on the government debt was paid partly in gold, partly in silver. Officials sometimes could use their positions to interpret the money of account in which their salaries had been stated so as to pay themselves in the most advantageous coin. Police magistrates levied fines collected either a oro or a monete, according to the size of the fine.[21]

Such splits changed the relations between the values of various commodities and services. For example, the split of the old lib. ven. into

---

[19]Papadopoli, 2:211–13; idem, "Sul valore della moneta veneziana," 680–91; idem, "Le monete trovate nelle rovine del Campanile di San Marco."

[20]See above, chap. 8.

[21]See above, chap. 16, secs. iv, v.

the lira di piccoli and the lira a grossi increased the value of government bonds compared with that of wages by about 30 percent. A split had such effects because after the split, obligations and prices previously recorded in a single money of account were payable partly one way, partly the other way.

In contrast, the shift of a money of account from one base coin to another, such as the shift of the lira di piccoli from the piccolo to the soldino in the mid-fourteenth century, did not alter the statement of the values of goods and services in relation to each other. It altered only the relation of all of them to the money of account's metallic base. Salaries and tariffs established by law, prices that had become customary, and wages that were "sticky" were not changed ipso facto by changing the link coin from the piccolo to the soldino. Nor were they changed automatically by later successive reductions in the amount of silver in the soldino. To call such changes in the metallic base the creation of a new money of account would serve no good purpose. Usage goes rather to the opposite extreme in accepting the unity and continuity of a money of account even if it shifts from one metal to another, as is clearly illustrated by the history of the English pound sterling. Economists refer to "unbroken continuity in the value of the pound"[22] in spite of changes in its value in gold and silver. Feavearyear, the historian of the pound sterling, extolled that continuity in sweeping terms: "Though at one period based upon a silver standard, later upon a gold standard, and in three periods upon no metallic standard at all, the pound has a continuous history and has never ceased to be accepted in any period in full settlement of debts incurred in the pounds of an earlier period."[23]

The mobility of the moneys of account created ambiguities, leading to disputes that were settled only after appeal to the law courts to decide on the relation between moneys of account and coins in use. The instance cited above concerning a payment due in 1396 in gold ducats of a legacy recorded sixty years earlier in lire di piccoli illustrates one way in which courts approached the problem. When several moneys of account were being used simultaneously, some based on gold coin, some on silver or billon, their decisions sometimes favored creditors, sometimes debtors.[24] By creating such ambiguities, the mobility of moneys of account limited or undermined the unity and continuity of monetary standards.

A change in a money of account's metallic equivalent was in most cases due to governmental action. But not in all cases and not altogether

---

[22]Harrod, *Money*, 8.

[23]*The Pound Sterling*, 2.

[24]See above, chap. 16, sec. iv. The Procurators of San Marco decided many such questions in their administration of estates and trust funds, for they were daily converting sums recorded in moneys of account into coins which they handed to legatees or beneficiaries. Cf. above, chap. 7, sec. ii, esp. n. 15.

by governmental action, which often merely recognized and gave legal status to a change that had occurred previously in business practice. Van Werveke's approach risks underestimating the extent to which market forces, rather than governmental initiatives, could shift the base of a money of account.[25] Venetian experience suggests that many changes originated in commercial markets and that official action was a mere approval of rates already established in practice.

Consider the process that detached the lira di grossi from the coin that was its original base, the silver grosso containing 2.1 grams of silver. The same process applied to the lira a grossi, although it involved more complicated arithmetic. The position of the grosso as the link coin of those moneys of account was not threatened immediately by the coinage of the gold ducat in 1284–85 or by the attempt to give them a bimetallic base by equating 1 ducat with 18–18 1/2 grossi. When that attempt was abandoned after 1296, the lira di grossi remained based on the grosso. One lira di grossi was still equal to 240 grossi coins, while the ducat rose to become worth 24 grossi coins and therefore worth in money of account 1/10 of a lira di grossi. Only after the ducat had stayed at about that level for some twenty years was the position of the grosso as the link coin weakened. As is indicated both by papal accounts and by Pegolotti's merchant manual, the grosso began to share its basic position with the ducat before the government made any move to change either the coins issued or the legal value of coins.

Other coins began taking the place of the grosso in making payments recorded in lire di grossi or lire a grossi because grossi coins, especially good grossi coins, became relatively scarce. They were being exported to the Levant, where silver commanded a better price in gold than it did in Venice. After the bimetallic ratio peaked in the 1320s and began to fall, full-weight grossi were more and more used in the Levant to make purchases of eastern wares. Much of the silver bullion brought to Venice was shipped east and used to buy gold there. In Venice, prices and obligations in lire di grossi were paid very largely in coin other than grossi. They were paid with ducats valued at about 24 grossi or with silver coin inferior in content to the old grossi. The change was nearly complete by 1335. It was speeded up before that date by two governmental actions: (1) the law of 1328 declaring the ducat legal tender for 24 grossi, and (2) the issuance in 1331 of the new silver coins, the mezzanino and soldino, which had higher legal value compared with their silver content than did the old grosso. These official actions completed the divorce between the lira di grossi and the grossi coins.

---

[25]van Werveke, "Monnaie di compte et monnaie réelle," 124, 125, 128. On the other hand, he correctly stressed the inability of governments to force the market place to value coins above their intrinsic value.

Although the completion of the change may be attributed to governmental action, the process had been started previously by private traders. A way of paying a lira di grossi without using grossi coins was recognized in commercial contracts that refer to obligations in "lira di grossi a monete" even before the new Venetian silver issues called "monete" appeared in 1331–32. Such references imply the extensive use in paying lire a grossi of such silver coins as the groats of Verona, Tyrol, and Rascia before the new Venetian silver coins began to circulate. Thus the shift away from the grosso as link coin to either the gold ducat or inferior silver coins had begun in commercial usage before it was accelerated and formalized by action of the Communal authorities.[26]

### iii. A MIDDLE PERIOD

The mobility of moneys of account and their bifurcation occurred most notably between about 1250 and 1650, an intermediate period in the millennium between Charlemagne and the French Revolution. That millennium can usefully be divided into three periods, featuring three stages of development. The first extends from Charlemagne to the mid-thirteenth century and is characterized by the minting of denarii only; "solidus" and "libra" meant, respectively, simply 12 and 240 of the units called "denarii." These denominations were used in making calculations even in the many instances in which actual payment was expected to be made in other forms than coin, such as services or commodities.

The second, or intermediate, period was inaugurated by what Marc Bloch called the great monetary revolution of the thirteenth century, namely, the appearance of a variety of new coins.[27] In that period, running from about 1250 to the late sixteenth or the seventeenth century, new questions arose concerning how the payments calculated in denarii, solidi, and libbre were to be paid. It was in this intermediate period that "a true system of money of account was created, tied to real coins only by a continually varying equivalence, by an 'imaginary' money, as it was called after the sixteenth century."[28]

The attachment of moneys of account to the coins from which they originated faded until in the third period, to use Bloch's phrase, "le decrochement de la monnaie de compte et de la monnaie réelle s'était veritablement opéré."[29] In other words, only after the complications and the mobility of an intermediate period did money of account become so de-

---

[26]On the preceding paragraphs see above, chaps. 15, sec. ii, and 16.

[27]Bloch, *Esquisse,* 44. Note that contrary to the general French usage explained above, in chap. 1, sec. ii, Bloch there used "monnaie de compte" in the same broad meaning that we have adopted here.

[28]Ibid.

[29]Ibid., 46–47.

tached from any particular coin as to become fixed in the minds of men as a measure of monetary value useful in stating the relative values of all the sundry coins in circulation. The third period was inaugurated in some areas already in the sixteenth century by the addition of numbers to the design of some coins stating their value in money of account, whereas previously coins had been known by such features as a cross or a crown. In Venice the start of the third period was signalized by the minting in 1562 of the silver ducat with its value in soldi di piccoli, 124, stamped on the reverse side.[30] That a coin was struck with such a statement of its value shows that the money of account referred to was readily recognizable as the generally accepted numerical statement of monetary value. Only after varied experiences in the course of the intermediate period—lasting in some places centuries, in others a relatively short time—did a money of account become established in a community as a measure of exchange value, no longer tied to any particular coin but useful in stating the relative values of all the coins in use.

This development was thoughtfully summarized by Allan Evans, whose skillful edition of Pegolotti's treatise has earned the grateful admiration of students of medieval trade and numismatics. In an incomplete, unpublished draft for a history of coinage (or perhaps of Florentine coinage) on which he worked before his diversion from medieval studies by the war in 1940,[31] after discussing debasement in the later Middle Ages, he continued:

> The fact is that by the seventeenth and eighteenth
> centuries the old pound had sunk to such remarkably low
> levels that it was almost inconceivable that the denier of
> account had ever had a calculable value, far less been minted
> as a coin of intrinsic value. Even in the fifteenth century,
> it had become useless in many places to coin deniers, and in
> Italy the quattrino, fourpenny bit, became the basis of
> value; after all it made little difference whether the pound
> should be valued as 240 actual physical units or as 240
> fourths of a quattrino. In this way it was possible for the
> system of account to continue sinking, deriving its value
> from whatever multiple of the denier of account the

[30]Papadopoli, 2:212–13; 3:pl. 31, no. 11; cf. pls. 32, nos. 1–2, and 34, no. 124.

[31]Evans was a senior tutor and instructor at Harvard from 1931 to 1938, overlapping the years during which Florence Edler and Raymond de Roover were making the acquaintance of Medici accounts books through the Selfridge collection at the Baker Library of the Harvard Business School and Abbott Payson Usher was preparing his *The Early History of Deposit Banking in Mediterranean Europe*. On Evans's service in the Office of Strategic Services and the Department of State from 1940 to 1970 see *Harvard Class of 1924, Fiftieth Anniversary Report*, 168.

government chose at any given time to set as the standard. Evidently there came a critical moment when a change took place in people's understanding of this institution. At some point it became apparent that the rating of *all* coins in terms of £ s. d. of account could be altered simultaneously. The £ could as easily be 240 sixths of a sixpenny piece, twelfths of a shilling, as quarters of a fourpenny piece. From this time, there grew up slowly the concept of the system of account as something distinct and apart from the actual pattern of coins which represented at any given moment multiples of accounting units; the system of account being in effect the expression of the price complex in the commodity market, upon convenient pegs of which coins might be hung at discretion of the authority which published tariffs of currency. And since the accounting system had sunk so low that the £ was now the term most often used in current bargaining, the system became known as the £ system, a fact which added to the abstract quality it already enjoyed, for the pound had seldom been for long embodied in an actual coin, and I think never represented by a coin of that name. The possibilities and interrelations between the system of account and the system of coins thus in the eighteenth and nineteenth centuries gave rise to much ingenious theorizing, and it is this situation which has been so skillfully and exactly described by Signor Einaudi.

Even so, it is clear that at any given moment the system of account must have derived its valuations from some one coin.[32]

---

[32]Evans's handwritten draft was kindly placed at our disposal by David Herlihy, who had received it from Mrs. Evans. Of interest also in this connection is a paragraph that Evans drafted apparently as part of an introduction or preface. It is indicative of his wariness towards the term "money of account":

To define in one word the subject with which this work is to deal offers difficulties. Money to the well-trained modern world conveys large implications, and may include the cheque on an equal footing with the treasury note; coinage on the other hand suggests a concern with no more than the tangible pieces of metal, and one must nowadays add paper, which form the common vehicle of petty exchange. For want of a better term I shall press into use the word currency to indicate the different kinds of units, tangible or intangible, in terms of which at a given time exchange transactions on a monetary basis may be calculated. In this study of currency, then, the unit will be regarded neither as the insignificant atom in a vast mass of purchasing power, nor as the artifact with external and compelling individuality. Rather the emphasis must be

During the intermediate period, the development that Evans sketched was only beginning. Moneys of account were more closely associated with particular coins, and no money of account so dominated as to be the one "device" useful in stating the value of coins compared one with another, at least not at Venice. Elsewhere also many moneys of account were used simultaneously, some briefly, some for long periods. Bloch generalized, "Il n'est presque aucune monnaie réelle d'usage un peu général que n'ait tendu à se transformer à son tour en monnaie de compte."[33]

At Venice the lira a grossi was for some time the money of account most used to indicate the relative values of coins. It was more used for that purpose than was the lira di piccoli, not only in rating foreign coins and moneys of account, as in the conversion tables of the Ternaria,[34] but also in rating Venice's own gold coin. When the value of the ducat as legal tender was first specified, it was stated as 40 soldi a grossi.[35] After the bimetallic ratio had risen from about 11 to 1 to about 14 to 1, Pegolotti stated the relative values of the gold ducat and the silver grosso by valuing the ducat at 52 soldi a grossi and the grosso at 26 denari a grossi.[36] Frequently he stated the relative values of ducats and grossi more simply by equating 1 ducat with 2 soldi di grossi.[37] He used the lira, soldo, and denaro di piccoli to give the relative values of different coins only when comparing the Venetian grossi and the friesachers (fregiacchesi) coined in Friuli. He valued the friesacher at 14 denari piccoli and the grosso at 32 piccoli ("denari 32 piccioli bagattini 1 grosso d'ariento di Vinegia").[38]

At Florence, as Mario Bernocchi has recently shown, after the gold florin was introduced in 1252, for several years its value relative to other coins was stated in soldi a fiorini as well as in soldi di piccioli, that is, in the money of account based on Florence's silver groats as well as in the money of account based on Florentine pennies. Only after 1279 did the lira a fiorini become tied to the gold florin by being valued always at 29 soldi a fiorini. Only then did the lira di piccioli become the one money of account used to express the relative values of all Florence's coins.[39] At Milan other moneys of account, such as the lira terzuola, were overshadowed from an

---

upon the interrelations of the units, upon the characteristics they derive from the effort of communities, in which monetary exchange has developed, to make that exchange more convenient by fitting diverse units of currency into a system, a ladder of denominations.

[33]Bloch, Esquisse, 48.
[34]See above, chap. 14, sec. iii; and below, app. G, doc. 1.
[35]See above, chap. 13, sec. iv.
[36]Pegolotti, Pratica, 50, 97.
[37]Ibid., 152.
[38]Ibid., 155.
[39]See above, chap. 13, sec. iii. See also Bernocchi, 3:78, 263–66; 4:v–vi.

early date by the lira imperiale.[40] Thus the intermediate period was very much shorter at Florence and Milan than at Venice, although separate, gold-based moneys of account appeared in all three cities.

Luigi Einaudi focused his attention on the third of the three periods between Charlemagne and the French Revolution. His "theory of imaginary money" arose from his analysis of the situation in Milan after its monetary system had reached the third stage of development. He described the situation in 1762, when there were 22 different gold coins and 29 different silver coins in circulation, each rated in lire, soldi, and denari imperiali. None of the coins in circulation was called a lira or had the value of 1 lira.[41] Applying to the denominations of money of account names that were different from the names of coins seemed to Einaudi an essential, as was noted in describing his simplified model. It enabled money of account to function as a "device" that permitted coins of different metals to continue to circulate even when the relative values of the metals changed markedly. So long as only one of the kinds of coins in circulation had a fixed legal tender value in money of account, the values of the others would rise or fall according to the changes in the market value of the kind of metal they contained.[42]

Of course, not all the assumptions clarified in a model can be expected to match conditions actually existing in a particular historical situation, but a model suggests what to look for in considering the decisions of policymakers. Einaudi's model helps in analyzing the possibilities facing Venetian senators when formulating monetary policy. Specifically, it suggests various different policies that they might have adopted and without any need to mint a new kind of coin with a different metallic content about 1330, when grossi began to disappear.

One of the conditions required for the operation of the "device" as suggested in Einaudi's model was present. The Venetian market was sufficiently free that the prices of coins could respond to changes in supply and demand. The official prices which the government gave the coins constituted a floor of minimum value. Coins had to be accepted as worth at least the legally specified amounts in payment of debts, but the decrees did not prevent coins from rising above their official values. During the second, or intermediate, period, at least during its early centuries, evidence of

---

[40]Zerbi, *Moneta effettiva*, 13–22, 33–37, 57–58.

[41]Einaudi in *Enterprise*, 241–43. The essentials of Einaudi's description of the monetary situation in Milan at that time have been confirmed by Aldo De Maddalena, who describes the lira imperiale of that period as being a denomination of account that was used for accounting purposes to reduce "to homogeneous accounting values the heterogeneous values expressed in coins that differed in their intrinsic and extrinsic characteristics" (*Prezzi e mercedi a Milano dal 1701 al 1860*, Studi e ricerche di storia economica italiana nell'età del Risorgimento, Banca Commerciale Italiana, 2 vols. [Milan, 1974], 1:38).

[42]Einaudi, "The Medieval Practice," 260–62.

"draconian" enforcement of official prices is lacking, at least at Venice.[43] The official value of the ducat was set at about 18 1/2 grossi in 1285, but as we have seen, that did not prevent its rise almost immediately to 20 grossi and its general acceptance after 1305 at 24 grossi.[44] Similarly, the official valuation of the grosso coin as 1/24 of a ducat in 1328 seems not to have prevented the grosso coin from acquiring a market value of 1/20 of a ducat when silver rose in value. Certainly, while still officially valued at 32 piccoli during the third and fourth decades of the fourteenth century, the grosso coin of the old standard rose above 40 piccoli. The government recognized and in a way approved such a rise above the "legal value" of 32 piccoli by forbidding officials, who generally paid their salaries to themselves out of the coins they took in, to pay themselves in grossi valued at 32 piccoli.[45] Although the Venetian money market was not free from government intervention, it was free enough to make the consideration of Einaudi's model enlightening.

Comparing historical actuality with some other assumptions of Einaudi's "theory of imaginary money" confirms the importance of names. Suppose that instead of issuing new series of silver coins the government had continued to mint grossi at their traditional weight and fineness but had cried up their value and made a grosso coin worth legally 1/20 of a ducat instead of 1/24. How would that increase in the legal value of grossi be expressed in money of account? It could not be expressed in the lira a grossi or the lira di grossi without an abrupt, difficult change in the meaning of "grosso." A banker or any merchant who received a grosso coin would have had to record its receipt as that of 1 1/5 of the denari grossi of which 240 constituted the lira di grossi in which he kept his accounts. Could popular usage in the 1330s have quickly accepted the thought that the grosso coin, which for generations had been identical in value with the denaro of the lira di grossi, was now worth 1 1/5 of those denari grossi? and in the next month perhaps 1 1/4? and then 1 1/2?

To be sure, that is what happened over the course of a generation. After the issuance of the new silver coins, the name "grosso" became detached from its former identification with the coin to which it had been attached for more than a century. By the time of the coinage of the new grosso with a slightly changed design in 1379, three separate meanings of "grosso" were in use. One referred to the coin, the others to moneys of

---

[43]Bloch, *Esquisse*, 57, refers to "interdictions les plus draconiens" for violations of decrees fixing the values of coins but admits that they were completely ineffective. Is there really much evidence in early centuries of inflicting heavy penalties for the bidding up of domestic coins of high metallic value? Were not the penalties really directed against foreign coins, especially those passed off at values not justified by their metallic content (for example, at Venice the groats of Rascia), and against counterfeits?

[44]See above, chap. 14, sec. ii.

[45]See above, chap. 15, sec. iii.

account. By the 1380s it was not confusing, apparently, for the Venetians to use a "grosso" coin that was worth 1 1/2 times as much as a "grosso a monete" and 1 1/5 times as much as a "grosso a oro."[46] That usage became well established, but not clearly so until about a half-century after the grosso had ceased to be Venice's main silver piece, after the denomination of account had become detached from its original link coin, and after the minting of any kind of grosso had been suspended for more than two decades, 1356–79. Back in the 1330s the moneys of account based hitherto on the grosso had been too firmly associated in men's minds with that coin. The distinctions accepted later would have been too difficult or confusing.[47]

The easy way to avoid the exodus of grossi when the value of silver rose would have been, according to Einaudi's model, a repeal of the law of 1328 that made the ducat legal tender for 24 grossi. All Venice's moneys of account would then have remained based on silver. Repealing that law and letting the ducat fall in legal value as fast as the bimetallic ratio fell would have had the same effect as crying down the ducat. If the market quotations for the ducat had fallen from 52 soldi a grossi to 45 1/2, then 1 gold ducat coin would have become equal in value to 21 silver grossi coins, which would have represented a bimetallic ratio of 12.4 to 1 (44.1/3.55). When the bimetallic ratio declined further in the 1340s and went down to 10 to 1, the ducat might have dropped to 36 1/5 soldi a grossi. Such low values of the ducat would have removed the reason for choosing grossi instead of ducats for export to the Levant. Lowering the value of the gold coin would seem to have been the practical way to keep silver in circulation without any new coinage.

It is understandable that devaluing the ducat in this way seemed far more objectionable to Venice's rulers than did issuing new coins. To have let the ducat fall to, say, 20 grossi after it had been circulating at 24 for a generation would have meant that a banker who owed a depositor 10 lire di grossi because he had received as a deposit 100 ducat coins could be called on to pay off the depositor by giving him 120 ducats unless he could find 2,400 grossi to pay out instead. Anyone who had accumulated ducats in order to meet obligations, such as paying forced loans or fulfilling the dowry terms of a marriage contract, would be in much the same difficulty as our imagined banker.

Opposition to such devaluing of gold was to be expected especially from those classes that were wealthy enough to be able to save money.

---

[46]See above, chap. 16, sec. iv.

[47]As Bloch said after stressing the separation of the two functions of money (as quoted above, n. 12), "Cependant, la dissociation ne fut jamais absolue. Les prix avaient beau être fixé en livres, sous, et deniers; il était impossible que, sous ces mots, les hommes manquassent à évoquer l'image de réalitées matérielles: pièces d'or ou d'argent d'une certaine apparence et d'une certaine teneur" (Esquisse, 49).

Before gold began falling in value about 1325, it had been rising for about three generations. Men and women with sufficient income to provide for their earthly futures by hoarding or multiplying their commercial investments had reason to believe that gold coin, or credits recorded in moneys of account based on gold, were the best "store of value." Among the kinds of money available, gold seemed ideal for preserving and accumulating wealth. Therefore the rich had a vested interest in opposing the devaluation of gold coins or of moneys of account tied to gold coin. Some way of inflating the silver currency was more in accord with their interests.[48]

In addition to class interests attached to gold values, a more general obstacle to maintaining bimetallism by using moneys of account in the manner outlined by Einaudi was that it involved devaluation of precisely those coins most in circulation. It encountered the same opposition that made intensely unpopular a recoinage that was accompanied by crying down coins so as to strengthen the money of account.[49] It made the payment of debts and traditional prices more difficult.

Considerations of prestige were also important. To declare any coin worth less for meeting obligations than the value previously given it as legal tender was an obvious breach of faith likely to destroy trust in the state's coins. Foreign coins could be devalued without loss of reputation, but not one's own coins—certainly not the Venetians' golden ducat. It was much easier to issue new silver coins.

The simultaneous use of several independently based moneys of account had another important consequence. Each money of account had developed in connection with assigning exchange values to a particular range of goods and services. As a result, one money of account was used to express the values compared with one another of a certain group of goods or services, while a different money of account was used to express the relative values of a somewhat different group of goods and services. At Venice about 1350, lire a grossi were used to compare the value of the capital and the interest on the public debt and to compare the salaries of a doge and a mintmaster. The lira di piccoli was used to state the relative values of the wages of a ship's carpenter and the wages of a caulker or a mason. When separate moneys of account that expressed the relative values of different sets of commodities were differently based—one on gold, the other on silver, or one on white money, the other on black money— changes in the coin on which they were based did not change the relative values of the goods and services within the set. But it might well change the value of one set compared with that of another. It could change the

---

[48]Cipolla, *Il fiorino*, 32–39, 73. Opposition in England to the government's efforts to reduce the value of the guinea when the bimetallic ratio was falling is described in Feavearyear, *The Pound Sterling*, 144–45.

[49]See above, chap. 3.

income received by different classes, for example, the income of wage earners compared with that of employers when prices set in silver-based or billon-based moneys of account moved differently than did prices set in gold-based moneys of account.

When men and women priced articles in lire and soldi, they had in mind not only the coins that were the basis of a particular money of account but also various articles and obligations priced in those denominations of account, such as the price of a loaf of bread or a bottle of wine. When a dispute between shipowners and caulkers was settled by fixing the daily wage at 32 or 22 soldi di piccoli, the caulkers were probably thinking less about the metallic content of the piccoli or soldini in which they would be paid than about how many loaves of bread or bottles of wine 32 soldi would buy.[50] When the Great Council voted that 3 lire a grossi should be the base salary of the watchmen to be appointed by the Signori di Notte, the councillors were probably thinking less about the metallic content of grossi than about the salary of the noble Signori di Notte themselves, which was about 6 lire a grossi.[51] Once a money of account had been used for a long time to price a set of basic commodities and services, those prices could determine the value of the money of account as much as did the coin or coins on which it was based.

In short, a denomination of account called to mind originally a specific coin or a multiple or fraction of a specific coin. After it had been used again and again to indicate the relative values of many commodities and services, it called to mind not only a specific coin or a specific amount of precious metal but also the amount of various commodities and services that the coin had been able to buy. To that extent, moneys of account became independent of their link coins in the third period.

A full treatment of the transition to the third stage in the history of Europe's experience with money of account is beyond the scope of this book, as is the question whether "money of account" ever became a standard of value so detached from anything that had intrinsic or commodity value that it should be compared to a notch in a stick of wood, as the discussion in our introductory chapter of bartering cows for horses, cowhides, and so on, may have seemed to suggest. Notched sticks of wood were in fact used in medieval England in settling accounts between the Lords of the Exchequer and the kings' sheriffs.[52] But in any case, such a symbol could be used only when it had acquired an agreed-upon meaning by long association with items judged inherently valuable—a cow or a

[50]Lane, *Navires et constructeurs*, 74. Cf. Goldthwaite, *The Building of Renaissance Florence*, 315–16.

[51]Roberti, ed., *Le magistrature giudiziarie*, 3:25, 94.

[52]According to the *Encyclopaedia Britannica*, 11th ed., s.v. "exchequer," the Exchequer used notched sticks until 1826.

horse, a coin or a royal writ. In primitive societies something widely used served as money because the users had a common feeling about its usefulness compared with that of other things. Later a coin of little intrinsic value could serve as the standard of value when there was general agreement based on common experience concerning how much it could buy in useful goods and services.

In characterizing money of account as a "device" and in clarifying eighteenth-century views of it, Einaudi quoted an author who said that money of account had been conceived with the use of bills of exchange when they were devised to avoid the expense of transporting specie.[53] But Einaudi was not misled by any such historical distortion. On the contrary, he correctly asserted that "money of account was not created by decree but grew spontaneously out of men's habit of keeping accounts in monetary units."[54] Our previous chapters have shown how it developed, as spontaneously as language, out of the monetary conditions amongst which the Venetian city-state originated. To assume that the later leaders of Venice had in mind concepts similar to those in Einaudi's model, or "theory of imaginary money," when formulating their monetary decisions would be absurdly anachronistic. Nevertheless, even though Venetian councillors did not think of moneys of account as "instruments" that they could use to avoid changes in the currency, Einaudi's model helps us to understand the alternatives they faced and some of the effects of their decisions.

[53]Einaudi's introduction to *Paradoxes inédits,* 56.
[54]Einaudi in *Enterprise,* 233. Cf. Bloch, "Mutations monétaires," 149.

# 21

# MOTIVATIONS IN
# VENETIAN MONETARY POLICY

HE BASIC ASSUMPTIONS underlying decisions about the minting of coins and their legal values were not expressed by Venetian legislators in any integrated way. They were not debated in pamphlets or refined in treatises. They have to be inferred, partly from the results and partly from preambles, which specify ills to be remedied, however, rather than expound general principles.

To judge from such sources, monetary policies from 1200 to 1500 were dominated by three concerns: (1) the bullion market, that is, the profitable marketing in Venice of precious metals; (2) maintenance in circulation of adequate supplies of gold and silver coins; and (3) maintenance of a unifying bimetallic monetary standard. We will discuss them in that order, without meaning to indicate thereby their relative importance, which is difficult to judge.

Venice's position as a market for silver from across the Alps was enhanced by Venice's first notable monetary innovation, the coinage of the grosso by Enrico Dandolo. It encouraged silver imports by promoting the export of silver coins from Venice eastward, at first to pay for the expenses of the Venetian and French Crusaders (before they reimbursed themselves liberally by their sack of Constantinople in 1204 and their subsequent division of conquered Greek lands) and later to pay for imports from the east. During Venice's subsequent leadership in the trade of the Levant, so much silver went to the Levant in the form of Venetian grossi that the grosso acquired international acceptance. In Romania, most notably in Crete, it became the basic link coin determining the value of the money of account derived from the Byzantine perpero. Having the Levant as its market, Venice itself became the best market for the silver extracted from the mines of Germany, Bohemia, and Hungary, and she profited from the impressive expansion of the output of those mines during the next century and a half.

Before the end of the thirteenth century the export of silver ingots whose fineness was guaranteed by the Venetian mint rivaled in importance that of grossi. Restrictions on exporting uncoined silver in order to increase the mint's production had no place in Venetian policy. On the contrary, the export of silver bullion for coinage in foreign mints, such as those of Armenia and Cyprus, was encouraged by special provision in 1273 for certifying ingots of the fineness of sterling, a standard made familiar in the Levant by western Crusaders, as well as ingots certified to be of the somewhat higher fineness of the Venetian grosso.

When Venice entered into competition with the Florentine, Genoese, and Neapolitan mints in the coinage of gold, it did so on terms that priced silver higher at Venice than elsewhere. By declaring in 1285 that its ducat was worth 40 soldi di grossi, Venice set its bimetallic ratio between coined silver and coined gold at 10.9 to 1, at a time when the Florentines were valuing gold at about 11.6 times the value of silver. Venice left her bullion market free to set a higher price on the ducat, to be sure, and when the output of German silver mines expanded rapidly in the opening years of the fourteenth century and silver fell in value, the ducat rose from 40 soldi a grossi to 52, reflecting a ratio of 14.2 to 1, higher even than the general Italian level of about 13 to 1. When silver production leveled off and then began to decline and gold became relatively more plentiful, Venice in the 1330s returned to her policy of offering coinage under regulations that valued silver more highly at Venice than elsewhere. The minting of the mezzanino and the soldino, which led the way in a general lowering of the bimetallic ratios expressed in European coinage, constituted a return to the earlier policy of stimulating silver imports by favoring high prices for silver.

The gold that Venice used to coin its ducats came partly from Hungary or indirectly from Africa but most clearly from the eastern Mediterranean. The importation of gold from the Levant was favored. On gold from overseas the mint's charge, including both seignoirage and production costs, was about 0.8 percent, whereas the gold from "within the Gulf," which meant mainly that coming from across the Alps, paid a charge of about 2 percent until about 1340. Some of the gold that came by sea to Venice to be made into ducats came in the form of Byzantine or Saracen coins of gold and silver mixed, especially in the years immediately following the introduction of the 24-carat ducat. The importation and recoinage of such coins from the east was promoted by specifying that none of these coins was to be accepted as worth more than the legal value assigned the ducat, although many were heavier than the ducat.

The amount of gold available for coinage in Italy and other countries of western Europe increased markedly in the third and fourth decades of the fourteenth century. The sources of that flood of gold were varied and their comparative importance debatable. Increased productivity of mines in the Carpathians, the Urals, and the Armenian highlands may have been less important than shifts in the trade routes in Africa leading from the Sudan to Egypt or across the western Sahara or changes in the coinages of Hindu princes and Mongol khans. Wherever it came from, Venetians were able to profit from the increased amount of gold being offered on Mediterranean markets, primarily for two reasons: (1) they had the silver to offer in exchange for the gold, and (2) their shipping lines gave them superior connections with the ports where silver could be marketed and gold obtained. The decades of the gold glut immediately followed the decades in which innovations in shipbuilding and improvements in navigational techniques, especially in the use of portolan charts and the mariner's compass, enabled Venice to organize her celebrated fleets of merchant galleys. The changes in shipbuilding and navigation were not at all restricted to Venice—they occurred all around the Mediterranean—but Venice was especially successful in using them to provide quicker and more secure passage to and from such eastern ports as Tana, Trebizond, Constantinople, Famagosta, Laias, Beirut, and Alexandria. This network of shipping, backed by war fleets, drew gold to Venice.

The change in the bimetallic ratio forced Venice to make changes in her money in order to maintain bimetallism, not only to keep both gold and silver coins available in circulation but also to keep a unified monetary system. Keeping an adequate supply of silver coin as well as gold coin in the city was not a serious problem as long as the bimetallic ratios expressed in mint prices favored silver. Moreover, foreign silver and billon coins, especially those from the Veronese and Tyrolese mints, were allowed to circulate so as to replace Venetian silver coins if the latter were drained out by exports to the east. To be sure, foreign coins containing less precious metal than the Venetian coins that they closely resembled, such as the groats of Rascia, were banned, as were of course counterfeits of foreign coins. But foreign silver that was up to the standard of the country minting it was acceptable at rates appropriate to its content of precious metal.

Keeping a monetary standard unified and bimetallic was more difficult. As gold fell and silver rose in value, grossi coins disappeared. With the new silver coins—the soldini and mezzanini introduced in 1331–32—a new bimetallic standard was established by assigning fixed values in lire di piccoli to the gold ducat and the new silver coins. A bimetallic ratio as low as 11.5 to 1 was set by equating 1 gold ducat and 64 silver soldini. When, after more than a decade, that bimetallic ratio diverged too far from the market value of the two metals, efforts were made to stabilize the relations of ducats and soldini at new levels.

Venice's repeated attempts to unify her monetary system so as to have one standard based on both metals resulted in a series of different bimetallic standards expressing different bimetallic ratios: 10.9 to 1 in 1285, 14.2 to 1 in 1305–30, 11.5 to 1 about 1332–46. In intervening years, even though an earlier official standard had not been repealed by any decree, it came to be ignored. Then Venice operated with two distinct monetary standards, one based on gold, the other based on silver or on a combination of silver and billon. Even in years in which the official bimetallic standard was close to expressing the free market values of the gold and silver coins and was fully enforced in many official transactions, exchanges at rates implying a different ratio were not suppressed.

Venice's tenacious striving for a bimetallic standard had both beneficial and negative results. Positively, it promoted high turnover on the bullion market and favorable terms of trade in many sectors of Venice's Levantine commerce. On the negative side, it contributed to the spawning on the Venetian market place of a remarkable number of ghosts, moneys that were not what they seemed.

An extraordinarily complex system of moneys of account developed at Venice largely as a result of the need for frequent adjustments in the pursuit of a unified bimetallic standard. A mid-fifteenth-century lawyer studying the claims, gifts, and contracts accumulated during generations by a foundation or a family might well have encountered almost a dozen.

1. Libra denariorum venetialium—equal to 240 of the denarii parvi minted by Sebastiano Ziani (1172–78); linked to the denarii grossi, first minted by Enrico Dandolo (1192–1205) and valued at 26 denarii parvi (until ca. 1254).
2. Lira di grossi (libra grossorum), 1194–ca. 1356—inaugurated by Enrico Dandolo and equal to 240 grossi.
3. Lira di grossi manca, 1256–ca. 1356—equal to 239 grossi.
4. Lira a grossi (libra ad grossus), 1254–ca. 1356—based on valuing, according to a decree of 1254, 9 grossi 5 piccoli as 1 lira a grossi.
5. Lira di piccoli—based on the piccoli minted by Lorenzo Tiepolo (1268–75) and similar coins issued by his successors; prescribed for the retail trade in and after 1269; based on valuing the piccolo as 1 of the 240 denari in this lira; after 1331 based on the soldino equal to 12 piccoli; after 1382 based on the soldino and on the grosso, type 2 (equal to 48 piccoli).
6. Bimetallic lira di grossi, ca. 1305–ca. 1335—linked both to the silver

grosso and to the gold ducat by valuing the gold ducat at 2 soldi di grossi and the silver grosso, type 1, at 1 denaro grosso.

7. Lira di grossi a oro, 1332–1797—linked to the gold ducat by valuing the ducat at 2 soldi di grossi.

8. Lira a grossi a oro, 1332–ca. 1405—linked to the gold ducat by valuing the ducat at 52 soldi a grossi.

9. Lira di grossi a monete—after 1332 linked to the soldino valued at 12 piccoli a monete; after 1382 linked also to the grosso, type 2, valued at 48 piccoli a monete.

10. Ducato d'oro, 1332–1797—of the same value as the gold ducat coin and divided for accounting purposes into 24 grossi a oro, each of which divided into 32 piccoli a oro.

11. Ducato a monete, 1332–ca. 1420—linked to the soldino by valuing 1 ducato di monete at 64 soldini or 16 grossi, type 2.

This listing of the moneys of account used at Venice, not counting those used in its subject territories, emphasizes the extreme contrast between Venice's experience and that of England. In those two centuries the English used only one money of account and changed its metallic base only slightly. Florence and Milan, like Venice, used several moneys of account based on different coins and on different bimetallic ratios, but since those cities abandoned efforts to maintain a single monetary standard embodying a fixed bimetallic ratio, they soon settled down to the use of two monetary standards, one based on silver, the other based on gold. Traces of the earlier effort at a single standard survived in the Florentine distinction between fiorini a oro and fiorini a fiorini, but after both became based on gold, that distinction became a mere matter of nomenclature, as was the distinction at Venice between lira a grossi and lira di grossi, when the lira di grossi (or the "lira di grossi manca") was consistently worth 26 times as much as the lira a grossi. But in Venice those lire were based at first on silver, later on both silver grossi and gold ducats, and then on the gold ducat alone, with the addition of "a oro." For a time the distinction between "a oro" and "a monete" was employed to provide flexibility in the use of the bimetallic standard legalized by making 1 ducat equal to 64 soldini. Then, in the mid-fourteenth century, Venetians began using at least a half-dozen different moneys of account simultaneously.

The disadvantages of having so many different moneys of account in common use are obvious. Much time and mental effort had to be expended in converting from one to another. In their ledgers bookkeepers had to reduce to whichever money of account they selected for use all the various prices to be recorded, including the values of coins and governmental credits originally stated in several different ways. Merchants, too, had to make similar calculations to guide their purchases of various commodities and their investments, some of which were valued in one money of account, some in another. The time and energy thus expended may be considered an unnecessary addition to transactions costs and in that sense a negative factor in productivity.

Venetians themselves may have been little concerned with that aspect, because the conversions were of the same kind that all international traders had to make. They were accustomed to buying and selling in the many different moneys of account used in the many market places where they carried on their commerce. A similar complexity in transacting business in Venice may have enabled some Venetians in bargaining with foreigners occasionally to profit from their expertise in handling their own moneys of account. While Venetians had an obvious advantage, no foreign merchant would be—or could afford to be—hoodwinked for long. Foreign merchants, too, had to come to grips with the complexities of Venetian usage, and the Tuscan expert dealers in bills of exchange certainly did so. Both local and foreign merchants were probably ahead of governmental authorities in simplifying accounting procedures. Both— but especially foreign merchants—had difficulty understanding the lira a grossi used by customs officials, and they "always felt deceived" ("putant semper esse decepti") when, as late as 1390, 10 ducats were entered as 26 lire 2 soldi 2 denari a grossi. One can sense a sigh of relief from the Datini correspondent who reported in 1404 the replacement of that lira a grossi in wholesale transactions by the simpler lira di grossi a oro (or ducato a oro), noting that the new pricing system would be "more expeditious" ("più spacciativo"), making clear his appreciation of resulting reductions in transactions costs.

By that time Venice had lapsed from her attachment to a single bimetallic standard. Admission of retreat from a unified bimetallism made possible a simplification of accounting. The trend towards simplification in the early fifteenth century gave pride of place to just three moneys of account, one based on silver, the other two on gold—the lira di piccoli, the lira di grossi a oro, and the ducato a oro. In the later fourteenth century, efforts were no longer made to stabilize the relationship between gold- and silver-based moneys of account, and the price of the ducat in domestic exchange was left free to respond to both market pressures and official devaluations. It was the market that defined the next unified standard when, at the conclusion of the wars against the Milanese, the ducat stabilized at 124 soldi, a price later strongly supported by the government.

While Venice's moneys of account may have been the most complex in medieval and Renaissance Europe, the coins on which those moneys of account were based formed a pattern simpler than in most cities. A rapid glance at the coin lists included in the merchant manuals suffices to measure the complexity with which a professional moneychanger had to deal; on those lists the items dedicated to Venice are minimal. In Italy, to be sure, and in contrast to German lands in the fifteenth century, the gold coin of the many independent mints was uniform from city to city and rarely manipulated. At Venice it was not changed at all from the first issue of the ducat in 1285 to the fall of the republic. Low-grade billon pennies, in contrast, were highly variable generally, but in ways that made black money function increasingly as token coinage. In Venice, that became more clearly the case after the sharp reduction in the silver content of the piccolo in 1385 (see table A.5). It was in her coinage of fine silver that Venice showed an exceptional simplicity and consistency. Below the surface of Milan's seemingly simple single money of account, the lira imperiale repeatedly shifted its links to a variety of silver coins, of which the content and relative values frequently were changing. In such complexities Genoa followed closely the example of Milan. Florence, as we have seen, made a habit of changing frequently the names, content, and legal values of its fine silver coins. The changes at Venice from the introduction of the soldino and mezzanino in 1332 to the minting of a slightly changed grosso in 1379 seem moderate indeed by comparison.

Seen in perspective within the three hundred years between 1200 and 1500, or between Sebastiano Ziani and Nicolò Tron, even the moderate changes of those fifty years 1332–82 seem an unusual episode—a brief interlude of confusion. In spite of the maze of moneys of account which had begun with the lira a grossi and accumulated more and more complications, the coins minted at Venice kept to the same basic pattern for three centuries. In that perspective, the Venetian grosso had an almost unmatched constancy. Except between 1356 and 1382, under every doge of those three centuries it was coined with practically no change in fineness and, until after 1378, with no change in weight. Even then, the slight modifications in weight successively authorized were little more than what was needed to compensate for deterioration of former issues through wear and tear and culling. Only during the decades when the sharp fall in the value of gold was creating both unusual difficulties and unusual opportunities did Venice complicate the fineness of her silver coins. The changes in the monetary system made inevitable by the falling bimetallic ratio appeared in the moneys of account more than in coins. Men and women who dealt with money only as coins which they passed from hand to hand had few adjustments to make; the burden of adaptability fell on accountants and on the merchants quoting prices on the Rialto.

# APPENDIX A

# MINT CHARGES

## i. METHOD

int charges before 1394 have been determined by comparing the number of coins made from a given weight of metal with the number of the same coins paid to the supplier of the metal, or by comparing the value of the coins made per mark with the value of the coins paid out. Stated as a percentage of the money coined, the mint charge was the same whether calculated according to the number of coins or according to the statements of their value in money of account.

After 1394, the mint charges as a percentage can be obtained when both the fee per mark and the value of the coins made from a mark were specified. Seigniorage, brassage, and costs of labor and alloy are all included in the mint charges thus calculated.[1]

---

[1]In accordance with the way their minting was administered, the Venetians distinguished between "lucrum Comuni," here rendered as profit or seigniorage, and "expense et callum," here rendered generally as costs of minting or manufacture. In 1349, for example, the mintmaster was instructed that he "deberet dare de lucro Comuni nostro, deductis omnibus expensis et callo . . ." (*PMV*, doc. 107, p. 91). Genoese usage seems to have been quite different. In his reconstruction of the accounts, Felloni charges administrative and incidental expenses to "signoraggio" (which contemporaries called "emolumento di sacrestia") and manual labor of artisans to "monetaggio," and he calls the total of the two "brassaggio" (see his "Ricavi e costi," 144–45, 149, and tables 2 and 3. For French usages cf. Einaudi, ed., *Paradoxes inédits*, 151–52).

Mint charges in England were divided by Feavearyear (*The Pound Sterling*, 346–47) into "seigniorage" and "expenses." Craig (*The Mint*, 92–93) speaks of a king's share and the mint's

Minting regulations sometimes stated directly how many coins of a particular kind were to be cut from a mark of metal, but more often both the yield and the amount to be paid to the supplier were stated in terms of the value of the coins, sometimes in lire di grossi, sometimes in lire a grossi, sometimes in lire di piccoli. Our interpretations of the meaning of the decrees and the relevant calculations are presented as an appendix because they require more explanation than could be clarified in separate notes to individual figures presented in the text or in the tables.

For the old grosso the number of coins was stated directly by saying how many should be cut from a mark; this statement was also a statement of the value of the coins made from a mark, since the coin embodied the denaro of the lira di grossi as a money of account. In the thirteenth century, saying "9 soldi di grossi" was the same as saying "9 dozen grossi coins."

In regard also to piccoli, when the weight was regulated by stating how many were to be cut from a mark, "soldo" in some cases was used to mean simply "twelve," or as Papadopoli said, "soldo vuol dire l'agglomerazione di 12 pezzi."[2] But in some other cases it is not used in that simple arithmetical sense; it refers to the values of the coins in the soldo of a money of account such as the lira a grossi. Whether it has a simple arithmetical meaning or is a denomination of value in a money of account, and if so, in which money of account, are questions for which the answers differ from one regulation to another.

When the prices of silver coin and bullion are stated in different moneys of account, it is necessary to reduce them for comparative purposes to a lowest common denominator. The lowest common denominator is the piccolo as a unit of account, that is, the denaro of the lira di piccoli. Its value after 1282 is explained by the following equations:

$$\text{1 grosso coin} = 26.\text{III denari a grossi} = 32 \text{ piccoli}$$
$$\text{1 piccolo} = 0.816 \text{ denari a grossi } (26.\text{III}/32)$$
$$\text{1 denaro a grossi} = 1.225 \text{ piccoli } (32/26.\text{III})$$

Thirty-two piccoli of the lira di piccoli and 32 piccoli of the lira di grossi a monete were the same.[3]

---

share of a "combined charge" or "levy." And he does not include the "king's seigniorage" as part of mint charges (pp. 423–24). Craig's usage is a result of his primary concern with the administration of the mint. What Feavearyear called expenses might include a large rake-off by officials of the mint, an aspect Craig wished to emphasize. But it is likely to be misleading in other contexts, and we have followed Feavearyear's usage, including seigniorage as part of mint charges. Included also is brassage, whether defined as "a charge levied to cover the cost of coinage" (*Webster's Dictionary,* 2d ed.) or as the "profit made by a moneyer" (Grierson, *Numismatics,* 193).

[2]Papadopoli, 1:176. For similar usage in the Florentine mint see Bernocchi, 3:133.

[3]Explanations of these and other relationships between the different moneys of account are elaborated in chaps. 8, sec. iii, and 16.

In a fourteenth-century mathematical treatise in the Marciana,[4] a conversion from denari di piccoli to denari a grossi shows that use was made of the following equations:

$$
\begin{array}{rcl}
16 \text{ denari di piccoli} & = & 13 \text{ denari a grossi} \\
16 & = & 13 \\
10 & = & 8 \\
\hline
42 \text{ denari di piccoli} & = & 34 \text{ denari a grossi}
\end{array}
$$

Presumably the mintmasters also worked by putting together such approximations, but being bound by habit to decimals, we have generally converted from denari di piccoli to denari a grossi by multiplying by 0.82, and from denari a grossi to denari di piccoli by multiplying by 1.22. (In view of the degree of inaccuracy of measurements, going beyond one or two decimals serves in most cases only to identify the arithmetical derivation of the figures.)

The prices the mint paid for silver are here considered to be prices for silver of the fineness of the grosso, called "argento di bolla," which was 0.965 fine before 1355, 0.952 fine from 1355 to 1421, and 0.949 thereafter.[5] In calculating the fineness of piccoli and the number that could be made with a mark of pure silver, we have not adjusted figures to allow for the fact that the laws stating the proportion of silver refer not to 100 percent pure silver but to argento di bolla. That adjustment and an adjustment of the prices of bullion to apply to 100 percent pure silver would approximately cancel each other out. For example, in 1379 the alloy to be made for coining piccoli was supposed to be composed of 160 carats of argento di bolla and 992 carats of copper. That works out as 0.1388888 fine, which Papadopoli rounds off to 0.138. If we allow for the fact that the argento di bolla was then 0.952 fine, we find that the content of pure silver was only 152.3 carats and the fineness of the coin only 0.1322. The number of coins that could be made from a mark of pure silver, consequently, is the number cut from a mark of alloy, namely, 1,200, divided by 0.132, not 0.138, that is, 9,090 instead of 8,696. On the other hand, the price of the mark of pure silver should be similarly adjusted for comparative purposes. For unfree silver it was given as 13 1/2 soldi di grossi, equal to 5,184 piccoli. The price of 100 percent pure silver should then have been 5,184/0.952, or 5,445.4. While paying 5,445.5 piccoli to the supplier, the mint could retain 3,645 piccoli (9,090 − 5,445), a mint charge of 40.1 percent. Calculations without adjustments for the fineness of the argento di bolla indicate that the mint charge was 40.3 percent.[6] The difference seems to be of no significance for present purposes. Some slight variations in the figures result from round-

---

[4]Trattato di Aritmetica.
[5]See below, app. C; above, chap. 10, sec. i; and below, table A.2.
[6]See below, sec. viii.

ing off at the first decimal in statements of conclusions but using the third or fourth decimal in most of the processes of calculation. Extant data concerning the early fractional coins listed in table A.2 are insufficient for calculating the mint charges.

## ii. CERTIFIED SILVER INGOTS

From the thirteenth century to the sixteenth, silver ingots the fineness of which had been certified by the mint were very important among the mint's products. Two grades of certified ingots are referred to ca. 1270–1320. The higher grade, which was 0.965 fine, was of the same fineness as grossi coins and was called argento di bolla. The other grade was called sterling and was 0.925 fine, as were the English pennies. The mint charge is not stated for ingots of either type, but the charge for sterling bars can be derived from the price credited the supplier of the silver and the price charged him for the certified bars that he received.

When silver was refined by the mint into sterling ingots or bars, the mint credited the supplier of the bullion with 11 lire 13 soldi a grossi for each mark of fine silver in the bullion he supplied. For the convenience of using decimals, we refer to this price as 233 soldi a grossi. The mint priced the sterling bars that it returned to the supplier in the same money of account. In 1273 it debited him with 11 lire 5 1/2 soldi per mark, and after the year 1274, with 11 lire 5 soldi (225 soldi).[7] Figuring, for convenience, in soldi, we may say that for 100 marks of silver of the fineness of grossi the supplier was owed 23,300 soldi. When he had received back 100 marks of sterling ingots, he was still owed 800 soldi, since the 100 marks of ingots were worth only 22,500 soldi. If the 800 soldi were paid him in additional sterling bars at 225 per mark, he would get 3.55 marks more, making a total weight of 103.55 marks. Since these bars were only 0.925 pure silver, they contained only 0.958 times as much silver as did a mark of bars of the standard of grossi, since grossi were 0.965 pure silver (0.925/0.965 = 0.958). In giving back 103.55 marks of sterling for each 100 marks of argento di bolla received, the mint was giving back only 99.2 (103.555 × 0.958) marks of silver of the fineness of grossi out of every 100 marks it received. The mint charge therefore was 0.8 percent.

A similar computation of the weight to be returned in sterling bars for a hypothetical amount of fine silver can be found in the fourteenth-century mathematical treatise mentioned above.[8] Using the same prices (those stipulated in the regulations) but calculating with fractions instead of decimals, it showed that slightly less than 194 marks 3 ounces (here

---

[7]PMV, docs. 20, 22; DMC, 2:245; Stussi, ed., Zibaldone da Canal, 6; and above, chap. 10, sec. i.

[8]Trattato di Aritmetica, fol. 34v.

figured as 194.35 marks) of sterling were due in return for a trifle over 187 marks 5 ounces of grossi silver (here figured as 187.63). Calculating, as above, that the 194.35 sterling bars contained 0.958 as much pure silver as did grossi (0.925/0.965) indicates that the sterling bars that the mint returned to the supplier contained 186.19 (194.35 × 0.958) marks of silver of the fineness of grossi, and the mint kept the difference, namely, 1.44 (187.63 − 186.19) marks, a mint charge of 0.77 percent (1.44/187.63). In table A.5 we have entered the mint charges as 0.8 percent.

The price of 233 soldi for silver to be cast into bars may well have remained unchanged, even after other prices for silver changed (i.e., in purchases by the mint for making coins and in private sales for export or industrial use). So long as the value that the mint set on silver bars in paying them out to the supplier also remained unchanged, the significance of both figures consisted simply in their relation to each other.

Although the sterling bars were subject to Venetian regulation in the thirteenth century and were mentioned in merchants' manuals in the early fourteenth century, later references to the silver ingots certified by the Venetian mint all seem to refer to argento di bolla, that is, silver of the fineness of grossi.[9]

Early direct evidence of the mint charge on the assaying and certifying of these bars or sheets of the fineness of grossi is lacking. Very probably the silver was refined by bullion merchants before being presented to the mint, as was true later. Quite possibly before 1417 only a minimal fee was collected for assaying and certifying silver already refined to the standard of the grosso.[10] The assaying fee was reduced to 2 grossi per mark on bullion submitted for coinage but was not being exacted on silver made into bars until 1442, when its collection was then specifically ordered.[11]

### iii. PICCOLI, 1269–1343

#### Piccoli, 1269–78

The piccoli minted under Lorenzo Tiepolo and Jacopo Contarini are said by Papadopoli to weigh 0.289 grams and be 0.250 fine.[12] In that case, 825.3 coins (238.5/0.289) could be cut from 1 mark of metal, and 1 mark of silver would suffice to make 4 marks of the alloy used and would yield 3,301.2 piccoli (825.3 × 4). How many of those 3,301.2 piccoli would the mintmaster have to give the supplier in order to pay him for the silver bullion? For the purposes of indicating the impact of changes in mint

---

[9]Stussi, ed., *Zibaldone da Canal,* 5–6; Pegolotti, *Pratica,* 291; *Tarifa zoè noticia,* 24, 41; above, chap. 17.

[10]On the refining fee that was then instituted on all silver see above, chap. 12, sec. iii.

[11]*Cap. Broche,* fol. 27v; Papadopoli, 1:258.

[12]Papadopoli, 1:112, 118.

regulations on the mint's profits, it is worthwhile to calculate what the mint charges would have been if the silver bullion had cost 233 soldi a grossi for a mark of grossi fineness. Using any fixed price would indicate the directions in which such changes affected mint charges, and the figure of 233 soldi is probably close to what really was generally paid, since it is referred to in later merchant manuals as the mint's price for silver bullion.[13]

Two hundred thirty-three soldi a grossi equal 2,796 (233 × 12) of the denari a grossi which had become units of account distinct from the denari piccoli when the grossi were given the official value of 26 1/9 piccoli ca. 1256. The denaro a grossi remained at 1/26.111 of a grosso when the official value of the grosso was raised to 28 piccoli in 1274.[14] Consequently, after 1274 the value of 1 denaro a grossi was for a while 28/26.111 denari piccoli, and the value of 2,796 denari a grossi was 2,998.3 piccoli (2,796 × [28/26.111]). In paying the supplier those 2,998.3 piccoli and keeping the balance, 302.9 piccoli (3,301.2 − 2,998.3), the mint was taking a mint charge of 9.2 percent (302.9/3,301.2).

That mint charge includes the cost of the copper. The earliest quotations of the price of copper in Venice indicate that it cost about 1 1/2 soldi per mark when silver cost 233 soldi per mark,[15] so that fluctuations in the price of copper would not seriously affect the ratio of expenses and seigniorage.

### Piccoli, 1278–82

During the next five years, the silver content of piccoli was reduced from about 1/4 to about 1/5, and the weight was changed slightly, but the dates of the changes are uncertain. The earliest surviving text of instructions regarding the fine silver content of the piccoli is in cap. 80 of the capitolare of the mintmasters, which comes just after *capitula* 1–78, approved in March 1278. It ordered that the alloy from which the piccoli were made should contain, in each mark of 1,152 carats, 228 carats of fine silver and 924 carats of copper. That made them 0.198 fine (228/1,152). (The 228 carats of silver are expressed as 1 1/2 oncie plus 12 carats "argenti tam boni sicut est grossus," the 924 carats of copper as 6 1/2 oncie minus 12 carats.)[16] From the alloy thus composed were to be cut 786–90 coins from each mark ("vadant isti denarii per marcham unam libras III et soldos V 1/2 usque ad denarios X," i.e., [240 × 3] + [12 × 5] + 6–10 = 786–90). Since a mark then weighed 238.5 grams, such a piccolo weighed 0.303 grams (238.5/788). This agrees well enough with the evidence of the surviving

---

[13]See above, chap. 10, nn. 13, 14, 28.
[14]Papadopoli, 1:110; and above, chap. 8, sec. iii.
[15]See below, app. C.
[16]Papadopoli, 1:325–26.

piccoli minted under Giovanni Dandolo (1280–89),[17] but Papadopoli indicates that the coinage of lighter piccoli of 0.292 grams also began under Giovanni Dandolo, and the records dating the changes are confusing.[18]

Taking 788 as the number made from a mark that was 1/5 silver indicates that 1 mark of silver sufficed to make 3,940 coins (5 × 788). So long as the silver was purchased for 233 soldi a grossi and the grosso was still valued at 28 piccoli, the number of piccoli paid the supplier of silver was the same as in 1274, namely, 2,998.3 piccoli. But the number of piccoli retained by the mint became 941.7 piccoli (3,940 − 2,998.3) after 1278, more than it had been in 1274, so that the mint charge about 1280 went up to 24.0 percent (941.7/3,930).

[17]A numismatist could refine the problem by a study of the surviving coins. According to Papadopoli's descriptions, it is clear that the fineness was reduced from almost exactly 1/4 silver to 1/5 about 1280 (Papadopoli, 1:118, 138). That reduction by 1/20 would account for much of the reduction of "sol. V et denar. II ad grossos" referred to in a law that Papadopoli cited as of 1282 (see below, n. 18), for 62 denari a grossi is 1/20 of 1,240 denari a grossi, which is more than 1/3 of the cost of a mark silver. According to the *CNI*, 7:45–54, the weights of surviving piccoli are, roughly:

| Issue of | Maximum Weight (in grams) | Weight Range (in grams) |
|---|---|---|
| Lorenzo Tiepolo | 0.30 | 0.18–0.30, many ca. 0.28 |
| Jacomo Contarini | 0.33 | 0.25–0.33, mostly ca. 0.28 |
| Giovanni Dandolo | 0.36 | 0.16–0.36, many ca. 0.30 |
| Pietro Gradenigo | 0.33 | 0.21–0.33, many ca. 0.28 |

[18]The regulations governing the weight and fineness of the piccoli between 1279 and 1289 have been printed or interpreted with errors by Papadopoli and Cessi. Papadopoli, 1:121, prints a regulation dated 6 October 1282 (not in Cessi's *PMV*) in which the weight of piccoli is specified by stating "fiant denarii qui vadant soldos VIII et denarios II per unziam qui sumabunt Libras III et soldos V et denarios IIII pro marcha." That is, 98 ([8 × 12] + 2) to an ounce, which amounts to 784 ([3 × 240] + [5 × 12] + 4) to a mark. He summarizes the document as ordering "3 lire, 5 soldi, e 2 [*sic*] denari e cioè 784 pezzi" (p. 122). Cessi dates as "1279 (dopo Settembre)" (*PMV*, doc. 30) a regulation almost identical with that printed by Papadopoli as cap. 80 of the "Capitolare Massariorum monete," 326. Cessi and Papadopoli both cite as the source for the capitolare the document in ASV, now classified as Secreta, Capitolari diversi (ex Misc. cod. 133). In the two printings the weight is reported differently. In Cessi's doc. 30 (*PMV*, 37) one reads: "vadant isti denarii per marcham unam libras III et soldos V usque ad denarios X." In Papadopoli, 1:326, one reads: "vadant isti denarii per marcham unam, libras III et soldos V ÷ usque ad denarios X" (that is, 5 soldi and 6–10 denari). Consulting the ex Misc. cod. 133 revealed that Papadopoli's is the correct reading. Hence we have used 786–90 denarii. But Papadopoli's statement (p. 123) assigns cap. 80 in his printing of the capitolare to a date later than 11 December 1289 by implication, without indicating a new source, and gives as an indication of weight what appears to be a garbled version of cap. 80 of the capitolare, namely, a yield of "fra lire 3, soldi 5 1/2 [786 pic] e lire 3 soldi 10 per marca [840] con una media di 813 pezzi per marca."

APPENDIX A

*Piccoli, 1282–1343*

Although the dates of change in the weight and fineness of the piccolo in the period 1279–82 are doubtful, clearly in May 1282 its legal value was reduced from 1/28 of a grosso to 1/32.[19] Since the number of coins made from a mark of alloy was by then certainly 788 and the alloy was only 1/5 silver, 1 mark of fine silver sufficed to make 3,940 piccoli, as before,[20] but the number of piccoli to be returned to the supplier was now (32 × 2,796/26.111), or 3,426.6 denari piccoli. In paying the supplier those 3,426.6 piccoli and keeping the balance, 513.4 piccoli (3,940 − 3,426.6), the mint was taking a mint charge of 13 percent (513.4/3,930).

All the piccoli minted under the doges between Giovanni Dandolo (1280–89) and Andrea Dandolo (1343–54), including notably the large coinage ordered when the mint was enlarged in 1317–19 under Doge Giovanni Soranzo (1312–28),[21] were of 0.292 grams, 0.198 fine, according to Papadopoli's compilation.[22]

---

Marino Sanuto (in his *Vite de' Duchi,* col. 574) reports for about 1282–83: "In questo tempo furono fatti stampare bagattini di rame chiamati piccoli, cioè messi per ogni marca once 6 e mezza di rame e once una e mezza d'argento. Sicchè vadano lire 3, soldi 5, denari 4 [784 piccoli] per marca e che questi bagattini si spendano nella Terra a ragione di dodici al soldo." The figures given by Pegolotti (*Pratica,* 292) for about 1320 indicate that the fine silver content of the lira di piccoli was 13.1 grams instead of the 13.92 grams shown in table 10, which is derived from the earlier documents described above.

[19]Papadopoli, 1:120–23; *DMC,* 2:75. The decree of 6 October 1282 (*DMC,* 3:10; not in Cessi's *PMV* but printed in Papadopoli, 1:121) states the proportions of silver and copper, but it seems unintentionally to make a change in the proportion. Its statement is the same as that in the capitolare partially quoted above, except that it reads "uno grosso" and "grosso uno di peso" where in cap. 80 of the capitolare (Papadopoli, 1:326) one reads "karatis duodecim." Since grossi were cut 109.4 from a mark, the weight of a grosso was 10.5 carats (1,152/109.4). Using that figure instead of 12 carats indicates 226.5 carats of fine silver instead of 228, and a fineness for the piccolo of 0.1966 instead of 0.1979, resulting in no significant difference in the mint charge.

[20]Although not agreeing with all of Cessi's argument in *PMV,* xxxix n. 2, in criticism of Papadopoli's interpretation, we reject, for reasons explained in n. 18, the conclusions that Papadopoli expressed (1:123), namely, that a decree of 1289 raised the average number cut from a mark to 813. On the other hand, Papadopoli's printing of the text of the capitolare (1:326) is the more accurate, as explained in n. 17 above, and is the basis for using the figure 788. If Papadopoli's figure of 813 is correct, then the mint charge was 638.4 piccoli out of 4,065, or 15.7 percent.

Papadopoli (1:145) gives the weight of the piccoli minted under Pietro Gradenigo (1289–1311) as 0.292 grams, which is consistent with cutting 813 on the average from a mark of 238.5 grams (238.5/813 = 0.293), but the *CNI,* 7:50–55, while indicating 0.28 as the average for specimens of that doge's issues, as for Giovanni Dandolo's, lists heavier specimens, the heaviest weighing 0.33 grams. Pegolotti, *Pratica,* 292, indicates a fineness of 0.189.

[21]See below, app. B, sec. iii.
[22]1:145, 155, 164, 169.

## iv. GROSSI, TYPE I, 1194–1356

The yield from a mark of silver of the required fineness (0.965) is stated in the capitolare of 1278 as 109 1/2 to 109 1/3 coins per mark (109.4 used here in calculating). Surviving coins confirm the adherence to that standard from the first issue. The same capitolare makes clear that there was no fixed price at which the mintmasters accepted all silver offered for coinage into grossi. They were to buy at the best prices they could, and presumably that had been the arrangement since the first issue, although in 1202 the "buying" had been done through Doge Enrico Dandolo's treaty by which the Crusaders promised to supply 85,000 marks of silver in return for the ships and services furnished by the Venetians.

If in 1273 and later the mintmasters paid for silver to be made into grossi the same price that was being paid for silver to be made into certified sterling bars, they could pay the 233 soldi a grossi due the supplier by giving him 107.1 grossi, because each grosso was worth 26 1/9 denari a grossi, as explained in chapter 8, section iii (233 × [12/26.111] = 107.1). That left the mint with 2.3 grossi (109.4 − 107.1), a mint charge of 2.1 percent (2.3/109.4). Out of each mark, 2 soldi a grossi, 0.84 percent, was the minimal profit for the Commune required from the mintmaster in charge.[23] That would leave for the cost of minting 1.25 percent of the yield.

The possibilities of buying grossi for less than 233 soldi a grossi before 1300 are discussed above, in chapter 10, section iii. After 1300, the market price of silver rose far above 233 soldi a grossi per mark, and yet the mint could continue to mint grossi. The value of grossi coins had also risen. One way, then, to issue grossi at a moderate profit was to find suppliers who would deliver a mark of bullion for 233 soldi as a purely institutional price, because the mint in return would value the grossi it paid them at only 32 piccoli even though moneychangers were charging 36, 40, or 48 piccoli for 1 grosso coin. Pegolotti implies that this is what happened.[24] Pegolotti's report may have been out of date, and Florentines actually operating in Venice, such as the Covoni, certainly paid more attention to awkward fractions.

Another way in which the mint could have continued to issue grossi at a moderate profit may have been applied at mid-century, when the price of silver bullion began to be quoted in lire di grossi a monete and when moneychangers were offering 42 or even 44 denari di piccoli for a freshly minted grosso. Although the legal value of the grosso remained fixed at 32 piccoli, the market price of grossi coins was at 36 in 1331–32 and then rose

---

[23]Ibid., 1:311–12; above, chap. 10, sec. iii and n. 21.
[24]Pegolotti, *Pratica,* 140; see also above, chap. 10, sec. iii.

to 42 and finally 48.[25] Assuming that their price was 44 piccoli in 1353 and the silver bullion for minting them was bought for the price offered at that time to all suppliers presenting free silver to be made into soldini, as explained in section vi, namely, 4,800 piccoli, then the mark of silver could have been paid for with 109.1 grossi (4,800/44). The mint would then have retained only 0.3 grossi out of every 109.4 cut from a mark, a mint charge of only 0.27 percent (0.3/109.4). Or, if by 1353 the grosso was already valued by moneychangers at 48 piccoli, and the mint valued them at that price in paying the suppliers of silver bullion, then the 4,800 piccoli could be paid with 100 grossi and 9.4 grossi kept by the mint, a mint charge of 8.6 percent. But such calculations are no more than hypothetical, since no prices have been found in the records of minting.

In the preamble to a motion—subsequently defeated—which he made on 10 January 1362, Senator Marco Capello told the senators that their ancestors had not tried to make great profits from the coins struck in the mint and that the profit on grossi used to "parvulos viginti ad grossos" per mark and was then "parvuli viginti sex ad grossos," although because of the obligation to consign the quinto to the mint, grossi were no longer being coined.[26] When the profit (seigniorage) was 20 and then 26 denari a grossi for a mark, from which were struck 109.4 grossi each worth 26.111 denari a grossi (a total value of 2,856.5 denari a grossi), the profit was 0.7 percent and 0.9 percent (20/2,856.5 and 26/2,856.5). The 0.84 percent profit called for in the capitolare of 1278 was indeed within that range.[27]

Although they do not reveal exact figures for exact dates, or the precise methods of accounting used during those centuries, the scattered diverse sources agree in indicating that the total mint charge on the coinage of grossi of the old type was about 2 percent, of which about 0.8 percent was seigniorage, the rest expenses.


## v. GOLD DUCATS

Under the first rules—which provided that 67 ducats be cut from a mark of gold, that 2,600 soldi a grossi be paid for a mark, and that each ducat be worth 40 soldi a grossi—the total yield of a mark would be 2,680 soldi (40 × 67), and the supplier would receive 2,600 soldi worth of ducats. The mint would keep 80 soldi worth, a mint charge of 3 percent (80/2,680). In the practice very soon adopted, the mint paid 2,592 soldi for a mark of pure gold (24 × 108 soldi per carat of fineness) and set two different values on the ducat when paying the supplier of the gold. If the

[25]See above, chap. 15, nn. 61–69.
[26]*PMV*, doc. 139.
[27]See above, n. 23.

gold had come from within the Gulf, the ducat was valued at 39 1/2 soldi; if it had come from outside the Gulf, the ducat was valued at 39 soldi.[28] When the ducat was valued at 39 1/2 soldi, 65.62 ducats (2,592/39.5) were required to pay the 2,592 soldi owed the supplier. The mint kept 1.38 ducats out of each 67, a mint charge of 2 percent (1.4/67). When the ducat was valued at 39 soldi, the number of ducats required to pay the supplier 2,592 soldi was 66.46 (2,592/39). Beginning in the 1340s, the Germans who brought gold considered to be from "within the Gulf" were also paid in ducats valued at 39 soldi.[29] On all coinage of ducats, the mint was then able to keep only 54/100 ducats out of each mark, that is, out of the 67 ducats made from a mark. That made a mint charge of 0.8 percent (0.54/67). About half of that was the cost of manufacture, half seigniorage, for the law of 1285 ordered that for export some gold already refined be turned into ducats with a charge "pro laboratura et expensis" at only 5 grossi per mark.[30]

The soldo used in these calculations, it should be emphasized, was a special kind of mint soldo a grossi a oro (as explained above, in chap. 14, sec. i).

After the establishment in common usage of yet another accounting unit called a "grosso a oro," of which there were 24 to a ducat (as explained in chap. 16, sec. i), the mint price of gold was stated in ducats and grossi a oro. Thus, the 66.461 ducats just mentioned were referred to in resolutions of 1414–21 and later as 66 ducats 11 grossi.[31] It was raised from

[28]See above, chap. 10, nn. 43–49.

[29]The *Zibaldone da Canal* (Stussi, ed.), like nearly all merchant manuals of later date, says simply (p. 71) that the mint paid out at 39 soldi. But the *Zibaldone da Canal* is concerned especially with overseas trade, as are most of the manuals. They indicate the early general use of that rate, but the provisions made in 1336 to encourage import of gold by the Germans and the explicit statement in the old capitolare of the massari al oro in ASV, Zecca, b. 6tris, indicate that the Germans were paid at 39 1/2 until 1338. At that date, apparently, the Quarantia, of which only a part of the minutes survive and which was then in charge of the mint, gave temporary permission to use the rate of 39 soldi in paying the Germans (ASV, Zecca, b. 6bis, fol. 26). The permission was extended again and again without any specification that it was limited to the Germans (*DQ*, vol. 1, docs. 17 [1342] and 275 [1343]). In some copies made after 1340 the provision dated 1338 is given with the 1/2 omitted, probably by a clerical error ignored because no longer relevant, as in the copy of the capitolare of the mintmasters for silver made in the eighteenth century by copying an earlier one (ASV, Zecca, b. 6bis, fol. 27).

[30]Papadopoli, 1:342. For comparison it may be noted that the total mint charge at Florence in 1294 was lowered to 3/5 of a florin for each 96 florins, 0.625 percent (see Pegolotti, *Pratica*, 191; and Bernocchi, 3:40).

[31]The equivalence appears from the following calculations: 67 ducats (67 × 24) = 1,608 grossi, and 66 ducats 11 grossi ([66 × 24] + 11) = 1,595 grossi, giving a mint charge of 13 grossi (1,608 − 1,595); and 13/1,608 = 0.008. Prices of the gold bullion in ducats and grossi appear in two defeated motions in April 1414 (ASV, Senato, Misti, reg. 50, fols. 95–98). In June 1416 one of the defeated motions called for adding 4 grossi per mark to the 5 lire 8 soldi currently

that figure to 67 ducats by the Council of Ten in 1473, when the council was favoring the coinage of gold and restricting that of silver. Gold was then coined without any mint charge; the cost of coining ducats was covered by charges on silver.[32]

An additional expense, the "calo," connected with the impurities of the bullion, might be considered part of the mint charges. Its existence is made clear in connection with privileges or regulations granted the Germans in 1362. If their gold was less than 23 carats, they were to be paid 10 soldi per mark as compensation for the dross which was extracted in refining it to 24 carats and which was kept by the mint. But if the gold was better than 23 carats fine, there was to be no such payment.[33] In the latter case, was the mint really levying an additional charge by keeping the impurities extracted?

Whether the dross was of much value depended on three factors:

1. The proportion of impurities in the bullion. As a general rule, the Venetian mint did not accept gold that was less than 23-1/2 carats fine.[34] The provision made in 1362 regarding payment for gold that was less fine was a special measure for the benefit of Germans only.

2. The value of the impurities extracted by the flux, whether mainly silver or copper or other less valuable substances. When the impurity was silver, the value of the dross might be considerable, even if the bullion was 23 1/2 carats gold. Since silver was worth approximately 1/10 as much as gold, if it amounted to 1/2 carats out of 24 (1/48 of the weight of the metal supplied), its retention by the mint might be considered an additional mint charge of 1/480 of the value of the metal, an additional mint charge of 0.2 percent.

3. The extraction—by the flux used in refining—of some of the gold so that it remained in the dross. If the value of the dross was derived only from a slight amount of gold adhering to the flux, the cost of extracting that gold by re-refining the dross might be more than the value of the gold that could be removed, especially if the gold had been refined to

---

being paid for gold (ibid., reg. 51, fol. 143v). The successful motion raised the price by 3 grossi for one category of suppliers (as explained below, vol. 2). That made the minting charge for them only 10 grossi. On the other hand, a defeated motion that proposed increasing minting charges stated the proposed amount as 16 grossi (fol. 142v).

[32]When the Council of Ten raised the price to 67 ducats in 1473 (ASV, Consiglio dei Dieci, Misti, reg. 18, fol. 36v [15 December 1473]), it referred to the previous price as 66 ducats 11 grossi.

[33]In *PMV*, docs. 141 and 142, the distinguishing fineness is stated consistently as 23 carats. In the publication by Thomas of the *Cap. Fontego*, cap. 73, p. 25, it is given as 13 carats in one place, obviously a mistake.

[34]According to Stussi, ed., *Zibaldone da Canal*, 71, the mint would not accept gold less fine. But exceptions may have been made for some other foreign importers as well as the Germans, for the possibility of the mint itself refining such gold is strongly suggested by the reforms of 1414–21.

23 1/2 or 23 3/4 carats before being delivered to the mint. According to a Venetian merchant's manual of the mid-fourteenth century, an importer paid 1 grosso per mark for having his gold melted down ("a far cholar el so oro").[35] One grosso per mark added only 0.06 percent (1/24 × 1/67) to the mint charge of 0.8 percent, imposed by returning only 66.46 ducats out of the 67 ducats made from a mark of pure gold, as explained above. The fee of 1 grosso may have been added when the gold was melted and recast into a form to facilitate the assaying, or it may have been charged when the mint melted and refined the gold and returned the dross to the supplier. In the latter case, the refining was said to have been done "a calo di mercanti." When the mint kept the dross, the refining was said to be done "a calo di comun."

Admittedly the interpretation of these two terms, "a calo di comun" and "a calo di mercanti," is sometimes difficult.[36] The costs and gains involved led to complicated controversies in 1414–22, which will be more fully described in volume 2. They become understandable when "a calo di comun" is interpreted as meaning that the government paid a price determined by the official assay and kept the dross, the calo. It must have had that meaning in the regulation for the Germans in 1362. In buying from a German importer, the mint was obligated to pay him within three days out of a special fund or chest of ducats set aside for the purpose. In paying so quickly, the mint could not pay him back with ducats made from the same gold that he had supplied. It was paying him before his gold had been through the slow process of refinement to 24 carats purity and of elaborate inspections which confirmed that that purity had been attained. Since he was paid before refining was completed, the amount he was paid had to be determined by the degree of purity assigned his bullion by the assayers at the Rialto.[37]

[35]*Tarifa zoè noticia*, 13–14, 54, 69. On the varied uses of the term "calo" see n. 36; and chap. 12, sec. iii.

[36]*PMV*, doc. 37, p. 42; ASV, Zecca, 6tris, cap. 105. The "callum" of silver referred to in the capitolare of 1279 probably was either the loss of weight of the silver being refined or the dross therefrom (Papadopoli, 1:323, cap. 66). The "calo" for the smith casting the silver, mentioned in ASV, Consiglio dei Dieci, Misti, reg. 18, fol. 101v, may refer to metal scraps that he retained or to silver that he retained as payment. In *PMV*, doc. 141, providing payment of callum to the Germans in 1362, "callum" refers to their compensation, for the passage reads:"solvatur mercatori callum ad rationem s. X grossos [*sic*] pro marcha." Borlandi, ed., *Manuale de' Ricci*, 135–36, refers to a loss of weight of 0.694 percent in melting down coins for recoinage.

[37]*PMV*, doc. 141. That the Germans be paid a price based on the fineness estimated by the assayers at the Rialto was specified earlier in the capitolare dei massari all'oro (*PMV*, doc. 37, cap. 2). Indeed the resolution of the Great Council in 1285 governing the coinage of the ducat provided that the 108 soldi per carat be paid for according to the number of carats estimated by the assayers at the time when the gold was sold at Rialto; if, on the other hand, the merchant had the gold melted down subsequently, the mintmasters were not to buy it until they had first refined and assayed it (*PMV*, doc. 40).

"A calo de mercanti" must have meant, in contrast, that the merchant received the dross. It would seem to follow that he would be paid, not according to the assay made at the Rialto prior to the refining, but according to the amount of 24-carat gold obtained after refining.

The assaying before refining was done with touchstones and was less accurate than assaying by means of a process resembling the refining method described in chapter 12, section iii, namely, roasting the gold in a "lasagna," so called because it consisted of alternate layers of gold and of material called "cimento," which extracted the silver mixed into the gold. The roasting process was in many cases likely to result in a lower amount of 24-carat gold than that estimated by the use of the touchstone and needles.[38]

An official account of one mintmaster's term as managing mintmaster (May–June 1485), a "quaderno della quindexena," serves to illustrate how large the difference might be between the amount of 24-carat gold obtained and the amount expected according to the assay.[39] During his term in charge the mintmaster whose account survives had handled the conversion into coin of two lots, both from men associated with banking, for whom the coinage was done "a suo calo," that is, "a calo di mercanti." Both batches of bullion were entered as being 23 carats 2 grains fine (an impurity of 2 grains, or 2.08 percent). The first lot weighed 162,090 carats before being refined, and the 24-carat gold produced from it weighed 153,702 carats, a loss of 8,388 carats, or 5.17 percent. The second lot weighed 119,232 carats before being refined, and the 24-carat gold produced from it weighed 115,149, a loss of 4,083, or 3.4 percent. The difference between the assay (2.08 percent) and the actual figures of 5.19 percent and 3.42 percent illustrates how much the assay might differ from the product of the refining process.

The difference was not necessarily due to errors in assaying, calculating, or weighing. It might arise intentionally or unintentionally from the process of refining. If the impurities in the gold had really been only 2 grains out of the 96 grains in 24 carats, the loss of weight need have been no more than 2.08 percent (2/96). For each half-grain of impurity in the bullion, at least 0.52 percent of the weight (1/192) would be removed by refining. This relationship between loss of weight and the proportion of impurities is referred to with the following formula: a mark of metal loses 6 of the units of weight called carats (of which 1,152 composed 1 mark) for each half-grain of impurity to be removed (the "grain" last referred to being 1/4 of one of the 24 carats in which the degree of fineness was

[38]Described above, in chap. 9, sec. iii.
[39]"Quaderno de mi Zuan Trivixan dela quindexena de mazo e zugno 1485, fatta per misser Piero Quirini fo de Misser Biasio," ASV, Zecca, serie finale, b. 3.

measured). Accordingly, the mint for some time operated on the general rule that gold assayed as 23 carats, 3 1/2 grains would lose at least 6 carats of weight; gold of 23 carats 3 grains would lose 12 carats of weight; and so on.[40]

At the beginning of the fifteenth century, Venetian nobles who acted as bankers and bullion merchants bought gold from importers and themselves supervised the refining of the gold to 23 carats 3 grains or even 23 carats 3 1/2 grains before taking it to the mint to be made into coin. It was processed "a suo calo," that is, "a calo di merchandanti," which presumably gave them the right to receive the dross with the cimento and extract what they could from it. But so long as the reduction in weight was only 6 carats per mark, the cost of doing so may have exceeded the return. By refining up to 23 3/4 or even 23 7/8 carats themselves, they had already recovered much silver and gold from the fluxes and dross.

There were protests and boycotts when in 1414–21 the minimum required loss of weight was raised from 6 carats per half-grain to 9 carats per half-grain, and the change was linked first with refining "a calo di comun," later with refining "a calo di mercanti." The minimal loss of weight of 9 carats per mark was reaffirmed in 1421 even though it was admitted that most of those additional 3 carats of weight would be gold that adhered to the purifying flux. The minimal total loss of weight required was accordingly 0.78 percent (9/1,152) per half-grain. With bullion 23 carats 2 grains fine, such as that recorded in the "quaderno della quindexena," the loss of weight would be 3.12 percent ($4 \times 0.78$), not very different from the 3.89 percent that the second lot did in fact lose by being refined but substantially less than the 5.17 percent loss in weight suffered by the first lot when it was refined. It would have been more accurately assayed as 23 carats 1 grain fine.

In the motion that in 1421 finally raised the required minimum reduction of weight from 6 carats per half-grain to 9, the amount that the mint paid to bankers supplying gold was raised by 3 grossi: from 66 ducats 11 grossi a oro to 66 ducats 14 grossi a oro.[41] That compensated the suppliers affected, for 3 carats (their possible loss of gold through the additional refining "a calo di mercanti") was only 0.26 percent (3/1,152), whereas the increase in price was 0.19 percent (3/1,595).

Considering the complexity and the variability of the "calo," it seems best not to include it in calculating the mint charges for table A.5. On the other hand, the addition in 1416 and 1421 of 3 grossi to the price that the mint paid to certain categories of suppliers is also not included in tabulating the mint charges.

[40]See above, chap. 12, sec. iii.
[41]ASV, Zecca, b. 6tris, cap. 105, and Senato, Misti, reg. 53, fols. 154–55.

## vi. SOLDINI AND MEZZANINI, 1331–79

### *Soldini, Type 1, with Lion Rampant, ca. 1331–46*

The text of the decree specifying the weight and fineness of soldini when first coined is not extant, but surviving specimens indicate that they weighed about 0.957 grams and were 0.67 fine, so that each soldino contained 0.641 (0.957 × 0.67) grams of fine silver.[42] Consequently 1 mark of silver sufficed to coin 372.1 soldini (238.5/0.641).

The silver was obtained at a cost of 233 soldi a grossi by requiring the sale to the mint at that price of 1/5 of all silver imported. This "quinto" was called unfree silver, "argento servo."[43] At that price, 285.5 soldini could pay for a mark, since each soldino was worth 1 soldo di piccoli, which equaled 0.816 soldi a grossi, so that 285.5 soldi di piccoli equaled 233 soldi a grossi. Paying the supplier those 285.5 soldini left the mint with 86.6 soldini (372.1 − 285.5), which was a mint charge of 23.3 percent (86.6/372.1).

In 1353 it was said that the soldini then being coined contained 5 ounces of silver and 3 ounces of copper, which would make them only 0.625 fine.[44] A change may have occurred between 1331 and 1353 of which

[42]Papadopoli, 1:160, 163. In the *CNI*, 7:64–69, soldini issued under Francesco Dandolo (1329–39) vary from 1.01 to 0.77 grams; soldini issued under Bartolomeo Gradenigo (1339–42) vary from 0.89 to 0.95. On the date of the authorization of the soldino and mezzanino see above, chap. 15, sec. iii and n. 47.

[43]References to the quinto in the ASV, Grazie, reg. 5, and Senato, Misti, reg. 16, fols. 29, 85, show that it was instituted at the time of the new silver coinage, not in 1369 as Papadopoli (1:207) implies. Cf. above, chap. 11, n. 39.

On the origin of the price of 233 soldi a grossi per mark see secs. ii and iv of this appendix. In his description of Venetian coinage as it was before 1331, Pegolotti says simply that the mint paid 233 soldi (*Pratica*, 140).

An assertion in a defeated resolution of 1362 that the mint paid 11 lire 13 soldi a grossi for silver (233 soldi) (in *PMV*, doc. 139; ASV, Senato, Misti, reg. 30, fol. 50v) is in a context that suggests that this price was paid for silver brought to the mint voluntarily ("argentum franchum"), that is, after the quinto had been consigned, but other reports of market and mint prices for free silver (app. C) make that reading unreasonable. The context permits an alternative reading, namely, that the only coins being made were those minted from the servile silver and therefore cost only 233 soldi a grossi.

When the mint price for silver from the quinto was changed in 1369, prices were stated in soldi di grossi, and the price was raised from 11 soldi 3 grossi to 12 soldi 3 grossi (*PMV*, doc. 157). Since 11 soldi 3 grossi is the equivalent of just about 290 soldi a grossi, this is solid evidence that sometime before 1369 the price had been raised above 233 soldi a grossi. Perhaps Capello's resolution misrepresented the situation. But the price paid for the quinto may have been raised between 1362 and 1369. The gaps in the records of the Quarantia (see prefaces to Lombardo's *DQ*, esp. 3:vi) leave open that possibility. The many proposals about the quinto that were made in the years for which we do have the record make it seem likely that other changes were made in years for which the record is lost. True, the Quarantia then shared control of the mint with the Senate and such a change should be recorded in Senato, Misti, but some actions by the Quarantia are not to be found in Senato, Misti, e.g., *Cap. Broche*, fol. 7v.

[44]*PMV*, doc. 115, p. 103.

we lack the record. Soldini weighing 0.957 grams that were 0.625 fine instead of 0.67 fine would contain only 0.598 (0.957 × 0.625) grams fine silver each, so that 1 mark of fine silver would suffice for 399 (238.5/0.598) coins. Since, as calculated above, only 285.5 soldini had to be used to pay 233 soldi a grossi for the silver, the mint would keep 113.5 (399 − 285.5), a mint charge of 28.4 percent.

After 1350, prices for silver bullion are so often given in soldi di grossi that it becomes convenient to use that money of account instead of the soldi a grossi. The equivalent of 233 soldi a grossi is 9 soldi di grossi, assuming that soldi di grossi a monete were meant.[45] Nine soldi di grossi equals 3,456 piccoli (9 × 12 × 32), and since each soldino coin was worth 12 piccoli, the silver could be paid for by giving the supplier 288 soldini (3,456/12). By this way of figuring, the mint kept 84.1 soldini (372.1 − 288), and the mint charge was 22.6 percent (841/372.1) of the money coined.

### Mezzanini, Type 1, ca. 1331–39

According to Papadopoli's assay, the first mezzanini were 0.780 fine. They weighed 1.242 grams, so that each coin contained 0.969 grams (1.242 × 0.78) of pure silver.[46] Consequently 1 mark of silver sufficed to coin 246.1 (238.5/0.969) mezzanini. Since the silver was obtained from the quinto, 1 mark cost the mint 233 soldi a grossi, the equivalent of 285.4 soldi di piccoli (233 × 1.225). With each mezzanino valued at 16 piccoli, 214.1 mezzanini (285.4 × [12/16]) sufficed to pay for the 1 mark of silver. Paying those 214.1 mezzanini left the mint with 32 (246.1 − 214.1) mezzanini, a mint charge of 13 percent (32/246.1).

### Mezzanini, Type 2, 1346–53

The mezzanini issued in 1346 were of the same fineness as the grossi of type 1 then being coined, and they weighed 0.774 grams each, so that a mark of silver of the fineness of grossi sufficed to mint 308.1 coins (238.5/0.774).[47] The silver was "argento servo," which, like the silver then being used to make soldini, cost only 285.4 soldi di piccoli, as just explained, that is, 3,425 piccoli. Since each mezzanino had the legal value of 16 piccoli, the mark could be paid for with 214.1 mezzanini (3,425/16). Paying the supplier those 214.1 mezzanini left the mint with 94 mezzanini (308.1 − 214.1), which was a total mint charge of 30.5 percent (94/308.1).

A decree issued in 1349 declared that in minting these mezzanini some mintmasters had made a profit for the Commune of 17 grossi 20 piccoli per mark of bullion coined, and others had made a profit of 17 grossi 28 piccoli. The report suggested that the mintmasters who had made

---

[45]See above, chap. 16; and below, app. C.
[46]Papadopoli, 1:160, 163.
[47]Ibid., 1:173, 181; CNI, 7:69–73. On the date of issue see above, chap. 15, sec. iii and n. 47.

APPENDIX A

only the lower of the two amounts must have been guilty of fraud or negligence. The Quarantia voted that thereafter all mintmasters must make at least 17 grossi 24 piccoli of profit per mark or pay the difference themselves.[48] Another statement of the same year says that the expenses of minting were at least 21 "denari grossi" per mark.[49] These figures permit the following tabulation in the denari grossi of the lira di grossi a monete:

Receipts from a mark of silver
  308.1 mezzanini worth 4,758.4 piccoli
    (308.1 × 16/32)                             = 154.05 grossi
Disbursements
  Bullion at 233 soldi a grossi = 3,425 piccoli      = 107.0 grossi
  Minimal costs of labor in manufacture
    (13.6 percent)                                 21.0
  Profit required for the Commune (11.6 percent)    17.8
    Total disbursements accounted for          145.8
Additional expenses or discrepancy in these estimates   8.25
      Total                                154.05 grossi

### Soldini, Type 2, with Lion Rampant, 1353–69

When it was ordered in 1353 that soldini also be made of silver of the fineness of traditional grossi, it was ordered that they be cut "ad soldos XXXVI per marcha."[50] Here also soldos means "twelve," for cutting 12 × 36, that is, 432, from a mark resulted in coins that weighed 0.552 grams (238.5/432), which is about the weight indicated by the lighter specimens of soldini with lion rampant issued between 1353 and 1369.[51]

Since for the unfree silver obtained through the quinto, the mint still paid the traditional price of 233 soldi a grossi, equivalent to 285.4 soldi di piccoli (233 × 1.225), it could pay 285.4 soldini for a mark of silver and keep 146.6 (432 − 285.4), so that the mint charge on minting soldini from unfree silver was 33.9 percent (146.6/432).

For all silver freely offered, the mint was ordered to pay 12 soldi 6 denari of the lira di grossi.[52] Being of the lira di grossi a monete, 12 soldi 6 denari grossi equaled 4,800 piccoli ([12 × 12 × 32] + [6 × 32]). Each soldino coin being worth 12 piccoli, the mint paid the supplier 400 soldini and kept 32 soldini, making the mint charge for minting soldini from free silver 7.4 percent (32/432).

[48]PMV, doc. 107, p. 91.
[49]Ibid., doc. 110.
[50]Ibid., doc. 115.
[51]Papadopoli, 1:182, 191. In the CNI, 7:72–78 and 83–85, the "soldi nuovi" of ca. 0.54 grams contrast with the "soldi vecchi," also issued under Andrea Dandolo, which weigh 0.85–0.95 grams.
[52]PMV, doc. 117.

510

### Soldini, Type 3, with Lion Crouching, 1369–79

In the resolution lightening the soldino in December 1369, the number to be cut from a mark was stated in terms of the value of the coins as 14.5 soldi per mark.[53] "Soldi" in that decree did not mean "twelve," as it had in various earlier decrees. A little calculation shows that the reference must be to the soldi of the lira di grossi a monete, which is the money of account used in the same decree in setting the price of silver bullion.[54] Since 1 soldo di grossi a monete equaled 12 denari grossi, each of 32 piccoli, 14 1/2 soldi equaled 14 1/2 × 12 × 32, or 5,568 piccoli. Since each soldino coin equaled 12 piccoli, the yield from a mark was 5,568/12, or 464 soldini. Making that many coins from a mark of 238.5 grams would give each coin a weight of 0.514 grams (238.5/464), which is close to the weight (0.513) of the second type of the surviving soldini minted after Andrea Contarini became doge in 1368.[55]

The yield, and consequently the mint charge as figured below, would appear to be slightly higher if allowance were made for the changed fineness of the soldino and other coins of fine silver struck thereafter. Chemical analysis showed it to have been 0.952 instead of the 0.965 of the grosso hitherto.[56] But there is no record of that change in the surviving documents, and uncertainty consequently remains as to whether it applied also to the mark of metal from which the 464 coins were cut. If it applied to both, as seems probable, the above calculations are applicable.

For unfree silver the price paid to the supplier was raised in December 1369 to 12 soldi 3 denari grossi ([12 × 12 × 32] + [3 × 32]), or 4,704 piccoli.[57] Each soldino being worth 12 piccoli, the mint paid the supplier 4,704/12, or 392, soldini and kept 72 soldini (464 − 392), or 15.5 percent (72/464). For free silver the price fixed in 1353—4,800 piccoli—was presumably still offered, which meant giving the supplier 400 soldini (4,800/12). Out of the yield of 464 soldi, the mint would keep 64 (464 − 400), or 13.8 percent (64/464).

### vii. SOLDINI AND GROSSI

### Soldini, Type 4, Lion Crouching with One Star, 1379–80

The number of soldini to be cut from a mark was stated in 1379 by giving their value as 15 soldi of the lira di grossi a monete, which is the same as 180 denari grossi a monete of 5,760 piccoli (15 × 12 × 32). With

---

[53]Ibid., doc. 157.
[54]Papadopoli, 1:207.
[55]Ibid., 1:216; *CNI,* 7:95–97.
[56]Papadopoli, 1:215n, 216.
[57]*PMV,* doc. 157.

each soldino worth 12 piccoli, that made 480 coins (5,760/12). A weight of 0.497 grams (238.5/480) is about that indicated by surviving coins.

For unfree silver the mint was ordered to pay 12 soldi 3 denari, or 4,704 piccoli, so that the mint gave the supplier 392 soldini (4,704/12) and kept 88 (480 − 392), which was a mint charge of 18.3 percent (88/480).[58] For free silver of certified fineness, Venetian citizens were offered 14 soldi 7 1/2 denari grossi, or 5,616 piccoli, which could be paid with 468 soldini (5,616/12), leaving 12 soldini (480 − 468) as a mint charge of 2.5 percent (12/480).

### Grossi, Type 2, with One Star, 1379–80

The number of grossi to be cut from a mark was stated in 1379–80 by giving the value of the coins, and was the same value per mark as the yield in soldini, namely, coins worth 5,760 piccoli. Each of the new grossi was to be worth 48 piccoli, so that the number made from a mark was 120 (5,760/48). The weight of 1.99 grams (238.5/120) is about that indicated by surviving specimens. For unfree silver the mint paid the same as for silver for the soldino, 4,704 piccoli per mark, so that the mint gave the supplier 98 grossi (4,704/48) and kept 22, which was also a mint charge of 18.3 percent (22/120). For free silver the offer was the same as that for silver for soldini, namely, 5,616 piccoli, which could be paid with 117 grossi, leaving 3 grossi, the same mint charge of 2.5 percent (3/120).[59]

### Soldini and Grossi, Both with Star, 1380–85

The alloy and number of soldini and grossi cut from a mark in 1380–85 was as specified in 1379, namely, 480 soldini or 120 grossi, worth in either case 15 soldi di grossi a monete (5,760 piccoli). For unfree silver the price paid was raised to 14 soldi. The mint charge can be figured directly from the prices: 15 − 14 = 1 soldo, which was 6.7 percent (1/15). For free silver, importers were offered 14 soldi 7 1/2 grossi (5,616 piccoli), so that out of the 5,760 piccoli worth coined, the mint kept only 144 piccoli (5,760 − 5,616), a mint charge of 2.5 percent.[60]

### Soldini and Grossi, Both with Star, 1385

The value, fineness, and weight of the soldini and grossi were not changed in 1385, but the price paid for unfree silver was lowered to 13.5 soldi, so that the mint kept coin worth 1.5 soldi (15 − 13.5), a mint charge on unfree silver of 10 percent (1.5/15).[61] On free silver the mint charge was unchanged, at 2.5 percent.

[58]Ibid., doc. 164; Papadopoli, 1:164; *CNI*, 7:95–101.
[59]*PMV*, doc. 164; Papadopoli, 1:215–16; *CNI*, 7:95–101.
[60]*PMV*, doc. 166.
[61]Ibid., doc. 172.

## Soldini, 1385–91, and Grossi, 1386–87, Both with Star

The value, fineness, and weight of soldini of 1385–91 and grossi of 1386–87 were not changed, but the price paid for unfree silver was reduced further to 13.25 soldi,[62] so that the mint kept coin worth 1.75 (15 − 13.25), a mint charge on unfree silver of 11.7 percent (1.75/15). On free silver the mint charge was unchanged.

## Grossi, Type 2, with One Star, 1387–91

The value, fineness, and weight of grossi of 1387–91 were officially unchanged, and on unfree silver there was no change in the mint charge, but for free silver a price of 14 soldi 8 denari grossi 20 piccoli per mark was offered for refined silver, but not to moneychangers or those buying silver at the auctions. The stated purpose was the general welfare and especially "pro bono et subvencione illorum pauperum qui laborant ad monetam."[63] After paying out grossi worth 5,652 piccoli ([14 × 12 × 32] + [8 × 32] + 20), the mint could keep coin worth 108 piccoli (5,760 − 5,652), a mint charge of only 1.9 percent (108/5,760).

## Soldini, Type 4, with One Star, 1391–94

On 19 May 1391 the above-mentioned higher price for free silver (equal to 5,652 piccoli) was offered also for all false or clipped coin freely turned in to the mint as bullion.[64] On 30 May the tolerance permitted in the number of soldini cut from a mark was fixed by the Senate as 24 lire 16 soldi to 25 lire 4 soldi.[65] To fit with other figures, the money of account must be assumed to be lire di piccoli, so that the range is 496–504 soldi, or 5,952–6,048 piccoli. Making coins of that value from each mark of silver bullion and paying for free bullion the price of 5,652 piccoli provided for in the regulation of 19 May, the mint would have retained coins worth from 396 piccoli (6,048 − 5,652) to 300 piccoli (5,952 − 5,652), representing a mint charge of between 6.5 percent and 5 percent of free silver.

This charge was probably higher than intended by those who had hoped the regulation would cause bad money to be turned in for re-coinage. Accordingly, a few days later (9 June) the price offered for bad coins turned in as bullion was raised to 15 soldi 3 grossi if return payment was made in soldini, while no change in price was ordered if repayment was made in grossi.[66] When paying 15 soldi 3 grossi, or 5,856 piccoli ([15 × 12 × 32] + [3 × 32]), and minting the maximum number of soldini per

[62]Ibid., doc. 178.
[63]Ibid., doc. 179; Papadopoli, 1:224–25.
[64]PMV, doc. 185; Cap. Broche, fol. 7.
[65]ASV, Senato, Misti, reg. 41, fol. 141v; Cap. Broche, fol. 7v. Cf. Papadopoli, 1:225.
[66]PMV, doc. 186; Cap. Broche, fol. 7v.

mark (worth 6,048 piccoli), the mint could keep 192 piccoli (6,048 − 5,856), a mint charge of 3.2 percent.

As this resolution of the Quarantia indicated, the decision of the Senate of 30 May regarding tolerances had in fact permitted soldini to be struck lighter than before ("sunt facte leviores consueto"): from 0.473 to 0.481 grams, down from a previous 0.496.[67] On 20 July a mean standard of 0.469 grams was established, the weight used by Papadopoli.[68] At that weight, 508.5 soldini could be struck from 1 mark (238.5/0.469). Their value in piccoli would be 6,102 piccoli, slightly more than the maximum indicated by the law of 30 May.

When the silver for those 6,102 piccoli was obtained from the quinto at 13 soldi 8 grossi (13.667), the price set in the law of 30 May, the mark cost the mint 5,248 piccoli (13.667 × 12 × 32). The mint kept 854 piccoli (6,102 − 5,248), a mint charge on unfree silver of 14 percent. When paying 5,856 piccoli for free silver, as set on 9 June, the mint charge would have been 4 percent (6.102 − 5,856 = 246; 246/6,102 = 4.0).[69]

### Soldini, Type 4, with One Star, 1394–99, and Grossi, Type 3, with Two Stars, 1394–97

In 1394, grossi were ordered made according to the same procedure as had been set for the soldino in 1391, in order to reinstate the parity of 1 grosso and 4 soldini. Each mark was to yield between 126 1/2 and 127 1/2 grossi (506–10 soldini). At 48 piccoli per grosso, that was a yield worth between 6,072 and 6,120 piccoli. It indicates grossi of the mean weight of ca. 1.88 grams (238.5/127) and soldini weighing exactly 1/4 as much (0.47 grams) as they had since 1391; both figures agree with Papadopoli's description of these coins in 1394–99.[70]

For unfree silver the amount paid seems to be that fixed on 30 May 1391, namely, 13.667 soldi di grossi a monete, equal to 5,248 piccoli. Out of the 6,072 or 6,120 that were the yield, the mint could keep coin worth 824– 872 piccoli (6,072 − 5,248 = 824; 6,120 − 5,248 = 872), a mint charge of 13.6–14.2 percent. For free silver seigniorage was abolished, at least nominally. The mint was ordered to return coin containing the same weight of silver as the bullion received ("pondus pro pondere") and to charge the merchant only for the costs of manufacture ("omnes expensas et callum"),

---

[67]The maximum number was 504 soldini (6,048/12), and the weight, 0.473 grams (238.5/504); the minimum number was 496 (5,952/12), and the weight, 0.481 grams (238.5/496).

[68]Papadopoli, 1:230.

[69]On the effects of the failure to narrow further the range of tolerance on soldini see above, chap. 18, secs. i and ii.

[70]Papadopoli, 1:229, 230. For the text see ibid., doc. 17; *PMV*, doc. 187; and *Cap. Broche*, fol. 8v.

in which was included the pay of officials as well as of craftsmen. The costs totaled 9 soldi di piccoli per mark. Since 127 grossi or 508 soldini were made from a mark, the mint charge was 1.8 percent (9/508).

### Grossi, Type 3, with Two Stars, 1397–99

According to a decree of the Senate dated 7 October 1399, recorded in volgare in a capitolare of the mintmasters, the mint had begun cutting 131 grossi instead of 127 from a mark two years earlier ("da do anny in qua"), apparently without any authorization, unless such authorization was somehow connected with using all the silver derived from the quinto for soldini[71] and the need to attract free silver in order to coin grossi. Accordingly, we date from 1397, not from 1399 as does Papadopoli, the change in weight that—after 1399—applied to soldini as well as grossi.

### Soldini and Grossi, 1399–1407

The decree of 7 October 1399 approved and confirmed the practice of cutting 131 grossi per mark and ordered that soldini be changed proportionally so as to be exactly 1/4 the weight of grossi. That made the weights 1.820 grams for the grosso and 0.454 for the soldino.[72]

Cutting 131 grossi from a mark gave a yield of coins worth 6,288 piccoli (131 × 48). Assuming that the price for unfree silver was unchanged at 5,248 piccoli, the mint could keep coins worth 1,040 piccoli, a mint charge of 16.5 percent (1,040/6,288) on unfree silver, for both grossi and soldini. On free silver, increasing the number of coins made from a mark reduced the mint charge to 1.77 percent of the yield, as long as it remained at the 9 soldi that had been set as the amount needed to cover the costs of production, called the "fattura" (9/[131 × 4] = 9/508 = 0.0177). In 1401 this fattura was increased to 9 soldi 4 piccoli, so that the mint charge was 1.8 percent (9 1/3/508 = 0.01837).[73] A decree of February 1406 regarding the striking of mezzanini for Verona and Vicenza mentioned that the fattura on soldini was then 13 soldi, which meant a charge of 2.56 percent.[74]

---

[71]PMV, doc. 191; *Cap. Broche*, fol. 8v (11 August 1395).

[72]PMV, doc. 192; *Cap. Broche*, fol. 10; Papadopoli, 1:227, 229–30. The *CNI* (7:106–12), while distinguishing among the three kinds of grossi of different weights and designs issued under Antonio Venier (1382–1400), does not clarify the dates of the changes. Although the next change clearly dated is that of 1407 (Papadopoli, 1:238), the *CNI* suggests that all the soldini of Doge Michele Steno (1400–1413) were of the lighter weight sanctioned only in 1407.

[73]ASV, Senato, Misti, reg. 45, fol. 95.

[74]Papadopoli, 1, doc. 19.

APPENDIX A

## Soldini and Grossi, 1407–14

In 1407 the Senate ordered silver coin made at "136 manus" per mark. By "manus" is meant a batch of coins, either grossi or soldini, here of the value of 136 grossi, a yield per mark of 6,528 piccoli (48 × 136). This meaning is confirmed by a marginal note to the law in the capitolare and by the law of 1416, where it is stated that the standard for grossi and soldini was 27 lire 4 soldi (similarly, 6,528 piccoli) per mark.[75]

Assuming that unfree silver was still paid for at 13.667 soldi di grossi, or 5,248 piccoli, the mint could keep coin worth 1,280 piccoli (6,528 − 5,248), a mint charge of 19.6 percent. In fact, the mint charged even more by minting more than the stipulated number of soldini per mark.[76] Free silver was ordered coined into grossi without charge, that is, the Commune was to pay the fattura whether the silver was imported by a Venetian or a foreigner, provided it was argento di bolla, sealed with the seal of San Marco. The mint would give back to the supplier the same weight in grossi as he deposited in bullion. If the supplier wished soldi instead of grossi, he had to pay only the difference between the production costs of soldi and grossi.[77]

## Soldini and Grossi, 1414–17

The only change that took place in 1414 was a shift of the costs of production to the supplier of free bullion. He was required to pay 10 soldi a mark on grossi, 14 soldi on soldini,[78] which represent mint charges of 1.8 percent ($10/[136 \times 4] = 10/544 = 1.84$) and 2.6 percent ($14/544 = 2.57$).

## Soldini and Grossi, 1417–21

The quinto was abolished in 1417, and with it the high charges on unfree silver. The mint was to coin all silver presented by any Venetian or foreigner into grossi and soldi. Suppliers would pay only 8 soldi per mark out of a fattura (expenses) totaling 14, the remaining 6 soldi being covered by the government. Coins to the value of 589 or 590 soldi were to be made from a mark,[79] so that the fee of 8 soldi constituted a mint charge of only 1.36 percent.

As some compensation for covering part of the cost of manufacture,

---

[75]Ibid., 1:234, 245; doc. 18, p. 350; also in *Cap. Broche*, fol. 15v and the editor's note "a."
[76]Papadopoli, 1:245, regarding the law of 1416 cited in the previous note.
[77]Papadopoli, 1, text of the law, p. 350.
[78]ASV, Senato, Misti, reg. 50, copia, fol. 247; in Venetian in *Cap. Broche*, fol. 17; cf. Papadopoli, 1:245.
[79]Papadopoli, 1, doc. 21, pp. 356–59. On p. 360 the document specified "livre XXVIIII, soldi VIIII" (389 soldi) from a mark. A decree of February 1420/21 says that silver coin was being made at "£ 29, soldi 10" per mark (390 soldi) (ibid., 363; also in *Cap. Broche*, fols. 18v–20v).

the government levied a refining charge of 4 1/2 grossi, or 3.08 percent per mark, on silver refined in the mint under a new office established there for that purpose. That and later decrees imply that the refining could have been done more cheaply, if not as accurately, elsewhere. Only a part of that refining charge, 8 1/3 soldi, has been considered part of the minting charge (as explained in chap. 2),[80] so that the mint charge is estimated as 2.7 percent.

### Soldi and Grossi, 1421–29

In February 1420/21 the weights were lightened by ordering 29 lire 16 soldi (596 soldi) cut from a mark. The fineness was also reduced slightly, from 0.952 to 0.949.[81] As long as a fee of only 8 soldi was collected as "cost" (fattura) from the supplier, the mint charge was 1.34 percent (8/596).

### viii. PICCOLI, 1343–1442

### Piccoli, 1343–54

During the dogeship of Andrea Dandolo, many piccoli weighed about 0.3 grams, although some were issued that Papadopoli describes as being 0.190 fine and weighing 0.336 grams.[82] At that weight they were considerably heavier than those that previously had been coined but had just about the same fineness. From a mark of alloy, 709.8 could be cut (238.5/0.336), and a mark of pure silver sufficed to make 3,735.8 coins (709.8/0.190).

A price of 12 soldi 6 denari of the lira di grossi a monete was offered in 1353 for all silver freely presented to the mint for manufacture into soldini,[83] and a similar price had been quoted in 1350.[84] If the mintmasters had to pay a somewhat similar price in buying silver to make piccoli, the Commune would have lost substantially, for

$$12 \text{ soldi } 6 \text{ denari grossi} = (12 \times 12 \times 32) + (6 \times 32)$$
$$= 4,800 \text{ piccoli}$$

which is 1,064.2 piccoli more (4,800 − 3,735.8) than the number coined from the mark. In contrast, if the silver was obtained at the price then paid

---

[80]See above, chap. 12, nn. 53, 54; chap. 11, n. 28. The decree specifies both the percentage and the amount, namely, 4 1/4 grossi, which indicates that the price of silver was 5 3/4 ducats, in line with other evidence.

[81]Papadopoli, 1:248, 250–51.

[82]Ibid., 1:183; *CNI*, 7:55.

[83]Papadopoli, 1:175; *DQ*, vol. 3, doc. 33.

[84]Cessi, in *PMV*, lxxix n.

for unfree silver, 233 soldi a grossi (the equivalent of 3,426.6 piccoli), the mint kept 309.2 coins (3,735.8 − 3,426.6), which was a mint charge of 8.2 percent (309.2/3,735.8) of the money coined.

Those were years when Venice was flooded with both gold and silver, the voyage to Tana was interrupted, the direct line to Alexandria was opened, and the unfree silver—until 1350—was reduced to 1/10 of the amounts imported.[85] It is not clear how under Andrea Dandolo the mintmasters obtained the silver to mint some piccoli that contained much more silver than those issued under the immediately preceding or succeeding doges. Probably it came either from unfree silver by specific direction of a superior council or from foreign coins collected at the customs or worn or clipped coins confiscated by officials.

### Piccoli, 1355–68

Specimens of piccoli 0.190 fine but weighing only 0.284 grams are listed for this period by Papadopoli.[86] Those figures indicate that 839.8 (238.5/0.284) were cut from a mark of alloy, and a mark of pure silver sufficed for 4,420 piccoli (839.8/0.190). How the silver was obtained remains doubtful. If obtained at the price at which free silver was accepted by the mint for minting soldini, 150 denari grossi (4,800 piccoli), it would have involved a loss of 380 piccoli on each mark. If obtained at the price of unfree silver, 233 soldi a grossi or 3,426.6 piccoli, the mint could have kept 993.4 (4,420 − 3,426.6) piccoli out of each mark, a mint charge of 22.5 percent (993.4/4,420).

### Piccoli just before April 1369

Just before April 1369 a mark of alloy was yielding 3 lire 15 soldi,[87] which can be read in a purely arithmetical sense or as lire di piccoli, which amounts to the same thing here, namely, 900 coins ([3 × 240] + [15 × 12]). Since no change in the alloy is indicated, a mark of pure silver sufficed for 4,736.8 coins (900/0.190). Even that large a yield would not quite cover the amount the mint was offering since 1353 for a mark of free silver to be coined into soldini, namely, an amount equal to 4,800 piccoli, but coinage would be profitable if unfree silver, still obtained at 3,426.6 piccoli, was used for piccoli instead of soldini. The mint could then keep 1,310.2 (4,736.8 − 3,426.6), a mint charge of 27.7 percent (1,310.2/4,736.8). But neither Papadopoli nor the CNI lists specimens of piccoli coined between 1368 and 1385.

[85]See above, chap. 17.
[86]Papadopoli, 1:192, 196, 200, 203.
[87]PMV, doc. 158.

## Piccoli, 1369

An increase in the number of piccoli cut from a mark of alloy was ordered on 13 April 1369 so as to make the yield 4 lire (i.e., 960 piccoli).[88] Since no change in alloy was indicated, it will be assumed that a mark of silver sufficed for 5,052.6 piccoli (960/0.190). The mint was said to be losing 7 soldi per mark because silver was worth 16 1/2 lire (presumably lire a grossi, equivalent to 330 soldi a grossi, equal to 3,960 denari a grossi, which equaled 4,853.1 piccoli). Hence the 7 soldi are presumably soldi a grossi equal to 102.9 piccoli (7 × 12 × [32/26.111]). The loss of 102.9 piccoli on each mark implies a total cost of 5,155.5 piccoli, that is, the yield of 5,052.6 plus the loss of 102.9. Since out of the 5,155.5 piccoli the cost of silver equaled 4,853.1, the amount left for other expenses was 302.2, or 6.2 percent (302.2/4,853.1), which covered the cost of manufacture but left no seigniorage.

## Piccoli, 1370–79

The Senate voted on 14 February 1370 to raise the number of piccoli cut from a mark to 4 lire 12 soldi, or 1,104 coins. A mark of silver then sufficed for 5,810.5 piccoli (1,104/0.190). When the mintmasters used silver derived from the quinto for piccoli, they were to charge the piccolo account for it at the rate of 16 1/2 lire (4,353.3 piccoli) per mark.[89] The piccolo account would then have to its credit for expenses and profit on each mark 957.2 piccoli (5,810.5 − 4,853.3), a mint charge on piccoli of 16.5 percent (957.2/5,810.5). It is doubtful whether these piccoli were actually struck, since no specimens of any kind of piccoli coined between 1368 and 1385 seem to be extant.[90]

## Piccoli Ordered in 1379, Minted 1385–90

A new issue of piccoli ordered in 1379 to replace the old was to be cut 3 soldi 1 1/2 denari grossorum from a mark of alloy, or 1,200 coins per mark (37 1/2 × 32). The fineness was specified as 1 ounce 16 carats of argento di bolla (160 carats) and 6 ounces 3 quartieri 20 carats (992 carats), of copper for the total of 1,152 carats in a mark, in short, 0.139 fine.[91] Papadopoli gives the weight as 0.198 (instead of 0.199) and the fineness as 0.138.[92]

[88]Ibid., doc. 158.

[89]That is, the mintmaster in charge of soldini for that period was to charge the mintmaster in charge of piccoli 16 1/2 lire (*PMV*, doc. 158).

[90]Neither Papadopoli nor the *CNI* lists any specimens of piccoli issued between 1368 and the issues under Antonio Venier, the first of which Papadopoli (1:200, 231) identifies with those ordered struck by a law of 4 June 1385.

[91]*PMV*, docs. 163, 164, 175; Papadopoli, 1:231.

[92]Papadopoli, 1:231.

Accepting his way of rounding off, we find that the number of piccoli that could be made from a mark of silver of fineness of 0.952 was 8,695.6 (1,200/0.138). The value of the money coined would be the same, 8,695.6 piccoli. The expenditure for the new coins ("omnibus chalis et omnibus expensis") was not to exceed 3 grossi 28 piccoli per mark, about 1.4 percent of their value (124/8,695.6).

In 1385 a decree acknowledging in its preamble that the decree of 1379 had not been observed called for enforcement, especially for turning in of all pennies minted elsewhere. It also provided additional silver for piccoli by stating that for a while ca. 7 percent of the silver received through the quinto should be used to make piccoli (1 soldo out of every 13 1/2 soldi worth of coin made from a mark).[93] By paying for that unfree silver only the 13 1/2 soldi di grossi a monete (equal to 5,184 piccoli) ordered in 1385[94] but coining the 8,695.6 piccoli made possible by the decree of 1379, the mint retained 3,511.6 piccoli (8,695.6 − 5,184), a mint charge of 40.4 percent.

### Piccoli, 1390–1417

In 1390 it was ordered that piccoli be made 10 soldi from an ounce and with 16 carats of silver.[95] That meant 960 from a mark (10 × 12 × 8) and 0.111 fine (16/144), figures that agree with Papadopoli's description.[96] The weight was 0.248 grams and remained unchanged under several doges. Since the fineness was 0.111, the number of piccoli that could be made from a mark of silver was 8,648 (960/0.111). Small amounts of the quinto were assigned to the making of piccoli in 1390 and 1391.[97] The price for the quinto was lowered in 1386 to 13 soldi 3 grossi, the equivalent of 5,088 piccoli (13 × 12 = 156; 156 + 3 = 159; 159 × 32 = 5,088).[98] The mint could keep 3,560 piccoli (8,648 − 5,088) out of every mark, a mint charge of 41.2 percent (3,560/8,648).

For free silver, a price was fixed in 1387 equivalent to 5,652 piccoli, although the possibility of buying for less was not excluded. As long as it paid that price, the mint could keep 2,996 piccoli (8,648 − 5,652) out of each mark, a mint charge of 34.6 percent. Higher prices were offered for some kinds of bullion or old coin, the highest amounting to 5,856 piccoli. At that price, the mint kept 2,792 piccoli (8,648 − 5,856), or 32.3 percent.[99]

The silver for this issue of piccoli was supposed to be derived from

[93]PMV, doc. 175.
[94]Ibid., doc. 172.
[95]Ibid., doc. 182.
[96]Papadopoli, 1:231, 239, 253, 271.
[97]PMV, docs. 181, 184.
[98]Ibid., doc. 178.
[99]Ibid., docs. 179, 185, 186, 187.

calling in all the old piccoli and redeeming them at face value. The piccoli coined in 1355–68 had been 0.190 fine and had weighed 0.284 grams (thus Papadopoli, as cited above) and each contained 0.053 grams of fine silver, whereas by Papadopoli's figures the prospective coins were to contain 0.027 grams (0.198 × 0.138) of fine silver. By the exchange the mint would have gained 0.026 grams of silver per coin, about enough to make two coins for each one received, but in fact old pennies must have been sufficiently deteriorated to have reduced profit from the exchange. If they had been in use for ten years and had deteriorated at an annual rate of 0.3 percent, they would have lost 3.3 percent of their weight (cf. table 16). That would have reduced their silver content from 0.053 to 0.051. The gain for the mint from the exchange would still have been large, 0.024 grams. Gain could also be hoped for from demanding surrender—at the mint's price— of foreign pennies, of which the circulation was forbidden.

Since these coins were almost 90 percent copper, the amount of actual profit obviously depended also on the price of copper. When, as in 1390, the expensive grade of copper, rame di bolla, cost about 82 ducats per migliaio grosso (2,000 marks) and the ducat stood at 84 soldi di piccoli, the cost of copper in piccoli constituted less than 4 percent of their legal value.[100] With gross mint charges at 32 percent, labor and seigniorage therefore came to about 28 percent.

### Piccoli, 1417–42

After the quinto was abolished, profits on coining piccoli varied with the market prices of silver and copper. At this time the price of silver is reported in ducats, and in 1417 it was officially given as 5 ducats 18 grossi,[101] when the ducat's price in soldi di piccoli had risen to 100 soldi.[102] For a rough estimate for the period 1417–42 the price of a mark is taken as equivalent to 6,900 piccoli (5.75 × 100 × 12). Since the weight and fineness of the piccolo was the same as in 1390–1417, 1 mark of silver sufficed to make 8,648 piccoli. The number retained by the mint was 1,748 (8,648 − 6,900), a mint charge of 20.2 percent (1,748/8,648).

## ix. DEPENDENCIES

### Torneselli, 1353–1442

For use in Romania, primarily for paying governmental expenses in Crete, Coron, Modon, and Negroponte, the Quarantia voted in July 1353

[100]See below, apps. C and D.
[101]Papadopoli, 1:357. Cf. ASV, Miscellanea Gregolin, b. 14, Soranzo libro real nuovo, fols. 13, 14, 38, 113, 115; and below, vol. 2.
[102]See below, app. D.

for the minting of "turonenses," commonly called torneselli. It was then ordered that they be 8/9 copper, 1/9 silver, and cut 320 from a mark. That would make them 0.111 fine with a weight of 0.75 grams.[103] Examination of the hundreds of torneselli (turonenses) found in hoards and in excavations shows that they were in fact minted at a fineness consistently close to 0.111 from 1353 until 1442, but their weight was from the beginning much below 0.75 grams. It was about 0.60–0.65 grams before 1382 and 0.55–0.60 grams after 1382. Alan Stahl examines and finds reasons to reject most of the plausible explanations of the lower weight.[104] Probably the drop from 0.75 to 0.65 is to be explained by a vote in the Quarantia to that effect, a vote recorded in the lost registers of the Quarantia.[105]

The vote of July 1353 stipulated that the tornesello should have the legal value of 3 "denari" (piccoli) in Romania; it does not seem to have been legal tender within Venice. A basis for calculating—in gold ducats—the mint charge and the profit as a percentage of the yield is provided by a statement in 1385 giving the annual production of torneselli as 12,000 marks, with an official value of 14,000 ducats, from which a revenue of 3,000 ducats was expected.[106] Since the alloy was only 0.111 fine, the silver contained in 12,000 marks of torneselli amounted to only 1,332 marks (12,000 × 0.111). At the price of 6 ducats per mark,[107] that amount of silver would cost 7,992 ducats (1,332 × 6). The yield of 14,000 ducats breaks down as follows:

| | | |
|---|---|---|
| Cost of silver | 7,992 ducats | 57.1 percent |
| Profit for Commune | 3,000 ⎞ | |
| Manufacturing cost | ⎟ | 42.9 |
| (including the cost of copper) | 3,008 ⎠ | ____ |
| Total | 14,000 ducats | 100.0 percent |

An estimate of the percentage of mint charges can also be calculated from the mint's regulations. Since a tornesello was 1/9 silver and weighed about 0.64 grams, each contained only about 0.07 grams of silver, and 1 mark of silver (238.5 grams) sufficed for making 3,407 torneselli (238.5/0.07). If each tornesello was worth 1/4 of a soldino, as it was in Romania, then the 3,407 torneselli had the value of 852 soldini (i.e., 852 soldi di piccoli). To compare this value of the yield with the value of the silver used requires

---

[103]PMV, doc. 119.

[104]Stahl, The Venetian Tornesello, secs. 5 and 6. The reduction of the tornesello, as well as of the piccolo, to a fineness of only 0.055 in 1442 is reported by Papadopoli, 1:227, 231, 258–60, 272.

[105]DQ, vol. 3; and Lombardo, "La ricostruzione." There are gaps after July 1353, namely, between December 1353 and February 1354 and after March 1354, while Andrea Dandolo was still doge.

[106]PMV, doc. 177.

[107]See below, app. C.

converting from the soldo di piccoli into the money of account that was coming into use in Venice in the mid-fourteenth century and was used by the mint in pricing the silver bullion it acquired (as explained in chapter 16 and appendix C). In that money of account, 1 soldo di grossi a monete equaled 32 soldini. Consequently 852 soldini equaled 26.6 soldi di grossi (852/32).

In contrast to 26 soldi di grossi as the yield from a mark was the cost of a mark of silver bullion, namely, 12.5 soldi di grossi, if bought at the price that the mint in 1353 was ordered to offer for all silver presented to be made into soldini. The difference between 26.6 soldi and 12.5 soldi left plenty of room for profit as well as for meeting the costs of manufacture.

In practice, the mint probably paid somewhat more than 12.5 soldi per mark, but not more than it offered after 1379 when accepting free silver for coinage as grossi, namely, 14 soldi 7 1/2 denari grossi.[108] The breakdown of the yield is similar whether the estimate starts from the summary figures in gold ducats or from the mint prices. In either case the legal value of the tornesello was about twice the value of its silver content. Using different methods, Alan Stahl estimates that "its extrinsic value" ranged from 50 percent to 100 percent above "its intrinsic value."[109]

### Soldi for Zara, 1410 and 1414

On 31 May 1410 the Senate ordered the mint to strike a coin for Zara, just reacquired by Venice, where Venetian grossi and soldini were being "chased" by Hungarian coins and especially by Aquileian "frignacchi" ("friesachers"), which circulated at the same value as the Venetian soldino, while containing only 2/3 the fine silver contained in the latter.[110] The decrees do not indicate precisely how the new coin (called a "soldo" in 1414) was to be paid out, but it can be inferred that it was to circulate as 1 soldo of the money of account used in Zara and the surrounding territory.[111] In fact, the friesacher of Aquileia was the basic coin of the Aquileian money of account used at Udine (where it constituted a "denaro" worth 14 Venetian piccoli);[112] and the quotations of the ducat at Udine in those

---

[108]See above, sec. vii.

[109]*The Venetian Tornesello,* sec. 3. Stahl implies that the soldo di grossi was still based on the old grosso coin even after that coin had risen in value to 46 or 48 piccoli. On the difficult problem of the silver equivalents of the "soldo di grossi" in the period 1331–1400 see below, app. C, sec. i.

[110]Papadopoli, 1:293–99 and doc. 34.

[111]Papadopoli (1:295–96) speaks of a "lira dalmata," which, on the basis of information dating from the eighteenth century, was supposed to be worth 2/3 as much as the Venetian lira. Under earlier Venetian domination, in 1293, "Sclavonia" was ordered to keep accounts in lire and no longer in perperi (*DMC,* 3:331).

[112]Pegolotti (*Pratica,* 154–55) wrote "e a minuto si mette il fregiacchese per denari 14 bagattini piccioli di Vinegia l'uno." That relationship continued over the following century (see Bernardi, *Monetazione;* and app. D).

years, converted into soldi di piccoli, are very close (higher by only about 4 percent) to the rates current in Venice.[113] The new coins were to imitate the friesacher as closely as possible (". . . ita modica differencia"), both in fine silver content and in design, while still being clearly Venetian issues.

The coin ordered struck in 1410 contained 0.266 grams of fine silver; 336 (42 × 8) were cut from a mark of alloy, and 897 from a mark of silver. The cost of manufacture, not including the "calo," was given by the Quarantia in August 1410 as a low 7.3 Venetian soldi (compared with the "fattura" of 14 soldi per mark [probably including calo] charged to purveyors for the coinage of soldini or 10 soldi for grossi in the period 1414–17, as indicated above).[114] Sometime after August 1410 the decree to issue the coin was revoked, as is stated in the decree of 1414, next to be considered.

In 1414 production was begun again—or begun in earnest for the first time—now at a slightly higher content of fine silver, 0.274 grams, in a slightly lighter coin: 352 (44 × 8) were struck from a mark of alloy, 870 from a mark of silver.[115] In both cases the soldo of Zara contained close to 2/3 the fine silver of the Venetian soldino (actually 0.638 in 1410, 0.657 in 1414). Since the new coin was meant to take the place of both the Venetian soldino and its foreign competitors in the region of Zara, it may be assumed that it was paid out to officials, who were to put it into circulation, as worth a soldino. In that case, the gross mint charge was about 35 percent.

## Mezzanini or Soldi for Verona and Vicenza, 1406

In February 1406 the mint was ordered to strike a coin sometimes called a mezzanino and sometimes a soldo, since it was worth 1 soldo in the money of account used in the newly acquired territories of Verona and Vicenza, where the lira was 1/3 larger than the Venetian lira di piccoli.[116] The fineness was that of Venetian grossi and soldini (0.952), and the weight of fine silver 0.577 grams. The mint offered to pay suppliers for free silver and for coins of the previous Milanese rulers of the area "pondus pro pondere," with the purveyor paying only 8 Venetian soldi or 6 Veronese soldi for "factura, callo et expensis." Any further costs incurred were to be absorbed by the Commune. Since 413.3 mezzanini were cut from a mark of silver (238.5/0.577), the charge was 1.45 percent (6/413.3). The same decree ordered that as of September the charge be raised to 13 soldi (9.75 mezzanini), the same fee then charged on soldini, which comes to 2.36

[113]See below, app. D.
[114]*Cap. Broche,* fol. 16v.
[115]Papadopoli, 1:295–99 and doc. 35.
[116]Papadopoli, vol. 1, doc. 19, which bears the correct date of 1405/6, as against the error in the text (pp. 235–36) of 1404/5.

percent (9.75/413.3).[117] For unfree silver the conditions holding for soldini were to be in effect, namely, a charge of 16.5 percent (see above, sec. vii, Soldini and Grossi, 1399–1407). The Venetian grosso was also to be current in Verona and Vicenza, where its legal value was 3 soldi veronesi.

### Piccoli for Verona and Vicenza, 1406

The same set of decrees that initiated the striking of the mezzanino in February 1406 also ordered production of a piccolo to fit the Veronese accounting system, so that 12 were to be current for 1 soldo veronese. They were to be of the same fineness as Venetian piccoli and torneselli, namely, 0.III, and 770 were ordered cut from a mark.[118] Thus, 6,937 Veronese piccoli were struck from 1 mark of silver (770/0.III). Since the Veronese lira was 1/3 larger than the Venetian lira di piccoli, that number of piccoli was equal to 9,226 Venetian piccoli (6,937 × 1.33), or 768.8 soldi. The fattura for the new Veronese piccoli was given as 94 piccoli per oncia or 752 piccoli (62.67 soldi) per mark; that meant costs of 8.2 percent.[119]

Since unfree silver seems still to have been figured at 5,248 Venetian piccoli (see above, sec. vii, Soldini and Grossi, 1399–1407), the mint could keep coins worth 3,978 piccoli (9,226 − 5,248), a mint charge of 43 percent. Assuming that free silver was purchased at 5,856 piccoli (see above, sec. viii, Piccoli, 1390–1417), the mint could keep coins worth 3,370 piccoli (9,226 − 5,856), which represents a mint charge of 36.5 percent.

[117]Fatture and other provisions are given in *Cap. Broche,* fols. 14v–15, and are dated September 1405, perhaps an error for 1406. There the mezzanino, unnamed, has a charge of 13 soldi per mark. The quattrino mentioned seems never to have been struck.

[118]Papadopoli, vol. 1, doc. 19.

[119]*Cap. Broche,* fol. 14v.

TABLE A.I.

Venetian Units of Weight Used for Precious Metals and Coins

| 1 marco = | 8 oncie = | 32 quarti = | 192 denari = | 1,152 carati = | 4,608 grani = | 238.49936 grams |
|---|---|---|---|---|---|---|
| | 1 oncia = | 4 quarti = | 24 denari = | 144 carati = | 576 grani = | 29.81242 grams |
| | | 1 quarto = | 6 denari = | 36 carati = | 144 grani = | 7.45311 grams |
| | | | 1 denaro = | 6 carati = | 24 grani = | 1.24218 grams |
| | | | | 1 carato = | 4 grani = | 0.20703 grams |
| | | | | | 1 grano = | 0.05176 grams |

*Lesser used units:*

| 1 sacco | = 6 marchi, 3 oncie | = 1,520.4334 grams |
|---|---|---|
| 1 libbra grossa | = 2 marchi | = 476.9987 grams |
| 1 oncia | = 6 saggi | |
| 1 saggio | = 24 carati | = 4.9687 grams |

NOTE: Regarding the mark, Louise Buenger Robbert ("The Venetian Money Market," 16, 28, 45, 54; "Reorganization," 56 n. 33) considers that the mark at Venice weighed 238.499 grams and that it was equal to the mark of Cologne, as do Papadopoli (1:ix n) and Arnold Luschin von Ebengreuth (*Allgemeine Münzkunde und Geldgeschichte* [Munich, 1926], 83). However, somewhat smaller and variable weights for the Cologne mark at earlier dates were also given by Luschin von Ebengreuth (pp. 165, 167) and Bruno Hilliger ("Studien zur mittelalterlichen Massen und Gewichten," *Historische Vierteljahresschrift*, n.s., 3 [1900]:171–99). Cipolla (*Le avventure della lira*, 41, n. 32) accepted a lower figure, 215 grams, for the Cologne mark in 1164, but in his table (p. 127) gave 238.49936 grams as its weight at a later date. See also Angelo Martini, *Manuale di metrologia* (Turin, 1883), 818; Gallicciolli, *Delle memorie*, 1:366–90; Carli, *Delle monete* (Mantua, 1754–60), vol. 1, par. 22, p. 73; Ronald Edward Zupko, *Italian Weights and Measures from the Middle Ages to the Nineteenth Century*, Memoirs of the American Philosophical Society, 145 (Philadelphia, 1981), 140; and Müller, ed., *Welthandelsbräuche*, 182–83. The *Memoria de tucte le mercantie*, ed. Lopez and Airaldi, gives the Cologne mark as 9 oncie of Genoa; at 26.3983 grams per oncia (Cipolla, *Le avventure della lira*, 127), the weight would be 237.56247 grams. All calculations here assume 1 Venetian mark equal to 238.5 grams.

Regarding the subdivisions of the mark, see esp. the *Tariffa zoè noticia*, 12, 68, for the division of the mark into 8 oncie, the oncia into 4 quarti, and the quarto into 36 carati. The quarto is sometimes called a "carato (grande)" (Stussi, ed., *Zibaldone da Canal*, 17), sometimes a "cartier" or "quartiero" (ibid., 7; *Trattato di aritmetica*, fol. 35). Cf. Bertelè, "Moneta veneziana," 4.

For the division of the oncia into 6 saggi (sazi) and the sazo into 24 carati see *Zibaldone da Canal*, 17; and Bertelè, "Moneta veneziana," p. 4 and app. 3. The "saggio" is defined as 6 saggi (sazi) in *Cap. Broche*, fol. 16v, in a provision dated 13 August 1410.

For conversions into the metric system see Martini, *Manuale*, 818; and Cipolla, *Le avventure della lira*, 127. Note that the carati mentioned above are to be distinguished from the carats used for measuring the fineness of gold, where 24 carats means 100 percent fine. On the use of oncia, denaro, and carato as measures of fineness, see below, app. E.

TABLE A.2.

## Content of Venetian Silver Coins, 1194–1429

| Period | Weight (in grams) | Fineness | Silver Content (in grams) | Page References to Papadopoli, 1 |
|---|---|---|---|---|
| *Grossi* | | | | |
| 1194 −1356 | 2.178 | 0.965 | 2.102 | 86, 191, and passim |
| 1379 −94 | 1.987 | 0.952 | 1.892 | 215, 220, 229 |
| 1394 −97 | 1.877 | 0.952 | 1.787 | 229 |
| 1397 −1407 | 1.820 | 0.952 | 1.733 | 229, 238 |
| 1407 −17 | 1.753 | 0.952 | 1.669 | 238 |
| 1417 −21 | 1.619 | 0.952 | 1.541 | 251 |
| 1421 −29 | 1.600 | 0.949−0.952 | 1.521 | 251, 248, 257, 270 |
| *Mezzanini* | | | | |
| 1331 −39 | 1.242 | 0.780 | 0.969 | 163 |
| 1346 −53 | 0.802 | 0.965 | 0.774 | 181 |
| *Soldini* | | | | |
| 1331 −ca. 1350 | 0.957 | 0.670 | 0.641 | 163, 168, 182 |
| 1353 −69 | 0.552 | 0.965 | 0.533 | 182, 187, 191, 196, 200, 203, 216 |
| 1369 −79 | 0.513 | 0.952 | 0.488 | 216 |
| 1379 −91 | 0.496 | 0.952 | 0.472 | 216, 220, 230 |
| 1391 −99 | 0.469 | 0.952 | 0.446 | 230 |
| 1399 −1407 | 0.454 | 0.952 | 0.432 | 230, 238 |
| 1407 −17 | 0.438 | 0.952 | 0.417 | 238, 252 |
| 1417 −21 | 0.404 | 0.952 | 0.385 | 252 |
| 1421 −29 | 0.400 | 0.949−0.952 | 0.380 | 252, 270 |

NOTE: The dates given are those of the laws authorizing the issues, where this is possible; in many cases, especially the early ones, the dates are those of the doges under whom the coins were issued. Occasionally we have corrected the dates given by Papadopoli; for the evidence see the relevant sections of app. A.

The figures for weight and fineness are those given by Papadopoli. The figures for the silver content have been calculated from the data in the two preceding columns.

## TABLE A.3.

### Content of Venetian Billon Coins, 1156–1442

| Period | Weight (in grams) | Fineness | Silver Content (in grams) | Page References to Papadopoli, 1 |
|---|---|---|---|---|
| *Piccoli* | | | | |
| 1172 −92 | 0.362 | 0.270 | 0.098 | 74, 78 |
| 1192 −1205 | 0.362 | 0.250 | 0.091 | 86 |
| 1269 −78 | 0.289 | 0.250 | 0.072 | 112, 118 |
| 1280 −1343 | 0.292 | 0.198 | 0.058 | 138, 145, 155, 164, 169 |
| 1343 −54 | 0.336 | 0.190 | 0.063 | 183 |
| 1355 −69 | 0.284 | 0.190 | 0.054 | 192, 196, 200, 203 |
| 1385 −90 | 0.198 | 0.138 | 0.027 | 231 |
| 1390 −1442 | 0.248 | 0.111 | 0.027 | 231, 239, 253, 271 |
| *Mezzodenari or Bianchi* | | | | |
| 1156 −72 | 0.414 | 0.070 | 0.030 | 67 |
| 1178 −92 | 0.465 | 0.070 | 0.033 | 78 |
| 1192 −1205 | 0.517 | 0.050 | 0.026 | 86 |
| 1205 −29 | 0.440 | 0.050 | 0.022 | 93 |
| 1229 −49 | 0.569 | 0.050 | 0.028 | 99 |
| 1249 −68 | 0.465 | 0.050 | 0.023 | 103, 107 |
| 1268 −75 | 0.420 | 0.050 | 0.021 | 113 |
| 1275 −80 | 0.414 | 0.050 | 0.021 | 118−19 |
| 1280 −89 | 0.336 | 0.040 | 0.013 | 138−39 |
| 1289 −1311 | 0.388 | 0.040 | 0.015 | 144−45 |
| 1312 −28 | 0.414 | 0.040 | 0.017 | 154−55 |
| 1329 −54 | 0.362 | 0.040 | 0.014 | 164, 169, 183 |
| *Quartaroli* | | | | |
| 1192 −1205 | 0.776 | 0.003 | 0.002 | 87 |
| 1205 −29 | 1.035 | 0.003 | 0.003 | 94 |
| 1229 −49 | 1.086 | 0.003 | 0.003 | 99 |
| 1249 −53 | 0.828 | 0.003 | 0.002 | 104 |
| 1253 −68 | 1.086 | 0.003 | 0.003 | 107 |
| 1268 −75 | 1.449 | 0.003 | 0.004 | 113 |
| 1275 −80 | 0.828 | 0.003 | 0.002 | 119 |
| 1280 −89 | 1.086 | 0.003 | 0.003 | 139 |
| 1289 −1311 | 0.983 | 0.003 | 0.003 | 145 |
| 1311 −12 | 0.828 | 0.003 | 0.002 | 148 |
| 1312 −28 | 0.854 | 0.003 | 0.003 | 154−55 |
| *Doppi Quartaroli* | | | | |
| 1268 −75 | 2.328 | 0.003 | 0.007 | 113 |
| 1275 −80 | 1.656 | 0.003 | 0.005 | 119 |
| 1280 −89 | 1.500 | 0.003 | 0.004 | 138−39 |
| 1289 −1311 | 3.105 | 0.003 | 0.009 | 144−45 |

NOTE: Dates and figures for weight and fineness are those given in Papadopoli. Figures for fine silver content have been calculated from the data in the two preceding columns.

TABLE A.4.

Content of Coins Issued for Dependencies, 1353–ca. 1417

| Designation | Period | Weight (in grams) | Fineness | Silver Content (in grams) | Page References to Papadopoli, 1 |
|---|---|---|---|---|---|
| *For Romania* | | | | | |
| Torneselli | 1353–68 | 0.724[a] | 0.130 | 0.094 | 183, 187, 192, 197, 201, 204 |
| Torneselli | 1368–1442 | 0.724[a] | 0.111 | 0.080 | 217, 221, 231, 240 |
| *For Verona and Vicenza* | | | | | |
| Mezzanini or soldi | 1406–13 | 0.606 | 0.952 | 0.577 | 235, 239 |
| Piccoli | 1406–42 | 0.309 | 0.111 | 0.034 | 235, 239, 253, 273 |
| *For Zara* | | | | | |
| Soldi | 1410–141[?][b] | 0.710 | 0.375 | 0.266 | 293–95, 299, 375–76 |
| Soldi | 1414  14[??] | 0.677 | 0.406 | 0.274 | 295–96, 299 |

[a]For corrected figures on the weight of torneselli see above, chap. 19, sec. ii.
[b]The soldo for Zara of 1410 may not actually have been issued; Papadopoli gives no specimen with the characteristics specified by the law of 1410.

TABLE A.5.

Mint Charges as a Percentage of Yield, 1194–1429

| Coins | Period | Mint Charges | |
|---|---|---|---|
| | | On Requisitioned Silver | On Free Silver |
| *Ingots of sterling fineness* | 1273–ca. 1345 | * | 0.8 |
| *Grossi, type 1* | 1194–1356 | * | ca. 2.1 |
| *Piccoli, ca. 1274–1343* | ca. 1274 | * | 9.2 |
| | 1278–82 | * | 24.0 |
| | 1282–1343 | * | 13.0 |
| *Piccoli, 1343–1417* | 1343–54 | 8.2 | * |
| | 1355–68 | 22.5 | * |
| | 1369 | 27.7 | * |
| | 1370–79 | 16.5 | * |
| | 1385–90 | 40.4 | * |
| | 1390–1417 | 41.2 | 32.3–34.6 |
| | 1417–42 | * | 20.2 |
| *Soldini, Mezzanini, and Grossi, 1331–1417* | | | |
| Mezzanini, type 1 | 1331–39 | 13.0 | * |
| Soldini, type 1 | 1331–46 | 23.3 | * |

(*continued*)

TABLE A.5.(*continued*)

| Coins | Period | Mint Charges | |
| | | On Requisitioned Silver | On Free Silver |
|---|---|---|---|
| Mezzanini, type 2 | 1346–53 | 30.5 | * |
| Soldini, type 2 | 1353–69 | 33.9 | 7.4 |
| Soldini, type 3 | 1369–79 | 15.5 | 13.8 |
| Grossi, type 2 | 1379–80 | 18.3 | 2.5 |
| Soldini, type 4 | 1379–80 | 18.3 | 2.5 |
| Grossi, type 2 | 1380–85 | 6.7 | 2.5 |
| Soldini, type 4 | 1380–85 | 6.7 | 2.5 |
| Grossi, type 2 | 1385 | 10.0 | 2.5 |
| Soldini, type 4 | 1385 | 10.0 | 2.5 |
| Soldini, type 4 | 1385–91 | 11.7 | 2.5 |
| Grossi, type 2 | 1386–87 | 11.7 | 2.5 |
| Grossi, type 2 | 1387–91 | 11.7 | 1.9 |
| Soldini, type 4 | May 1391 | * | 5.0–6.5 |
| Soldini, type 4 | June 1391–1394 | 14 | 4.0 |
| Grossi, type 3 | 1394–97 | 13.6–14.2 | 1.8 |
| Soldini, type 4 | 1394–99 | 13.6–14.2 | 1.8 |
| Grossi, type 3 | 1397–99 | 16.5 | 1.8 |
| Grossi, type 3 | 1399–1407 | 16.5 | 1.8 |
| Soldini, type 4 | 1399–1407 | 16.5 | 1.8–2.6 |
| Grossi, type 3 | 1407–14 | 19.6 | 0 |
| Soldini, type 4 | 1407–14 | 19.6+ | * |
| Grossi, type 3 | 1414–17 | 19.6 | 1.8 |
| Soldini, type 4 | 1414–17 | 19.6+ | 2.6 |
| Grossi | 1417–21 | * | 2.7 |
| Soldini | 1417–21 | * | 2.7 |
| Grossi | 1421–29 | * | 1.34 |
| Soldini | 1421–29 | * | 1.34 |

SOURCES: Sources and calculations are explained in app. A.

NOTE: Asterisks indicate that no silver was requisitioned or that evidence about the coinage from free silver is lacking. The fractional coins and coins for dependencies listed in tables A.3 and A.4 have not been included here, since the documentation concerning them is largely insufficient for calculating mint charges.

# APPENDIX B

# VOLUME AND RATE OF PRODUCTION

ince we have not found any series of figures on the amount of bullion received at the mint or the amount of coins issued, we are not confronted with the problem of having to estimate, by averaging figures over several periods, the rates of production actually achieved. At best we can make only rough estimates of the scale of operations at a few dates. For that purpose, admittedly dubious interpretations or assumptions have to be made in order to connect or compare the few well-attested facts. The problem is to choose those interpretations and assumptions that yield the most plausible general picture, since some conception of the scale of operations, albeit with a large margin of error, is needed.

## i. THE NUMBER OF EMPLOYEES IN THE MINT

Estimates of output about 1280 depend in part on figures concerning the number of workmen employed. For the categories of craftsmen identified in the description of the processes of production in chapter 12 the following figures have been found:

1. Diemakers. Until near the end of the fifteenth century there were only 2 or 3 diemakers, counting both engravers and ironsmiths, and they were often employed elsewhere and summoned to work in the mint when needed.[1]

---

[1]Papadopoli, 1:332; *PMV*, doc. 112; and above, chap. 12, sec. iv.

2. Moneyers or minters ("monetarii" or "stampidori"). The capitolare of 1278 ordered that there be no more than 20 moneyers or minters. They were to be Venetians.[2] In 1498 the maximum to be employed was set at 25.[3]

3. The workers who checked and corrected the weight of the blanks before they were given to the moneyers were generally called "mendadori." Following the usage of Charles Johnson and John Craig, we here call them sizers.[4] The capitolare of 1278 ordered the number of mendadori reduced to 28.[5] The term "mendadori" may sometimes be replaced by "lavoranti"[6] or "ovrieri."[7] In the gold mint it covered also the shearers.[8]

4. Shearers, to use Johnson's term, seems the best name for the craftsmen who cut the square pieces of metal from sheets or ribbons and clipped or heated and beat them to make them round. Making them round is explicitly said to be the task of ovrieri in the long senatorial decree of 1417 reforming procedures in the mint and setting a new list of costs, the fattura.[9] That is consistent with the use of the term "ovrieri" in the capitolare of 1278. The capitolare composed for the mintmasters for gold (probably in the next century) provided for mendadori but used the term "lavoranti" for those who beat the gold into sheets and cut it into squares before it was given to the mendadori and workers who then finished preparing the blanks before they were struck.[10]

The number of shearers (ovrieri) who might be employed, unlike the number of mendadori and monetarii, was not limited in 1278. The only basis for estimating their number is considering the limits on the number of sizers and moneyers and comparing the expense charged to those crafts with the expense charged to shearers.

A comparison of labor costs for minting shows that payments per mark to shearers (ovrieri) amounted to about twice as much as payments to moneyers.[11] Judging from the nature of their crafts, there is reason to assume that a moneyer earned at least as much per day as did a shearer. To do so, a moneyer had to process twice as many marks per day as a shearer. The piece rates paid in 1417 for work on grossi (shown in table 7) will serve as an example. In order to earn 144 piccoli a day, a moneyer had to strike 9

[2]Papadopoli, 1:324, cap. 74.
[3]*Cap. Broche,* fol. 72v.
[4]Johnson, ed. and trans., *The De moneta,* xxxv; and Craig, *The Mint,* 42–44.
[5]*PMV,* doc. 25, cap. 45.
[6]Ibid., doc. 37, cap. iv.
[7]"Quaderno della quindexena."
[8]*PMV,* doc. 37, cap. iv.
[9]Papadopoli, 1:362.
[10]*PMV,* doc. 37, cap. iv.
[11]See above, table 7.

marks, for each of which he was paid 16 piccoli ($9 \times 16 = 144$). A shearer had to shape only 4 marks, for each of which he was paid 36 piccoli ($4 \times 36 = 144$). The 144 piccoli, or 12 soldi, per day can be considered a low minimum for skilled labor. To earn even that much, a moneyer had to process more than twice as many marks of grossi as did a shearer, and to do so he had to be supplied each day with more than twice as many blanks as 1 shearer earning that amount would shape in a day. To keep the minters thus occupied, there had to be at least 2 shearers for each moneyer. To have a steady flow of work from one craftsman to another, when 20 moneyers were employed, 40 shearers were needed.[12] To be sure, the proportion may have changed with changes in the techniques of the two crafts.

5. One or 2 casters ("fondadori") received the metal after it was refined. They cast it into ingots to be assayed, and if it was to be coined, they cast it into sheets or rods, from which were cut the squares that the shearers rounded into blanks.

6. The refiners of the metal are referred to by the general terms "ovrieri" and "lavoranti"; only in a few cases are they called "affinadori." The number employed *by* the mint and the number employed *in* the mint pose two separate problems. According to statements as to their number in 1393–99, there used to be 6 who had much work, but there were then 12 who had very little work and were too poor to take apprentices. To maintain the "useful art," they were to be given 400 baskets of charcoal a year (at a cost of 60 ducats) on the condition that they took 4 apprentices.[13] At about that same time there were complaints that the refiners never came to the mint, and they were ordered to do so.[14] In the fifteenth century the employees of the silver mint's refinery were listed as follows:

1435:   6 affinadori; 4 vecchi maistri; 2 mezo maistri
1440:   7 affinadori—tutto maistro; 4 mezo maistri; 4 fanti[15]

How much of the refining was done inside the mint and how much was

---

[12]Cf. above, chap. 12, n. 71. From fifteenth-century regulation of the Burgundian mints, Peter Spufford concluded that "monnayeurs" were outnumbered in a proportion of 4 to 1 by the "ouvriers," there a broad category that seemingly included sizers and refiners as well as shearers (Spufford, "Mint Organisation," 242). From figures concerning the mint at Messina in 1471–72, Trasselli concluded, in contrast, that there the moneyers were twice as numerous as the "operai" and that their task took twice as long! It seems more likely that his figures—derived from the number of "operai" named in his document—refer to heads of work teams (called "capi bottega" in Venice) rather than to a total number of men (Trasselli, *Zecche e monete*, 124–27).

[13]ASV, Grazie, reg. 18, fol. 77v, and Zecca, b. 6bis, fol. 44.

[14]ASV, Zecca, b. 6bis, fol. 43.

[15]*Cap. Broche*, fols. 36v, 37, 20.

done outside at various dates seems impossible to determine, but it seems reasonable to consider that the process contributed no more than 12 to the total number of master craftsmen employed within the mint about 1280, and probably fewer. These indications are the basis for a guess that the maximum number of persons employed about 1280, when—and if—the silver mint was operated at full capacity, was close to 100, distributed approximately as follows:

| | |
|---|---|
| Supervisory staff, including the "famuli" of the mintmasters | 5–6 |
| Diemakers, ironsmiths | 2–3 |
| Casting foundrymen | 2 |
| Refinery workers | 6–12 |
| Shearers | 20–40 |
| Sizers | 18–28 |
| Moneyers | 10–20 |
| Apprentices | 10–30 |
| Total | 73–141 |

Even the lower figures are estimates of employment when the mint was busy. In contrast, there must have been periods of relative inactivity when only a few besides the supervisory personnel were in the mint.

At a very much later date, 1484, when the output of the mint was more varied and presumably larger considering the variety of coins being produced, there is reference to dividing revenues from a fee charged to merchants among 50 persons in the silver mint.[16] That number, the way the manufacture was organized, and the evidence on wages suggest the probability that the mint had a core of regular employees who had a steady income from the mint and that when there was more work than that core could handle, other craftsmen were employed at piece rates either in the mint or in their homes.[17]

When the gold mint was instituted in 1284–85, its work force was much smaller. Fifty years after its creation its moneyers numbered only 3, and those who prepared the blanks for them numbered only 7. When in 1342 its furnaces were increased from 4 to 8, the number of moneyers was raised to 5, and the number of preparers of blanks to 10.[18] Its supervisory staff and the refiners and casters with apprentices probably raised the total engaged to nearly 30.

In spite of the probability of a wide margin of error in these figures, especially in regard to apprentices, they are better than no figures at all when thinking about the mint as a form of industrial organization. Moreover, limits placed on the number of sizers and moneyers, figures derived

[16]Ibid., fol. 54v.
[17]See above, chap. 12, sec. iv.
[18]See above, chap. 17, sec. ii.

directly from the sources, are useful as a basis for estimating the size of the output of the silver mint about 1280.

## ii. FULL CAPACITY ABOUT 1280

A starting point for estimating the mint's production at "full capacity" in the sense explained in chapter 12 is given by the limits placed on the numbers of craftsmen to be employed and on the amount of metal to be given them. Since striking the design into the blanks was the last stage in the process of manufacture, the amount of coin struck by the moneyers in a day was the day's production of finished product. The number of craftsmen to be employed and the amounts of metal to be given them were specified in the early capitolare, the limits for piccoli and for grossi being set differently.

In coining piccoli the mintmasters were enjoined (in chapters added to the capitolare immediately after those approved in March 1278) to employ no more than 8 moneyers and the same number of shearers (ovrieri). They were to be supplied daily with amounts of metal limited by the seasons as follows:

February 1–April 30:  6 marks to ovrieri, 5 marks to moneyers
May 1–August 31:  7 marks to ovrieri, 6 marks to moneyers
September 1–October 31:  6 marks to ovrieri, 5 marks to moneyers
November 1–January 31:  5 marks to ovrieri, 4 marks to moneyers[19]

Since 1 mark of alloy sufficed to make 786–90 piccoli,[20] the *daily* production envisaged was 3,940 (788 × 5) coins during spring and fall; 4,728 (788× 6) coins during summer; and 3,152 (788 × 4) coins during winter. From these rates of daily output an annual production when at full capacity of 1,001,401 piccoli weighing 1271 marks, that is, 303 kg, can be calculated by assuming that there were 250 working days in the year spread equally over the 12 months. The total number of piccoli produced annually is reached by multiplying the daily production in each of the four seasons by the number of months specified for that seasonal rate and by the number of days in an average month of working days, which was estimated to be 20.833 (250/12). Thus,

3,940 coins per day
for 5 months  $= 3{,}940 \times 5 \times 20.833 = $  410,410.1
4,728 coins per day
for 4 months  $= 4{,}728 \times 4 \times 20.833 = $  393,993.7
3,152 coins per day
for 3 months  $= 3{,}152 \times 3 \times 20.833 = $  196,996.8
                                                    1,001,401.6 piccoli

[19]Papadopoli, 1:326, cap. 80; *PMV,* doc. 30.
[20]See above, app. A.

The total weight of piccoli produced annually was:

| | | | |
|---|---|---|---|
| 5 marks per day for 5 months | = | 5 × 5 × 20.833 = | 520.825 |
| 6 marks per day for 4 months | = | 6 × 4 × 20.833 = | 499.992 |
| 4 marks per day for 3 months | = | 4 × 3 × 20.833 = | 249.996 |
| | | | 1,270.813 marks |

The output of grossi was limited in the capitolare of 1278 by restricting the number of blanks to be given to the moneyers daily.[21] The restriction was stated in lire, obviously lire di grossi, each of 240 grossi, as follows:

| | |
|---|---|
| May 1–September 29: | 2,160 (9 lire × 240) blanks |
| October 1–February 28: | 1,440 (6 lire × 240) blanks |
| March 1–April 30: | 1,680 (7 lire × 240) blanks |

Assuming that the number of working days in a year was as above and calculating by the method used for piccoli gives:

| | |
|---|---|
| 2,160 blanks for 5 months of 20.833 days = | 224,996 |
| 1,440 blanks for 5 months of 20.833 days = | 149,998 |
| 1,680 blanks for 2 months of 20.833 days = | 69,999 |
| | 444,993 blanks |

This figure can be taken for the total number of grossi struck annually. Since 109.4 grossi were cut from 1 mark of silver, the weight of a year's output of grossi can be calculated to be 4067.6 marks (444,993/109.4). If calculated from the weight of each grosso, 2.18 grams, the total weight in either case is 4,067.4 marks (444,993 × [2.18/238.5]), or 970 kg (4,067.6 × 238.5 = 970,122.6 g). The annual output at full capacity about 1280 of piccoli and grossi combined can accordingly be summarily estimated as follows:

| | | | |
|---|---|---|---|
| Piccoli: | 1,001,401 coins, | weighing 1,271 marks, i.e., | 303 kg |
| Grossi: | 444,993 coins, | weighing 4,067 marks, i.e., | 970 kg |
| Total: | 1,446,394 coins, | weighing 5,338 marks, i.e., | 1,273 kg |

These rates of output and the restrictions on the number of craftsmen to be employed can be used to make an estimate of the speed with which the moneyers were expected to strike the coins (see table B.1). For piccoli, the total production at "full capacity" was 394 piccoli per hour, assuming that the working day was 12 hours in summer, 10 hours in spring

[21]Papadopoli, 1:319; *PMV*, doc. 25, cap. 2.

TABLE B.I.

The Mint's Production at "Full Capacity" ca. 1280

|  | Piccoli | Grossi | Total |
|---|---|---|---|
| *Number of Coins* |  |  |  |
| Per year | 1,001,401 | 444,993 | 1,446,394 |
| Per average month | 83,450 | 37,083 | 120,533 |
| Per working day | 3,152–4,728 | 1,680–2,160 | — |
| (low and high season) |  |  |  |
| Per hour | 394 | 180 | — |
| Per moneyer |  |  |  |
| Per hour | 49.25[a] | 15[b] | — |
| Per minute | 0.82 | 0.25 | — |
| *Weight of Coins in Marks (and kg)* |  |  |  |
| Per year | 1,271[c] (303) | 4,068[c] (970) | 5,339 (1,273) |
| Per average month | 106 | 339 | 445 |
| Per working day | 4–6[c] | 13.2–19.7[c] | — |
| *Value in Lire a Grossi*[d] |  |  |  |
| Per year | 3,404.8 | 48,415.1 | 51,819.9 |
| Per average month | 283.7 | 4,034.6 | 4,318.3 |

[a]394/8.

[b]180/12.

[c]Derivation explained in this appendix.

[d]Values are computed by figuring that 1 piccolo = 0.0034 lire a grossi (26.III/[32 × 240]); and 1 grosso = 0.1088 lire a grossi (26.III/240) (see above, chap. 8, sec. iii, and app. A).

and fall, and 8 hours in winter (4,728 piccoli/12 hours). If all the 8 moneyers whom the mintmasters were authorized to assign to striking piccoli were so employed, to produce that much, each had to average only 49–50 per hour (394/8), that is, 1 piccolo about every 72 seconds (60 × [60/50]).

For grossi the pace envisaged was much slower. The number of moneyers was not strictly limited, for some of the 8 who might be assigned to striking piccoli could be assigned to striking grossi. But the total number of moneyers employed in the mint was limited to 20.[22] If 12 were assigned to make the 2,160 grossi per day that was the limit set in summer, they could do so by averaging merely 15 grossi per hour (2,160 grossi/12 hours = 180 per hour; 180 per hour/12 moneyers = 15 grossi per hour per moneyer), that is, by each moneyer striking 1 grosso every 4 minutes (60/15).

Unless very cautiously interpreted, the figures in table B.I are more misleading than helpful. It would be utterly misleading to assume that in fact the whole work force was employed day after day for a whole year of 250 days or that any of the craftsmen worked a full day steadily at an

[22]Papadopoli, 1:324, cap. 74; 329, cap. 85.

average indicated speed, as can be imagined on a power-driven assembly line. On the contrary, we should assume great irregularity in the individual production from hour to hour and great irregularity in the total output from day to day and especially from month to month.

The probable irregularity of operations is suggested by comparison with operations in Bologna, where there are some surviving early records of the volume of production of the Bolognese mint, although no figures on the number of craftsmen employed. When the Visconti took over Bologna in October 1350, they sent 2 moneyers from Milan to replenish the city's supply of silver coin, which was said to have been drained away by the pilgrims going to Rome for the jubilee of 1350. Much silver coin may have been shipped to the Levant also.[23] The production of Bolognese grossi was pushed to a peak of 660 marks during the first 10 days of February 1351. It remained very high until the end of February; thereafter it declined rapidly. The total issued by September 23 was 2,829 marks. Since 176 Bolognese grossi were made from a mark of metal, the peak production for 10 days was 11,616 coins per day ($660 \times [176/10]$).[24] With a 10-hour day, that required striking 19.36 coins per minute (11,616/600). If the number of moneyers employed had been 20, the maximum number allowed for both grossi and piccoli at Venice under the statutes of 1278–80, each moneyer would have had to strike 1 coin per minute, a rate of production 4 times as fast as the limit set for full capacity in Venice about 1280. But the actual number of moneyers employed at Bologna is unknown.

The Bolognese comparison suggests that the moneyers' technique and physical dexterity were quite sufficient to strike many more coins per hour than indicated in table B.1. D. J. Sellwood, a modern engineer who enjoys making coins by medieval methods and has made thousands, estimated that a minter aided by 2 assistants, one to place and remove the blanks, the other to hold the upper die, could probably turn out 1 coin every 5 seconds.[25] At a constant pace, that would mean 720 per hour! There is no evidence that any such 3-man teams were employed in the Venetian mint; indeed, the regulations strongly imply that each master minter (i.e., moneyer) worked alone, perhaps sometimes aided by an apprentice. But the historian of the British mint, Sir John Craig, describes striking by primitive methods in modern India as also done with "incredible rapidity."[26] Striking a coin every 5 seconds for a few minutes is of course very different from striking 720 coins an hour for 10 hours per day.

[23]See above, chap. 17, sec. i.

[24]Salvioni, "Il valore della lira bolognese," in *Atti e memorie* 16:23–24, 31.

[25]Sellwood, "Medieval Monetary Technique," 64. Of course the speed of striking varied with the type of coin, but the differences between the Venetian grossi and the Anglo-Saxon silver coins with which Sellwood was more familiar do not seem sufficient to make the comparison irrelevant.

[26]Craig, *The Mint*, 43.

Sellwood gives no estimate of how long a moneyer could maintain the output of 1 coin every 5 seconds. Even allowing for long rest periods and slower methods than he envisaged, Sellwood's expert estimate strongly suggests that the Venetian regulations of 1278–80 were designed to set a limit on the mint's production at "full capacity" well below the output technically possible if the full number of craftsmen-employees were at work. The total number of coins and the total weight of metal that would be processed in a year at full capacity under the regulations of 1278–80 also seem relatively small. When compared with other figures for total production, they too indicate that the purpose of the regulations was to limit the mint's output of coin. The totals are very low compared with Venetian figures for silver coinage at a later date, such as that of about 10,000 kg (20 million coins) in a peak year about 1423.[27] They are very low compared with Craig's estimate that the annual production of the English mint late in the thirteenth century reached in some years 50 million pennies.[28] To be sure, the contrast is not only between a kingdom and a city but also between the recoinage in England in 1279–81 and, in Venice, an annual emission when there was no recoinage. But the comparison with totals from Bologna for some years when that mint was most active also make the Venetian totals seem low, considering the lesser importance of Bologna as an urban center and as a bullion market. Between October 1350 and October 1351 the number of Bolognese grossi minted was 497,904; the number of piccoli was 782,000.[29] Scattered figures of yearly production of

[27]On production about 1423 see Frederic C. Lane, "Exportations d'or et d'argent de Venise, 1200–1450," in Day, ed., *Etudes d'histoire monétaire*. Ugo Tucci in his "Die Mechanisierung der Münzpragung und die Münze von Venedig," in Schneider, ed., *Wirtschaftskräfte und Wirtschaftswege*, vol. 1, *Mittelmeer und Kontinent*, 721–23, Beiträge zur Wirtschaftsgeschichte, ed., Hermann Kellenbenz und Jürgen Schneider, 4–8 (Stuttgart, 1978), indicates that in the late sixteenth century large silver ducats were struck by a moneyer at the rate of about 300 a day (10 kg of coins each weighing about 33 grams), which would be an average of 1 every 2 minutes in a 10-hour day, although copper coins weighing about 2 grams were struck at the rate of 3,000 coins a day, which would be 5 every minute in a 10-hour day. The estimates made by Brunetti in "Del quantitativo" and in his "Sulle quantità di moneta di argento emesse sotto Anna di Savoia, imperatrice di Bisanzio (1341–1347)" in *RIN*, 5th ser., 11, no. 65 (1963):143–68 (including a letter to Brunetti from Bertelè), are based on assumptions about several unknowns: whether the coins examined formed an adequate sample for statistical purposes of those minted; how many coins were struck from a single die; and how to distinguish the products of one die from the products of another through slight involuntary differences in the coins (cf. Grierson, "Byzantine Coinage as Source Material," 321–22). Brunetti estimated the number of soldini coined under Andrea Dandolo as about 30 million ("Del quantitativo," 67–68).

[28]Craig, *The Mint*, 39–40, 52. In "Monetary Contraction," 149, table 10, Munro gives the annual mean output of silver coin in England in 1270–1369 as 9,095.69 kg; and in Flanders and the Burgundian low countries in 1335–69 as 6,262.59 kg.

[29]Salvioni, "Il valore della lira bolognese," 54.

grossi at Bologna in the early fifteenth century do not rise that high, but the manufacture of piccoli in the peak year 1403 was more than 644,000.[30] Considered altogether, these comparisons reinforce the conclusion that one purpose of the Venetian regulations of 1278–80 was to restrict the amount of coinage.

Indeed, some of the figures in table B.1 are so low as to raise the question whether the table is not based on a misinterpretation of some restrictive clauses. The possibility deserves full discussion because the interpretation of passages in some other regulations is influenced by the figures estimated.

One may ask, first of all, whether the limitation of the amount of metal to be given moneyers, 4–6 marks for piccoli according to the season, applied not to the group as a whole but to the amount to be given each individual moneyer. In the latter case, the 8 moneyers that the mintmasters were allowed to assign to striking piccoli would produce at 8 times the rate shown in table B.1. Second, one may ask whether the limitation on the number of blanks for making grossi applied not to the moneyers as a group, as assumed in table B.1, but to each moneyer individually. That comparison is suggested also by a comparison of the wages paid about 1420 with the amount of silver processed in a day at full capacity about 1280. But certainly moneys of account (the "piccoli" and "soldi di piccoli" in which piece rates and salaries were calculated) and possibly techniques changed so much between 1280 and 1420 that the comparison is not compelling.

Such reservations may be countered by four considerations. First, multiplying the estimates of piccoli production by 8 and estimates of grossi production by 12 (the number of moneyers left to work on grossi when 8 were assigned to making piccoli) would indicate an excessively high rate of output. It would assume that in summer each moneyer could strike 6–7 piccoli every minute and keep it up for a working day of 12 hours. That does not imply the longer time for striking an individual coin than Sellwood estimated, but keeping up that speed steadily for 12 hours does seem incredible. Second, the number of separate shops and furnaces in the

---

[30] Reports of the weight, fineness, and number of coins delivered by the Bolognese mint in 1401–6 were tabulated by Salvioni. He used them to estimate the value of the Bolognese lira; but he reported that the condition of the documents led him to conclude that the record was far from complete (ibid., 367, 375–81). Nor can the figures be used as an accurate minimum figure of production for the period between delivery dates, since some coins struck earlier may have been delivered at later dates. Even if so used, they would not indicate rates of production of silver bolognini nearly as rapid as that of 1351. For example, in 1406, the year in which the largest production, a total of 190,786 silver bolognini, is recorded, deliveries of over 36,000 coins were recorded on 13 July and 26 July. If we assume that the 36,000 that were delivered on 26 July had been struck during 12 of the preceding days, that would have been a rate of production of 3,000 a day, much below the peak production of 11,616 coins per day recorded for 1351.

silver mint implied by this interpretation also seems too large compared with the number indicated by other sources.[31] Third, most persuasive is the language of the pertinent paragraphs in the regulations. When each master is clearly meant, as in specifying the amount of metal to be given to each master in charge of one of the furnaces in which blanks for grossi were prepared for striking, "alicui maestro" is specified. But in setting the limit on the number of blanks to be given the moneyers, "alicui" is not used. Instead, the plural is used to refer to them as a group.[32] Finally, the rates of output per month and year or day shown in table B.1 are reconcilable with later, spotty references to the volume of output as it expanded between 1280 and 1350.[33]

In conclusion, it must be reemphasized that the figures in table B.1 are not estimates of what was actually produced nor of any kind of average from records of the actual rate of production. They are estimates of what production would have been if the mint had operated at "full capacity" and if full capacity had been maintained for the durations indicated. Moreover, "full capacity" is defined by regulations originating at various dates before 1280, regulations the enforcement and even the precise applicability of which may well be doubted. An extreme example is the figure for the number of grossi struck per hour by a moneyer. It is reached by dividing by 12 the maximum number of blanks the mintmasters were authorized to give the moneyers as a group. The figure 12 is reached by deducting from the 20 which was the maximum number of moneyers to be employed the 8 who could be assigned to piccoli. But even when 20 moneyers were considered employees of the mint (approved or appointed by the mintmasters), the average number showing up each day must have been less. If we had contemporary estimates of how many moneyers were actually at work, and how many coins they actually struck, it would not be surprising if the average figure per moneyer was about 30 grossi per hour, twice that indicated in the table, and if the yearly output consequently was much higher. In spite of its potentially misleading features, table B.1 is of value in estimating roughly the mint's scale of operation at the earliest date for which there is any numerical information about the number of its employees.

The comparison with rates of production at other times and other places leads to the conclusion that the limitations in force about 1280 were imposed in order to prevent production at as rapid a rate as was technically feasible with the specified labor force. Together with the limitation of the number of moneyers to be employed, the regulations embodied a policy of restricting coinage and encouraging instead the export of certified silver

---

[31]See above, chap. 12, sec. iv.

[32]Papadopoli, 1:319, cap. 42; 326, cap. 82. *PMV*, doc. 30.

[33]See below, sec. iii.

ingots.[34] Moreover, the really tight restrictions applied to piccoli, not grossi, and they are in the clauses added to the capitolare about 1278–82. The limitation to 8 of the number of moneyers and of shearers that could be assigned to making piccoli was added to the capitolare after March 1278, when other clauses about piccoli were added. They may be considered part of a reaction against the coinage policy of Lorenzo Tiepolo (1268–75). A different attitude towards grossi is evident in the passage by the Great Council in December 1278 of a resolution explicitly permitting the mintmasters to employ in striking grossi the 8 moneyers who on other days might be employed in striking piccoli.[35] And the number of shearers who could be assigned to the making of grossi was not limited. If all 20 moneyers had been assigned to striking grossi, as many as 40 shearers would have been necessary to keep them sufficiently occupied so that a moneyer could earn as much per day as a shearer, if piece rates were proportionally the same in 1280 as they were in 1417. To be sure, only 8 shearers had been provided for to prepare blanks to be struck as piccoli by 8 moneyers. Since 8 shearers would hardly have produced enough blanks to keep 8 moneyers busy, restricting to 8 the number of shearers assigned to piccoli was the tightest restriction on their production. Some of the 8 moneyers must have lacked blanks to strike. That such was indeed the case is suggested by the new rule made in December 1278 providing that such moneyers could be assigned to making grossi.

How completely these restrictions—both those made before March 1278 and incorporated then in the capitolare and those added in 1278–80—were ignored in later years is uncertain, but certainly many restrictions were brushed aside when the mint's activity expanded.

### iii. EXPANSION

Before the end of the 1280s there was felt to be a shortage of Venetian-minted coins of lesser value than the grosso, and a series of steps (summarized above, in chapter 10, section v) was then taken to remedy that situation. The first step was the decision made in November 1287 concerning the use of a fund of 2,000 lire which the mintmasters had available for making silver coin. The Great Council ordered the mintmasters to use 1,200 lire of it for piccoli ("moneta parva") and 800 for "moneta grossa." The purpose of the decree is most clearly revealed in the last sentence, which orders the mintmasters to provide as much as 50 lire per day to any Venetian requesting piccoli and to replenish the reserve of 2,000 lire with the payment received. The 1,200 lire of piccoli and 800 lire of grossi were to be kept in special chests, with special keys, special ac-

---

[34]Reasons for such a policy at that time are suggested above, in chap. 10, sec. v.
[35]Papadopoli, 1:329, in cap. 85.

counts, and so on.[36] The coining of piccoli continued to be a problem, however, for in September 1289 the mintmasters were ordered to devote 100 lire per month, apparently to be obtained from the coinage of grossi, to building up a fund of 500 lire for buying silver and copper for piccoli.[37]

How much silver could be bought with 500 lire? or with the earlier appropriations of 1,200 and 800 lire? The kind of "libra" referred to in all these decrees can be assumed to be the lira a grossi from which the lira di piccoli had only recently split off.[38] Prices of silver bullion were at that time quoted in lira a grossi. To acquire silver on the open market in 1289, the mintmasters probably had to pay a price somewhere between the 233 soldi a grossi per mark that they offered in 1273 for silver to be cast into certified bars and the 260–80 soldi per mark referred to as market prices in 1311 and 1315.[39] If for rough calculation we take 250 soldi as the price to be paid in 1287 or 1289, the amount of fine silver that could be bought with 500 lire (10,000 soldi) was 40 marks. The 1,200 lire assigned in 1287 for the making of piccoli would have bought 96 marks, and the 800 lire assigned for the making of grossi would have bought 64 marks (1,200 × [20/250] = 96; 800 × [20/250] = 64).

Since in coining piccoli the silver was mixed with four times as much copper, the weight of the alloy was five times as much, and since 788 piccoli were made from a mark of alloy, the output of piccoli can be estimated thus: from the 500 lire, 40 marks silver, 200 marks alloy, 157,600 piccoli coins; from the 1,200 lire, 96 marks silver, 480 marks alloy, 378,240 piccoli coins. To allow for the expense of labor and copper, these figures for the output in coins should be reduced somewhat. The lowest the mint ever charged for the coinage of piccoli was 8–10 percent.[40] Applying that reduction gives about 340,000 as the number of coins called for in ordering the assignment of 1,200 lire to the making of piccoli. At the winter and spring rates of output, that production would take the mint about 4 months of operation at full capacity (340,000/83.450 = 4.07).

For grossi, the law of 1287 was much less significant. Since grossi were of 0.965 fine silver, the 64 marks bought to make grossi would yield only 7,001.6 grossi (64 × 109.4), 4 to 5 days' work, according to table B.1. These figures confirm the impression that the number of grossi manufactured from silver purchased by the government with appropriated funds in order to have a supply with which to pay for defaced or forbidden foreign coins was trivial compared with the number of grossi manufactured for merchants who had their bullion coined into grossi for export.

[36]Ibid., 332, cap. 100, dated 31 November but citing MC, Zaneta, under the date 22 November. In *PMV*, doc. 48, it is dated 11 November 1287.

[37]Papadopoli, 1:326–27, cap. 83.

[38]See above, chap. 8, sec. iii.

[39]See below, app. C, sec. i.

[40]See above, table A.5.

Neither the 1,200 lire for making piccoli in 1287 nor the fund of 500 lire to be built up by the 100 lire per month provided for in 1289 produced enough piccoli to satisfy the ruling councils. On 21 May 1291 the Quarantia ordered the mintmasters to coin at least 250 marks of piccoli every two months, somewhat more than our estimate of output at full capacity. At the same time, the Quarantia offered incentives for a higher rate of production, implicitly lifting the restrictions in the regulations previously in effect. It offered the mintmasters a bonus for increased production. The bonus could not amount to much, however, unless the full capacity was doubled or tripled, which indicates that it could be done. The bonus offered was 1 piccolo for each mark beyond the 250.[41] A mintmaster who tripled production during his quindena would receive 500 piccoli in extra pay (worth less than 2 lire a grossi) to add to his yearly salary of 100 lire a grossi.

Tripling production would have produced about 250,000 piccoli per month, and some such rate of production seems to have been the goal in the next recorded spurt of piccoli production, that of 1318. A decree issued in May of that year said that the mintmasters had been ordered the year before to employ at least 8 ovrieri and 8 monetari on piccoli and to make all they could. It said that because previously no figure had been set for the volume of output, they were not making enough. The Quarantia ordered them to make 1,000 lire per month.[42] Probably 1,000 lire di piccoli, and thus 240,000 coins, were meant; if lire a grossi were meant, the number of coins would have been 292,800. Assuming 21 working days per month, that required an output of 11,500–14,000 coins per day, 2.5–3.0 times the summer daily rate at full capacity as envisaged in 1280.

Significantly, this demand for a tripling of the minting of piccoli in May 1318 was followed in January 1319 by an expansion of the mint.[43]

During the 1320s the replacement of deteriorated, underweight grossi was a major concern, as described above, in chapter 15, section i. In the 1330s and 1340s, although the supply of silver became plentiful,[44] it went mainly into the new coins—mezzanini and soldini—which were replacing grossi of the old standard. The soldini were of such small size and value that their circulation diminished the need for piccoli. As long as imports of silver were as large as they certainly were in the 1340s, the quinto (or decimo) assured the mint of silver for coining soldini and for

---

[41]Papadopoli, 1:327, cap. 89. On the misdating of this decree as of 1281 in *PMV*, doc. 32, see above, chap. 10, n. 73.

[42]Nani-Mocenigo, ed., *Capitolare dei Signori di Notte*, doc. 180. Under the limitations recorded in the capitolari, the work force described would not have been adequate for so large a production, but this decree does not specifically forbid employing more craftsmen in the production of piccoli, and in fact it implies permission to employ more.

[43]See above, chap. 12, n. 4; and MC, Fronesis, fol. 13 (7 January 1318/19).

[44]See above, chap. 17, sec. i.

coining the new kind of grossi introduced after 1379.[45] But figures are lacking from which to calculate the output of silver coins in mid-century, or the presumably smaller output during the "silver famine" in the last decade of the century.

The gold mint had meanwhile increased its output, especially during the 1340s, when the number of moneyers making ducats was increased from 3 to 5, the number of sizers (mendadori) from 5 to 7, and the number of refining furnaces from 4 to 8.[46] In 1343 provision was made for processing more than 600 marks of gold in the mint at one time, and extra staff appointed.[47] Six hundred marks were the makings of 40,200 ducats (600 × 67). Later in the fourteenth century it was asserted that the managing mintmaster was occasionally responsible for as much as 100,000 ducats in the process of being coined,[48] and in recommending—in 1370—a higher salary for a weigher who had served twenty years, the mintmasters said that he had recently been kept constantly at work from morning till night because the gold received during a "quindena," which used to be 400 marks, had risen to 1,500 marks.[49] That was enough to make 100,000 ducats (1,500 × 67). If the term of office called a quindena was then two months, as seems likely (see below, app. F), yearly production at that rate would have been 603,000 ducats.

The output of gold coin rose to twice that figure and exceeded the silver output in value about 1422, if the statistics included in the "Death Bed Oration" of Doge Tommaso Mocenigo are to be believed. They certainly do not report yearly averages or even a typical year of about that date. They are credible only as reflecting peak activity resulting from a recoinage of silver and an unusually abrupt swing upwards of gold exports at the conclusion of Venice's trade war with Emperor Sigismund (which will be described in volume 2). So interpreted and compared with other figures from that period, they appear to be as credible as his much used figures about the government's finances and the size and composition of the fleet and of the population.[50]

Table B.2 shows the number of coins of various kinds or purposes indicated by the figures that Doge Mocenigo listed according to their value in ducats. He gave the value of the annual coinage of silver as 800,000 ducats and indicated the following breakdown:

[45]See above, chap. 10, sec. iii; and app. A.

[46]See above, chap. 17, sec. ii.

[47]A figure of only 6 marks is given in *PMV*, doc. 100, but in the parchment source it is clearly *600* marks ("VI^C") (ASV, Quarantia Criminal, reg. 15, fol. 29v, where it is ahead of the chronological order in which it has been printed with the correct reading in *DQ*, vol. 1, doc. 173).

[48]ASV, Zecca, b. 6tris, cap. 68.

[49]ASV, Grazie, reg. 16, fol. 111 (1369/70).

[50]Lane, "Exportations."

APPENDIX B

TABLE B.2.

A Year's Output of Gold and Silver Coins ca. 1422

| Coins | Number | Value (in ducats) | Total Value (in ducats) |
|---|---|---|---|
| Gold ducats, mostly for export | 1,200,000 | 1,200,000 | 1,200,000 |
| Silver | | | |
| For export | | | |
| Grossi for Syria and Egypt | 785,000 | 30,000 | |
| Grossi, mezzanini, and soldini for Terraferma | 7,500,000 | 100,000 | |
| Grossi and soldini to the overseas empire | 3,125,000 | 50,000 | |
| Soldini to England | 10,000,000 | 100,000 | |
| Total exported | | 280,000 | 280,000 |
| Remaining in Venice | | | |
| Recoinage of grossi and soldini | | 520,000 | 520,000 |
| Total silver | | | 800,000 |
| Total gold and silver | | | 2,000,000 |

NOTE: Figures are estimates based on the "Death Bed Oration" of Doge Mocenigo in 1423.

1. To Syria and Egypt, 5,000 marks, or 1,192,500 grams (5,000 × 238.5). The silver coins sent these lands were grossi, the new lighter variety which in 1421–29 contained 1.521 grams of silver; thus, 1,192,500 grams were sufficient for striking 784,023.66 coins (1,192,500/1.521 = 784,023.66). Or, calculating from the value of a mark of silver bullion[51] and allowing something for the cost of manufacture, one may estimate that 1 mark of grossi coin was worth about 6 ducats, and 5,000 marks therefore were worth about 30,000 ducats. Since the ducat was declared legally worth 100 soldi in 1417 (and was worth only a little more on the market five years later),[52] 1 ducat was worth about 25 grossi, and a total of 30,000 ducats would require at least 750,000 grossi coins.
2. To the Terraferma, 100,000 ducats' worth of "grossetti, mezzanini, and soldini." The mezzanino was a special coin issued in 1406 after Verona and Vicenza were acquired and was worth 1 1/3 soldini.[53] If by value this export had been 50 percent soldini, 25 percent grossi, and 25 percent mezzanini, as suggested by the law of 1406, the total number of coins would have been:

[51]On the content of coins see above, table A.2; on the prices of silver see below, app. C. We have added 4 percent to the well-attested price of 5 3/4 ducats.
[52]See below, table D.3.
[53]Papadopoli, 1:235, 239, and doc. 19, p. 352; see also above, app. A, sec. ix. Use of the term "grossetto" suggests a version of Mocenigo's speech from after 1429, when "grossoni" were first coined and the diminutive was applied to the grosso (cf. Papadopoli, 1:250).

50,000 ducats' value in  5,000,000 soldini
25,000 ducats' value in    625,000 grossi
25,000 ducats' value in  1,875,000 mezzanini
                         7,500,000 coins

3. To Venice's overseas empire, 50,000 ducats' worth of grossi and soldini. With the ducat at about 100 soldi in these years, and assuming that
the total was evenly divided between soldini and grossi, 25,000 ducats
meant 2,500,000 soldini, and the other 25,000 ducats meant 625,000
grossi, for a total of 3,125,000 coins.
4. To England (or way stations), 100,000 ducats' worth of soldini, which
could be disposed of in England as worth a half-penny each, in spite of
English laws against that.[54] At 100 soldi to a ducat, 100,000 ducats
meant 10 million soldini coins. Mocenigo's figures when thus interpreted indicate an annual export of about 20 million silver coins,
worth 280,000 ducats.
5. Since he said that the total value of the silver coined annually was
800,000 ducats, this leaves coin worth 520,000 ducats, which he says
remained in Venice ("reman in Veniesia"). That figure is so high as to
be incredible if interpreted as an annual addition to the city's money
supply, but it is credible as a report on the recoinage that had been
ordered just a year earlier.[55] Moreover, in view of Venice's monetary
relations with its dependencies Treviso and Padua, which used the same
money of account and the same coins as Venice, one may suspect that
the coins going there were recorded together with those entering into
use or being recoined in Venice.

There is partial confirmation of Mocenigo's figures in a senatorial
decree of 1419 about the effects of the trade war which states that normal
annual imports of bullion had amounted to 40,000 marks.[56] The market
price for silver bullion at that time was 5 ducats 18 grossi, so that 40,000
marks were worth only 230,000 ducats (40,000 × 5.75). About 20 percent
below Mocenigo's figure of 280,000 ducats, this figure of 230,000 indicates that normal imports were insufficient for the production for export
of as much coin as Mocenigo recorded, unless the silver had gained more
than 20 percent in value in Venice between its arrival and departure as a
result of the refining, minting, and transaction costs or middlemen's
profits.

If instead of starting with the price of bullion we start with the value

[54]Peter Spufford, "Continental Coins in Late Medieval England," *British Numismatic
Journal* 32 (1964):132–36.
[55]Lane, "Exportations"; *Cap. Broche*, fol. 23v; ASV, Senato, Misti, reg. 54, fols. 6v–7 (7
March 1422).
[56]Papadopoli, 1:246–47.

in lire di piccoli of the 280,000 ducats' worth that Doge Mocenigo said were exported, the discrepancy is less. The market quotations for the ducat in 1419–23 were close to 103 soldi di piccoli. The coins Mocenigo valued at 280,000 ducats therefore had the value of 28,840,000 soldi di piccoli (280,000 × 103). If in all the coins that were exported the relation between their silver content and their legal value was the same as it was in the soldino (it certainly was the same in the Venetian grosso of those years), then since 1 soldino contained 0.380 grams of silver, the coins worth 28,840,000 soldi di piccoli contained 10,959,200 grams (28,840,000 × 0.38), which equals 45,951 marks of silver (10,959,200/238.5). That constitutes over 10 percent more than the 40,000 marks "normally" imported. This suggests that in the boom years after the end of the trade war with Sigismund imports rose well above the 40,000 marks. The rest of the 800,000 ducats, namely, the 520,000 ducats' worth of silver that according to Doge Mocenigo's report remained in Venice, might have been obtained from coins sent to the mint for reminting.

Mocenigo's figures for silver exports in Egypt and Syria are very much lower than the figures given elsewhere for the amounts of specie carried out by the galley fleets. Whereas he mentions an annual silver export of 5,000 marks, which would be worth only about 30,000 ducats, the galleys to Beirut and Alexandria are recorded in the chronicle of Antonio Morosini as carrying 200,000 to 620,000 ducats in cash in the years around 1423. Their cash may well have been mostly gold, however, in that period. The figures on galley cargoes certainly do nothing to cast doubt on Mocenigo's figures; they are significant chiefly as evidence of the reversals in the flows of precious metals.[57]

As evidence for the eminence of the Venetian mint, Mocenigo's figure for the coinage of gold—1.2 million ducats yearly—is most impressive. It implies averaging 4,800 gold coins each working day throughout the year. It is roughly three times the output of the Florentine mint when it led in coining gold.[58] It amounted to 4,260 kg of gold a year (1,200,000 × [3.55/1,000]), whereas the yearly output of the mints of the Burgundian low countries were, for 1420–24, 14.4 kg; for 1425–29, 910.4 kg; and for 1430–34, 1,729.3 kg, and never again in the century rose above 1,000 kg.[59] Mocenigo's figure is so high that even if all the specie loaded on galleys for the Levant had been gold, there still would have been as much again left to be exported elsewhere, presumably to buy grain for consumption, cloth for reexport, and so on. It is four times Venice's

[57]Lane, "Exportations."

[58]Robert S. Lopez, Harry A. Miskimin, and Abraham Udovitch, "England to Egypt, 1350–1500: Long-term Trends and Long-distance Trade," in *Studies in the Economic History of the Middle East, from the Rise of Islam to the Present Day,* ed. M. A. Cook (New York, 1970), III, n. 66.

[59]Munro, "Monetary Contraction," 140, table 3.

production of gold coin reported by a well-informed French observer at the beginning of the sixteenth century.[60]

On the other hand, the figure of 1.2 million ducats per year is quite in accord with various references made in Mocenigo's time to the amount of gold that was in the process of being coined. A contemporary diarist who described a fire in the butcheries near the mint in 1414 said that the fire threatened the more than 120,000 ducats of gold and silver coin then in the mint,[61] and in that same year the Senate, in adjusting the duties of the mintmasters for gold, referred to the managing mintmaster as having during his two-month term as manager more than 100,000 ducats "in manibus suis." To produce 1.2 million ducats per year would require a turnover of twice that amount every two months.[62]

In order to estimate the total number of coins issuing from the mint in the course of a year, a quantity of black money should be added to the above estimate of gold and silver coinage. The number of billon coins called torneselli issued for use in Greece, and especially Crete, reached at least 4 million annually beginning in the 1380s.[63] In the mid-fifteenth century there was a great increase in the output, for use in Venice's large mainland empire, of piccoli and other billon coins of which the silver content was reduced to almost nothing and also of debased coins of larger denominations introduced during the monetary wars with Milan.[64] Considering the coinage for both Venice's overseas colonies and the subject territories on the mainland, it seems safe to say that many millions of largely copper coins issued from the Venetian mint in many years during the fifteenth century.

[60]"Traité du gouvernement," Bibliothèque nationale, Paris, Fonds français 5599, fol. 117v.
[61]Morosini, *Cronica,* fol. 885.
[62]ASV, Senato, Misti, reg. 50, fol. 99. But cf. below, app. F.
[63]Stahl, *The Venetian Tornesello.*
[64]Mueller, "L'imperialismo monetario"; idem, "Guerra monetaria tra Venezia e Milano nel Quattrocento"; and below, vol. 2.

# APPENDIX C

# SILVER
# AND COPPER PRICES

## i. SILVER PRICES, 1273–1509

able C.1 (located at the end of this section) requires explanation especially because of the heterogeneous nature of the sources from which the data were derived. The prices tabulated are assumed to be comparable by presuming that they all refer, as many clearly do, to silver of a standard fineness, namely, argento di bolla, and that when silver that was less fine was sold, the price was discounted appropriately.[1] Convention probably standardized also the kind of lire and soldi referred to in quoting prices, so that it seemed unnecessary to specify the kind of lire or soldi meant (i.e., whether a grossi or di grossi, whether a monete or a oro), but these conventions must have changed over the centuries. Just when and how the changes occurred is seldom clearly stated; it has often to be inferred. Exceptional is the clear change from lire a grossi to ducats and grossi a oro which occurred in 1404.[2]

Since the majority of silver prices in the period that interests us here

[1]ASV, Grazie, reg. 5, fol. 57, reports that mintmasters said "argentum non finum valebat illo tempore [16 July 1334, the date of a violation] usque ad recessum galearum lib. xv." We interpret "non finum" to mean prior to refining but the price to be that for the amount of fine silver that would be obtained from unrefined silver. The mint's price for gold, as explained above, in app. A, sec. v, was set in terms of pure gold, and comparison of the various quotations for silver suggests that silver prices similarly were in terms of fine silver, i.e., argento di bolla. Thus, on 11 June 1340 there is reference to a moneychanger selling silver when the market price was 14 lire 13 soldi 6 denari per mark (ASV, Grazie, reg. 8, fol. 62v).

[2]See above, chap. 16, sec. v.

were quoted in lire a grossi, that money of account, reduced to soldi and denari a grossi, has been used as the common denominator in order to facilitate comparisons. Prices quoted in other moneys of account have been tabulated in their original form and then converted into soldi a grossi (multiplying soldi di grossi by 26) and entered in table C.1 in brackets. Prices not directly quoted in documents but derived from various sources as described below in this introductory note are marked by an asterisk.

## Mint Prices

Mint prices are all given in moneys of account based on silver coins, whether given in soldi a grossi or di grossi.

Before 1331, mint prices were given in moneys of account based on the old grosso. After 1331 they seem to have been based on the new silver coinage; that is, they were given in lire a monete. The lower price for unfree silver, the quinto, a price that had the effect of an import duty on all silver (as explained above, in chapter 15), ended with the abolition of the quinto in 1417. Beginning in 1417 all the silver minted, including the 1/4 that an importer of bullion was required to have coined, was subject to the same mint charge, which was specified in soldi per mark, as explained in appendix A.

Before 1353 there was no fixed price at which the mintmasters had to accept for coinage all free silver offered, although in 1273 they were required to accept at 233 soldi per mark all silver offered for refining or certification in ingots of standard fineness, as explained in chapter 10.

The sources for mint prices for both free and unfree silver at the dates indicated are given in appendix A.

## Market Prices in Ducats

All market prices given in ducats are in gold-based moneys of account. (The market prices stated in soldi a grossi are partly gold-based, partly silver-based.) For the early decades of the fourteenth century, the market prices here entered in ducats are estimates calculated from figures found in coinage regulations. The prices are derived from the content and legal values of coins and are entered in table C.1 with an asterisk.

In deriving prices for silver bullion from the content and either the legal value or the exchange value of coins, consideration was given to the difference in value between coined and uncoined silver and the resulting differences in three kinds of bimetallic ratio: (1) between uncoined silver and uncoined gold; (2) between uncoined silver and the gold coined into ducats; and (3) between silver that had been coined into coins of fine silver such as grossi and gold that had been coined into ducats. Silver gained more in value by being coined than did gold. Consequently, the first and second of these three ratios were higher than the third ratio, which is the ratio most easily determined from mint regulations. It will be estimated here that the extent of the difference was such that when the ratio between the coined metals was 10.9 to 1, the ratio between uncoined silver and coined gold was 11.5 to 1. Part of that difference reflected the costs of manufacture, which were higher (compared with the value of the product) for silver than for gold.[3]

The extent of the difference in prices between uncoined and coined silver can be calculated for 1285. The mint price for silver bullion was then 233 soldi per mark. A mark sufficed to coin 109.4 grossi each worth 2.18 soldi a grossi,[4] so that the 109.4 grossi were worth 238.49 soldi a grossi. The difference between the mint's price and the value produced was 5.49 soldi, that is, 2.3 percent (5.49/238.49) of the value of the grossi made from the mark of bullion. The price of bullion was thus 2.3 percent lower than the value of the coin made from the bullion.

A similar percentage difference is indicated by the calculations embodied in a proposal of 1417 to reduce the weight of soldini and grossi in such a way that the value of a mark of coined silver would exceed the cost of the bullion, while the price paid for the uncoined silver was kept high enough to attract silver imports. The senatorial resolution stated that the current ("usado") price of a mark of silver was 5.75 ducats. It provided that the number of soldini cut from a mark of silver be 589 so that the value of the coined silver made from a mark would be 589 soldi di piccoli. Since the ducat at that time was valued at 100 soldi, the 589 coined soldini were worth 5.89 ducats, 0.14 ducats (5.89 − 5.75) more than the uncoined silver, that is, 2.4 percent. The difference was entirely accounted for by the expense of manufacture of the 589 coins, which was stated as 16 soldi (16/589 = 0.272).[5]

These estimates for Venice and the differences in Florence between the mint charges on fine silver and on gold indicate that the gold price for coined silver was 2–3 percent higher than the price for uncoined silver. Because the value of coined silver was higher than that of uncoined silver, for coined silver the bimetallic ratio was lower than that for uncoined silver. In 1285 the bimetallic ratio between uncoined silver and coined gold was 11.5 to 1, for the decree of that year made the ducat worth 40 soldi.

$$1 \text{ mark} = 238.5 \text{ grams silver bullion} = 233/40 = 5.825 \text{ ducats}$$
$$238.5 \text{ grams silver} = 5.825 \times 3.55 \text{ grams gold}$$
$$238.5/20.68 = 11.53 \text{ silver to 1 gold}$$

At the same time, the ratio between coined silver and coined gold was only 10.9 (as calculated above, in chapter 13, section iv) as follows:

[3]On ratios calculated using the silver content of billon coins see above, chap. 5, nn. 15–16; and cf. the ratios distinguished in Watson, "Back to Gold," 22–23.

[4]PMV, doc. 25, cap. 1, last sentence; and in Papadopoli, vol. 1, doc. 4.

[5]Papadopoli, 1:360.

$$18.38 \text{ grossi} = 18.38 \times 2.1 \text{ grams silver} = 1 \text{ ducat} = 3.55 \text{ grams gold}$$
$$= 38.598 \text{ grams silver} \quad = 3.55 \text{ grams gold}$$
$$= 38.598/3.55 \quad = 10.873 \text{ silver to 1 gold}$$

The difference of 0.6 (11.5 − 10.9), 5 percent, which these calculations show between the two bimetallic ratios has been used in estimating prices of bullion, although perhaps 2 percent would have been better. But the 2.0–2.4 percent indicated by the decrees of 1285 and 1417 may not have allowed sufficiently for seigniorage or other factors that might increase the relative value of silver once it had been coined.[6] Adding 5 percent to the ratio of 14.2 to 1 between coined silver and coined gold in 1305–30 gives a ratio for those dates of 14.9 to 1 as the relative value of uncoined silver to coined gold. When gold was valued that high, a mark of silver bullion must have cost only about 4.5 ducats, for if 1 ducat = 3.55 grams gold = 53 grams silver (14.9 × 3.55), then 1 mark (238.5 grams) silver = 238.5/53 ducats = 4.5 ducats (4 ducats 12 grossi a oro).

Small differences in bimetallic ratio, even a difference as large as that between 9.9 to 1 and 9.4 to 1, cannot be considered significant when estimating the price of silver in this manner, given the lack of accuracy in such calculations and the likelihood of error, but as large a difference in ratios as that between 14 to 1 and 12 to 1 is significant. A change of that magnitude occurred when gold began to fall after the bimetallic ratio had been between 14 to 1 and 15 to 1 for about twenty-five years. When the soldini issued in 1331–35 were accepted as worth 1/64 of a gold ducat, the bimetallic ratio between the coined metals was as low as 11.5 to 1.[7] That ratio between coined silver and coined gold indicates a ratio between uncoined silver and coined gold of 12.1 to 1. At that ratio, a mark of silver bullion would command 19.7 grams (238.5/12.1) of coined gold, which was the weight of gold contained in 5.6 ducats (19.7/3.55), or 5 ducats 14 grossi a oro.

The bimetallic ratio went yet lower, and the gold price of silver went yet higher, after the coinage of Andrea Dandolo's mezzanino in 1346.[8] The ratio between coined gold and coined silver was then 10.5 to 1, so that the estimate of the ratio between coined gold and uncoined silver is 11.1 to 1. The price for a mark of silver bullion corresponding to that ratio was 6.1 ducats (238.5/11.1 = 21.4865; 21.4865/3.55 = 6.05). A confirmation of the degree of accuracy of these estimates calculated from bimetallic ratios is

---

[6]Some mint charges at Venice (as compiled above, in app. A) include substantial profits as well as expenses, but the mint charges referred to in the decrees of 1285 and 1417 do not. The defeated proposal of Pietro Steno in 1362 would have established a bimetallic ratio of 11.3 to 1 between silver bullion and gold coin and a ratio of 10.9 to 1 between coined silver and coined gold (see above, chap. 18, sec. ii).

[7]See above, chap. 15, sec. iii; and table 18.

[8]See above, chap. 16, sec. iii.

the price of 6 ducats recorded in 1349. That is the first of our prices for a mark of silver bullion that is given in gold.[9]

A few years later, in 1362, Piero Steno's proposals to stabilize the bimetallic ratio at the price to which silver had then risen would have put a ceiling on the value of coined gold by giving the new silver coinage that he proposed a value as legal tender that would make the ratio between coined metals 10.9 to 1. At the same time, he proposed putting a floor under the price of uncoined silver at the ratio of 11.7 to 1. The "floor" was to be assured by making a certified mark of silver bullion legal tender for 5.75 ducats.[10] Steno's "floor" seems to have been a little under the prices current at about that time, but only a little lower, so we have entered 5 ducats 20 grossi. For several dates between 1397 and 1417 market prices of silver bullion are clearly recorded in a gold-based money of account and generally at a little less than 6 gold ducats.[11]

### Market Prices Given in Soldi a Grossi

Some of the market prices entered in soldi a grossi refer to gold-based moneys of account, and some refer to silver-based. Three different periods can usefully be distinguished: (1) before 1331; (2) 1331–79; and (3) after 1379.

In the latest of the three periods the market prices are given sometimes in ducats, sometimes in soldi di grossi, sometimes in lira a grossi; but the market prices in these moneys of account were all based on the gold ducat coin. Occasionally that is explicitly stated by adding "a oro." In other cases it can be inferred from the relation of the market price to the mint price and to the changes in the silver content of the coins. The mint price for silver rose after 1380 because the mint price for silver was then based on the soldo di grossi a monete, which was based on silver coins, and the quantity of silver in those coins was being reduced. The market price did not rise similarly. While the mint price for free silver rose to over 380 soldi a grossi in the 1380s, the market price hardly rose above 320.

After 1391 there was no officially set mint price because each supplier

---

[9]PSM, Misti, b. 62A, commis. G. Stornado. Bimetallic ratios differing one from another as calculated above, in chap. 5, sec. i, and in chaps. 8, 13–15, and 17, can be reconciled by recognizing the differences between ratios calculated in four different ways. The ratio between silver bullion and gold coin was the highest. If, for example, the ratio between the coined metals was 10 to 1, the four ratios were likely to be generally: uncoined silver to coined gold, 10.5 to 1; coined silver to coined gold, 10.0 to 1; uncoined silver to uncoined gold, 9.8 to 1; and coined silver to uncoined gold, 9.3 to 1.

[10]See above, chap. 18, sec. ii.

[11]For example, Papadopoli, 1:360; PSM, Misti, b. 189, commis. G. Condulmer.

was given back silver coin of the same weight as the bullion delivered minus a fee of a fixed amount per mark. But if the market price had been expressed in a silver-based money of account, it would have increased after 1390, because the quantity of silver in soldini and grossi was diminished, so that the silver equivalent of the soldo a grossi a monete was diminished, just as was the silver equivalent of the soldo di piccoli (as shown in table 10). In fact, the market price did not increase; on the contrary, it fell between 1391 and 1417 from about 320 soldi to below 300. The contrast between the movements of market and of mint prices shows that the market prices, which are from merchant's records, were recorded in lire a grossi a oro.

In the earliest period, however, before 1331, the moneys of account used, both soldi a grossi and lire or soldi di grossi, were linked to the old grosso, of which the silver content was unchanged. Why during that earliest period did the price of silver bullion rise from 233 soldi a grossi to 300 soldi a grossi? The rise must have been due to demand in the Venetian bullion market of buyers other than the Venetian mintmasters. The upward push must have come from buyers seeking silver for export. As explained in chapter 10, secs. ii and iii, the regulations governing the mint prevented the mintmasters from buying silver at such a high market price but did not prevent them from valuing the coins with which they paid for the bullion in such a way as to continue to attract some silver, especially for the minting of the grossi, which were in turn extensively exported. On the other hand, the disparity between the conventional mint prices and the current market price may have influenced the institution of the quinto in 1331–32 and probably had something to do with the discontinuance of the minting of the old grosso about 1356.

The middle period, 1331–79, raises more questions than can be satisfactorily answered without a more continuous and homogeneous series. During those years the lira a grossi and the lira di grossi ceased to be based on the grosso coin. That was the period during which the lire di grossi split, as explained in chapter 16. There came into use a lira di grossi a oro based on the gold ducat and a lire di grossi a monete based on the same silver coins that were the bases for the lira di piccoli, that is, especially on the soldino and—after 1379—on the new grosso.

While mint prices between 1331 and 1380 seem to be stated in money of account based on the new silver coinage, market prices in these years were partly gold prices. Those quoted in 1352 and 1368 at about 300 soldi must have referred to soldi a oro, because the mint was then under orders to pay 325 soldi a monete for all silver offered to make soldini. But the earlier rise of the market price from 291 soldi 6 denari in 1340 to 308 soldi in 1348 can refer to either soldi a oro or soldi a monete. One would expect a market price quoted in soldi a oro to rise because the bimetallic ratio fell

TABLE C.I.

## Market and Mint Prices of Silver Bullion Compared, 1273–1509
### (Per Mark of Argento di Bolla)

| | Market Prices | | | | Mint Prices | | | | | | | | |
| | In Soldi a Grossi | | In Ducati a Oro | | Free Silver[a] | | | | | Unfree Silver[b] | | | |
| | | | | | In Soldi a Grossi | | In Soldi di Grossi | | | In Soldi a Grossi | | In Soldi di Grossi | |
| Period | Sol. | Den. | Du. | Gr. | Sol. | Den. | Sol. | Den. | Pic. | Sol. | Den. | Sol. | Den. |
|---|---|---|---|---|---|---|---|---|---|---|---|---|---|
| 1273 | | | | | 233 | | | | | | | | |
| 1284–85 | | | *5 | 20 | | | | | | | | | |
| 1305–25 | | | *4 | 12 | | | | | | | | | |
| 1311 | 260 | | | | 233 | | | | | | | | |
| 1315 | 280 | | | | | | | | | | | | |
| 1320 | | | | | 233 | | | | | | | | |
| 1331 | | | | | | | | | | 233 | | | |
| 1331–35 | | | *5 | 14 | | | | | | | | | |
| 1334 | 300 | | | | | | | | | | | | |
| 1337–40 | 295 | 6 | | | | | | | | | | | |
| 1340 | 291 | 6 | | | | | | | | 233 | | | |
| 1343 | 295 | | | | | | | | | | | | |
| 1344 | 300 | | | | | | | | | 233 | | | |
| 1346–48 | | | *6 | 2 | | | | | | | | | |
| 1348 | 308 | | | | | | | | | | | | |
| 1349 | [312] | | 6 | | | | | | | 233 | | | |
| 1352 | 292–300 | | | | | | | | | 233 | | | |
| 1353 | | | | | [325] | | 12 | 6 | | 233 | | | |
| 1362 | | | *5 | 20 | [325] | | 12 | 6 | | 233 | | | |
| 1368 | 307 | | | | | | | | | [292] | 6 | 11 | 3 |
| 1369–70 | | | | | [330] | | 12 | 6 | | [318] | 6 | 12 | 3 |

| Year | | | | | | | | | | | | |
|---|---|---|---|---|---|---|---|---|---|---|---|---|
| 1370 | | | | 330 | | | | | | | | |
| 1379 | | | | [380] | 5] | 14 | 7 | 16 | [318] | 6] | 12 | 3 |
| 1380 | 308 | | | [380] | 5] | 14 | 7 | 16 | [364] | 6] | 14 | 3 |
| 1386 | | | | [382] | 6] | 14 | 7 | 16 | [344] | 6] | 13 | 3 |
| 1387 | 308 | | | [396] | 2] | 15 | 8 | 20 | | | | |
| 1391 | 320 | | | | | | 3 | | [344] | 6] | 13 | 8 |
| 1391 | | | | | | | | | [355] | 4] | 13 | 8 |
| 1397–1400 | 294–326 | | | | | | | | [355] | 4] | 13 | 8 |
| 1400–1403 | 302 | 6 | | | | | | | | | | |
| 1405–9 | [296] | 5 | 17 | | | | | | [355] | 4] | 13 | 8 |
| 1417 | [299] | 5 | 18 | | | | | | | | | |
| 1463–64 | [295] | 5 | 16 | | | | | | | | | |
| 1509 | [325] | 6 | 6 | | | | | | | | | |

SOURCES: For mint prices see the sources (mostly printed in *PMV*) as cited in app. A, under the relevant dates.

For market prices:

1311: Zanetti, *Nuova raccolta,* 4:170.

1315: Predelli, ed., *I libri commemoriali,* vol. 1, no. 676.

1334: ASV, Grazie, reg. 5, fol. 57.

1337–40: PSM, Ultra, b. 180, fasc. 7, commis. Nigrino de la Rossa.

1340: ASV, Grazie, reg. 8, fol. 62v.

1343: PSM, Misti, b. 100, 100A, commis. Fresco Querini, Cf. *PMV,* lxxix n.

1344: Ibid.

1348: Ibid.

1349: PSM, Misti, b. 62A, commis. Giovanni Stornado.

1352: Ibid., as well as b. 66, commis. P. Michiel, and b. 172, commis. P. Gradenigo.

1368: *PMV,* doc. 151.

1386–1409: Rough averages from extensive price data compiled mostly from PSM, Misti, b. 189, commis. G. Condulmer, and integrated with quotations from ASP, letters from Venice in the Archivio Datini (presented in detail in vol. 2).

1417: Papadopoli, vol. 1, doc. 21, p. 360.

1463–64: ASV, Raccolta Grimani-Barbarigo, b. 43, reg. 5, fols. 41, 49, 57, 65.

1509: BMCV, Ms. PD. C. 912/2, Journal of Lorenzo Priuli.

aIn 1397–1509 an equal weight of silver was returned minus fee (see above, app. A, sec. vii).

bIn 1417–1509 there was none (see above, app. A, sec. vii).

*See explanation above, *Market Prices in Ducats.*

during the 1340s, making silver cost more in gold. One would expect also a rise in the silver price because of the high legal value of the new coin issued between those dates, namely, Andrea Dandolo's mezzanino.

Further reductions after 1350 in the silver equivalents of the silver-based moneys of account were not matched by further increases in the market prices of silver. The lack of increase shows that in commercial markets silver bullion was not then being priced in a silver-based soldo a grossi.

That the market price of silver bullion was given in lire and soldi a oro as soon as the old grossi disappeared is suggested also by the drop in price in 1352. Later in the century the market price in the gold-based lire a grossi remained fairly stable at about 300. Its stability contrasts with the price the mint paid for a mark of free silver. That silver-based price reached almost 400 because of reductions in the silver content of the silver coins.

The long decree of 1417 which abolished the different mint charges for unfree and free silver clearly expressed the perception by Venetian senators of the close interconnections between (a) the content of coins and their value as legal tender, (b) the market's ducat price for silver, and (c) attracting silver imports. (Their concern at that time was prompted by the trade war with Emperor Sigismund, who was seeking to cut Venice off from its supplier of bullion.) The relevant paragraph begins:

> Because in the regulations of the silver mint it is ordered
> that coins worth 27 lire, 4 soldi be cut from a mark, a rule
> made when the ducat was worth 93 soldi; and for some time
> now that rate has not been followed nor could it be
> because with the coins at that weight no one would bring
> silver to the mint, because he would lose heavily, the ducat
> being worth 100 soldi; and in these circumstances no
> silver would ever be brought to Venice.[12]

The decree proposed to raise the number of coins cut from a mark, so their value would be 29 lire 8 soldi, which would permit making good money and give work to the craftsmen of the mint, and "will give good reason to cause silver to be brought to Venice at a profit and maintain silver at its usual price of 5 ducats, 18 grossi the mark."

## ii. COPPER PRICES

The copper prices given in tables C.2, C.3, and C.4 also require explanation. It is sometimes forgotten that copper is a monetizable metal.

[12]Papadopoli, 1:360, doc. 21.

TABLE C.2.

## Copper Prices at Selected Dates, 1324–1519: Rame di Bolla in Gold Ducats

| Date | Per Migliaio Grosso[a] | Per 100 kg |
|------|------------------------|------------|
| 1324 | 61 ducats | 12.8 ducats |
| 1367 | 87 | 18.2 |
| 1384 | 80 | 16.8 |
| 1398 | 90 | 18.9 |
| 1407 | 66 | 13.8 |
| 1418 | 70 | 14.7 |
| 1480 | ca. 56 | 11.7 |
| 1519 | 44 | 9.2 |

SOURCES: The prices for 1324–1418 are taken from table C.4, below. That for 1480 comes from ASV, Miscellanea Gregolin, b. 15, ledger of Alvise Michiel, fols. 129, 146, 155. The figure for 1519 is derived from calculations made at the mint concerning the costs of producing coins called bezi or mezzanini (mezzo soldi). The alloy was to be 422 carats of silver per mark; the rest (730 carats out of the 1,152 in a mark) were to be of copper. The price of silver was calculated at 6 ducats 12 soldi. Since the ducat was then quoted at about 132 soldi di piccoli, that silver price amounted to 804 soldi. The silver required for a mark of coin was estimated at 14 lire 15 soldi 2 denari, or 295.1 soldi; and in fact $804 \times (422/1,152) = 294.5$. The copper required was estimated at only 1 soldo 10 piccoli, or 1.83 soldi, which implies that the price of copper was only about 3 soldi per mark ($1.83 \times [1,152/730] = 2.9$). Since there were 2,000 marks in 1 migliaio grosso, the traditional weight for quoting copper prices, the mint was working with a copper price of ca. 44 ducats per migliaio ($2.9 \times [2,000/132]$). The document, in ASV, Consiglio dei Dieci, Misti, reg. 43, fols. 17–18, was published by Padovan in *AV* 17 (1879):86, and in his *Le monete dei veneziani*, 228–30 (13 April 1519). It should be noted that the libbra grossa, 1/1,000 of the migliaio grosso, equals 2 marks, the unit of weight used for gold and silver.

[a]1 migliaio grosso = 1,000 libbre grosse = 2,000 marks = 477 kg.

While its importance in producing the alloy of largely silver coins such as grossi and soldini is minimal, the metal becomes crucial in the production of largely copper coins, such as piccoli and torneselli. The profit the Commune could make on such coins depended in part on the price of copper. That this was understood by contemporaries is clear from the proposal made in 1391 by Marco Sanuto, mintmaster for torneselli. Sanuto sought to increase the Commune's profits by saving very considerable sums of money in the refinement and preparation of the kind of copper needed by the mint.[13] A graphic idea of the huge quantities of copper necessary for the production of torneselli and of the black money issued for the Terraferma dependencies can be had from the report that nearly 5 metric tons

[13]*Cap. Broche,* fol. 7; and above, in chap. 12, sec. ii.

TABLE C.3.

Bimetallic Ratios of Copper to Silver at Selected Dates, 1324–1519

| Year | Silver (Argento di Bolla) | | Copper (Rame di Bolla) | | Ratio of Copper to Silver |
|---|---|---|---|---|---|
| | Price in Ducats per Mark (0.2385 kg) | Amount Worth 1 Ducat (in kg) | Price in Ducats per Migliaio Grosso (477 kg) | Amount Worth 1 Ducat (in kg) | |
| 1324 | 4.5 | 0.0530 | 61 | 7.82 | 148:1 |
| 1367 | 5.9 | 0.0404 | 87 | 5.48 | 136:1 |
| 1384 | 5.92 | 0.0403 | 80 | 5.96 | 148:1 |
| 1398 | 5.69 | 0.0419 | 90 | 5.30 | 126:1 |
| 1407 | 5.69 | 0.0419 | 66 | 7.23 | 173:1 |
| 1418 | 5.75 | 0.0415 | 70 | 6.81 | 164:1 |
| 1480 | 6.5 | 0.0367 | 56 | 8.52 | 232:1 |
| 1519 | 6.1 | 0.0391 | 44 | 10.84 | 277:1 |

SOURCES: Prices of copper are from the same sources as those in table C.2. Prices of silver are taken from table C.1, from the date closest to the year in column 1. The figure for 1480 was taken from the mint's offer to pay 6–7 ducats per mark in the years 1480–83, as discussed in vol. 2. For 1519 see the source note to table C.2.

of copper were recovered from counterfeit piccoli withdrawn from circulation in 1463. The metal was requisitioned by the arsenal for the production of large cannon.[14] The amounts of copper used by the Egyptian mint in the fifteenth century, when it produced little other than copper coins, is even more astounding. (Much of that copper was probably imported from Venice.)[15]

It became necessary, therefore, to consider copper prices and their relationship to silver prices. Venetian prices of copper are generally quoted for the type called "rame di bolla." We have compiled those as the only data available, although the mint may have used copper refined somewhat differently.

Table C.2 summarizes major price changes.

Table C.3 summarizes the changes in the bimetallic ratios of copper to silver, pairing the price of copper at given dates with the price of silver at the closest possible date. The results, in the last column, indicate clearly that the cost of copper used in the alloy of largely silver coins was in fact of little significance for determining the mint charges, as has been assumed in appendix A. Throughout, silver cost much more than 100 times as much as an equal weight of copper.

[14]Mueller, "L'imperialismo monetario," 289.
[15]See Shoshan, "From Silver to Copper."

TABLE C.4.

## Copper Prices, 1324–1419
### (Per Migliaio Grosso of Rame di Bolla)

| Date | | In Lire di Grossi | | In Ducati d'Oro[a] | Sources[b] |
|------|---|------|-------|--------|---------|
| | | Lire | Soldi | | |
| 1324 | January–October | ca. 6 | — | 59.8–61.5 | Ashtor, *Les métaux*, 116–17. The prices quoted range from 155.5 to 160 lire a grossi, here converted in both columns. |
| 1367 | 16 September | 8 | 14 | 87 | PSM, Misti, b. 67, commis. P. Soranzo, reg. 1, fol. 4. |
| 1383 | 16 January | 8 | 16 | 88 | D, 1171. |
| | 10 December | 7 | 10 | 75 | D, 548, Inghilese to Pisa. |
| 1384 | 6 February | 7 | 13 | 76.5 | Ibid., Z. Gaddi to Pisa. |
| | 12 March | 7 | 13 | 76.5 | D, 1171. |
| | 31 March | 7 | 14 | 77 | Ibid. (in Heers, "Il commercio"). |
| | 15 April | 7 | 12 | 76 | D, 548, Z. Gaddi to Pisa. |
| | 1 August | 8 | | 80 | D, 1171. |
| | 5 August | 8 | | 80 | D, 548, Z. Gaddi to Pisa; "for cash." |
| | 18 August | 8 | | 80 | D, 548, Z. Gaddi to Pisa. |
| | 15 September | 8 | | 80 | Ibid. |
| 1385 | 17 January | 8 | 6 | 83 | Ibid. |
| 1386 | 5 January | 7 | 18 | 79 | D, 1171. |
| | 31 December | 8 | 5 | 82.5 | Ibid. (in Ashtor, *Les métaux*). |
| 1387 | 9 January | 8 | 8 | 84 | Ibid. |
| 1390 | 21 February | 8 | 6.25 | 83.125 | Ibid. |
| 1391 | 6 February | 8 | 16 | 88 | D, 1171. |
| 1393 | 8 August | 8 | 3 | 81.5 | D, 549, Z. Gaddi to Pisa. |
| | | | | 77 | Ibid.; "afinato in Ungheria." |
| | 16 August | 8 | 3–4 | 81.5–82 | Ibid.; "for cash." |
| | | 8 | 9 | 84.5 | Ibid.; "on terms." |
| | 31 December | — | | 81 | D, 1171. |
| 1394 | 31 December | — | | 80 | D, 549, Z. Gaddi to Pisa. |
| 1395 | 31 December | 8 | 6 | 83 | D, 1171/19. |
| 1396 | 3 December | — | | 85 | Ibid. |
| | 22, 23 December | 8 | 13 | 86.5 | Ibid. (incorrect in Ashtor, *Les métaux*). |
| 1397 | 16 December | 9 | | 90 | Ibid. (in Ashtor, *Les métaux*). |
| 1398 | 16 January | 9 | | 90 | Ibid. |
| 1399 | 8 March | 8 | 12 | 86 | D, 712, Z. Gaddi to Florence; "for cash, none available on terms." |
| | 24 May | — | | 85 | D, 1171, and D, 550, Z. Gaddi to Pisa. |
| | | — | | 90 | Ibid.; "in tole." |
| | 26 July | 8 | 12 | 86 | D, 712, Z. Gaddi to Florence. |
| | | 9 | | 90 | Ibid.; "in tole." |

(*continued*)

TABLE C.4. (*Continued*)

| Date | | In Lire di Grossi | | In Ducati d'Oro[a] | Sources[b] |
|---|---|---|---|---|---|
| | | Lire | Soldi | | |
| 1400 | 10 January | 8 | 16 | 88 | Ibid. |
| | | 9 | | 90 | Ibid.; "in tole." |
| | 27 March | 8 | 12 | 86 | D, 1083, in letter of 13 September to Maiorca. |
| | | 9 | 5 | 92.5 | Ibid.; "in tole." |
| | 20 November | — | | 87 | D, 713, commis. Gaddi to Florence. |
| 1401 | 15 January | 8 | 10 | 85 | Ibid., Simone di Lapaccino to Florence; same price "in tole" and "del'angnolo." |
| | 16 July | — | | 90 | Ibid., commis. Gaddi to Florence, "up from 84 du." |
| | | 9 | | 90 | Ibid.; "in tole." |
| 1403 | 26 May | 8 | 10 | 85 | Ibid., "in tole," "up from £8 s3." |
| | 22 June | 8 | 12 | 86 | D, 714, commis. Gaddi to Florence; bought in "bolla," transformed into "tole" to send to Valencia. |
| | 6 October | — | | 86 | D, 714, commis. Gaddi to Florence. |
| | | — | | 85.5 | Ibid.; "in tole." |
| | 20 October | 8 | 10 | 85 | Ibid.; "di bolla in pani." |
| 1404 | 1 March | 8 | 10 | 85 | D, 715, Paoluccio to Florence. |
| | 24 December | 8 | 0–2 | 80–81 | D, 1171. |
| 1405 | 11 April | — | | 72–73 | D, 715, Giov. di Ser Nigi and Gherardo Davizi to Florence. |
| | | | | 58–60 | Ibid.; "fine." |
| | 24 October | 7 | | 70 | D, 929, Paoluccio to Barcelona. |
| | | 6 | 10 | 65 | Ibid.; "in tole." |
| | 23 December | — | | 70–72 | Ibid., commis. Gaddi to Barcelona. |
| 1407 | 23 July | — | | 62–63 | D, 930, commis. Gaddi to Barcelona. |
| | | | | 64–67 | Ibid.; "in tole." |
| | 29 October | — | | 66–67 | Ibid.; "for cash." |
| 1408 | 18 May | — | | 70 | Ibid., Alberti to Barcelona; "in tole." |
| 1409 | 3 August | — | | 66–67 | Ibid., Lamberti to Barcelona; "in tole"; "c'è pocho venuto buon pezzo fa d'Ungheria." |
| | | | | 48–49 | Ibid.; "schazato." |
| | | | | 63–64 | Ibid.; "fine." |
| 1418 | 12 November | — | | 70 | Ashtor, *Les métaux*, 117–18. |
| 1419 | 31 May | — | | 70 | Ibid. |
| | 20 June | — | | 68 | Ibid. |
| | 30 June | — | | 68 | Ibid. |

[a]By conversion if given in lire in the source.
[b]D = ASP, Archivio Datini.

In contrast to silver coins, coins that were largely copper bore high mint charges and had a legal value far above their commodity value. In the case of the piccolo struck between 1390 and 1417, almost 90 percent copper, we have calculated that the cost of copper constituted only about 4 percent of its legal value. When the gross mint charge was 32 percent, deducting that 4 percent left 28 percent for the cost of labor and seigniorage.[16]

Table C.4 is a full compilation of our Venetian copper prices during the period treated in this volume. They come mainly from the Archivio Datini in Prato, which covers the years 1383–1409.

[16]See above, app. A, sec. viii.

# APPENDIX D

# DOMESTIC EXCHANGE

his appendix presents data collected on domestic exchange, the movement of exchange between local currencies on local markets. Since Venetian authorities seem not to have registered daily market quotations, as did Florentine authorities, no single source could be used to compile tables. Besides the body of data collected for Venice (still not without gaps), we present six other series for an area that in monetary terms might be called Venice's sphere of influence. No pretense of completeness is intended, either in terms of geography or in terms of data. Other material remains to be uncovered. (The total number of quotations entered, excluding those in the source column, is 1,007, i.e., for Venice 461, for Treviso 80, for Udine 200, for Padua 86, for Verona 72, for Zara 71, for Greece 37.)

## VENICE

Table D.1 gives the value of the grosso in denari piccoli. Only after 1379 was the grosso made legal tender for 48 piccoli. It was then linked to the soldino in the relationship of 1 to 4, which lasted as long as the grosso was coined.[1]

Table D.2 gives the value of the florin or ducat in silver grossi and in soldi di piccoli. Although most of the quotations come from the accounts

---

[1]Cf. Robbert, "Monetary Flows," 56.

TABLE D.1.

Domestic Exchange: The Grosso in Denari Piccoli, 1194–1379

| Period | Price | Source[a] |
|---|---|---|
| 1194–1202 | 24 | Chap. 8, sec. ii (cf. Spufford and Wilkinson, *Interim Listing,* 138–39) |
| 1202–54 | 26 | Chap. 8, sec. ii |
| 1254–68 | 26. 11 | Ibid., sec. iii |
| 1268–80 | 28 | Ibid. (official in 1274) |
| 1280–1331 | 32 | Ibid.; and Schäfer, *Die Ausgaben,* 126* |
| 1307 | 30 | Chap. 15, sec. i |
| 1331–32 | 36 | Ibid., sec. ii |
| 1344 | 41 | Ibid., sec. ii and n. 61 |
| 1352 | 41 | Ibid. |
| 1362? | 48? | Chap. 18, sec. ii (Pietro Steno proposal) |
| by 1370 | 44–48 | Chap. 10, sec. iii |
| 1379 (–1468) | 48 | Chap. 16, sec. iv; and Papadopoli, 1:174 (legal tender value) |

[a]Chapters in text, above.

TABLE D.2.

Domestic Exchange: The Florin or Ducat in Grossi and Soldi di Piccoli, 1275–1305

| Year(s) | Date | Grossi | Soldi di Piccoli | Source |
|---|---|---|---|---|
| 1275–76 | | | 52 | Schäfer, *Die Ausgaben,* 897 (also 40 soldi a grossi) |
| 1277–79 | | 20 | 53.3 | Ibid. |
| 1280 | | 18.3 | 49 | Ibid. |
| 1280 | | 20 | 53.3 | Ibid. |
| 1284–86 | | 19 | 50.6 | Ibid. |
| 1284–86 | | 20 | 53.3 | Ibid. |
| 1284 | 31 October | 18 | 48 | *PMV,* doc. 36, official rate when coinage of ducato ordered |
| 1285 | 30 May | 18.3 | 49 | *PMV,* doc. 40 (which gives 40 soldi a grossi, here converted), official. Gallicciolli, Padovan, Cipolla, and Stella seem to reproduce earlier errors when they quote 60 or 62 soldi for 1285, 1287, 1289. |
| 1288–89 | | | ca. 52 | Schäfer, *Die Ausgaben,* 898 |
| 1290 | | 18.5 | 49.3 | Ibid., 898 and 127* |
| 1290 | | 20 | 53.3 | Ibid., 898 and 127* |
| 1291 | | 18.5 | 49.3 | Spufford and Wilkinson, *Interim Listing,* 143 |
| 1292–98 | | 20 | 53.3 | Schäfer, *Die Ausgaben,* 898 |
| 1300–1302 | | 24 | 64 | Ibid., 898–99 |
| 1305 | | 24 | 64 | Ibid. |

of the papal Camera, they can be taken as indicative of the situation in Venice.[2]

Table D.3 gives the value of the ducat in soldi di piccoli, from 1305 to the War of the League of Cambrai, 1509–16. Quotations for the capital city have been gleaned especially from account books, beginning with those kept by the Procurators of San Marco for the estates they administered. Unless otherwise indicated, all data come from the ASV. Estate papers in the archives of the PSM are cited in short form: M, C, and U for the series Misti, Citra, and Ultra, followed immediately by the number of the busta and the name of the person. Exceptions are two private account books preserved by the PSM, cited simply as Talenti and Da Pozzo. The first (in PSM, Citra, b. 141, commis. Tommaso Talenti) covers much of the critical year 1380, during the War of Chioggia, and presents a nearly weekly picture of the domestic exchange.[3] The second (in PSM, Misti, b. 80A, commis. Andrea da Pozzo) covers the years 1397–1403. As explained above, in chapter 16, section iv, this small account book was kept largely in lire di grossi a monete, and the method used for the entries there reproduced and transcribed was applied to all entries in which a conversion was recorded, in order to arrive at the current quotation of the ducat; only the last few entries recorded the quotation directly. Some private account books not kept by the PSM are listed simply by name: Barbarigo = ASV, Raccolta Grimani-Barbarigo, bb. 41–42, journal A and ledgers A and B; Soranzo = ASV, Miscellanea Gregolin, b. 14, Libro real nuovo. (Since the latter was prepared for a civil suit, the dates of the quotations from the household accounts are often inexact and were entered in the table as indicative only of the year, with the notation "ex-post accounting.") Cases heard before the commercial court of the Giudici di Petizion sometimes present extracts from account books, which can include quotations of the ducat (series Sentenze a Giustizia, abbr. Petizion, S. a g.). Tuscan archives indicated in the source column also have provided some data.

Wherever possible, day and month have been specified. Where this was not possible, the quotation was inserted at the year, under "s.d." (sine data).

Printed lists of quotations of the ducat are myriad. Cipolla cited two for Venice and one for Treviso (*I movimenti*, 44–48). Most are eighteenth-century, and many of them are based on the manuscript list prepared by Domenico Brusasette in 1703 (of which there are several copies, e.g., ASV, Ospedali e Luoghi Pio Diversi, b. 551, fasc. 1, fol. 14), most recently pub-

[2]For this table, as well as table D.3, see both sections in Schäfer, *Vatikanische Quellen*, 126*–127*, 896–905. Cf. Robbert, "Monetary Flows," 61.
[3]Some quotations were already extracted in Mueller, *The Procuratori*, 203.

lished by Louise Buenger Robbert in her contribution to Richards, ed., *Precious Metals*, 63. The best of the old lists are G. Burani, *Giornale solario e pronostico perpetuo* . . . (Venice, 1794), 12–13; and Galicciolli, *Delle memorie*, 1:376–77. Previously published lists provide 15–50 quotations at most for the entire history of the republic, and the rates are reported only by year; some are based on official decrees, but many are inaccurate or obviously wrong, as errors and misprints were copied by later compilers. Padovan (*Le monete dei veneziani*) published three lists: 135–36 (Brusasette), 273–77 (from a sixteenth-century compilation), and 365–67 (supposedly "taken from documents of the mint"). Cipolla, in *I movimenti*, used primarily such old lists, although not the most accurate; he did not use the last edition of Padovan, but one of 1879. For the sake of completeness, such quotations have been entered in table D.3 under the year, even when doubtful or erroneous; they have not been included in the data used to make graph 3.

Not all figures extracted from account books of the PSM are equally reliable. Those from active estates are reliable. Those taken for the sake of inventory or for fiscal purposes are not always so and have generally been identified in the table by the notations "accounting convention" or "register-cover" (for figures found on the parchment covers of the account books). One has the impression that the bookkeeper for the estate of Polo Signolo (PSM, Ultra, b. 88) sometimes hung on to quotations like 100 or 110 soldi longer than he ought to have done in order to simplify his arithmetic (see, e.g., under the years 1424 and 1445).

For the period 1330–50 it is often impossible to know whether a document used the legal rate of 64 soldi or a market rate at the same figure.

The rate of 124 soldi per ducat (6 lire 4 soldi) was firmly established by the market in 1455–56 after a sharp rise beginning in 1452, a development made very clear by the private account books of the Giustinian family and of Marino Sanuto's father and uncle (cited in table D.3). The rate, in short, did not begin with the policy decision of 1472 to support the ducat at that level, the impression created by most lists, including Cipolla's. (The only exception seems to be Argelati, *De monetis*, 2:69, where the rate is given for 1453–1508).

Just when the ducat resumed its rise is not clear, although it was connected with the War of the League of Cambrai, which began in 1508. It has been assumed that the ducat climbed to 6 lire 10 soldi (130 soldi) during the war on the basis of an order reported by Sanuto in his diaries. Under the date 19 January 1517/18, he wrote that the ducat was again to circulate at 124 soldi: "Item, li ducati d'oro che si toleano per lire 6 pizoli 10, si toy per 6, 4, e cussì le altre monede si toy per quello valevano avanti la guera." In 1519 the Council of Ten fixed the rate at 6 lire 14 soldi (134 soldi).[4] Perhaps during the war the rate floated in some moments, but perusal of the Priuli accounts has turned up four conversions, always at 124 soldi, for 1512–17.[5]

## TREVISO

The quotations for Treviso conscientiously collected by Azzoni-Avogaro in his contribution to Zanetti, *Nuova raccolta* (4:169–76), have been added to from the Archivio di Stato of Treviso (AST). The relevant series are Ospedale di S. Maria dei Battuti (Osp.) and the Pergamene dell'Ospedale (PO). For the latter, there exists a fine, four-volume inventory done in the nineteenth century by an archivist interested enough in economic matters to note domestic exchange rates; many of the rates cited "PO" were culled from this inventory, after appropriate checking.

## UDINE

The existence of data for Udine was made known by Bernardi, *Monetazione,* who included a graph (at p. 23) but did not publish the figures. The source is an eighteenth-century list compiled by Carlo Fabrizi, "Tavola del Valore del ducato d'oro ovvero Zecchino . . . ," Biblioteca Civica di Udine, Ms. 599. That list was drawn from unique treasury records, the Quaderni dei Camerari della Città di Udine, in 20 volumes, 1297–1417 (Biblioteca Civica, Ms. 882/I–XX). The list has been checked for accuracy against the originals. Fabrizi gave the values in two columns, one for the Aquileian money of account which rates 1 denaro (or friesacher) at 14 small denari, the other a translation of that figure into traditional soldi of 12 denari. For the sake of uniformity, only the second column is reproduced here.[6]

## PADUA

The first quotations for Padua are derived by calculation from Sapori, ed., *Libro giallo dei Covoni* (abbr.: *Covoni*), when the Covoni did business in Padua. The conversions into lire a fiorini made by the accountant are generally not for simple exchanges of coin, and the vacillating rates

---

[4]Sanuto, *I diarii,* vol. 23, col. 496. Cf. Papadopoli, 2:750, tavola 2.

[5]BMCV, P.D. C. 911 (19 October 1512, 19 February 1512/13, 29 February 1515/16) and P.D. C. 912, fol. 85 (21 March 1517). According to a Friulian chronicler, the ducat began rising in 1515 (Roberto di Spilimbergo, *Cronaca de' suoi tempi [1499–1540],* ed. V. Joppi [Udine, 1884], 35 [kindly passed on by G. Del Torre]).

[6]Pegolotti, *Pratica,* 154–55, rates the frisachese of Aquileia at 14 bagattini piccoli di Vinegia, and the florin at 60 frisachesi (which would be 70 soldi).

may include unexplained factors, such as interest or discount. Quotations from the Archivio notarile (AN) at the Archivio di Stato, Padua (ASPD), were kindly made available by Benjamin Kohl; others were collected by Silvana Collodo for a future publication to be entitled "La compagna del cittadino. Proprietari—produzione—terra a Padova tra Tre e Quattrocento," the appendix to which she kindly made available.

## VERONA

The quotations for Verona were most generously provided by Gian Maria Varanini. The lira of account used in Verona and Vicenza was larger than the Venetian lira di piccoli, so that 4 lire ven. = 3 lire ver. (1 lira ven. = 0.75 lira ver.; 1 lira ver. = 1.33 lire ven.). The abbreviations used are the following:

At the Archivio di Stato, Verona,
    AAC = Archivio Antico del Commune
    SIL = Ospedale dei SS. Iacopo e Lazzaro alla Tomba
    AUR = Antico Ufficio del Registro
    CF = Camera Fiscale
    SMO = S. Maria in Organo
    SMSC = S. Maria della Scala
    ACV = Archivio Capitolare di Verona
    Simeoni = Luigi Simeoni, "L'abside di San Zeno di Verona e gli ingegneri Giovanni e Nicolò da Ferrara," *Atti dell'Istituto Veneto di Scienze, Lettere ed Arti* 67 (1907–8):1286.

Varanini culled the rates from bound volumes; where there is no pagination the reference is to the date, as indicated by the notation "alla data."[7] Several of the rates cited "CF" were provided by John Law.

[7]Not always do rates given in the sources correspond to known moneys with known equivalences. Vicenza, which passed from Paduan to Veronese domination in 1311, presents such a case in accounts kept in Vicenza and Venice in 1342–44, where one Venetian ducat was quoted at

| 1342 | 31 October | 77 soldi |
| | 31 December | 80 |
| 1343 | 31 January | 80 |
| 1344 | 24 January | 75 |
| | 23 April | 77 |

(see Gallo, "Contributi," 28, 32, 37; and Natascia Carlotto, "Pietro Nan da Marano, miles e civis veneto: Accumulazione e restituzione di un patrimonio nel primo Trecento" [Laurea thesis, Faculty of Letters and Philosophy, University of Venice, 1982–83], 110, 130).

## ZARA

The quotations for Zara are the only ones here entered that were previously published as a complete list.[8] They cover the years 1366–1400, when Zara was free from political domination by Venice. But the close relationships between Zara and Venice are documented, by the same author, by the business dealings of Jews in the two cities in the late fourteenth century. Teja's sources were notarial, and the rates may occasionally include some kind of interest or discount.

## GREECE

The figures for Greece (that is, for Romania and the Morea) were generously made available by Alan Stahl prior to their publication as appendix 3 of his *The Venetian Tornesello*. The rates are given in soldi per ducat, but the base coin of the soldo becomes the tornesello by the end of the fourteenth century; as a consequence, the rates diverge from those in Venice.

In Corfu business was sometimes done in Venetian soldi di piccoli, at exchange rates close to those current in Venice although lagging behind, as well as in soldi di torneselli. For example, an account book kept in Corfu by the Venetian Alvise Giustinian (PSM, Misti, b. 10, fasc. 11) records the following rates for the ducat as current there ("chome ad ora chore qui in Chorfu") in 1440–44:

| | | | |
|---|---|---|---|
| 1440 | 19 October | 110 soldi | (fols. 1–3) |
| | | | |
| 1441 | 6 March | 111 | (fol. 27v) |
| | 26 March | 111 | (fol. 26v) |
| | 10 May | 113 | (fol. 34v) |
| | 25 September | 114 | (fols. 38v, 39v) |
| | 9 December | 114 | (fol. 41v) |
| | | | |
| 1444 | February | 114 | (fol. 45v) |

Since the Giustinian rates diverge so widely from the rates in soldi di torneselli collected by Stahl, they have not been included in table D.3.

Some final general guidelines to reading the table: In order to limit the length of the source column, reference to published lists is made solely by name of the author, usually without indicating the pages. (For Burani, Cipolla, Gallicciolli, Padovan, and Schäfer see above, under Venice. Carli:

---

[8]Teja, *Aspetti della vita economica di Zara*, vol. 1, *La pratica bancaria*, 23–24; the same list is reproduced in vol. 2, *La schiavitù domestica ed il traffico degli schiavi* (Zara, 1942), 72. For quotations of the ducat in Ragusan grossi, 1351–1500, see Krekić, "Italian Creditors," 253.

edition of 1754, 1:447–48. Papadopoli: vol. 1, tavola 2. Spufford and Wilkinson: 138–44. Stella: table 3 [used only until 1370, since thereafter it is based on Cipolla]. Archivio Prop. Trevisan: ASV, Secreta, Archivio Proprio Trevisan, filza 17, anonymous "Trattato per render lo stato copioso di danari . . . ," no pagination. Zon: 32. The works are easily found in the bibliography.) Zanetti is the abbreviation used for Zanetti, *Nuova raccolta*, vol. 4. Quotations calculated from other figures are indicated as "by calc." Further and alternative quotations (abbr.: "q"), beyond those in the data columns, are entered in the source column. *Soldi* is rendered as "s." Where more than one city is quoted for a single date, the sources for each are separated by a period. Finally, for the sake of facilitating manipulation of the data by computer, fractions of soldi were converted to decimals.

Graph 3, which concludes appendix D, represents the movement of domestic exchange rates and plots the annual averages (undated quotations excluded, except at the two extremes of the curve for Venice) of the cities with most data: Venice, 1305–1510, and Udine, 1333–1421.

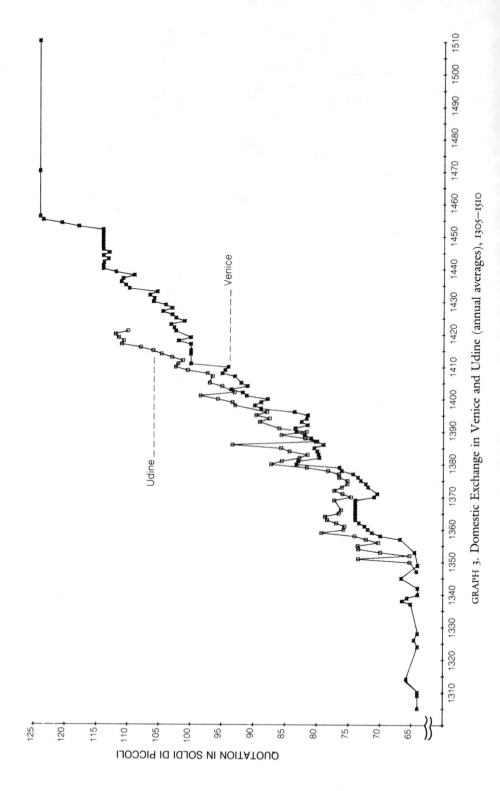

GRAPH 3. Domestic Exchange in Venice and Udine (annual averages), 1305–1510

QUOTATION IN SOLDI DI PICCOLI

TABLE D.3.

Domestic Exchange: The Ducat in Soldi di Piccoli, 1305–1508

| Year Day/Month | Place | | | | | | | Sources |
|---|---|---|---|---|---|---|---|---|
| | Venice | Treviso | Udine | Padua | Verona | Zara | Greece | |
| **1305** s.d. | 64 | | | | | | | Schäfer, 127*. |
| **1308** s.d. | | 64 | | | | | | Zanetti, 169. |
| **1309** s.d. | 64 | | | | | | | Schäfer. |
| **1310** s.d. | 64 | | | | | | | Gallicciolli; Padovan; Cipolla; Stella. Zanetti, 170, gives 61.3 s. for 1311 (from a commentary by B. Henrici). |
| **1314** 30/10 | 65.83 | | | | | | | Monticolo, ed., *I capitolari delle arti*, 3: 320, doc. 42 (1 du. = 24 gr. 22 pic.). |
| **1317** s.d. | 67.167 | | | | | | | Schäfer, 127* (also 64 s.). |
| **1318** 28/12 | | 64 | | | | | | Zanetti, 170. |
| **1319** s.d. | 64 | | | | | | | Schäfer (1 du. = 24–26 gr.; thus 1 du. = 64–69.3 s.). |
| **1320** s.d. | 66 | | | | | | | Gallicciolli; Padovan; Cipolla; Stella. |
| s.d. | 64 | | | | | | | Schäfer. |
| **1322** s.d. | 64 | | | | | | | Ibid. |

*(continued)*

TABLE D.3. (Continued)

| Year | Place | | | | | | | Sources |
|------|-------|--|--|--|--|--|--|---------|
| Day/Month | Venice | Treviso | Udine | Padua | Verona | Zara | Greece | |
| **1323** s.d. | 64 | | | | | | | Ibid. |
| **1324** 28/07 | 64 | | | | | | | PSM, M79, N. Paolini, in Ashtor, *Les métaux précieux*, 118. |
| **1326** s.d. | 64 | | | | | | | Schäfer, 901, gives ca. 24–25 gr. for 1326–27, i.e., 64–66.67 s. |
| 18/02 | 64.6 | | | | | | | Spufford and Wilkinson (from Roberti, ed., *Le magistrature giudiziarie*). |
| **1328** 12/09 | 64 | | | | | | | Cipolla; Stella, s.d.; Papadopoli: the Quarantia set 64 s. as the official rate. Teja says that Zara quoted the du. at 53.3 s. until 1328, at 64 s. from 1328 to ca. 1360. |
| **1329** s.d. | 66.10 | | | | | | | Stella. *PMV*, lx, gives 66.83 s., incorrectly citing Zanetti, 170, as the source. |
| 09/09 | | 68 | | | | | | Zanetti, 170 (3q, of which 2 s.d.). |
| **1330** s.d. | 67.9 | | | | | | | Stella. |
| **1331** s.d. | 70 | | | | | | | Ibid. |
| 17/09 | | 70 | | | | | | Zanetti, 170; s.d., 187–89. |
| **1333** s.d. | 64 | | 64 | | | | | Spufford and Wilkinson (from *Rationes Decimarum*, by calc.). Fabrizi. |

| Date | | | |
|---|---|---|---|
| *1335* | | | |
| s.d. | 64 | | Spufford and Wilkinson (from *Rationes Decimarum*, by calc.). |
| *1336* | | | |
| 01/10 | | 64.5 | *Coroni*, 22, 262: the ducat is "a ragione di £3 s4 d6 picc. l'uno." |
| *1337* | | | |
| 01/03 | | 65.12 | Ibid., 78 f., 267 (per florin). |
| 26/04 | | 65.167 | Ibid., 58 (per florin). |
| 16/05 | | 62.7 | Ibid., 3 entries, 79–81, 277, 281. |
| 19/05 | | 65.167 | Ibid., 62 (per florin). |
| 28/07 | | 62.5 | Ibid., 282–84 (per florin). |
| 04/08 | | 62.5 | Ibid. (per florin). |
| 01/09 | | 63.56 | Ibid., 95; on the same day, a different transaction gives 65.12 s. (pp. 267 f.); both per florin. |
| 11/09 | 65.16 | | Ibid., 105, 289. Mandich, clxxxiii and n. l, gives 62.5 s. "Fiorini d'oro al peso di Vinegia" are ducats. |
| 04/12 | | 63 | *Coroni*, 120, 293. |
| *1338* | | | |
| 01/01 | | 65.12 | Ibid., 106, 291 (per florin). |
| 01/02 | | 63.78 | Ibid., 104, 294 (per florin). |
| 24/02 | | 66.285 | Ibid., 115 (per florin). |
| 25/02 | | 63.13 | Ibid., 158, 304 f. (per florin). |
| 26/05 | | 63.13 | Ibid., 305 (per florin). |
| 26/06 | 66.67 | | Mandich, cvii f., notes, from Duccio di Banchello ledger. |
| 01/09 | | 66.285 | *Coroni*, 117, 156 (per florin). |
| 15/11 | | 63.13 | Ibid., 191, 313 (per florin). |
| 28/11 | 66.5 | | Mandich, cvii f., notes, from Duccio di Banchello ledger. |
| 07/12 | 66.5 | | Ibid. |

(continued)

TABLE D.3. *(Continued)*

| Year Day/Month | Venice | Treviso | Udine | Padua | Verona | Zara | Greece | Sources |
|---|---|---|---|---|---|---|---|---|
| **1339** | | | | | | | | |
| s.d. | 64 | | | | | | | Schäfer. |
| 09/01 | 66.5 | | | | | | | Mandich, cix n, from Duccio di Banchello ledger. |
| 20/03 | 64.96 | | | | | | | Spufford and Wilkinson, from Melis, *Documenti per la storia economica*, 388, in turn from the Duccio di Banchello ledger. |
| 15/10 | | | | 61.3 | | | | *Covoni*, 192, 218 ("£ pic. bagattini, entranci ducati a ragione di £3 s1 d4 pic."). |
| **1340** | | | | | | | | |
| s.d. | 64 | | | | | | | Stella (also 65 s.). |
| 01/11 | 64 | | | | | | | Luzzatto, in *Studi*, 288, explaining the testament of Nicolò Morosini of that date; one figure works out to 64 s., another to 63.9 s. |
| **1341** | | | | | | | | |
| s.d. | 68 | | | | | | | Stella. |
| 06/09 | | 70 | | | | | | Zanetti, 170. |
| **1342** | | | | | | | | |
| s.d. | | 68 | | | | | | Ibid., 170 f.; and *PMV*, lxxv (also 68.3 s.). |
| 24/07 | 64 | | | | | | | PSM, M4, P. Nan da Marano, reg. 1, fol. 3, "prout solutis comunibus." |
| **1343** | | | | | | | | |
| s.d. | | | 64.167 | | | | | Fabrizi (also 70 s.). |
| **1345** | | | | | | | | |
| s.d. | 68.11 | | | | | | | Stella. Zanetti, 171, distinguishes between the legal rate of 64 s., at which the deposit was made, and the market rate of 70 s. "plus minus" current in Venice. |

576

(continued)

| Date | | | | | Source |
|---|---|---|---|---|---|
| 29/01 | 66.67 | | | | PSM, M70A, N. Morosini, reg. 1 (agio = 1 grosso per ducat). |
| **1346** | | | | | |
| s.d. | | 68.167 | | | Fabrizi. |
| 12/02 | | | 64.167 | | Zanetti, 171. |
| **1347** | | | | | |
| 14/11 | | | 64.167 | | Fabrizi. |
| **1348** | | | | | |
| s.d. | | | 64.167 | | Ibid. |
| **1349** | | | | | |
| s.d. | | 64 | | | Stella. Zanetti, 171. |
| 00/04 | 64 | | | 64 | SMSC, 2, 18r. |
| 04/05 | 64 | | | | PSM, M62A, G. Stornado, reg. 1. |
| **1350** | | | | | |
| 08/01 | | | 65.3 | | Fabrizi. |
| 00/07 | | 64 | | | Zanetti, 171 (same rate also s.d.) |
| **1351** | | | | | |
| s.d. | 63 | | | | Gallicciolli; and Carli: 63 s. Cipolla; Burani; Padovan, 273; and Stella: 64 s. |
| 22/11 | | | 73.5 | | Fabrizi. |
| **1352** | | | | | |
| s.d. | 66 | | | | Burani; Padovan, 273; Cipolla; Stella. |
| 17/02 | | | 65.3 | | Fabrizi. |
| 00/09 | | | | 64 | Stahl (Crete, Modon). |
| **1353** | | | | | |
| s.d. | 66 | | | | Cipolla; Stella. |
| 18/02 | 64.5 | | | | PSM, M62A, G. Stornado (by calc.); same for 23/02. |
| 24/06 | | | 70 | | Fabrizi. |
| **1354** | | | | | |
| s.d. | 71 | 71.92 | | | Stella. Zanetti, 171. |
| 18/06 | | | 72.3 | | Fabrizi. |
| 20/10 | | | 74.67 | | Ibid. |

TABLE D.3. (Continued)

| Year | | | | Place | | | | |
| Day/Month | Venice | Treviso | Udine | Padua | Verona | Zara | Greece | Sources |
|---|---|---|---|---|---|---|---|---|
| *1355* | | | | | | | | |
| 02/05 | | | 75.83 | | | | | Ibid. |
| 21/09 | | | 72.3 | | | | | Ibid. |
| 18/10 | | | 72.67 | | | | | Ibid. |
| *1356* | | | | | | | | |
| s.d. | 66 | | | | | | | Gallicciolli. Cipolla; Burani; Stella give 68 s. |
| 30/01 | | 70 | | | | | | Zanetti, 171 f. |
| 24/07 | | | 70 | | | | | Fabrizi. |
| 30/09 | | | 70.583 | | | | | Ibid. |
| *1357* | | | | | | | | |
| s.d. | 70 | | | | | | | Schäfer; Cipolla; Stella. |
| 27/01 | 69.7 | | | | | | | *PMV*, lxxxi (by calc.). |
| 11/04 | | | 72.3 | | | | | Fabrizi. |
| 00/09 | 64 | | | | | | | A. Borlandi, "Moneta e congiuntura," 416 n. 2 (from ASV, Commemoriali, regarding a mercenary's pay). |
| 23/10 | | | | 76 | | | | ASPD, AN, 100, fols. 323–24. |
| *1358* | | | | | | | | |
| s.d. | 70 | | | | | | | Schäfer. |
| 17/08 | 70 | | | | | | | PSM, Mizo, C. da Canal. |
| 20/09 | | | 74.67 | | | | | Fabrizi. |
| 28/12 | | | 73.5 | | | | | Ibid. |
| *1359* | | | | | | | | |
| s.d. | 68 | | | | | | | Gallicciolli; Padovan, 365. Burani; Padovan, 273; Cipolla; and Schäfer give 70 s. |
| 05/04 | 71 | | | | | | | PSM, Mizo, C. da Canal. |
| 17/08 | 71.67 | | | | | | | Ibid. (The rate of 56 s. given in Spufford and Wilkinson, 140, refers to Negroponte.) |

(continued)

| Date | | | | | Sources |
|---|---|---|---|---|---|
| 27/08 | | 79.3 | | | Fabrizi. |
| 03/10 | 66 | | | | Stahl (Negroponte). |
| **1360** | | | | | |
| s.d. | | | 72 | 70 | Cipolla; Stella. For Treviso: Zanetti, 172, for the 14th indiction (1/09/1360–31/08/1361); while Zanetti lists 72 s., the doc. on which he bases the figure would give 76 s. |
| 25/02 | | 79.3 | | 70 | Fabrizi. |
| 08/03 | | 73.5 | | | Ibid. |
| 23/03 | | 74.67 | | | Ibid. |
| 27/06 | | | | 72 | PSM, C230, Reniero Zen, reg. 4, fol. 9v. |
| **1361** | | | | | |
| s.d. | 73 | | | 70 | Galliciolli, Padovan, 365. Burani; Padovan, 273; Cipolla; and Stella give 72 s. Stahl, also 74 s. (Vostitsa). |
| 00/01 | | | | 73 | PSM, M67, G. Gabriel, reg. 2, fol. 14. |
| 17/06 | | 75.83 | | 73 | Fabrizi. |
| 20/09 | | | | 72 | PSM, M4, M. Giustinian, reg. 3, fol. IV (several entries same day), also at 72.5 s. |
| 05/10 | | | | | Fabrizi. |
| 02/11 | | 75.583 | | 72 | |
| **1362** | | | | | |
| s.d. | | | | 72 | Stella. P. Sten tried to fix the rate at 72 s. by law on 22/01 but failed (see PMV, cx). |
| 10/03 | | 77 | | 72 | Fabrizi. |
| 29/04 | | | | 72 | PSM, M67, G. Gabriel, reg. 2, fol. 11. |
| 30/04 | | | | 73 | Ibid., fol. 15v (2q). |
| 00/05 | | | | 74 | Ibid., fol. 18v. |
| 10/06 | | | | 73.5 | Ibid., fol. 14. |
| 28/07 | | | | 74 | Ibid., fol. 15. |
| 27/08 | | | | 74 | AST, PO, n. 8957. |
| 01/12 | | | 74 | | PSM, M67, G. Gabriel, reg. 2. |
| **1363** | | | | | |
| 06/05 | | | | 74 | Ibid., fol. 14. |

TABLE D.3. (*Continued*)

| Year | Place | | | | | | | Sources |
|------|-------|---------|-------|-------|--------|------|--------|---------|
| Day/Month | Venice | Treviso | Udine | Padua | Verona | Zara | Greece | |
| 21/09 | | | 79.917 | | | | | Fabrizi. |
| 28/09 | | | 77 | | | | | Ibid. |
| **1364** | | | | | | | | |
| 10/10 | 74 | | | | | | | PSM, M67, G. Gabriel, reg. 2, fol. 14. |
| 22/06 | 74 | | | | | | | Ibid. |
| 05/10 | 74 | | | | | | | Ibid. |
| 15/10 | | | 79.3 | | | | | Fabrizi. |
| 21/11 | | | 78.167 | | | | | Ibid. |
| **1365** | | | | | | | | |
| s.d. | 72 | | | | | | | Cipolla; Stella. |
| 19/04 | | | 77 | | | | | Fabrizi. |
| 13/05 | | | 75.83 | | | | | Ibid. |
| 21/08 | | | 77 | | | | | Ibid. |
| 23/08 | 74 | | | | | | | Three q for 23/08–30/08 in PSM, M88, J. Scrovegni; ibid, F. Ridolfi; ibid, M67, G. Gabriel. |
| **1366** | | | | | | | | |
| s.d. | 74 | 74 | | | | | | Stella. Zanetti, 172, 2q. |
| 13/06 | | | 76.25 | | | | | Fabrizi. |
| 20/06 | 74 | | | | | | | PSM, M120, C. da Canal, reg. 2. |
| 26/12 | | | | | | 74 | | Teja. |
| **1367** | | | | | | | | |
| 12/04 | 74 | | | | | | | PSM, M88, J. Scrovegni. |
| 27/08 | | | | | | 74 | | Teja. |
| 06/10 | | | | | | 74 | | Ibid. (also for 11/10). |
| **1368** | | | | | | | | |
| s.d. | | 74 | | | | | | Zanetti, 172. |
| 01/07 | 74 | | | | | | | PSM, M67, P. Soranzo, reg. 2, fol. 4v. |

| | | | | | Sources |
|---|---|---|---|---|---|
| **1369** | | | | | |
| s.d. | 73 | | | | Stella. Zanetti, 172. |
| 10/02 | 74 | 67 | | | PSM, M73, P. Soranzo, reg. 2, fol. 7; ibid., M126, M. Pagan, reg. 2. |
| | | | | | Fabrizi. |
| 12/05 | | | 77 | | Ibid. |
| 26/05 | | | 77.583 | | PSM, M126, M. Pagan, reg. 2. |
| 02/06 | 74 | 73 | | | Zanetti, 172. |
| 11/11 | | 67 | | | Ibid. |
| 30/12 | | | | | |
| **1370** | | | | | |
| s.d. | 72 | | | 88 | For Venice: Gallicciolli; Padovan, 365; Cipolla; Stella. Carli; Burani; and Padovan, 273, give 73 s. Zagata (in Argelati, vol. 2) gives 74 s. For Padua: Cessi, "Nuovi documenti," 148. |
| 12/02 | 72 | | 75.3 | | PSM, C232, R. Zen, reg. 5. |
| 02/03 | | | 75.83 | | Fabrizi. |
| 06/04 | 70 | | | | Ibid. |
| 31/05 | | | 72.917 | | PSM, M120, C. da Canal, reg. 3. |
| 15/07 | | | 74.67 | | Fabrizi (also 72.67 s.). |
| 28/09 | | | | | Ibid. |
| 15/11 | | 70 | | | Zanetti, 172. |
| **1371** | | | | | |
| 24/02 | 70 | 71.8 | | | PMV, lxxxi n. 1 (by calc.). |
| 12/04 | | | | 67.5 | Zanetti, 173 |
| 21/04 | | | | | Ibid., 364, 400. |
| 01/05 | | | 77 | | Fabrizi. |
| 15/10 | | | 75.083 | | Ibid. |
| 14/11 | 71 | | | | PSM, M120, L. Celsi. |
| 21/11 | | 71 | | | Zanetti, 173. |
| **1372** | | | | | |
| 06/01 | 72 | | | 67 | SMSC, 4, alla data. |
| 30/01 | | | | | Zanetti, 173. |

*(continued)*

581

TABLE D.3. (*Continued*)

| Year | Place | | | | | | | Sources |
| Day/Month | Venice | Treviso | Udine | Padua | Verona | Zara | Greece | Sources |
|---|---|---|---|---|---|---|---|---|
| 26/04 | | | 77 | | | | | Fabrizi. |
| 26/06 | | | 77.83 | | | | | Ibid. |
| 21/10 | | | | | | 72 | | Teja. |
| 00/11 | | | | | 67.33 | | | SMSC, 4, alla data. |
| 23/12 | | | | | 67 | | | ACV, atti capitolari, n. 249. |
| **1373** | | | | | | | | |
| 04/02 | 72.3 | | | | | | | PSM, M141, B. Dallesmanini, reg., fol. 13r–v. |
| 05/02 | | | | | | 72 | | Teja. |
| 09/02 | 72.3 | | 77 | | | | | Fabrizi. |
| 11/02 | 72.3 | | | | | | | PSM, M141, B. Dallesmanini, reg., fol. 13r–v (also 72.5 s.). |
| 19/02 | 72.3 | | | | | | | PSM, M141, B. Dallesmanini. |
| 24/02 | | 70 | | | | | | AST, PO, no. 9712. |
| 05/03 | 72.3 | | | | | | | PSM, M141, B. Dallesmanini. |
| 27/04 | 72.3 | | | | | | | Ibid. |
| 14/05 | | 72 | | | | | | AST, PO, no. 5250. |
| 11/06 | | | 75.83 | | | | | Fabrizi. |
| 26/06 | | | 77 | | | | | Ibid. |
| 05/07 | | | | | | 72 | | Teja. |
| 09/08 | 70.3 | | | | | | | PSM, M88, G. de Soria (also 3q at 70 s. on 12/08). |
| 19/09 | | | 74.67 | | | | | Fabrizi. |
| 16/10 | | 73 | | | | | | AST, PO, no. 6204. |
| **1374** | | | | | | | | |
| 09/01 | | | 75.83 | | | | | Fabrizi. |
| 17/02 | 72 | | | | | | | PSM, M141, B. Dallesmanini. |
| 00/03 | 72 | | | | | | | Ibid. |
| 21/03 | | 73 | | | | | | Zanetti, 173 (several q at 73 s., s.d.). |

582

| Date | | | | Source |
|---|---|---|---|---|
| 30/05 | 73 | | | PSM, M88, F. Ridolfi. |
| 03/06 | | | 72 | ASPD, AN, 34. fol. 30. |
| 08/08 | 73 | | | PSM, M88, F. Ridolfi. |
| 20/08 | 72.3 | | 67.5 | SMSC, 6, alla data. |
| 25/08 | | 74.67 | | PSM, M120, L. Celsi. |
| 10/09 | 71 | | | Fabrizi. |
| 13/09 | | 75.83 | | PSM, M88, G. de Soria (4q). |
| 20/09 | | 74.67 | | Fabrizi. |
| 06/11 | | | | Ibid. |
| 22/11 | 73 | | | PSM, M88, G. de Soria (4q). |
| **1375** | | | | |
| s.d. | 72 | | | Spufford and Wilkinson, 140 (from Cibrario). |
| 16/02 | 73 | | | PSM, M141, B. Dallesmanini. |
| 19/03 | | 75.83 | | Fabrizi. |
| 03/05 | | 74.67 | | Ibid. |
| 21/05 | | | 71 | Stahl (Crete). |
| 16/06 | 73.3 | | | PSM, M120, L. Celsi. |
| 12/07 | 73.167 | | | Ibid. |
| 26/10 | 73 | | | Ibid., M88, G. de Soria |
| **1376** | | | | |
| 22/01 | | 75.83 | | Fabrizi. |
| 15/03 | 73.25 | | | PSM, M120, L. Celsi. |
| 24/04 | | 77 | | Fabrizi. |
| 11/06 | 74 | | | PSM, M120, L. Celsi. |
| 16/06 | | | 72 | Teja. |
| 06/07 | | | | Zanetti, 173. |
| 13/08 | 73.5 | | | PSM, M88, F. Ridolfi. |
| 01/09 | | 76.25 | | Fabrizi. |
| 08/11 | | 77 | | Ibid. |
| 03/12 | | 76.25 | | Ibid. |
| 04/12 | | 77 | | Ibid. |

(continued)

TABLE D.3. (Continued)

| Year Day/Month | Place | | | | | | | Sources |
|---|---|---|---|---|---|---|---|---|
| | Venice | Treviso | Udine | Padua | Verona | Zara | Greece | |
| **1377** | | | | | | | | |
| s.d. | 73 | | | | | | | Gallicciolli; Padovan, 365; Cipolla. Carli; Burani; and Padovan, 273, give 74 s. Zagata (in Argelati, vol. 2) gives 76 s. |
| 02/04 | 74.67 | | | | | | | PSM, M67, G. Gabriel. |
| 04/04 | | | | | 67.5 | | | SMSC, 6, alla data. |
| 02/05 | 74 | | | | | | | PSM, M88, F. Ridolfi. |
| 11/07 | | | | | | 72 | | Teja. |
| 04/08 | | | | | | 72 | | Ibid. |
| 14/08 | | | 77 | | | | | Fabrizi. |
| 12/11 | | | 77 | | | | | Ibid. |
| 26/11 | | | 75.83 | | | | | Ibid. |
| 27/11 | | | | | | 72 | | Teja. |
| 04/12 | | | | | | 72 | | Ibid. |
| **1378** | | | | | | | | |
| s.d. | 74 | | | | | | | Gallicciolli; Padovan, 365; Cipolla. Carli; and Burani give 76 s. Zagata (in Argelati, vol. 2); and Padovan, 273, give 78 s. |
| 15/01 | | | | | | 72 | | Teja. |
| 05/04 | | | | | | 72 | | Ibid. |
| 17/04 | | | | | | 76 | | Ibid. |
| 07/05 | 76.3 | | | | | | | PSM, M67, G. Gabriel, reg. 2, fol. 28. |
| 18/05 | | | | | | 76 | | Teja. |
| 28/05 | | | | | | 72 | | Ibid. |
| 01/06 | | | | | | 72 | | Ibid. |
| 10/06 | | | | | | 76 | | Ibid. |
| 29/06 | | | 78.167 | | | | | Fabrizi. |
| 20/07 | | | | | | 74 | | Teja. |

| Date | | | | | Source |
|---|---|---|---|---|---|
| 24/07 | | 76 | | | Zanetti, 173. |
| 28/07 | | | 77 | | Teja. |
| 28/09 | 76 | | | | Fabrizi. |
| 27/10 | | | | | PSM, M67, G. Gabriel. |
| 31/11 | | | 78.75 | | Teja. |
| 12/12 | | | | | Fabrizi. |
| 16/12 | | | | | Teja. |
| 21/12 | | | 79.3 | | Fabrizi. |
| 24/12 | | 72 | | | Collodo. |
| *1379* | | | | | |
| s.d. | 76 | | | | Gallicciolli; Padovan, 365; Cipolla. Carli; Burani; and Padovan, 273, give 78 s. Zagata (in Argelati, vol. 2) gives 80 s. |
| 18/02 | 76 | | | | PSM, M88, F. Ridolfi. |
| 08/03 | | 72 | | | Teja. |
| 31/05 | | | 72 | | Collodo. |
| 15/06 | | | 72 | | Ibid. |
| 18/06 | | | 80.5 | | Fabrizi. |
| 05/07 | | | | 67.5 | SMSC, 6, alla data. |
| 09/07 | 77 | | | 67.5 | Cap. Broche, fol. 3v; Papadopoli, 1: 206 (rate at which mint repays borrowed silver). |
| 02/08 | | 76 | | | Teja (also for 23/08). |
| 09/08 | | | 81.67 | | SMSC, 6, alla data (same for 10/09). |
| 28/08 | | | 82.83 | | Fabrizi. |
| 13/09 | | | | | Ibid. |
| 00/11 | | | | 75 | Stahl (Achaia). |
| *1380* | | | | | |
| s.d. | 78 | | | | Padovan, 366; Cipolla. Burani; Zon; and Padovan, 273, give 80 s. Zagata (in Argelati, vol. 2) gives 82 s. |
| 16/01 | | 76 | | | Teja. |

(continued)

TABLE D.3. (Continued)

| Year | Place | | | | | | | Sources |
|---|---|---|---|---|---|---|---|---|
| Day/Month | Venice | Treviso | Udine | Padua | Verona | Zara | Greece | |
| 18/02 | 81 | | | | | | | Talenti, fol. 4v. |
| 03/03 | 81 | | | | | | | Ibid. |
| 08/03 | | | | | | 76 | | Teja. |
| 10/03 | 82 | | | | | | | Talenti, fol. 6. |
| 14/03 | 81.83 | | | | | | | Ibid., fol. 4v (also 81.5 s.). |
| 17/03 | 82 | | | | | | | Ibid., fol. 4. |
| 22/03 | 82 | | | | | | | Ibid. (same on fol. 6v for 21/04). |
| 04/04 | 82.5 | | | | | | | Ibid., fol. 7v (8q). |
| 14/04 | 82.67 | | | | | 78 | | Ibid., fol. 6v (8q). Teja. |
| 19/04 | 82.67 | | | | | | | Ibid., fol. 4v. |
| 01/05 | | | 88.083 | | | | | Fabrizi. |
| 04/05 | | | | | 67.5 | | | SMSC, 6, alla data (same for 7/05). |
| 18/05 | 83.5 | | | | | | | Talenti, fol. 5v. |
| 28/05 | 83.5 | | | | | | | Ibid., fol. 4v (2q) (same on fol. 5v for 23/05). |
| 05/06 | | | 87.5 | | | | | Fabrizi. |
| 06/06 | 83.5 | | | | | | | Talenti, fol. 5 (also 83.417 s., fol. 5v). |
| 17/06 | | | 86.167 | | | | | Fabrizi. |
| 26/06 | 83.5 | | | | | | | Talenti, fol. 21 (same for 28/06; on both days also 83.583 s., fols. 18v–19). |
| 03/07 | 83.5 | | | | | | | Ibid., fol. 20v. |
| 17/07 | 83.5 | | | | | | | Ibid. (5q; same for 18/07 and 20/07). |
| 29/07 | 83.5 | | | | | | | Ibid., fol. 2s (same for 30/07 and 1/08). |
| 11/08 | 83.917 | | | | | | | Ibid., fol. 22v. |
| 13/08 | 83.5 | | | | | | | Ibid., fol. 22 (same on 14/08 and 17/08; also 83.917 s. on 17/08). |
| 22/08 | 83.917 | | | | | | | Ibid., fol. 22v (on 28/08 same and 83.5 s.). |
| 00/09 | | | | | 67.5 | | | SMSC, 6, alla data. |
| 01/09 | 83.917 | | | | | | | Talenti, fols. 21, 22v. |

| Date | | | | Source |
|---|---|---|---|---|
| 04/09 | 84 | | | Ibid., fol. 22v. |
| 10/09 | 84 | | | Ibid., fol. 26v (same for 12/09, 13/09, 15/09). |
| 11/09 | | | | Teja. |
| 17/09 | 84 | | 80 | Talenti, fol. 27 (same for 19/09). |
| 28/09 | 85 | | | Ibid., fol. 19. |
| 01/10 | 84 | | | Ibid., fol. 25v (3q; also 2q at 83.917 s.). |
| 04/10 | 85 | | | Ibid., fol. 19. |
| 25/10 | 86 | | | Papadopoli (1:210 f., from BMV, Ms. Lat., Cl.X, cod. 259, for Oct. to Dec.) |
| 28/12 | | | 78 | Teja. |
| *1381* | | | | |
| 31/01 | | | 78 | Ibid. |
| 06/02 | | | 77 | Ibid. |
| 11/02 | | | 76 | Ibid. (same for 14/02). |
| 28/03 | | | 78 | Teja. |
| 08/04 | | | 76 | Ibid. (also 78 s.). |
| 30/04 | | | 78 | Teja. |
| 09/05 | 85 | | | PSM, M88, R. Bon (also 86 s.). |
| 19/05 | | 84 | | Fabrizi. |
| 08/06 | | | 76 | Teja. |
| 09/06 | | | 80 | Ibid. |
| 20/06 | | 81.67 | | Fabrizi. |
| 03/07 | 82.5 | | | Papadopoli, 1:210 f. (also 82.67 s.). |
| 06/07 | 82.5 | | | Ibid. (and Cipolla, s.d.). |
| 11/07 | 82.25 | | | Ibid. |
| 23/07 | 82.67 | | | Ibid. |
| 25/07 | | 89.83 | | Fabrizi. |
| 15/08 | | 86.167 | | Ibid. |
| 23/08 | | 88.67 | | Ibid. |
| 27/08 | | | 80 | Teja. |
| 18/10 | | 83.167 | | Fabrizi. |

*(continued)*

587

TABLE D.3. (*Continued*)

| Year Day/Month | Place Venice | Treviso | Udine | Padua | Verona | Zara | Greece | Sources |
|---|---|---|---|---|---|---|---|---|
| **1382** | | | | | | | | |
| s.d. | 80 | | | | | | | Gallicciolli; Padovan, 366; Cipolla. Carli; Burani; and Padovan, 273, give 84 s. |
| 28/01 | | | 82.83 | | | | | Fabrizi. |
| 13/03 | | | | | | 80 | | Teja. |
| 06/04 | | | 84 | | | | | Fabrizi. |
| 21/06 | 80 | | | | | | | PSM, M120, A. Contarini. |
| 27/06 | 79.5 | | | | | | | Ibid. |
| 08/07 | 79.58 | | | | | | | Papadopoli, 1:210 f. (8/07–25/07). |
| 23/07 | 80 | | | | | | | PSM, M120, A. Contarini. |
| 25/07 | 79.5 | | | | | | | Papadopoli, 1:210 f. (25/07–31/07). |
| 05/09 | 79 | | | | | | | PSM, M120, A. Contarini. |
| 01/10 | 80 | | | | | | | Ibid. |
| 11/10 | | | | | | | | SMSC, 6, all data. |
| 18/10 | | | 81.67 | | 68 | | | Fabrizi. |
| 22/10 | | | | | | | 75 | Stahl (Zante). |
| **1383** | | | | | | | | |
| 21/02 | 80 | | | | | | | PSM, M120, A. Contarini. |
| 06/03 | | | 82.83 | | | | | Fabrizi. |
| 14/03 | 80 | | | | | | | PSM, M120, A. Contarini (several q from 14/03 to 16/05). |
| 24/03 | | | | | | 80 | | Teja. |
| 16/05 | 80 | | | | | | | PSM, M120, A. Contarini. |
| 17/06 | 79 | | | | | | | Ibid., M88, R. Bon (also 80 s.). |
| 29/06 | | | | | | 80 | | Teja. |
| 05/09 | 80 | | | | | | | PSM, M120, A. Contarini. |
| 20/10 | | | 80 | | | | | Fabrizi (also 80.5 s.). |
| 02/11 | | | 81.67 | | | | | Fabrizi. |
| 20/11 | | | 81.67 | | | | | Ibid. |

588

| Date | | | | | | Reference |
|---|---|---|---|---|---|---|
| *1384* | | | | | | |
| s.d. | 84 | | | | | Galicciolli; Padovan, 274, 366; Cipolla. |
| 26/01 | | | | | 82.83 | Fabrizi. |
| 06/02 | | 68 | | | | SMSC, 6, alla data. |
| 21/03 | | | | | 85.167 | Fabrizi. |
| 13/04 | 80 | | | | 83.417 | PSM, M120, A. Contarini. |
| 23/04 | | 68 | | | | Fabrizi. |
| 00/05 | | | | | 82.83 | SMSC, 6, alla data. |
| 15/06 | | | | | | Fabrizi. |
| 13/08 | | 73 | 73 | | | Rizzoli and Perini, *Le monete di Padova*, 35 and doc. 6. The rate of 73 s. was for silver carraresi and soldi padovani; for quattrini padovani the rate was 73.5 s., for piccoli 74.5 s. The Carrarese ordinance for Padua, Treviso, Conegliano, and Belluno was repeated in 1386 (21/03 and 12/10) and 1387 (12/07). |
| 29/08 | | | | 80 | | Teja. |
| 12/10 | 80 | | | | 86.83 | PSM, M88, F. Ridolfi. Fabrizi. |
| 01/11 | | | | | 85.167 | Ibid. |
| *1385* | | | | | | |
| 02/01 | | | | | 85.167 | Fabrizi. |
| 18/02 | 80.5 | | | | | PSM, M120, A. Contarini. |
| 04/03 | 81 | | | | | Ibid. |
| 25/03 | 81 | | | | | Secreta, Collegio, Secreti, 1382–85, fols. 68v–69; in Istria the rate was 86 s. or, in "monetis hungaris," 88 s. |
| 27/03 | | | | | 80 | Fabrizi. |
| 02/04 | | | | | 88.67 | Ibid. |
| 12/04 | 80 | | | | | PSM, M120, A. Contarini. |
| 16/06 | 80 | | | | 91 | Ibid. |
| 05/09 | | | | | | Fabrizi. |
| 09/10 | | | | 80 | | Teja. |

*(continued)*

TABLE D.3. (*Continued*)

| Year Day/Month | Place | | | | | | | Sources |
|---|---|---|---|---|---|---|---|---|
| | Venice | Treviso | Udine | Padua | Verona | Zara | Greece | |
| 07/12 | | | 84 | | | | | Fabrizi. |
| 15/12 | | | 85 | | | | | Ibid. |
| 16/12 | | | 86 | | | | | Fabrizi (also 84 s.) |
| **1386** | | | | | | | | |
| 17/01 | | | 90 | | | | | Fabrizi. |
| 20/01 | | | 80 | | | | | Ibid. |
| 30/01 | | 73 | | | | | | Zanetti, 173. |
| 07/02 | | | | | | 80 | | Teja. |
| 02/03 | | | 92 | | | | | Fabrizi. |
| 21/03 | | 73 | | 73 | | | | Zanetti, 168; and as above under 13/08/84. |
| 21/04 | | | 108 | | | | | Fabrizi. |
| 05/05 | | | 110 | | | | | Ibid. |
| 10/06 | | | 90 | | | | | Ibid. |
| 03/07 | | 76 | | | | | | Zanetti, 173. |
| 05/10 | 80 | | | | | | | PSM, M88, F. Ridolfi. |
| 08/10 | | | 92 | | | | | Fabrizi. |
| 11/10 | | | 96 | | | | | Ibid. |
| 12/10 | | | 94 | | | | | Ibid. |
| 19/10 | | | 95 | | | | | Ibid. |
| 05/11 | 78 | | | | | | | PSM, M120, A. Contarini. |
| 19/11 | | | 80 | | | | | Fabrizi. |
| 27/12 | | | | | | 84 | | Teja. |
| **1387** | | | | | | | | |
| 12/01 | | | 78 | | | | | Fabrizi. |
| 15/01 | 80 | | | | | 84 | | ASP, D. 709, Zanobi Gaddi to Florence. |
| 28/03 | | | | | | 86 | | Teja. |
| 18/06 | | | | | | 80 | | Ibid. |
| 27/07 | | | | | | 80 | | Ibid. |
| 08/09 | | | | | | 80 | | Ibid. |

| Date | | | | | | Source |
|---|---|---|---|---|---|---|
| 13/09 | | | 81 | | | Fabrizi. |
| 24/09 | | | 80 | | | Ibid. |
| 04/10 | | | | | 86 | Teja. |
| 10/10 | | | 80 | | 80 | Ibid. |
| 04/11 | | | 82 | | | Fabrizi. |
| 28/11 | | | | | | Ibid. |
| 27/12 | | | 80 | | 80 | Teja. |
| **1388** | | | | | | |
| 17/02 | | | | | 86 | Teja. |
| 20/03 | | | | | 80 | Ibid. |
| 10/04 | | | | | 86 | Ibid. |
| 21/04 | | 82.4 | | | | Zanetti, 173 f. (also 82.58 s.). |
| 13/05 | | 83 | | | | Zanetti, 173 f. |
| 12/06 | | | | 68 | | SMSC, 6, alla data. |
| 04/09 | | | 81 | | | Fabrizi. |
| 06/09 | | | 81.67 | | | Ibid. |
| 24/09 | 81 | | | | | ASP, D. 709, Giorgio Nicoli and Co. to Florence. |
| 04/10 | | | | | 90 | Teja. |
| 08/10 | | | 83 | | | Fabrizi. |
| 25/10 | | | | 73 | | Argelati, 1:252. |
| 10/11 | 81 | | | | | ASP, D. 709 G. Nicoli and Co. to Florence. |
| 20/11 | | | | 88 | | ASPD, AN, 106, fols. 347–48. |
| 10/12 | | | | | 90 | Teja. |
| **1389** | | | | | | |
| s.d. | | | | 67.5 | | Cessi, "Documenti inediti," 110–11. |
| 20/02 | | 82.67 | | | | AST, PO, no. 5079. |
| 22/02 | | | 84 | | | Fabrizi. |
| 13/03 | | 82 | | | | Zanetti, 173 f. (also for 24/03). |
| 07/05 | | | | 68 | | SMSC, 6, alla data. |
| 13/05 | | 83 | | | | Zanetti, 174 ("quia ipse ivit Venecias recuperando offertorium," thus conceivably referring to Venice rather than Treviso). |

(continued)

TABLE D.3. (Continued)

| Year | | | | Place | | | | Sources |
| Day/Month | Venice | Treviso | Udine | Padua | Verona | Zara | Greece | |
|---|---|---|---|---|---|---|---|---|
| 19/06 | 82 | | | | | | | ASP, D. 710, G. Nicoli and Co. to Florence (also 26/06): "right now it is 82 s, but let us reckon at 83 s." |
| 16/08 | | | 86 | | | | | Fabrizi. |
| 22/08 | | | | | | 84.0 | | Teja. |
| 14/09 | | | 87 | | | | | Fabrizi. |
| *1390* | | | | | | | | |
| s.d. | | | | | | | | Zanetti, 174. |
| 10/06 | | 84 | | | | | | Teja. |
| 14/06 | 80 | | | | | 95 | | PSM, M88, F. Ridolfi, fols. 3v, 10v (also 81 s.). |
| 13/07 | | | 81.67 | | | | | Fabrizi. |
| 12/08 | 84 | | | | | | | PSM, M115, J. Bragadin (also 18/08). |
| 06/09 | | | | | | 100 | | Teja. |
| 23/09 | 84 | | | | | | | PSM, M148, R. De Caresinis. |
| 04/10 | 84 | | | | | | | Ibid. (7q 4/10–24/11). |
| 15/10 | | | | | | | 83 | Stahl (Crete). |
| 19/10 | | | | | | 100 | | Teja. |
| 24/11 | 84 | | | | | | | PSM, M148, R. De Caresinis. |
| 10/12 | | | | | 65 | | | Simeoni, 1286. |
| 30/12 | 84 | | | | | | | PSM, M148. Between 7/12 and 12/12, the rate in Trieste was 85 s. ASF, Del Bene, 49, no. 162, letter from Trieste to Venice. |
| *1391* | | | | | | | | |
| 00/01 | | | | 84 | | | | Collodo. |
| 14/01 | 83.5 | | | | | | | ASF, Del Bene, 49, no. 229, letter from Venice to Padua. |
| 02/03 | 84 | | | | | | | PSM, M148, R. De Caresinis. |
| 03/03 | | | 86 | | | | | Fabrizi. |

| Date | | | | | Source |
|---|---|---|---|---|---|
| 11/03 | 84 | | | | AST, PO, no. 5789. |
| 15/03 | | | 84 | | ASF, Del Bene, 20, fol. 6, and 19, fol. 13 (also 84.5 s.). |
| 10/04 | | | 83.5 | | Ibid., 20, fol. 13. |
| 19/04 | | | 84 | | Ibid., fol. 15. |
| 22/04 | | | 82 | | Ibid., fols. 16, 28, 27 (also 83 s.). |
| 27/04 | | | 84 | | Ibid., fol. 17. |
| 05/05 | 84 | | | | Ibid., 49, no. 239, letter from Venice to Padua (also 84.16 s.). |
| 23/06 | 84 | | | | Zanetti, 174. |
| 11/08 | 82 | | | | PSM, U128, fasc. 5, reg. cover. |
| 12/09 | 84 | | | | PSM, M88, F. Ridolfi. |
| *1392* | | | | | |
| s.d. | 82 | 87.5 | | | Zanetti, 174 (also 83 s.). Fabrizi. |
| 02/02 | 82 | | | 96 | Teja. |
| 23/02 | 82 | | | | PSM, M88, F. Ridolfi. |
| 16/05 | | | | 90.75 | Teja. |
| 01/06 | 83 | | | | ASP, D. 710, Gaddi to Florence. |
| 08/06 | 83 | | | | Ibid. |
| 08/06 | | | 84 | | Collodo. |
| 26/07 | 80 | | | | PSM, M145, R. De Caresinis. |
| 01/08 | 82 | | | | Ibid. |
| 20/08 | 80 | | | | Ibid., M120, A. Contarini. |
| 16/10 | 81 | | | | Ibid. |
| 31/10 | 81 | | | | Ibid., M145, R. De Caresinis. |
| *1393* | | | | | |
| 11/03 | | | | 96 | Teja. |
| 30/04 | | | | 90 | Ibid. |
| 03/05 | | 88.67 | | | Fabrizi. |
| 08/05 | 81 | | | | PSM, M148, R. De Caresinis. |
| 14/07 | | 93.3 | | | Fabrizi. |
| 07/10 | | 85.167 | | | Ibid. |
| 21/10 | 84 | | | | PSM, M148, R. De Caresinis. |

*(continued)*

TABLE D.3. (Continued)

| Day/Month | Venice | Treviso | Udine | Padua | Verona | Zara | Greece | Sources |
|---|---|---|---|---|---|---|---|---|
| **1394** | | | | | | | | |
| s.d. | 84.3 | | | | | | | PMV, cl, incorrectly citing Zanetti, 174 f. Zanetti, 174. |
| 10/01 | | 83 | 85.167 | | | | | Fabrizi. |
| 25/01 | | 81 | | | | | | AST, PO, no. 7482. |
| 10/03 | | | 86.917 | | | | | Fabrizi. |
| 04/04 | 82 | | | | | | | PSM, M67, G. Gabriel, reg. 3. |
| 09/04 | 81.67 | | | | | | | Ibid. |
| 27/04 | | | | | 66 | | | Simeoni, 1286. |
| 03/05 | | | 87.5 | | | | | Fabrizi. |
| 22/06 | 81 | | | | | | | PSM, M67, G. Gabriel, reg. 3. |
| 26/08 | | | | | | | 86 | Stahl (Crete). |
| 30/10 | 82 | | | | | | | PSM, M67, G. Gabriel, reg. 3. |
| 01/12 | | 82 | | | | | | Zanetti, 174 (also 22/12). |
| 17/12 | | | 88.67 | | | | | Fabrizi. |
| 31/12 | | | 89.25 | | | | | Ibid. |
| **1395** | | | | | | | | |
| 05/02 | | | 93.3 | | | | | Fabrizi. |
| 25/02 | 81 | | | | | 90 | | PSM, M148, R. De Caresinis, registration on same day of past expenditures (2q at 81 s., 2q at 82 s.). |
| 01/04 | | | 94.5 | | | | | Teja. |
| 20/04 | | | 88.67 | | | | | Fabrizi. |
| 00/09 | | | 85.167 | | | | | Ibid. |
| 09/10 | | | | | | | | Ibid. |
| 19/10 | 82 | | 86.3 | | | | | PSM, M67, G. Gabriel, reg. 3. |
| 09/12 | | | | | | | | Fabrizi. |
| **1306** | | | | | | | | |
| s.d. | | 85 | | | | | | Zanetti, 174 f |

| Date | | | | | Source |
|---|---|---|---|---|---|
| 07/03 | 83.2 | | | | Zerbi, *Il mastro a partita doppia*, 74. |
| 17/05 | 84 | | | | ASV, S. M. Gloriosa dei Frari, b. 128 (see below, app. G, doc. 7). |
| **1397** | | | | | |
| 00/09 | | | 87.5 | | Fabrizi. |
| 08/09 | | | 87.5 | | Ibid. |
| 11/09 | | | 88.67 | | Ibid. (also 87.5 s.). |
| 07/11 | | 85 | | | Zanetti, 174 f. |
| 25/04 | | 87 | | | Ibid., 175. |
| 08/06 | 88 | | | 90 | Teja. |
| 26/07 | 88 | 88 | | | PSM, M148, R. De Caresinis, reg., fol. 15, calculation of loss between receipts at 80 s., payments at 88 s. The accounting convention ("invenimus in saculo") used 80 s. on 17/07 (PSM, M67, G. Gabriel, reg. 3) and 24/09 (PSM, M120, A. Contarini). |
| 01/09 | 89 | 89 | | | Da Pozzo (2q; also 90 s.). |
| 27/09 | 89.6 | | | | Da Pozzo. |
| **1398** | | | | | |
| 26/01 | | | 91 | 90 | Bernardi, *Monetazione*, 204. |
| 09/02 | 89 | 89 | | | AST, Osp., b. 356, fol. 5 (also 28/02). |
| 14/02 | 89 | | | | Da Pozzo. |
| 04/03 | 90 | | | | Ibid. |
| 20/04 | 90 | | | | Ibid. |
| 30/04 | | 89 | | | AST, Osp., b. 356, fol. 5. |
| 11/05 | 90 | 90 | | | Da Pozzo. |
| 25/06 | | | | | Zanetti, 175. |
| 01/07 | 90 | | | | Argelati, 1:252. |
| 26/07 | | 90 | | | Da Pozzo (89.75 s. for 31/07). |
| 09/08 | 90 | 90 | | 100 | AST, Osp., b. 356, fol. 5. |
| 13/08 | | | | | Teja. |
| 21/08 | 90 | 90 | | | AST, Osp., b. 356, fol. 5. |
| 28/08 | 90 | 90 | | | PSM, M88, F. Ridolfi. |

TABLE D.3. (Continued)

| Year | Place | | | | | | | Sources |
|---|---|---|---|---|---|---|---|---|
| Day/Month | Venice | Treviso | Udine | Padua | Verona | Zara | Greece | |
| 01/10 | 90 | | | | | | | Da Pozzo (same for 7/10). |
| 09/10 | | | 93.3 | | | | | Fabrizi. |
| 29/10 | | | 94.5 | | | | | Fabrizi (also 80 s.). |
| 17/12 | 90 | | | | | | | Da Pozzo; an accounting convention used 85 s. on 15/11 (PSM, U128, fasc. 5), on 20/11 (PSM, U121, fasc. 4) and on 7/12 (PSM, U162, fasc. 1) on the register covers. |
| *1399* | | | | | | | | |
| s.d. | 93 | | | | | | | Cipolla; Cecchetti; Carli. This (dubious) figure is referred to the date 7/10 by Gallicciolli; Papadopoli (tav. 2); and Padovan (p. 366). |
| 26/01 | | | | | 79.167 | | | Zanetti, 367, 400. |
| 11/02 | | | | | | 90 | | Teja. |
| 23/02 | | | 95.67 | | | | | Fabrizi. |
| 04/04 | 90 | | | | | | | PSM, M148, R. De Caresinis. |
| 22/04 | | | | | 64 | | | CF, b. 27, no. 217, "florenos 1400 ad computum librarum trium, soldorum quatuor tertiolorum." |
| 24/04 | 90 | | | | | | | Da Pozzo. |
| 09/05 | | | 88.67 | | | | | Fabrizi. |
| 13/05 | 90 | | | | | | | Da Pozzo. |
| 07/08 | 89 | | | | | | | Ibid. |
| 31/08 | | | | 90 | | | | ASPD, AN, b. 525, fól. 125. |
| 01/09 | 89 | | | 90 | | | | Da Pozzo. |
| 21/09 | | | | 90 | | | | ASPD, AN, b. 525, fol. 76v. |
| 30/09 | 89 | | | 90 | | | | Da Pozzo. |
| 14/10 | | | | 90 | | | | Argelati, 1:252. |
| 15/12 | 85 | | | | | | | PSM, M67, G. Gabriel, reg. 3 (concerning a purchase of wheat for charity) |

| Date | | | | | | | Source |
|---|---|---|---|---|---|---|---|
| 29/12 | | | | | | 95.67 | Fabrizi (also 91 s.). |
| *1400* | | | | | | | |
| s.d. | 93 | | | | | | Cipolla; *PMV*, cl, erroneously citing Zanetti, 173 f., as the source. |
| 00/01 | 89.5 | | | | | | Petizion, S. a g., 6, fol. 28v, for Jan.–Apr. |
| 01/02 | | 90 | | | | | Zanetti, 175. |
| 12/02 | 85 | | | | | | Da Pozzo. |
| 08/03 | | | 88 | | | | Argelati, 1:252. |
| 19/03 | 86 | | | | | | Da Pozzo. |
| 00/05 | 86 | | | | | | Petizion, S. a g., 6, fol. 28v. |
| 10/05 | | | 87 | | | | Collodo. |
| 11/05 | | | 87 | | | | ASPD, AN, b. 525, fol. 164. |
| 29/05 | 87 | | | | | | Da Pozzo (86.65 s. on previous day). |
| 26/06 | | | | | 90 | | Teja. |
| 27/06 | | 87 | | | | | AST, PO, no. 9337. |
| 06/07 | | | 88 | | | | ASPD, AN, b. 525, fol. 168. |
| 10/07 | 90 | | | | | | Da Pozzo. |
| 13/07 | 87 | | | | | | Ibid. (same for 17/07). |
| 26/08 | 90 | | | | | | Da Pozzo. |
| 01/09 | 87.6 | | | | | | Ibid. |
| 12/10 | 90 | | | | | | Ibid. |
| 15/11 | | | | | | 95.67 | Fabrizi. Teja. |
| *1401* | | | | | | | |
| s.d. | 93 | | 90 | | 90 | 95.67 | Cipolla (from Zagata, for 1401–7, all at 93 s.). Gallicciolli; and Padovan, 366, give the even more erroneous figure of 98 s. For Padua: Collodo. |
| 01/01 | | | 90 | | | | Argelati, 1:252; Rizzoli and Perini, doc. 10. |
| 26/01 | | | 90 | 98 | | | Fabrizi. |
| 29/01 | 90 | | | | | | Misc. carte non appartenenti a nessun archivio, b. 28, account book of D. Soranzo, fol. 57. |
| 05/02 | | 90 | 90 | | | | AST, Osp., b. 334, fol. 5 (same on 9/02 and 27/02). |

*(continued)*

TABLE D.3. (Continued)

| Year | Place | | | | | | | Sources |
|---|---|---|---|---|---|---|---|---|
| Day/Month | Venice | Treviso | Udine | Padua | Verona | Zara | Greece | |
| 22/02 | | | 101.5 | | | | | Fabrizi. |
| 01/03 | | | 100.3 | | | | | Ibid. |
| 07/03 | | | 103.83 | | | | | Ibid. |
| 24/03 | | | 102.67 | | | | | Ibid. |
| 11/04 | | | 105 | | | | | Ibid. |
| 18/04 | 91 | | | | | | | PSM, U162, L. Visconti, reg. 1, fol. 31v, same for 20/04 in Da Pozzo. PSM, M67, G. Gabriel, reg. 3, gives 84 s. for a purchase of wheat under the date 7/04. |
| 05/05 | 91 | | | | | | | Da Pozzo; on 27/05 80 s. in PSM, M70A, N. Morosini, "invenimus in saculo" convention. |
| 26/05 | | | 92 | | | | | Fabrizi. |
| 21/06 | 91 | | | | | | | Da Pozzo. |
| 09/07 | 91 | | | | | | | Ibid.; same in PSM, U162, L. Visconti, fol. 35, while the copy of the same in ASF, Conv. soppr., 51, b. 217, gives 90 s. Da Pozzo gives 91 s. also for 16/07. |
| 20/07 | | | 91 | | | | | Fabrizi. |
| 28/08 | | 92 | | | | | | AST, PO, no. 5801. |
| 09/09 | | | | 91 | | | | Collodo. |
| 28/09 | | | 92 | | | | | Fabrizi. |
| 31/10 | 92 | | | | | | | Da Pozzo. |
| 19/11 | 92 | | | | | | | Ibid. |
| 15/12 | | | | 91 | | | | Collodo. |
| *1402* | | | | | | | | |
| s.d. | 93 | | | 91.5 | | | | Cipolla. Collodo. |
| 08/02 | 92 | | | | | | | Da Pozzo. |
| 20/02 | | 93 | | | | | | Zanetti, 175. |

| Date | | | | | | Source |
|---|---|---|---|---|---|---|
| 21/03 | | | 93 | | | Fabrizi (also 93.3 s. for the "somma generale"). |
| 20/04 | | | | | 100 | Stahl (Corfu). |
| 28/04 | | | | 92 | | Collodo. |
| 06/05 | 91.25 | | | | | ASP, D. 714, B. Piaciti to Florence. |
| 20/05 | 89.8 | | | | | Da Pozzo. |
| 27/05 | 92 | | | | | ASP, D. 714, B. Piaciti to Florence, conto di lana. |
| 02/06 | 92 | | | | | Da Pozzo. |
| 15/09 | 92 | | | | | Ibid. |
| 00/10 | | | | 92 | | Collodo. |
| 01/10 | 93 | | | | | Da Pozzo. |
| 06/11 | 92 | | | | | Ibid. |
| *1403* | | | | | | |
| s.d. | 93 | | | | | Cipolla. |
| 20/03 | 92 | | | | | Da Pozzo. |
| 11/04 | 94 | | | | | Ibid. |
| 02/06 | 94 | | | | | ASP, D. 714, Bindo Piaciti to Florence. |
| 28/07 | 94 | | | | | Ibid., published in Melis, *Documenti per la storia economica*, 250. |
| 31/08 | 94 | | | | | PSM, M88, F. Ridolfi. |
| 07/09 | | | | | 102 | Stahl (Crete). |
| 01/10 | | 94 | | | | Zanetti, 175. |
| 02/10 | | | | | 100 | Stahl (Coron, Modon). |
| *1404* | | | | | | |
| s.d. | 93 | | | | | Cipolla. |
| 06/02 | | | 95 | | | Fabrizi. |
| 12/03 | | | 95 | | | Ibid. |
| 20/05 | | | | | 96 | Stahl. |
| 24/05 | 91 | | | | | ASP, D. 715, Piaciti to Florence (re. the account of an insurance underwriter). |
| *1405* | | | | | | |
| s.d. | 93 | 95 | | | | Cipolla. Zanetti, 175. |
| 02/01 | 92 | | | | | PSM, U128, fasc. 5, reg. cover. |

*(continued)*

TABLE D.3. (*Continued*)

| Year | Place | | | | | | | Sources |
|---|---|---|---|---|---|---|---|---|
| Day/Month | Venice | Treviso | Udine | Padua | Verona | Zara | Greece | |
| 29/06 | | | | | 78 | | | AAC, 56, fol. 5. |
| 28/09 | | | | | 77 | | | SIL, 664, f. 22v. |
| 17/10 | | | | | 77 | | | Ibid., fol. 24v. |
| 25/10 | | | | | 77 | | | Ibid., fol. 25v. |
| 07/11 | | | | | 77 | | | Ibid., fols. 26, 26v (same for 13/11). |
| 11/11 | | | 97 | | | | | Fabrizi. |
| *1406* | | | | | | | | |
| s.d. | 93 | | | | | | | Cipolla. Collodo. |
| 18/01 | | | | | 82 | | | SIL, 664, fol. 30v. |
| 05/04 | | | | | 83 | | | Ibid., fol. 34. |
| 17/04 | | 95 | | | | | | AST, PO, no. 569s. |
| 21/05 | | | | | 73 | | | SIL, 664, fol. 36. |
| 15/06 | | | | | 71 | | | Ibid., fols. 37v, 38r (same for 12/06). |
| 10/07 | | | | | 71 | | | Ibid., fol. 39. |
| 20/08 | | | | | 70 | | | Ibid., fol. 41v. |
| 06/09 | | | | | 71 | | | Ibid., fol. 43. |
| 29/10 | | | | 95 | | | | Collodo. |
| 13/11 | | | | 95 | | | | Ibid. |
| 29/11 | | | | 95 | | | | Ibid. |
| 10/12 | | | | 95 | | | | Ibid. |
| 20/12 | | | | 95 | | | | Ibid. |
| *1407* | | | | | | | | |
| s.d. | 93 | | | | | | | Cipolla. SIL, 577, fol. 25v. |
| 19/04 | 93 | | | | 71 | | | CF, b. 26, no. 177. |
| 10/05 | 93 | | | | 70 | | | Papadopoli, 1, doc. 21 of 11 Nov. 1417, which quotes the rate current at the time of the 10 May 1407 law. |
| 13/06 | 92 | | | | | | | PSM, U128, fasc. 5, reg. cover. |

| Date | | | | | | Reference |
|---|---|---|---|---|---|---|
| 24/07 | 95 | | | | | AST, PO, no. 5739. |
| 04/08 | 92 | | 97 | | | PSM, U162, fasc. 1, reg. cover. |
| 00/09 | | 95 | | | | Fabrizi. |
| 12/09 | | 95 | | 70 | | Collodo. |
| 20/09 | | | 96 | | | CF, b. 26, no. 177, and b. 27, no. 217. |
| 11/10 | 95 | | | | | Fabrizi. |
| 31/10 | | 95 | | | | PSM, M88, F. Arimondo. |
| 02/11 | | | | 70 | | SIL, 578, fol. 3v. |
| ***1408*** | | | | | | |
| s.d. | 96 | | | | | Cipolla (from Papadopoli). |
| 09/02 | | 95 | | | | Collodo. |
| 07/05 | | 95 | | | | Ibid. |
| 27/05 | | | | 71 | | SIL, 577. |
| 31/05 | | | | | 111 | Stahl (Corfu). |
| 00/06 | 95 | | | | | PSM, U139, B. Pisani, galley accounts of A. Arian. |
| 03/06 | | | 97 | | | Fabrizi. |
| 30/08 | | | 98 | | | Collodo. |
| 09/10 | | | 97 | | | Fabrizi. |
| 30/10 | | 95 | | | | Ibid. |
| ***1409*** | | | | | | |
| s.d. | | 100 | | | | Ibid. |
| 13/03 | 94.5 | 95 | | | | Collodo. |
| 30/03 | | 95 | | | | Ibid. |
| 01/05 | | 95 | | | | Petizion, S. a g., 18, fol. 56v seg. (28/06/1410). |
| 21/09 | | 95 | 100.5 | | | Collodo. |
| 20/10 | | 95 | | | | Fabrizi. |
| 26/11 | | 95 | | | | Collodo. |
| ***1410*** | | | | | | |
| s.d. | | 100 | | | | Ibid. SIL, 577, fol. 29. |
| 23/01 | 96 | | | 75 | 100 | Stahl (Crete). |
| 25/01 | 96 | | | | | AST, PO, no. 7808. |
| 28/02 | | | 101.5 | | | Fabrizi. |

*(continued)*

TABLE D.3. (*Continued*)

| Year | Place | | | | | | | Sources |
|---|---|---|---|---|---|---|---|---|
| Day/Month | Venice | Treviso | Udine | Padua | Verona | Zara | Greece | |
| 00/03 | | | 101 | | | | | Ibid. |
| 26/04 | | | | | | | | SIL, 578, fol. 12. |
| 10/06 | 94 | | | | 72 | | | PSM, U162, L. Visconti, reg. 1, fol. 27. |
| 03/07 | | | 104 | | | | | Fabrizi. |
| 24/07 | | | | | | | 120 | Stahl (Negroponte). |
| 27/08 | | | | | | | 109 | Ibid. (Crete). |
| 05/09 | | | | | | | 105 | Ibid. (Crete). |
| 06/10 | | | 103 | | | | | Fabrizi. |
| 09/10 | | | 103 | | | | | Ibid. |
| 16/10 | | | 102.5 | | | | | Ibid. |
| 07/11 | | | 102 | | | | | Ibid. |
| *1411* | | | | | | | | |
| 14/01 | | | | | | | 120 | Stahl (Corfu). |
| 29/03 | | | | 100 | | | | Collodo. |
| 09/05 | | | | 100 | | | | Ibid. |
| 07/07 | | | | | 75 | | | SIL, 1013, fol. 2. |
| 22/08 | | | 102 | | | | 116 | Stahl (Crete). |
| 02/10 | | | 102 | | | | | Fabrizi. |
| 09/10 | | | | 100 | | | | SIL, 1013, fol. 2. |
| 26/10 | | | | | 75 | | | Collodo. |
| 29/10 | 100 | | | | | | | PSM, M88, F. Ridolfi. |
| 25/11 | | 100 | | | | | | AST, PO, no. 6052. |
| 28/11 | | | | | 75 | | | SIL, 1013, fol. 2. |
| 30/12 | | | | 100 | | | | Collodo. |
| *1412* | | | | | | | | |
| s.d. | 93 | | | 100 | | | | For Venice: Gallicciolli. Carli; and Cipolla (from Zagata) give 94-67 s. For Padua: Collodo. |

| Date | | | | | | Source |
|---|---|---|---|---|---|---|
| 02/10 | | | | 102 | | Fabrizi. |
| 07/10 | | | | 101 | | Ibid. |
| 12/10 | | | | 100 | | Ibid. |
| 20/10 | | | | 102 | | Ibid. |
| *1413* | | | | | | |
| s.d. | 100 | | 100 | | | Carli; Gallicciolli gives 94 s. Collodo. |
| 09/03 | 100 | | | 103 | | Fabrizi. |
| 15/08 | | 100 | | | | AST, PO, no. 5379. |
| 07/10 | 100 | | | 103 | | Fabrizi. |
| *1414* | | | | | | |
| s.d. | 100 | 100 | 100 | | | Gallicciolli. Zanetti, 175. Collodo. |
| 28/04 | | 100 | | | | AST, PO, no. 5643. |
| 15/06 | | | | 105 | | Fabrizi. |
| 16/06 | | | | 104 | | Ibid. |
| 10/11 | 100 | | | | | PSM, U128, fasc. 5, reg. cover. |
| 03/12 | | | | 105 | 74.5 | AUR, vol. 41, fol. 1307. |
| 27/12 | | | | | | Fabrizi. |
| *1415* | | | | | | |
| s.d. | 100 | | | | | Collodo. |
| 29/01 | 100 | | | 106 | | PSM, U162, L. Visconti, reg. 1, fol. 11v. |
| 08/08 | 100 | | | | | Fabrizi (also 107 and 108 s.). |
| 30/10 | | | | | | PSM, U128, fasc. 1, reg. 2, back cover. |
| *1416* | | | | | | |
| s.d. | 100 | | | | | Collodo. |
| 08/06 | | | | 108 | | Fabrizi. |
| 21/06 | | | | | 74.8 | AUR, vol. 47, fol. 45ov. |
| *1417* | | | | | | |
| s.d. | 100 | | | | | For Venice: Gallicciolli; Burani; Cipolla. Luzzatto, *Storia*, 214 f. gives 101 s. For Padua: Collodo. |
| 11/03 | | | | | | Fabrizi. |
| 21/04 | | | | 112 | 116 | Stahl (Crete). |

(continued)

TABLE D.3. (*Continued*)

| Year Day/Month | Venice | Treviso | Udine | Padua | Verona | Zara | Greece | Sources |
|---|---|---|---|---|---|---|---|---|
| 09/05 | 100 | | 111 | | | | | Fabrizi. |
| 11/06 | 100 | | | | | | | PSM, U88, P. Signolo. |
| 11/07 | 100 | | 110 | | | | | Fabrizi. |
| 11/11 | | | | | | | | Papadopoli, 1, doc. 21; Padovan, 366 (decision to debase soldini and grossi by 7.7 percent). |
| *1418* | | | | | | | | |
| s.d. | 100 | | | 100 | | | | For Venice: Archivio Prop. Trevisan, filza 17, Trattato. Cipolla (from Zagata) gives 101 s. For Padua: Collodo. |
| 22/02 | 100 | | | | | | | PSM, U88, P. Signolo. |
| 27/02 | | | 112 | | | | | Fabrizi. |
| 09/03 | 104 | | | | | | | Collegio, Notatorio, 5, fol. 192v: "sicut presentialiter currunt (monete)"; the Bond Office will pay interest at 100 s. |
| 19/07 | | | 110 | | | | | Fabrizi. |
| 31/10 | | | 110 | | | | | Ibid. |
| *1419* | | | | | | | | |
| s.d. | | | | 100 | | | | Collodo. |
| 14/05 | | | 110 | | | | | Fabrizi. |
| 25/05 | | | 112 | | | | | Bernardi, *Monetazione*, 207. |
| 16/07 | | | 112 | | | | | Fabrizi. |
| 09/08 | | | 112 | | | | | Ibid. |
| 27/12 | 100 | | | | | | | BMV, Ms. It., cl. vii, cod. 2049 (8332-1), fol. 236. Soranzo ledger, fol. 86, uses 100 s. in registering old accounts (1419–20). |
| *1420* | | | | | | | | |
| s.d. | | | 111 | 100 | | | | Fabrizi. Collodo. |
| 00/06 | | | 112 | | | | | Fabrizi. |

| Date | | | | | Reference |
|---|---|---|---|---|---|
| 20/06 | | | | 140 | Stahl (Negroponte). |
| 26/07 | | | | 128 | Ibid. (Crete). |
| **1421** | | | | | |
| s.d. | 103 | | 111.5 | | Padovan, 366; the Soranzo ledger uses 104 s. Zanetti, 175. Fabrizi. |
| 17/01 | 103 | 104 | 101.5 | | AST, Osp. b. 334, fol. 43 (by calc.). |
| 30/04 | 103 | | | | PSM, M182, G. Condulmer. |
| 17/06 | 100 | | | | Ibid., U88, P. Signolo. |
| 30/06 | 103 | | 110 | | Fabrizi. |
| 19/08 | 103 | | | | AST, PO, no. 13, 380. |
| 22/08 | 103 | | | | Petizion, S. a g., 65, fol. 113v (4/08/1433), extract. |
| 30/09 | 103 | | | | PSM, M182, G. Condulmer. |
| 22/10 | 103 | | | | Ibid. |
| **1422** | | | | | |
| s.d. | 104 | | | | Soranzo ledger, fol. 86 (ex post accounting). |
| 07/03 | 108 | | | | Deliberation of the Senate, mentioned by Papadopoli, 1: 248; in *Cap. Broche*, 23v: old worn coins circulating at 108 s. to be called in and replaced with the new, ordered in 1421. |
| 26/03 | 100 | | | | Petizion, S. a g., 74, fol. 36 (private act as evidence in case of 19/02/1436/37). |
| 31/08 | 100 | | | | PSM, U88, P. Signolo. |
| **1423** | | | | | |
| s.d. | 104 | | 103 | | Soranzo ledger, fol. 86. Collodo. |
| 14/01 | 104 | | | | Petizion, S. a g., 90, fol. 56v (21/08/1443), quoting a contract of 1423; the exchange was set "como semo stadi de achordo de mettere el ducato." |
| 13/03 | 104 | | | | BG, 1, doc. 80. |
| 16/07 | 100 | | | | PSM, U88, P. Signolo. |
| 19/07 | | | | 75 | CF, reg. 3, fol. 8v (also 78.5 s.). |

*(continued)*

TABLE D.3. (Continued)

| Year Day/Month | Place Venice | Treviso | Udine | Padua | Verona | Zara | Greece | Sources |
|---|---|---|---|---|---|---|---|---|
| 15/09 | 104 | | | | | | | PSM, M10, fasc. ix, A. Giustinian. U88, P. Signolo. |
| 01/10 | | | | | 78 | | | SIL, 668, fol. 55r (same for 13/10 and 18/10). |
| 12/10 | 104 | | | | | | | PSM, U88, P. Signolo. |
| 24/11 | | | | 104 | | | | Collodo. |
| 01/12 | | | | | 78 | | | SIL, 668, fol. 55r (same for 2/12). |
| *1424* | | | | | | | | |
| s.d. | 103 | 103 | | | | | | Gallicciolli; Cipolla. Zanetti, 175. |
| 15/02 | 100 | | | | | | | PSM, U88, P. Signolo. |
| 15/03 | | | | | 78 | | | CF, reg. 3, fol. 11 (also 75 s.). |
| 21/07 | 100 | | | | | | | PSM, U88, P. Signolo. |
| 27/09 | 103 | | | | | | | BMV, Ms. It., cl. vii, cod. 2049 (8332–1), fols. 509–10 (farm of the dazio becharia); similar in *BG*, 1, doc. 84 (from another chronicle), with the date 17/10/1424. |
| 04/12 | | | | | | | 130 | Stahl (Crete, Modon). |
| 20/12 | | | | | | | 122 | Ibid. (officially reduced to 120 s.). |
| *1425* | | | | | | | | |
| s.d. | 104 | | | | | | | Soranzo ledger, fol. 86 (ex post accounting). |
| 07/02 | | | | | | | 140 | Stahl (Crete). |
| 12/02 | | 103 | | | | | | AST, PO, no. 5697. |
| 00/05 | | | | | 77 | | | SMSC, reg. 8, alla data. |
| 03/07 | 103 | | | | | | | PSM, U128, fasc. 3, reg. cover. |
| 02/08 | 100 | | | | | | | Ibid., U88, P. Signolo. |
| 31/08 | 104.167 | | | | | | | Soranzo ledger, fol. 122, for grossi di zecca. |
| *1426* | | | | | | | | |
| s.d. | | | | 104 | | | | Collodo. |
| 28/06 | 103 | | | | | | | PSM, U128, fasc. 5. |

| Date | | | Source |
|---|---|---|---|
| 00/11 | | | CF, reg. 3, fol. 22v. |
| **1427** | | | |
| 08/02 | 104 | | Petizion, Framm. ant., b. 13, fasc. 1445, sub Febr. (copy of account) |
| 13/07 | 105 | | Collegio, Notatorio, reg. 6, fol. 38 (wages of oarsmen). |
| **1428** | | | |
| s.d. | 104 | | Soranzo ledger, fol. 86 (ex post accounting). |
| 05/01 | 104 | 103 | Collodo. |
| 20/01 | 104 | | Petizion, S. a g., 76, fol. 68v (case of 29/03/1438). |
| 16/02 | 103 | 102 | Collodo. |
| 11/03 | 100 | 103 | PSM, U88, P. Signolo. The Collegio fixed 100 s. as the rate at which salaries of Venetian rectors were to be paid (Semi, *Capris, Iustinopolis, Capodistria*, 165). |
| 08/08 | 104 | 100 | Petizion, Framm. ant., b. 13, fasc. 1445, sub Febr. (copy of account). |
| 18/08 | 104 | | PSM, U88, P. Signolo. |
| 29/10 | 104 | | |
| **1429** | | 140 | Stahl (Negroponte). |
| 10/03 | 104 | | Collodo. |
| 10/03 | | 104 | Petizion, S. a g., 85, fol. 6iv (6/03/1441, citing private accounts of 1429). |
| 11/04 | 104 | | Petizion, Framm. ant., b. 13 (sub Febr. 1444/45). |
| 13/04 | 104 | 100 | Collodo (for one "ducato scarso"). |
| 00/07 | 104 | | Papadopoli, 1, doc. 23, and on all lists; all coinage then ordered (soldini and grossi, debased by 4 percent, and new grossoni and grossetti for Venice and the Terraferma) to circulate at 104 s., the then current rate. |
| 09/07 | | | Petizion, S. a g., 85, fol. 6iv. |
| 30/07 | 104 | | |

(*continued*)

TABLE D.3. (Continued)

| Year Day/Month | Place Venice | Treviso | Udine | Padua | Verona | Zara | Greece | Sources |
|---|---|---|---|---|---|---|---|---|
| 01/08 | 104.25 | | | | | | | BMV, Ms. It., cl. vii, cod. 2049 (8332/2), fol. 103 (for grossi). |
| 23/08 | 104 | | | | | | | Petizion, S. a g., 85, fol. 61v. |
| 07/10 | | | | | 78 | | | AAC, 57, f. 132. |
| 07/12 | 104 | | | | | | | Petizion, S. a g., 85, fol. 61v. |
| 21/12 | 104 | | | | | | | Ibid. |
| *1430* | | | | | | | | |
| 22/09 | 106 | | | | | | | Soranzo ledger, fol. 120. |
| *1431* | | | | | | | | |
| 13/02 | 106 | | | | | | | Petizion, S. a g., 61, fol. 33. |
| 18/05 | | 106 | | | | | | AST, PO, no. 14,451. |
| 14/08 | 106 | | | | | | | Barbarigo ledger A, fol. 34 (by calc.); (same on fol. 40 for 30/08). |
| 06/11 | 105.3 | | | | | | | Ibid., fol. 34 (by calc.). |
| 21/11 | 106 | | | | | | | PSM, U88, P. Signolo. |
| *1432* | | | | | | | | |
| 00/03 | | | | | 80 | | | SIL, 752, alla data. |
| 10/03 | 106.4 | | | | | | | Barbarigo ledger A, fol. 49 (by calc.). |
| 16/08 | 107 | | | | | | | Ibid., fol. 44. |
| 03/09 | 104 | | | | | | | PSM, U88, P. Signolo. |
| 08/09 | | | | 103 | | | | Collodo. |
| 25/10 | 107.5 | | | | | | | Barbarigo ledger A, fol. 43. |
| 00/12 | | | | 108 | | | | Collodo. |
| 29/12 | 108 | | | | | | | Barbarigo journal A. |
| *1433* | | | | | | | | |
| s.d. | 110 | | | | | | | Gallicciolli; Padovan, 366; Cipolla. |
| 12/02 | 108 | | | | | | | Petizion, S. a g., 65, fol. 84v (26/03/1433). |
| 03/04 | 108 | | | | | | | Senato, Misti, 58, fols. 191v–192; rate at which sailors were to be paid. |

| Date | | | | Source |
|---|---|---|---|---|
| 17/05 | | | 100 | MC, Ursa, fol. 93v; reiteration of the rule of 1428 (see above, 8/08/1428) that rectors receive their salaries at this rate. |
| **1434** | | | | |
| s.d. | 110 | | | Zanetti, 175. |
| 12/08 | | | 110 | Barbarigo ledger A, fol. 93; interest was paid on government bonds at 107 s. |
| 01/09 | | | 109.5 | Ibid., fol. 120. |
| 27/09 | | | 110 | Ibid., fol. 131. |
| **1435** | | | | |
| 12/03 | | 82 | | SIL, 1020, fol. 4. |
| 00/07 | | 80 | | Ibid., fol. 6v. |
| 20/07 | | | 110.4 | Barbarigo ledger A, fol. 170 (by calc.); another calc. for the same day reflects a rate of 116.2 s. (see ibid.). |
| 21/12 | | 82 | | SMO, reg. 26, fol. 70v. |
| **1436** | | | | |
| 15/03 | | | 111.2 | Barbarigo ledger A, fol. 160 (by calc.). |
| 13/12 | | | 111 | MC, Ursa, fol. 109, in *BG*, 1, doc. 89, and in *PRV*, doc. 23. |
| **1437** | | | | |
| 15/09 | | | 111 | Barbarigo ledger A, fol. 217. |
| 08/10 | | | 111 | Petizion, framm. ant. b. 13, fasc. 1445 (sub 4/06/1445), copy of accounts of Marchio di Colti (Dare). |
| 17/10 | | | 110 | Ibid. (Avere); same for 19/10. |
| 30/10 | | | 111 | Ibid. (Dare). |
| 04/11 | | | 111 | Ibid. (Dare). |
| **1438** | | | | |
| s.d. | | | 110 | Gallicciolli. |
| 13/05 | | 152 | | Stahl, also 153 s. (Modon). |
| 19/11 | | | 109 | PSM, U128, fasc. 3. |

*(continued)*

TABLE D.3. (*Continued*)

| Year Day/Month | Venice | Treviso | Udine | Padua | Verona | Zara | Greece | Sources |
|---|---|---|---|---|---|---|---|---|
| **1439** | | | | | | | | |
| s.d. | | | | | | | | Zanetti, 175. |
| 00/05 | 112 | 113 | | | | | | Senato, Misti, 60, fol. 143v, 12/05, but refers to an undated earlier transaction. |
| 16/07 | 112 | | | | | | | PSM, U88, P. Signolo. |
| 21/07 | 113 | | | | | | | Ibid. |
| 15/12 | 110.67 | | | | | | | Barbarigo ledger A, fol. 268 (by calc.). |
| **1440** | | | | | | | | |
| s.d. | 114 | | | | | | | Avogaria di Comun, 3649, fols. 76v–77; an audit of the accounts of the Treasury of Verona, effected in 1449, demonstrated a form of embezzlement: sums received at 114 s. were entered in the books at 116 s. |
| 22/04 | 114 | | | | | | | Senato, Misti, 60, fol. 209v, regards an impositio payable "de grossonis ad soldos 114 pro ducato." |
| 05/12 | 114 | | | | | | | Barbarigo ledger B, fol. 30 (by calc.) |
| **1441** | | | | | | | | |
| s.d. | 113 | 114 | | | | | | Cipolla. Zanetti, 176. In the same case as cited above, the Avogadori discovered that sums recorded at 112–14 s. were payed out at 115–16 s. |
| 00/07 | 114 | | | | | | | PSM, C189, fasc. 6, several q for July, Aug., Sept. |
| 04/10 | | | | | | | 154 | Stahl (Crete). |
| 17/10 | | | | | | | 160 | Ibid. (Negroponte). |
| 05/11 | | 114 | | | | | | AST, Osp, b. 1, loose sheet at fol. 4s. |
| **1442** | | | | | | | | |
| s.d. | 114 | | | | | | | Gallicciolli. |

(continued)

| Date | | | | Reference |
|---|---|---|---|---|
| 13/01 | | | 86 | SIL, 1024, fol. 90. |
| 07/02 | 114 | | | PSM, C189, fasc. 6. |
| 08/02 | | | 85.5 | SIL, 1024, fol. 90v. |
| 11/02 | 113.7 | 154 | | Stahl (Crete). |
| 15/02 | | | 86 | Barbarigo journal B (by calc.). |
| 24/02 | | | | SIL, 1024, fol. 91. |
| 05/03 | | 114 | | AST, Osp., b. 1, loose sheet at fol. 45 (by calc.). |
| 24/03 | | | 86 | SIL, 1024, fol. 91v. |
| 03/08 | 113.8 | | | Barbarigo journal B (by calc.). |
| 21/11 | 114 | | | PSM, C189, fasc. 4. |
| 17/12 | | 152 | | Stahl (Crete). |
| **1443** | | | | |
| s.d. | 114 | | 86 | Burani; Archivio Prop. Trevisan, filza 17, Cecchetti; and Cipolla, but their reference is to Jan. more veneto, i.e., 1444. For Verona: SIL, regs. 1027–29, passim. |
| 22/03 | 113.5 | | | Barbarigo ledger B, fol. 109 (by calc.). |
| 09/05 | 114 | | | PSM, C189, fasc. 6. |
| 07/06 | 111 | | | Ibid., fol. 25v. The Barbarigo ledger B, fol. 109, gives 118 s. for 29/06 (by calc.). |
| 24/12 | 114 | | | Barbarigo ledger B, fol. 109 (by calc.). |
| **1444** | | | | |
| s.d. | | | 86 | SIL, regs. 1027–29, passim. |
| 23/01 | 114 | | | Gallicciolli; Padovan, 135, 366; Papadopoli, 1, doc. 24. |
| 30/04 | 114 | | | Petizion, framm. ant. b. 13, fasc. 1445 (sub. 8/04/1445), copy of an account for a debt of 10 du.: 4 are paid in gold, 6 in "monede" at 112 s., while the total is calculated at 114 s. |
| 06/10 | 114 | | 86 | Barbarigo ledger B, fols. 121, 130 (3q); for 10/03 at 117 s., fol. 121 (by calc.). |
| **1445** | | | | |
| s.d. | | | 86 | SIL, regs. 1027–29, passim. |

TABLE D.3. (Continued)

| Year Day/Month | Place | | | | | | | Sources |
|---|---|---|---|---|---|---|---|---|
| | Venice | Treviso | Udine | Padua | Verona | Zara | Greece | |
| 23/08 | 114 | | | | | | | Barbarigo ledger B, fols. 130, 145 (2q). |
| 23/08 | 110 | | | | | | | PSM, U88, P. Signolo; inventory of the sack, "computando monetas ad refusum s. 110 per duc." |
| 05/12 | 114 | | | | | | | PSM, M10, fasc. x, A. Giustinian household accounts, fol. 3 (hereafter A. Giustinian). |
| 07/12 | 114 | | | | | | | Barbarigo ledger B, fol. 161 (2q). |
| *1446* | | | | | | | | |
| s.d. | | | | | 86 | | | SIL, regs. 1027–29, passim. |
| 04/03 | 114 | | | | | | | A. Giustinian, fol. 3. |
| 23/08 | 114 | | | | | | | Scuola Grande della Misericordia, b. 198, Notatorio, fol. 8; interest on bonds paid out at 111 s. |
| *1447* | | | | | | | | |
| 17/01 | 114 | | | | | | | A. Giustinian, fols. 3, 8. |
| 03/02 | 114 | | | | | | | Ibid. (also Barbarigo ledger B, fol. 130, 28/02). |
| 19/03 | | | | | 86 | | | SIL, 1029, fols. 58r-v, 59 (same for 20/03 and 22/03). |
| 29/03 | 114 | | | | | | | A. Giustinian, fols. 3, 8. |
| 04/04 | 114 | | | | | | | Ibid. |
| 20/05 | 114 | | | | | | | Ibid. |
| 12/09 | | | | | 85.5 | | | SIL, 1030, fol. 17v. |
| *1448* | | | | | | | | |
| 18/01 | 114 | | | | | | | A. Giustinian, fols. 3, 8. |
| 16/03 | 114 | | | | | | | Ibid. |
| 02/06 | 114 | | | | | | | Barbarigo ledger B, fol. 180. |
| 25/07 | 114 | | | | | | | A. Giustinian, fols. 3, 8. |
| 03/08 | 114 | | | | | | | Barbarigo ledger B, fol. 209. |
| 11/09 | 114 | | | | | | | Ibid., fol. 218. |

| Date | | | Reference |
|------|------|------|-----------|
| 11/10 | | 114 | A. Giustinian. |
| 03/11 | | 114 | Barbarigo ledger B, fol. 217. |
| **1449** | | | |
| 14/02 | | 114 | A. Giustinian, fol. 8. |
| 18/04 | | 114 | *PRV*, doc. 265; *BG*, 1, doc. 93. |
| 02/05 | | 114 | A. Giustinian, fol. 8. |
| 07/06 | | 114 | Barbarigo ledger B, fol. 222. |
| 12/11 | | 114 | PSM, M145, L. Corner (4q). |
| 24/12 | | 114 | A. Giustinian, fol. 8. |
| **1450** | | | |
| 09/02 | | 114 | Ibid., fols. 3, 8, 12 (also for 25/02). Gallicciolli and Zon give 124 s., s.d.; they mistook the year, which should be 1455. |
| 04/03 | | 114 | A. Giustinian, fols. 3, 8, 12 (also for 23/03). |
| 11/03 | 174 | | Stahl (Crete). |
| 10/06 | | 114 | A. Giustinian, fols. 3, 8, 12. |
| 06/07 | | 114 | Misericordia, 198, Notatorio, fol. 10; interest on bonds, paid at 113 s., is entered at 114 s. |
| 01/08 | | 114 | A. Giustinian, fols. 3, 8, 12. |
| 07/09 | | 114 | Ibid. |
| 22/09 | 152 | | Stahl (Crete). |
| **1451** | | | |
| 18/01 | | 114 | A. Giustinian, fols. 3, 8, 12. |
| 28/06 | | 114 | Ibid. |
| 06/08 | | 114 | Ibid. (4q from 6/08 to 28/08). |
| 28/09 | | 114 | A. Giustinian, fols. 3, 8, 12. |
| 05/10 | | 114 | Ibid. |
| 03/12 | | 114 | Ibid. |
| **1452** | | | |
| s.d. | 116 | 116 | Burani; Cipolla. Zanetti, 176. |
| 07/01 | | 114 | A. Giustinian, fols. 12–14. |
| 07/02 | | 114 | Ibid. |

*(continued)*

TABLE D.3. (Continued)

| Year / Day/Month | Venice | Treviso | Udine | Padua | Verona | Zara | Greece | Sources |
|---|---|---|---|---|---|---|---|---|
| 05/03 | 114 | | | | | | | PSM, M63, F. Marcello ("deducto lazio sachulorum monetarum a s. III usque ad s. 114"). |
| 16/06 | 114 | | | | | | | A. Giustinian. |
| 12/07 | 114 | | | | | | | Ibid. |
| 17/07 | | | | | 86 | | | SIL, 1031, fol. 59. |
| 05/08 | 114 | | | | | | | A. Giustinian. |
| 05/09 | 114 | | | | | | | Ibid. (same for 17/09). |
| 00/10 | | | | | 86 | | | SIL, 1031, fol. 17v. |
| 21/11 | 114 | | | | | | | A. Giustinian. |
| 15/12 | 114 | | | | | | | Senato, Terra, 3, fol. 48v; the mint was ordered to pay in piccoli a loan of 1,000 du. to a Jew of Vicenza; by calc. |
| **1453** | | | | | | | | |
| s.d. | | 120 | | | | | | Zanetti, 176. |
| 22/01 | 114 | | | | 87 | | | A. Giustinian, fol. 4. SIL, 1031, fol. 88. |
| 25/01 | 115 | | | | 86 | | | A. Giustinian, fol. 12. SIL, 1031, fol. 88. |
| 12/04 | 120 | | | | | | | A. Giustinian, fol. 20. |
| 10/07 | 116 | | | | | | | Ibid., fol. 4. |
| 04/08 | 116 | | | | | | | Ibid., fol. 18. |
| 23/08 | 120 | | | | | | | Senato, Terra, 3, fol. 75v: "parvuli veneti" ordered coined and passed to the Arsenal to pay for construction of galleys: 3,000 ducats' worth "at £ 6 per du." |
| 30/09 | 120 | | | | | | | A. Giustinian, fol. 12. On 18/09 the Senate took note that many silver coins and piccoli were being minted, but little gold (Senato, Terra, 3, fol. 79). |

| Date | s. | | Reference |
|---|---|---|---|
| 09/10 | 118 | | A. Giustinian, fol. 13. |
| 05/11 | 118 | | PRV, doc. 270; immediate payment of a forced levy could be made "in grossetis" at 116 s.; after one week, payment was to be rendered half in silver at 118 s., half in ducats. |
| 15/11 | 120 | | A. Giustinian, fol. 12. |
| 10/12 | 120 | | Ibid., fol. 13 (also 28/12). |
| **1454** | | | |
| s.d. | 124 | | Zanetti, 176 (perhaps an error for 1455). |
| 02/01 | 120 | | A. Giustinian, fol. 18. |
| 22/01 | 120 | | Senato, Terra, 3, fol. 97v: taxes and dues may be paid half in gold, half in grossetti, at £ 6 per du. |
| 23/05 | 120 | | A. Giustinian, fol. 4. |
| 23/08 | 120 | 90 | Ibid. |
| 14/09 | 120 | | SIL, 1031, fol. 8. |
| 08/10 | 120 | 90 | A. Giustinian, fol. 13 (un unghero d'oro). |
| 31/10 | 120 | | SIL, 1031, fol. 174. |
| 30/11 | 120 | | Senato, Terra, 3, fol. 137: some dues may still be paid at 120 s., "but those who owe the State for bills of exchange must pay in gold, for they used our money meanwhile, and should not benefit from the low rate permitted for 'monete'." Arts professors at Padua are paid at 100 s.; ibid., fol. 137. |
| 03/12 | 122.29 | | A. Giustinian, fol. 20. |
| 04/12 | 122 | | Ibid. |
| **1455** | | | |
| 15/01 | 123 | | Ibid. On 7/01 the Salt Office was ordered to pay importers "sicut currit ducatus" and not at 120 s., the rate at which tax farms were sold (Senato, Terra, 3, fol. 142). |

(continued)

TABLE D.3. (Continued)

| Day/Month | Venice | Treviso | Udine | Padua | Verona | Zara | Greece | Sources |
|---|---|---|---|---|---|---|---|---|
| | | | | | | | | **Place** |
| 25/01 | 122 | | | | | | | A. Giustinian, fols. 16, 20 (also 123 s.). |
| 20/02 | 123 | | | | | | | Ibid., fol. 20. |
| 01/03 | 123 | | | | | | | Petizion, b. 955, cash book of Leonardo Sanudo (hereafter simply L. Sanudo). |
| 03/03 | 124 | | | | | | | L. Sanudo (same on 6/03). |
| 08/03 | 123.5 | | | | | | | L. Sanudo. |
| 10/03 | 123 | | | | | | | Ibid.; same entry, fol. 4v, also gives 124.5 s. |
| 12/03 | 124 | | | | | | | A. Giustinian, fol. 12. |
| 17/03 | 123 | | | | | | | Ibid., fol. 16. |
| 20/03 | 122.8 | | | | | | | Ibid., fol. 21. |
| 26/03 | 123 | | | | | | | A. Giustinian; and L. Sanudo. |
| 14/04 | 124 | | | | | | | L. Sanudo. |
| 16/05 | 124 | | | | | | | A. Giustinian, fol. 17. The Sanudo accounts give 125 s. |
| 18/05 | 124 | | | | | | | L. Sanudo (also 125 s.). |
| 13/06 | 124 | | | | | | | A. Giustinian, fol. 17. |
| 02/08 | 124 | | | | | | | BG, 1, doc. 109: State offices were to take in revenues all in gold, or half in gold, half in monete at 124 s. per du. In his footnote, Besta quite correctly calls this the "fixing" of rates dated by Papadopoli and others (later also by Cipolla) only from the reforms of 1472. |
| 20/08 | 124 | | | | | | | A. Giustinian, fol. 4. |
| 23/09 | 124 | | | | | | | PSM, C189, fasc. 6, fol. 56. |
| 07/12 | 124 | | | | | | | A. Giustinian, fol. 4. |

| Date | | | Source / Notes |
|---|---|---|---|
| 1456 s.d. | 124 | | A. Giustinian; and L. Sanudo, all months. |
| 1457 s.d. | 124 | | Ibid., several months. Exception: 14/05, ducats at 126 s. with "fiorini" at 124 s. (L. Sanudo, fol. 72). |
| 15/02 | | 175.5 | Stahl (Nauplia). |
| 1458 s.d. | 124 | 152 | A. Giustinian, several months; also Mensa patriarcale, b. 154. Stahl (Crete). |
| 1459 s.d. | 124 | | A. Giustinian, June and Oct. |
| 1460 s.d. | 124 | | Ibid., Jan. and June. |
| 1461 s.d. | 124 | | Ibid., Jan.; and PSM, U217, fasc. 4, Dec. By this time the rate of 124 s. was taken for granted (see, e.g., PSM, M78, account books of Gerolamo Morosini). |
| 1464 26/09 | | 156 | Stahl (Crete). |
| 1466 02/03 | | 198 | Stahl (Corfu). |
| 1472 06/06 | 124 | | After a brief dip in rates resulting from demonetization, the rate of 124 s. was reaffirmed by the monetary reform, on which see below, vol. 2. |
| 1472–1508 | 124 | | The rate remained stable until the period of the War of the League of Cambrai (1509–16). |

# APPENDIX E

# SILVER: SPECIAL PROBLEMS

## i. STANDARDS OF FINENESS

A good general explanation of various medieval methods of defining and measuring the fineness of refined silver is in Carlo Cipolla's *Le avventure della lira*.[1]

The fineness of the Venetian grosso is given by Papadopoli as 0.965 in the modern system of thousandths by starting from Pegolotti's statement of its fineness in the duodecimal system in use in his native Florence (explained by Cipolla). Papadopoli converted that first into the Venetian system, which described fineness according to the number of copper (or nonsilver) carats in the 1,152 carats that constituted 1 Venetian mark.[2]

Grossi were thus described as "peggio 40," meaning that 40 out of 1,152 carats were not silver. Since $(1,152 - 40)/1,152 = 0.965$, and since that agreed well enough with chemical analyses of coins, Papadopoli used that figure. He ignored the statement in the first chapter of the mintmasters' statute of 1278 that, in addition to specifying how many grossi were to be cut from 1 mark of metal, specified that the metal be "de tam bono argento, quod non callet ultra medium quarterium pro marcha vel inde inferius,

[1]Pp. 126–31, esp. nn. 22 and 23, to which it may be added that Venetians occasionally expressed fineness using their system of ounces, of which there were 8 in a mark; a fineness of 0.9525 was stated as "d'onc. 7, q.2-1/2."

[2]See above, table A.1; Papadopoli, 1:84–86; and Pegolotti, *Pratica*, 289. Pegolotti gives the fineness as 11 oncie 14 denari; 12 oncie = 288 denari (of 24 to the oncia); 278/288 = 0.96527.

ad racionem boni argenti."[3] Since a quarterio, or quarto, a fourth of the Venetian ounce, contained 36 carats, this clause of the statute required that grossi be of the fineness of (1,152 − 18)/1,152, or 0.984, if "ad racionem boni argenti" meant pure silver. But an alternative interpretation of the clause quoted might be that "bonum argentum" meant silver of the standard of the grosso (argento di bolla) and that a margin of error in attaining exactly that standard was allowed, a tolerance (remedy) of 18 carats, or 1.6 percent. It seems best to accept Papadopoli's—and Pegolotti's—figure, 0.965. Craig gives the "remedy" for fineness at the English mint as 10.4 parts in 1,000, reduced in 1350 to 8.3 parts.[4]

A later statement prohibited the mintmasters from accepting "aliquod argentum factum in Veneciis quod sit peius de denariis sex pro marcha."[5] A reference to 6 "denari parvi" appears earlier in a decree of 1273 which can be rendered as follows: "Motion passed: that silver should not be used to cast ingots unless of the fineness of grossi. And if it is less fine but not worse by more than 6 small denari per mark [that is, 6 denari out of a mark of 192 denari, giving a fineness of 0.969], the masters of the mint of the Commune of the Venetians should pay 11 lire 13 soldi for silver for [making] grosso coins. And if the silver be of higher fineness than a grosso coin, the mintmasters are to pay accordingly."[6]

The same decree goes on to state how much copper should be added to make the kind of silver bars that in later decrees were called "sterling." The fineness of sterling was peggio 86, so that 46 carats of copper were added to the silver of the fineness of grossi (for 46 is to 1,152 as 32 is to 800).

The Venetian standard in 1335 for industrial silver was 0.903, namely, less pure by 72 carats per mark than the grosso ([1,152 − 40 − 72]/1,152 carats). A change in October 1335 permitted industrial silver to be only 18 carats less fine than sterling, namely, 0.910 ([1,152 − 40 − 46 − 18]/1,152). A motion passed in December, however, restored the old standard by requiring that the jewelers' silver be 72 carats less fine than the grosso.[7]

To summarize, the standards of fine silver were as follows:

| | | |
|---|---|---|
| Grossi | 1,112/1,152 = | 0.965 fine |
| Sterling | 1,066/1,152 = | 0.925 fine |
| Industrial | 1,040/1,152 = | 0.903 fine |

A merchant's list of 1418 gives 0.875 as the fineness of the silver used for silverware in Venice. That indicates a decline somewhat greater than

[3]Papadopoli, 1:311; *PMV*, doc. 25, p. 16.
[4]Craig, *The Mint*, 51.
[5]Papadopoli, 1:334, cap. 112.
[6]*PMV*, doc. 20.
[7]ASV, Zecca, b. 6bis, fols. 23, 25v.

the decline in Venice's finest silver coins, for which 0.953 is indicated by the figures in that manual.[8]

## ii. THE INCOME FROM THE QUINTO

How much the import tax embedded in the quinto amounted to can be roughly estimated in four ways:

1. For the period 1331–69 the mint charge on the soldini made from the quinto averaged about 30 percent.[9] Three percent seems a liberal allowance for the cost of minting, since on grossi the mint charge had been only about 2 percent and additional cost for the smaller coin probably did not exceed 1 percent. Subtracting 3 percent from the mint charge leaves 27 percent as a minimum estimate of the mint charge on unfree silver in excess of costs. Collecting an additional 27 percent on 1/5 was equivalent to collecting 5.4 percent on the whole amount of silver imported.

2. In 1353 the mint was ordered to coin all free silver that might be offered by purveyors for a mint charge of 7.4 percent. The charge seems very high compared with contemporary Florentine charges or with the 5.3 percent charged on the English penny.[10] The mint charge on soldini struck from unfree silver was also set very high in 1353, at 33.9 percent. Applying the difference of 26.5 percent ($33.9 - 7.4$) to 1/5 of all imports amounted to collecting 5.3 percent on total imports.

3. Enforcement officials asserted in 1344, when the quinto had been cut in half to a decimo, that the Commune lost 3 grossi on each mark of imported silver that avoided being registered and thus escaped the decimo.[11] Three grossi equal about 6.5 soldi a grossi (3 grossi = 3 × [26.111/12] = 6.5), which is 2.167 percent of the price of a mark of silver (6.5/300).[12] The quinto's yield would have been twice that, 4.3 percent.

4. In contrast, the figures concerning the mezzanini of 1349 (analyzed above, in app. A, sec. vi) indicate that out of a total mint charge of 26 percent on the unfree silver, about 14 percent was "cost" and about 12 percent "profit," but there are indications that the figure for "cost" was padded.

---

[8]Borlandi, ed., *Manuale de' Ricci*, 146–48. On the reduction in the fineness of grossi from 0.965 to 0.952 see above, table A.2.

[9]See above, table A.3.

[10]See Bernocchi, 3:181, 188; and Feavearyear, *The Pound Sterling*, 346.

[11]ASV, Grazie, reg. 11, fol. 11.

[12]See above, table C.1.

## iii. THE BIMETALLIC RATIO ABOUT A.D. 1250

According to A. Nagl, there was no evidence from which to determine the bimetallic ratio at Florence in 1252.[13] In his "Memoria" presented in the same year, Desimoni found evidence that it was 8.3555 to 1 and that at Genoa it was 8.542 to 1.[14] Robert S. Lopez follows Desimoni and adds evidence regarding Genoa and the general credibility of the lower ratio. From one contract in Genoa in 1253 he works out a ratio of 8.16 to 1.[15] But the figures that Desimoni used were criticized by Robert Davidsohn,[16] and Carlo Cipolla gives the ratio at Florence in mid-century as 10 to 1.[17] The disagreement arises from the difficulty in determining the silver content of the silver coin on which the Florentine lira was based when the gold florin was first coined. David Herlihy has written on the silver coinage in Tuscany previously,[18] and recently M. Bernocchi has presented a full display and analysis of coins and documents.[19] Supplemented by statements in later merchant manuals about the fineness of Florentine coins, these sources permit the conclusions that sometime between 1250 and 1260, Florence minted a silver groat called the "fiorino vecchio da denari 12" and that when 1 lire equaled 20 of these and also 1 gold florin, the bimetallic ratio was 8.99 to 1.[20] Bernocchi gives figures indicating a ratio of 8.96 to 1.[21] If the Florentine lira was based on 240 of the Pisan denari as minted in 1258, the bimetallic ratio was 8.81 to 1. Bernocchi concludes that when the florin was coined, the bimetallic ratio was certainly below 9 to 1.[22]

A ratio of 8.5 to 1 for 1252 is supported if we assume that the Florentine lira was based on those silver and billon coins of about that date that had the lowest silver content compared with their value in the money of account. The figure 8.5 represents also about the low point at which a long downward trend ended and gold began to increase in value in Europe. Probably it represented a dip occasioned by the crusade of Louis IX of France that ended with his capture in Egypt. The whole crusade involved

---

[13]"Die Goldwährung," 113–29, 139.

[14]"La moneta e il rapporto dell'oro all'argento," 32–35.

[15]See his *Settecento anni fa*, 36–37; see also idem, "Back to Gold," 234.

[16]*Forschungen*, 4:321.

[17]*Le avventure della lira*, 56, 132.

[18]"Pisan Coinage and the Monetary Development of Tuscany, 1150–1250." *American Numismatic Society Museum Notes* 6 (1954):143–66, revised in *Le zecche minori toscane fino al XIV secolo* (Pistoia, [1975]), 169–92.

[19]*Le monete della repubblica fiorentina*.

[20]Bernocchi, 3:134–35.

[21]Ibid., 60.

[22]Ibid., 59–60.

sending much silver east. Even then, giving the gold florin the legal value of only 1 Florentine lira probably intentionally undervalued gold and thus encouraged the export of florins from Florence.

Giuseppe Felloni, by compiling prices of gold and silver bullion, found that the bimetallic ratio touched its lowest point, at 8.5, in 1253.[23] The calculations above[24] concerning the values implied in the Venetian maritime statutes of 1255 contain so many questionable assumptions that they cannot claim to be *proof* that a similarly low ratio was used at Venice, but those calculations and the establishment in Crete of the ratio of 1 perpero to 12 grossi[25] do indicate that assuming a ratio of about 8.5 to 1 at Venice also about 1252 is, in light of the evidence at present available, more reasonable than assuming a higher ratio.

[23]"Profilo," 222, 246–47.
[24]In chap. 13, nn. 39–47.
[25]Ibid., nn. 31–35.

# APPENDIX F

# THE "QUINDEXENA"

s explained in chapter 12, in the thirteenth century in the silver mint each mintmaster served in rotation as managing mintmaster ("massaro della quindena" or "quindexena"), associate mintmaster, and then backup mintmaster. The length of the term of duty called a "quindena" or "quindexena" is important not only for understanding the administration of the mint but also for making estimates of the mint's rate of production.

The meaning of the term "quindexena" changed over the centuries. Obviously the length was originally two weeks—fifteen days—but its length was already much longer at least as early as the compilation of the mint's capitolare of 1278. Among its provisions is the requirement that the mintmasters render accounts at the end of six months and turn over the profits due the Commune within fifteen days of the end of their term. One might be tempted to interpret the clause as meaning that the term of the managing mintmaster was six months, but the statement of obligation is modified at the beginning and end of the sentence by the phrase "simul cum sociis meis."[1] That phrase suggests that the three mintmasters reported together at the end of six months, after each of them had served as managing mintmaster for a quindena two months in length.

Although this interpretation might seem strained if it stood alone, other early indications of a two-month quindena make it preferable. In the

---

[1] Papadopoli, 1:312; *PMV*, doc. 25, caps. 27, 28.

gold mint in 1410 and presumably earlier the length of the quindena or quindexena was clearly two months.[2]

The earliest explicit statement of the length of the quindena in the silver mint is in a decree of the Quarantia in 1349. It says that a mintmaster had then in his quindena forty days in which to accept silver from merchants, twenty days in which to pay the merchants, and then a month to settle his account with the Commune. It ordered that thereafter he would have thirty days for receiving silver and must settle his accounts more quickly.[3] Excluding that final settling-up month from his terms as the managing mintmaster left him thirty days as massaro della quindena, but the sixty days might sometimes all be referred to as in his quindena.

In agreement with the indications that the quindena was two months already in the thirteenth century is the order in 1291 for the production of 250 marks of piccoli each quindena. That amount is not much more than the mint's production of piccoli when operating at "full capacity" for two months, as estimated from the regulations of that time.[4]

In 1416 a new rotation of duties among three mintmasters was defined as follows: one of the three was to be in charge of silver for one month, another in charge of silver the next month, the third in charge of torneselli for two months. Then they were to rotate so that none stayed in charge of silver for more than one month or of torneselli for more than two months. After his term as managing mintmaster, each was to submit his completed accounts to the Offitiales Rationum Novarum. In that assignment of duties, "quindexena" clearly referred to the one month of managing; it did not include the following month for the submission of accounts.[5] The need of that added time for rendering accounts was recognized shortly thereafter by giving the mintmaster who had been managing the making of torneselli as much as four months in which to complete his accounts.[6]

It seems that when the Council of Ten took over and ordered the "quindexena" reduced from six months to four months, they were including the whole series of rotating terms, including the accounting periods.[7]

---

[2]ASV, Zecca, b. 6tris, cap. 66 and fol. 37, which says of the mintmaster, "Il qual debea far la sua quindexena de mexi II." Cf. ASV, Avogaria di Comun, Raspe, reg. 3646, II, fols. 106–7 (1414–15).

[3]*PMV,* doc. 107.

[4]Papadopoli, 1:327, cap. 89; above, app. B, sec. i.

[5]ASV, Senato, Misti, reg. 51, fols. 124v–125r, printed in *Cap. Broche* in footnote to fol. 17v: "Itaque aliquis ipsorum non possit stare in quindecena ad argentum nisi per unum mensem et ad tornexios mensibus duobus."

[6]*Cap. Broche,* fols. 17v–18r.

[7]Ibid., fol. 45v.

"Quindexena" was then used also in a generic sense for any rotating term of office, as in the assignment of duties to the gastaldi.[8]

Earlier the accounts of the nobleman Alvise Giustinian, who served for many years as the pesador in the silver mint, indicate terms of six months from one rendering of accounts to the next.[9]

[8]Ibid., end of fol. 47r.
[9]PSM, Misti, b. 8, fasc. 2.

# APPENDIX G

# DOCUMENTS

*1. Regulation of ca. 1268 regarding the exchange rates to be applied by the customs officials of the Ternaria when making their collections.* Capitulare Visdominorum Ternarie, *BMV, Ms. Lat., cl. V, cod. 6 (2380), cap. 17, fols. 10v–11v. See above, chap. 14, n. 25.*

apitulum ad petendum et excuciendum datium de una pro centenario et de denariis sex pro libra.
Item studiosus ero cum sotiis meis vel cum uno eorum bona fide sine fraude ad petendum et excutiendum ab omnibus illis qui mercationes adduxerint de Romania, Levante, Barbaria, Cicilia, Calabria, Apulia, Marchia, Ancona, Romagna, Ystria et Sclavonia[1] dacium quod ordinatum est tolli de ipsis mercationibus, videlicet, s. xx pro centenario [de lib.] de omnibus mercationibus supradictis, Salvo de pelamine quod debeo accipere sex denarios pro lib., excepto pelamine quod veniet ad fonticum, de quo non me intromittam. Et ex[ce]ptis caseo et carnibus salatis, et de olio de quibus aliud datium ordinatum est tolli sicut dictum est supra. Sciendum est etiam quod de amidalis, nucibus, ficubus et nucellis et castaneis, datium aliquod accipere non debemus.
Et supradictum datium exigam et executiam hoc modo, videlicet, de mercationibus que venient de ultramare, si aducte fuerint per Venetum exigam et accipiam a Veneto qui aduxerit de s. xxxii biç. ad s. xxxii.

Item biç. Armenie fiat ad d[i]remis x pro biç. saracenato fiat ad sol. xxxii.

Item pro biç. de Cepro saracenato s. xxxii.

Item pro biç. de Alexandria sol. Lv.

Item pro yperpero de Crete, de Nigroponte et quocumque parte quod habeant yperpero ad grossos xii, sol. xxx.

Item de yperpero de Clarentia et Corone et Motone et de omnibus partibus ubi currunt asterlini xx pro yperpero fiant s. xxvi.

Item de yperpero [de] Constantinopoli et de Sanlonica et toto imperio s. xxxiii.

Item de yperpero de Sclavania [sic] ad grossos xii, sol. xxx.[2]

Item de biç. Barbarie s. xiii.

Item de Apulia lib. x pro unçia.

Item xviii libr. Anchontanorum valoris s. xx de grossis permaneat in sua firmitate.

Item asperi biritati de Gaçaria currunt xx pro yperpero de Constantinopoli veniunt sol. xxxiii pro yperpero.

Item asperi cummanati currunt xi pro yperpero.

Item asperi soldanini de Turchia currunt x÷ pro yperpero de Constantinopoli veniunt triginta tres sol. pro yperpero, accipiendo sacramentum de faciendo solucionem de rebus quas adduxerint tam pro se quam pro aliis veruntamen si dictum datium erit a xx sol. infra, accipiam fidantiam sicut michi bonum videbitur. Si vero dicte mercationes adducte fuerint per forasterium accipiam a foresterio pleçariam de manifestando michi illum qui eas ement et pesum et quantitatem et numerum. Et studiosus ero ab illo emptore predictum datium excutere ut dictum est.

[1]From *Marchia* to *Sclavonia* not in *DMC*, 2:284.
[2]Contrast *DMC*, 3:331 (February 1292/93).

*2. Decree of the Senate, 1333, regarding the payment in various Levantine moneys of freights fixed in grossi. ASV, Senato, Misti, reg. 15, fol. 66v. See above, chaps. 10, sec. iii, and 15, sec. iii.*

13 March 1333
+ Capta[1]

Quod meçanini et soldini debeant curere in Creta e in aliis partibus nobis subdictis que videbuntur et sic scribatur nostris rectoribus.

+ Capta

Cum sepissime questiones venient inter patrones galearum et navium et mercatores de restis nabulorum et occasione mensarum, Vadit pars quod si dictis patronis restaret aliquid habere de naulis in Constantinopoli aut occasione mensarum debeant recipere in solutionem yperperum unum pro grossis xiii÷; et similiter in Tana et per totam Gazariam debeant recipere aspros xv pro grossis xii; et similiter recipiant in Trapesunda aspros cavalarios xiiii pro grossis xii. Et hec scribantur rectoribus nostris ad quos spectant, ut ius tribuant habentibus si questio coram eis moveretur.[2]

+ Capta

Et simili modo observetur in Cypro et Harmenia de nabulis et mensa quod accipi debeant in Cypro pro grossis xii bisancios albos ii÷, et in Harmenia pro grossis xii taculinos xiii.[3]

---

[1]Here and below a single cross signifies that the law was passed.

[2]In the margin at this point is the following notation: "die xvi marcii facte fuerunt littere baiulo Constantinopoli et consuli Tane."

[3]See the calendars published in Cessi, Sambin, and Brunetti, eds., *Le deliberazioni dei Rogati*, 2:138–39, nos. 485–87, which contain one misprint: *11* rather than *12* grossi for Tana and Gazaria; printed partially in *L'armeno-veneto*, 103.

*3. Decree of the Council of Forty, 1338, regulating the sale of bullion and coin by German merchants at the banks of campsores on the Rialto, mediated by brokers at the Fondaco dei Tedeschi. ASV, Secreta, Capitolare dei Capi Sestiere, cap. 134, fols. 50–52. The original decree was in a register of the Quarantia that is no longer extant. See above, chap. 9, sec. iv.*

10 December 1338

Captum fuit in XL

Quod missete fontici theotonicorum teneantur ducere suos mercatores ab argento cum toto suo argento per tabulas canbij ad vendendum cui sibi plus dederit, et penes quas incurunt missete contrafacientes et alie persone ementes vel consulentes emere argentum vel monetam cuniatum alibi quam inter duas scalas.

Cum sit totis viribus intendendum quod ordines statu[i]ti per terras inviolabiliter observentur nec ullatenus subrumpantur. Et quidam ordo factus est et stabillitus fuisset in MCCLXXXII die XXVIII octubris per maius conscilium super facto argenti quod non posset vendi nisi inter duas scallas,[1] qui ordo violari videntur et frangi per nonnullos qui non timea[n]t in comunis preiudicium atentare, de quo comune non modicum dampni patitur pro suo quinto quod deberet poni in cecca; eciam campsores senciunt dampnum propter magnos affictus quos solvunt ad presens, et eciam mercatores qui deberent habere argentum pro navigando, quod propterea habere non possunt.

Capta fuit pars ut tot maliciis obvietur quod quicunque misseta tractaverit, fecerit sive operam dederit de vendendo argentum sive vendi faciendo contra ordinem antedictum, perdere debeat libras XXX, soldos XII÷ et priventur perpetuo de messataria et cridatur sperçurus in scallis, prout in dicto conscilio continetur. Et teneantur missete fontici ducere suos mercatores per tabulas canbii cum toto argento quod habuerint dicti mercatores, pro vendendo illud argentum illis qui plus eis dederit.

Item, quod si aliquis mercator quecumque condicionis existat videre[t] argentum vel alia[m]² monetam cuniatam que vendatur ad marcham alibi quam inter dictas duas scalla[s], ubicumque fuerit, tam pro emendo quam consullendo de dicto argento, cadat de libris trecentis, non faciendo mercatum; et si mercatum aliquo modo conpleretur vel fieret, perdat emptor totum illud argentum et monetam sic emptum [sic], si illud argentum ascendet trecentis libris supra vel vallorem dicti argenti; et si dictum argentum ascendet a libris trecentis infra, cadat solum de libris trecentis, non perdendo illud argentum. Et comittatur vicedominis fontici, pesatoribus argenti, consulibus, officialibus missetarie, officialibus grossorum tonsorum, provisoribus comunis, capitibus postarum, cataveribus, dominis de nocte, capitibus sexteriorum, justiciis novis et veteribus, quod inquirant et inquiri faciant de predictis et excuciant dictas penas. Et officiales ad quorum officium primo facta fuerit accusacio et exacta pena habeant tercium, tercium comune et tercium accusator, si accusator inde fuerit, per cuius accusacionem veritas habeatur, intelligendo quod si venditor talis argenti fuerit accusator habere debeat dictam partem prout alius qui accusaret. Verum, si aliquis homo prout condicionis contra comissit et non haberet unde valleret solvere dictam poenam stet uno anno in carcere vel solvat penam predictam.

Item, quod quicunque videret argentum sive emeret, modis quibus dictum est superius, scilicet contra ordinem antedictum,³ [banitur] de fontico per quinque annos, ita quod non possit conversari vel ire in fontico sub pena standi medio anno in carcerem [sic] vel solvendi penam librarum centum, quam penam vicedomini fontici excutere teneantur, non intelligendo hunc ordinem in eam [campsores] platee, quibus non sit prohibitum emere argentum super suis tabullis, tantum prout facere consueverunt. Et de predictis non possit fieri gracia, nisi per sex consciliarios, tria capita de XL et XXXV de XL. Et comittatur vicedominis fontici quod predicta omnia cridari faciant singulis tribus mensibus in fontico semel ad minus. Et provisores teneantur omni medio anno ipsa publice cridari

facere semel ad minus in scallis Rivoalti et Sancti Marci, ut possint omnibus clare manifesta.

[1]See the text in *DMC*, 3:12, doc. 55.

[2]The words *vel alia* and *quecumque* were repeated on two lines and out of place by the copyist, here corrected.

[3]*Ordinem* repeated.

4. *Decree of the Council of Forty, 1344, prohibiting forestalling
practices in the sale of bullion on the Rialto. No Venetian bullion
merchant ("i.e., one who has bullion refined") may enter the
room of a German merchant at the Fondaco without a broker of
the Fondaco or make any deal outside of the designated area.*
*ASV, Secreta, Capitolare dei Capi Sestiere, caps. 192–95, fols. 81–
83. See above, chap. 9, sec. iv.*

25 October 1344
Capta in conscilio de XL
De ordine argenti et theotonicorum
      Cum ducali dominio fuerit querella deposita per vicedominos fontici
theutonicorum continens de modo inlicito et inhonesto quod tenent et
observant in ipso fontico mercatores argenti et ut obvietur predictis, comissum fuerit per capita de XL nobilibus viris Petro Piçamani, Paulo
Mudacio et Johanio [*sic*] Lauredano, iunori Quadraginte, quod super predictis consulerent de remedio opportuno et propterea ipsi considera quod
ipse fonticus est quicquid utilius terre et volentes apponere tanto bono
sicut est conservacio ipsius fontici, provisionem utilem et totaliter neces-
sariam sic providetur concorditer consulendo, et ita:
      Capta fuit pars quod nullus mercator argenti, intelligendo mer-
catorem argenti illum qui facit afinari argentum, ne aliqua alia persona
nomine ipsius mercatoris, que ita subiaceat poenis infrascriptis, sicut ille
qui mitteret, non audeat nec debeat modo aliquo ingenio vel causa intrare
cameram alicuius mercatoris theotonici sine proprio misseta ipsius mercatoris theotonici, sub pena librarum III^c pro quolibet et qualibet vice; qui
sic intraverit et si faceret mercatum argenti cadat, ultra penam predictam,
ad penam mittendi argentum sic emptum sicut in conscilio capto super
facto argenti in MCCCXXXVIIII[1] plenius continetur. Et nichillominus
stet duobus mensis in uno carcere inferiorum et per decem annos banitus
fontico antedicto et quociens intraverit ipsum fonticum infra terminum
banni cadat pro qualibet vice de libris Centum. Et ut predicta melius
observentur et fiant, comittatur tribus famulis fontici quod sub pena priva-

cionis officiorum et beneficiorum perpetuo comunis veneciarum et standi uno anno in uno carcere inferiorum teneantur et debeant inquirere diligenter si quis mercator argenti vel alia aliqua persona nomine ipsius intraverit cameram alicuius mercatoris theotonici sine suo proprio misseta et si quis invenerint [*sic*] vel viderint [*sic*] vel eis accussatum fuerit aliquem mercatorem argenti vel alia persona nomine ipsius intrasset ut dictum est supra, debeant ipsum accusare vicedominis fontici habendo tercium condempnacionis, tercium vicedomini et reliquum tercium comune. Et comittatur omnibus missetis, ligatoribus et quibuscumque aliis officialibus dicti fontici quod sub penis privacionis officiorum et standi in carcere ut dictum est, teneantur accusare si viderint aliquem mercatorem intrante ut dictum est, habendo de ipsa condempnacione partem, et cetera.

## Cap. 193

Item, quod aliquis mercator argenti vel aliquis qui presumeretur mercator argenti nec aliqua persona nomine ipsius mercatoris ut dictum est supra, non audeat nec debeat modo aliquo vel ingenio conducere nec conduci facere, recipere nec recipi facere aliquem mercatorem theutonicum in aliquam suam domum, voltam, stacionem vel locum nec alterius persone nomine, sub pena librarum CCC pro quolibet et qualibet vice, qua sic receperit vel conduxerit, et si faceret mercatum cadat ad penam supradictam. Et nichillominus stet in carcere et banditur fontico ut superius dictum est.

## Cap. 194

Item, quod aliqua persona non audeat nec debeat modo aliquo ingenio vel causa ire ad fonticum theutonicorum nec in stratam aliquam vel locum pro conducendo nec produci faciendo extra fonticum aliquem mercatorem theutonicum dicendo "Ego fui primus hic et propterea primo debeo videre argentum," sub pena librarum centum pro quolibet et qualibet vice, sed permittere mercatores theotonicos et sic ire debeant, ut tenentur, super tabulis cambii cum suo argento, sub penis ordinatis. Et hec omnia suprascripta addatur illis officialibus inquirenda quibus comissum fuit conscilium de MCCCXXXVIII quod si eis contrafacientes accusarentur exigant penam supradictam, habentes tercium, accusator tercium si inde fuerit, et reliquum tercium sit comunis. Et si maiores pene essent pro conservacione predictorum, subiaceant ipsis maioribus.

## Cap. 195

Item, quod omnes suprascripte provissiones observentur et fiant, intelligantur de argento ragusiensium et lonbardorum, que omnia publice cridari debeant in scalis Rivoalti ut per omnes scire possint. Et vicedomini fontici theotonicorum teneantur quolibet mense semel ad minus hec omnia in fontico facere proclamari et scribani eorum sub debito sacramenti teneantur ducere ad memoriam dictis vicedominis de proclamacione predicta. Et hec omnia addantur conscilio antedicto de 1338 pro maiori observacione predictorum; et si conscilium [et cetera].

[1]This should be 1338; doc. 3, above, is meant.

*5. A pardon is granted in 1346 to Francesco Vielmo,*
*moneychanger in Piazza San Marco and sometime mint official,*
*who had been sentenced for allegedly buying bullion at San*
*Marco at a bank of which he was not currently a partner (since*
*he was employed at the mint). He had been accused of illicit*
*dealings by a competitor. ASV, Grazie, reg. 11, fol. 70. See above,*
*chap. 9, sec. iv.*

8 April 1346                                    Officiales grossorum tonsorum
     Cum Franciscus Vielmo campsor ut dicit semper habendo et tenendo cambium in platea excepto isto anno pro eo quod est officialis ad monetam, qui tamen nolens esse sine bancho accepit partem cum Checho Spirito de quodam bancho sibi scripto, dando ei ducatos quinque pro parte solutionis quod consuetum est fieri si quod duo vel tres habent partem in banchis platee in XL et alio tempore, nec umquam fuit hoc contradictum sed quia super dicto bancho quadam die emit argentum a quodam mercatore, petens ab eo si illud presentaverat et alia fecerat qui fieri debent. Respondit quod sic. Et fuit ad mercatum cum eo et illud habuit ponderatum, solutum, et positum quintum in cecha. Et quia officiales grossorum tonsorum dicunt quod nullus nisi campsores habentes tabulas eis scriptas possunt emere argentum, cum non habeat bancum ei scriptum, condempnaverunt eum in libris CCC secundum formam sui capitularis, dicentes insuper quod dictus Franciscus, sedens super tabulam dicti Chechi, vidit ad tabulam Thome de Borra quemdam mercatorem argenti facientem mercatum cum ipso Thoma, quem ad se vocavit et mercatum fecit cum eo de suo argento. Et quia dictus Thomas dixit quod male faciebat sic vocare mercatores, tunc ductus sua superbia ivit et dedit unam alapam ipsi Thome. Et quia non est campsor nec habens tabulam sibi scriptam et emerit argentum contra suum capitulare, requisiverunt ab eo dictam penam et condempnationem etiam habuerunt. Qua de causa recursum habuit ad dominos auditores et audiverunt partis [sic] et viderunt capitulare et testificationes et scriptam etiam de manu sua et testificationem dicti Chechi qui dixit suo sacramento nullam societatem habuisse

cum eo nec ei etiam aliquam libertatem dedisse. Et dixerunt quod eorum sentencia erat bona et iusta.

Considerata condicione Francisci, fiat sibi gratia, et quod dictus Franciscus absolvatur totaliter a predicta condempnatione.[1]

[1]In the margin at this point are a double cross, signifying full approval, and the following notation: "capta in XL 16 jun. et habuit XXXV XL, posita in 40 se. 29 maii."

*6. Extract of the account opened in 1380 by Tommaso Talenti with the Venetian grain magistracy. The second entry, which records a transfer to Talenti's account at the bank of Gabriele Soranzo, is an example of accounting in ducati a monete and lire di piccoli. PSM, Citra, b. 141, Account Book of Tommaso and Zaccaria Talenti, fol. 20r. See above, chap. 16, sec. ii and n. 15; cf. Mueller,* The Procuratori, *chap. 2, pt. 3.*

1380

Signori Provededori dalla Biava de' avere a dì 28 zugno i quali me****[1] contanti gli uficiali dal fontego per loro cambiati con ser Bertuzi Valier, per ducati CC d'oro a s. 83 pic. 6 l'uno e posti a intrata a c. 19, val di pic. e cosi v'entra al ditto presio in somma di pic.    £ VIII^C XXXV

E de' avere dicto dì £ 78 di grossi a monete le qual me fe' prometere a ser Gabriel Sovranzo, posti a suo conto a c. 21 che debia dar, val a s. 64 per ducato in summa di piccoli,    £ II^M IIII^C LXXXXVI

E de' avere dicto dì £ 19 s. 10 gr a monete i quali fe dare per mi a Bartholomeo d'Acarixi contanti dal qual gli tolsi in oro a s. 83 pic 6 il ducato entrovi ducati 149, gr. 11, pic. 2 ad oro e posti al entrata a c. 19. . . .
    £ VI^C XXIIII

[1]Word illegible due to a hole in the folio.

*7. Sentence handed down in 1396 by the Giudici del Procurator, ordering the Procurators to pay the bequest of Marsilio da Carrara of 50 lire di piccoli in ducats at 64 soldi, even though the*

*current rate was 84 soldi. ASV, Santa Maria Gloriosa dei Frari,*
*b. 128 (formerly b. 129), fasc. Marsilio da Carrara, sentence of*
*the Curia del Procurator, 17 May 1396. See above, chap. 16.*

Comparuerunt in iudicio nobilis vir ser Petrus Lauredano procurator et procuratoris nomine conventus et monasterii Sancti Stephani de Venetiis, nec non venerabiles viri frater Nicolaus Durante procurator conventus Sancte Marie ordinis minorum, frater Anthonius de Avantio, procurator conventus fratrum Sancte Marie Carmelitarum de Venetiis prout de ipsis procuratoribus plene constavit officio, exponentes in hanc formam, Quod cum magnificus dominus Marsilius de Cararia olim Padue dominus per suum testamentum legavitur eisdem monasteriis libras quinquaginta parvorum pro quolibet anuatim in perpetuum, certis modo, conditione et ordine in ipsius testamento insertis, quibus procuratoribus volentibus dictas libras Lᵃ parvorum exigere a dominis procuratoribus de ultra comissariis dicti testatoris ad rationem librarum trium, soldorum quatuor pro ducato ut semper in huiusmodi legatis extitit observatum. Et ipsi domini procuratores recusant solvere legatum nisi ad libras quatuor et soldos quatuor pro ducato quod quidem est contra ius et patrie consuetudinem, Ea propter petunt quatenus ipsi domini judices procuratorum per eorum iusticiam et suum officium, attento quod beneficia huiusmodi semper ampliantur. Insuper quod ab initio ducatus vallebat solum libras iii et soldos iiii or parvorum, quod sic et per preteritum et futurum in hiis causibus interpretatum est et interpretari debet, dicere, declarare et terminare dignentur dictas libras Lᵃ parvorum solvi debere ad libras tres soldos quatuor pro ducato.

Ex adverso autem vir nobilis ser Raphael Grimani, advocatus dictorum dominorum procuratorum de ultra comissariorum antedictorum respondens dicebat dictum legatum non debere solvi aliter quam ad libras quatuor et soldos quatuor pro ducato prout vallet ad presens ducatus, ex eo quod sic vult et mandat testus carte dicti testamenti, cum loquitur libre quinquaginta parvorum, a quo quidem textu carte minime recedendum est.

UNDE prefacti domini iudices procuratorum videlicet domini Jacobi Georgio, Franchus Chaucho, tercio iudice curie vacante, visis auditis petitione et responsione partium premissarum, viso textu puncti testamenti predicti dicente libre quinquaginta parvorum, consideratis interpretationibus hiusmodi fieri solitis, quod si vulgariter loquitur "lasso cinquanta libre" non aliter loquendo, intelliguntur libre ad grossos. Et si loquitur "lasso libre Lᵃ de piçoli" inteligitur ad libras tres et soldos quatuor pro ducato, et sic ab initio extitit observatum et potissime in beneficiis que semper ampliantur et ampliari debent. Super hoc habito consilio dilligenti per eorum iusticiam et eorum officium et diffinitionem et determinationem et determinando et declarando dixerunt, terminaverunt et declaraverunt, quod dictum legatum factum per dictum condam Magnificum dominum Marsilium de Chararia, olim dominum Padue, de libris quinquaginta parvorum dandis et persolvendis annuatim singulis dictorum trium conventuum et monasteriorum, videlicet fratrum minorum, fratrum sancti Stephani et fratrum Carmelitarum, Intelligatur et intelligi debeat ad libras tres et soldos quatuor pro ducato, causis et rationibus antedictis.

# BIBLIOGRAPHY

PRIMARY SOURCES

*Manuscript Sources*

The reader is referred to the footnotes for exact references to documents culled from the extensive collections of deliberative, judicial, administrative, and private records preserved at the Archivio di Stato, Venice; of chronicles, tracts, and private papers at the Biblioteca Marciana, the Biblioteca del Museo Civico Correr, and the Seminario Patriarcale of Venice, and at the Bibliotèque Nationale, Paris; of business records and commercial and diplomatic correspondence at the Archivi di Stato of Florence, of Prato, and of Mantua. The following codices are listed here to facilitate their full identification, since they are cited in some footnotes in shortened form.

ASV, Zecca, b. 6tris. Capitolare dei Massari della Moneta d'Oro (formerly in the Raccolta Papadopoli).

Capitulare Visdominorum Ternarie. BMV, Ms. Lat., cl. V, cod. 6 (2380).

Cronaca (Pseudo-) Zancaruolo. BMV, Ms. It., cl. VII, cod. 50 (9275) (regarding both this and the real Cronaca Zancaruolo and their changed and misleading classifications at the BMV, see the article by Giulio Zorzanello cited in full in the bibliography).

Morosini, Antonio. Cronica. BMV, Ms. It., cl. VII, cod. 2048–49 (8331–32) (a nineteenth-century transcription in two codices [each of two tomes with consecutive numbering of folios]).

Quaderno della quindexena. "Quaderno de mi Zuan Trivisan della quindexena de mazo e zugno 1485, fatta per Misser Piero Quirini fo de Misser Biasio." ASV, Zecca, serie finale (white buste), b. 3.

Sanuto, Marino [il giovane]. Notes on registers of the *parti* of the Quarantia Criminal, with transcriptions and paraphrases of decisions, 1333–1515, many from registers no longer extant. ASV, Quarantia Criminal, reg. 14bis (ex Misc. cod. 678).

"Traité du gouvernement de la cité et seigneurie de Venise." Bibliothèque Nationale, Paris, Fonds français, 5599.

Trattato di Aritmetica. BMV, Ms. It., cl. IV, cod. 497 (5163).

## Published Sources

Agricola, Georgius, *De re metallica.* Translated, with notes, by Herbert C. Hoover and Lou N. Hoover. London, 1912.

Alighieri, Dante. *The Divine Comedy.* Edited and translated by Charles S. Singleton. 6 pts. in 3 vols. Bollingen Series, 80. Princeton, 1970.

*L'armeno-veneto. Compendio storico e documenti delle relazioni degli armeni coi veneziani. Primo periodo: secoli XIII–XIV.* Venice, 1893.

Baroni, Manuela, ed. *Notaio di Venezia del secolo XIII (1290–1292).* FSV. Venice, 1977.

*Bilanci generali della Repubblica di Venezia.* Edited by Fabio Besta. DF, 2d ser., 1, tomo 1. Venice, 1912. Abbr.: *BG.*

Biringuccio, Vannuccio. *De la pirotechnia.* Edited by Adriano Carugo. Facs. ed. Milan, 1977.

———. *De la pirotechnia libri X.* Venice, 1550.

———. *The Pirotechnia of Vannuccio Biringuccio.* Edited and translated by Cyril Stanley Smith and Martha Trach Gnudi. New York, 1942.

Bondi Sebellico, Andreina, ed. *Felice de Merlis, prete e notaio in Venezia ed Ayas (1315–1344).* Vol. 1. FSV. Venice, 1973.

Bonfiglio-Dosio, Giorgetta, ed. *Il "Capitolar dalle broche" della Zecca di Venezia (1358–1556).* Verona, forthcoming. Abbr.: *Cap. Broche.*

Borlandi, Antonia, ed. *Il manuale di mercatura di Saminiato de' Ricci.* Università di Genova, Istituto di Storia Medievale e Moderna, Fonti e studi, 4. Genoa, 1963.

Borlandi, Franco, ed. *El libro di mercatantie et usanze de' paesi.* Documenti e studi per la storia del commercio e del diritto commerciale italiano, edited by F. Patetta and M. Chiaudano, 7. Turin, 1936. Reprint. 1970.

Camerani Marri, Giulia, ed. *Statuti dell'Arte del Cambio di Firenze (1299–1316).* Florence, 1955.

Cessi, Roberto, ed. *Deliberazioni del Maggior Consiglio di Venezia.* 3 vols. Bologna, 1931–50. Abbr.: *DMC.*

———. *Problemi monetari veneziani fino a tutto il secolo XIV.* DF, 4th ser. Padua, 1937. Abbr.: *PMV.*

————. *La regolazione delle entrate e delle spese (sec. XIII–XIV)*. DF, 1st ser. Padua, 1925. Abbr.: *RES*.

Cessi, Roberto, and Fanny Bennato, eds. *Venetiarum historia vulgo Petro Iustiniano Iustiniani filio adiudicata*. Monumenti storici, n.s., 18. Venice: Deputazione di Storia Patria, 1964.

Cessi, Roberto, Paolo Sambin, and Mario Brunetti, eds. *Le deliberazioni del Consiglio dei Rogati (Senato), serie "mixtorum."* 2 vols. Monumenti storici, n.s., 15–16. Venice: Deputazione di Storia Patria, 1960–61.

Chiaudano, Mario, and Antonino Lombardo, eds. *Leonardo Marcello, notaio in Candia (1278–1281)*. FSV. Venice, 1960.

Chinazzo, Daniele di. *Cronica de la guerra de Veniciani a Zenovesi*. Edited by Vittorio Lazzarini. Monumenti storici, n.s. 11. Venice: Deputazione di Storia Patria, 1958.

Ciano, Cesare, ed. *La "pratica della mercatura" datiniana (secolo XIV)*. Biblioteca della rivista *Economia e storia*, 9. Milan, 1964.

Cotrugli, Benedetto. *Della mercatura et del mercante perfetto*. Venice, 1573.

da Canal, Martin. *Les estoires de Venise: Cronaca veneziana in lingua francese dalle origini al 1275*. Edited by Alberto Limentani. Civiltà veneziana, Fonti e testi, 12. Florence, 1972.

Dandolo, Andrea. *Andreae Danduli Chronica per extensum descripta*. Edited by E. Pastorello. Rerum Italicarum Scriptores, 2d ed., 12, pt. 1. Città di Castello and Bologna, 1938–58.

Dante Alighieri. *See* Alighieri, Dante.

degli Azzi, Giustiniano, ed. "Un frammento inedito della cronaca di Benedetto Dei." *Archivio storico italiano* 110 (1952).

de Gravina, Dominicus. *Chronica de rebus in Apulia gestis*. Edited by Albano Sorbelli. Rerum Italicarum Scriptores, 2d ed., 12, pt. 3. Città di Castello, 1903.

de Monacis, Lorenzo. *Chronicon de rebus venetis. . . .* Venice, 1758.

Dini, Bruno, ed. *Una pratica di mercatura in formazione (1394–1395)*. Pubblicazioni dell'Istituto Internazionale di Storia Economica "Francesco Datini," 1st ser., 2. Florence, 1980.

Documenti finanziari della Repubblica di Venezia. 4 ser. Series 1, 3, and 4 issued by R. Accademia dei Lincei, Rome, Commissione per gli atti delle Assemblee Costituzionali Italiani. Ser. 1 edited by Roberto Cessi; ser. 3 edited by Gino Luzzatto; ser. 4 edited by Roberto Cessi. Ser. 2, issued by the R. Commissione per la Pubblicazione dei Documenti Finanziarii della Repubblica di Venezia in 3 volumes, edited by Fabio Besta. Abbr.: DF.

Dorini, Umberto, and Tommaso Bertelè, eds. *Il libro dei conti di Giacomo Badoer, 1436–1440*. Il Nuovo Ramusio, 3. Rome, 1956.

Favaro, Elena, ed. *Cassiere della bolla ducale: Grazie—novus liber (1299–1305)*. FSV. Venice, 1962.

Firpo, Luigi, ed. *Relazioni di ambasciatori veneti al Senato*. Vol. I, *Inghilterra*. Turin, 1965.

Gaudenzi, A., ed. *Statuti delle società del popolo di Bologna*. 2 vols. Fonti per la Storia d'Italia, 2. Rome, 1896.

Johnson, Charles, ed. and trans. *The De moneta of Nicholas Oresme and English Mint Documents*. London, 1956.

Lisini, A., et al., eds. *Cronache senesi*. Rerum Italicarum Scriptores, 2d ed., 15. Bologna, 1931–39.

Lombardo, Antonino, ed. *Le deliberazioni del Consiglio dei Quaranta della Repubblica di Venezia*. 3 vols. Monumenti storici, n.s., 9, 12, 20. Venice: Deputazione di Storia Patria, 1957–68. Abbr.: *DQ*.

————. *Documenti della colonia veneziana di Creta, I: Imbreviature di Pietro Scardon (1271)*. Documenti e studi per la storia del commercio e del diritto commerciale italiano, edited by F. Patetta and M. Chiaudano, 21. Turin, 1942.

————. *Nicola de Boateriis, notaio in Famagosta e Venezia (1355–1365)*. FSV. Venice, 1973.

Lopez, Robert S., and Gabriella Airaldi, eds., "Il più antico manuale italiano di pratica della mercatura [*Memoria de tucte le mercantie*]." In *Miscellanea di studi storici*, vol. 2, pp. 99–133. Genoa, 1983.

Luzzatto, Gino, ed. *I prestiti della Repubblica di Venezia nei sec. XII–XV*. DF, 3d ser. Padua, 1929. Abbr.: *PRV*.

Melis, Federigo. *Documenti per la storia economica dei secoli XIII–XVI*. Pubblicazioni dell'Istituto Internazionale di Storia Economica "Francesco Datini," Prato, 1st ser., 1. Florence, 1972.

Monticolo, Giovanni, ed. *I capitolari delle arti veneziane sottoposte alla Giustizia e poi alla Giustizia vecchia (dalle origini al 1330)*. 3 vols. Istituto Storico Italiano, Fonti per la Storia d'Italia, 26–28. Rome, 1896–1914.

Morozzo della Rocca, Raimondo, ed. *Lettere di mercanti a Pignol Zucchello (1336–1350)*. FSV. Venice, 1957.

Morozzo della Rocca, Raimondo, and Antonino Lombardo, eds. *Documenti del commercio veneziano nei secoli XI–XIII*. 2 vols. Documenti e studi per la storia del commercio e del diritto commerciale italiano, edited by F. Patetta and M. Chiaudano, 19–20. Turin, 1940.

————. *Nuovi documenti del commercio veneto dei secoli XI–XIII*. Monumenti storici, n.s., 7. Venice: Deputazione di Storia Patria, 1953.

Motta, E. "Documenti visconteo-sforzeschi per la storia della zecca di Milano." *RIN* 6 (1893)–9 (1896).

Müller, Karl Otto, ed. *Welthandelsbräuche (1480–1540)*. Deutsche Handelsakten des Mittelalters und der Neuzeit, Historische Kommission bei der Bayerischen Akademie der Wissenschaften. Stuttgart and Berlin, 1934.

Musper, H. Th., ed. *Kaiser Maximilians Weisskunig*, vol. 1, *Textband*. Stuttgart, 1956.

Nani-Mocenigo, Filippo, ed. *Capitolare dei Signori di Notte*. Venice, 1877.

Noiret, Hippolyte, ed. *Documents inédits pour servir à l'histoire de la domination vénitienne en Crete, de 1380 à 1485, tirés des archives de Venise*. Bibliothèque des Ecoles Françaises d'Athènes et de Rome, 21. Paris, 1892.

*Novissimum statutorum ac venetarum legum volumen duabus in partis divisum Aloysio Mocenigo*. Venice: Pinelliana, 1729.

Pacioli, Luca. *Summa de arithmetica, geometria, proportioni e proportionalità*. Venice, 1494.

Pegolotti, Francesco Balducci. *La pratica della mercatura*. Edited by Allan Evans. Cambridge, Mass., 1936. Reprint. New York, 1970.

Predelli, Riccardo, ed. *I libri commemoriali della Repubblica di Venezia— Regesti*. 8 vols. Monumenti storici, 1st ser. (Documenti). Venice: Deputazione di Storia Patria, 1876–1914.

Predelli, Riccardo, and Adolfo Sacerdoti, eds. *Gli statuti marittimi veneziani fino al 1255*. Venice, 1903. The edition also appeared in *NAV*, n.s., 4–6 (1902–3).

Priuli, Gerolamo. *I diarii*. Edited by Arturo Segre and Roberto Cessi. Rerum Italicarum Scriptores, 2d ed., 24, pt. 3. Città di Castello and Bologna, 1912–36.

*A Relation or rather a True Account of the Island of England . . . about the Year 1500*. Edited and translated by C. A. Sneyd. London, 1847. Reprinted in Firpo, ed., *Relazioni di ambasciatori Veneti*.

Roberti, Melchiore, ed. *Le magistrature giudiziarie veneziane e i loro capitolari fino al 1300*. 3 vols. Monumenti storici, 2d. ser., 16–18. Venice: Deputazione di Storia Patria, 1909–11.

Sanudo, Marin, il giovane. *See* Sanuto, Marino.

Sanuto, Marino, [il giovane]. *De origine, situ et magistratibus urbis venetae ovvero la città di Venetia (1493–1530)*. Edited by Angela Caracciolo Aricò. Milan, 1980.

———. *I diarii*. Edited by Rinaldo Fulin et al. 58 vols. Venice, 1879–1903.

———. *Vite de' Duchi di Venezia*. In Rerum Italicarum Scriptores, 22, edited by Ludovico Antonio Muratori. Milan, 1733.

Sanuto, Marino ("Torsello"). *Liber secretorum fidelium crucis super Terrae Sanctae recuperatione et conservatione*. In *Gesta Dei per Francos*, edited by J. Bongars, vol. 2. Hanover, 1611. Facs. reprint. Jerusalem, 1972.

Sapori, Armando, ed. *I libri degli Alberti del Giudice*. Milan, 1952.

———. *I libri di commercio dei Peruzzi*. Milan, 1934.

———. *Libro giallo della compagnia dei Covoni*. Milan, 1970.

Schäfer, K. H. *Die Ausgaben der Apostolischen Kammer unter Johann XXII. nebst dem Jahresbilanzen von 1316–1317*. Vol. 2 of *Vatikanische Quellen*

*zur Geschichte der Päpstlichen Hof- und Finanzverwaltung, 1316–1378.*
Paderborn: Görres-Gesellschaft, 1911.

Sella, Pietro, and Giuseppe Vale, eds. *Rationes Decimarum Italiae nei secoli XIII e XIV, Venetiae-Histria-Dalmatia.* Studi e testi, 96. Vatican City, 1941.

Simonsfeld, Heinrich. *Der Fondaco dei Tedeschi in Venedig und die deutsch-venezianischen Handelsbeziehungen.* 2 vols. Stuttgart, 1887. Reprint. Aalen, 1968.

Spilimbergo, Roberto di. *Cronaca de' suoi tempi (1499–1540).* Edited by V. Joppi. Udine, 1884.

Stussi, Alfredo, ed. *Zibaldone da Canal, manoscritto mercantile del sec. XIV.* FSV. Venice, 1967.

*Tableaux des principaux evenemens de la vie et du regne de l'Empereur Maximilian I en une suite de deux cent trente sept planches gravees en bois sur les dessins et sous la conduite de Hans Burgkmaier.* Vienna and London, 1799.

Tafel, G. L. F., and Georg Martin Thomas, eds. *Urkunden zur älteren Handels- und Staatsgeschichte der Republik Venedig mit besonderer Beziehung auf Byzanz und die Levante vom IX. bis zum Ausgang des XV. Jahrhunderts.* 3 vols. in 2. Fontes Rerum Austriacarum, Diplomata et acta, 12–14. Vienna, 1856–57. Reprint. Amsterdam, 1964.

*Tarifa zoè noticia dy pexi e mexure di luogi e tere che s'adovra marcadantia per el mondo.* Edited by the Istituto Superiore di Scienze Economiche e Commerciali di Venezia. Venice, 1925.

Thiriet, Freddy, ed. *Délibérations des assemblées vénitiennes concernant la Romanie.* 2 vols. EPHE-6, Documents et recherches, edited by P. Lemerle, 8, 11. Paris, 1966–71.

———. *Regestes des délibérations du Sénat de Venise concernant la Romanie.* 3 vols. EPHE-6, Documents et recherches, edited by P. Lemerle, 1, 2, 4. Paris and The Hague, 1958–61.

Thomas, Georg Martin, ed. *Capitolare dei Visdomini del Fontego dei Todeschi in Venezia/Capitular des Deutschen Hauses in Venedig.* Berlin, 1874. Abbr.: *Cap. Fontego.*

———. *Diplomatarium Veneto-Levantinum, sive acta et diplomata res Venetas Graecas atque Levantis illustrantis, a. 1300–1350.* Monumenti storici, 1st ser. (Documenti), 5. Venice: Deputazione di Storia Patria, 1880.

Tiepolo, Maria Francesca, ed. *Domenico prete di S. Maurizio, notaio di Venezia (1309–1316).* FSV. Venice, 1970.

Villani, Giovanni. *Cronica.* Edited by F. G. Dragomanni. 4 vols. Florence, 1844–45.

Yule, Sir Henry, ed and trans. *The Book of Ser Marco Polo, the Venetian, concerning the Kingdoms and Marvels of the East.* Rev. ed. by Henri Cordier. 4 vols. Reprint. New York, 1966.

Zago, Ferruccio, ed. *Consiglio dei Dieci—Deliberazioni Miste—Registri III–IV (1325–1335)*. FSV. Venice, 1968.

## SECONDARY WORKS

Ames, Edward. "The Sterling Crisis of 1337–1339." *JEcH* 25 (1965):496–522. Reprinted in Roderick Floud, ed., *Essays in Quantitative Economic History*. New York, 1974.

Andreades, A. "De la monnaie et de la puissance d'achat des métaux précieux dans l'Empire Byzantine." *Byzantion* 1 (1924).

Argelati, F., ed. *De monetis Italiae variorum illustrium virorum dissertationes*. 6 vols. Milan, 1750–59.

Arnaldi, Girolamo. "Andrea Dandolo doge-cronista." In *La storiografia veneziana fino al secolo XVI: Aspetti e problemi*, edited by Agostino Pertusi. Civiltà veneziana, Saggi, 18. Florence, 1970.

Ashtor, Eliyahu. *Histoire des prix et des salaires dans l'orient médiéval*. EPHE-6, Monnaie, prix, conjoncture, 8. Paris, 1969.

———. *Les métaux précieux et la balance des payements du Proche-Orient à la basse époque*. EPHE-6, Monnaie, prix, conjoncture, 10. Paris, 1971.

———. "Observations on Venetian Trade in the Levant in the Fourteenth Century." *JEEcH* 5 (1976):533–86.

———. *A Social and Economic History of the Near East in the Middle Ages*. Berkeley, 1976.

Attman, Artur. *The Bullion Flow between Europe and the East, 1000–1750*. Acta regiae societatis scientiarum et litterarum gothoburgensis, Humaniora, 20. Göteborg, 1981.

Aymard, Maurice. *Venise, Raguse et le commerce du blé pendant la seconde moitié du XVIe siècle*. EPHE-6, Ports-routes-trafics, 20. Paris, 1966.

Bacharach, J. L. "The Dinar versus the Ducat." *International Journal of Middle East Studies* 4 (1973).

Balard, Michel. *La Romanie génoise (XIIe–début XVe siècle)*. Bibliothèque des Ecoles Françaises d'Athènes et de Rome, 1st ser. 235. 2 vols. Rome, 1978. Published in collaboration with the Società Ligure di Storia Patria.

Barbagli Bagnoli, Vera, ed. *La moneta nell'economia europea, secoli XIII–XVIII*. Florence, 1982. Papers presented at the seventh "Settimana di Studio" of the Istituto Internazionale di Storia Economica "Francesco Datini," Prato, 1975.

Barbieri, Gino. "Le dottrine monetarie dal XIII al XVIII secolo (schema di una ricostruzione panoramica)." *Economica e storia* 22 (1975):319–55. Also in Barbagli Bagnoli, ed., *La moneta nell'economia europea*, 309–49.

Barker, Wharton. *Bimetallism, or the Evils of Gold Monometallism and the Benefits of Bimetallism*. Philadelphia, 1896.

Battistella, Antonio. *La Repubblica di Venezia nei suoi undici secoli di storia.* Venice, 1921.

Bautier, Robert-Henri. *The Economic Development of Medieval Europe.* London and New York, 1971.

———. "Les rélations économiques des pays occidentaux avec les pays d'Orient au Moyen Age. Points de vue et documents." In *Sociétés et compagnies du commerce en Orient et dans l'Ocean Indien, Actes du 8e Colloque Internationale d'Histoire Maritime* (Beirut, 1966), edited by Michel Mollat, 263–331. Paris, 1970.

Becker, Marvin B. *Florence in Transition.* 2 vols. Baltimore, 1967–68.

Bendall, Simon, and P. J. Donald. *The Later Paleologan Coinage, 1282–1453.* London, 1979.

Berchet, Federico. "Contributo alla storia dell'edificio della veneta zecca prima della sua destinazione a sede della Biblioteca Nazionale Marciana." *Atti dell'Istituto Veneto di Scienze, Lettere ed Arti* 69, pt. 2 (1910):337–86.

Bergier, Jean-François. "From the Fifteenth Century in Italy to the Sixteenth Century in Germany: A New Banking Concept?" In *DMB.*

Berindei, M., and C. Veinstein. "La Tana-Azaq, de la présence italienne à l'empire ottomane." *Turcica: Revue d'études turques* 8, no. 2 (1976).

Bernardi, G. *Monetazione del Patriarcato di Aquileia.* Trieste, 1975.

Bernocchi, Mario. *Le monete della repubblica fiorentina.* 4 vols. Florence, 1974–78. Abbr.: Bernocchi.

———. "Le monete di conto e il fiorino di suggello della repubblica fiorentina." In Barbagli Bagnoli, ed., *La moneta nell'economia europea.* Also in Bernocchi, vol. 3.

Bertelè, Tommaso. "L'iperpero bizantino dal 1261 al 1453." *RIN,* 5th ser., 5, no. 59 (1957):70–89.

———. "Moneta veneziana e moneta bizantina (secoli XII–XV)." In Pertusi, ed., *Venezia e il Levante,* vol. 1, pt. 1.

———. *Numismatique byzantine, suivie de deux études inédites sur les monnaies des Paléologues.* Paris, 1978.

Besta, Enrico. *Il Senato veneziano (origine, costituzione, attribuzione, e riti).* Miscellanea di storia veneta, 2d ser., 5. Venice: Deputazione di Storia Patria, 1899.

Besta, Fabio. Introduction to *BG.*

Bisson, Thomas N. "Coinages and Royal Monetary Policy in Languedoc during the Reign of St. Louis." *Speculum* 32 (1957).

———. *Conservation of Coinage.* Oxford, 1979.

Blake, Robert P. "The Circulation of Silver in the Moslem East down to the Mongol Epoch." *Harvard Journal of Asiatic Studies* 2 (1937).

Blancard, L. "Le besant d'or sarracinas pendant les Croisades." *Mémoires de l'Académie des Sciences, Lettres et Beaux Arts de Marseilles,* 1879–80.

Bloch, Marc. *Esquisse d'une histoire monétaire de l'Europe.* Edited by Lucien Febvre and Fernand Braudel. Cahiers des *Annales,* 9. Paris, 1954.

———. *Land and Work in Medieval Europe: Selected Papers.* London, 1967. New York, 1969.

———. *Lineamenti di una storia monetaria d'Europa.* Edited by Lucien Febvre and Fernand Braudel, Italian translation of the *Esquisse,* with a preface by Ugo Tucci. Turin, 1981.

———. "La monnaie de compte." Review of "Monnaie de compte et monnaie réelle," by Hans van Werveke. *Annales d'histoire économique et sociale* 7 (1935):323–25.

———. "Mutations monétaires dans l'ancienne France." *Annales, ESC* 7 (1953):145–58, 433–56.

———. "Le problème de la monnaie de compte." Review of "La teoria della moneta immaginaria nel tempo da Carlomagno alla rivoluzione francese," by Luigi Einaudi. *Annales d'histoire économique et sociale* 10 (1938):358–60.

———. "Le problème de l'or au Moyen Age." *Annales d'histoire économique et sociale* 5 (January 1933). Reprinted in Marc Bloch, *Mélanges historiques,* 2. Paris, 1963. Translated in Marc Bloch, *Land and Work,* chap. 7.

Blomquist, Thomas. "The Dawn of Banking in an Italian Comune: Thirteenth Century Lucca." In *DMB.*

Bogaert, Raymond. "Ursprung und Entwicklung der Depositenbank im Altertum und Mittelalter." In Bogaert and Hartmann, *Essays.*

Bogaert, Raymond, and Peter Claus Hartmann. *Essays zur historischen Entwicklung des Bankensystems.* Mannheim, 1980.

Bollati di Saint Pierre, F. *Illustrazioni della spedizione in Oriente di Amadeo VI, il Conte Verde.* Biblioteca storica italiana per cura della Deputazione di Storia Patria, 5, pt. 6. Turin, 1900.

Bonfiglio-Dosio, Giorgetta. "Lavoro e lavoratori nella Zecca veneziana attraverso il 'Capitolar dalle broche' (XIV–XVI sec.)." In *Viridarium floridum: Studi in onore di Paolo Sambin,* edited by Giorgio Cracco, Maria Chiara Billanovich, and Antonio Rigon. Padua, forthcoming.

Borelli, Giorgio, ed. *Uomini e civiltà agraria in territorio veronese.* Verona, 1982.

Borlandi, Antonia. "Moneta e congiuntura a Bologna, 1360–1369." *Bollettino dell'Istituto Storico Italiano per il Medio Evo e Archivio Muratoriano* 82 (1970):390–478.

Bovill, E. W. *Caravans of the Old Sahara.* London, 1933.

———. *The Golden Trade of the Moors.* 2d ed. New York and Oxford, 1969.

Braudel, Fernand. "La vita economica di Venezia nel secolo XVI." *La civiltà veneziana del Rinascimento.* Florence, 1958.

Braudel, Fernand, and Frank C. Spooner. "Les métaux monétaires et l'économie du XVIe siècle." *Relazioni del X⁰ Congresso Internazionale di Scienze Storiche,* vol. 4, *Storia moderna.* Rome, 1960.

――――. "Prices in Europe from 1450 to 1750." In *The Cambridge Economic History of Europe,* vol. 4, pp. 378–486. Cambridge, 1967.

Braunstein, Philippe. "Pénurie et cherté à Venise pendant la guerre de Chioggia (1378–1380)." *Beiträge zur Handels- und Verkehrsgeschichte,* 17–31. Grazer Forschungen zur Wirtschafts- und Sozialgeschichte, 3.

――――. "Remarques sur la population allemande de Venise à la fin du Moyen Age." In *Venezia centro di mediazione tra oriente e occidente (secoli XV–XVI): Aspetti e problemi,* edited by H. G. Beck, M. Manoussacas, and A. Pertusi, 1:233–43. Civiltà veneziana, 32. Florence, 1977.

――――. "Wirtschaftsliche Beziehungen zwischen Nürnberg und Italien im Spätmittelalter." *Beiträge zur Wirtschaftsgeschichte Nürnbergs* 1 (1967):377–406.

Bridrey, Emile. *La théorie de la monnaie au XIVe siècle. Nicole Oresme. Etude d'histoire des doctrines et des faits économiques.* Paris, 1906.

Broglio d'Ajano, Romolo. "L'industria della seta a Venezia." In *Storia dell'economia italiana,* edited by Carlo M. Cipolla, vol. 1. Turin, 1959.

Brunello, Franco. "La *Pyrotechnia* di Vannuccio Biringuccio." In *L'editoria scientifica a Venezia nel '500.* Venice: Università Internazionale dell'Arte, forthcoming.

Brunetti, Lodovico. "Del quantitativo coniato di soldini di Francesco Dandolo." *RIN,* 5th ser., 6, no. 60 (1958):63–68.

――――. "Sulle quantità di moneta di argento emesse sotto Anna di Savoia, imperatrice di Bisanzio (1341–1347)." *RIN,* 5th ser., 11, no. 65 (1963):143–68.

Brunetti, Mario. "Venezia durante la peste del 1348." *Ateneo veneto* 32, no. 1, fasc. 3; no. 2, fasc. 1 (1909).

Brunner, K., and A. H. Meltzer. "Uses of Money: Money in the Theory of an Exchange Economy." *American Economic Review* 61 (1971):784–805.

Brunschvig, Robert. "Esquisse d'histoire monétaire Almohado-Hafside." In *Mélanges William Marcais.* Paris, 1950.

Bucher, Karl. *Industrial Organization.* Translated by S. Morley Wickett. New York, 1901. Reprint. 1968.

Buenger Robbert, Louise. *See* Robbert, Louise Buenger.

Burani, G. *Giornale solario e pronostico perpetuo. . . .* Venice, 1794.

Burkhard, Arthur. "Hans Burgkmair." *Speculum* 7 (1932).

Carabellese, Francesco. *Carlo d'Angiò nei rapporti politici e commerciali con Venezia e l'Oriente.* Bari, 1911.

Cardini, Franco. "I costi della crociata: L'aspetto economico del progetto di Marin Sanudo il Vecchio (1312–1321)." In *Studi in memoria di Federigo Melis,* vol. 2, pp. 179–210. Naples, 1978.

Carile, Antonio. *La cronachistica veneziana (secoli XIII–XVI) di fronte alla spartizione della Romania nel 1204.* Florence, 1968.

———. *La rendita feudale nella Morea latina del XIV secolo.* Bologna, 1974.

Carli, GianRinaldo. *Delle monete e dell'istituzione delle zecche d'Italia.* Mantua, 1754–60. Also vols. 2–8 of his *Opere.* Milan, 1784.

Carlotto, Natascia. "Pietro Nan da Marano, miles e civis veneto: Accumulazione e restituzione di un patrimonio nel primo Trecento." Unpublished laurea thesis, Faculty of Letters and Philosophy, University of Venice, 1983.

Casaretto, Francesco. *Le monete genovesi in confronto con le altre valute mediterranee.* In Atti della Società Ligure di Storia Patria, 55. Genoa, 1928.

Casini, Bruno. "Il corso dei cambi fra il fiorino e la moneta di piccioli a Pisa dal 1252 al 1500." In *Studi sugli strumenti di cambio a Pisa nel medioevo,* by G. Garzella et al. Pisa, 1979.

Cassandro, Giovanni. "Concetto, caratteri e struttura dello stato veneziano." *Rivista di storia del diritto italiano* 36 (1963). Also published, but without notes, in *Bergomum* 38 (1964):33–55.

———. "I porti pugliesi nel medio evo." In his *Saggi di storia del diritto commerciale.* Rome, 1974.

Cazelles, R. "Quelques réflexions à propos des mutations de la monnaie royale française (1295–1360)." *Le Moyen Age* 72 (1966):83–105.

Cecchetti, Bartolomeo. "Saggio sui prezzi delle vettovaglie e di altre merci in Venezia nei secoli XII–XIX." *Atti del R. Istituto Veneto di Scienze, Lettere ed Arti,* 4th ser., 3 (1874):1465–91.

Center for Medieval and Renaissance Studies, University of California, Los Angeles, ed. *The Dawn of Modern Banking.* New Haven, 1979. Abbr.: *DMB.*

Cessi, Roberto. "Documenti inediti sulla zecca padovana dell'epoca carrarese." *Bollettino del Museo Civico di Padova* 9 (1906): 109–14.

———. Introduction to *DMC* (in vol. 1).

———. Introduction to *PMV* (in vol. 1).

———. Introduction to *RES* (in vol. 1).

———. "Nuovi documenti sulla zecca padovana dell'epoca carrarese." *Bollettino del Museo Civico di Padova* 10 (1907):145–51.

———. *Politica ed economia di Venezia nel Trecento.* Rome, 1952.

———. "Le relazioni commerciali tra Venezia e le Fiandre nel secolo XIV." *NAV,* n.s., 27 (1914). Reprinted in his *Politica ed economia.*

———. *Storia della Repubblica di Venezia.* Rev. ed. 2 vols. Milan and Messina, 1968.

———. "Studi sulla moneta veneziana: I. Il denaro *piccolo* ed il denaro *grosso* fino alla coniazione del ducato." *Economia. Rassegna mensile di politica economica* (Trieste) 1 (1923):371–89.

———. "Studi sulla moneta veneziana: II. La coniazione del ducato aureo." *Economia. Rassegna mensile di politica economica* (Trieste) 2 (1924):42–52.

Cessi, Roberto, and Annibale Alberti. *Rialto: L'isola—il ponte—il mercato.* Bologna, 1934.

Challis, Christopher E. "The Circulating Medium and the Movement of Prices in Mid-Tudor England." In *The Price Revolution in Sixteenth-Century England,* edited by Peter H. Ramsey, 117–46. London, 1971.

Chandler, Lester V. *The Economics of Money and Banking.* 3d ed. New York, 1959.

Cipolla, Carlo M. "Argento tedesco e monete genovesi alla fine del Quattrocento." *RIN,* 5th ser., 4, no. 58 (1956):100–107.

———. *Le avventure della lira.* 2d ed., rev. Bologna, 1975.

———. "Currency Depreciation in Medieval Europe." *EcHR,* 2d ser., 4 (1963):413–22.

———. *Il fiorino e il quattrino: La politica monetaria a Firenze nel 1300.* Bologna, 1982.

———. *Money, Prices, and Civilization in the Mediterranean World, Fifth to Seventeenth Century.* Princeton, 1956.

———. *Moneta e civiltà mediterranea.* Venice, 1957.

———. *Les mouvements monétaires dans l'Etat di Milan (1580–1700).* EPHE-6, Monnaie—Prix—Conjoncture, 1. Paris, 1952.

———. *Studi di storia della moneta.* Vol. 1, *I movimenti dei cambi in Italia dal secolo XIII al XV.* Pubblicazioni dell'Università di Pavia, Studi nelle scienze giuridiche e sociali, 101. Pavia, 1948. Abbr.: Cipolla, *I movimenti.*

———. "La svalutazione monetaria nel Ducato di Milano alla fine del Medioevo." *Giornale degli economisti e annali di economia,* n.s., 6 (1947):540–50.

Ćirković, Simar. "The Production of Gold, Silver, and Copper in the Central Parts of the Balkans from the 13th to the 16th Century." In Kellenbenz, ed., *Precious Metals,* 41–69.

Clough, Shepard, T., and Richard T. Rapp. *European Economic History.* 3d ed. New York, 1975.

Corazzol, Gigi. *Fitti e livelli a grano: Un aspetto del credito rurale nel Veneto del '500.* Milan, 1979.

*Corpus Nummorum Italicorum.* 19 vols. Rome, 1910–40. Vol. 7, *Veneto.* Abbr.: *CNI.*

Cox, Eugene. *The Green Count of Savoy.* Princeton, 1967.

Cox, H. *The Caporelli Hoard.* Numismatic Notes and Monographs, 43. New York, 1930.

Cracco, Giorgio. "Relinquere laicis que laicorum sunt. Un intervento di Eugenio IV contro preti notai di Venezia." *Bollettino dell'Istituto di Storia della Società e dello Stato Veneziano* 3 (1961):179–89.

———. *Società e stato nel medioevo veneziano.* Florence, 1967.

Craig, John. *The Mint: A History of the London Mint from A.D. 287 to 1948.* Cambridge, 1953.

Crump, C. G., and C. Johnson. "Tables of Bullion Coined under Edward I, II, and III." *Numismatic Chronicle,* 4th ser., 13 (1913):200–245.

Curtin, Philip D. "Africa and the Wider Monetary World, 1250–1850." In Richards, ed., *Precious Metals,* 231–52.

Cuvillier, J. P. "Notes on the Royal Coinage in France from the Fourteenth to the Fifteenth Centuries." *JEEcH* 8 (1979):117–30.

Dal Pane, Luigi. *Storia del lavoro in Italia dagli inizi del secolo XVIII al 1815.* Storia del lavoro in Italia, edited by Amintore Fanfani, 4. Milan, 1958.

Da Mosto, Andrea. *L'Archivio di Stato di Venezia.* Bibliothèque des "Annales Institutorum," 5, bks. 1 and 2. Rome, 1937.

Davidsohn, Robert. *Forschungen zur Geschichte von Florenz.* 4 vols. Berlin, 1896–1908.

———. *Geschichte von Florenz.* 4 vols. Berlin, 1896–1927.

Day, John. "La circulation monétaire en Toscane en 1296." *Annales, ESC,* 23 (1968):1054–66.

———. "The Great Bullion Famine in the Fifteenth Century." *Past and Present,* no. 79 (May 1978):3–54.

———. "The Question of Monetary Contraction in Late Medieval Europe." *Nordick Numismatick Årsskrift* (Nordik Numismatic Journal [Copenhagen]), 1981. 12–29.

———. "Terres, marchés et monnaies en Italie et en Sardaigne du XIIème au XVIIIème siècles." *Histoire, économie et société* 2 (1983):187–203.

———, ed. *Etudes d'histoire monétaire.* Lille, forthcoming.

de la Roncière, Charles M. *Un changeur florentin du Trecento: Lippo di Fede del Sega (1285 env.–1363 env.).* EPHE-6, Affaires et gens d'affaires, 36. Paris, 1973.

———. *Prix et salaires à Florence au XIVe siècle, 1280–1380.* Collection de l'Ecole Française de Rome, 59. Rome, 1982. Published earlier in typescript form with additional chapters as *Florence: centre économique régional au XIVe siècle.* Thesis in 6 vols. Aix-en-Provence, 1976.

De Maddalena, Aldo. *Prezzi e aspetti di mercato in Milano durante il secolo XVII.* Milan, 1949.

———. *Prezzi e mercedi a Milano dal 1701 al 1860.* Studi e ricerche di storia economica italiana nell'età del Risorgimento, Banca Commerciale Italiana. 2 vols. Milan, 1974.

———. "Uomini e monete preindustriali: Personaggi in cerca d'autore." In Barbagli Bagnoli, ed., *La moneta nell'economia europea,* 497–527.

Demarco, Domenico. "Origini e vicende dei banchi pubblici: I banchi napoletani." Paper presented at the fourth "Settimana di Studio" of the Istituto Internazionale di Storia Economica "Francesco Datini," Prato, 1972.

de Roover, Raymond. "Banking and Credit in the Formation of Capitalism." *Fifth International Conference of Economic History, Leningrad 1970.* Vols. 4–5, pp. 9–17. Paris, The Hague, and New York, 1979.

———. *The Bruges Money Market around 1400.* Verhandelingen van de Koninklijke Vlaamse Academie voor Wetenschappen, Letteren en Schone Kunsten van Belgie, Klasse der Letteren, 30, no. 63. Brussels, 1968.

———. *Business, Banking, and Economic Thought in Late Medieval and Early Modern Europe.* Edited by Julius Kirshner. Introductory essays by Julius Kirshner and Richard A. Goldthwaite. Chicago, 1974.

———. "Early Banking before 1500 and the Development of Capitalism." *Revue internationale d'histoire de la banque* 4 (1971):1–16.

———. *Gresham on Foreign Exchange: An Essay on Early English Mercantilism with the Text of Sir Thomas Gresham's Memorandum for the Understanding of the Exchange.* Cambridge, Mass., 1949.

———. *Money, Banking, and Credit in Mediaeval Bruges: Italian Merchant-Bankers, Lombards, and Money-Changers. A Study in the Origins of Banking.* Cambridge, Mass., 1948.

———. "New Interpretations of the History of Banking." *Journal of World History* 2 (1954):38–76. Reprinted in de Roover, *Business, Banking, and Economic Thought.*

———. "The Organization of Trade." In *The Cambridge Economic History of Europe,* vol. 3. Cambridge, 1963.

———. *The Rise and Decline of the Medici Bank, 1397–1494.* Harvard Studies in Business History, 21. Cambridge, 1963.

———. "La structure des banques au Moyen Age." *Third International Conference of Economic History, Munich 1965,* vol. 5, pp. 159–69. Paris, 1974.

———. "La struttura della banca fiorentina nei secoli XIV e XV e la tesi Salvemini-La Sorsa." *Economia e storia* 11 (1964):190–98.

Desimoni, C. "La moneta e il rapporto dell'oro all'argento nei secoli XII al XIV." *Atti della R. Accademia dei Lincei, Classe delle scienze morali,* 5th ser., 3:3–6. Rome, 1896.

Dewey, Davis R. *Financial History of the United States.* New York, 1934.

Deyell, John. "The China Connection: Problems of Silver Supply in Medieval Bengal." In Richards, ed., *Precious Metals,* 207–13.

Di Tucci, Raffaele. *Studi sull'economia genovese del secolo decimosecondo. La nave e i contratti marittimi. La banca privata.* Turin, 1933.

Doehaerd, Renée. *Les relations commerciales entre Gênes, la Belgique, et l'Outremont d'après les archives notariales genois au XIIIe et XIVe siècles.* 3 vols. Institut Historique Belge de Rome, Etudes d'histoire économique et sociale, 2–4. Rome and Brussels, 1941.

Dubois, Henri. "Commerce international, métaux précieux et flux monétaires aux confins orientaux du Royaume de France (XIIIe–XVe siècles)." In Barbagli Bagnoli, ed., *La moneta nell'economia europea*, 681–97.

———. *Les foires de la Saône à la fin du Moyen Age (vers 1280–vers 1430)*. Paris, 1976.

Du Cange, Charles Du Resne. *Glossarium mediae et infinae latinitatis*. Rev. ed. 10 vols. Niort, 1883–87.

Ederer, Rupert J. *The Evolution of Money*. Washington, D.C., 1964.

Edler, Florence. *Glossary of Mediaeval Terms of Business, Italian Series, 1200–1600*. Cambridge, Mass., 1934.

Einaudi, Luigi. Introduction to *Paradoxes inédits du Seigneur de Malestroit touchant les monnoyes, avec la response du President De la Tourette*. Collezione di scritti inéditi e rari di economisti, edited by Luigi Einaudi, 3. Turin, 1937.

———. "The Medieval Practice of Managed Currency." In *The Lessons of Monetary Experience: Essays in Honor of Irvin Fisher*, edited by A. D. Gayer. New York, 1937.

———. "La teoria della moneta immaginaria nel tempo da Carlomagno alla rivoluzione francese." *Rivista di storia economica* 1 (1936):1–35. Reprint. Turin, 1976.

———. "The Theory of Imaginary Money from Charlemagne to the French Revolution." Edited with the assistance of Raymond de Roover. In Lane and Riemersma, eds., *Enterprise and Secular Change*. A translation by Giorgio Tagliacozzo of "La teoria della moneta immaginaria." Abbr.: Einaudi in *Enterprise*.

Eucken, Walter. *The Foundations of Economics*. Translated by T. W. Hutchison. London, 1950.

Fanfani, Amintore. *Storia del lavoro in Italia dalla fine del secolo XV agli inizi del secolo XVIII*. Storia del lavoro in Italia, edited by Amintore Fanfani, 3. 2d ed. Milan, 1959.

Fasoli, Gina. "La 'Cronique des Veniciens' di Martino da Canale." *Studi medievali*, 3d ser., 2 (1961).

Favier, Jean. "Etat et monnaie." In Barbagli Bagnoli, ed., *La moneta nell'economia europea*, 171–84.

———. *Philippe le Bel*. Paris, 1979.

Feavearyear, A. E. *The Pound Sterling: A History of English Money*. Oxford, 1931.

Fedalto, Giorgio. "Rationes decimarum Romanie, sec. XIV." *Studi veneziani* 12 (1970):157–98.

Felloni, Giuseppe. "Profilo economico delle monete genovesi dal 1139 al 1814." In Pesce and Felloni, *Le monete genovesi*.

———. "Ricavi e costi della zecca di Genova dal 1341 al 1450." In *Studi in memoria di Federigo Melis*, vol. 3, pp. 141–53. Naples, 1978.

Finlay, Robert. *Politics in Renaissance Venice*. New Brunswick, N.J., 1980.

Fisher, F. J. "The Development of London as a Centre of Conspicuous

Consumption in the Sixteenth and Seventeenth Centuries." Reprinted in *Essays in Economic History,* edited by E. M. Carus-Wilson, vol. 2, pp. 197–207. London, 1962.

Forberger, Rudolf. "Zur Auseinandersetzung über das Problem des Übergangs von der Manufaktur zur Fabrik." In *Beiträge zur deutschen Wirtschafts- und Sozialgeschichte des 18. und 19. Jahrhunderts,* edited by Deutsche Akademie der Wissenschaften. Schriften des Institut für Geschichte, 1st ser., 10. East Berlin, 1962.

Fournial, Etienne. *Histoire monétaire de l'occident médiéval.* Paris, 1970.

Freudenberger, Herman. "Die Struktur der frühindustriellen Fabrik in Umriss (mit besonderer Berücksichtigung Böhmens)." Reprinted in *Wirtschafts- und Sozialgeschichtliche Probleme der frühen Industrialisierung,* edited by Wolfram Fischer. West Berlin, 1968.

Freudenberger, Herman, and Fritz Redlich. "The Industrial Development of Europe: Reality, Symbols, Images." *Kyklos* 17 (1964):375–403.

Friedman, Milton. *Encyclopaedia Britannica, Macropaedia,* 15th ed., s.v. "money" (1980).

Fryde, Edmund B. "Edward III's Wool Monopoly: A Fourteenth-Century Royal Trading Venture." *History,* n.s., 37 (1952). Reprinted in Fryde, *Studies.*

————. "The Financial Policies of the Royal Governments and Popular Resistance to Them in France and England, c. 1290–c. 1420." *Revue belge de philologie et d'histoire* 57 (1979):824–60. Reprinted in Fryde, *Studies.*

————. "Financial Resources of Edward I in the Netherlands, 1294–1298; Main Problems and Some Comparisons with Edward III in 1337–1340." *Revue belge de philologie et d'histoire* 40 (1962):1168–87. Reprinted in Fryde, *Studies.*

————. "Financial Resources of Edward III in the Netherlands, 1337–40." *Revue belge de philologie et d'histoire* 45 (1967). Reprinted in Fryde, *Studies.*

————. "Loans to the English Crown, 1328–1331." *English Historical Review* 70 (1955):198–211. Reprinted in Fryde, *Studies.*

————. *Studies in Medieval Trade and Finance.* London, 1983.

Fryde, Edmund B., and M. M. Fryde. "Public Credit, with Special Reference to North-Western Europe." In *The Cambridge Economic History of Europe,* vol. 3. Cambridge, 1963.

Gallicciolli, G. B. *Delle memorie venete antiche profane ed ecclesiastiche.* 8 vols. Venice, 1795.

Gallo, Rodolfo. "Contributi alla storia della scultura veneziana. Andriolo de Santi." *AV* 44–45 (1949).

Geremek, Bronislaw. *Le salariat dans l'artisanat parisien aux XIII–XV siècles.* The Hague, 1969.

Giomo, Giuseppe. "Regesto di alcune deliberazioni del Senato Misti già esistenti nei primi 14 volumi distrutti (1290–1332). . . ." *AV* 17 (1879)–31 (1886).

Girard, Albert. "Un phénomène économique: La guerre monétaire (XIVe–XVe siècles)." *Annales d'histoire sociale* 2 (1940):207–18.

Goldthwaite, Richard A. *The Building of Renaissance Florence: An Economic and Social History*. Baltimore, 1980.

———. "Italian Bankers in Medieval England." Review of *Bankers to the Crown: The Riccardi of Lucca and Edward I*, by Richard W. Kaeuper. *JEEcH* 2 (1973):763–71.

Gough, John W. *The Mines of Mindip*. Oxford, 1930.

Gould, J. D. *The Great Debasement: Currency and Economy in Mid-Tudor England*. New York and Oxford, 1970.

Gras, N. S. B. *Industrial Evolution*. Cambridge, Mass., 1930.

Graus, F. "La crise monétaire du XIVe siècle." *Revue belge de philologie et d'histoire* 29 (1951):445–54.

Grierson, Philip. *Byzantine Coinage*. Dumbarton Oaks Collection, 41. Washington, D.C., 1982.

———. "Byzantine Coinage As Source Material." In *Proceedings of the XIIIth International Congress of Byzantine Studies, Oxford, 5–10 September, 1966*, edited by J. M. Hussey et al. Oxford, 1967.

———. *Byzantine Coins*. London, Berkeley, and Los Angeles, 1982.

———. "Byzantium and the Christian Levant." In *Coins: An Illustrated Survey, 650 B.C. to the Present Day*, edited by Martin J. Price. New York and London, 1980.

———. "Coinage and Money in the Byzantine Empire." *Moneta e scambi nell'alto medioevo*. Atti delle settimane di studio, 8. Spoleto, 1961.

———. "The Coin List of Pegolotti." *Studi in onore di Armando Sapori*, vol. 1, pp. 485–92. Milan, 1957.

———. *Dark Age Numismatics: Selected Studies*. London, 1970.

———. "Deux fausses monnaies vénitiennes au Moyen Age." *Schweizer Münzblätter*, August 1954, 86–90.

———. "La moneta veneziana nell'economia mediterranea del '300 e '400." In *La civiltà veneziana del Quattrocento*, 75–97. Florence, 1957. Reprinted in *Storia della civiltà veneziana*, edited by Vittore Branca, vol. 2. Florence, 1979.

———. *Monnaies du Moyen Age*. Fribourg, 1976.

———. "Note on Stamping of Coins and Other Objects." In *History of Technology*, edited by Charles Singer, 5 vols. Oxford, 1954–78. Vol. 2, pp. 485–92.

———. *Numismatics*. New York and Oxford, 1975.

———. "Numismatics." In *Medieval Studies*, edited by James A. Powell. Syracuse, 1976.

———. "The Origins of the Grosso and of Gold Coinage in Italy." *Numismaticky Sbornik* 12 (1971–72).

————. "Pegged Venetian Coin Dies." *Numismatic Chronicle,* 6th ser., 12 (1952):99–105.

————. "Problemi monetari dell'Alto Medioevo." *Bollettino della Società Pavese di Storia Patria* 54 (1954).

————. "The Weight of the Gold Florin in the Fifteenth Century." *Quaderni ticinesi di numismatica e antichità classiche* [Lugano] 10 (1981): 421–31.

Grunzweig, Armand. "Les incidences internationales des mutations monétaires de Philippe le Bel." *Le Moyen Age* 59 (1953).

Halm, George N. *Monetary Theory.* Philadelphia, 1942.

Harrod, Roy. *Money.* London, 1969.

Hart, Albert Gaylord. *International Encyclopedia of the Social Sciences,* edited by David L. Sills, s.v. "money." New York, 1968.

————. *Money, Debt, and Economic Activity.* New York, 1948.

Hazard, H. W. *The Numismatic History of Late Medieval North Africa.* Numismatic Studies, 8. New York: Numismatic Society, 1952.

Heers, Jacques. *Il clan famigliare nel medioevo.* Naples, 1976.

————. "Il commercio nel Mediterraneo alla fine del secolo XIV e nei primi anni del XV secolo." *Archivio storico italiano* 113 (1955).

————. *Gênes au XVe siècle: Activité économique et problèmes sociaux.* EPHE-6, Affaires et gens d'affaires, 24. Paris, 1961.

Hendy, Michael F. *Coinage and Money in the Byzantine Empire, 1081–1261.* Dumbarton Oaks Studies, 12. Washington, D.C., 1969.

Henneman, John Bell. *Royal Taxation in Fourteenth Century France: The Development of War Financing, 1322–1356.* Princeton, 1971.

————. *Royal Taxation in Fourteenth Century France: Captivity and Ransom of John II, 1356–1370.* Memoires of the American Philosophical Society, 116. Philadelphia, 1976.

Herlihy, David. *Medieval and Renaissance Pistoia: The Social History of an Italian Town, 1200–1430.* New Haven, 1967.

————. *Pisa in the Early Renaissance.* New Haven, 1958.

————. "Pisan Coinage and the Monetary Development of Tuscany, 1150–1250." *American Numismatic Society Museum Notes* 6 (1954):143–66. Revised version in *Le zecche minori toscane fino al XIV secolo,* 169–92. Pistoia, [1975].

Herlihy, David, Robert S. Lopez, and V. Slessarev, eds. *Economy, Society, and Government in Medieval Italy: Essays in Memory of Robert L. Reynolds.* Kent, Ohio, 1969. (The vol. previously appeared as a special issue of *Explorations in Economic History* 7 [1969].)

Heyd, Wilhelm. *Storia del commercio di Levante nel Medioevo.* Biblioteca dell'Economista, 5th ser., 10. Turin, 1913.

Hibbert, A. B. "The Economic Policies of Towns." In *The Cambridge Economic History of Europe,* vol. 3. Cambridge, 1963.

Hill, Christopher. *The Century of Revolution, 1603–1714.* London, 1961.

Hill, George F. *A History of Cyprus.* 4 vols. Cambridge, 1948.

Hilliger, Bruno. "Studien zur mittelalterlichen Massen und Gewichten." *Historische Vierteljahresschrift,* n.s., 3 (1900):171–99.

Hóman, Bálint. "La circolazione delle monete d'oro in Ungheria dal X al XIV secolo e la crisi europea dell'oro nel secolo XIV." *RIN,* 2d ser., 5, no. 1 (1922):109–56.

———. *Geschichte des ungarischen Mittelalters.* Translated for the Ungarische Institut of the University of Berlin by Hildegard von Roosz and Max Pfotenhauer. 2 vols. Berlin, 1940–43.

Horsefield, J. Keith. "The Beginnings of Paper Money in England." *JEEcH* 6 (1977):117–32.

———. *British Monetary Experiments, 1650–1710.* Cambridge, Mass., 1960.

Howard, Deborah. *Jacopo Sansovino: Architecture and Patronage in Renaissance Venice.* New Haven, 1975.

Ives, Herbert E., and Philip Grierson. *The Venetian Gold Ducat and Its Imitations.* American Numismatic Society, Notes and Monographs, 128. New York, 1954.

Janáček, Josef. "L'argent tchèque et la Méditerranée (XIVe et XVe siècles)." In *Mélanges en l'honneur de Fernand Braudel,* vol. 1, pp. 245–61. Toulouse, 1973.

Jevons, W. Stanley. *Money and the Mechanism of Exchange.* London, 1876.

Kellenbenz, Hermann. *Deutsche Wirtschaftsgeschichte.* 2 vols. Munich, 1977–81.

———. "Final Remarks: Production and Trade of Gold, Silver, and Lead from 1450 to 1750." In Kellenbenz, ed., *Precious Metals.*

———, ed. *Precious Metals in the Age of Expansion: Papers of the XIVth International Congress of the Historical Sciences. Introduced and Edited on behalf of the International Economic History Association.* Beiträge zur Wirtschaftsgeschichte, edited by Hermann Kellenbenz and Jürgen Schneider, 2. Stuttgart, 1981.

Keynes, John Maynard. *A Treatise on Money.* 2 vols. London, 1930.

Kirshner, Julius. "Raymond de Roover on Scholastic Economic Thought." In de Roover, *Business, Banking, and Economic Thought.*

Kovačević, Desanka. "Dans la Serbie et la Bosnie médiévales: Les mines d'or et d'argent." *Annales, ESC,* 15 (1960):248–58.

Krekić, Bariša. *Dubrovnik (Ragusa) et le Levant au Moyen Age.* EPHE-6, Documents et recherches, edited by P. Lemerle, 5. Paris, 1961.

———. "Italian Creditors in Dubrovnik (Ragusa) and the Balkan Trade, Thirteenth through Fifteenth Centuries." In *DMB,* 241–54.

Kretschmayr, Heinrich. *Geschichte von Venedig.* 3 vols. Vols. 1 and 2, Gotha, 1905 and 1920; vol. 3, Stuttgart, 1934.

Kriedte, Peter. *Spätfeudalismus und Handelskapital.* Göttingen, 1980.

Kriedte, Peter, Hans Medick, and Jürgen Schlumbohm. *Industrialization before Industrialization: Rural Industry in the Genesis of Capitalism.* Translated by Beate Schempp. Cambridge, 1981.

Landes, David. "Technological Change and Development in Western Europe, 1750–1914." In *The Cambridge Economic History of Europe,* vol. 6, pt. 1. Cambridge, 1965.

———. *The Unbound Prometheus.* Cambridge, 1969.

Lane, Frederic C. "The Enlargement of the Great Council of Venice." In *Florilegium Historiale: Essays Presented to Wallace K. Ferguson,* edited by J. G. Rowe and W. H. Stockdale. Toronto, 1971.

———. "Exportations d'or et d'argent de Venise, 1200–1450." In Day, ed., *Etudes d'histoire monétaire.*

———. *Navires et constructeurs à Venise pendant la Renaissance.* EPHE-6, Oeuvres étrangères, 5. Paris, 1965.

———. *Profits from Power: Readings in Protection Rent and Violence-Controlling Enterprises.* Albany, 1979.

———. "Le vecchie monete di conto veneziane ed il ritorno all'oro." *Atti dell'Istituto Veneto di Scienze, Lettere ed Arti, Classe di scienze morali e lettere,* 117 (1958–59).

———. "The Venetian Galleys to Alexandria, 1344." In Schneider, ed., *Wirtschaftskräfte und Wirtschaftswege,* vol. 1, *Mittelmeer und Kontinent,* 431–40.

———. "Venetian Maritime Law and Administration, 1250–1350." In *Studi in onore di Amintore Fanfani,* vol. 3, pp. 21–50. Milan, 1962. Reprinted in Lane, *Venice and History,* 227–52.

———. "Venetian Merchant Galleys, 1300–1334: Private and Communal Operation." *Speculum* 38 (1963):179–203. Reprinted in Lane, *Venice and History,* 193–226.

———. "Venetian Seamen in the Nautical Revolution of the Middle Ages." In Pertusi, ed., *Venezia e il Levante,* 403–29.

———. *Venetian Ships and Shipbuilders of the Renaissance.* Baltimore, 1934.

———. *Venice: A Maritime Republic.* Baltimore, 1973.

———. *Venice and History: The Collected Papers of Frederic C. Lane.* Baltimore, 1966.

———. "Wages and Recruitment of Venetian Galeotti, 1470–1580." *Studi veneziani,* n.s., 6 (1982):15–43.

Lane, Frederic C., and Jelle C. Riemersma, eds. *Enterprise and Secular Change: Readings in Economic History.* Homewood, Ill., 1953.

Lapeyre, Henri. "La banque, les changes et le credit au XVIe siècle." *Revue d'histoire moderne et contemporaine* 3 (1956):284–97.

La Sorsa, Saverio. *L'organizzazione dei cambiatori fiorentini nel medio evo.* Cerignola, 1904.

Lattes, Alessandro. *Il diritto commerciale nella legislazione statutaria delle città italiane.* Milan, 1884.

Laughlin, J. Lawrence. *History of Bimetallism in the United States.* New York, 1897.

Laurent, Henri. *La loi de Gresham au Moyen Age: Essai sur la circulation monétaire entre la Flandre et le Brabant à la fin du XIVe siècle.* Brussels, 1933.

LeBras, Gabriel. *Dictionnaire de théologie catholique,* edited by A. Vacant, E. Mangenot, and E. Aman, s.v. "usure." Paris, 1903–72.

Le Goff, Jacques. *Marchands et banquiers du Moyen Age.* Paris, 1956.

―――. *La nascita del purgatorio.* Turin, 1983.

―――. "The Usurer and Purgatory." In *DMB,* 25–52.

Lenin, V. I. *Imperialism: The Highest Stage of Capitalism.* New York, 1939. Reprint. 1970.

Léonard, Émile G. *Histoire de Jeanne I, reine de Naples, contesse de Provence (1343–1382): La jeunesse de Jeanne I.* 2 vols. Monaco and Paris, 1932–37.

Letwin, William. "Monetary Practice and Theory of the North American Colonies during the 17th and 18th Centuries." In Barbagli Bagnoli, ed., *La moneta nell'economia europea,* 439–69.

Li Ming-Hsun. *The Great Recoinage of 1696–1699.* London, 1963.

Limentani, Alberto. "Cinque note su Martino da Canal." *Atti dell'Istituto Veneto di Scienze, Lettere ed Arti, Classe di scienze morali, lettere ed arti* 124 (1965–66).

Lloyd, Terence H. *The English Wool Trade in the Middle Ages.* Cambridge, 1977.

―――. "Overseas Trade and the English Money Supply in the Fourteenth Century." In Mayhew, ed., *Edwardian Monetary Affairs.*

Lombardini, G. *Pane e denaro a Bassano tra il 1501 ed il 1799.* Vicenza, 1963.

Lombardo, Antonino. "La ricostruzione dell'antico archivio della Quarantia veneziana." In *Miscellanea in onore di Roberto Cessi,* vol. 1, pp. 239–53. Rome, 1958.

Lopez, Robert S. "An Aristocracy of Money in the Early Middle Ages." *Speculum* 28 (1953):1–43.

―――. "Back to Gold, 1252." *EcHR,* 2d ser., 9 (1956):219–40.

―――. "Continuità e addattamento nel medio evo: Un millennio di storia delle associazioni di monetieri nell'Europa meridionale." In *Studi in onore di Gino Luzzatto,* vol. 2, pp. 74–117. Milan, 1949.

―――. "The Dawn of Medieval Banking." In *DMB.*

―――. "La prima crisi della banca in Genova (1250–1259). Milan, 1956.

―――. "Prima del ritorno all'oro nell'occidente duecentesco: I primi denari grossi d'argento." *Rivista storica italiana* 79 (1967):174–81. Reprinted in his *Su e giù per la storia di Genova.*

―――. "I primi cento anni di storia documentata della banca a Genova." In *Studi in onore di Armando Sapori,* vol. 1, pp. 215–53. Milan, 1957.

―――. "Il problema della bilancia dei pagamenti nel commercio di Levante." In Pertusi, ed., *Venezia e il Levante,* vol. 1, pt. 1.

————. *Settecento anni fa: Il ritorno all'oro nell'occidente duecentesco.* Quaderni della *Rivista storica italiana,* 4. Naples, 1955.

————. "Stars and Spices: The Earliest Italian Manual of Commercial Practice." In Herlihy, Lopez, and Slessarev, eds., *Economy, Society, and Government in Medieval Italy,* 35–42.

————. *Su e giù per la storia di Genova.* Genoa, 1975.

————. "Un texte inédit: Le plus ancien manuel italien de technique commerciale." *Revue historique* 94 (1970):67–76.

Lopez, Robert S., Harry A. Miskimin, and Abraham Udovitch. "England to Egypt, 1350–1500: Long-term Trends and Long-distance Trade." In *Studies in the Economic History of the Middle East, from the Rise of Islam to the Present Day,* edited by M. A. Cook, 93–128. New York, 1970.

Lopez, Robert S., and Irving W. Raymond. *Medieval Trade in the Mediterranean World.* New York, 1955.

Lunt, William E. *Papal Revenues in the Middle Ages.* 2 vols. New York, 1934.

Lupprian, Karl-Ernst. *Il Fondaco dei Tedeschi e la sua funzione di controllo del commercio tedesco a Venezia.* Centro Tedesco di Studi Veneziani, Quaderni, 6. Venice, 1976.

————. "Zur Entstehung des Fondaco dei Tedeschi in Venedig." In *Grundwissenschaften und Geschichte. Festschrift für P. Acht,* 128–34. Münchner Historische Studien, Abteilung Geschichtliche Hilfswissenschaften, 15. Kallmünz, 1976.

Luschin von Ebengreuth, Arnold. *Allgemeine Münzkunde und Geldgeschichte.* Munich, 1926.

————. "Goldgeschäfte Meinhards II. Grafen von Tirol und seine Söhne: Ein Beitrag zur Geschichte der Edelmetalle (1289–1303)." *Veröffentlichungen des Museum Ferdinandeum in Innsbruck* 8 (1928):441–58.

Luzzati, Michele. *Giovanni Villani e la compagnia dei Buonaccorsi.* Rome, 1971.

Luzzatto, Gino. *Enciclopedia italiana,* s.v. "banca—dal medioevo ai nostri giorni." 35 vols. Rome, 1929–36. Reprint. Rome, 1949.

————. "Il costo della vita a Venezia nel Trecento." *Ateneo veneto* 125 (1934). Reprinted in his *Studi.*

————. Introduction to *PRV.* Reprinted as *Il debito pubblico della Repubblica di Venezia, dagli ultimi decenni del XII secolo alla fine del XV.* Milan, 1963.

————. "L'oro e l'argento nella politica monetaria veneziana dei sec. XIII–XIV." *Rivista storica italiana,* 1937. Reprinted in his *Studi,* 259–70.

————. "Sindacati e cartelli nel commercio veneziano dei sec. XIII e XIV." *Rivista di storia economica,* 1943. Reprinted in his *Studi,* 195–200.

————. *Storia economica di Venezia dall'XI al XVI secolo.* Venice, 1961.

————. *Studi di storia economica veneziana.* Padua, 1954.

————. "Sull'attendibilità di alcune statistiche economiche medievali." *Giornale degli economisti,* 1929. Reprinted in his *Studi,* 271–84.

Macaulay, Thomas Babington. *The History of England from the Accession of James II,* 5 vols. Boston, 1856–61.

Majer, Giovannina. "L'officina monetaria della Repubblica di Venezia." *AV,* 5th ser., 52–53 (1954).

Mandich, Giulio. "Formule monetarie veneziane del periodo 1619–1650." *Il risparmio* 5 (1957):634–82.

————. "Per una ricostruzione delle operazioni mercantili e bancarie della compagnia dei Covoni." In Sapori, ed., *Libro giallo della compagnia dei Covoni.*

Maranini, Giuseppe. *La costituzione di Venezia,* 2 vols. Vol. 1, *Dalle origini alla serrata del Maggior Consiglio.* Vol. 2, *Dopo la serrata del Maggior Consiglio.* Venice, Perugia, and Florence, 1927–31. Reprint. Florence, 1974.

Marchesi, Raffaello. *Il cambio di Perugia: Considerazioni storico-artistiche.* Prato, 1853.

Markham Schulz, Anne. *Niccolò di Giovanni Fiorentino and Venetian Sculpture of the Early Renaissance.* New York, 1978.

Martin, David A. "1853: The End of Bimetallism in the United States." *JEcH* 33 (1973).

Martini, Angelo. *Manuale di metrologia.* Turin, 1883.

Martinori, Edoardo. *La moneta: Vocabolario generale.* Rome, 1915. Reprint. 1977.

Marx, Karl. *Capital.* Translated by Ernest Untermann. 3 vols. Chicago, 1906–9.

Mas Latrie, Le conte de. *Rélations et commerce de l'Afrique Septentrionale ou Magreb avec les nations chrétiennes au Moyen Age.* Paris, 1886.

Mate, Mavis. "High Prices in Early Fourteenth Century England: Causes and Consequences." *EcHR,* 2d ser., 28 (1975).

————. "The Role of Gold in the English Economy, 1338–1400." *Numismatic Chronicle,* 7th ser., 18 (1978).

Mattozzi, Ivo. "Il politico e il pane a Venezia (1570–1650)." *Società e storia* 20 (1983):271–303.

Mayhew, Nicholas J. "Numismatic Evidence and Falling Prices in the Fourteenth Century." *EcHR,* 2d ser., 27 (1974):1–15.

————, ed. *Edwardian Monetary Affairs (1279–1344).* British Archaeological Reports, 36. Oxford, 1977.

*Mélanges en l'honneur de Fernand Braudel.* 2 vols., Toulouse, 1973.

Melis, Federigo. "La grande conquista trecentesca del 'credito di esercizio' e la tipologia dei suoi strumenti fino al XVI secolo." Paper presented at the fourth "Settimana di Studio" of the Istituto Internazionale di Storia Economica "Francesco Datini," Prato, 1972.

———. *Note di storia della banca pisana nel Trecento.* Pisa, 1956.

Metcalf, David Michael. *Coinage in South-Eastern Europe, 820–1396.* Royal Numismatic Society Special Publications, 11. 2d ed. London, 1979.

———. *Coinage in the Balkans, 820–1355.* Thessalonike, 1965. Chicago, 1966.

———. "The Currency of Deniers Tournois in Frankish Greece." *Annual of the British School at Athens* (London) 55 (1960):38–59.

Middeldorf, Ulrich, and Dagmar Stiebral. *Renaissance Medals and Plaquettes.* Florence, 1983.

Misbach, Henry L. "Genoese Commerce and the Alleged Flow of Gold to the East, 1159–1253." *Revue internationale de l'histoire de la banque* 3 (1970):67–87.

———. "Genoese Trade and the Role of Sicilian Coinage in the Mediterranean Economy, 1154–1253." *Revue internationale de l'histoire de la banque* 5 (1972):305–14.

Miskimin, Harry A. "L'applicazione della legge di Gresham." Paper presented at the Fourth "Settimana di Studio" of the Istituto Internazionale di Storia Economica "Francesco Datini," Prato, 1972.

———. "Monetary Movements and Market Structure—Forces for Contraction in Fourteenth and Fifteenth Century England." *JEcH* 24 (1964):470–90.

———. *Money, Prices, and Foreign Exchange in Fourteenth Century France.* Yale Studies in Economics, 15. New Haven, 1963.

———. "Le problème d'argent au Moyen Age." *Annales, ESC,* 17 (1962):1125–30.

———. "Two Reforms of Charlemagne: Weights and Measures in the Middle Ages." *EcHR,* 2d ser., 20 (1967):35–53.

Mollat, Michel. *Le commerce maritime normand à la fin du Moyen Age.* Paris, 1950.

Molmenti, Pompeo. *La storia di Venezia nella vita privata.* 3 vols. Bergamo, 1927.

Mor, Carlo Guido. "Il procedimento 'per gratiam' nel diritto amministrativo veneziano del sec. XIII." In Favaro, ed., *Cassiere della bolla ducale.*

Morison, Samuel Eliot, and Henry Steele Commager. *The Growth of the American Republic.* 2 vols. New York, 1937.

Morozzo della Rocca, Raimondo. "Cronologia veneziana del '300." In *La civiltà veneziana del Trecento.* Florence, 1956.

Mosher Stuard, Susan. "The Adriatic Trade in Silver, c. 1300." *Studi veneziani* 17–18 (1975–76):95–143.

Mueller, Reinhold C. "Aspetti sociali ed economici della peste a Venezia nel Medioevo." In *Venezia e la peste, 1348–1797.* Venice, 1979.

————. "'Chome l'ucciello di passagio': La demande saisonnière des es-pèces et le marché des changes à Venise au Moyen-Age." In Day, ed., *Etudes d'histoire monétaire*.

————. "Effetti della Guerra di Chioggia (1378–1381) sulla vita economica e sociale di Venezia." *Ateneo veneto* 19 (1981):27–41.

————. "Guerra monetaria tra Venezia e Milano nel Quattrocento." Paper presented at the international congress "La Zecca di Milano," Milan, May 1983.

————. "L'imperialismo monetario veneziano nel Quattrocento." *Società e storia* 8 (1980):277–97.

————. *The Procuratori di San Marco and the Venetian Credit Market: A Study of the Development of Credit and Banking in the Trecento*. New York, 1977.

————. "The Procurators of San Marco in the Thirteenth and Fourteenth Centuries: A Study of the Office as a Financial and Trust Institu-tion." *Studi veneziani* 13 (1971).

————. "The Role of Bank Money in Venice, 1300 1500." *Studi veneziani*, n.s., 3 (1979):47–96. A revised and expanded version of "Bank Mon-ey in Venice, to the Mid-Fifteenth century," in Barbagli Bagnoli, ed., *La moneta nell'economia europea*, 77–104.

Muir, Edward. *Civic Ritual in Renaissance Venice*. Princeton, 1981.

Munro, John H. "Bullion Flows and Monetary Contraction." In Rich-ards, ed., *Precious Metals*.

————. "Bullionism and the Bill of Exchange in England, 1272–1663: A Study in Monetary Management and Popular Prejudice." In *DMB*.

————. "Medieval Monetary Problems: Bimetallism and Bullionism." *JEcH* 43 (1983):294–98.

————. "Mint Policies, Ratios, and Outputs in the Low Countries and England, 1335–1420: Some Reflections on New Data." *Numismatic Chronicle* 141 (1981):71–116.

————. "Monetary Contraction and Industrial Change in the Late-Medi-eval Low Countries, 1335–1500." In *Coinage in the Low Countries, 880–1500*, edited by Nicholas J. Mayhew. British Archaeological Reports, International series, 54. Oxford, 1979.

————. *Wool, Cloth, and Gold: The Struggle for Bullion in Anglo-Burgun-dian Trade, 1340–1478*. Toronto, 1972.

Murari, Ottorino. "Il cosidetto mezzo-denaro o bianco del Doge Vitale Michiele II." *RIN*, 5th ser., 15 (1967):115–22.

Nagl, A. "Die Goldwährung und die handelsmässige Geldrechnung im Mittelalter." *Numismatische Zeitschrift* 26 (1895):41–258.

Nef, John U. "Mining and Metallurgy in Medieval Civilization." In *The Cambridge Economic History of Europe*, vol. 2. Cambridge, 1952.

Noonan, John T. *The Scholastic Analysis of Usury*. Cambridge, Mass., 1957.

Nussbaum, Arthur. *A History of the Dollar.* New York, 1957.

Origo, Iris. *The Merchant of Prato: Francesco di Marco Datini.* London, 1957.

Padovan, Vincenzo. *Le monete dei veneziani: Sommario.* 3d rev. and expanded ed. Venice, 1881. (This is a collection of many notes and documents previously published by the author in the *AV.*)

Panvini Rosati, Franco. *La monetazione comunale in Italia.* Archivio di Stato di Bologna, Quaderni della Scuola di Paleografia ed Archivistica, 5. Bologna, 1963.

Papadopoli-Aldobrandini, Nicolò. *Le monete di Venezia.* 4 vols. Venice, 1893–1919. Abbr.: Papadopoli.

———. "Le monete trovate nelle rovine del Campanile di San Marco." *Atti dell'Istituto Veneto di Scienze, Lettere ed Arti,* 20 March 1904. Reprint. Venice, 1905.

———. "Sul valore della moneta veneziana." *Atti del R. Istituto Veneto di Scienze, Lettere ed Arti,* 6th ser., 3 (1884–85).

Patterson, C. C. "Silver Stocks and Losses in Ancient and Medieval Times." *EcHR,* 2d ser., 25 (1972).

Paulinyi, Oszkár. "The Crown Monopoly of the Refining Metalurgy of Precious Metals and the Technology of the Cameral Refineries in Hungary and Transylvania in the Period of Advanced and Late Feudalism (1325–1700) with Data and Output." In Kellenbenz, ed., *Precious Metals,* 27–39.

Peragallo, Edward. "Jachomo Badoer, Renaissance Man of Commerce and His Ledger." *Accounting and Business Research* 10, no. 37A, *Special Accounting History Issue* (1980).

Perret, Paul M. *Histoire des relations de la France avec Venise du XIIIe s. à l'avènement de Charles VIII.* 2 vols. Paris, 1896.

Perroy, Edouard. "Le 'décrochage' des monnaies en temps de mutations: Le cas des viennois faibles en 1304–1308." *Le Moyen Age* 64 (1958).

Perroy, Edouard, and Etienne Fournial. "Réalités monétaires et réalités économiques." *Annales, ESC,* 13 (1958).

Pertusi, Agostino. "Quedam regalia insignia." *Studi veneziani* 7 (1965).

———, ed. *Venezia e il Levante fino al secolo XV.* 2 vols. Florence, 1973.

Pesce, G., and Giuseppe Felloni. *Le monete genovesi—Storia, arte ed economia delle monete di Genova dal 1139 al 1814.* Genoa, 1975.

Pierotti, Romano. "La circolazione monetaria nel territorio perugino nei secoli XII–XIV." *Bollettino della Deputazione di Storia Patria per l'Umbria* 78 (1981):81–151.

Pinto, Giuliano. "Note sull'indebitamento contadino e lo sviluppo della proprietà fondiaria cittadina nella Toscana tardomedievale." *Ricerche storiche* 10 (1980):3–19. Reprinted in his *La Toscana nel tardo Medio Evo.*

————. *La Toscana nel tardo Medio Evo: Ambiente, economia rurale, società.* Florence, 1982.

Piquet-Marchal, Marie-Odile. "Doctrines monétaires et conjonctures aux XIVe et XVe siècles." *Revue internationale de l'histoire de la banque* 4 (1971).

Pistorino, Geo. "Banche e banchieri del '300 nei centri genovesi del Mar Nero." *Cronache Finmare* 5–6 (May–June 1974):8–13.

Pohl, Artur. *Ungarische Goldgulden des Mittelalters (1325–1540).* Graz, 1974.

Poliakov, Léon. *Les banchieri juifs et le Saint-Siège du XIIIe au XVIIe siècle.* Paris, 1967.

Postan, Michael M. "The Trade of Medieval Europe: The North." In *The Cambridge Economic History of Europe,* vol. 2, pp. 119–256. Cambridge, 1952.

Powell, Ellis T. *The Evolution of the Money Market, 1385–1915: An Historical and Analytical Study of the Rise and Development of Finance as a Centralised, Co-ordinated Force.* London, 1915.

Prestwich, Michael. "Currency and the Economy of Early Fourteenth Century England." In Mayhew, ed., *Edwardian Monetary Affairs,* 45–58.

————. "Edward I's Monetary Policies and Their Consequences." *EcHR,* 2d ser., 22 (1969).

————. "Italian Merchants in Late Thirteenth and Early Fourteenth Century England." In *DMB.*

————. *The Three Edwards: War and State in England, 1272–1377.* London, 1980.

Previté-Orton, C. W. *A History of Europe from 1198–1378.* London, 1951.

Pullan, Brian. *Rich and Poor in Renaissance Venice: The Social Institutions of a Catholic State, to 1620.* Oxford, 1971.

————. "Service to the Venetian State: Aspects of Myth and Reality in the Early Seventeenth Century." *Studi secenteschi* 5 (1964).

————. "Wage-Earners and the Venetian Economy, 1550–1630." *EcHR,* 2d ser., 16 (1964). Reprinted in Brian Pullan, ed., *Crisis and Change in the Venetian Economy in the 16th and 17th Centuries.* London, 1968.

Queller, Donald E. *The Fourth Crusade.* Philadelphia, 1977.

————. "A Note on the Reorganization of the Venetian Coinage by Doge Enrico Dandolo." *RIN* 77 (1975):167–72.

Queller, Donald E., and Francis R. Swietek. "The Myth of the Venetian Patriciate: Electoral Corruption in Medieval Venice." In Donald E. Queller and Francis R. Swietek, *Two Studies in Venetian Government.* Etudes de philosophie et d'histoire, 33. Geneva, 1977.

Ravagnani, Giorgio. *Dizionario biografico italiano,* s.v. "Dandolo, Andrea" and "Dandolo, Francesco." Rome, forthcoming.

Reddaway, Thomas F. "The King's Mint and Exchange in London, 1343–1543." *English Historical Review* 82 (1967):1–23.

Reiss, Timothy J., and Roger H. Hinderliter. "Money and Value in the Sixteenth Century: The *Monete Cudendo Ratio* of Nicholas Copernicus." *Journal of the History of Ideas* 40 (1979):293–313.

Renouard, Yves. "Le commerce de l'argent au Moyen Age." *Revue historique* 203 (1950):41–52.

———. *Les relations des papes d'Avignon et des companies commerciales et bancaires de 1316 à 1378.* Bibliothèque des Ecoles Françaises d'Athènes et de Rome, 151. Paris, 1941.

Richards, John F., ed. *Precious Metals in the Later Medieval and Early Modern Worlds.* Durham, N.C., 1983.

Richards, R. D. *The Early History of Banking in England.* London, 1929.

———. "The First Fifty Years of the Bank of England (1694–1744)." In van Dillen, ed., *History of the Principal Public Banks.*

Riu, Manuel. "Banking and Society in Late Medieval and Early Modern Aragon." In *DMB,* 131–67.

Rizzoli, Luigi, and Quintillio Perini. *Le monete di Padova.* Rovereto, 1903.

Robbert, Louise Buenger. "Monetary Flows—Venice, 1150 to 1400." In Richards, ed., *Precious Metals,* 53–78.

———. "Reorganization of the Venetian Coinage by Doge Enrico Dandolo." *Speculum* 49 (1974).

———. "The Venetian Money Market, 1150–1229." *Studi veneziani* 13 (1971):3–94.

———. "A Venetian Naval Expedition of 1224." In Herlihy, Lopez, and Slessarev, eds., *Economy, Society, and Government in Medieval Italy.*

Robertson, D. H. *Money.* Rev. ed. Chicago, 1949.

Rodkey, G. *Encyclopedia of the Social Sciences,* edited by E. R. A. Seligman and Alvin Johnson, New York, 1930–35. Sv. "bank deposits."

Rodolico, Niccolò. *I ciompi: Una pagina di storia del proletariato operaio.* Florence, 1945.

———. *La democrazia fiorentina nel suo tramonto.* Bologna, 1905.

Romanin, Samuele. *Storia documentata di Venezia.* 10 vols. Venice, 1853–61. Reprint. Venice, 1925.

Romano, Ruggiero, ed. *I prezzi in Europa dal XIII secolo a oggi.* Turin, 1967.

Romano, Ruggiero, Frank C. Spooner, and Ugo Tucci. "Le finanze di Udine e della Patria del Friuli all'epoca della dominazione veneziana." *Memorie storiche forogiugliesi* 44 (1960–61):235–67.

Romano, Ruggiero, and Ugo Tucci, eds. *Storia d'Italia. Annali.* Vol. 6, *Economia naturale, economia monetaria.* Turin, 1983.

Rösch, Gerhard. *Venedig und das Reich: Handels- und verkehrspolitische Beziehungen in der deutschen Kaiserzeit.* Bibliothek des Deutschen Historischen Instituts in Rom, 53. Tübingen, 1982.

———. "Die Wirtschaftsbeziehungen der Ostalpenländer zu Venedig am Beginn des 13. Jahrhunderts und ein Raubzug babenbergischer Ministerialen nach Ungarn." *Zeitschrift des historischen Vereines für Steiermark* (Graz), 1979, 71–82.

Ruggiero, Guido. "Modernization and the Mythic State in Early Renaissance Venice: The Serrata Revisited." *Viator* 10 (1979).

Ruiz Martin, Felipe. "Demanda y oferta bancarias, 1450–1600." In *Mélanges en l'honneur de Fernand Braudel*, vol. 1. Toulouse, 1973.

Sacerdoti, Alberto. "Venezia e il regno hafsida di Tunisi. Trattati e relazioni diplomatiche (1231–1534)." *Studi veneziani* 8 (1966).

Salvioni, Giovanni Battista. "Il valore della lira bolognese dalla sua origine alla fine del secolo XV." *Atti e memorie della Deputazione di Storia Patria per la Romagna*, 14–18 (1896–1900). Rev. offprint, Bologna, 1902. Reprint. Turin, 1961.

Salzman, Louis F. *English Industries of the Middle Ages.* London, 1913.

Sapori, Armando. "Le compagnie italiane in Inghilterra." In his *Studi di storia economica (sec. XIII, XIV, XV)*. 3d enlarged ed. 3 vols. Florence, 1955–79. vol. 2.

———. *La crisi delle compagnie mercantili dei Bardi e dei Peruzzi.* Florence, 1926.

———. *Enciclopedia italiana*, s.v. "cambiatori." 35 vols. Rome, 1929–36. Reprint. Rome, 1949.

———. *La mercatura medievale.* Florence, 1972.

Sayous, André-E. "Les operations des banquiers italiens en Italie et aux foires de Champagne pendant le XIIIe siècle." *Revue historique* 170 (1932).

Schaube, Adolf. "Ein italienischer Coursbericht von der Messe von Troyes aus dem 13. Jahrhundert." *Zeitschrift für Sozial- und Wirtschaftsgeschichte* 5 (1897).

Schick, Léon. *Un grand homme d'affaires au début du XVIe siècle, Jacob Fugger.* EPHE-6, Affaires et gens d'affaires, 11. Paris, 1957.

Schlumberger, G. *Numismatique de l'orient latin.* Paris, 1878.

Schneider, Jürgen, ed. *Wirtschaftskräfte und Wirtschaftswege: Festschrift für Hermann Kellenbenz.* Beiträge zur Wirtschaftsgeschichte, edited by Hermann Kellenbenz and Jürgen Schneider, 4–8. Stuttgart, 1978.

Sellwood, D. G. "Medieval Monetary Technique." *British Numismatic Journal* 31 (1962).

Semi, Francesco. *Capris, Iustinopolis, Capodistria.* Trieste, 1975.

Setton, Kenneth M. *The Papacy and the Levant (1204–1571).* Vol. 1, *The Thirteenth and Fourteenth Centuries.* Memoirs of The American Philosophical Society, 114. Philadelphia, 1976.

———, general editor, *A History of the Crusades.* Vol. 1, *The First Hundred Years,* edited by Marshall W. Baldwin. Vol. 2, *The Later Crusades, 1189–1311,* edited by Robert Lee Wolff and Harry W. Hazzard. Madison, Wis., 1969.

Shaw, William A. *The History of Currency, 1252–1894.* New York, 1895.

Shoshan, Boaz. "From Silver to Copper: Monetary Changes in Fifteenth Century Egypt." *Studia Islamica* 56 (1982).

Sieveking, Heinrich. "Das Bankwesen in Genua und die Bank von S. Giorgio." In van Dillen, ed., *History of the Principal Public Banks*.

———. *Genueser Finanzwesen*. Vol. 2, *Die Casa di S. Giorgio*. Volkswirtschaftliche Abhandlungen der Badischen Hochschulen, 3. Freiburg, 1899.

Simeoni, Luigi. "L'abside di San Zeno di Verona e gli ingegneri Giovanni e Nicolò da Ferrara." *Atti dell'Istituto Veneto di Scienze, Lettere ed Arti* 67 (1907–8).

Sisto, Alessandra. *Banchieri-feudatari subalpini nei secoli XII–XIV*. Pubblicazioni della Facoltà di Lettere e Filosofia, Università di Torino, 14/I. Turin, 1963.

Smith, Adam. *The Wealth of Nations*. New York, 1930.

Soldi Rondinini, Gigliola. "Politica e teoria monetarie dell'età viscontea." *Nuova rivista storica* 59 (1975):288–330. A slightly revised version of the paper with the same title published in Barbagli Bagnoli, ed., *La moneta nell'economia europea*, 351–408.

Sombart, Werner. *Der Moderne Kapitalismus*. 2 vols. Munich and Leipzig, 1924.

Spallanzani, Marco. "A Note on Florentine Banking in the Renaissance: Orders of Payment and Cheques." *JEEcH* 7 (1978):145–68.

Spengler, Joseph J. "Coin Shortage: Modern and Premodern." *National Banking Review* 3 (1965).

Spufford, Peter. "Coinage and Currency." Appendix to *The Cambridge Economic History of Europe*, vol. 3, Cambridge, 1963, pp. 576–602.

———. "Continental Coins in Late Medieval England." *British Numismatic Journal* 32 (1964).

———. "Mint Organisation in the Burgundian Netherlands in the Fifteenth Century." In *Studies in Numismatic Method Presented to Philip Grierson*, edited by C. N. L. Brooke, Ian Stewart, J. G. Pollard, and T. R. Volk. Cambridge, 1983.

———. *Monetary Problems and Policies in the Burgundian Netherlands, 1433–1496*. Leiden, 1970.

Spufford, Peter, and Wendy Wilkinson. *Interim Listing of the Exchange Rates of Medieval Europe*. Keele, 1977.

Stahl, Alan M. *The Venetian Tornesello: A Medieval Colonial Coinage*. American Numismatic Society, Numismatic Notes and Monographs, 161. New York, forthcoming.

Stella, Aldo. *Politica ed economia nel territorio trentino-tirolese dal XIII al XVIII secolo*. Padua, 1958.

Strayer, Joseph R. Review of *Money, Prices, and Foreign Exchange*, by Harry A. Miskimin. *JEcH* 24 (1964).

———. *The Reign of Philip the Fair.* Princeton, 1980.

Studenski, Paul, and Hermann E. Krosos. *Financial History of the United States.* New York, 1952.

*Studi in memoria di Federigo Melis.* 5 vols. Naples, 1978.

Supple, Barry E. "Currency and Commerce in the Early Seventeenth Century." *EcHR,* 2d ser., 10 (1957).

Sutherland, C. H. U. *The Art of Coinage.* London, 1955.

Sylla, Richard. "Monetary Innovation in America." *JEcH* 42 (1982).

Tafuri, Manfredo. *Jacopo Sansovino e l'architettura del '500 a Venezia.* Padua, 1972.

Teja, Antonio. *Aspetti della vita economica di Zara dal 1289 al 1409.* Vol. 1, *La pratica bancaria.* Vol. 2, *La schiavitù domestica ed il traffico degli schiavi.* Zara, 1936–42.

Tenenti, Alberto, and Corrado Vivanti. "Le film d'un grand système de navigation: Les galères vénitiennes, XIVe–XVIe siècles." *Annales, ESC.,* 16 (1961):83–86.

Thiriet, Freddy. *La Romanie vénitienne au Moyen Age: Le developpement et l'exploitation du domaine colonial vénitien (XIIe–XVe siècles).* Bibliothèque des Ecoles Françaises d'Athènes et de Rome, 193. Paris, 1959.

Topping, Peter. "Le régime agraire dans le Péleponnèse latin au XIVe siècle." *Hellenisme contemporain,* 2d ser., 10 (1956).

Trasselli, Carmelo. "Le aree monetarie nel Mediterraneo centro-occidentale (secc. XIII–XVI)." In Barbagli Bagnoli, ed., *La moneta nell'economia europea,* 49–75.

———. *Note per la storia dei banchi in Sicilia nel XIV secolo.* Banco di Sicilia, Fondazione "I. Mormino," Quaderno no. 1. Palermo, 1958.

———. *Note per la storia dei banchi in Sicilia nel XV secolo.* Pt. 1, *Zecche e monete.* Banco di Sicilia, Fondazione "I. Mormino," n.s., Quaderno no. 2. Palermo, 1959.

———. *Note per la storia dei banchi in Sicilia nel XV secolo.* Pt. 2, *I banchieri e i loro affari.* Banco di Sicilia, Fondazione "I. Mormino," n.s., Quaderno no. 6. Palermo, 1968.

Tucci, Ugo. "Il Banco della Piazza di Rialto, prima banca pubblica veneziana." Reprinted in his *Mercanti, navi, monete nel Cinquecento veneziano.* Bologna, 1981.

———. "Die Mechanisierung der Münzprägung und die Münze von Venedig." In Schneider, ed., *Wirtschaftskräfte und Wirtschaftswege,* vol. 1, *Mittelmeer und Kontinent.*

———. "Le monete in Italia." In *Storia d'Italia,* vol. 5, *I documenti,* 533–79. Turin, 1973.

Unwin, George, "The Economic Policy of Edward III." In *Finance and Trade under Edward III,* edited by George Unwin. Manchester, England, 1918. Reprinted in Unwin, *Studies.*

————. "London Tradesmen and Their Creditors." In *Finance and Trade under Edward III,* edited by George Unwin. Manchester, England, 1918. Reprinted in Unwin, *Studies.*

————. *Studies in Economic History: The Collected Papers of George Unwin.* Edited by Richard H. Tawney. London, 1927.

Usher, Abbott Payson. *The Early History of Deposit Banking in Mediterranean Europe.* Harvard Economic Studies, 75. Cambridge, Mass., 1943. Reprint. New York, 1967.

————. "The Origins of Banking: The Primitive Bank of Deposit, 1200–1600." *EcHR* 4 (1943):399–428. Reprinted in Lane and Riemersma, eds., *Enterprise and Secular Change.*

van der Wee, Herman. *The Growth of the Antwerp Market and the European Economy.* 3 vols. The Hague, 1963.

————. "Monetary, Credit, and Banking Systems." In *The Cambridge Economic History of Europe,* vol. 5. Cambridge, 1977.

————. Review of *The Bruges Money Market around 1400,* by Raymond de Roover. *Business History Review* 43 (1969).

van Dillen, J. G., ed. *History of the Principal Public Banks.* The Hague, 1934. Reprint. London, 1965.

van Werveke, Hans. "Currency Manipulation in the Middle Ages: The Case of Louis de Mâle, Count of Flanders." *Transactions of the Royal Historical Society,* 4th ser., 31 (1949).

————. "The Economic Policies of Governments: The Low Countries." In *The Cambridge Economic History of Europe,* vol. 3. Cambridge, 1963.

————. "Monnaie de compte et monnaie réelle." *Revue belge de philologie et d'histoire* 13 (1934):123–52.

Vinaver, Vuk. "Der venezianische Goldzechin in der Republik Ragusa." *Bollettino dell'Istituto di Storia della Società e dello Stato Veneziano* 4 (1962):106–75.

Viner, Jacob. *Studies in the Theory of International Trade.* New York, 1937.

Violante, Cinzio. *La società milanese nell'età precomunale.* Rome, 1953. Reprint. Bari, 1974.

von Stromer, Wolfgang. *Bernardus Teotonicus e i rapporti commerciali tra la Germania meridionale e Venezia prima della istituzione del Fondaco dei Tedeschi.* Centro tedesco di studi veneziani, Quaderni, 8. Venice, 1978.

————. "Hartgeld, Kredit und Giralgeld. Zu einer monetären Konjunkturtheorie des Spätmittelalters und der Wende zur Neuzeit." In Barbagli Bagnoli, ed., *La moneta nell'economia europea,* 105–25.

————. "Nuremberg in the International Economics of the Middle Ages." *Business History Review* 44 (1970):210–25.

————. "Oberdeutsche Unternehmer im Karpatenraum, 1335–1435." In

*Fourth International Conference of Economic History, Bloomington, 1968.* EPHE-6, Congrès et colloques, 14. Paris, 1973.

————. "Oberdeutschland als Geld- und Wechselmarkt." In *Fifth International Conference of Economic History, Leningrad, 1970,* vol. 4, pp. 130–50. EPHE-6, Congrès et colloques, 15. Paris, 1976.

————. "Die Struktur von Produktion und Verteilung von Bunt- und Edelmetallen an der Wende vom Mittelalter zur Neuzeit und ihre bestimmenden Faktoren." In Kellenbenz, ed., *Precious Metals,* 13–26.

Vryonis, Spero. "The Question of the Byzantine Mines." *Speculum* 37 (1962).

Walker, Thomas. "The Italian Gold Revolution of 1252: Shifting Currents in the Pan-Mediterranean Flow of Gold." In Richards, ed., *Precious Metals,* 29–50.

Watson, Andrew M. "Back to Gold—and Silver." *EcHR,* 2d ser., 20 (1967):1–34.

Weiss, Roberto. "La medaglia veneziana del Rinascimento e l'umanesimo." In *Umanesimo europeo e umanesimo veneziano,* edited by Vittore Branca. Florence, 1963.

Whitting, Philip D. *Byzantine Coins.* London, 1973.

Wirobisz, Andrè. "L'attività edilizia a Venezia nel XIV e XV secolo." *Studi veneziani* 7 (1965):307–43.

Wirth, Peter. "Das Ende der römisch-byzantinischen Goldwährung." *Jahrbuch für Numismatik und Geldgeschichte* (Munich) 25 (1975):113–22.

Wolff, Philippe. *Commerce et marchands de Toulouse, vers 1350–vers 1450.* Paris, 1954.

Yang Lien-shing. *Money and Credit in China.* Cambridge, Mass., 1961.

Yeoman, R. S. *A Guide Book of United States Coins.* 27th ed. Racine, Wis., 1974.

Yvon, J. "Deux trésors médiévaux de la Méditerranée orientale." Congresso Internazionale di Numismatica, Rome, 1961, *Atti,* vol. 2.

Zanetti, Guid'Antonio. *Nuova raccolta delle monete e delle zecche d'Italia.* 4 vols. Bologna, 1775–89.

Zerbi, Tommaso. *Il mastro a partita doppia di una azienda mercantile del Trecento.* Como, 1936.

————. *Moneta effettiva e moneta di conto nelle fonti contabili di storia economica.* Milan, 1955.

Zon, A. "Zecca e monete di Venezia." In *Venezia e le sue lagune,* vol. 1, pt. 2. Venice, 1847.

Zordan, Giorgio. *L'ordinamento giuridico veneziano: Lezioni di storia del diritto veneziano, con una nota bibliografica.* Padua, 1980.

————. *I Visdomini di Venezia nel sec. XIII.* Pubblicazioni della Facoltà di Giurisprudenza dell'Università di Padova, 59. Padua, 1971.

Zorzanello, Giulio. "La cronaca veneziana trascritta da Gasparo Zancaruolo." *AV*, ser. 5, 114 (1980):37–66.

Zupko, Ronald Edward. *Italian Weights and Measures from the Middle Ages to the Nineteenth Century*. Memoirs of the American Philosophical Society, 145. Philadelphia, 1981.

# INDEX

NOTE: *Coins and moneys of account are entered under their names, not under their places of origin, which, however, are indicated after the items.*

Serbia: coins in, 430; mines of, 288, 373; mint of, 262–67, 315. *See also under* Grosso, foreign, in Venice

Sesino, of Milan, 8, 54

Sesto: family, 240; Luca, 240; Marco, 241

Sforza, Francesco, ducat of, 239

Shilling, English, 7, 48, 52. *See also* Soldo, coin of Venice

Ships, round, 368. *See also* Galleys, voyages of

Sicily: gold coins of, 11, 285; and gold flow, 135, 141, 156, 312, 374; mints of, 245 n. *See also* Oncia; Tarì, of Sicily

Siena: and banking, 74, 87 n; and domestic exchange, 319

Sigismund, Emperor, 199–200, 210, 249, 545, 548, 558

Signoria, 95–97, 184, 233

Signori di Notte, 152, 483

Silesia, gold from, 376

Silver. *See also* Bimetallic ratios; Bullion; *names of mining and trading areas;* Refining

—certified ingots of, in Venice, 155–56, 162–67, 219; export of, 162–68, 170, 368–71, 486; mint charge on, 495–97, 529; prices of, 164–74, 461–62, 550–58

—fall of, 286–313

—fineness of, in Venice, 618–20

—flows of, 114–16, 120, 123, 134–60, 208, 313, 324–26, 365–73, 438, 485–87

—"free," defined, 346–47

—price of, in Florence, 462 n

—rise of, 314–32, 351, 364–79, 416–65

—"servile" (*see* Quinto)

Sissa, mint at, 370

Smith, Adam, 244

Soldino, of Venice: and bimetallic ratios, 445, 456–60; circulation of, in Crete, 424–27, 430–33, 449; devaluation of, 382–412 *passim;* export of, 389, 453, 465, 546; first issue of, 169, 326–32, 367, 486–87, 491; linked to grosso type 2, 174; mint charge on, 200, 508–17, 529–30; minting of, 210, 389; and money of account, 333–54, 470, 473–74; output of, 546–47; silver content of (1331–1429), 527; tolerance of, 225–26, 384, 513–14

Soldo, coin of Venice. *See also* Lira, of Venice; Marchetto, of Venice; Soldino, of Venice

—a oro di zecca, of account, 287 n, 288–89, 305–7, 503

—soldino renamed, 248, 338

—for Verona, 248, 524–25, 529, 546–47

—for Zara, 248, 524–25, 529

Solidus. *See also* Monetary system, Carolingian; Soldo, coin of Venice

—of Byzantium, 105, 268. *See also* Perpero

—Roman, 7

Sommo, of Tana, 164, 300 n, 369, 371

Soranzo, Giovanni (doge), 240, 388, 500

Sou, of France, 11

Sovereign, of England, 52

Spain: coins of, 11, 37; and gold flow, 135, 141, 312, 374

Specie: flows, 145–46; points, 21–22

Spooner, F., 32

Spufford, P., 468

Stahl, A., 430, 522–23, 570

Stavraton, of Byzantium, 405, 419, 422

Stefan Uros II, 264–66

Steno, Pietro, reform proposal of, 395–97, 403

Sterling: bars, in Venice, 163, 165; of England, 10

Stornato, Giovanni, 320, 351–52

Strasbourg, and silver flow, 436

Strayer, J., 60

Sudan, and gold flow, 141, 142, 319, 487

Supraconsules Mercatorum, 145

Symmetallism, 268–73, 295, 416

Syria: coins of, 271; mints of, 325; and silver flow, 368; Venetian coins in, 405, 427, 453; and Venetian trade, 91, 159

Tabriz, and silver flow, 370

Tabula Maris, 356

Taccolino, of Armenia, 302–3

Talenti, Tommaso, 335, 358 n, 359, 633

Tana (Azov): and bullion flow, 368–70, 378, 487; coins of, 300; galleys to, 273; Venetian coins in, 164. *See also* Sommo, of Tana

Tana (rope factory), 235

Tarì, of Sicily, 45, 158, 274–76, 311–12

Tartars, 164, 369, 371, 453

Taula, of Valencia, 82

Taxes, in Venice: brokerage, 187–91, 197–99, 356; on bullion imports, 186–87, 191–201; on imports, 191, 356; sales, 187. *See also* Decimo; Quinto

*Silver Mezzanino of Andrea Dandolo:*
*The doge receives a candle from*
*St. Mark*

*sopitis omnibus solus vigilia*
(though others may sleep, you alone must remain vigilant)
—Petrarch, letter to A. Dandolo, 1351
(*Fam.* XI, 8, 23)

FREDERIC C. LANE was professor of history at the
Johns Hopkins University. Among his many books is
*Venice, a Maritime Republic,* also available
from Johns Hopkins, and now translated
into three foreign languages.
REINHOLD C. MUELLER is a professor at the
Università degli Studi in Venice.

THE JOHNS HOPKINS UNIVERSITY PRESS

*MONEY AND BANKING IN MEDIEVAL*
*AND RENAISSANCE VENICE*

This book was set in Bernhard Roman display type and
Galliard text by the Composing Room of Michigan, Inc.
The text initials are reproductions
of 15th-century ornamental Venetian letters.

The book was designed by Cynthia W. Hotvedt,
printed on 50-lb Eggshell Cream paper, and bound in
A grade Arrestox cloth by the
Maple Press Company, York, Pennsylvania.